21世纪英语专业系列教材

A Survey of the United Kingdom and the United States of America
新编英美概况教程

(第二版)

周叔麟
〔美〕C. W. Pollard 主编
June Almes

图书在版编目(CIP)数据

新编英美概况教程/周叔麟等主编. —2版. —北京:北京大学出版社,2009.4
(21世纪英语专业系列教材)
ISBN 978-7-301-15085-6

Ⅰ. 新… Ⅱ. 周… Ⅲ.①英语－阅读教学－高等学校－教材 ②英国－概况－英文 ③美国－概况－英文 Ⅳ. H319.4:K

中国版本图书馆 CIP 数据核字(2009)第 043966 号

书　　名：新编英美概况教程(第二版)
著作责任者：周叔麟　〔美〕C. W. Pollard　June Almes 主编
责 任 编 辑：徐万丽
标 准 书 号：ISBN 978-7-301-15085-6/H · 2235
出 版 发 行：北京大学出版社
地　　址：北京市海淀区成府路 205 号　100871
网　　址：http://www.pup.cn
电 子 邮 箱：编辑部 pupwaiwen@pup.cn　总编室 zpup@pup.cn
电　　话：邮购部 62752015　发行部 62750672　编辑部 62759634
印 刷 者：北京虎彩文化传播有限公司
经 销 者：新华书店
　　　　　787 毫米×1092 毫米　16 开本　23.5 印张　641 千字　彩插 4 页
　　　　　2004 年 5 月第 1 版　2009 年 4 月第 2 版
　　　　　2023 年 12 月第 19 次印刷(总第 30 次印刷)
定　　价：58.00 元

未经许可,不得以任何方式复制或抄袭本书之部分或全部内容。
版权所有,侵权必究　举报电话：010－62752024
　　　　　　　　　　电子邮箱：fd@pup.cn

Buckingham Palace

The Houses of Parliament

Big Ben

London

Church

Rural Area

An England Suburb

Palace Guards

The Stonehenge

The White House

The Statue of Liberty

The Capitol

Mount Rushmore

The Golden Gate Bridge

Hollywood

A Midwestern House

Hiker

Baseball

School Bus

总 序

北京大学出版社自2005年以来已出版《语言与应用语言学知识系列读本》多种，为了配合第十一个五年计划，现又策划陆续出版《21世纪英语专业系列教材》。这个重大举措势必受到英语专业广大教师和学生的欢迎。

作为英语教师，最让人揪心的莫过于听人说英语不是一个专业，只是一个工具。说这些话的领导和教师的用心是好的，为英语专业的毕业生将来找工作着想，因此要为英语专业的学生多多开设诸如新闻、法律、国际商务、经济、旅游等其他专业的课程。但事与愿违，英语专业的教师们很快发现，学生投入英语学习的时间少了，掌握英语专业课程知识甚微，即使对四个技能的掌握也并不比大学英语学生高明多少，而那个所谓的第二专业在有关专家的眼中只是学到些皮毛而已。

英语专业的路在何方？有没有其他路可走？这是需要我们英语专业教师思索的问题。中央领导关于创新是一个民族的灵魂和要培养创新人才等的指示精神，让我们在层层迷雾中找到了航向。显然，培养学生具有自主学习能力和能进行创造性思维是我们更为重要的战略目标，使英语专业的人才更能适应21世纪的需要，迎接21世纪的挑战。

如今，北京大学出版社外语部的领导和编辑同志们，也从教材出版的视角探索英语专业的教材问题，从而为贯彻英语专业教学大纲做些有益的工作，为教师们开设大纲中所规定的必修、选修课程提供各种教材。《21世纪英语专业系列教材》是普通高等教育"十一五"国家级规划教材和国家"十一五"重点出版规划项目《面向新世纪的立体化网络化英语学科建设丛书》的重要组成部分。这套系列教材要体现新世纪英语教学的自主化、协作化、模块化和超文本化，结合外语教材的具体情况，既要解决语言、教学内容、教学方法和教育技术的时代化，也要坚持弘扬以爱国主义为核心的民族精神。因此，今天北京大学出版社在大力提倡专业英语教学改革的基础上，编辑出版各种英语专业技能、英语专业知识和相关专业知识课程的教材，以培养具有创新性思维的和具有实际工作能力的学生，充分体现了时代精神。

北京大学出版社的远见卓识，也反映了英语专业广大师生盼望已久的心愿。由北京大学等全国几十所院校具体组织力量，积极编写相关教材。这就是说，这套教材是由一些高等院校有水平有经验的第一线教师们制定编写大纲，反复讨论，特别是考虑到在不同层次、不同背景学校之间取得平衡，避免了先前的教材或偏难或偏易的弊病。与此同时，一批知名专家教授参与策划和教材审定工作，保证了教材质量。

当然，这套系列教材出版只是初步实现了出版社和编者们的预期目标。为了获得更大效果，希望使用本系列教材的教师和同学不吝指教，及时将意见反馈给我们，使教材更加完善。

航道已经开通，我们有决心乘风破浪，奋勇前进！

胡壮麟
北京大学蓝旗营

Forward to the Second Edition

This revised edition follows the U. K. and the U. S. well into the twenty-first century. Authors and experts have updated all information, and some chapters have been thoroughly revised so that readers can picture the current condition of these two nations. The United States, particularly, changed significantly after 2001, and this book will help. readers see the effect of these changes.

We regret the death of June Almes, whose deep commitment to Sino-American friendship helped to bring together the many scholars and experts who wrote the book. She also contributed as editor and expert. Fortunately, she lived long enough to revise her sections and to see the completed revisions for this work. May the scholarship and the friendships both flourish.

Preface

Yang Zhizhong

A Survey of the United Kingdom and the United States of America is a collection of articles written by American, British and Chinese professors in the related fields. It covers many topics including philosophy, history, geography, politics, economy, education, culture and society. While the information is authentic and up-to-date, the language, being tailored to the needs of learners of English, is easy to read, and even to remember. At the end of each chapter, there are questions offered for reflection or discussion, and notes provided for better understanding. When reading the chapters, learners can not only gain knowledge but improve their English proficiency.

I was privileged to be the first reader of the manuscripts, and in the course of reading them, I found myself benefiting from it. Therefore, I recommend without slightest hesitation or reservation this collection to lovers of English, learners of English and all those who wish to know more about the USA and Great Britain.

Foreword

The purpose of this survey of the United Kingdom of Great Britain and Northern Ireland and the United States of America is to provide an overview of the geography, history, government, economy, sociology, culture and education of the two countries, as well as of the philosophical traditions that have shaped much of western thought, including that of the United Kingdom and the United States.

The textbook is designed to assist people studying the English language, people studying British or American literature and culture, people planning to study in or travel to the United Kingdom or the United States, or people planning to work with British or American people.

This book is the result of a unique Sino-British-American cooperative effort. Professor Zhou Shulin at Nanjing University as well as Professors C. W. Pollard and June Almes at Lock Haven University of Pennsylvania were chief editors on the Chinese and American sides.

Each chapter was either written by or reviewed by a specialist in the field and contains up-to-date, factual material. Each chapter was written in standard English, using the vocabulary of the appropriate academic field.

Professors June Almes and C. W. Pollard wrote the philosophy chapter. Shen Peixin from Changsha University of Science and Technology wrote the UK geography chapter, and US geography chapter in consultation with Professor John Way of Lock Haven University. Judy Ochs, M. Ed. of the South Middleton School District and C. W. Pollard wrote the UK history chapter; Prof. Lawrence T. Farley of Lock Haven University described the UK and US Governments. Prof. Steven D. Soderlund of St. Olaf College wrote the British economy chapter, and Gillian Masemore, ex-London newspaper staff, and C. W. Pollard wrote the chapters on British culture and education. Zhou Shulin wrote the American history chapter. Prof. Philip Sprunger of Lycoming College wrote the chapter on the US economy. Professors Judy Brink and Renuka Biswas, both of Lock Haven University, wrote the chapters on US culture and society. Prof. Almes wrote the American education chapter.

We would like to extend our hearty thanks to Yang Zhizhong, President, College English Teaching and Research Association of China, Professor of Nanjing University, for writing the preface of the book and for his great concern and valuable advice about the writing and publishing of the book. Special thanks go to Xiao Li, Zhang Yiyun and Sang Xiaoli of Nanjing University for making notes for the book, and Shawn Smith for her editorial suggestions.

Table of Contents

CHAPTER 1 PHILOSOPHY OF WESTERN CIVILIZATION 1
   Ⅰ. Introduction 1
   Ⅱ. Greek Rationalism 1
   Ⅲ. The Middle Ages 6
   Ⅳ. The Renaissance 7
   Ⅴ. Modern Philosophy 11
   Ⅵ. Modern Philosophical Trends 13
   Ⅶ. Summary 17

CHAPTER 2 GEOGRAPHY OF THE UNITED KINGDOM 21
   Ⅰ. Introduction 21
   Ⅱ. General Characteristics of the United Kingdom 22
   Ⅲ. Water: The Key Geographical Feature 26
   Ⅳ. Geographical History 26
   Ⅴ. Surface Features and Geography—by Political Region 27
   Ⅵ. Current Situation 38
   Ⅶ. Commonwealth 39

CHAPTER 3 HISTORY OF THE UNITED KINGDOM 43
   Ⅰ. Prehistory to the Norman Conquest 43
   Ⅱ. The Making of a Nation: From the Norman Conquest to the Renaissance 48
   Ⅲ. The Tudors: Sea Power and Protestantism 54
   Ⅳ. Founding of the British Empire 63
   Ⅴ. England in Revolution: Representative and Constitutional Government 67
   Ⅵ. England in the Eighteenth Century: The Age of Reason 76
   Ⅶ. Napoleonic Wars and a Century of Slow Reforms 84
   Ⅷ. Nineteenth Century Imperialism 89
   Ⅸ. Twentieth-Century England: Crisis of Identity 92
   Appendixes 102

CHAPTER 4 BRITISH ECONOMY 112
   Ⅰ. Introduction 112
   Ⅱ. Highlights of Britain's Economic Development 112
   Ⅲ. Britain's Prosperity Today 115
   Ⅳ. Britain's Economic System: A Unique Mix 118
   Ⅴ. Consumer Expenditure 123
   Ⅵ. Industrial Structure and Output 124

- Ⅶ. International Trade ······ 125
- Ⅷ. Taxation and Public Spending ······ 126
- Ⅸ. Economic Policy ······ 128

CHAPTER 5 BRITISH CULTURE ······ 132
- Ⅰ. Introduction ······ 132
- Ⅱ. The British People—General Traits ······ 132
- Ⅲ. Entertainment ······ 139
- Ⅳ. Conclusion ······ 144

CHAPTER 6 BRITISH EDUCATION ······ 146
- Ⅰ. Introduction ······ 146
- Ⅱ. Medieval England—Church and Class ······ 146
- Ⅲ. Renaissance Education ······ 150
- Ⅳ. Eighteenth Century—What Is Correct English ······ 153
- Ⅴ. Nineteenth Century—Class Struggle and Change ······ 154
- Ⅵ. Twentieth Century—Reform, Socialism and Conservatism ······ 157
- Ⅶ. Conclusion ······ 162

CHAPTER 7 GEOGRAPHY OF THE UNITED STATES ······ 164
- Ⅰ. Introduction ······ 164
- Ⅱ. Economic Activities ······ 164
- Ⅲ. Rural, Suburban, and Urban Living Patterns ······ 168
- Ⅳ. Physiographic Subdivisions of the United States ······ 172
- Ⅴ. Geologic Processes Shape the Nation's Physical and Human Geography ······ 197
- Ⅵ. Energy and Mineral Resources Required for a Modern Society ······ 198
- Ⅶ. Summary: The United States—"A Land of Contrasts" ······ 198

CHAPTER 8 HISTORY OF THE UNITED STATES ······ 204
- Ⅰ. Introduction ······ 204
- Ⅱ. Native Americans ······ 204
- Ⅲ. Colonial North America ······ 205
- Ⅳ. The Founding of the United States ······ 208
- Ⅴ. Forming A New Nation ······ 210
- Ⅵ. Nationalism and the Economy ······ 215
- Ⅶ. Westward Expansion ······ 216
- Ⅷ. The Industrial Revolution and Social Reforms ······ 219
- Ⅸ. The American Civil War and Reconstruction ······ 221
- Ⅹ. Industrialization, Capitalism, and Monopolies ······ 226
- Ⅺ. The United States Becomes a World Power ······ 231
- Ⅻ. The Post World War Ⅰ Period ······ 233
- ⅩⅢ. World War Ⅱ ······ 237
- ⅩⅣ. The Post World War Ⅱ Period (1945-1989) ······ 239
- ⅩⅤ. Modern Times ······ 248

XVI. Conclusion ········ 252
Appendixes ········ 252

CHAPTER 9 BRITISH AND AMERICAN GOVERNMENT ········ 259
I. Introduction ········ 259
II. Politics ········ 260
III. Political Legitimacy ········ 262
IV. Absolutism and Constitutionalism ········ 265
V. Democracy ········ 268
VI. Indirect or Representative Democracy ········ 271
VII. Elections ········ 273
VIII. The Assembly Model ········ 275
IX. Conclusion ········ 276
Appendixes ········ 276

CHAPTER 10 THE ECONOMY OF THE UNITED STATES ········ 286
I. Introduction and Overview ········ 286
II. History and Growth ········ 286
III. Commercial and Nonprofit Firms ········ 287
IV. Households ········ 291
V. Government and the Economy ········ 293
VI. International Trade ········ 299
VII. Problems and Challenges for the U. S. Economy ········ 301

CHAPTER 11 AMERICAN SOCIETY ········ 305
I. Introduction ········ 305
II. Individuals ········ 305
III. Families ········ 310
IV. Groups ········ 310
V. Organizations ········ 311
VI. Socioeconomic Classes, Status and Roles ········ 313
VII. Race and Ethnicity ········ 315
VIII. Other Social Issues ········ 319
IX. Social Changes and Global Connections ········ 322

CHAPTER 12 AMERICAN CULTURE ········ 326
I. Introduction ········ 326
II. Materialism and the Mass Media ········ 326
III. Individual Style and Personal Rites of Passage ········ 327
IV. Manners ········ 330
V. Food and Meals ········ 331
VI. Housing ········ 333
VII. Pets ········ 334
VIII. Leisure Activities ········ 335

Ⅸ. Holidays ·· 337
Ⅹ. American Values ··· 342

CHAPTER 13 EDUCATION IN THE UNITED STATES ············ 344
Ⅰ. Introduction ··· 344
Ⅱ. Issues in American Basic Education ······································ 348
Ⅲ. Higher Education ·· 352
Ⅳ. Conclusion ··· 357

后记 ·· 359

CHAPTER 1 PHILOSOPHY OF WESTERN CIVILIZATION

Prof. June Almes and Dr. Carol W. Pollard

I. Introduction

The word "philosophy" is Greek for "love of wisdom" and has come to mean a systematic search for answers to life's great questions. Universal questions were asked independently by great thinkers in all civilizations: "What is man?" "Why are we here?" "What is truth?" To simplify the contrasts between eastern and western philosophical traditions, three characteristics can be identified. In the East, philosophy has had a longer history; it was founded on the oral tradition; and it contained principles to live by. In the West, philosophy is "younger"; it was recorded in written form; and it made claims supported by logical or *empirical[1] arguments.

Early western philosophers living near the eastern Mediterranean Sea, including the ancient kingdoms of *Sumeria[2], *Mesopotamia[3], Syria, Persia and *Phoenicia[4], made valuable contributions. However, it was the early Greeks who changed the history of philosophy in the West.

Beginning with some of the major contributions of these Greeks, this chapter summarizes several important philosophical questions and arguments to the end of the 20th century. The primary purpose of this chapter is to provide a foundation for understanding the other chapters in this book.

II. Greek *Rationalism [5]

Not only did the ancient Greeks ask universal questions, but they also made important assumptions. One major assumption was that something has always existed. They also believed that a unity underlies the diversity of people, animals, plants and inanimate objects. Today, this search for a unifying, unchanging theory of the universe continues through the work of modern physicists, including the German-Swiss-American, *Albert Einstein[6] (1879 – 1955) and Britain's *Stephen Hawkings[7] (1942 –   ).

Equally important, the Greeks theorized about this unity. In other words, they made reasonable guesses about natural causes, based on their studies of Nature itself. This combination of assumptions and theories dramatically differed from previous philosophical approaches which relied on mythology and divine beings to describe the world. The end result was that early Greeks defined the true task of philosophy as system building: How does the "whole of things" emerge from this "tiny seed of self"?

The first major Greek philosopher was *Thales[8] (624 – 550 B.C.). Thales claimed that Nature is rational; therefore, human beings could use their reasoning abilities to understand Nature. He asked, "From what do all things come and to what do all things return?" Once Thales asked this question, Greek thinkers wondered if our changing world was based on something unchanging? To answer this riddle, they were challenged to discover answers which avoided mythology. Furthermore, this was the origin of *metaphysics[9], the philosophical study which probes the nature of reality itself.

Thales reasoned that water is the basis of everything. Like the philosophers who followed Thales, what was important was not his answers, but the questions he asked. Thales' student, *Anaximander[10] (611 - 547 B. C.) disagreed that water or any single substance could explain everything. Instead, he viewed the world *in terms of[11] opposites: hot and cold; dry and moist; and light and dark. As part of his search for simple concepts that explained the entire universe, he incorporated mathematical ideas to describe the rational world.

Convinced that mathematical truths do not depend on day-to-day contingencies, *Pythagoras[12] (570 - 500 B. C.) explained the entire natural world with numbers. His *"Pythagorean Theory"[13] which demonstrates the relationships among the sides of a triangle is studied in modern geometry. Today, using mathematics as a method to describe the universe is prevalent.

*Heraclitus[14] (535 - 475 B. C.) is remembered because he introduced the concept of change as the only unchanging reality in the universe. He compared life to a flowing river: A person cannot step into the same river twice. As part of his universal theory of change, Heraclitus claimed that opposites are inherently connected. Heat cannot exist without cold; night cannot exist without day. The tension created by "Unity in opposition" is the principle which accounts for perpetual change. Therefore, the physical world is not what it seems to be; *static[15] appearance is not the same as reality (change).

*Parmenides[16] (515 - 440 B. C.) disagreed. He argued that change was an illusion. The world may appear to change, but actually everything was the same. To Parmenides, human reasoning could discover the hidden universal truth(s) which was disguised by the facade of change.

Like Heraclitus and Parmenides, *Democritus[17] (460 - 390 B. C.) was intrigued by the phenomenon of change. He argued that everything in the universe obeys the laws of necessity. Events are not random; they are the result of mechanical laws. Like Parmenides, he believed that nothing actually changes. To explain this, he and his colleagues developed the atomic theory: the building *blocks[18] of physical objects are collections of indestructible and invisible particles of matter called atoms. Nature consisted of an unlimited number and variety of atoms. When a plant or animal died, its atoms disperse and could be used again in new bodies. In English translation, the Greek word, "Atom" means "uncuttable", even though modern scientists have "cut" the atom into smaller particles: electrons, *protons[19] and *neutrons[20]. Ironically, Democritus' mechanistic view of the world was accepted by western thinkers as early as the 16th century, but his modified atomic theory was not adopted until the 20th century.

At the time when Chinese scholars, *Confucians[21] and *Taoists[22], were concerned with social relationships and human harmony with the natural world, Greek philosophers were arguing about what Nature itself was. By the 5th century B. C., certain concepts were familiar to most Greek thinkers. The world of human experience differed somehow from ultimate reality. Rationalism, the belief that reason is the primary source of knowledge, was firmly entrenched. Human beings could understand Nature through reasoning, because Nature followed rational laws.

Not all Greek philosophers agreed with the Rationalists. One major group who doubted that human reason could understand Nature were called *Skeptics[23]. Their question, "What is Knowledge?" led to the development of *epistemology[24], the philosophical study of knowledge itself.

One group of Skeptics were the *Sophists[25], wandering teachers who would teach anyone willing to pay for their services. Like other Skeptics, the Sophists did not believe that reasoning could solve the riddles of Nature. Unlike other skeptics, the Sophists concentrated on the individual and the individual's relationship to society. Their debates about what was socially induced and what was naturally induced led them to the conclusion that there were no absolute norms for right or wrong actions. The individual had to decide. The importance of the individual dramatically shaped future philosophical discourse in the West.

The Sophists and other thinkers gravitated to the Greek city-state of Athens, a city which dominated western civilization for nearly 250 years (594 – 338 B.C.). Athens was famous for its writers, architects, sculptors, thinkers and sports contests, including the origins of the modern-day Olympic Games. When Athens was conquered by the Italian Romans, many of its contributions were incorporated into the *Roman Empire[26]. In turn, the Roman Empire laid the political and cultural foundations of Western Europe. The influence of this small city went far beyond its physical size.

1. SOCRATES (470 – 399 B.C.)

*Socrates[27], one of the three great ancient Greek philosophers, also lived in Athens. Today, we know Socrates primarily through the writings of his famous student and the second of the great Greek philosophers, *Plato[28]. Therefore, it is not easy to distinguish Socrates' philosophy from Plato's ideas.

Socrates strongly disagreed with the Sophists. He argued that some norms are universally valid and absolute. He did not teach for money, and he did not believe that he was a wise person. He knew that he knew nothing about life and the world. It troubled him that he knew so little. According to Plato, Socrates once said, "One thing only I know, and that is that I know nothing".

He was also a rationalist who had unshakable faith in human reason. He distinguished between two types of knowledge: innate or *a priori* knowledge and empirical or *a posteriori*[29] knowledge. *A priori*, or prior to birth, each person has Virtue which is not learned through the physical senses. Virtue transcends both the individual and time and is the same for all people and all time. Paradoxically, Virtue cannot be taught and is lost at birth.

Empirical or *a posteriori* knowledge is learned through the physical senses. Empirical knowledge includes virtues in the ordinary meaning, such as helping a sick friend. This distinction between the abstract concept of Virtue and the everyday concept of virtues is important because Socrates' theory generated a thousand-year controversy about the nature of scientific knowledge. Today, there is general agreement that scientific knowledge is always based on first principles (Virtue) which are not subject to change. Human beings may make mistakes, but once a scientific truth has been discovered, it does not change.

Another major contribution was his question-and-answer technique, called the Socratic method, which is still used today. Instead of telling the student the answer, Socrates engaged his student in a dialogue. He never criticized the student, but led the student to understand his own self-contradictions and to a better understanding of himself and his values.

He believed that everyone could understand philosophy if a person used common sense. Right insights lead to right action. Socrates said, "He who knows what good is, will do good". Only a person who does right can be virtuous and happy. We do wrong because we do not know better; that is why it is important to continue to learn.

The Socratic question-and-answer method angered people who did not understand its purpose. When his enemies had him condemned to death for his beliefs, Socrates could have escaped from Athens. Valuing truth more than his life, he remained and was forced to drink poison.

2. PLATO (428—347 B.C.)

Plato considered (that) the death of his beloved teacher, Socrates, marked the difference between actual human society and the ideal society. He sought the ideal, the reality which is eternal and unchanging for both society and Nature. The earlier natural philosophers asked, "What allows our changing world to be based on something that is unchanging?" Plato now asked, "What is eternally true", "eternally beautiful" and "eternally good"?

Like Democritus, Plato believed that everything in the material world dies, decomposes and disintegrates. Unlike Democritus, Plato observed that many animate and inanimate objects in the material world are very similar. He reasoned that there were a limited number of forms (ideas), transcending the sensory world. For example, a particular chair can be destroyed, but the idea of a chair cannot be destroyed.

Since empirical knowledge of physical things is knowledge of unreliable objects, which change and decay, empirical knowledge is not the road to true knowledge. Therefore, true, absolute and eternal knowledge must be *a priori*, or innate within human beings. This amazing view is the basis of Plato's theory of ideas.

Plato's theory, called *Idealism[30], was that human senses provide inexact concepts of things; only human reason can give us true knowledge about the world. To clarify his Idealism, Plato told a story about prisoners in a dark cave. This story is often called the *Allegory[31] of the Cave.

Plato asked his listeners to imagine that the prisoners in the cave spent their entire lives facing the back wall of the cave. Behind them was a path where people walked, talked and carried objects. Behind the path was a fire, which cast the people's shadows on the back wall of the cave. The prisoners could see the shadows, but not the people. They believed that the shadows were real people walking, talking and carrying real objects.

Then, Plato asked his listeners to imagine that one of the prisoners managed to look at the path behind him. At first, the prisoner would be blinded by the light from the fire. Gradually, he would see the real people and the real objects, not the shadows. Eventually, he would understand that the shadows were not real.

Finally, Plato asked his listeners to imagine that the prisoner went outside the cave. Again, the prisoner would be blinded by the light, but this time it would be the light of the sun. There he would see shadows and real people and objects. In time, he would look beyond this scene and realize that there are causes for events, even in caves.

In Plato's story, human beings are the prisoners trapped in the cave of their physical senses, which shows them only shadows of reality. The brighter, outside world is the true world, the world of ideas which are absolute and eternal realities. Understanding the world of ideas leads to understanding the ultimate cause of the physical world. This *dualistic[32] view of reality is sometimes called "Mind over Matter".

Plato advocated an ideal society which he described in his work, *The Republic*. Ideally, every person could reach the highest level of wisdom and virtue possible in his society. He believed such people would be led by "philosopher kings" who would serve their fellow citizens unselfishly because they would be the people with the most wisdom. Today, this concept of an ideal republic is unique, but it was even more amazing that it appeared in the Athenian society of Plato's day.

In summary, Plato used earlier philosophical contributions to develop his Idealism into a comprehensive system which became a pillar of western thinking. *Alfred North Whitehead[33], a 20th-century British philosopher, wrote, "The safest general characterization of the European tradition is that it consists of a series of footnotes to Plato".

3. ARISTOTLE (385 – 323 B.C.)

As differing Confucian and Taoist views affected feudal China, so the views of Plato and Aristotle, Plato's most famous student and the third great Greek philosopher, affected feudal Europe.

Although *Aristotle[34] accepted the division of human thought into the empirical world of the senses and the ideal world of thought, he believed that Plato had turned reality upside down.

To Plato, the highest reality was gained through reason. To Aristotle, the highest reality was gained through the physical senses. Unlike Plato who described the natural world as a poor imitation of the world of ideas, Aristotle believed that nothing exists in consciousness that has not first been experienced through the senses.

For Plato, our senses lead us to understand the eternal ideal forms in our mind which exist without any physical object. Even if there were no chairs in the world, the eternal, ideal form of a chair would exist, awaiting the mind that could think of it. Aristotle agreed that specific objects represented an ideal form, but he disagreed that an ideal form could exist without a specific form. At least one chair had to exist in the world. If Plato's motto was "Mind over Matter", then Aristotle's motto was "Matter over Mind".

Aristotle acknowledged that man has the innate ability to reason, his most distinguishing characteristic, but reason depended on the senses. Since man had reasoning ability, he could organize physical experiences into categories. Aristotle categorized all known living and non-living objects, as well as the fields of knowledge of his time. Although these categories have changed since Aristotle's day, his major contribution was his articulation of criteria for his categories. Reality consisted of "substance", what objects are made of, and "form", each object's specific characteristic or what it can do. For example, a hen's "form" is that it lays eggs, cackles and flutters. When the chicken dies, it cannot lay eggs, cackle or flutter. All that remains is the hen's "substance", but then it is no longer a chicken.

As a result of Aristotle's search for causes of events, he created a pattern which continues to be debated today. He developed four causes for why events occur in the natural world. To answer the question, "Why does it rain?", Aristotle would agree with the modern explanation that moisture in the clouds cool and condense into raindrops which fall to the earth by the force of gravity. However, only three of Aristotle's causes were included in the answer. The "material" cause is the clouds; the "efficient" cause is the cooling of the cloud's moisture; the "formal" cause is the form of water which falls as raindrops. Aristotle added a fourth and "final" cause, which is the purpose of the rain; namely that plants grow so people can eat them. Today, people who believe in a final cause or a benign purpose for the universe argue with those who believe that only the material, efficient and formal causes can be scientifically analyzed.

By defining a structure which validated or invalidated deductive reasoning, Aristotle founded the science of logic. His method is called a *syllogism[35] which argues from a general principle to a specific example:

General Principle: All men are mortal.
Connection: I am a man.
Deductive Conclusion: I am mortal.

Aristotle's theories dominated Western philosophy for more than a *millennium[36]. Some of his ideas, such as the belief that women were "incomplete" men and that the earth was the center of the universe (*geocentric[37] theory), held western thinking back for a very long time. Despite contemporary criticism of Aristotle's theories, his influence was enormous. Modern science is richer for overcoming his arguments. He was a *seminal[38] thinker, and his consistent, systematic approach to the philosophical problems he faced serves as a model for all times.

III. The Middle Ages

The Greeks were conquered by the Romans who adopted and modified much of the Greek culture. These two ancient civilizations are often studied together as the *Greco-Roman Age[39]. After its first introduction to the Roman Empire, three or four hundred years passed before Christianity dominated western philosophy. The Christian dominated era in Western Europe is called "the Middle Ages"(ca 476 A.D. - ca 1400 A.D.), or the Medieval Period, a thousand-year-feudal era which occurred between *Antiquity[40] and the Modern Age.

The Christian tradition generally assumed that Christianity, based on the life and teaching of *Jesus Christ[41], was true. During this era, non-Christian thinkers and their writings were often burned. Both Plato and Aristotle were born before Christ, and, therefore, were not Christians. However, Christians did accept earlier ideas which did not contradict Christian thought, such as the dual nature of the world; the separation of humans from the natural world; the need to promote virtue and goodness as human goals;

and the importance of each human being. Ironically, much of the Greco-Roman heritage was lost until the Islamic scholars in the Near East, who had preserved many writings from Antiquity, reintroduced them to western Europe during the *Renaissance[42].

Throughout the Middle Ages, most thinking was devoted to religious interpretation, or the study of *theology[43]. Unlike philosophers, who are not restricted to thoughts based on a particular religious belief, theologians are more limited in their studies. Two medieval theologians have also been called philosophers. The major philosophical problem for them was whether a person should simply believe the Christian doctrines or whether these doctrines could also be analyzed through reason. One of these theologian philosophers was *St. Augustine[44] (354 - 430), who was influenced by Plato's Idealism. According to St. Augustine, man has a body and a soul; all human history is a struggle between the materialistic and the spiritual worlds. The other significant philosopher was *St. Thomas Aquinas[45] (1225 - 1247). If St. Augustine *christianized[46] Plato's philosophy, then St. Thomas christianized Aristotle's philosophy. Aquinas believed that he could demonstrate the existence of God (*Aristotle's Final Cause[47]), based on both innate reason and faith.

Despite the materialism and *secular[48] nature of most modern European and American culture, the medieval Christian millennium shaped western thinking. To some extent, contemporary western philosophy is an attempt to refute or replace much of medieval religious thought.

Ⅳ. The Renaissance

The Middle Ages gradually ended with the emergence of the Renaissance (ca 1400 - 1700), the precursor of the Modern Age. The French word "renaissance" means "rebirth" in English. It refers to the rebirth of knowledge in Europe, particularly the rediscovery of the Greco-Roman texts. This era was characterized by changes in all areas of human endeavor, based on a new humanism which focused on Man. However, Man was seen differently than the earlier views held by the Sophists and Socrates. Man became part of the natural world, an object of investigation as much as any other animal. Gradually observation and systematic experimentation expressed in mathematical terms replaced medieval *scholasticism[49] and religious faith.

Medieval philosophers, primarily church men, built on the traditions of previous generations. Starting with the Renaissance, the modern history of philosophy became a procession of outstanding individuals from the secular world, each with a personal style, each proud of marking an epoch.

Three important scientists refuted Aristotle's geocentric universe by recording observations of the planets and stars. The Polish *astronomer[50], *Nicholaus Copernicus[51] (1473 - 1543); the Italian scientist and mathematician, *Galileo Galilei[52] (1564 - 1642); and the German astronomer, *Johann Kepler[53] (1571 - 1630) demonstrated that the earth was only a small part of an infinite universe. Once they had established that there was no absolute center of the universe, a person could imagine that he was the center of his own universe.

*Isaac Newton[54] (1642 -1772), a British mathematician, surpassed both

Anaximander and Pythagoras in his use of mathematics to describe the universe. Newton's laws of motion explained all visible motions, from those of stars to those of tiny pebbles.

*Francis Bacon[55] (1561 – 1626), a British statesman and writer, wrote the first description of the modern scientific method: constructing a hypothesis; conducting an experiment to test the hypothesis; and reaching conclusions based on the experiment. Unlike Aristotle who merely observed, Bacon and western scientists actively manipulated nature in order to understand and control it.

*Thomas Hobbes[56] (1588 – 1679), a British mathematician and political writer, described human society and hypothesized about its future. His harsh description of the materialistic, selfish society is very different from either Plato's Republic or Christianity's idealism.

These thinkers adopted Democritus' mechanistic world view. They compared the universe to a huge machine which followed laws, with changes that could be measured accurately. The dramatic shift to the scientific method challenged the authority of both church and state. In parts of the contemporary western world, the scientific method is still regarded as inferior to religious authority as a source of knowledge.

1. RENE DESCARTES (1596 – 1650)

There is a direct line from Socrates and Plato via St. Augustine to the French logician and mathematician, *Rene Descartes[57]. All of these men were Rationalists who claimed that reason was the only path to knowledge. Descartes applied reason to the question, "What can we know for certain?" Descartes insisted that a philosopher must begin by doubting all that can be doubted. At the same time, the philosopher must avoid skepticism when doubting doubt itself.

Descartes agreed with earlier thinkers who relied on mathematics, rather than the evidence provided by our senses. He used mathematical logic to reason through complex problems in other fields of knowledge. By first dividing the problem into its smallest components, he moved progressively to more complex issues.

Descartes did not believe that man knew nothing. This belief led him to ask another important question, "What is the relationship between the body (matter) and the mind (spirit)?" According to Descartes, the human body is a perfect machine, following natural laws. But man also has a mind which interacts or operates independently from the body. Descartes' dualism separated mind and matter (body) into two great, mutually exclusive and mutually exhaustive divisions of the universe. In his search for the simplest component of truth, he said, "I think; therefore, I am".

To the question, "What am I?" Descartes answered that I am a thinking, conscious being for as long as I am thinking. His *epitaph[58] was a most Socratic motto: "No man is harmed by death, save he who is known too well by all the world, and has not yet learned to know himself".

Throughout the West, Descartes' view of the nature of the mind is still the most widespread view among educated people who are not philosophers. Descartes has also been called the father of modern Rationalism and the father of modern western philosophy.

As Aristotle challenged some of Plato's Idealism, Descartes' contemporaries challenged his Rationalism. The major disagreement came from the 17th and 18th century

Empiricists who concurred with Aristotle that all ideas are the result of sense experiences grounded in the physical world. *John Locke[59], *David Hume[60] and *George Berkeley[61] were the most influential Empiricists of their time. Because all three men were British, modern day Empiricism is sometimes called British Empiricism.

2. JOHN LOCKE (1632—1704)

If Descartes, the mathematician, was the modern father of Rationalism, then Locke, once a medical student, was the modern father of Empiricism. Both men asked the same questions: "Are there innate ideas?" and "Is the world really the way we perceive it?" However, their answers to these questions radically differed.

First and foremost, the Empiricist claims that man's physical senses are the only source of knowledge. Locke's empirical answer to the question, "Are there innate ideas?" was, "There is nothing in the mind... except what was first in the senses". At birth, the mind is a blank tablet, much like a classroom black board is blank until a person writes on it. Locke believed that ideas come from sense experiences and are processed in the mind through thinking. Locke combined thinking, reasoning, believing and doubting into a single concept which he named "reflection".

Locke's concept of the blank mind represented one side of a deep division in western social thought which is concerned with how much knowledge is given *a priori* (from the individual's reason) and how much is learned *a posteriori* (from the individual's sensory experience). If humans only derive ideas from their experiences, then a child's environment is responsible for shaping the child. On the other hand, if the Rationalists are correct about innate ideas and concepts, then the child is also responsible for his actions. This continuing debate is often summarized as "Nurture" versus "Nature".

Then Locke asked his next question, "Is the world really the way a person perceives it?" His answer was both "Yes" and "No". "Yes", the world does consist of primary qualities, such as motion and weight, which can be measured objectively. Therefore, primary qualities are truly the way they are perceived (Correspondence Theory). The world also consists of secondary qualities, such as colors and flavors which are subjective and depend on the individual. Locke's answer was also "No"—the world is not as it is *perceived[62] when these secondary, subjective qualities are analyzed.

Like many other philosophers who preceded and followed him, Locke was not always consistent in his views. In addition to his contributions to Empiricism, Locke is also famous for his political views which relied less on the senses and more on reasoning. He advocated the equality of the sexes; the separation of powers within a government; and the natural rights of man. The American Declaration of Independence reflects Locke's arguments for the natural rights of man. The United States' Constitution and national and state governments are organized by the separation of powers: executive, legislative and judicial branches.

3. DAVID HUME (1711—1776)

Hume, a Scot, was the most important Empiricist of his age. He was skeptical about all we claim to know. He began by asking, "How do humans experience the everyday world?" He argued that people have two types of perception: impressions and ideas. Based on sense experiences, impressions are original and immediate. Reflections, or reasoning processes, are an imitation of impressions and occur later. To Hume, a true idea was one which could be measured. He opposed all ideas and appearances that could not be traced to sense perceptions, including religious knowledge. Hume's philosophy broke the final link between medieval faith and contemporary knowledge.

Hume agreed with Locke that a child has no preconceived opinions. A child perceives the world as it is, based on his experiences. Since the child has not yet developed habits, the child is more open-minded than an adult. The concept of open mindedness is critical to understanding Hume's important analysis of the law of causation.

The law of causation means that everything that happens has a cause. The expectation of one thing following another is a universal human characteristic. For example, it appears that lightening causes thunder because thunder follows lightening. Today, scientists claim that light travels faster than sound which is why lightening appears to occur first. Hume further argued that both thunder and lightening are the results of a third event, electric discharge. The expectation of one thing following another only exists in our minds and is the result of our habits. In other words, the laws of nature are what we expect, rather than what is reasonable.

Hume did recognize the existence of unbreakable and eternal natural laws, but, because these laws cannot be experienced through our senses, wrong conclusions could be made. After Hume, scientists could not say with certainty that one event causes another event. The best claim is that one event probably causes another one. Probability became critical in scientific discourse. The mathematical field of statistics has become one way to describe probability in a cause-and-effect relationship. To this day, the agenda for a discussion of the causal relationship is the one set by David Hume.

4. GEORGE BERKELEY (1685-1753)

Berkeley was a religious leader who decided that the materialism of his day was a threat to the Christian way of life. He agreed with Locke and Hume that knowledge is based on experience, and material objects only exist in their physical forms. He differed from them about the source of ideas. Locke and Hume said that ideas come from the mind's reflection on the physical world; Berkeley argued that ideas come from the mind of a supernatural *All-Perceiver[63]. Since the human mind can think of objects that human senses cannot perceive, such as an object hidden in a box, there must be another source of ideas. Ideas come from other ideas and the minds that possess these ideas. All things exist in the eternal mind of the All-Perceiver. In this way, Berkeley attempted to reconcile Empiricism and religion.

In spite of their differences, Locke, Hume and Berkeley agreed that the foundation of all scientific knowledge is sense experience. Unlike Descartes and the Rationalists, they argued that reason is secondary to sense-experience. To the Empiricists it was "Matter over Mind".

5. THE MODERN *PARADIGM[64]

Earlier, philosophers focused on the question, "What?" They asked what was the nature of the world around them and what caused the world to be that way. To explain causation, thinkers often claimed that a supernatural source or *deity[65] had a purpose for the world. Examples would be Aristotle's fourth and "Final Cause", Aquinas' "God", and Berkeley's "All Perceiver". When thinkers try to explain events in the physical world in terms of goals or purposes, this is called a *teleological[66] explanation.

Beginning with the Renaissance, and certainly after Hume, most western philosophers no longer asked what caused the world to act as it does. Instead, they asked "How does the world act?" They replaced teleological explanations with mechanical explanations. For example, the teleological explanation to the question, "Why does it rain?" might be to grow plants for animals to eat. The mechanistic explanation might be that the rising air could no longer hold the moisture. Given the seemingly universal application of Newton's laws of motion, perhaps it is not surprising that thinkers studying physical objects adopted this paradigm before those studying human beings.

V. Modern Philosophy

The 18th century is sometimes called *the Age of Enlightenment[67] or the Age of Reason. It was the last period before powerful political and social upheavals gave new directions to western thought. Several famous philosophers, mostly French, contributed to the Enlightenment, including *Montesquieu[68] (1689 – 1755), *Voltaire[69] (1694 – 1778), and *Rousseau[70] (1712 – 1778). These men wrote about Nature, Rationalism and human rights based on natural law.

1. IMMANUEL KANT (1724 – 1804)

The most influential Enlightenment philosopher was the German thinker, *Immanuel Kant[71]. He combined elements of both Rationalism and Empiricism into one new comprehensive system to explain how humans know the world.

Kant agreed with the Empiricists that knowledge came from sensory experiences. However, he did not believe that sensory experiences were recorded on a blank mind. Instead, he agreed with the Rationalists that the mind had *a priori* knowledge which influenced the interpretation of sensory experiences. For example, humans universally interpret their sensory experiences in terms of space and time. Kant claimed that both space and time are *a priori* categories imposed on sensory experience by the human mind. They do not exist in the physical world, but they do exist as categories of perception in the human mind.

If human beings cannot perceive the world, other than through their perceptions grounded in a particular location at a particular period of time, Kant had difficulty answering his question, "How can we know truth about the world?" Kant argued that sensory experiences can be true knowledge since the mind's categories both shape and conform to these experiences. As long as people recognize the structure of the human mind and restrict themselves to sensory experience, they may be able to achieve provable knowledge. This was Kant's first category of knowledge.

"What happens when both reason and experience fail?" he then asked. Kant believed that God, free choice, and immortality probably exist, since they are all necessary for mortality to exist. This was Kant's second category of knowledge which could never be proven; this knowledge could only be taken on faith.

Because Kant believed that the law of causality was one of the *a priori* categories of the human mind, he differed with David Hume. Hume claimed that humans could only achieve a degree of probability in determining the cause of a given event. Kant believed that all change has a cause and that the law of causality was eternal and absolute. Human reason perceives everything that happens as cause-and-effect, because the law of causality is inherent and innate in us. Since the law of causality is known *a priori* in a person's mind, it precedes experience.

According to Kant, humans have a dual nature. They are subject to the laws of causality, but they are free to make choices because they have reasoning ability. Kant argued that people must assume the existence of God and behave morally. He is famous for his *"categorical imperative"[72]: "Act as if the *maxim[73] from which you act were to become through your will a universal law". If a person is kind, then he has chosen to act as though kindness should be required of everyone. If a person steals, then he has chosen to act as though stealing should be required of everyone.

Kant's words on morality still resonate today. "Morality. . . is the only thing that has dignity. Skill and diligence in work have a market price; wit, lively imagination and humor have a fancy price; but fidelity to promises and kindness have an *intrinsic worth[74]."

2. *ROMANTICISM[75] (1780 – 1840)

The Romantic Age was a reaction to the Enlightenment and to the bloody French Revolution (1789 – 1794). Although no great philosopher spoke for this movement, it was very influential on writers, artists and musicians. The Romantic Movement allowed greater exploration of feelings, imagination, and ideas from other cultures. Now, the individual was free to interpret life in his own way, and artists created their own realities. One characteristic of Romanticism was the yearning for Nature and Nature's mysteries. Some Romantics considered that the natural and spiritual worlds were actually the same thing. It was the duty of the Romantic to experience life or dream himself away from it.

Two types of Romanticism dominated: Universal Romanticism and National Romanticism. The Universal Romantics were mainly interested in love, Nature and art. The National Romantics focused on the history, language and culture of "the people". In this way, folklore told by ordinary people became part of the national literature.

3. GEORG HEGEL (1770 – 1831)

The philosophy of the German thinker *Georg Hegel[76] is extremely difficult to understand. His two most important contributions were his treatment of the *paradoxical[77] nature of change and the concept of *dialectical[78] change.

Since Plato, western philosophy struggled with a paradox: change is the only reality (Heraclitus), and change is only an illusion (Parmenides). Both of these views seemed to be true, and both seemed to contradict each other. Solving this paradox is important to explain the changes of history, and the extent to which the mind affects the physical world and history. Hegel was particularly interested in the questions, "How do the two views of change interact?" "How do Mind and Matter interconnect?" and "How could that which is historical be real in any universal sense?"

Unlike his predecessors, Hegel did not attempt to develop universal laws for what man can know about the world, because he did not think eternal truths existed. Instead, Hegel developed a method to answer the questions he asked about change, mind-matter, and the reality of history. His method is called the dialectical process.

According to Hegel, all philosophical theories are correct, at least in their historical time. Hegel viewed the history of philosophy like a flowing river which constantly changes. Thoughts are imbedded in past traditions as well as in the prevailing physical conditions. Therefore, a thought is not correct forever, but it is correct in relationship to its historical context. Like the flowing river, human knowledge is constantly expanding and progressing. Humanity is moving toward greater rationality and freedom. Only the historical process can determine what is most reasonable.

The historical process is dialectical. An idea existed, and because it existed, its opposite idea was created. The two ideas fuse and produce a third idea. Hegel called this triad of elements *"thesis[79], antithesis and *synthesis[80]". Pure Reason (thesis) is in opposition to Nothing (antithesis). The two come together as Becoming (synthesis). In other words, a thought is usually based on previous thoughts. When the new thought (thesis) is proposed, it is contradicted by another thought (antithesis). Tension which occurs between the two is resolved by a third thought which *accommodates[81] the best of both points of view (synthesis). Then the process begins again.

Hegel took Plato's Idealism to its logical conclusion in an attempt to demonstrate that the real is the ideal. Not only does the Ideal exist as an absolute, but it also exists in the physical world. The changing physical world is the very process by which the Absolute Idea realizes itself in history. Hegel's dialectic and his attempt to resolve the paradox between what changes and what is eternal are important to understanding western philosophy.

Hegel influenced some important thinkers who followed him. *Karl Marx[82] used Hegel's concept of dialectical materialism, and *Soren Kierkegaard[83] borrowed the idea of paradox, although both men hated Hegel's philosophy.

Ⅵ. Modern Philosophical Trends

Hegel was the last western philosopher to develop a comprehensive system. Generally, thinkers after Hegel limited the kinds of questions they asked. The result was that they focused on narrower, more specialized issues.

Modern western thought has been influenced by several great thinkers who, although not categorized as philosophers, have radically changed the assumptions made by philosophers. *Charles Darwin[84] (1809 – 1882), an English biologist, demonstrated that human beings were members of the animal kingdom. Karl Marx (1818 – 1883), a German writer, profoundly changed the way thinkers view the ideal political state. *Sigmund Freud[85] (1856 – 1939), an Austrian *cognitive[86] *psychologist[87] and his colleagues refuted any possibility of a new born child possessing a blank mind. *Max Planck[88] (1858 – 1947), a German Nobel Prize winning physicist, developed the *quantum[89] theory which mathematically described the structure and behavior of atoms and molecules. Albert Einstein (1879 – 1955), a German-Swiss-American, demonstrated a whole new set of universal laws that portrayed a universe very differently from the mechanical universe described in Newton's laws.

1. EXISTENTIALISM

Modern philosophical trends were dominated by *Existentialism[90] and *Positivism[91]. Existentialism, a philosophy concerned with an individual's moral actions, is a collective term for several philosophical movements. Soren Kierkegaard (1813 - 1855), a Dane, was the first Existentialist. He argued that the Romantic's idealism and Hegel's dialecticism obscured the individual's responsibility for his own life. He asked, "What kinds of truths are relevant?" His answer was those truths which have meaning to a particular individual. Meaning requires action. The individual experiences his own existence when he acts. Unlike the early Greeks, for whom knowledge meant happiness, Kierkegaard argued that as an individual became more aware of the gap between his actual existence and eternal values, the individual would fall into despair. For Kierkegaard, truth was subjective, individual and personal. Objective truths, such as mathematical statements, are irrelevant to each person's existence.

*Friedrich Nietzsche[92] (1844 - 1900), a German, believed that moral action should come from a strong superhero. He influenced Adolf Hitler (1889 - 1945) with his ideas that the weak should not hamper the life force of the strongest and that "God is dead".

*Henri Bergson[93] (1859 - 1941), a French philosopher who won the Nobel Prize for literature, believed that Reason perceives the material world, but Intuition could perceive the life force which pervades the world. He is considered to be an irrationalist who stressed intuition and feeling. He believed that life is a flow, an undivided process which is only endured, not understood.

*Jean-Paul Sartre[94] (1905 - 1986) was a French Existentialist who claimed that man is the only living creature that is conscious of its own existence. Existence takes precedence over all other experiences. Sartre did not believe in the supernatural, the Ideal or externally derived values. Each person must make choices without any frame of reference in an alien, meaningless world. Because humans have freedom, they must constantly make choices and accept the consequences of their choices. Because there are no external values and norms, an individual's choices become more significant. To Sartre, excuses, such as "human nature", are not acceptable. It is imperative that the individual decides what is meaningful by selecting what is significant. Sartre defined a philosophical question as one that each generation and each individual must ask over and over again. Sartre was nominated for the Nobel Prize for Literature for his novels and plays. He declined on the grounds that it would make his writings too influential!

2. POSITIVISM

Unlike the Existentialists who were concerned with meaning and morality, the Positivists were concerned with Nature and science. They searched for common elements among the various branches of science. To do this, the Positivists "reduced" one field of science to another, such as biology to chemistry or chemistry to physics.

All Positivists were Radical Empiricists who opposed all forms of dualism, especially mind-body, matter-spirit and *physical- metaphysical[95] debates. For example, *Ernst Mach[96] (1838 - 1916), an Austrian physicist and philosopher, argued that phenomena are neutral, having neither physical nor mental status. He claimed that science should only describe phenomena that could be perceived through the senses.

Analysis of the relationship between logic and language intrigued some modern Positivists. In the spirit of Descartes, *Bertrand Russell[97] (1872 - 1970), an English mathematician, philosopher and writer, developed the theory of logical atomism. First applying the theory to mathematics and later to logic, Russell argued that concepts and arguments are constructed of "atomic", or smallest propositions, that have their roots in the world of experience. In collaboration with Alfred North Whitehead (1861 - 1947), another English mathematician, Russell wrote a monumental three-volume work titled *Principia Mathematica*. They argued that mathematics can be reducible to pure logic. Since logic had to be a rigorous formal system, the language of logicians had to be analyzed.

Relationships between logic and language interested other modern philosophers. *Ludwig Wittgenstein[98] (1889 - 1951), an Austrian-Englishman, was an engineer who became a philosopher. He developed a theory to explain how language, mind and reality are related. According to Wittgenstein's Picture Theory, the essential character of every sentence is painting a picture of the real world. Anything that we can say in words or pictures will depend upon other things which cannot be said. Since these unspoken things can only be shown, they are taught by example, not by lecture. Wittgenstein did not reject the existence of metaphysical qualities. Like Kant, he said that we cannot know some ideas by direct physical experience. However, unlike Kant, he argued that many problems in philosophy are not problems related to ideas or sensory experience, but to language.

He inspired *the "Vienna Circle"[99], a group of influential Austrian scientists, mathematicians and philosophers who founded the movement known as Logical Positivism. Their goal was to purge philosophy of all speculations about issues that could not be established by empirical investigations. They applied the Verification Principle: statements can be true, false or meaningless. True and false statements must be verifiable. The conditions which establish the truth or falsity of the statement must be able to be stated. Otherwise, the statement is meaningless. For example, since statements about God or *ethics[100] cannot be experientially verified, they are meaningless. Critics responded that the verification principle was too narrow. Eventually, the more radical elements of Logical Positivism were modified or abandoned, although the Positivists' ideas were important in the continuing debate about language and philosophy.

During the early half of the 20th century, two approaches to philosophy and language emerged. One approach to achieving a language for philosophers was to create an ideal language which would express the truths of science exactly. Since language consists of the relationship between *syntax[101] and *semantics[102], the relationship between the two took on philosophical importance. The extreme view was that all philosophical problems involve semantics, the meanings of terms. Advocates believed that if an ideal language could be developed, scientific and mathematical terms could be expressed without confusion. Any idea that could not be expressed in this ideal language would be meaningless.

A second approach claimed that such an ideal language was impossible to construct. Instead, philosophers should analyze how philosophy is expressed in language that is currently used. *Proponents[103] of this approach were not concerned with analyzing particular languages, such as Chinese or English, but rather with analyzing existing languages in general. Like those who hoped to develop an ideal language, the purpose of this analytic movement was to avoid the confusion the use of language had traditionally caused in philosophical discourse.

Of the two branches of modern philosophy, Existentialism was more prevalent on the European mainland, and Positivism was more prevalent in England and the United States. Two trends within American linguistic thought have separated the United States from European philosophy. Some American linguists agree with *the Sapir-Whorf hypothesis[104], based on the work of two linguists who studied Native American languages. This hypothesis claims that "language influences thought". Many of the attempts to impose favorable names for people are made by those who agree with this concept. For example, people with a "low intellect" might be called "mentally handicapped". Other American linguists agree with *Noam Chomsky[105] (1928 –   ) and those who view language as an innate product of the mind, somewhat like Kant's *a priori* knowledge. Many of these linguists consider the Mind to be a machine that is a product of the material nature of the human brain.

Such approaches are countered by philosophers such as *Jacques Derrida[106] (1930 –   ), the French philosopher who argues that language does not refer to the real world at all, but only to other language. Therefore, a single statement has many meanings, depending upon the reader.

3. PRAGMATISM IN THE UNITED STATES

As a relatively young country, America did not have a history of philosophy. Instead, it became a "melting pot" for the philosophies of the world. However, Western European philosophy dominated, probably because the majority of immigrants came from that region. America did contribute one important idea called *Pragmatism[107].

*Charles Peirce[108] (1839 – 1940) was never a part of the Logical Positivist movement, but he shared the Positivists' concern for logic, meaning and the philosophy of science. He named his theories "Pragmatism". Pragmatism defines meaning as the total observable consequences of a course of action. Peirce was an Empiricist who rejected Descartes' Rationalism. Instead, Peirce argued that ideas are clear only when we show which actions establish their meaning. Unless words and phrases can be empirically tested, they are meaningless.

Peirce developed four methods people use to hold onto their beliefs, even when these beliefs are in doubt. First, people cling to their beliefs by refusing to consider alternatives or counter-arguments. Peirce called this method *tenacity[109]. Second, people believe what persons in authority believe. He labeled this authority. Third, people *appeal to reason[110] in the manner of Plato, Descartes, and Hegel. He named this method *speculation[111]. Fourth, people use the scientific method. Peirce believed that this method was acceptable because scientific statements could be empirically tested.

*William James[112] (1842 – 1910) adopted Peirce's pragmatism as a way to investigate beliefs and theories. "Does it make any difference whether you do or do not believe it?" was James' question about any claim. If it makes no difference, then the belief is meaningless. A meaningful belief must always have consequences to life and action. The truth of a theory means that it "works", and expectations are fulfilled.

Earlier, Descartes, Locke and others adhered to *the Correspondence Theory[113] of truth. This theory claimed that a true statement is one that "corresponds" or copies a fact. James disagreed with this definition. He claimed that such a relationship is static and in opposition to the pragmatic view based on life and action.

Pragmatism influenced other disciplines in America, including education. *John Dewey[114] (1859 – 1952) was a controversial American educator because he implemented his version of Pragmatism in the education system.

Pragmatism has had many interpretations. Its overall effect was to support the scientific method of understanding the world. Pragmatism helped to move the direction of science to practical goals. Increasingly in the United States, the major purpose of science is not to develop new theories; it is to develop new technologies.

The philosophies of the latter half of the 20th century are too recent to make a definitive judgment, even those that already seem to be ephemeral. Great ideas can permeate every aspect of human thought and endeavor. They take a long time to do so, and an even longer time is necessary for their influence to be established.

Ⅶ. Summary

Historically in the West, science and philosophy were one and the same. The primary concern of these philosophers/scientists was "Truth". The search for truth led them to ask questions about the phenomena of knowledge. The basic assumption was that reality exists. No matter what human beings think, reality is what it is. Skeptics denied that knowledge of reality is possible, because individuals see and understand the world differently.

Beginning with the Renaissance, philosophers/scientists began to ask the question, "How?" rather than "What?" Once the basic question changed, the scientific method dominated the discussion. The use of the senses was required in all scientific investigations. The philosophical problem then became the correct use of the senses.

To avoid the additional confusion of ordinary language in discussions, results of scientific experimentation were stated in mathematical terms. However, the use of mathematics as a universal language caused new philosophical problems.

During the 19th century, science became fragmented into special fields, such as physics, chemistry and biology. Each of the sciences developed its own set of questions and its own methods for searching for answers. It was also the time when the last comprehensive system of philosophy was constructed. Systematic philosophical theories were replaced by studies of specific issues, including Existentialism, Positivism and Pragmatism. The end result was that philosophy and science separated into two distinct fields of knowledge.

By the beginning of the 21st century, most westerners were interested in the useful and the practical which would make their lives easier. The average person had difficulty making the connection between universal questions and their everyday world. Nevertheless, they are the recipients of thousands of years of philosophical speculations and controversies. These speculations and controversies provide a foundation that encourages an individual approach to morality; an investigator's approach to nature; and a skeptical approach to knowledge and authority.

As for the philosophers themselves, the American philosopher, Thomas Nagel, cautioned them in his book, *The View from Nowhere*, "Even those who regard philosophy as real and important know that they are at a particular, and, we may hope, early stage of its development, limited by their own primitive intellectual capacities, and relying on the partial insights of a few great figures of the past. As we judge their results to be mistaken in fundamental ways, so we must assume that even the best efforts of our own time will come to seem blind eventually".

Study Questions

1. How did the ancient Greeks change the history of western philosophy?
2. Why has Plato been called one of the world's greatest philosophers?
3. What are the differences between a teleological and mechanical explanation of the universe? Why did mathematics became the language of science?
4. Characterize the three ages of western philosophy: the Age of Antiquity, the Middle Ages, and the Modern Age.
5. Compare and contrast Rationalism and Empiricism.
6. Why do we study philosophy?

Selected Bibliography

Gaarder, Jostein. *Sophie's World*. NY: Farrar, Strauss and Giroux, 1991.
Irwin, John P. "Philosophical Foundations of Western Civilization". Unpublished manuscript, 1998.
Oxford History of Western Philosophy. Oxford: Oxford University Press, 1994.
Russell, Bertrand. *A History of Western Philosophy*. NY: 1961.

注　　释①

〔1〕经验主义的。
〔2〕苏美尔(西南亚一地区,在现今伊拉克境内,公元前4000至3000年间有繁盛的文明)。
〔3〕美索不达米亚(西南亚一地区,底格里斯河和幼发拉底河之间,曾为阿卡德、亚述、巴比伦等文化的所在地)。
〔4〕腓尼基(地中海东岸一古国,相当于现今的黎巴嫩及叙利亚沿海地区)。
〔5〕唯理论,理性主义。
〔6〕爱因斯坦,相对论的创立者;1921年获诺贝尔物理奖。
〔7〕霍金,英国理论物理学家。
〔8〕泰利斯,古希腊哲学家,数学家,天文学家,米利都学派创始人。
〔9〕形而上学。
〔10〕阿那克西曼德,古希腊哲学家,科学家。
〔11〕用……来说明,以……观点来考虑。
〔12〕毕达哥拉斯,希腊哲学家,数学家,天文学家,毕达哥拉斯教派创始人,对西方的数学

---

① 本书所有注释所解释的对象均介于注释编号前的＊号和该注释编号之间。——编者注

与哲学发展有巨大影响。
〔13〕勾股定理。
〔14〕赫拉克利特,古希腊哲学家,认为宇宙处于不断的对立统一的变化中,相信火是万物的本原。
〔15〕静态的。
〔16〕巴门尼德,古希腊哲学家,著有诗体哲学著作《论自然》。
〔17〕德谟克利特,古希腊哲学家,原子论创始者。
〔18〕材料。
〔19〕质子。
〔20〕中子。
〔21〕孔子信徒。
〔22〕道家学说的信徒。
〔23〕怀疑论者,不可知论者。
〔24〕认识论。
〔25〕智者派,诡辩派,通常教授辩论术、修辞等知识;他们的论点影响后来的道德相对论,因而常常不被人们赞同。
〔26〕罗马帝国(公元前 27 年到公元 476 年罗马统治下的广大地域,势力范围东达美索不达米亚,西至伊比利亚半岛,北部直到莱茵河及多瑙河流域,向南延伸到埃及和地中海沿岸地区)。
〔27〕苏格拉底,古希腊哲学家,用发问的方法寻求真理,暴露谬误,探讨哲学和伦理等方面的问题。
〔28〕柏拉图(428—347B.C.),古希腊哲学家,创建雅典学园;其思想体系对基督教哲学和西方哲学有深远的影响。
〔29〕实证主义。
〔30〕理念论,始于柏拉图,他认为理念是唯一的认知对象。
〔31〕寓言。
〔32〕二元论的。
〔33〕怀特海(1861—1947),英国哲学家,数学家。
〔34〕亚里士多德(385—323B.C.),古希腊哲学家和科学家,柏拉图的学生,创建雅典逍遥学派。
〔35〕三段论法。
〔36〕千年。
〔37〕地球中心说。
〔38〕开创性的,有重大影响的。
〔39〕希腊和罗马时代。
〔40〕(尤指中世纪以前之)古代。
〔41〕耶稣基督(基督教的创始人,传道时间为公元 28—30 年间)。
〔42〕文艺复兴(14—17 世纪欧洲之古希腊文学、艺术、思想的重新发现与繁荣)。
〔43〕神学。
〔44〕圣奥古斯丁,著有《上帝之城》、《忏悔录》等书,其思想主导后来的西方神学。
〔45〕圣阿奎那,意大利哲学家,神学家,经院哲学的代表人物。
〔46〕使基督教化。
〔47〕亚里士多德的生前讲稿,经后人整理出版的自然哲学和自然科学著作。
〔48〕世俗的。
〔49〕经院哲学。
〔50〕天文学家。
〔51〕哥白尼,波兰天文学家,他提出的日心说最终推翻了地心说。
〔52〕伽利略,意大利天文学家,物理学家,现代科学的奠基人之一。
〔53〕开普勒,德国天文学家,发现行星运动三大定律。
〔54〕牛顿,英国数学家,物理学家,爱因斯坦之前对理论物理学最有影响的科学家。
〔55〕培根,英国政治家和哲学家,其激进的哲学思想在其死后的一个世纪仍影响巨大。
〔56〕霍布斯,英国哲学家,唯物论者。
〔57〕笛卡尔,法国哲学家,数学家,现代哲学之父。
〔58〕墓志铭。
〔59〕洛克(1632—1704),英国哲学家,经验论和政治自由主义奠基人。著有《政府论》(1690),反对"天赋君权";在《人类理解论》(1690)中提出所有知识由知觉经历而来。
〔60〕休谟(1711—1776),苏格兰哲学家,经济学家,历史学家,不可知论代表人物。
〔61〕贝克莱(1685—1753),爱尔兰唯心主义哲学家,主教。否认物质的存在,认为存在即被感知。
〔62〕感知。
〔63〕全知者。
〔64〕程式,规范。
〔65〕神性。
〔66〕宇宙目的论的。
〔67〕启蒙运动(欧洲 17 世纪和 18 世纪文化思想运动,深受笛卡儿、洛克、牛顿等人的思想影响,崇尚理性,认为理性是人类知识和进步的核心)。
〔68〕孟德斯鸠,法国政治哲学家。
〔69〕伏尔泰,法国作家,剧作家,诗人,启蒙运动

的领导人物。
〔70〕卢梭,法国哲学家,作家,相信人性本善。
〔71〕康德,德国哲学家,在《纯粹理性批判》(1781)中指出人类思维不可能证实、否定或科学地论证现实的最终本质;他的哲学思想在黑格尔身上得到很大的继承。
〔72〕绝对命令。
〔73〕行为准则,基本原理。
〔74〕本身价值。
〔75〕浪漫主义。18世纪开始的艺术与文化运动,抵制理性主义;尊崇灵感、非理性;代表人物有作曲家舒伯特、舒曼,诗人华兹华斯、雪莱、济慈等。
〔76〕黑格尔,德国哲学家,马克思在他的基础上发展出唯物主义辩证法。
〔77〕自相矛盾的。
〔78〕辩证的。
〔79〕正题。
〔80〕合题。
〔81〕容纳。
〔82〕马克思(1818—1883),德国政治哲学家、经济学家;著有《共产党宣言》《资本论》等。
〔83〕克尔凯郭尔(1813—1855),丹麦哲学家,存在主义先驱。
〔84〕达尔文,英国自然主义历史学家,地理学家,自然选择进化论的倡导者。
〔85〕弗洛伊德,奥地利精神病学家,精神分析学家,精神分析学奠基人。
〔86〕以实际经验为依据的。
〔87〕心理学家。
〔88〕普朗克,德国物理学家,量子力学的开创者。
〔89〕量子论。
〔90〕存在主义,强调个人作为有自由意识而存在的个体的哲学流派。
〔91〕实证主义。
〔92〕尼采,德国哲学家,轻视基督教,提倡超人哲学。
〔93〕柏格森,法国哲学家,二元论思想,抨击科学唯物主义,反对达尔文的进化论。
〔94〕萨特,法国哲学家,小说家,剧作家,批评家,存在主义的主要发言人。
〔95〕机械的,形而上学的。
〔96〕马赫,奥地利物理学家和哲学家,认为世界的所有知识源于感觉。
〔97〕罗素,英国数学家,哲学家,逻辑学家,社会改革家。
〔98〕维特根斯坦,英国哲学家,对逻辑实证主义和语言哲学有卓越的贡献。
〔99〕维也纳学会。
〔100〕伦理学,道德学。
〔101〕句法。
〔102〕语义。
〔103〕支持者。
〔104〕萨皮尔-沃尔夫假说。
〔105〕乔姆斯基,美国理论语言学家,政治活动家,转换生成语法奠基人。
〔106〕德里达,法国哲学家,评论家,解构主义先驱。
〔107〕实用主义。
〔108〕皮尔斯,美国哲学家,逻辑学家,实用主义奠基人之一,对当代符号学和语义学的发展有重大影响。
〔109〕坚持,顽强。
〔110〕诉诸于理论。
〔111〕推测。
〔112〕詹姆斯,美国哲学家,心理学家,实用主义创始人之一,心理学方面介绍意识流的概念。
〔113〕符合说,认为一切和对象相符合的就是真理。
〔114〕杜威,美国实用主义哲学家,教育家,将知识定义为成功的实践。

CHAPTER 2 GEOGRAPHY OF THE UNITED KINGDOM

Dr. Carol W. Pollard

I. Introduction

1. NAMES

The United Kingdom of Great Britain and Northern Ireland is generally referred to as the United Kingdom or the UK. Geographically, most of the UK is located on the British *Isles[1]: the main island, Britain, containing England, Wales, and Scotland; part of the Irish island; and a host of nearby smaller islands. Politically, the UK consists of the separate political *entities[2] of England, Scotland, Wales and Northern Ireland, as well as the many islands around Britain and the few remnants of the British Empire, such as *the British Virgin Islands[3] or the British region of *Antarctica[4]. The United Kingdom is sometimes called Britain, or Great Britain, although strictly speaking, the terms "Britain" or "British" refer only to the main island, not Ireland. UK Citizens refer to themselves as English, Welsh, Scots or Irish; they take pride in their own regions. If a person's native region is unknown, it is best to refer to a person from the UK as British.

2. LOCATION AND CONSTITUENTS

The British Isles are located off the northwest coast of Europe. They consist of two large islands and 2,000 smaller islands lying between 50 and 60 degrees north *latitude[5]. The island of Britain is crossed by the 0 degree *meridian[6] of *longitude[7]. The 0 degree meridian was established at the original site of * the Royal Greenwich Observatory[8]. "Greenwich" is pronounced "grennich" in modern English. *"Greenwich Mean Time"[9] is the time at *the prime meridian[10].

The islands sit on the European *continental shelf[11], which extends west 160 km beyond Britain. The surrounding seas are shallow, less than 200 m deep, and so provide good conditions for fishing.

The English Channel and the North Sea separate Britain from Europe, and the shallow Irish and *Celtic[12] seas separate Britain and Ireland. The Irish Sea is only 65 m deep. The largest section of the Irish Island belongs to the Republic of Ireland, a separate country. Northern Ireland, the UK portion, occupies only the northeastern corner of the island.

Most of the smaller UK islands are found near western and northern Scotland. These northern islands occur in three main groups, each with its own regional character. The *Hebrides[13], or Western Islands, are formed of old *granite[14], *gneiss[15] and *metamorphic rocks[16] that resist the harsh weather and seas. These rocks are some of the oldest in Europe. *The Orkneys[17], about 70 small islands off northern Scotland, have a mild climate due to the warm water from *the Atlantic Drift Current[18], a branch of *the Gulf Stream[19]. They are a major agricultural area. *The Shetlands[20], about 100 small islands found north of the Orkneys, also have a mild climate, but poorer soil. Being close to *Scandinavia[21], both the Shetlands and the Orkneys have been influenced historically by the *Vikings[22] and *Norse[23] culture.

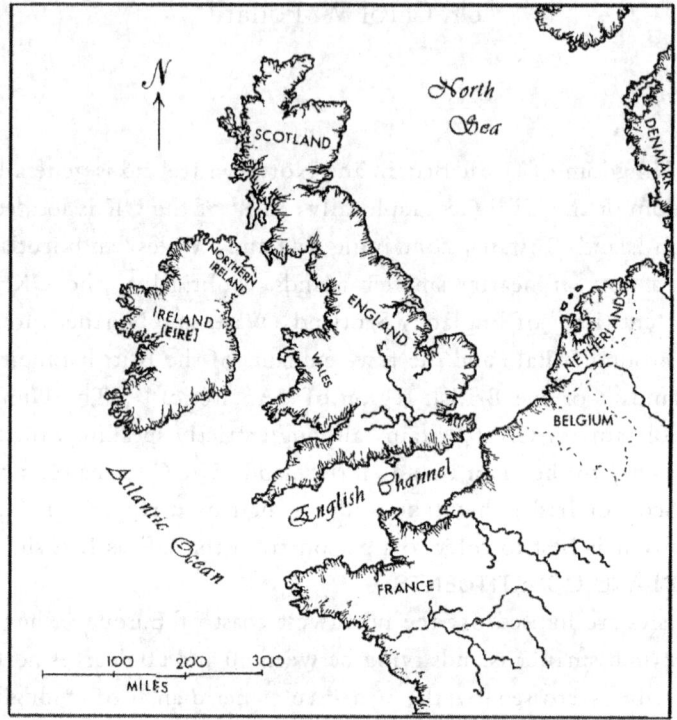

Figure 1　Map of the United Kingdom of Great Britain and Northern Ireland

Southern small islands include the Isle of Angelsey off Wales; *the Scilly Isles[24] off the south west coast of England; and *the Isle of Wight[25] in the English Channel. *The Isle of Man[26] in the Irish Sea and *the Channel Isles[27] near the Coast of France are UK dependencies, not UK members, and have semi-autonomous status. The softer terrain off eastern Britain was eroded by the pounding of the North Sea, so that no islands of any size are found east of Britain.

Ⅱ. General Characteristics of the United Kingdom

1. LAND AREA

The land area of the UK is approximately 242,000 sq km. From the northern point of Scotland to the southern coast of England, the island of Britain measures 1,000 km. Its width varies from 500 to 150 km.

2. CLIMATE

Despite its northern location—southern England is at approximately the same latitude as North China—the UK has a remarkably mild climate. This climate is a gift of the North Atlantic Drift Current, which flows west of the UK. When the temperature rises above 29 degrees centigrade or drops below minus 7 degrees centigrade, the news media report the unusual event. Western winds coming across the Atlantic waters warm Ireland and western Britain in winter and cool them in summer, while eastern winds crossing the European Continent and the cold North Sea bring a raw, damp cold to eastern Britain.

The annual rainfall varies little from year to year, and droughts are rare. Heaviest rains fall in the western uplands. Upland Britain normally receives 1,020 mm of rain per year; much of lowland Britain receives less than 760 mm per year. The wettest areas in the United Kingdom—parts of the Lake District and the eastern Scottish Highlands—receive 2,540 mm per year. The difference between areas can be striking. Mt *Snowdon[28], in Wales, may have ten times the rainfall of Rhyl, an area 40 km to the southeast.

British weather is rather dreary because much of the rain comes in a protracted drizzle, not in heavy showers. Often many days go by without the sun being visible. The loss of sunshine is worse in winter. Because the UK is located in the far north, winter days are short. In January, the southern coast of England averages only two hours of sunshine a day; in north of *Birmingham[29], the average drops to an hour and a half. The opportunity for sunlight improves during the long days of a northern summer. In July, the south coast averages 7 hours of sunlight a day, although northern Britain has less than 5 hours. The lack of sunshine is due to overcast skies rather than to fog. The infamous London *"pea soup fogs"[30] of the past were really smog caused by pollution rather than by *meteorological[31] conditions. Despite strict pollution measures, London still has mild fog for about 45 days a year, mainly in January and February. Most ports in the UK have 15 to 30 foggy days each year, which may halt sea traffic for two or more days.

3. MOUNTAINS

UK mountains are not high by world standards. *Ben Nevis[32] in Scotland, the highest peak in the UK, reaches only 1,343 meters. The highest in Wales, *Gwynedd[33], is lower, only 1,085 meters; the highest in England, Scafell Pike in the Lake District, is 978 meters. The highest point in Northern Ireland, Silieve Donard is 852 meters. The mountainous regions along the west coast of Britain were formed earliest. Because they received moisture from the Atlantic, they were the most heavily *glaciated[34]. Spectacular landscapes resulted in the northwest portions of all three regions of Britain. These mountains attract many climbers and tourists each year. Farther east, the mountains were not as severely cut by glacial erosions; instead, they were scraped and rounded, providing excellent terrain for hiking and sheep *rearing[35].

Glaciers and continuing heavy rains have removed the soil and *limestone[36] cover from the rocks of all of the uplands. As a result, upland lakes and pools are *oligotrophic[37]. Recent air pollution has increased the *acidity[38] of rain, intensifying the acidity of upland soil and waters.

4. POPULATION

At the start of the 21st century, the UK population was nearly 61,000,000. The increase is due in part to immigration. The population is aging. In 2008, there were more people over 60 than people under 16. Because the population is located in a small region, the UK contains some of the most densely populated areas of Europe.

5. TRANSPORTATION

The UK possesses an extensive network of highways and railroads. Many ports and airfields serve both inland and foreign commerce.

A) Shipping

The heavily indented coastlines and many short rivers of the British Isles provide many harbors and waterways suitable for boats and small ships. Currently, there are nearly 80 commercial ports with continuing development of port facilities and harbors. Major deep-water ports are located at London, *Liverpool[39], *Glasgow[40], *Southampton[41], *Cardiff[42] and *Belfast[43].

B) Canals and Railroads

With the beginning of *the Industrial Revolution[44] in the mid-8th century, many canals were built, including several linking Britain's west and east coasts. Nearly 2,300 km of inland waterways remain. The smaller canals are now used for pleasure boating since railroads and motorways have replaced them for goods transport. The world's first public railway for passengers and freight opened in the north of England in 1825. During the 19th century, railway lines were extended to all parts of the UK. In the 20th century, the smaller routes were supplanted by motorways. Today there are about 17,000 km of railways. Major passenger routes linking the principal cities of England, Scotland and Wales are served by trains traveling at 200 km per hour, with at least one train per hour on most routes. Service to smaller cities is slower and less frequent. In 1994, *the Chunnel[45] opened. A major engineering achievement, this *Anglo-French[46] railway tunnel under the English Channel links England with France. By providing a reliable connection to Europe, the Chunnel has helped to strengthen commercial ties to the European Continent. Previously, shipping depended on ferries, which were sometimes prevented from sailing by storms in the Channel or the North Sea.

C) Roads and Motorways

The Romans built the first highways in Britain during the first to fourth centuries A.D. These well-engineered roads, designed to move soldiers rapidly, remained the best built roads in Britain for over 1,500 years. During the nineteenth century, well-drained roads surfaced with gravel or crushed stone became common. In 2005, there were 388,006 km of paved roads, with 3,520 km of high-speed motorways or limited-access, divided highways. As a result, more freight and passengers move by road than by rail. Cars and lorries in the UK have the driver's seat on the right-hand side of the car and drive on the left-hand side of the road, unlike vehicles in Europe and America. This causes some problems to overseas visitors and to companies shipping goods between the UK and Europe by ferry.

D) Airports

As of the start of the 21st century, the U.K. had nearly 60 airports with scheduled flights. There were 11 heliports. The London airports handled 140 million passengers in 2007; the regional airports handled 101 million. Increasing passenger traffic and heightened security measures have created long queues and delays. *Heathrow[47] one of the three main London airports, is one of the busiest international airports in the world.

6. PIPELINES AND TELECOMMUNICATIONS

An extensive network of pipelines is used to transport petroleum products and natural gas. Almost every home or business is connected to the technologically advanced telecommunications system. The system uses a mix of buried cables, microwave and optical fiber systems, supplemented by satellite ground stations for international communications. Most households have television sets, which are served by several government-operated channels and a variety of commercial broadcasters using ground-based and satellite transmitters.

7. INDUSTRY AND AGRICULTURE

In general, the economy has shifted from manufacturing (now 18% of the workforce) to service industries (80%). The UK is self-sufficient in energy through the discoveries of North Sea oil and natural gas, and exploiting nuclear power and water power. Both water and air pollutions are major concerns in all areas of the country. Major efforts are being made to reduce pollutants; polluting firms are being required to pay for anti-pollutant measures, although this policy is not always successful. Still, by 2007, the U.K. had met its greenhouse emissions target under the Kyoto Protocol and significantly reduced the amount of industrial and commercial waste sent to landfill sites.

The UK is not self-sufficient in food, although it is a food-exporter as well as importer. Only 23.2% of the land is arable, but it is worked by one of the most efficient systems of agriculture in the European Union. The agricultural workforce (1.4% of the population) is involved in food and forestry, mainly in fishing, cattle and sheep rearing, forestry, as well as grain, potato, *rapeseed[48] and sugar *beet[49] production. Southern lowlands in England, Scotland, Wales and Northern Ireland are main agricultural sites.

The European Community has designated over thirty areas in the UK as Environmentally Sensitive Areas (ESAs); in an ESA, farmers are asked to adopt farming methods to reduce pollution and erosion. Despite such efforts, pollution from organic wastes remains a problem throughout the UK. Most uplands in the UK are defined by the European Community as Less Favored Areas (LFA's). An LFA is an agricultural area with "permanent natural *handicaps[50]" and low crop yields. Such areas may receive more government benefits.

8. WILDLIFE

Plant and animal life in the United Kingdom has been so influenced by human activities that it is difficult to find truly native wildlife although some species still survive. After the glaciers retreated, the land was covered with forests, *mostly deciduous[51]. *Neolithic[52] farmers, thousands of years ago, felled the forests to grow crops and introduced sheep that have since kept hills open and grassy. The *Normans[53], in 1066, introduced rabbits as food and fur animals. When these escaped from captivity and grew wild, they also kept lands open and grassy. The influence of rabbits can be seen when they were removed, for a time, in the late 20th century. In 1953, the rabbit disease, *myxomatosis[54], reached Britain, destroying much of the wild rabbit population. The result was a change in animal and plant life, as larger plants, usually eaten by rabbits, grew and overshadowed the smaller plants. Animals and insects dependent on the smaller plants decreased in numbers, while those favored by the taller plants increased. Other imported animals such as *reindeer[55] from Scandinavia, the grey *squirrel[56] from North America and deer from China are altering the ecology.

In addition, the UK government is sponsoring major reforestation efforts to increase wood production. Since certain varieties of trees grow faster than others, the new forests are often *monocultures[57] that do not support animal life well. To help support remaining wildlife, efforts are being made to diversify types of reforestation.

III. Water: The Key Geographical Feature

The UK does not have *catastrophic[58] weather or many kinds of spectacular geographical features. There are no high mountain ranges, no deserts, no active volcanos, no rivers likely to flood, no *monsoons[59], few *hurricanes[60] or *tornados[61] or earthquakes. The key feature that marks Great Britain is water. Water has shaped the climate, the landscape, the history and the industrial resources of Britain.

Although the United Kingdom's land area is less than 3% of the land area of the People's Republic of China, its 8,800 km coastline (when the coasts of all the little islands are included) is more than 60% of that of the People's Republic of China. The study of British geography is the study of how profoundly water can influence a land and its people.

Apart from the land border with the Republic of Ireland, the UK is surrounded by the sea, with no part more than 125 kilometers from *tidal[62] water. Even though the English Channel narrows to 35 kilometers near its eastern end, it has barred invasion by European armies for over 900 years. (Some Europeans may argue that the cold, rainy climate may also have served as a barrier!) The dependence upon ships for international trade and for defense led Britain to become a major maritime power.

The warmth of the Atlantic Drift Current attracts fish; the inshore waters teem with *mackerel[63], *cod[64] and *herring[65]. The current causes the waters near the Shetland and Orkeney islands to be warmer than the waters near Southeast England over a thousand kilometers to the south. The warm, moist air from the Atlantic encountering the cooler air of northern Europe also provides the rain that has kept agriculture flourishing. However, despite the abundant rainfall, the dense population in southern England sometimes lacks enough water. Even though one percent of Britain's land area is covered by freshwater lakes, rivers and wetlands, water shortages are developing. Furthermore, pollution of rivers and nearby ocean water is a continuing problem.

Finally, the *deposits[66] from ancient seas and oceans influenced the nature of Britain and its land. Because of silts carried in rivers and deposited in the rivers' mouths, some port cities are now inland cities. The rising waters of today's warm oceans may have an influence in the years to come.

IV. Geographical History

The UK's natural resources were created during the shifting dance of the earth's *plates[67], the solid matter that floated on the liquid *magma[68]. Because the region that is now the UK lies on the edge of a European plate, it was affected as plates collided and moved apart. For a time, parts of the British Isles were connected to the plate containing

North America. The uplands in Britain are the result of two collisions. The first, over 345 million years ago, created the high hills of Scotland, Wales and Southwest England. These first hills tend to run southwest to northeast across Britain. The second collision, over 220 million years ago, created *the Pennines[69] and regions of southwestern England. These hills tend to run north and south.

Because the region that is now the UK lies on the continental shelf, when the ocean levels rose, much of the land was covered by water. Small creatures living in the water left their shells on the sea floor, forming the large *chalk[70] and limestone deposits of southern England. In addition, rains eroded the mountains so that the region was covered with *quartzites[71], sandstones and limestone, providing later resources for agriculture and building.

Then, when the glaciers advanced and retreated over much of northern and mountainous Britain, they smoothed the mountains and dropped *debris[72] in the valleys. As a result of erosion from glaciers and from rain, the hills of the UK lack soils and are poor agricultural areas. The lowlands have richer soils from erosion and marine deposits.

These early forces created a rich diversity of terrain types in a relatively small area. A person traveling more than 100 kilometers in the UK is likely to encounter two or more totally different types of landscape.

The rising waters after the last ice age have slowly separated the British Isles from the European Continent. The last land bridge was submerged about 6,000 B.C. Between the retreat of the glaciers and the separation from Europe, plants and animals crossed from Europe to fill the empty land. Since Ireland was the first to be isolated from Europe, fewer animals had time to cross from Europe before the waters rose. Thus, Ireland does not have the same wildlife diversity as Britain. However, the Irish are proud of one difference: they have no snakes. The poisonous snake, the *adder[73], found in Britain, is not found in Ireland. Great Britain is known for its very harsh animal quarantine laws to preserve this freedom from *rabies[74] although the European Union has forced a slight easing of these restrictions.

Even after the Chunnel has restored the link between Britain and the continent, the British are still watching the sea. If global warming continues, much of the current coastline will be flooded, particularly on the eastern coasts, and inland cities may once again be ports! Finally, any alteration of the Atlantic Ocean Currents could be disastrous, since the mild UK climate depends upon this current.

V. Surface Features and Geography—by Political Region

1. SCOTLAND

Scotland has a population of over 5 million people in an area of nearly 80 thousand sq km. Some Scots still speak their native language, *Gaelic[75], although most speak English, the official language. Geologically, Scotland is divided into three main regions: the Highlands and Western Isles, *the Lowlands[76], and the southern Uplands.

A) Scotland—The Highlands and Western Isles

The northern Uplands and Western Isles (Hebrides) of Scotland contain soils so thin that "the poor bare bones of the country show through" in many places. Tough gneisses, *schists[77] and metamorphic rocks are common. The dark, windswept stones of the Outer Hebrides are over 3 billion years old. On these islands remote from the Scottish mainland, farmers and weavers still manage to make a living. The Inner Hebrides, closer to Scotland, are not as old. They were formed from volcanic eruptions 60 million years ago. On both *Inner and Outer Hebrides[78], the heavy rains typical of northwestern Scotland have eroded much of the soil. The Shetlands and Orkneys, to the north of the Scottish mainland, are more recent still and have not suffered as much erosion.

Figure 2   Map of Scotland

The northern Uplands are also called the Highlands of Scotland, although sometimes the term is reserved for the northernmost Uplands. The Uplands are divided into two regions: the Highlands in the far north and the southern *Grampians[79] and *Cairngorms[80].

The Highlands, or far northern region, form a craggy, desolate land. The acid quartzite rocks are poor for agriculture. Heavy glaciation further reduced soils while cutting deep valleys through the jumbled mixture of rock types, in part igneous and in part granite or limestone. Along the west coast of Scotland these steepsided valleys became *firths[81] or sea lochs when they were flooded by the ocean. The treacherous seas and the jagged mountains have protected many groups fleeing from the south. People from this region call themselves "highlanders" and speak a different dialect of English from southern Scotland. Because transportation is so difficult, this region is not developed.

The boundary between the Highlands and the Grampians is *the Great Glen[82], a *fault[83] line crossing Scotland southwest to northeast. A major attraction for modern visitors is the *Caledonian Canal[84], an artificial waterway, following this fault line. It links the long lakes or lochs (including *Loch Ness[85]) with the deeply indented bays or firths. In earlier days, the Canal offered a trans-Highland passage that avoided many dangers of the north Scottish coasts. The Grampian uplands are more *homogeneous[86] than the Highlands, being a plateau that has been deeply cut by faults that were further enlarged by glacial erosion. On the southwest coast, ancient volcanic activity created a region of higher mountains, including Ben Nevis. To the southeast lie the Cairngorm Mountains, named for the beautiful, yellow cairngorm quartz found there.

The Scottish Uplands have been designated as a Less Favored Area (LFA) by the European Community. However, despite the lack of agricultural resources, these northern Uplands do produce oats and sheep; reforestation of pine and *spruce[87] woods is increasing timber supplies. Many parts of the Scottish Highlands are still wilderness, supporting a variety of *montane[88] (arctic-environment) plants, birds and herds of the red deer, native to Britain. The great beauty of the Highlands attracts many summer tourists despite the heavy rainfall.

Two plants are particularly important: *sphagnum[89] *moss[90] and *heather[91]. Sphagnum moss is found in moist, poorly drained areas. When it decays under pressure, the moss forms *peat[92], which is used in agriculture and as a fuel. Heather is found on the drier hill slopes, transforming the grey stones into rosy beauty. In addition to attracting tourists, heather also provides a good environment for *grouse[93], a bird that is hunted for sport and food.

There is little industry in the Scottish Highlands. For many years, the only exports were granite rock, wool, fish, whiskey and textiles. After the discovery of oil and natural gas in the North Sea, the eastern Grampian coast, particularly the city of *Aberdeen[94] with nearly 211,000 people, has become an industrial center.

B) Scotland—Lowlands

In contrast to the scarcely populated Highlands, the Lowlands of Scotland contain some of the most densely populated areas in the UK. The capital of Scotland, *Edinburgh[95] (population 500 thousand) and the industrial port of Glasgow (population 700 thousand) are located in this belt.

The term "lowlands" is a comparative term. The region rarely drops below 100 metres and contains several hills above 300 metres. The landscape of steep hills and strangely winding rivers was created by volcanic activity and severe glacial erosion. The result was a region with many resources for early development of industry. In the east, *the Firth of Forth[96] cut deeply into the coastline, allowing boats to reach deep into the countryside. Opposite, on the west, the winding *Clyde River[97] did the same. The distance between the two waterways was only about 35 km. Glacial scraping brought coal and iron deposits close to the surface. Clay, sand for glassmaking and good agricultural soil were also located near the coasts.

At first, industry centered on the eastern region as trade with Europe was important. The city of Edinburgh was located on the Firth of Forth with its natural shelter from the rough North Sea. And as the city was located near the head of one of the few land routes to England, it has become the banking and legal center of Scotland. It is also home to the famous, centuries-old Edinburgh University and a major paper and publishing industry. Edinburgh also promotes tourism, particularly through the yearly "Edinburgh Festival"— the Edinburgh International Festival of Music and Drama. The city has many ancient buildings and possesses a majestic dignity that makes it one of the finest cities in Europe.

With the canal linking the Firth of Forth and the Clyde River, the base of industry has shifted west toward the canal. Here are found major oil refineries and many oil-elated industries that transform refinery by products into plastics, dyestuffs and other materials, which are shipped from the major port of Grangemouth.

Glasgow, on the west coast, is located inland from the mouth of river Clyde, which originates in the southern Uplands. Although Atlantic tides affect Glasgow, it is still a major port, in part due to large-scale dredging of the river. Once the American markets became important to the UK, western-facing Glasgow grew into a major industrial center and port, famous for its shipbuilding and heavy industry. With the loss of heavy industry, Glasgow is currently turning more to light industry and electronics. Also, the city is fighting its old image of once containing some of the worst slums in the United Kingdom. Building on its major educational institutions, Glasgow has turned to culture, competing with Edinburgh. In 1990 Glasgow was named a European City of Culture by the European Community. Then, after spending more millions of pounds on the arts, the city was named the 1999 European City of Architecture and is coming to rival Edinburgh in tourist popularity.

C) Scotland—The Southern Uplands

These uplands are rounded, rolling hills, no more than 900 meters high. Sheep, the main agricultural product, graze the hills and keep them bare, so that their gentle contours are visible. The hills follow the older southwest to northwest orientation, except near the English border. There, the Scottish Uplands merge with the north-south running Pennine Uplands. The Pennine Uplands extend east to *the Cheviots[98], another famous sheep-raising area of Britain. The place where the two lines of hills intertwine is known as the "Border Country". Since no natural boundary divides Scotland from England, the two countries spent much of their history fighting over this territory. This explains why the "Border Country" contains so many old castles and fortifications.

Tucked on either side of the southern Uplands of Scotland are two small lowland areas, one on each coast. The warmer, western section is used for stock farming, orchards and other agricultural products. The cooler east can only support cool weather crops, such as wheat and oats, as well as sugar beets and potatoes.

2. NORTHERN IRELAND

Northern Ireland, administrative division of the United Kingdom of Great Britain and Northern Ireland, is situated in the northeastern portion of the Island of Ireland. Northern Ireland is sometimes referred to as *Ulster[99], the name of an ancient kingdom including the territory of current Northern Ireland. In 2006, its estimated population was 1,741,619. Most people live in the major cities of Belfast and *Derry[100] (Londonderry). The capital of Northern Ireland is Belfast.

A) Land and Resources

The total area of Northern Ireland is 14,160 sq km, of which 628 sq km is inland water. The region's topography is often described as saucer-shaped: A low-lying central area is surrounded by the Antrim Mountains and Glens of Antrim to the north and northeast, the Mourne Mountains to the southeast, the uplands of south *Armagh[101] to the south, and the Sperrin Mountains to the northwest. A number of broad river valleys run from the central region to the sea. The highest mountain is Slieve Donard (852 m), located at the eastern end of the Mourne Mountains in County *Down[102]. Near the northernmost point of Northern Ireland is Giant's *Causeway[103], an unusual formation of 40,000 *basalt[104] columns created by the cooling of an ancient lava flow. Rathlin Island and several smaller islands lie off the northern coast.

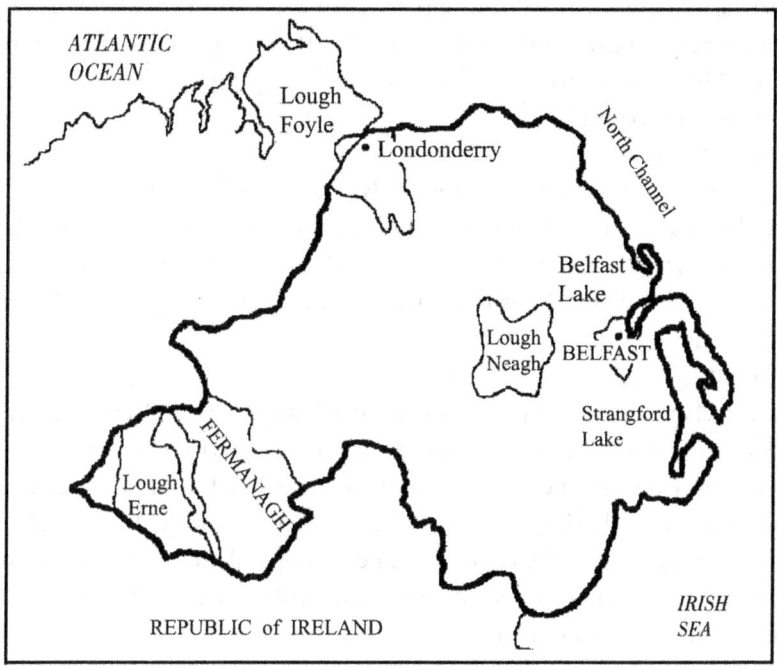

Figure 3 Map of Northern Ireland

Northern Ireland shares much of its geology with Scotland, because it was formed by similar processes. Its highlands have ancient rocks and thin soils, but attract many tourists to the beautiful lakes (called *loughs[105], particularly in the southwestern region of *Fermanagh[106]. The upland *bogs[107] provide plentiful peat, still an important source of fuel and agricultural material. The rugged and misty uplands of Northern Ireland have many fast-flowing rivers with beautiful waterfalls and dramatic gorges.

B) Natural Resources

Ireland is not rich in minerals. Small-scale coal mining has been pursued sporadically at Coalisland, in central Northern Ireland, and at Ballycastle in the north. Limestone and gravel are extensively quarried. Some 6% of Northern Ireland's land area is forested, much of it planted in recent times.

C) Industry and Agriculture

Linen manufacture is the main industry of Northern Ireland. Synthetic fibers are also manufactured in Northern Irish factories. Other manufactures include aircraft, textile machinery, electrical and electronic equipment, processed food, liquor, carbonated beverages, tobacco products and chemicals.

Most farms in Northern Ireland are small. Agriculture in Northern Ireland largely revolves around livestock production—cattle, pigs, sheep, and poultry are the main animals raised. Barley is the most important crop, followed by potatoes and oats.

D) Energy

Northern Ireland's main sources of energy are imported oil and coal, which are used primarily to run electric power stations. Bottled *propane[108] gas is widely used for domestic heating, as are oil, coal and peat. Natural gas from the North Sea, which has been a major source of power in Britain since the 1970s, was denied to Northern Ireland until the late 1990s owing to the high cost of laying pipes across the North Channel between Scotland and Ireland.

E) Transportation

The province's railway system connects Bangor, Larne, Coleraine, and Londonderry with one another and with *Dublin[109]. The highway system is well developed. Belfast International Airport, Belfast City Airport, and Londonderry Airport have established themselves effectively in the British and Irish markets. Ferries connect Belfast and Larne to ports in Scotland.

F) Tourism

Northern Ireland is an attractive tourist destination for golfers, fishers, horseback riders, hikers and campers. The province has many magnificent sandy beaches, although the water is too cold and the weather too unreliable for beach tourism to develop on a large scale. Some important heritage centers have been established, notably in Belfast, Londonderry, Armagh and *Omagh[110]. These supplement Northern Ireland's world-renowned natural attractions, the most famous of which are the Glens of Antrim in the northeast, the Mourne Mountains in the southeast.

The coastline of Northern Ireland particularly attracts tourists. Jagged cliffs plunge dramatically to the sea.

3. WALES

Wales (also known by its Welsh language name of Cymru) is home to nearly three million people living on 20,764 sq km.

Located in the southwestern corner of Britain, Wales is a land of mountains; nearly 40% of Wales lies above 240 meters. In the northern and central regions, ancient *Cambrian[111] rocks underlie the bleak, windswept moorlands. In the northern region, the mountains sides drop sharply from dramatic, jagged peaks into narrow valleys. Sheep and tourism are the main industries. The mountains of central Wales are smoother and less dramatic. Isolated sheep farms and occasional slate *quarries[112] are strung along the narrow valleys. Welsh slate is a major source of roofing material. The longest river in Britain, *the Severn River[113], rises in these central mountains, tumbling and dashing through the mountain valleys in a fast flow into England before reaching the Irish Sea at *the Bristol Channel[114]. In South Wales, the Black Mountains draw many tourists.

In the past, the word "Wales" made people think of the word "mines", because of the extensive coal fields in southern Wales, which once attracted heavy industry. However, the mines are now exhausted, and where streams sliced deep valleys on the sides of the mountains and exposed seams of coal, only the remnants of mines are evident. As a result, unemployment is a major problem in Wales. The government has worked to establish light industry, such as manufacture of paper, textiles, chemicals, electronics and mineral products. Although some agriculture exists on the coast of southern Wales, agriculture (including forestry) and fishing employ only 2% of the Welsh population.

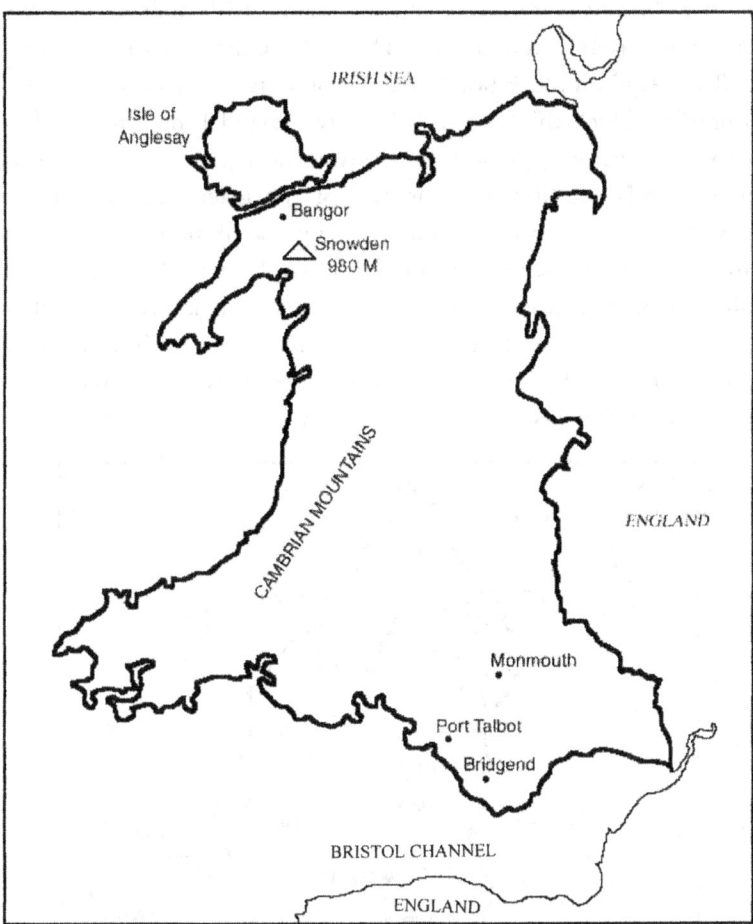

Figure 4 Map of Wales

Tourism is an important part of the Welsh economy. The beautiful valleys and challenging mountains have always lured nature lovers, and at the start of the 21st century the hotel and catering industry had grown into the fifth largest employment sector in Wales (after service industries, retail sales, health services and finances/business industries).

4. ENGLAND

In 2008, England had a population of nearly 61 million, living in an area of 130,836 sq km. This made it the most crowded country in Europe. England consists of many different geological regions: the Pennines, a range of mountains coming down the center of England, like a large T; the Lake District in the northwest of England; *Vale of

Eden[115]; Lowlands of Central England (Midlands); the hills of Southwestern England and the bands of different soil types (*Oolite[116] Limestone, chalk and soil) that constitute south central and south eastern England, along with the London Basin.

A) England—The Pennines

The Pennines form the *backbone[117] of central northern England, extending from the Scottish border almost as far south as Birmingham. With their north eastern extension, the Cheviots and their near neighbor, the Hills of *Cumberland[118], are known as the Lake District. The Pennines block north-south ground travel in Britain. The range of hills consists of an uplifted block of *porous[119] sandstone and limestone, and that is divided into three sections by major gaps or water flows: northern, central and southern. The northern section reflects conditions at the end of the glacial retreat. The grit-covered, *Carboniferous[120] limestone rocks, combined with a bleak rainy and windy climate, produce one of England's most desolate moorland landscapes. One section, the Northern Yorkshire Dales, is known for sheep rearing. These windswept, treeless regions are covered either with wide expanses of tall coarse grasses or with heather interspersed with peat or bogs. Even more important, the northern Pennines are known for rare mountain plant species, surviving from the time of glacial retreat.

Figure 5 Map of England

The central Pennines are known for their *"karst"[121] plateaus, which harbor interesting plants. Karsts are grooves of the bare limestone caused by erosion. Since the limestone provides good nourishment and the grooves protect plants from wind, many unusual, low growing species of plants survive here.

The southern Pennines have suffered from human activity. Five centuries of overgrazing by sheep and two centuries of industrial pollution have greatly reduced plant diversity, affecting even the resistant sphagnum moss and heather. Furthermore, the southern Pennines are home to the Peak District Park, the first national park in Britain (1951). These hills are heavily trampled by tourists.

B) England—The Lake District

The Lake District of northwestern England is one of the most famous tourist regions in Britain because of its natural beauty. Located in *Cumbria[122] and northern *Lancashire[123], the Lake District consists of several geological types. In the south is moorland, in the north are weathered slate and *mudstone[124] hills, forming gently rounded mountains. The central section consists of the Lakeland Dome, a mixture of rock types through which glaciers have carved deep, steep-sided valleys, radiating out like *spokes[125] of a wheel. Many of the valleys contain long, narrow lakes which give the district its name. Although the hills in the district are not high, every year hikers are either injured or killed because they are unprepared for the dangers hidden by the beauty of the Lake District.

C) England—Vale of Eden

The fertile Vale of Eden lies east of the Lake District, at the foot of the Pennine *escarpment[126], one of Britain's grandest topographic features. An escarpment is a very long cliff. The edge of the Pennines towers 610 meters above the valley floor and is underlain by red sandstone. In the valley, the red sandstone was buried by glacial deposits of rich soil; the result is a very productive agricultural area. Because this narrow strip of lowland offers one of the few north-south routes through the mountainous north of England, it is also a major transportation corridor.

D) Lowlands of Central England

Surrounding the "T" of the Pennines is a lowland "V" of rich, red *marl[127]. Here, in three regions, are the major industrial cities of England. The red marl supported agriculture to feed the workers and the hills provided resources for industry. One group of industrial sites is located west of the Pennines in the Lancashire/ *Cheshire[128] Plain; a second lies south of the Pennines in the area known as "The Midlands"; and the third, known as the Vale of York, is found east of the Pennines. The second region, The Midlands, has been termed the Industrial Heart of England or the Black Country because of the heavy dependence upon coal. In the nineteenth-and twentieth-centuries, this area was black from coal dust and red from furnace fire. Heavy industry was supported by coal and iron from the Pennines, water from the Pennines, and clay in the soil. The western Midlands has the advantages of salt deposits and Liverpool's excellent port facilities. The East and Central Midlands had more difficulties with transport. First, they used canals to reach ports in Bristol, Southampton or London. Today, goods are shipped by road or rail.

Moving south from the breathtaking loveliness of the natural beauty of the Lake

District, a traveler on the western side of the Pennines moves through one industrial center after another: *Lancaster[129], *Manchester[130], *Liverpool[131], through *the Pottery Country of Staffordshire[132] to Birmingham. Then, still remaining in heavily industrialized country, the traveler could swing east along the bottom of the Pennines through *Coventry[133] and *Northampton[134], then turn north again through *Leichester[135], *Sheffield[136] to *York[137] on the eastern side of the Pennines. In recent years, these cities have faced rising unemployment, as heavy industries are shutting down and light industry is moving to southern England.

E) England—Southwestern Uplands

On the southwestern *peninsula[138] of England the hills of *Devon[139] and *Cornwall[140] underlain by *sedimentary[141] rocks which contain great masses of granite. These granite areas form the windswept moorlands of the southwest, including *Dartmoor[142] and *Exmoor[143]. Rocks around the granite intrusions have partly mineralized. Prehistoric travelers from Mediterranean ventured the rough Atlantic Ocean to trade for *tin[144] from mines in southwestern England. However, the tin and copper mines have closed. Today the people in the region dig for clay which is used to make the famous Staffordshire pottery and quarry granite which is used for construction.

Southwest England boasts of its climate, one of the warmest and most pleasant regions in the UK. Many tourists are drawn to the beauty of the old fishing villages of Cornwall or the bleak charm of the Dartmoor granite uplands. These uplands offer unusual plants growing in the karst grooves and wild *Dartmouth[145] ponies grazing on the low, sparse moorland vegetation.

F) England—South and Southeast

The landscape of Southern England is lined with hedgerows. Planting lines of shrubs was first encouraged by King Edward Ⅳ in 1483 to protect small woodlands from cattle. Then, at the beginning of the 19th century, many rows of hedges were planted to mark new field boundaries. By the mid-twentieth century there were 2.5 million km of hedgerows, which supported many kinds of wildlife. With the change to mechanized agriculture requiring larger fields, over 300,000 km of hedgerows have been destroyed, but hedgerows still are visible throughout Southern England.

Geologically, Southern England can best be visualized as a broken bowl. This partial bowl contains several strips of different terrain. The rim of the bowl runs through the southern coast, along the southwestern uplands and Wales, north into Yorkshire. The bowl slopes east into the North Sea. Near the rim of the bowl is the *Jurassic[146] belt of oolitic limestone. Oolites are small particles of limestone deposited from the shallow, warm ancient seas. This belt runs from the edge of the Southwestern uplands to the Yorkshire Moors in Northeastern England. Although the belt is named for its oolites, it also contains deposits from muddy seas that compacted to become clay and slate. The clays make excellent bricks. Although the limestone found in the oolite belt forms better soil than the granites and gneiss rocks of the neighboring uplands, the soil is too thin for any agriculture, except sheep-raising. The *Cotswolds[147], on the west of this oolite belt, are known for their gentle beauty as the hills rise slowly from the east, then drop precipitously in scarps, or small cliffs, to the west, as though the earth has been pushed firmly from the west to make ridges. The limestone of this "stone belt" makes very good building material, and houses made from this stone have a beautiful yellowish color.

The next "ring" of Southern England is the chalk belt. This belt was important in the settlement of England. Millions of years ago, southeastern England was covered with chalk from calcium carbonate deposits. Over the years, erosion and *upheavals[148] removed all but this chalk strip, which also contained deposits of *silica[149]. Silca, under pressure, turned to *flint[150], a substance important for weapons and building material. The chalk belt itself was not good for agriculture, since the soil is thin and water sinks through the porous chalk into underground streams. The sparse vegetation of the chalk instead provided a clear road through the thick woods and *swampy[151] bogs of ancient England. Additionally, the chalk belt contained large sandstone blocks, sometimes called *sarsen[152] stones. These stones were most common along the southwestern portion of the chalk belt near the *Salisbury Plains[153]. Sarsen stones, along with other large stones drawn from farther away, were used to build the puzzling and awesome ancient stone circles found at *Stonehenge[154]. Stonehenge was constructed over a period of several millennia, beginning in 3000 B.C. with stones from Wales. The present set of rings has stones over 7 meters high dating from 1500 B.C.

The chalk belt is broken in several places, primarily by newer deposits that have not eroded, although at one point older rock intrudes through the chalk. Some geologists speculate that the intrusion of older rock is due to a far reaching effect of the collision of the Indian plate with the Asian plate, a collision that is building the Himalayas and causing major earthquakes in Asia and the Near East. England is on the far edge of the land area affected by the collision of these two plates, yet it is believed that the coast of Southern England was raised by this collision, creating the beautiful high white chalk cliffs, memorialized as "the White Cliffs of *Dover[155]". Whatever the cause, not only was the Channel coast raised, but a portion of land south of London as well, the southeastern break in the chalk ring. This section, known as *"the Weald[156]," divides the North and South *Downs[157], although the term "Weald" is sometimes applied to the whole general area. The Downs are gently rolling chalk hills. They do not support heavy agriculture, but instead are now part of the heavily populated area around London.

In Southern England, the chalk belt is broken on the south coast, near the cities of Southampton and *Portsmouth[158]. An ancient depression in the chalk was filled by water and debris, so that the chalk belt goes south east from the Isle of Purbeck, dips under the waters of the Solent, emerges as the dramatic white needles off the western edge of the Isle of Wight, dips under water again, and emerges above water east of Portsmouth. The unflooded part of the circle contains *Tertiary[159] rocks with a heavy concentration of sand. This soil is not good for heavy agriculture, but does support woodland. One of the unique sights in this sand-clay region is *New Forest[160], a region of replanting done in 1066 A.D. and now a small wilderness area, inhabited by wild ponies as on Dartmoor.

In the central part of the east coast, the chalk belt is broken by *the Fen[161] region of *East Anglia[162]. The northern portion of chalk forms the hilly region of the Yorkshire and Lincoln Wolds, chiefly used for livestock grazing. The broken portion, the Fen region, is unusual. The area was originally a nearly impenetrable swamp, preventing travel and agriculture. However, over the centuries, this area has been drained and now is some of the richest farmland in England. This area is the lowest part of Britain, at some points being below the level of the North Sea, because the land fell as water was removed.

The final strip in the "bowl" of Southern England consists of *the Broads[163] and farmlands of *Norfolk[164] and *Suffolk[165]. This area has rich soil, the result of eroded deposits from the higher western regions. The region consists of low hills, cut by many small streams. In Norfolk, these streams merge together in small lakes and broad expanses of water, called the Broads, home to a wide variety of marine plants and animals. The small lakes are often the sites of ancient peat bogs. As the medieval people excavated the peat for fuel, the land filled with water. As with the Fens, this area has been extensively ditched and drained, and now is a major site of agriculture, producing cattle, sugar beets, *barley[166] and other grains. However, because of agricultural pollution, the area has been designated an ESA (Environmentally Sensitive Area); farmers and pleasure boaters face restrictions as ecologists try to restore good water quality.

The London Basin is really part of the chalk belt. It lies part way up the coast on *the Thames River[167], the longest river in England and a major transportation route for Southern England. London is located upriver from the Channel, in part because the region nearer the Channel was very swampy and London was one of the few places where it was easy to approach the river by land.

London is built in a depression in the chalk north of the Weald; it is surrounded by richer clay soil which produced food for the citizens of London. Although the Thames is tidal at London, the river was deep enough and wide enough to serve as a major port, with the London docks stretching for miles beside the river. Nowadays, with container ships, more of the dock activity has shifted down river.

The chalk layer underlying the soil of the London basin collects water and also provides a base for buildings as well as a structurally safe medium for the miles of the London Underground, the subterranean train system. London is a sprawling city, occupying the most territory of any city in the world. It does not have striking *skyscrapers[168], but simply extends for miles in every direction. The clays do not support high buildings; in fact, London itself is slowly sinking. Since ocean waters and tides are slowly rising, this poses a major problem for the city.

The Thames River was once one of the most polluted rivers in the world, but massive efforts to reduce pollution have resulted in a major improvement. Fish now swim in what was dead water at the middle of the twentieth century. The Thames itself is a gentle river; unlike most other British river, its origin is not much higher than its mouth, and it drops only slowly as it flows. It passes through historic towns such as Oxford and *Windsor[169], and forms a major part of the south central landscape.

Ⅵ. Current Situation

The United Kingdom has many assets: the strong national characters of its component regions, a strong technological and education base, a good source of fuel from a variety of sources, and highly efficient agriculture.

The United Kingdom also faces many problems. One problem is reduced production from the oil fields in the North Sea, which peaked in 1999 and declined steadily since. Another major problem is a trade imbalance, as the UK must import food and raw materials where it was once self-sufficient. It must find new industries to replace the heavy industries that once dominated the central and northern areas of Britain. Despite the damp, rainy climate, Britain faces a water shortage.

Ⅶ. Commonwealth

For many years Britain thought its dominions and colonies were inexhaustible suppliers of raw materials and insatiable purchasers of manufactured goods. But political independence and the desire for economic *autonomy[170] has forced Great Britain to agree to limit its own commercial independence. While the UK's trade with *Commonwealth[171] nations increases, the value of exports to these former colonies continues to diminish. It may be that commercially the UK needs the Commonwealth nations more than these nationals need the UK, hence the increasing economic ties to the European Union.

The United Kingdom has occupied a curious position in world affairs. It lies on the periphery of Europe, and consists of an uneasy assembly of culturally distinct regions. Yet its military and economic *empire[172] once encircled the globe. It stands in a position looking west to the Americas and east to Europe, and in part has served as a bridge between the two. Although on the northern edge of Europe, international traffic streams through London airports. Perhaps Britain can best serve as an example of what determination can accomplish. If people from a small, wet cluster of islands can accomplish so much, how much more can others do?

Study Questions

1. In what ways has water been important to the UK?
2. The Welsh, Scottish, and Irish peoples have a "Celtic" culture in common. In what ways are their regions similar and dissimilar?
3. What geographic features aided the growth of Britain's industries?
4. How is the UK linked to Europe?

Selected Bibliography

Let's Go: Britain & Ireland. ed. Olivia Choe. New York: St. Martins, 1999.
Rothery, David A. *Geology*. Coventry: Hodder & Stoughton, 1997.
Chaffey, John. *A New View of Britain*. Bath: Hodder & Stoughton, 1994.
Angel, Heather et al. *The Natural History of Britain and Ireland*. London: Book Club Associates, 1981.
Great Britain: Geographical Essays. ed. Jean Mitchell. Cambridge: Cambridge University Press, 1962.
UK Statistics Authority. Office for National Statistics. www.statistics.gov.uk.

Welsh Assembly Government. Statistics. www.new.wales.gov.uk/topics/statistics.

注　释

[1] 岛。
[2] 独立存在体。
[3] 英属维尔京群岛，包括 40 个岛屿，首府罗德城。
[4] 南极洲。
[5] 纬度。
[6] 子午线。
[7] 经度。
[8] 皇家格林尼治天文台。
[9] 格林尼治时间，世界标准时间，格林尼治平均时。
[10] 本初子午线。
[11] 大陆架。
[12] 凯尔特的。
[13] 赫布力群岛，位于苏格兰西北部。
[14] 花岗岩。
[15] 片麻岩。
[16] 变质岩。
[17] 奥克尼群岛，位于苏格兰东北部，首府柯克沃尔。
[18] 大西洋暖流。
[19] 墨西哥湾流。
[20] 设得兰群岛，位于苏格兰北部，北海石油工业基地。
[21] 斯堪的纳维亚地区，指挪威、瑞典、芬兰、冰岛及法罗群岛地区。
[22] 8—11 世纪掠夺欧洲西北海岸的北欧海盗。
[23] 古斯堪的纳维亚的。
[24] 锡利群岛，位于英格兰西南部。
[25] 怀特岛，英格兰南部小岛，行政中心纽波特。
[26] 马恩岛，爱尔兰海上岛屿，首府道格拉斯。
[27] 海峡群岛，在英吉利海峡中，与法国相邻。
[28] 斯诺登峰，位于威尔士西北部。
[29] 伯明翰，英格兰中部城市。
[30] 黄色浓雾，形容伦敦的雾。
[31] 气象的。
[32] 本尼维斯山，位于苏格兰西部。
[33] 圭内斯山，位于威尔士北部。
[34] 受冰川作用。
[35] 放养。
[36] 石灰石。
[37] （湖泊、池塘等）缺乏营养的。
[38] 酸性。
[39] 利物浦，英格兰西北部工业城市。
[40] 格拉斯哥，苏格兰最大城市。
[41] 南安普敦，英格兰南部工业及海港城市。
[42] 加的夫，威尔士首府。
[43] 贝尔法斯特，北爱尔兰首府。
[44] 工业革命，18 世纪中期到 19 世纪发生在英国，当时工业迅猛发展，蒸汽动力代替人力等。
[45] 穿过英吉利海峡，连接英法两国的海底隧道。
[46] 英法。
[47] 伦敦的希思罗机场。
[48] 油菜子。
[49] 甜菜。
[50] 不利条件。
[51] 落叶性的。
[52] 新石器时代的。
[53] 诺曼人，10 世纪定居诺曼底的法国人与斯堪的纳维亚人的后裔。
[54] 多发性粘液瘤病。
[55] 驯鹿。
[56] 松鼠。
[57] 单一栽种。
[58] 灾难性的。
[59] 季风。
[60] 飓风。
[61] 龙卷风。
[62] 潮汐性的。
[63] 鲭鱼。
[64] 鳕鱼。
[65] 鲱鱼。
[66] 沉积物。
[67] （地）板块。
[68] 岩浆。
[69] 奔宁山脉，位于英格兰北部。
[70] 白垩。
[71] 石英石。
[72] 岩屑。
[73] 蜂蛇。
[74] 狂犬病。
[75] 盖尔语，主要用于爱尔兰和苏格兰等地。
[76] 苏格兰低地。

〔77〕片岩,页岩。
〔78〕赫布里底群岛被小明奇海峡分为内、外赫布里底群岛。
〔79〕格兰扁山,位于苏格兰北部。
〔80〕凯恩戈姆山脉,位于苏格兰北部。
〔81〕峡湾。
〔82〕大峡谷,位于苏格兰。
〔83〕断层。
〔84〕喀里多尼亚运河,位于苏格兰北部。
〔85〕尼斯湖,位于苏格兰西北部。
〔86〕同种的。
〔87〕枞树。
〔88〕山地森林的。
〔89〕(植)泥炭藓。
〔90〕苔藓。
〔91〕欧石楠,杜鹃花科植物。
〔92〕泥炭。
〔93〕松鸡。
〔94〕阿伯丁,苏格兰东北部海港城市。
〔95〕爱丁堡,苏格兰首府,位于苏格兰东南部。
〔96〕福斯湾,福斯河的河口流域。
〔97〕克莱德河,位于苏格兰中西部。
〔98〕切尔维特丘陵,英格兰和苏格兰边界上的一系列小山。
〔99〕阿尔斯特,爱尔兰的别称。
〔100〕德里,北爱尔兰主要城市,1613 年被献给伦敦作为其殖属地,即被称为伦敦德里。
〔101〕(北爱尔兰)阿尔马郡。
〔102〕(北爱尔兰)唐郡。
〔103〕堤道。
〔104〕(地)玄武岩。
〔105〕(爱尔兰语)湖,海湾。
〔106〕(北爱尔兰)弗马纳郡。
〔107〕沼泽,湿地。
〔108〕(化)丙烷。
〔109〕都柏林,爱尔兰共和国首都。
〔110〕奥马,北爱尔兰西部城镇。
〔111〕寒武纪的。
〔112〕采石场。
〔113〕塞文河,英国西南部河流。
〔114〕布里斯托尔海峡,南威尔斯和英格兰西南半岛间宽阔的湾口。
〔115〕伊甸山谷。
〔116〕缅粒岩。
〔117〕分水岭。
〔118〕坎伯兰,位于英格兰西北部。
〔119〕渗水的。
〔120〕石炭纪的。
〔121〕(地)喀斯特地形。
〔122〕(英格兰的)坎布里亚郡。
〔123〕兰开夏郡,位于英格兰西北部。
〔124〕泥岩。
〔125〕轮辐。
〔126〕悬崖。
〔127〕泥灰土。
〔128〕柴郡,位于英格兰中部。
〔129〕兰开斯特,兰夏郡城市。
〔130〕曼彻斯特,英格兰西北部港市。
〔131〕利物浦,英格兰西部港市。
〔132〕斯塔福特郡北部的一个区,为英国制陶工业中心。
〔133〕考文垂,英格兰中部的工业城市。
〔134〕北安普敦,英国中部城市。
〔135〕莱斯特,英格兰中部城市。
〔136〕谢菲尔德,南约克郡的工业城市。
〔137〕约克,英格兰北部城市。
〔138〕半岛。
〔139〕德文郡,位于英格兰西南部。
〔140〕康沃尔郡,位于英格兰岛最西南端。
〔141〕沉积的,沉积性的。
〔142〕达特穆尔,位于德文郡,曾为皇家森林,现为国家森林。
〔143〕埃克斯穆尔,为德文郡一高地,国家公园。
〔144〕锡。
〔145〕达特茅斯,位于德文郡的港市,皇家军事学院所在地。
〔146〕侏罗纪的。
〔147〕科茨沃尔丘陵地带,位于英格兰西南部。
〔148〕地壳隆起。
〔149〕硅石,二氧化硅。
〔150〕燧石,电石。
〔151〕多泥沼的,湿地的。
〔152〕砂岩,漂砾。
〔153〕索尔兹伯里平原,位于英国南部。
〔154〕巨石阵,索尔兹伯里附近一史前建筑遗址,公元前 5000—3000 年建成。
〔155〕多佛,为肯特郡港市,紧靠英吉利海峡,英国本土离欧洲大陆最近处。
〔156〕威尔德地区,位于英格兰东南部。
〔157〕英格兰南部白垩石山地区。
〔158〕朴次茅斯,英格兰南部港市。
〔159〕第三纪的。
〔160〕南汉普郡的一片林地,1079 年起为皇家林苑。
〔161〕英格兰东部沼泽地。
〔162〕英格兰东部,包括诺福克、萨福克等郡及

埃塞克斯郡、剑桥郡的部分地区。
〔163〕浅水湖区,指英格兰诺福克郡和萨福克郡的淡水湖群。
〔164〕诺福克郡,英格兰东部沿海一郡。
〔165〕萨福克郡,英格兰东部一郡。
〔166〕大麦。
〔167〕泰晤士河。
〔168〕摩天大楼。
〔169〕温莎,英格兰东南部城市。
〔170〕自主,自治。
〔171〕英联邦(1931年由原为英属殖民地获得独立的一些国家与英国及其自治领组成,英国君主为其象征性首脑)。
〔172〕帝国。

CHAPTER 3   HISTORY OF THE UNITED KINGDOM

Prof. Judith Ochs and Dr. Carrol W. Pollard

I. Prehistory to the Norman Conquest

1. *IBERIANS[1] (2500 B.C.) AND THE *CELTIC[2] INVASION (700 B.C. — 300 B.C.)

The geography of a country exerts a major influence on its history, and the history of Great Britain—determined by the sea—illustrates that truth. From earliest known history until the Norman Conquest in 1066 A.D., the British Isles were invaded by migratory tribes and pirates landing along the flat southern and eastern coastlines. Successive tides of warlike colonists, seamen, farmers and merchants, including the Iberians, Celts, Saxons, Danes, *Phoenicians[3], Romans and Normans swept across the English Channel and the North Sea to inhabit the British shores. These early people were drawn by the game-filled forests of Britain, as well as by *flints[4], tin, pearls and gold. These invasions have created a nation of mixed heritage. The first known inhabitants were collectively known as "Iberians", although they themselves consisted of different peoples. These Iberian tribes inhabited Great Britain during the Stone and Bronze Ages. Two of the early invading cultures underlie much of modern British history and culture: the *Celts[5] and the mixture of *Germanic[6] tribes commonly referred to as Anglo-Saxon. Their invasions were separated by time and other intruders, but these two cultures remained. From the 7th to the 3rd centuries B.C., the Celtic tribes arrived from territory that is now Germany and the Netherlands, pushing the Iberians into the highlands of Wales, Northwest England and Scotland. Celts were tall, blond warriors skilled in ironwork and art. Their intricately carved stone monuments still can be found in Britain. They imposed their own language and government on those inhabitants who remained in the south. Their government was based on extended families or clans, which were then loosely associated into tribes. The clan protected and punished its members, providing justice within the extended family.

Agriculture progressed slowly under the Celts during the Iron Age as it had under the Iberians in the Bronze Age. The Celts primarily obtained food by hunting, fishing although they also engaged in herding, weaving, bee-keeping, metalwork, carpentry, drinking mead (an alcoholic beverage made from honey), and, above all, fighting. No real town life existed during this period.

Celtic civilization in Britain was most advanced in the south and the southeast. In 150 B.C., these tribes used gold coins, imitating the gold *staters[7] produced by the kings of *Macedonia[8] (a *Mediterranean[9] kingdom). In 100 B.C., when these British tribes learned that the Romans were planning to subdue their kinsmen in Northern Gaul (modern France), they sent men and ships to aid their kin. That decision contributed to the Roman emperor *Julius Caesar[10]'s decision to invade Britain.

2. ROMAN BRITAIN—A TEMPORARY CIVILIZATION

The Roman occupation took place between the Celtic and Saxon invasions of Britain. Unlike other early invaders who slaughtered or expelled previous inhabitants and settled on their lands, the Romans came as imperialists to exploit and govern by right of being the superior civilization. After the Roman conquerors plundered Britain, they designated it as part of the Roman Empire and endeavored to assimilate the Britons into Roman life, an effort which ultimately failed. True Roman occupation was confined almost exactly to modern England and Wales. Britain was divided into two sharply contrasting regions: the *Latinized[11] south and east, and the Celtic north and west.

In 55 B.C., the Roman leader Julius Caesar decided to invade Britain. Politically he needed an important military victory as well as *tribute[12] and slaves to pay his partisans and soldiers. Additionally, since the Celtic tribes of North France and South Britain were allied, Caesar believed that North France might accept Roman rule if the British Celts were forced by Roman military power to pay tribute to Rome.

Caesar's first invasion of Britain was a failure. His second campaign in 54 B.C. was a military success, but it did not lead to Roman occupation. For the next hundred years, wars and civil unrest diverted the Roman leaders from further invasion. However, *Julius Caesar's conquest of North Gaul[13] brought the southern Britons into greater contact with Roman civilization. Roman traders and colonists from Romanized Gaul established settlements in Britain and gained influence with tribal kings.

In 43 A.D. the Roman Emperor *Claudius[14] ordered the full Roman conquest of Britain. Southern and eastern England, ruled by partially Romanized chiefs, were easily conquered. However, the Roman *legionnaires[15] met with serious resistance when they reached the Welsh mountains and the moors of northern England.

The Romans used a different method of conquest from the Celts and the Saxons, Danes and Normans that followed. Where others destroyed, brought in immigrant farmers, or built castles, the Romans built military roads and constructed forts to hold troops at strategic locations along the roads. Eventually this method enabled the Romans to occupy Wales although they were unable to Romanize the Celtic mountaineers in the north as they had the Britons in the South.

The Roman armies were never able to stabilize the fiercely defended and rugged northern frontier. Finally, in 123 A.D. the Emperor Claudius renovated Hadrian's Wall (118.3 km), a man-made barrier between modern England and Scotland. This marked the limit of Roman influence in Britain.

Roman civilization was based on city life in hundreds of walled towns linked by military roads. In southern Britain, the Romans first built cities, including London, which provided the best landing place for commerce going north along the Thames River. London Bridge was built over the river to connect the ports at Kent to the northern and western parts of Britain. This combination of port facilities and access to the heart of Britain made London an important geographic, economic and military center. *Bath[16], a city where the Romans constructed large hot water bathing facilities, became the center of fashion, luxury and leisure.

Roman roads were marvels of engineering. They were straight, were raised above ground level, and were wide enough for a troop of soldiers to travel. Even after two millennia, traces of these roads still remain in England and Wales. In all of the many towns, everyone spoke Latin, the language of the Romans. Within these towns were villas or large houses with heated floors, indoor plumbing, and many art works including beautiful mosaic floors.

Although the Roman culture bound the towns together, the government of Roman Britain was decentralized, and larger towns had self-government. Outside of the towns and in southeast England, the influence of Roman culture and government decreased because these areas were governed by tribal chiefs under Roman rule. The Romans tried to entice the chiefs to become Roman in dress, language and spirit. As Rome became more Christianized, the Romans brought Christian teachings to Britain. However, the Romans failed to impose their culture as too few Romans were willing to colonize Britain.

When the Roman Empire disintegrated in 476 A.D., and the Roman soldiers retreated toward Rome, they left behind only their roads, a few place names, and clusters of Christian converts.

3. NORDIC INVASIONS AND THE ANGLO-SAXON CONQUEST (300 – 1020 A.D.)

The retreat of the Romans opened the way for the second important invaders, the Germanic peoples loosely described today as "Anglo-Saxon". During the period between the Roman settlement and the Norman Conquest, many different peoples came from what is now *Scandinavia[17] as well as from Germany. The Angles, the group that gave England its name, and the Saxons were the most important of these Germanic invaders.

The Anglo-Saxons pushed the Celts into the mountains or overseas to Ireland, where a strong Celtic culture already flourished. The Celts assimilated with the original inhabitants, bringing their own language with them. *Gaelic[18], a term loosely used to describe the languages of modern Ireland and Scotland, is derived from the early Celtic language. The Welsh language, although different from Gaelic, is also derived from the early Celtic language.

The various Germanic tribes fought with each other, with the Celts, and with the increasing numbers of invaders from Denmark and Norway. Nevertheless, they established a dominant culture, a common religion and a common form of government. The Celtic clans were replaced by small kingdoms ruled by a single man chosen from the descendents of the previous king. However, the king did not have absolute power; many decisions were made by twelve of the most respected men within each village. Although few decisions were written down, they were recalled orally; these unwritten decisions eventually formed the body of law called Common Law, which still underlies British law and government. There was also a strong oral literary tradition, some of which survives today. *Beowulf[19] is a famous *epic[20] poem from the Anglo-Saxon period.

Pre-Christian Anglo-Saxon religion stressed the fellowship of heroes with the gods and emphasized manliness, generosity, loyalty and honesty. Gradually, the Anglo-Saxons were converted to Christianity. The Romans had introduced Christianity to the Welsh. Because the Welsh hated their Saxon conquerors so much, they refused to share their religion with them. Instead, Irish *missionaries[21] trained in the tradition of St. Patrick (389 – 461 A.D.) brought Christianity to northern England and Scotland, while *St.

Augustine (354 – 430 A. D.)[22] sent by the head of the Catholic Church in Rome converted southeastern England. The two versions of Christianity were not the same. The southern version insisted on government of all churches by the Roman Pope while the Celtic/Irish version had self-governed churches. Eventually St. Augustine's version prevailed in England, and St. Patrick's version prevailed in Ireland. As this history will show, England turned away from *Roman Catholicism[23] while Ireland was dominated by it. Ironically, the deep religious divide in modern Britain, characterized by terrorism and warfare, now results from Irish Roman Catholicism and British *Protestantism[24]!

The prevalence of Catholicism affected government in two ways. First, the emphasis upon a central religious authority paved the way for greater authority for *seculars[25], and the country was organized into small territorial units called *parishes[26], established in the 7th century. Church officials, called bishops, governed the parishes. As the population grew, a priest was assigned to govern a parish, which was usually a small town and its surrounding fields. Eventually the religious parish merged with the secular village system to form the foundation of the religious and political organizations which still exist today in rural England.

Anglo-Saxon kings supported the Roman Catholic Church by giving land to bishops and *monasteries[27]. The common people were forced to pay taxes to the church and to the king. The church taxes, called *tithes[28], were a tenth of the gross product of the land. These tithes placed a heavy financial burden on peasant farmers.

4. SECOND NORDIC INVASION

At the end of the eighth century, the Vikings from what is now Norway, Sweden and Denmark changed the history of Western Europe. Brilliantly navigating their keeled boats, they raided east along the Danube River, south to the Mediterranean, and west as far as North America. Marauders from Norway and Sweden attacked Ireland, Scotland and Northern England, while those from Denmark attacked southeastern England. The Vikings established small kingdoms in these regions. The territory ruled by the *Danes[29] was called the *"Danelaw[30]".

Later, these small kingdoms were united through the efforts of *Alfred the Great[31] (849 – 899), a remarkable leader and scholar, and his successors.

Alfred was king of Wessex, an Anglo-Saxon kingdom in southwestern England. He defeated Danish attempts to expand "the Danelaw", and regained land, including London. He built a navy and established strong garrisons for protection. He persuaded the Danes to become Christians and founded the first "public" schools for the sons of noblemen and magistrates. He also began what we now called the Anglo-Saxon *Chronicle[32], the first historical record composed in English.

His son, Edward the Elder, and his daughter, Lady Ethelfeda, reconquered more territory lost under the "Danelaw". Since only Celtic Wales and Celtic Scotland remained independent, Edward and his son Athelstan were the first true kings of England.

There was no permanent enmity between the Anglo-Saxons and the Danes, two Nordic groups which shared a kinship and common customs. After the Danes converted to Christianity, they easily merged with the English under the rule of the House of Wessex.

CHAPTER 3 HISTORY OF THE UNITED KINGDOM

5. LATER SAXON ENGLAND (900-1042)

In the 11th century, Sweyn Forkbeard, King of Denmark, invaded England. He encountered only weak resistance from the incompetent Anglo-Saxon king, Ethelred the Unready. Canute, Sweyn's son, was chosen as the King of England by the *Witan[33], the council of high officials who had, by custom, the right to choose the king's successor. Canute united England, Denmark and Norway.

His successors could not maintain this union, and the rule of England was given to Edward the *Confessor[34], the son of Ethelred the Unready. Edward's mother was connected to the *Normans[35], Viking descendents living in Northern France. Since Edward was more closely related to the Normans than to the Anglo-Saxons, he gave the Normans powerful positions in church and secular governments, positions that facilitated the Norman Conquest of Britain.

6. THE NORMAN CONQUEST (1042-1066)

As its name suggests, the Norman culture began when Vikings from the north settled in northern France. Over time, these Vikings were assimilated into France, and by the time of Edward the Confessor, the Normans spoke French and adopted the French method of government known as the feudal system. Under feudal government, all classes of society had fixed relationships with each other. At the top was the Duke, who gave lands to Barons, in return for military service. At the bottom were the peasants, some of whom were serfs or slaves bound to the land and its owner. These relationships were determined by birth; a son succeeded his father.

In 1066, Edward the Confessor died with no clear successor to the throne of England. The Witan selected Harold, Earl of Wessex. He was immediately challenged by Harald Hardarda, King of Norway, and William, Duke of Normandy, a nephew of Canute. Harold defeated the Norwegians at the Battle of Stamford Bridge and quickly headed south, only to be defeated in turn by William near Hastings. Harold's infantry was no match for William's archers and cavalry. On December 25, 1066, William was crowned William I at *Westminster Abbey[36] in London.

Fat, vigorous, intelligent and violent, William the Conqueror displayed the Norman genius for government. He took five steps which established him firmly in control of England, despite numerous rebellions, particularly in the north of England.

First, William ruthlessly crushed all resistance, devastating farms and villages and massacring the rebellious population. He built castles throughout England to protect garrisons. Second, he broke up the old Saxon *earldoms[37] and established centralized royal government managed by a new, French-speaking Norman aristocracy. He outlawed private warfare; now only the king could declare war. Third, he appointed administrative officers, called *vicomtes[38], who carried out a variety of government functions as tax collectors, troop leaders and judges. These functions overlapped with those of the Anglo-Saxon sheriff, and the vicomtes helped link the centralized Norman government with the localized Saxon government. Fourth, he developed a *solvent[39] royal *treasury[40]. Like a Norman Duke, he gave the confiscated territories to his followers in return for fealty and military service. He sold the rights to build castles to his supporters, while retaining the land and the buildings. He established royal *coinage[41] as the only legal money in

Britain. Fifth, he forged an alliance with the Roman Catholic Church. He appointed Normans as bishops. Although William refused to recognize the Pope as his overlord, he did agree to send money to the church leaders in Rome. This was the beginning of the centuries' long struggle between the English king, the national leader, and the pope, the international religious leader. Each needed the other; each was wary of the other's power.

The Norman Conquest was important for two other reasons: English law and language. Even though William created a stronger monarchy, he did not enjoy absolute despotic power. He was not a king above the law. He was bound by the feudal customs brought from continental Europe and also by the old, often unwritten Saxon laws, which became known as the "common law" of England. The union of the feudal and the Saxon laws became the basis for modern English law and civil liberties.

After the Norman invasion, people in Britain spoke three major languages. The *clergy[42] spoke and wrote Latin, the language of Rome; the rulers, military leaders and lawyers spoke French; and the common people spoke a variety of German dialects known as "*Old English[43]". To help the common people understand, the clergy and secular leaders would often use "doubling", in which a Latin or French term was paired with an Old English term. The final result was a *variant[44] of Old English, without many of its *inflections[45] or word changes, and with a greatly expanded vocabulary drawn from Latin, French and Old English.

7. WILLIAM THE CONQUEROR'S SONS (1087—1135)

When William I died in 1087, he was succeeded by his eldest son, William II, who was murdered. The next son, Henry I, altered the relationships between the English King and the Pope and between the King and his followers. Henry chose bishops who would give their loyalty to him; the Pope only gave ceremonial approval to these appointments. Henry also began accepting money from his Barons instead of requiring military service. To record these payments, he created the *exchequer[46], a specialized treasury department which continues to operate in England today.

II. The Making of a Nation: From the Norman Conquest to the Renaissance

1. STEPHEN/MATILDA AND HENRY II —CIVIL WAR

Henry I died in 1135 without a male heir. A dreadful civil war broke out when Henry's daughter Matilda fought Henry's nephew Stephen for the throne of England. After nearly twenty years of anarchy and the weakening of central authority, the cousins finally agreed that Stephen would rule; when Stephen died, Matilda's son Henry would succeed him as Henry II.

2. LEGAL REFORM AND HENRY II (1135—1189)

Henry II, energetic, quarrelsome, and scholarly, did great and lasting work. He influenced England in three major areas. The first was the area of law. Henry expanded common law to cover all Englishmen, regardless of their social class. He appointed able men as royal judges, who developed regular procedures and precedents which, when combined with Saxon law, formed Common Law. Moreover, these judges' decisions could become new law without requiring new legislation. During Henry II's reign, the idea of private property and the use of law to settle disputes was strengthened. For example, landowners could pay a fee to use the royal courts to initiate a legal inquiry.

Henry also introduced the *assize session[47] as a legal alternative to trial by combat (the stronger person was assumed to be right) or trial by compurgation (the person with the most supporters was right). An important element of the assize session was trial by jury. At first juries were merely panels of witnesses, but now modern juries judge trial evidence and determine guilt or innocence. Henry's reforms gave more people greater access to the legal system, and the fines from the courts increased his treasury.

Henry's second major legacy was the area of foreign territorial claims. William I had kept his properties in Norman France, as did many of his followers. William's grandson, Henry II claimed vast territories in France and Ireland through various family connections, and these claims involved England in many foreign wars.

Henry II altered the relationships between secular and religious authorities. Religious authorities had their own courts and their own legal system called *canon law[48]. Clerics, people *affiliated with the church[49], were tried in religious, not secular courts. Henry wished to reform the church courts, and to do this he appointed his chancellor and friend, Thomas Becket, to the highest church position in England, the * Archbishop of Canterbury[50].

When Henry tried to change the law so that clerics convicted in church courts would be punished by secular authorities, Thomas Becket opposed him. When Henry exclaimed, "Can no one rid me of this priest?" four of his knights murdered Becket in Canterbury Cathedral. Henry claimed that he never intended Becket's death, but to retain power he had to undergo humiliating *penance[51] and give up his attempts to reform canon law. Thomas Becket became revered as a holy person, and for centuries people traveled to visit his tomb.

Amid all his great reforms, Henry was also responsible for one of Britain's greatest and longest tribulations: he invaded Ireland and established an English kingdom there.

3. RICHARD I (1189－1199) AND JOHN (1199－1216): THE KING IS SUBDUED BY THE POPE AND IS SUBJECT TO ENGLISH LAW

A) King Richard I

Henry II was followed by his older son, Richard I, also known as *Richard the Lionhearted[52]. Richard spent less than six months of his ten-year reign in England. After fighting Muslims for control of holy sites in the Near East during the Third *Crusade[53], his Christian allies imprisoned him for *ransom[54]. After his release from prison, he fought in France, trying to retain control of some of the vast holdings claimed by his father. His ransom and his wars were expensive, and English people suffered from higher taxes and confiscation of their property.

B) King John and the Magna Carta

When Richard's younger brother John finally succeeded to the throne, he faced domestic and foreign enemies, and no money to resist them. John was opposed by Philip Augustus, a strong ruler of a large French territory previously claimed by Henry II. John raised property taxes and generally extorted money from the English people, who were already angered by the expensive lifestyle of Richard I. Since John was not an able military leader, he was unable to defeat Philip *Augustus[55], and large territories in

France passed from English control.

The military power of Philip Augustus became important during John's struggles with Pope Innocent Ⅲ, who chose his own candidate as Archbishop of Canterbury. John did not acknowledge this appointment and confiscated church property. In retaliation, the Pope placed England under an *Interdict[56] or religious ban. This meant that all church functions ceased, and every church was closed. Since the church was deeply involved in all areas of life, this immediately affected all English people. The Pope then declared John *excommunicated[57], or no longer a member of the Catholic Church, and therefore, ineligible to be king. All of the feudal oaths of loyalty were no longer valid. The Pope then ordered Philip Augustus to invade England. Fearing that his sworn supporters would no longer be loyal in the face of such an invasion, John capitulated and accepted the Pope's candidate as Archbishop of Canterbury. He also swore that he would restore the law of his predecessors, which to the barons meant returning property taxes to lower levels. But John had no intention of lowering their taxes.

The barons united in a "tenant's rights" movement which reflected their unhappiness with their landlord, the king. The barons overlooked their own oppression of the lower social classes. The barons wrote the famous document called the *Magna Carta[58], which they forced John to accept on June 15, 1215 at Runnymede. This Magna Carta, also called the Great Charter, was designed to obtain public liberties and to control the king's power through Common Law, baronial assemblies and alliances with other social classes in England.

Both English and American historians refer to the Magna Carta as the foundation of liberty. Actually the charter was a feudal contract, written in sixty-three chapters, to redress the barons' grievances. In the document, the King promised to reform taxes, to unify weights and measures and to make concessions to the Church.

Over the centuries certain provisions of the Magna Carta have proved to be important. For example, the provision, "No scutage or aid, save the customary feudal ones, shall be levied except by the common counsel of the realm," only meant that the king had to consult his council of barons and bishops before levying additional taxes. Later, this concept was interpreted by rebellious American colonists to mean "Taxation without representation is tyranny".

By writing "No freeman shall be arrested or imprisoned or dispossessed or outlawed or banished or in any way molested; nor will we set forth against him nor send against him, except by the lawful judgment of his peers and by the law of the land," the barons seemed to be trying to limit the king's power to have their cases tried by royal justices. However, that idea was later expanded into the doctrine that every citizen was entitled to a trial by a jury of his peers.

Originally the Charter was important because it assigned particular, practical remedies to temporary evils. Its modern importance lies in its abstract implications and later interpretations of the document. Two general principles pervaded the document: the King was subject to the law, and the King was forced to observe the law. The Magna Carta began the slow change of power from the king to the community-at-large.

Ironically, the practical remedies promised by the Charter were not immediately available. John instantly tried to break his promises, and the Pope declared the Charter null and void. When John died in 1216, the barons selected his nine-year-old son, Henry III, to be king and expelled the French from England.

4. HENRY III (1216—1272) AND THE ORIGINS OF PARLIAMENT

Henry III was a disastrous king. His French wife appointed her relatives from France and Italy to high positions in England. Henry III became embroiled in wars on the European Continent and made heavy demands on his people to support them. Finally, in 1258, a year of bad harvests, Henry asked for one-third of the revenues of England as an extra grant for the Pope.

The British nobles were infuriated with Henry's politics and openly rebelled. They came armed to the great council where they organized a baronial body of twelve men. In 1263, civil war began between Henry III and the baronial party headed by his brother-in-law, Simon de Montfort. In 1265 Montfort captured the King and called an assembly of his supporters as well as *burgesses[59], or wealthy urban *commoners[60]. This was the origin of the modern British Parliament.

The French word "parliament" means "talking" or parley, a conference of any kind. In the early thirteenth century the word referred to the assemblies summoned by the king, especially those that heard petitions for legal redress. It was a session of the king's large council acting as a court.

During the reign of Henry III, the barons gained experience in the practical work of government; and the Great Council, the assembly of barons, was strengthened. Yet this Council rarely met because the kings usually consulted a small group of personal advisors. Before Henry's troubles, it was the king's *privilege[61], not his duty, to receive counsel, and it was the baron's duty, not his privilege to offer it. When the barons took control of the government in 1258, they determined that the great council should meet three times a year, and they called it "parliament".

Henry III's son Edward I restored his father to the throne, and once again his father turned to his personal advisors; however, he also continued the practice of summoning the barons to parliament.

5. EDWARD I (1272—1307) AND EDWARD II (1307—1327): WALES IS JOINED TO ENGLAND, SCOTLAND STAYS INDEPENDENT, AND PARLIAMENT IS EXPANDED

By comparison, Edward I was an effective ruler. He tried to unite England, Wales and Scotland into one kingdom. After he defeated the Welsh rebels in 1283, he proclaimed his infant son Prince of Wales, a title reserved for the eldest British royal son ever since. In 1296, Edward I declared himself King of Scotland. He successfully crushed a Scottish rebellion by William Wallace. But after Wallace was executed, Robert Bruce led the Scots in a successful resistance, during which Edward I died. His son, Edward II, was defeated by Bruce at the Battle of Bannockburn (1314), and it was not until 1603 that England and Scotland were joined under James VI of Scotland, who became James I of England and Scotland.

Edward I expanded royal power in England. During his reign, the power of the royal courts increased and the power of the baronial courts decreased. He required all freemen to equip themselves for fighting and to serve in the military. He allowed the knights and other *subvassals[62] to represent themselves at his parliaments. Not only did this decision undercut the power of the barons, who taxed their vassals, but it also introduced the idea of paying taxes directly to the king.

However, the king also instituted practices that limited his power. His "model parliament" of 1295 included knights by right of owning estates and burgesses by right of positions in city government. In his summons to this parliament appeared the celebrated clause "What touches all should be approved by all". Echoing a famous provision in Roman law, this principle meant that taxation depended upon the consent of the people being taxed. The barons, earls, clergy, knights and burgesses representing the wealthier freemen in the kingdom, set a precedent that Parliament's confirmation was a condition to any grant of money to the king.

Edward II, Edward I's son, (1307 – 1327) was weak and inept. He was no more successful at ruling his barons than he was at conquering the Scots. The barons seized control in 1320, establishing twenty-one "Lord *Ordainers[63]" who controlled key decisions. Finally, Edward's wife led a revolt against her husband, who was imprisoned and murdered. She, in turn, was deposed by their fifteen-year-old son, Edward III (1327 – 1377).

6. EDWARD III (1327 – 1377): WAR WITH FRANCE PARLIAMENT DEVELOPS, NATIONALISM APPEARS

Edward III began his reign with great vigor and success. He reasserted English claims to French territory and began a series of wars, called the Hundred Years' War, in an attempt to regain control of France. This warfare took place in intervals over the next century. At first the English won great victories, even capturing the French King and holding him for ransom. However, these wars had the usual effect. To raise money for the war, Edward needed money. To raise money, he needed the help of Parliament; therefore Parliament increased its power.

In addition, England was devastated by the *Black Death[64] (1348 – 1349), the initial outbreak of the *bubonic plague[65] which decimated all of Europe and killed about three-eighths of the English population. The resultant labor shortage meant that crops rotted in the field; farm land was not cultivated; and food prices rose.

Feudal practice fixed the amount of pay given to farm laborers. The inflation of prices caused hardship to the workers, and they demanded higher wages and better working conditions. When these reforms did not happen, the farm laborers moved to the towns, which were not as strictly regulated. In 1351, Parliament passed the Statute of Laborers, a futile attempt to reinstate pre-plague wages and prices and to stop the migration to the towns. Instead, the labor shortage continued and was a major cause of the disintegration of the feudal system.

Military control over the laboring classes also underwent a change during this time. William the Conqueror had established strong castles and mounted knights to keep order. These knights, wearing metal armor on specially trained horses, were very effective in destroying men on foot. The power of knights lasted into the fourteenth century. When gunpowder, a Chinese invention, was used in cannons and mines, and archery also improved, the military system of the castle and the knight was no longer as effective.

English military victories in France were due more to expert archers and engineers than to knights.

The tensions between the classes were heightened by growing religious dissension. Paradoxically, the Christian Church was both a source of rebellion and an active agent in repressing rebellion. The life and teachings of Jesus stressed peace and poverty. One of his sayings was that it was easier for a camel to go through a needle's eye than for a rich man to enter heaven. Yet the upper-class clergy lived lives of great wealth and comfort which violated these teachings. Further, the Bible made no reference about social classes. One of the slogans used to unite the laborers was "When Adam delved and Eve span, who then was the gentry man?" The implication was that God created workers (Adam, the first man, dug the soil and Eve, his wife, spun yarn, not the nobility). These ideas caused rebellion among the laborers.

On the other hand, the upper-class clergy were ruthless in maintaining order. They massacred whole towns and villages in France and Italy in order to eliminate those who interpreted Christianity differently. They burned heretical Christians while they were still alive, and prevented translations of the Bible from Latin into languages that the common people could understand. Roman Catholicism united all of Europe by providing a common language (Latin), a common leader (the Pope), and a common culture (Christianity). However, this unity came under increasing attacks.

Despite the tensions between the classes, there was a surge of nationalism. Instead of being a nation of Norman rulers and Saxon peasants, there was a growing sense of being English. This process was strengthened by the war against France and hostility against the pope. English was now spoken by the upper classes and was used in the legal system. By 1399 it was the language of Parliament. *Geoffrey Chaucer[66]'s great literary works, including *The Canterbury Tales[67], were written in English and gave further prestige to the language.

7. RICHARD II (1377-1399): THE CAUSE OF THE WARS OF THE ROSES

Edward III's two most important sons were Edward, known as the Black Prince; and the Duke of Lancaster, known as John of Gaunt. When the Black Prince died, his ten-year-old son, Richard II, became king. His uncles, the remaining sons of Edward III, fought bitterly for power through and around Richard.

Richard II had one moment of false glory. His uncles imposed a head tax (1378-1380) which meant both rich and poor paid the same amount. The common people arose in a disorganized act of rebellion known as the *Peasant's Revolt[68] (1381). When the rebels marched on London, Richard rode out to meet them alone and promised to end *serfdom[69] and to seize the wealth of the upper-class clergy. The rebels dispersed without attacking the city. The king then rescinded his promises and persecuted the rebels.

When Richard was young, the barons increased their power; they defeated Richard's supporters and imposed their own counselors and members of parliament. However, when Richard came of age, he seized power and replaced the barons' supporters. He became extravagant and imposed heavy taxes. When his uncle, John of Gaunt died, Richard confiscated his estates, violating the law of inheritance. Richard's cousin, Henry, led a rebellion against him. Henry gained support because others feared the power of the king.

Richard was defeated, forced to abdicate and was murdered.

8. LANCASTER, THE HOUSE OF THE RED ROSE; AND YORK, THE HOUSE OF THE WHITE ROSE

Henry's rebellion set off a chain of important events called the War of the Roses (1455 – 1485). Henry's descendents, known as the *Lancastrians[70], used the red rose as their symbol. Henry's cousin Lionel and his descendents, known as *Yorkists[71], used the white rose as their symbol. Many English noblemen were killed; English control of France was nearly eliminated; and the middle-class came to dominate British politics. For thirty years the aristocracy slaughtered each other in droves, and the kingship changed sides repeatedly as the two branches of the family fought for the right to rule England.

9. LANCASTRIAN RULE: HENRY IV (1399 – 1413), HENRY V (1413 – 1422) AND HENRY VI (1422 – 1461):

Henry IV (1399 – 1413) spent much of his reign suppressing rebellions against him. By illegally seizing power, he lost the protection of the laws of inheritance and opened himself to challenges. His son, Henry V (1413 – 1422) also spent time asserting authority at home and in France. However, his untimely death in 1422 brought to the throne his infant son Henry VI (1422 – 1461), again giving England the problem of a weak King and divided governance.

Henry VI was increasingly mentally unstable, and his army was defeated in France. The Yorkists took advantage of this disastrous weak king to seize power, beginning the dreary War of the Roses (1455 – 1485). In 1461, Edward, the son of Richard of York, deposed Henry VI, who was eventually murdered along with his sons.

10. YORKIST RULE: EDWARD IV (1461 – 1483), EDWARD V, AND RICHARD III (1483 – 1485)

However, Edward IV (1461 – 1470, 1471 – 1483) did not reign easily. The baronial supporters who helped place him on the throne were untrustworthy allies, and Edward was not politically adept. He married disastrously and further alienated his supporters, who united with Edward's brother Clarence to briefly oust him from power in 1470. Edward's death in 1483 again left England with a child king, his twelve-year old son, Edward V. Edward V and his brother Richard (known as "the Princes in the Tower") were soon murdered, and Edward IV's brother, Richard III (1483 – 1485) became king. He was defeated in the Battle of Bosworth by Henry Tudor, Earl of Richmond (Henry VII), who strengthened his very tenuous Lancastrian claim to the throne by promptly marrying Elizabeth, a daughter of Yorkist Edward IV. This union of the Houses of Lancaster and York was marked by a new symbol, the Tudor rose. This remarkable man began a line of remarkable rulers, *known as the Tudors[72].

III. The Tudors: Sea Power and Protestantism

1. INTRODUCTION

The Tudor dynasty oversaw the transition of England from a feudal country to a modern state. This change was prompted, not by the king, but by "profound changes in the habits of the English people... the emancipation of the *villeins[73]; the growth of London; the rise of education and active-minded middle classes; the spread of textile manufacture and other trading activities outside the chartered town; the unifying effect of the Common Law, the royal administration and the national Parliament; the national pride engendered by the Hundred Years' War and the democratic triumphs of the English archer over the mounted aristocrat; the adoption of the English language by the educated classes; the invention of cannon to shatter the noble's stronghold, and of the printing-press to undermine the churchman's monopoly of learning...". (Trevelyan). This change was also prompted by the intellectual challenges from the rediscoveries of Greek and Roman artists and philosophers, from the Protestant *theologians[74], and from contact with new cultures discovered by British explorers.

2. THE RENAISSANCE

The *Renaissance[75] (literally "rebirth") is a term used to describe "classical" works of art, philosophy, science and government influenced by the rediscovery of Greek and Roman artists and philosophers. Knowledge of the classical works was lost in Europe, but it was preserved by Arabic scholars, who transmitted it to Mediterranean *Christendom[76]. From about 1300, these ideas percolated north through Europe, arriving in battle-torn England with Henry Tudor in 1485. However, the word "Renaissance" also describes the vigorous culture of Europe during this time of transition. The cutthroat economic and political competition of the Italian city-states schooled men in rugged individualism, and the successful business men of Italy left the stamp of their own enterprise and materialism upon the Renaissance.

This was a time when modern banking developed and capitalistic associations began. Christians and Muslims had been prevented from collecting interest on loaned money because of religious dogma. In order to provide this service, Jews were the money lenders in Europe. During the Renaissance, some Christians modified their beliefs and became bankers and owners of large *mercantile firms[77].

In spite of these radical changes, the Renaissance was still medieval in its concern for religion and its class-consciousness. It was the transitional period from the medieval to the modern age.

3. PROTESTANTISM

The fifteenth-century *papacy[78] was noted for its power, corruption and wealth. Many great artists and architects were supported from church funds. But the common people were more and more distressed by the wealth of "Christ's church" held by the corrupt clergy, and by doctrines favoring the wealthy. Finally, in 1517, Martin Luther was condemned by the Roman Catholic Church for his attacks on their religious dogma. He and his followers who protested abuses were known as protesters or *Protestants[79]. During the sixteenth century, other groups of Christians broke with the Roman Catholic Church, surviving only if they were able to find powerful nobility to protect them.

4. VOYAGES OF DISCOVERY

Most Americans can recite the short rhyme, "In fourteen hundred and ninety two, Columbus sailed the ocean blue". During the fourteenth and fifteenth centuries, southern European countries, particularly Spain and Portugal, explored the world, seeking trade routes to India and China. Looking for shorter routes, they inadvertently discovered the Americas and their native cultures. Although they ruthlessly destroyed the American native civilizations, these explorers brought back to Europe not only gold, but new plants, such as tobacco, potatoes and tomatoes. The contact with different cultures challenged their traditional ways of thinking. It was Henry Tudor who prompted England to compete with other European nations for global trade.

5. HENRY VII (HENRY TUDOR) 1485 – 1509: A SECURE COUNTRY AND A NEW CULTURE

Henry VII was a remarkable king. In some respects he was like William the Conqueror. He used a weak claim to the throne as an excuse for a successful military invasion. He then consolidated his position, established strong rule, and brought a new culture to the country. Henry quietly imprisoned or murdered all possible claimants to the throne. He saw to it that the nobles would not find it easy to make war by forbidding them to keep private armies. Nobles were also forbidden to interfere with royal justice.

Henry VII enforced these measures through a special committee of the King's Council, known as the Star Chamber, named for the room where the group usually met. This special committee formed an administrative court that was charged with ensuring that the law itself could not be used to promote local privileges, local abuses or local resistance to Henry's decisions. Since the *Star Chamber[80] bypassed the customary procedures of Common Law, including juries, the decisions were often arbitrary.

The men who worked for Henry were, for the most part, "new men", men of the prosperous urban merchant class or church men who owed their careers to him. Henry rewarded many of his advisors with lands confiscated from his feudal opponents at the end of the Wars of the Roses. The King and his councilors more than doubled the revenues of the central government, in part by using such high-handed methods as " *Morton's Fork[81] ". This fund-raising scheme victimized prelates when they were summoned to make payments to the King. One "tine" of the fork caught those church officials who dressed magnificently to plead exemption on the grounds of the cost of high ecclesiastical office. They were told that their rich clothing proved that they could make a high payment. The other "tine" caught those who dressed shabbily; they were told that their poor clothing demonstrated frugality and so they could afford a large contribution.

These sharp practices turned a treasury deficit into a surplus. This enabled Henry to avoid a clash with Parliament because he seldom had to raise taxes requiring parliamentary sanction.

Both the King's obvious efficiency and his commercial policy won support from the business community. At the time, foreign ships still carried the bulk of English foreign trade, so Henry did not dare to limit the privileges of foreign merchants. However, he used the threat of revocation to gain trading privileges for English merchants abroad, especially in Italy. He also buttressed his financial success by keeping England out of war. Henry VII left a well-filled treasury and a prosperous country; he had re-established law and order in an England weary of rebellion and civil war.

Further, Henry began the process, completed by his son, Henry VIII, of peacefully combining England and Wales into one political entity. Henry VII was a Welshman, educated in Wales. All his life he retained a love of Welsh poetry and tradition. Fellow Welshmen believed that they had recovered their independence by placing one of their own princes on the throne of England, and they flocked to his court. In 1535 Henry VIII incorporated Wales and England on equal terms in the first act of union in British history. Wales was divided into twelve counties which were locally governed according to the English model. Welsh gentlemen, who were natural leaders of their people, were appointed as magistrates or justices of the peace. These magistrates were subject to the order of the King's Council and the laws made in the English Parliament, but the Welsh *shires[82] and *boroughs[83] were represented in the English House of Commons.

One final benefit of the early Tudors came not from Henry VII, but from his mother, Lady Margaret Tudor. Lady Margaret was a strong believer in education. She provided funds for new colleges at the two English universities (Oxford and Cambridge) and supported Caxton, the first English printer. She funded John Cabot, one of the first English explorers and imported foreign artists and tutors for her grandchildren. As a result of her influence, the Tudor kings and queens were among the best educated of English monarchs.

6. HENRY VIII (1509—1547)

In 1509 Henry VIII succeeded to the throne at age eighteen. A powerful and intelligent man, Henry won the hearts of the English people from the beginning. He spoke several languages and was an excellent musician and composer. He was a *patron[84] of both sportsmen and of Renaissance scholars. These humanistic scholars, gentle critics of the Catholic Church, not only implanted in his mind a dislike of certain types of Roman Catholic clergy and doctrines, but also a respect for the Bible.

During the first part of his reign, the country was effectively governed by *Cardinal[85] Wolsey, the last Roman Catholic cardinal to rule England. A "new man", owing his position to royal favor, Wolsey was the first leader to establish the concept of "balance-of-power" as the basis of English foreign policy, a policy practiced for the next five centuries. Balance-of-power meant that Britain would support weaker countries in a conflict with a powerful country. In this way, no one nation could dominate Europe. This practical decision was in part dictated by the rising powers of the great monarchies in France and Spain. If either country overcame the other, little England would be in jeopardy. For several years, Wolsey skillfully played France against Spain, with almost no expenditure of money or English soldiers. Unfortunately, in 1521, he backed the Hapsburg Charles V, Monarch of Spain and the Netherlands and Emperor of Germany, when he should have supported France. Charles became too strong, eclipsing both France and England.

A) The Founding of the English Navy

The most important action of these early years was not taken by Wolsey, but by Henry VIII. He created the Royal Navy, which became the basis of future British sea power. His architects designed vessels especially adapted to ocean travel and to naval battle maneuvers. These vessels were bigger than the medieval *galleys[86], which depended on oarsmen, and they were armed with heavy cannon, mounted in rows. In addition, Henry decreed that these ships could only be used in public service. One of these great ships, the Mary Rose, has been salvaged and is publicly displayed in the English port of Portsmouth.

B) English Government under Henry VIII

Henry was not as frugal as his father. He loved display and all of the *trappings[87] of the Renaissance monarchy. One of his state visits to France was known as "the Field of the Cloth of Gold" because precious cloths were spread on the ground around the tents of the two monarchs. Like his mother, he supported the arts and brought famous artists, such as *Holbein[88], to England. He provided the finest tutors for his children.

During his reign England was stable and prosperous. On the whole, the middle class and the new upper class continued to thrive. Since Henry avoided sending large armies to the continent, national productivity was not unduly weakened. Henry continued the administrative policies of his father, strengthening the central administration and maintaining adequate supervision of local governments in order to prevent abuses by the magistrates or justices of the peace.

Parliament gave Henry money for his small wars and ultimately supported him when he decided to end the Roman Catholic Church's religious monopoly in England. Henry's parliaments were not elected legislatures based on universal *suffrage[89]. The Tudor House of Lords had a safe majority of men who were titled nobles. The House of Commons was composed of the knights chosen by the freeholders of the shires and the burgesses, representing the incorporated towns or boroughs. In most boroughs, a very small, elite, male *electorate[90] chose members of Parliament. Since the majority of the people living in the shires were farmers or tenants rather than freeholders of land, the county *franchise[91] was limited. In fact, knights of the shire were chosen from among and largely by the squires and lesser country gentlemen, known as the gentry. Royal favor and royal patronage as well as the patronage of the great lords molded the composition of the House of Commons, which represented the rural gentry and urban bourgeoisie, the middle class. Parliament did have the power to make laws, including tax laws, although the laws had to have royal approval.

C) The Founding of the Church of England

Through much of Henry's reign, religious opinion was not sharply divided between Catholicism and Protestantism (the word used for all Christian sects which are not Roman Catholic, and not Greek or Russian *Orthodox[92]). Honest men were perpetually altering their views. Public opinion was more interested in preserving the peace than arguing over religious differences, although Henry burned Protestants and executed Catholics during an *anti-clerical[93] revolution.

Despite the peace and security of the time, Henry became more and more obsessed with a threat to the stability of the Tudor dynasty. His wife, Katherine of Aragon, had only one surviving child, a daughter. It was increasingly clear there would be no son. Aunt to the powerful Hapsburg emperor Charles V, Katherine was popular in England. Ignoring these obstacles, Henry sought to divorce her on the grounds that she had been married to his older brother Arthur and that Henry's marriage to her was invalid. His case was not strengthened by the fact that it took him twenty years to discover this!

Hapsburg troops had recently conquered Rome and controlled the Pope, the only person able to grant Henry his divorce. Wolsey, who had promised Henry a divorce, was dismissed from office by the Pope. Then one of Henry's mistresses, Anne Boleyn, assured him that she was pregnant with his son. He appointed the enigmatic Protestant clergyman, Cranmer, Archbishop of Canterbury. In return, Cranmer gave Henry his desired divorce. When the furious Pope excommunicated Henry, he replied with the Act of Supremacy (1534), which recognized the king as supreme head of the Church in England. This decree dramatically and irrevocably separated England from the Roman Catholic Church.

Henry could not have secured the Act of Supremacy and other Protestant legislation from Parliament if there had not been a considerable number of people who agreed with him, particularly among the prosperous middle classes. Opposition to the pope, one aspect of English nationalism, had long existed. During Henry's reign, this opposition focused on religious monasteries. Individual monks vowed a life of poverty, but the monasteries to which they belonged were wealthy landowners. In earlier times, the monasteries were centers of scholarship, of medical care, and of support for the poor. However, during the fifteenth century, these monasteries had become corrupt, and many no longer served as *humanitarian[94] centers. At the start of the sixteenth century, there were approximately 800 monasteries in England. In the eyes of many Englishmen they needed to be reformed or abolished.

After the Act of Supremacy, Henry closed the monasteries and confiscated their property, doubling the nation's revenues. He distributed much of the money among the nobility and the country gentry, binding them to him and to his heirs. When Henry's Roman Catholic daughter, Mary, came to power, most of the nobility and gentry supported her. In turn, she did not try to reclaim the monastic lands for her church. Politics and religion were very closely interwoven during this time.

Despite the Act of Supremacy and the dissolution of the monasteries, Henry Ⅷ did not consider himself a Protestant. He did require weekly reading of the Bible in English in all churches, but otherwise retained Catholic doctrines and rituals. Inevitably, his policies aroused opposition. Roman Catholics rebelled, primarily in the north of England. This uprising, the *Pilgrimage of Grace[95], was forcibly suppressed. He also executed Catholic leaders, most notably his friend and intellectual leader, *Thomas More[96]. But Henry was also pressured by militant Protestants, who wanted to bring the English or Anglican church closer to that of the teachings of Martin Luther, the Protestant reformer. Henry responded to this pressure by appealing to Parliament, which obligingly passed the statute of the Six Articles, reaffirming doctrines held by the Roman Catholic Church. In this complex intermixture of religion and politics, the secular government determined which religious beliefs were heresy. However, there were too many Englishmen with divergent beliefs; the Six Articles were not effective.

This separation from the Roman Catholic Church had a disastrous effect on the relationship between England and Ireland. During the fifteenth century, the native Irish were governed by an Anglo-Saxon aristocratic landed class which did not mingle with the Irish people. The system began to disintegrate during the reign of Henry Ⅶ. In 1495, the Irish Parliament was allowed to make laws and send them to the English Parliament, which would enact them. This meant that all Irish laws were firmly controlled by England. This system came to a violent end in 1537 when Henry Ⅷ hanged the powerful

Fitzgerald, Earl of Kildare, and his five uncles at *Tyburn⁽⁹⁷⁾. Ireland had no government until 1542, when it was made a kingdom under the English Crown.

D) Relation with Ireland

At this point, Henry made things worse by importing his religious reformation to Ireland. The Anglo-Saxons had chosen St. Augustine's version of Christianity, not the Celtic version of *St. Patrick⁽⁹⁸⁾, which was used in Ireland. As a result, Protestant ideas did not flourish in Ireland. Further, the Irish monasteries had not degenerated as far as the English monasteries; they still served as important educational and cultural centers. The dissolution of the Irish monasteries destroyed these centers, and the English did not replace them with universities or schools. Unlike Wales, which moved smoothly into political union with England, Ireland remained broodingly hostile until modern times.

Ironically, *Anne Boleyn⁽⁹⁹⁾, who forced Henry into Protestantism, did not survive. Her promised son was a girl, Elizabeth; her next child, a boy, was born dead. Henry's interest in her quickly waned. Anne was executed, and Henry remarried immediately after her execution. This time, the desired son, Edward, lived, but the wife, Jane Seymour, died. Henry had three more wives: one was executed, one was divorced, and one survived.

7. EDWARD VI (1547 – 1553) AND MARY I (1553 – 1558): RELIGION AND POLITICS

Edward VI was nine years old at his coronation. As with most under-age kings, his uncles were supposed to rule until he became 21 years old. This time, the uncles were the "new men", the brothers of Jane Seymour, who were supporters of radical Protestantism. During Edward's brief reign, an effort was made to prescribe uniformity of religious worship through a prayer book and articles of faith imposed by Parliament. *Cranmer⁽¹⁰⁰⁾, who had overseen Henry VIII's divorce, wrote a Book of Common Prayer, a collection of services in English which was used in the Anglican Church into the twentieth century. More people converted to Protestantism after Henry's death.

Then, in 1553, the frail teenage king died. By Henry VIII's will, Edward was to be followed first by Mary and then by Elizabeth. Mary was a staunch daughter of Katherine of Aragon, Henry VIII's divorced first wife. Mary was a Roman Catholic who looked to powerful Spain for guidance. Panicked, Protestant intriguers unsuccessfully attempted to crown a Protestant great-granddaughter of Henry VII, Lady Jane Grey.

Since Mary had been raised by Katherine and Henry as a Catholic, she immediately began to restore the old ways. Of course, there was open rebellion, especially after Mary chose as her husband Philip II, the Catholic king of Spain. During the three years of this marriage, England was a vassal of the great Spanish monarchy. By supporting the Spanish war against France, England lost the last of its French lands, the port of Calais. Cranmer was burned at the stake; a Catholic replaced Cranmer as Archbishop of Canterbury. Catholic forms of worship returned to local churches. However, the monastic property remained in the hands of the nobility. Mary, nicknamed "Bloody Mary", died childless in 1558.

8. ELIZABETH I (1558-1603): THE FLOWERING OF ENGLISH CULTURE
A) Character of Elizabeth I

After both her brother and sister died childless, Elizabeth succeeded to the throne. She was, of necessity, a Protestant, since her mother's marriage to Henry VIII was not valid in the eyes of Roman Catholics; to Roman Catholics, she was illegitimate and, therefore, ineligible to be queen. This fact dominated all of Elizabethan politics.

England faced grim prospects during the early years of her reign. The troublesome reigns of Edward VI and Mary I had undone some of the statesmanship of her father and grandfather; dissension surrounded her. Yet Elizabeth ruled for nearly fifty years and gave her name to one of the greatest periods of English society, the Elizabethan Age.

Her personality was more like that of her grandfather than her father. She was intelligent, highly educated, proud, and calculating. She was never led astray by her emotions in great matters. This self-control may have been the result of her childhood. Her mother was executed amid great scandal for not bearing a son; her father's fourth wife was also executed for not pleasing him. Her sister's life was miserable because she could not bear a child and could not please Philip, her younger, stronger Spanish husband. While childless Mary was queen, Elizabeth's life was constantly threatened since she was the Protestant heir.

Elizabeth is often contrasted to Mary Queen of Scots, her rival, her cousin, and the Catholic heir to the English throne. Mary Queen of Scots was the daughter of Henry VIII's sister Margaret. A Roman Catholic, Mary was first married to the King of France. When he died, Mary was sent to Scotland, a kingdom she inherited from her father. There, she married an English nobleman with claims to the English throne, only to quarrel with him. Immediately after her husband was murdered, she married again. At this point, the Scots kept her infant son, James, and drove her out of Scotland into the hands of Elizabeth, who imprisoned and eventually executed her.

Elizabeth was a politician and a survivor. She surrounded herself with able civil servants, such as Burleigh and Walsingham, who served her loyally. She *played off[101] one foreign suitor against another, dangling the throne of England as a bribe to prevent war. She spent money lavishly on her clothing, making her appearance truly *regal[102], but she spent very little money for warfare or government service. As a result, the country remained *fiscally[103] sound.

B) War with Spain and the Spanish Armada

The dramatic crisis during Elizabeth's reign was the war with Roman Catholic Spain, caused by Catholic hatred of Protestantism and the rivalry between Spain and England for global trade and ultimate control of the world's oceans. The conflict was resolved when the Spanish fleet, known as the *Spanish Armada[104], was destroyed in 1588 by English ships and by storms. The destruction of the Spanish fleet demonstrated to the world that the rule of the oceans had passed from the Mediterranean to Northern European countries. Not only did this defeat ensure the survival of Protestantism in northern Europe, but it guaranteed the leadership of the Northerners, especially England, in the new oceanic age.

C) Relations with Ireland under Elizabeth I

Tragically, however, this war also sealed the hostility between England and Ireland, a hostility that continues today. Despite English bans on Roman Catholicism, Ireland remained firmly Catholic. The Catholic Pope, allied with Spain, sent *Jesuits[105] a militant order of Catholic priests to support loyal Catholics in their religion and in their hostility to England.

Their hatred was increased by two disastrous policies of Elizabeth. First, she raised money and gained support from the aristocracy by granting them commercial and real estate monopolies in Ireland. For example, Sir Walter Raleigh had the exclusive right to sell playing cards. These monopolies were often abused. Second, she sent poorly trained, highly ambitious, and highly avaricious favorites as military commanders in Ireland. Since the English feared that the Spanish forces would use Ireland as a staging ground for invasion, these policies were foolish. Her lieutenants killed or starved the Irish and obliterated districts which they could not hold. Other English "gentlemen adventurers" conquered and exploited the Irish to impose Protestant Christianity, which they identified with their own ethnic background, in order to maintain what they regarded as a solemn duty to England and to God.

The result was to unite the Irish in nationalistic fervor, binding together their love of Roman Catholicism with a passionate hatred of the English. In 1597, the Irish revolted under the leadership of Hugh O'Neill, Earl of Tyrone. Although his revolt was crushed in 1601, the pattern was set. The political and religious differences between the two peoples were firmly established as "the Irish Problem", which still plagues the British and Irish today.

D) The Elizabethan Age

The Elizabethan Age was not a quiet time. It was characterized by wars, rebellions, personal and party strife, and intense competition. However, there was a solid foundation under the British nation and society that produced the literature, music, architecture, science, wealth and victories that also characterized the Elizabethan Age.

This foundation contained a good administrative system based on a substantial degree of national unity, unlike countries on the European continent which were plagued with local differences and tensions. It also contained general economic prosperity, based on individual enterprise in many fields. This enterprise was often unscrupulous. Drake and *Hawkins[106], who are celebrated as English sea captains, were often piratical in their raids on foreign ships. Still, there was a sense of commonality. This is surprising since religious differences increased in the country, as Roman Catholics and a wide spectrum of Protestant sects came into conflict. However, Elizabeth promoted laws and policies that, as far as possible, reduced discord; regardless of religion, the English were united as "her subjects" and as English people.

The term "Elizabethan Age" is a loose term, which can be applied to poetry of *Skelton[107], Henry VIII's tutor, and to poems by *John Donne[108], who died in 1631. It applies to the arts, to the spirit of adventure in exploration and in business, to the stirrings of scientific discovery, and to the heady combination of limitless potential and of danger best represented in *Marlowe[109]'s play, Dr. Faustus (1588), whose hero is destroyed for seeking knowledge and power stretching as far as "the mind of man".

In general, European art was profoundly affected by the Renaissance rediscovery of classical arts and architecture. In England, the most lasting artistic works reflect a combination of classical with the native English tradition. Tudor and early *Stuart[110] architecture represents this combination. The new palaces and *manor[111] houses no longer imitated the medieval castles; they were more open and elegant. However, they still preserved all sorts of the earlier *Gothic[112] habits: arched windows with decorative stone inserts and elaborately carved woodwork. The great *madrigals[113] of Morley and Dowland were full of references to classical Greek and Roman deities, but the music was based on harmonies developed by the great English composers of the fifteenth century, such as *John Dunstable[114]. The plays and poetry of Shakespeare, Marlowe, *Spenser[115], Donne, Johnson, and a host of others used classical forms and references, but they also used elements from Chaucer and the religious dramatic tradition. Where there was no native English tradition, as in painting or sculpture, the age left no mark.

Although English science had no formal organization until the mid-seventeenth-century, the foundation was laid during the Elizabethan Age. *Francis Bacon[116] not only wrote fine essays, but the first work describing the scientific method. He died as the result of illness caused by exposure to cold weather as he tested the preserving qualities of snow on meat. *Harvey[117] described the circulation of the blood, and *Gilbert[118] produced a major treatise on magnetism.

The Elizabethan Age was also a time of great challenge and daring. An individual might rise to great wealth and position. *William Cecil (Lord Burghley)[119] rose from the ranks of the minor gentry to found a dynasty through his long and faithful service as chief minister to Elizabeth. On the other hand, those who sought wealth might lose their heads as did *Sir Walter Raleigh[120] and Elizabeth's beloved Essex, who so badly mismanaged the suppression of the Irish.

Appropriately, though, the most lasting product of the Elizabethan Age, apart from the works of William Shakespeare, is the *King James Bible[121] (1611). Translated by a committee of clergymen, this English translation of the Hebrew, Greek and Latin original versions of the Bible, is noted for its powerful and beautiful language. Tudor religious reforms required church attendance and required weekly readings from the King James Bible. Thus, these magnificent words were woven into the texture of all English lives, from ruler to peasant. Even today when newer translations of the Bible are commonplace, phrases from the King James Bible are found in literary works and in the common speech. Moreover, this was the book the British took with them when they traveled throughout their empire. Introducing the King James Bible in many countries partially explains why English is a world language today.

Ⅳ. Founding of the British Empire

1. INTRODUCTION

In order to understand the role of the British Empire in world affairs, it is necessary to understand its development (1600 - 1800), which began in the early seventeenth century. Until 1600, English kings gained new territory and power through conquest or marriage. Now, the English people, not the aristocracy, turned to commerce and to colonization, two practices which reinforced each other.

At first, Spain and Portugal held a virtual monopoly of trade between the East and the West. However, other European nations soon challenged them. The Netherlands was the first to seize commercial supremacy. Dutch successes during the first half of the seventeenth century taught the English how much wealth and power could be gained from a vigorous commercial policy. After a period of competition, culminating in the Dutch War of 1665 – 1667, England seized commercial supremacy from the Dutch.

Generally, British colonization was sponsored by chartered commercial companies, not by the English crown. The exception was the settlement of Scottish people in northern Ireland in an attempt to secure Protestant rule there. To some extent, the pattern of colonization reflects English religious politics. During times of Anglican rule, radical *Protestants[122] and Catholics left England. During the Puritan *Commonwealth[123], Anglicans fled. As a result, North America became a patchwork of religions, composed of Puritan, Catholic, *Quaker[124], Anglican and other religious sects. Each colony had its own laws and elected its own officials under the policies stated in its charter.

Colonists came from all parts of Great Britain. In addition to religious reasons, some of these colonists migrated because of poor economic conditions in Britain and the tales of American gold. Others searched for a northwest passage through Canada to Asia. The Crown, as well as businessmen, hoped that these settlements would provide markets for English goods and supply raw materials for English industry.

2. THE AMERICAS: FOUNDING OF THE COLONIES

After various abortive attempts, the first permanent English colony in North America was founded for commercial reasons on the Atlantic coast at Jamestown, Virginia in 1607. The second colony, at Plymouth Massachusetts, was founded by the *Pilgrims[125] in 1620 for religious reasons. The English were not the only European colonizers of the Americas. They also competed with Spain, France and the Netherlands, although the competition with Spain was primarily located in the Caribbean. As part of the settlement following the Dutch War, the English gained control of the mid-Atlantic Colonies. However, the French settlements created more problems for the British. In 1670, the English king gave a private commercial company, the *Hudson Bay Company[126], the exclusive right to trade on the shores of Hudson Bay in Canada. When the English traders came into contact with the Frenchmen who were also interested in the rich fur trade, clashes were inevitable.

A series of wars, often linked to wars in Europe, took place between France and England on North American territory. The turning point came in 1757, when General Wolfe's English army defeated the French forces led by General Montcalm at Quebec, Canada. In a desperate maneuver, Wolfe led 5,000 men in an attack up a high cliff against the 15,000 members of Montcalm's army. His victory led to the collapse of the French control of Canada. In the peace treaty of 1763, France ceded Canada to Great Britain. All French territory east of the Mississippi River now belonged to the British, except for New Orleans in Louisiana. Spain ceded Florida to Britain, in exchange for Havana in Cuba and Manila in the Philippines resulting in British sovereignty over the entire eastern part of North America, from the Gulf of Mexico to the polar regions, and from the Atlantic Ocean to the Mississippi River.

This sovereignty ended when the thirteen colonies along the Atlantic Ocean declared their independence from Britain. The causes of the revolt were complex. One reason was the commercial exploitation of the colonies. The British mercantile system assumed that the colonies were dependencies held for their commercial value. Colonists were prohibited from developing their own manufacturing. Instead, they had to ship raw materials to England, and then buy back the products from English manufacturers. They were required to send their goods in British ships and could only trade with British merchants.

Since the colonies were accustomed to self-government under the terms of their charters, they were angered by these restrictions. When the British government tried to raise additional money to pay for wars with the French and Spanish, the resulting taxes and enforcement of regulations infuriated the colonists to the point of rebellion. With assistance from France, particularly the French fleet, the colonists separated from England. In 1783, Great Britain acknowledged their independence and agreed that the boundaries of the new nation should be the Great Lakes and Canada on the north, Florida on the south, and the Mississippi River on the west. Great Britain later returned Florida to Spain.

The 1783 treaty left Great Britain with two groups of settlements in Canada. The first included the predominantly British maritime colonies: Newfoundland, Nova Scotia, Cape Breton and Prince Edward Islands. The second, situated along the St. Lawrence River, was populated almost entirely by French Roman Catholics. The Quebec Act (1774) granted the Catholics religious freedom and permitted French law to remain in force in all civil matters. Many loyalists, or colonists who supported the King against the American rebels, fled to Canada. They were absorbed easily into the maritime colonies. However, assimilation was not smooth in the inland settlements. The Loyalists, steeped in British tradition, could not easily accept French civil law. As a result, the Canada Act (1791) divided this settlement into two provinces, Ontario and Quebec, which were partially separated by the Ottawa River. Within a few years after the loss of the American colonies, six new Canadian states had been established. These states remained loyal to Britain. When United States forces invaded during the War of 1812, they were soundly repulsed by the Canadians.

England also founded a number of colonies on the islands in the Caribbean, later called the British West Indies. The primary crop was sugar-cane, which produced sugar, molasses, and *rum[127]. This gave rise to the infamous, highly profitable Atlantic trade "triangle". Slaves were brought from Africa and sold in the West Indies(on one side of the triangle). Slave labor grew the sugar canes and prepared the raw sugar. The first side of the triangle lengthened when the raw sugar was sold to *distillers[128] in the northern American colonies who turned the sugar into the powerful alcohol, rum. The second side of the triangle involved sending this rum to England, where it was popular among the poorer classes. Some of the profits from the rum were used to buy slaves, completing the trade triangle.

3. INDIA

At the end of the seventeenth century, the English had unsuccessfully challenged the Dutch East India Company in the Asian Eastern Archipelago. Thereafter, the English contented themselves with trade with the mainland of India, where they had already established a base. The first English factory was established in Surat (1609). Calcutta, Bombay and Madras became the three main centers for English expansion in India.

When the first Europeans arrived in India, most of the country was controlled by the Mogul emperor, who ruled through *nawebs[129] or *viceroys[130]. By the middle of the eighteenth century, the emperor's power had declined, and many of the nawebs sought protection from more powerful neighbors through alliances with the French. Francois Dupleix, a French leader with a fertile imagination, dreamed of establishing a great French empire in India. He used companies of natives called *sepoys[131], under the command of French officers who trained them to fight in the European manner. By 1750, Dupleix's policy was so successful that the nawebs of all of southeastern India were his allies. English prospects for control of India seemed poor.

At this point, Robert Clive arrived. He was a young British officer who was destined to end Dupleix's dream. Relying on speed and surprise, Clive was responsible for a series of victories against the French and native princes. His victory at Plassey firmly established British power in Begal. By 1761 the French empire in India had collapsed as completely as their empire in America had collapsed.

However, the government established by Clive was cumbersome and unsatisfactory. He gave the English *East India Company[132], a commercial firm, status as a territorial power. Parliament, concerned about giving such power to a trading company, passed the Regulating Act (1773) which placed the company under control of the Crown. This act, which may be regarded as the beginning of modern constitutional history in India, permitted the monarch to appoint a governor-general aided by four councilors and a supreme court comprising four judges who tried servants of the company. Prime Minister Pitt's India Act (1784) virtually made the governor-general supreme and created a Board of Control, which was directly responsible to Parliament and given direct supervision of the political and military affairs of British India.

Clive's successes were consolidated by the victories of Richard Wellesley, who was appointed governor-general in 1798. He believed that the British must be either supreme in India or be driven out. By the end of his regime, the British were close to controlling of all of India.

4. AUSTRALIA/NEW ZEALAND: COLONIZATION

British expansion in Australia also began in the second half of the eighteenth century. Abel Tasman, a Dutch sailor, circumnavigated Australia (1642 – 1643), but the Dutch East India Company did not pursue his discoveries. William Dampier, the first Englishman to explore the Australian continent, discouraged interest in the country. It remained for Captain James Cook (1728 – 1779), a British sea captain, to gather the first real knowledge of Australia. His discoveries might have been ignored if the English jails had not been crowded. Before the American Revolutionary War, convicts had customarily been transported to the American colonies, where they were sentenced to years of forced labor. After 1783, this option ended. To·relieve the congestion in the English prisons, 550 male and 200 female convicts were sent to Australia, accompanied by 200 marines as guards. In 1788 they settled in Sydney, where the colony soon became self-supporting.

Upon expiration of their sentences, convicts were given grants of land. Other settlers, particularly discharged soldiers, also received land. As further convicts and settlers arrived, other settlements began along the eastern coast. In 1813, a party of explorers discovered the interior fertile plains which assured the future of wool-growing, one of Australia's major industries. People also settled in Tasmania and New Zealand, but it was not until 1835 that the British government asserted sovereignty over these two islands.

V. England in Revolution: Representative and Constitutional Government
1. INTRODUCTION

One of the greatest contributions the British have made to the world is the combination of the abstract idea and the day-to-day operations of a representative and constitutional government. To the people of the seventeenth century, France seemed to be the home of a stable government and society, and England was the land of violence and change. Most European monarchs were *"divine-right"[133] monarchs; they claimed that God had given them the right to rule, not their people. Europeans living under these monarchies were scandalized when the English cut off the head of one king and drove another into exile. It is hard to realize that the orderly English of today were once regarded as rebellious people who were hard to govern. In spite of considerable turmoil, the English gradually modified their government, and their ideas and practices were adopted with varying degrees of success, in all western countries by the end of the nineteenth century.

This modification was not "democracy"; it was representative or parliamentary government. To the extent that the English government used the new methods of professional administration developed in the fifteenth and sixteenth centuries, it could be considered as "absolute" as any divine-right monarchy. But representative government grew in the West under historical conditions that provided a check on the potential absolutism it shares with divine-right monarchy. This control is the concept of a "constitution", a set of rules, written or oral, which cannot be altered by the ordinary processes of government. In modern western tradition, these rules act as limitations on a government, a government which is elected by a majority of its citizens. A constitution guarantees rights to individuals and groups, permitting them to do certain things even though some government officials may disagree. Without these rules or "civil rights", even a parliamentary government could be ruthlessly absolute.

English-speaking people throughout the world have come to believe that England has always had a representative and constitutional government. This belief is partially correct, but it would be more accurate to say: in the fifteenth and sixteenth centuries England began to develop a new model of centralized monarchy. Development of this process in the seventeenth century was checked and modified by the continued growth of representative institutions at both the local and the national levels.

During the seventeenth century, violent quarrels occurred between the King and Parliament, with Parliament the victor. This victory was due in part to one important difference between the English and continental parliaments: the British Parliament united both the aristocracy and the urban middle-class. This union resulted in a single ruling class with membership open to talented and energetic men from several social classes.

The medieval heritage of a unified ruling class was supplemented by another medieval legacy: the persistence of local magistrates who were not directly dependent on the Crown. Certainly, England had its bureaucrats on the royal *payroll[134], but the gentry and aristocracy continued to do important local work. The Elizabethan Poor Law of 1601 put the care of poor people squarely on the smallest local governmental units, the town parishes, where decisions lay ultimately with the amateur, unpaid magistrates or justices of the peace, recruited from the gentry.

Acting as justices of the peace meant that the privileged classes were active in government, but not as agents of the central government. Instead, they preserved a firm base in local government and an equally firm base in Parliament's House of Commons. When Charles I tried to govern without the consent of these privileged classes, and when he tried to raise money from them and their dependents to run a bureaucratic government without their help, they had a solid institutional basis to resist him.

The clashes between the king and parliament were intensified after the death of Elizabeth I. Since Elizabeth was childless, her cousin Mary's son, James Stuart, was invited to become the British king. The nature of the first Stuart kings, James I and his son Charles I, was not conciliatory. These two rulers lacked the great Tudor gift of statecraft and insight into the hearts of their people. The fundamental fact about the conflict between these two kings and their parliamentary opponents is that both were in a sense revolutionaries. Both were seeking to bend the line of English constitutional growth away from the Tudor compromise of a strong Crown working with and through a late medieval Parliament. James I and Charles I were expecting to be divine-right monarchs. The parliamentarians were seeking something quite new: the establishment of a legislative body possessing the final authority in the making and implementing law and policy.

Behind this struggle lay the fact that the business of state was gradually increasing both in scope and in cost. For example, foreign relations which had been rudimentary in the Middle Ages, had, by the end of the sixteenth century, begun to take on modern forms: a central foreign office, ambassadors and clerks who all needed additional money and personnel. The Stuarts needed money to run a government that was beginning to take over new functions. Basically, James I and Charles I failed to get the money they needed because the ruling classes succeeded in controlling the raising and spending of money through parliamentary supremacy.

Religious differences also played a major part in welding both sides into cohesive fighting groups. The struggle for power in England was in part a struggle to impose a uniform worship on the English people. The royalist cause was identified with High Church Anglicanism, a version of the English Church that closely resembled the Roman Catholic model. The parliamentary cause attracted a strong Puritan or *Calvinist[135] element.

The term "Puritan" comes from the desires of these English Christians to "purify" the Anglican Church by removing all traces of Roman Catholicism. Although they disagreed among themselves as to how much should be removed, they basically repudiated the Catholic *sacraments[136] and rejected music and church ornamentation. They emphasized sermons, simplicity in and out of church, and "purifying" the tie between the worshipper and God by removing Catholic "superstitions" and "corruptions".

2. THE CIVIL WAR

A) JAMES I (1603-1625): Rising Dissension

When Queen Elizabeth I died childless, the throne of England passed to her distant Stuart relative, James VI of Scotland, son of her cousin, Mary Queen of Scots. James Stuart was educated by radical Protestant tutors, whose views he later repudiated. He was highly educated, conceited and stubborn. Since he was already king of Scotland when he inherited the throne of England as James I of England, he peacefully brought Scotland into a political union with England. However, he also brought troublesome ideas to the government of England at a time when the king was faced with three major problems: lack of money, disagreement about foreign policies, and bitter religious dissension.

James I sought new ways to raise revenue without asking for parliamentary approval. Two ways he did this were by granting titles of nobility in payment for money or by awarding Elizabethan-type monopolies. Parliament insisted on the principle that any new revenue-raising had to be approved by Parliament. The Tudors had regarded foreign affairs as strictly a matter of royal prerogative. However, when James I openly sought a princess from hated Catholic Spain as a wife for his heir Charles, the English did more than grumble.

In 1621 the House of Commons publicly petitioned against the Spanish marriage. When James I rebuked the parliamentarians for meddling, the House drew up the Great Protestation, the first of the great documents of the English Revolution. The parliamentarians based their objections on historic liberties, franchises, privileges and jurisdictions; in reality they made a new claim for parliamentary control over foreign affairs. James I responded by dissolving Parliament and imprisoning four of its leaders. Ironically, the Spanish marriage did not occur. However, the betrothal of Charles in 1624 to a French Catholic princess was hardly more popular with the English people. James was simply pursuing the medieval tactic of allying with powerful neighbors through marriage, but he underestimated the strength of religious fervor in Britain. He was also blind to the growing strength of the mercantile class which did not draw its power from land and the king, but from money and commerce.

The religious policy of Elizabeth I had been broad and moderate. Although she persecuted both extremes of Roman Catholicism and Puritanism, she allowed a variety of actual practices within the Anglican Church. James I neatly summed up his new religious policy with a short phrase: "No bishop, no king," meaning that the bishops' absolute power in religion was essential to his own monarchical power. Immediately after becoming king, James I favored the *High Church[137] tightened up on *nonconformity[138], particularly the religious practices of the Puritans.

A minor event that occurred during James' reign gave England one of her more popular holidays, *Guy Fawkes Day[139]. Guy Fawkes, angered by laws against Roman Catholics, packed 36 barrels of gunpowder below the Houses of Parliament, intending to blow up both Parliament and the King when the King addressed Parliament. The plot was discovered, and Fawkes and his fellow conspirators were executed. Ever since, November 5th is memorialized as "Guy Fawkes Day". Images of Fawkes are burned on bonfires constructed by children, who beg for materials from their fellow townspeople by asking for "A penny for the Guy". Nowadays, restrictions on open air burning have reduced the number of these bonfires, but the rhyme still endures: "Please to Remember the Fifth of November, with gunpowder, treason and plot; We see no reason why powder and treason should ever be forgot".

B) CHARLES I (1625-1649): Successful Rebellion

a) New Limits on the Monarchy

When he was a child, no one expected Charles Stuart to be king of England. His older brother, Arthur, was intelligent and popular. However, Arthur was killed in an accident, and gracious, slow, stubborn, untrustworthy Charles became the heir to the throne. All of the problems that began under James I quickly came to a crisis under Charles I. Despite parliamentary opposition, England had been maneuvered into a war against Spain, a war Parliament was most reluctant to finance. Meanwhile, in spite of his French wife, Charles I became involved in a war against France. He forced his wealthier subjects to lend him money, and he housed his troops in private homes at the householders' expense. Consequently, in 1628, Parliament passed the Petition of Right, in which some of the most basic rules of modern constitutional government were first explicitly stated: No taxation without the consent of Parliament; no billeting of soldiers in private houses; no *martial law[140] in time of peace; no one is to be imprisoned except on a specific charge and subject to the protection and limitation of regular legal procedures. The Petition of Right placed new limitations on the Crown.

Charles consented to these provisions in exchange for money from Parliament, but he also collected unauthorized taxes. In protest, Parliament passed resolutions against Charles' illegal taxes and his religious policy. In 1629, the King retaliated by dissolving Parliament and imprisoning nine of its leaders in the Tower of London. John Eliot, the man responsible for introducing the resolutions, died, becoming the first parliamentary martyr. For the next eleven years (1629-1640), Charles I governed without a parliament. He relied on traditional royal revenues, although his opponents questioned some of his methods of taxation.

In church matters, Charles I was guided by a religious zealot, *William Laud[141]. In civil matters, Charles relied on Thomas Wentworth, another extreme *conservative[142]. During Charles' reign, England seethed with repressed political and religious passions underneath its domestic and colonial prosperity. The English people who revolted against the Crown were not despairing, downtrodden, poor peasants. They were hopeful, self-assertive people determined to achieve their goals: power, wealth, religious freedom—their own newly conceived rights.

b) The Road to Civil War (1638-1642)

The English Revolution actually began in Scotland. Perhaps Charles I could have managed his finances better if he did not have to contend with his fellow Scots. Although James I had united Scotland and England in one political body, the two regions differed sharply in law, culture and religion. Scotland was still a Celtic culture; England was an Anglo-Saxon one. Archbishop Laud attempted to enforce the Anglican Church's organization and rituals on the Scots. However, the Scots had their own religions: Roman Catholicism in the highlands and *Presbyterianism[143] in the lowlands. Presbyterian Scots elected their church leaders, unlike the Anglicans whose leaders were appointed by the king. In 1638, the Presbyterian Scots banded together to resist Charles. Charles marched north with an army, but declared a temporary peace when his army fled without fighting. Charles needed a paid army, which meant he needed substantial amounts of money. At last, he needed to reconvene Parliament.

Charles' requests for money were answered only by grievances. Parliament said that their problems had to be resolved before any money would be given. After Charles I angrily dismissed this "Short Parliament", the Scots invaded England. Lacking an effective army, Charles stopped the Scottish soldiers' advance by promising them 850 pounds *sterling[144] a day until peace was made. Since this substantial amount of money was the annual income of a moderately wealthy English person in the seventeenth century, Charles was forced to convene Parliament again. The result was the famous *Long Parliament[145] of the Revolution.

Charles I agreed to Parliament's demands for reform in order to pay the Scottish soldiers. Parliament abolished taxes and unpopular royal administrative courts, like the Star Chamber. Charles was forced to dismiss many of his favorite officials, including Archbishop Laud. More importantly, he was obligated to convene parliament every three years.

Meanwhile, the Irish rebelled against England's harsh policies, and thousands of Protestants living in Northern Ireland were massacred. Members of Parliament were unwilling to trust Charles I with an army to suppress the Irish rebellion. Instead, they summarized their grievances in the document called the *Grand Remonstrance[146] (1641). In response, Charles attempted to imprison the leaders, who took *sanctuary[147] in London where mobs of people prevented the king's forces from capturing them. Charles I fled to Nottingham in middle England where he rallied an army to fight Englishmen, not the Scots. In his absence, parliamentary leaders took control of the national government. The Civil War had begun.

c) The Civil War (1642—1649)

The English people's allegiance depended on their location and their social/economic status. Parliament's supporters were located in the south and east, including London. Royalists, supporters of the King, were strongest in the north and west, areas largely controlled by country gentlemen and the bishops. These gentlemen were skillful at riding horses, which gave the King's army a superior cavalry. These mounted soldiers also gave the royalists their popular name, *"Cavaliers"[148].

At first the struggle between the King's Cavaliers and supporters of parliament, usually political and religious radicals, was indecisive. This situation changed when Oliver Cromwell was appointed general of Parliament's army. Cromwell (1599 – 1658) was a Puritan gentleman, who became famous for his well-trained, well-disciplined army of Puritan soldiers. Eventually all of the soldiers fighting for Parliament were called

"Roundheads", because they had short hair, unlike the aristocratic Cavaliers, who wore their hair at shoulder-length. The Roundheads left a lasting legacy of destruction in England, since their hatred of Roman Catholic practices led them to destroy ancient church artifacts throughout the country. When Charles I was defeated (1645), he took refuge with his former enemies, the Scots, who sold him to Parliament in return for their soldiers' back pay of 400,000 pounds sterling!

The situation in England was similar to the French Revolution in 1792 and the Russian Revolution in 1917. The group of moderates who started the revolution and who controlled the national government were now confronted by a much more radical group who controlled the army. Generally, the moderates were Presbyterian or Low Church Anglicans, who supported a constitutional monarchy. The radicals were Puritans or *Congregationalists[149], who wanted to eliminate the monarchy and establish a republic.

When the moderates resisted dethroning the king, the leaders of the Roundheads purged Parliament of the moderates; only sixty radicals remained of the more than five hundred members of the original Long Parliament. These remaining members were called the *Rump Parliament[150] or "Rump", literally meaning what was left after the purge. It was the Rump which tried Charles I before a special high court of trustworthy radicals who condemned him to death. On January 30, 1649, Charles I was beheaded.

C) Cromwell and the *Interregnum[151] (1649-1660)

England was now a republic, called the Commonwealth (which is distinct from the later association of countries called the British Commonwealth). The Commonwealth was the dictatorship of a radical minority, which owed its power to the tight organization of the army. Cromwell was the dominating personality of the new government. In politics, he was a patriotic Englishman, strong-minded and stubborn, but without a pathological drive for power. In religion, he was an earnest and sincere Puritan, but not a fanatic. Since Cromwell was an unwilling dictator who was willing to compromise, he was a prisoner of his position.

Cromwell governed an England in which most people supported the monarchy but were weary of the civil war. He faced a hostile Scotland and an even more hostile Ireland. In addition to these difficulties Cromwell went to war with the Netherlands for commercial reasons. The Navigation Act (1651) stipulated that goods shipped to England or English colonies had to be transported in English ships or ships of the countries producing the goods. In reality, this Act was an embargo on Dutch shipping.

By 1654, Cromwell had solved these problems, but he solved them with violence. He suppressed the Irish rebellion with a ferocity and thoroughness that is still remembered. He achieved order in Ireland by replacing Irish landowners with Protestants, but he did not achieve peace.

When Charles II, eldest son of beheaded Charles I, landed in Scotland, he guaranteed that the Presbyterian religion would be the official religion of Scotland. He was defeated when he led an army against the English, but romantically escaped to France disguised as a woman. After English ships defeated the Dutch (1652), England became the master of the northern seas.

Cromwell's success in military matters was not duplicated in English politics. He could not master the Rump Parliament, which ignored his requests to increase its membership and reform its procedures. Using military force, Cromwell dissolved the Rump and set himself up as *Lord Protector[152] of the Commonwealth of England, Scotland and Ireland. A new parliament was chosen, based on the Instrument of Government, the only written constitution England ever had. Since no royalist dared to vote, the 460 new members were Puritan sympathizers. Even so, Cromwell had constant troubles with his Parliaments, and he finally accepted some modifications to his dictatorship in 1656.

After Cromwell's death, his son, Richard, succeeded him as Lord Protector. Unlike his father, he was ineffective, and the army soon seized control of the government. By now, some army leaders believed that restoration of the king would be the best hope for ending the political turmoil. To ensure the legality of the monarchy, several members from the Long Parliament and the Rump reconvened. In 1660, they invited Charles Stuart to England, where he was crowned King Charles II.

D) Effects of the English Revolution

Since the English Revolution was fought between two well organized armies, England was able to reunite after the war with fewer problems than those facing France after the French king, Louis XVI, was killed during the French Revolution's civilian Reign of Terror. However, there was a legacy of dislike in Britain toward extreme Puritanism.

a) Condemnation of "Puritanism"

At the height of their rule in the early 1650's, the Puritans attempted to enforce their difficult, austere life on the whole population. They passed "blue laws", which prohibited popular amusements, such as horseracing, gambling, and dancing. These laws created implacable enemies. The mistrust of motives leading to the blue laws is summarized in a comment by the historian Trevelyan on the prohibition of *bear baiting[153], a cruel sport which encourages dogs to attack a chained bear. Trevelyan said "The Puritans prohibited bear-baiting, not because it gave pain to the bear, but because it gave pleasure to the spectators". This exemplifies the population's continuing condemnation of the Puritan reign.

b) Parliament Now Controls Taxes

Many contemporary English people seem rather ashamed of their great revolution, preferring to call it the "Civil War" or the "Great Rebellion". Yet the events of 1648 – 1660 are important, not only to England, but also in Western history. For the first time, the absolute monarchy was decisively challenged, and a constitutional, representative government was firmly established based on a legislature supported by politically active private citizens. Though the Stuart king was restored, no English king ever again could hope to rule without a parliament, a parliament which limited the power of the monarchy by controlling the tax money.

c) Beginnings of Religious Toleration

Most importantly for England, the concept of religious toleration emerged from the revolution. A variety of Christian sects developed in the following century. One such sect was the Quakers, a Puritan sect, who today still practice religious toleration as one of their basic beliefs. Quakers are officially known as the Religious Society of Friends, but they are often called by their shorter name, "Friends". They are pacifists who refuse to fight and who work for peace.

d) Growth of Scientific Organizations and Activities

Another important concept, which did not have political consequences until later years, was the concept of scientific experimentation. Scientific amateurs banded together to perform experiments and publish their findings. In 1662, this group was formally organized as the *Royal Society[154], one of the earliest scientific organizations in Europe.

After the return of Charles II, the growing interest in science led to what many perceive as an even greater revolution in thought—the publication of Sir Isaac Newton's Principia (1687). Newton, an English mathematician, scientist and philosopher, mathematically described the physical world. His work was part of the western tradition of using mathematics to explain the physical world that began with the classical Greek philosophers. However, Newton developed this idea in greater detail in his "Three Laws of Motion", equations which are still used in modern physics to describe a wide variety of events, from the falling of an apple to the motions of the planets. His ordered universe was a major foundation of *rationalist[155] thought in the eighteenth century, a period known as the *Enlightenment[156] or the Age of Reason. *Alexander Pope[157], an eighteenth-century poet, wrote "Nature and Nature's laws lay hid in Night; God said, let Newton be! and all was light".

3. THE RESTORATION (1600 - 1688): THE MONARCHY RETURNS

A) Nonconformists

Parliament remained essentially supreme even though Charles II was restored as the British king. There were attempts to undo some of the results of the Revolution. Protestants who would not accept the Church of England were called *"dissenters"[158]. Although they were citizens, they were denied access to the major universities. Many dissenters were middle class merchants or members of the working class. Slowly these groups grew more powerful, so that the "nonconformist" conscience became a major factor in English public life.

The attempts of the Puritans to regulate morals were especially detested by the upper classes. The reign of Charles II was a period of public pursuit of pleasure, of loose morals, of festive court life, and indecent wit in Restoration literature and drama.

B) Disasters: The Black Death and the Great Fire Ravages London

Two disasters devastated England during the years 1665 and 1666. The first was the last great outbreak of the bubonic plague (Black Death) which killed over 70,000 people in London alone. This was followed by the Great Fire of London, which destroyed 40 percent of the city during a four-day blaze. This loss was only equaled by Hitler's bombing attacks of England during World War II. Many of the beautiful buildings and parks in London were built after the Great Fire, including St. Paul's Cathedral, designed by *Christopher Wren[159].

C) James II: Fears of Roman Catholicism

These natural disasters were not the Stuart kings' major problem. The real problem was their lack of political wisdom. Charles and his brother James, who later became James

II (1685 – 1688), were strongly influenced by their Roman Catholic mother. Although Charles II had many illegitimate children, he had no legal heir to the throne. When he died, his brother James, an outspoken Catholic, became king. Hoping to enlist the support of the dissenters for toleration of Catholics, James II issued a *"Declaration of Indulgence"[160] in 1687, granting freedom of worship to all denominations. In the abstract, James' idea was a step toward full religious freedom. The reality was quite different. Although only Irish Roman Catholics actively opposed the English, the majority of English people feared any Catholics and saw this act as a threat to their country. After a bastard son of Charles II staged a small rebellion, James' reactions reinforced the people's fears. First, his judges conducted trials in which suspected rebel sympathizers were unduly punished. Second, he created an army of 30,000 men, some of whom were stationed near London. It appeared as though James II was plotting to force Roman Catholicism and divine-right monarchy on an unwilling England. The result was the bloodless "Glorious Revolution".

4. THE GLORIOUS REVOLUTION (1688 – 1689): CATHOLIC JAMES II PEACEFULLY REPLACED BY PROTESTANT WILLIAM AND MARY

The Revolution was a coup d'état, a sudden attempt to remove James from the English throne. The leaders of the revolution were James' opponents from Parliament and their allies comprised the great lords and prosperous merchants who called themselves "*Whigs[161]". Those who supported James II and represented the conservative landed aristocracy called themselves "*Tories[162]". The Tory (Conservative) party still exists; the Whig Party does not.

A) William and Mary

James II married twice. By his first marriage he had two Protestant daughters: Anne and Mary, who married William of Orange, the leader of the Netherlands. Through his second marriage he had a Roman Catholic son who was the legal heir to the British throne. Because they feared having a Catholic king, Whig leaders began a propaganda campaign against James II and opened negotiations with William of Orange. William agreed to become king of England in order to cement the alliance between the Netherlands and England. This shift in alliances strained the relationship between France and England. William arrived in England in 1688 and was welcomed as a hero by the Protestant leaders. James fled to France where he remained in permanent exile.

William reigned as William III (1689 – 1702) with his wife Mary II (1689 – 1694). Because William owed his position to members of Parliament, he agreed to their demands, known as the *Bill of Rights[163]. This famous document summarizes the constitutional practices advocated by Parliament in the Stuart Era. It approximates a written constitution, for it states the essential principles of parliamentary supremacy: control of "the purse" or money, *dispensation[164] power, and frequent, regular meetings of Parliament.

After the Bill of Rights, only four major changes were needed to transform the seventeenth-century Parliament into the modern-day Parliament: concentration of executive power in the Prime Minister and cabinet; the extension of voting rights to all adults; salaries for members of Parliament (which meant that members of Parliament need not be wealthy); and weakening the House of Lords by removal of its veto power which finally occurred at the end of the 20th century.

B) Queen Anne Succeeded by George I

Since William and Mary were childless, Mary's younger sister Anne (1702 – 1714) became queen, but Anne was also childless. Two generations of exiled Catholic Stuarts tried to regain the throne, but they were not successful. Parliament, in 1701, passed the Act of Settlement, promising the crown to Sophia, Protestant granddaughter of James I and wife of the *Elector⁽¹⁶⁵⁾ of *Hanover⁽¹⁶⁶⁾. Because Sophia died before Anne, the Crown actually passed to Sophia's son, George, the German-speaking king of the House of Hanover in Germany. By regulating the succession, Parliament clearly established the fact that Parliament, not the monarch, determined who would rule England.

C) Act of Union, Scotland and England Join Together

During Queen Anne's reign, England and Scotland were formally united under the name of Great Britain (1707). The Scots sent representatives to Parliament, but they retained the right to make their own laws and keep their religion. The Union Jack, a new national flag, had superimposed crosses: St. George's, representing England, and St. Andrew's representing Scotland. At first the union was difficult, and some Scots supported the Stuart kings, but generally it proved beneficial to both nations. Still, it is wise never to call a Scottish person an Englishman.

D) Further Repression of Ireland

Unlike Scotland and Wales, Ireland was not peacefully assimilated into the Union. Irish Roman Catholics supported James II, but were defeated at the Battle of Boyne in 1690. William III tried to be moderate in governing the Irish, but the Protestant army stationed in Ireland soon forced him to be more severe. Although Roman Catholic worship was not directly forbidden, all sorts of restrictions were imposed on the Irish Catholic. Not only could they not send their children to Catholic schools, but they were not able to participate as equal members in Britain's rapidly growing commercial empire.

VI. England in the Eighteenth Century: The Age of Reason

1. GEORGE I (1714 – 1727)

A) Character of George I

To this point, English history was dominated by the actions of its kings and queens. Their personalities often determined the direction of events and the general character of their reigns. From the Hanoverian kings onward, events were shaped by prime ministers and dominant politicians.

The personality of George I dramatically contrasted with his predecessors, the flamboyant Stuarts. He was stolid in appearance, mediocre in ability, narrow in his interests, uncouth in his ways, and common in his tastes. To George, England was not as interesting as his home country of Hanover, Germany, where he spent as much time as possible. He never learned to speak English and was ignorant of British customs and life. However, he was fair and possessed considerable common sense. He rarely interfered in governmental affairs, a boon for England.

B) Emergence of the Prime Minister

George I believed that the Tories were loyal to the Stuarts, who still claimed to be rulers of England. Therefore, he chose his ministers from the Whig party. The first parliamentary election after George's accession gave the Whigs a majority which they held for nearly fifty years. Before George's reign, ministers had been the king's servants. They were chosen or dismissed by him, without the approval of Parliament, and were responsible only to him. During the reigns of George I and George II, the power of selecting ministers began to shift from king to parliament. The ministers, chosen from parliament, are collectively known as the Cabinet. Both George I and George II rarely attended Cabinet meetings; in fact, George I was willing to leave much of the responsibility for formulating policies to the Cabinet, contenting himself with accepting or rejecting their proposals.

The King's absence opened the way for one Cabinet member to take a leadership role and to act as an intermediary between the king and the rest of the Cabinet. This person gradually became known as the Prime Minster. *Robert Walpole[167], the first prime minister, was originally a member of the Cabinet in the important ministerial position of First Lord of the Treasury. Walpole was both the confidant of the King and the Leading Minister in the Cabinet; in addition, he was the most influential member of the Whig Party in the House of Commons. A coarse, bluff, good-humored, hard-drinking country squire, Walpole possessed considerable political wisdom. He became Prime Minister in 1721 and held this office for twenty years. His principal aim was to make the country more prosperous by encouraging trade and industry. Since England needed peace at home and abroad to achieve this goal, Walpole tried to reduce political and religious strife and to avoid foreign entanglements. On the whole, he was remarkably successful. Not only did the country prosper, but Walpole managed to reduce both the national debt and the property tax. In 1735, Walpole boasted that "Fifty thousand men were killed in Europe this year, and not a single Englishman". When war did break out in 1739, it was only because Walpole could not prevent it.

2. GEORGE II (1727-1760)

A) Character of George II

In 1727 George I died on one of his trips to Germany and was succeeded by his son, George II. The new King understood the English language and English affairs better than his father had, but George II also preferred Germany over England. Though honest and well-meaning, George II was a man of few talents; he was obstinate, quick-tempered and shallow-minded. His best quality was his personal courage; on the battlefield, no one displayed more bravery. In affairs of state, he was largely swayed by his wife, Queen Caroline, who had greater political ability. Following her advice, he retained Walpole in office; together the queen and the prime minister cleverly and tactfully managed the King. Since the king insisted that his will must prevail, the prime minister had to direct the royal will into the proper channels. Walpole confided his desired policies to the queen, who then skillfully instilled them in the King's mind. George then presented them to Walpole as the King's own policies, and the prime minister obediently carried them out. In this way, the King was beguiled into believing that he was the originator of Walpole's policies.

B) William Pitt and War with France

The death of Queen Caroline in 1737 weakened Walpole's position. He could not prevent war with Spain over the question of trade with the Spanish colonies. Walpole's famous motto was, "Any peace is preferable even to successful war". His opponents in Parliament, including a fiery, eloquent young man named William Pitt, forced Walpole to consent to war, first with Spain and then with France. Only when his majority in Parliament became so small that it would put his party out of power, did Walpole resign (1742).

In 1757, William Pitt the elder, who had contributed to Walpole's resignation, became a leader in the English government. In the previous year, the Seven Years' War began, the result of a dispute between Austria and Prussia (now a part of modern Germany) about the succession to the Austrian throne. France supported Austria; Britain, although not prepared for war, supported Prussia. The navy was in fair condition, but the army was poorly equipped, poorly disciplined and poorly led. The situation was so bad that *mercenaries[168] had to be imported from Germany to defend England. People feared that Britain itself might be invaded. The British government was forced to turn to Pitt as the only man who might save the situation.

Pitt, later known as the Earl of Chatham, was a man of eloquence, unselfish devotion and high ideals. From the beginning of his parliamentary career in 1735, he worked to eliminate corruption in the government. However, in addition to being arrogant, aloof and irritable, he was disliked by George Ⅱ. This delayed his selection as prime minister. The Seven Years' War left the King no choice; he was forced to turn to Pitt. This was the first instance of an English king being compelled to accept as prime minister a man whom he both disliked and distrusted.

Undismayed by the state of affairs, Pitt began with the characteristic vigor which moved *Frederick the Great[169] to remark that England had finally brought forth a man. Pitt was so confident of his own abilities that he said, "I am sure that I can save the country, and I am sure that no one else can". Britain was fighting France in Europe, America and India. Pitt knew that the European struggle was most important to achieving complete victory. He sent subsidies to Frederick the Great, who was opposing several countries, including France. He organized a militia for home defense, planned ways to oust the French from both Canada and India, and used the British navy to blockade French ports to stop supplies and reinforcements from reaching French forces overseas. Pitt's vigorous measures turned the Seven Years' War into the most successful war for England in the eighteenth century.

3. GEORGE Ⅲ (1760—1820)

A) Character of George Ⅲ

In the midst of the English success in the Seven Years' War, George Ⅱ died suddenly. He was succeeded by his eldest grandson, George Ⅲ. Only twenty-two years old when he ascended the throne, the new King could rightfully boast that he was "born and bred a Briton". George Ⅲ was conscientious, well-meaning, hard-working and religious. His private life was exemplary. He lived simply and thriftily, devoting considerable time to agriculture and earning for himself the nickname, "Farmer George".

On the other hand, he was obstinate and narrow-minded. He could not accept the views of others, and was harsh in his condemnation of all who disagreed with him. His mother, who had supervised his upbringing, taught him exaggerated ideas of royal power. Accordingly, he resolved to be every inch a king. This did not lead him to attack the sovereignty of Parliament, for he was not aiming for absolute power. Instead, he wanted the crown to resume administering affairs and determining government policy, activities which the two previous monarchs had ignored. George Ⅲ wanted to make the cabinet ministers responsible to him instead of to Parliament.

B) George Ⅲ Gathers Power

Conditions were favorable to him. The Whigs had grown lazy and no longer represented well-defined principles. They had split into a number of factions which quarreled with one another. They had lost popular support because the people were tired of the corrupt means the Whigs used to retain power. On the other hand, the Tories rallied around George Ⅲ, who warmly welcomed their support. With their aid, he resolved to break the power of the Whig *oligarchy[170] and to make himself the master of his own kingdom. His first move was to force Pitt to resign by refusing to declare war on Spain. The enemies of England were jubilant. "His (Pitt's) dismissal is a greater gain to us than the winning of two battles," said the French philosopher *Diderot[171]. In 1763, the Seven Years' War ended. At the resultant Peace of Paris, England gained a great deal, but might have gained much more if the king had retained and supported Pitt.

C) The Loss of the American Colonies

After Pitt resigned, George Ⅲ devoted himself to strengthening a group in Parliament known as the "King's Friends". He spent much of the royal revenues buying them votes or seats in the House of Commons. Even with these measures, he only gained control with difficulty. Between 1760 and 1770, ministers and cabinets changed often. Finally, Lord North (1770 – 1782) became prime minister. During North's ministry, George Ⅲ exercised personal power, prompting his mother to say, "Now, indeed, my son is king". George's personal rule had disastrous consequences for England. The American colonies were lost, and the national debt increased tremendously. Toward the end of Lord North's ministry, Parliament became alarmed over the king's power. In 1780, a resolution was passed which stated that "the influence of the crown has increased, is increasing, and ought not to be increased". The situation might have become serious, but in 1783 the king offered the position of prime minister to William Pitt's second son, known as William Pitt the younger. Because Pitt the younger was equally popular with the king and the people, he was able to mediate between the two factions.

D) Son of William Pitt Assumes Power

Pitt the younger was elected to Parliament in 1781, when he was only twenty-two years old. An accomplished orator, he was an instant success in the House of Commons. In 1782, he was made chancellor of the exchequer, an important fiscal position, and in 1783 he became the youngest prime minister in English history. At first, people ridiculed the idea of such a young man heading the government; they did not believe that he could remain as prime minister. However, Pitt the younger held his office, with a short gap in

1801–1803, until he died in 1806.

Pitt devoted himself to eliminating the national debt, cutting down on government expenditures, organizing a system of auditing the national accounts, and introducing order into the chaos of the national finances. Pitt's greatest achievement was his commercial treaty with France, concluded in 1787. Based on *Adam Smith[172]'s idea that two nations will benefit from a free exchange of goods, this treaty abolished the duties on most of the staple products of Great Britain and France, and both countries profited from it. Pitt also advocated the abolition of the slave trade, parliamentary reform and the removal of restrictions on Roman Catholics. He lacked sufficient support for the first two reforms, but he was able to remove barriers for Catholics so that they could enter the army and the legal profession.

E) Act of Union with Ireland

During Pitt's administration, the Act of Union (1800) merged the parliaments of Great Britain and Ireland. When the American colonies rebelled, the Irish realized that they were also ruled by a parliament in which they had no representation. The consequence was a widespread movement for a new relationship between Ireland and Great Britain. On the one hand, the Irish sought complete independence; on the other, Pitt sought to incorporate the Irish into the British system of government. His solution was the Act of Union, which was so unpopular that bribery and intimidation were needed to induce its passage through Parliament. The Irish were represented in both Houses of the British Parliament. Their representation in the House of Lords consisted of four Irish Anglican bishops and twenty-eight Irish nobles. Their representation in the House of Commons consisted of one hundred members. The name chosen for the combined nations was "the United Kingdom of Great Britain and Ireland". Pitt also worked for the emancipation of the Irish Roman Catholics, but George III said that he had taken an oath to maintain the privileges of the Anglican church, and such emancipation would violate his oath. Despite the Act of Union, relations between the Irish Catholics and British Protestants remained unfriendly.

F) Reaction to the French Revolution

After the revolutionary French beheaded their king and began the Reign of Terror (1793) in which mob rule prevailed, Pitt devoted himself to preventing the French revolutionary spirit from spreading to England. Haunted by the fear of a similar revolution in England, Pitt changed from a proponent of liberal reform to a reactionary, who advocated coercion and repression. For example, in 1794 he suspended the *Habeas Corpus Act[173], the parliamentary act which prevented arbitrary arrest without a trial. Moreover, he restricted the right of people to meet together freely, and he suppressed two small social groups which advocated revolutionary ideas.

These stringent measures were not necessary. In 1790, *Edmund Burke[174] launched his crusade against the French Revolution by publishing his Reflections on the Revolution in France, one of the most powerful and influential pamphlets ever written. It instantly became popular, and seven thousand copies were sold in six days. Burke described the French Revolution (1789–1799) as a "strange chaos of levity and ferocity, and of all sorts of crimes jumbled together with all sorts of follies". Burke's pamphlet provoked many rebuttals, among them was *Thomas Paine[175]'s Rights of Man, but it was Burke's conservative views that won the support of the upper and middle classes, setting the tone for English public opinion and making it easy for Pitt to prevent French revolutionary ideas from spreading into England.

Some historians argue that the French Revolution was the most important event in English history. That great social upheaval released forces which became decisive factors in establishing democratic government in England. But, for more than a generation, conservative opinion opposing revolutionary ideas halted urgently needed reforms at a time of industrial changes, called "the Industrial Revolution".

4. THE INDUSTRIAL REVOLUTION

At the beginning of the eighteenth century, England was chiefly an agricultural country; more than three-fourths of the population lived in rural districts. The cities, except London, were small. Bristol, the second largest city in the kingdom, could boast a population of only thirty thousand. Existing industry was mostly domestic. Since it took place in the homes or cottages of the workers, domestic industry was often called a "cottage industry". Cloth manufacture was often a cooperative activity shared by all members of the family. The wife and children prepared the wool and spun the yarn, and the weaver wove the cloth. Most products were made by hand; spinning and weaving were done on the old-fashioned spinning wheel and the hand loom.

During the eighteenth and nineteenth centuries, great changes took place. By the end of the eighteenth century, human power was rapidly being supplanted by machine power; the domestic system was being replaced by the factory system; and a substantial part of the population was moving to industrial towns and cities. England was well on its way toward becoming a major workshop of the world.

These great industrial changes are commonly called "The Industrial Revolution". This term must not be interpreted too literally. There was no revolutionary overturning of established practices. Instead, changes came slowly. Old ideas were modified, not swept away, and new ideas gradually took shape.

Many historians now believe that the Industrial Revolution began in 1709, the year in which a method for smelting iron with coal and lime was discovered; or at least by 1718, when a silk factory was equipped with power machinery. Certainly, by 1760, the industrial changes were far advanced. However, it was not until 1830, that even one British industry had completed all of the technical changes which defined the Industrial Revolution. This is why the beginning period of the British Industrial Revolution must be extended to the middle of the nineteenth century. Every step added another link to the chain of an industrial evolution which amounted to a "revolution".

The heart of the Industrial Revolution was the invention of machinery which could be applied to manufacturing processes. Earlier, machines had been used in manufacturing; for example, Italian silk manufacturers used machinery powered by horses and water as early as the fourteenth century. In the sixteenth century, an Englishman invented a machine to knit woolen stockings a hundred times faster than by hand. This machine was later adapted to knitting caps, gloves and cotton or silk hosiery. Also, there was a mechanical loom, which embodied the basic principles of automatic weaving, used to weave ribbons, tapes and braids. What separated such occasional use of machinery from the Industrial Revolution was the role of the machine, which now became central to the industry.

Several factors caused these changes to occur earlier in England than on the European Continent. First, overseas expansion by England had opened markets that were ready to absorb more manufactured goods. Second, England had vast deposits of coal and iron, both essential in manufacturing machinery. Third, the English inventors outstripped those of other countries. So pressing was the demand for certain types of machines that the British Royal Society of Arts offered money to those who would invent them. The result was new machine after new machine, until they dominated manufacturing. However, it is important not to overemphasize the role of inventors in the Industrial Revolution. These inventors were servants, not masters, of the new economic forces.

The direct result of manufacturing with machinery was the rise of the factory system. Factories had existed before the Industrial Revolution, but power machinery created a new system. Power machinery meant greater efficiency, more goods and greater freedom for manufacturers to locate plants where labor was scarcer. Power was originally supplied by animals or water. During the eighteenth century, steam power, a far greater force, was harnessed by several inventors, including Thomas Newcomen, who invented the steam pump, and James Watt, who invented the steam engine.

The factories produced goods with greater efficiency, but required more raw materials and more fuel. This created a demand for better means of transportation. In the second half of the eighteenth century, wagons replaced pack-horse trains, and new roads were built. However, the roads were poorly constructed and it was not until the turn of the century that macadam roads were built.

A network of canals further improved transportation in the 18th century. The development of the steamboat and the locomotive engine in the nineteenth century greatly enhanced the speed of shipping raw materials and manufactured products.

Better transportation meant more markets and more profits. However, it was not the workers who earned the profits. Profits went to the employers, or capitalists, people who invested their wealth to make more money. Capitalists provided the workers with the raw materials, paid them wages, and sold the finished products. At that time factory workers were entirely at the mercy of the factory owners.

The changes which occurred during the Industrial Revolution met with opposition from workers. From the very beginning, the hand-workers, fearing the loss of their livelihood, tried to halt the use of machines even by force. They attacked factories, smashed machinery, and sometimes even tried to harm the inventors. In spite of this futile resistance, the use of machines prevailed.

5. CHANGES IN AGRICULTURE

While the application of machinery was transforming industrial society, widespread changes were also taking place in the rural countryside—changes which some historians have called the "Agrarian Revolution". Better methods of farming were introduced; larger areas were put under cultivation; and scientific breeding improved the quality of cattle.

A number of agriculturists advocated applying scientific methods to improve productivity. John Tull, an outstanding pioneer in the scientific movement, devised the horse-hoe, horse-pulled blades which broke soil into small particles. He also invented a drilling machine which planted the seeds in straight rows.

In the eighteenth century, the serious difficulty of feeding cattle during the winter was eliminated by the cultivation of new varieties of grasses, turnips, clover, and other root crops. Overall, agricultural changes spread slowly and were mostly local.

6. LIFE AND CULTURE

Although a reaction against the loose morals of the Restoration period did take place and although polite society prided itself on its refinement, the early eighteenth century was an age of ignorance, brutality and drunkenness. Most people were uneducated, and only a few people had a higher education. Women were often illiterate; they had few legal rights. The poorer classes living in the cities suffered from crowded and unhealthy living conditions, along with the other effects of poverty. During the first half of the eighteenth century, political offices and votes were bought and sold openly. Drunkenness increased to such an extent that it came to be regarded as the national vice.

The brutality of the age was reflected in a general contempt for human suffering. Criminals on the way to be hanged were given brandy and cheered. The insane were confined in Bethlehem Hospital, better known as Bedlam, where they were chained, beaten and generally mistreated. The unfortunate insane provided amusement to their fellow Londoners, much as zoo animals are a spectacle today.

7. INTELLECTUAL LIFE IN EIGHTEENTH-CENTURY ENGLAND

A) *Methodism[176]

In 1729, a group of students at Oxford University founded a "Holy Club", which eventually became a major subdivision of the Church of England, and later a separate Christian denomination. Known as Wesleyanism or Methodism, this movement was important in helping the working classes to improve their condition through abstinence from self-destructive practices, such as drinking alcohol, and dedication to improvement of the human condition through education and reform. Like the Quakers and the fourteenth century peasants, they turned to the Bible with its message that all people are brothers and sisters in one human family. To the upper classes, this outrageous doctrine was based on a social concept that was unthinkable. Although no longer as politically important, Methodism continues to be a popular religion in both England and the United States.

B) *"Laissez Faire" [177] Economics

In 1776, Adam Smith published his important *An Inquiry into the Nature and Causes of the Wealth of Nations* (also known as *The Wealth of Nations*). Smith argued that a beneficent law or order of nature regulates human affairs. Smith's idea of nature owes much to the thinker, David Hume, and also to the general eighteenth century belief in the rational and orderly nature of the universe. This belief in a rational universe had its roots in the orderly world of Newtonian mechanics. Smith argued that nature's laws are more important than human laws and, therefore, that mercantilist restrictions on trade and industry are "unnatural", or contrary to the law of nature. Therefore, they defeated the very purpose for which they were designed. He declared that the greatest wealth can be obtained only through the free action of individuals, for nature has arranged that, by seeking his own welfare, an individual also promotes the welfare of his nation. He condemned the idea that prosperity of one nation must mean a loss to others, asserting that a prosperous neighbor offers a better market than an impoverished one. Unfortunately, this book did not produce an immediate change in the restrictions placed on Ireland or on colonized lands, but it did influence Pitt the younger in his treaty with France, and it did influence the future of western commerce through Smith's argument that government should stay out of business, an idea commonly known as "free trade" or laissez faire.

C) Newspapers and Literature

Another noteworthy event during the eighteenth century was the publication of the first English daily newspaper, the Daily Courant (1702). Newspapers became increasingly important as people became more literate, more involved in government, and more aware of the changes that affected business and their lives.

Those works of art and literature which remain important from this time tend to be satiric, poking fun at those who act irrationally. This satire could be politically savage, as in *Jonathan Swift[178]'s attacks on English cruelty in Ireland, or gentle and humorous as in the essays of *Joseph Addison[179] (1672 – 1719) or the novels of *Henry Fielding[180] (1707 – 1754). These authors criticized people from all social ranks. The most notable visual satirist was the engraver, *William Hogarth[181] (1697 – 1764), who portrayed the dissolute lives of both upper and lower classes.

Ⅶ. Napoleonic Wars and a Century of Slow Reforms

1. THE NAPOLEONIC ERA

The period 1793 – 1815 was marked by British preoccupation with events across the English Channel, while the internal changes of growing industrial and agricultural revolution went unmarked.

Provoked by an incompetent monarchy and harsh conditions for the common people, the French people revolted against their king and aristocracy. At first, English reformers supported this revolt, but after the royal family and middle-class people were executed, English reaction turned to disgust and fear. When the French people beheaded their king and declared France a republic, their armies swarmed out of France, intent on forcibly converting their neighbors to French beliefs, particularly the equality of people. The French military was strong on fervor, but weak on leadership, since the traditional leaders had been aristocrats and few aristocrats remained in France.

Napoleon Bonaparte filled this vacuum. Napoleon, a soldier from Corsica, a French-Italian island, quickly rose through the military ranks to become general, then political leader of France, and finally the emperor of conquered Europe. For a time, the only European power opposing him was Great Britain, protected by the English Channel and the British fleet. British sea power prevented a French invasion of England or the British territory in the Mediterranean Sea, and seriously interrupted French trade with its colonies. The British admiral, *Lord Nelson[182], is still renowned in England for his naval tactics and courage. His flagship, Victory, is on display in Portsmouth Harbor as a national shrine.

However, the British military was, in some ways, inferior to the French, since leaders were often chosen for their aristocratic connections or their wealth. The common soldier or seaman was treated as expendable "cannon fodder", or food for cannons. Conditions were particularly harsh in the British navy so that men either avoided conscription or joined the merchant fleet. As a result, the government allowed military gangs known as "the press" to capture men and force them into the navy. Sailors in the navy were discharged only by injury or death. Even these measures were not enough, so British warships seized sailors from American ships. This practice provoked the United States to declare war on England (War of 1812). Consequently, England was forced to fight on both the European and North American continents and on the seas wherever French ships were found.

The turning point came when Napoleon treacherously invaded his ally, Russia. This campaign was disastrous. The Russians refused to admit defeat and waited, letting the vast territory of Russia and the cold Russian winter fight for them. Napoleon invaded with 400,000 men in June, 1812. By December of that year, he and his remaining 20,000 men were driven out of Russia. European countries now joined with England in a common alliance, and aided by the military genius of Britain's Lord *Wellington[183], the Allied armies finally defeated Bonaparte in the Battle of Waterloo (1815).

England, Russia, Austria and Prussia signed the *Quadruple Alliance[184] in November, 1815 to ensure the quarantine of France. This was an experiment in government by international conference, a modest first step along the road leading to the League of Nations and the United Nations in the twentieth century. This agreement, known as the Vienna Settlement, marked one of those rare attempts at massive political reconstruction of Europe. There were few reprisals against France, which was ordered back to its pre-Napoleonic borders; forced to return plunder to its rightful owners; ordered to pay an indemnity to the Allies; and subject to an army of occupation for a few years. In many respects, the Vienna Settlement succeeded very well since there was no major European war until the *Crimean[185] conflict of the 1850's, and none involving all of Europe until 1914. Not until the end of the Second World War, did victors begin to treat the defeated aggressor more generously.

2. BRITAIN AS A DEMOCRACY: 1815-1901—A CENTURY OF SLOW REFORMS
A) The Aftermath of the Napoleonic Wars—the Need for Reform

Having successfully dealt with problems on the continent, England now turned to equally pressing matters at home. The following years were marked by social unrest followed by social and political reform. In 1815, England's economy was undergoing rapid changes. Improvements in agriculture, due to technology and revised practices, transformed the countryside into larger farms; fewer agricultural workers were needed, and the numbers of returning soldiers and sailors added to rural unemployment. In contrast, industrial cities were growing rapidly. More and more manufacturing processes moved from the home to large factories, where men, women, and children were often overworked and underpaid, as well as subject to all the insecurities of the economy. By 1851, over half the population was urban. Industrialization did not take place without a struggle. Luddites were nineteenth-century workers who rioted and destroyed the machinery that threatened their jobs. These protests became more intense after the Napoleonic Wars.

Problems were heightened by a series of bad harvests in the years immediately after the Napoleonic Wars; competition from European manufacturers who returned to business after the defeat of Napoleon; and a very restrictive tariff on foreign grain that kept agricultural prices high (which benefited the landed gentry) at a time when people were starving. Aid for the poor was still regarded a religious function, and was administered through the local parishes. At the end of the Napoleonic Wars, the social problems were too great, and the parish system could no longer meet the needs of the growing numbers of poor people.

All over Europe, this period was one of class conflict, culminating in the unsuccessful revolts of 1848. This conflict inspired Karl Marx to write *Das Kapital*[186] and *The Communist Manifesto*[187]. However, England did not suffer the severe class warfare that waged on the European continent, perhaps because strain had been reduced by parliamentary reform which began earlier in England. Although England was still under the nominal rule of a monarch, political power had now passed into the hands of Parliament. One monarch, Queen Victoria (1837 – 1901) came to symbolize nineteenth-century England, but in fact, she had little real power. The struggle was no longer between monarch and Parliament, but between social classes for representation in Parliament.

B) Parliamentary Reform—the Path to Universal Suffrage

Reform did not come quickly or easily. The landed aristocracy still controlled Parliament, because representation was based on the medieval census, not modern population. Old agricultural centers had few people, while the urban centers were rapidly expanding. Yet the old agricultural centers still had many parliamentary representatives while cities of millions, which needed new parliamentary legislation, had few representatives. The members of the House of Commons were chosen by less than one-sixth of the adult male population. Votes were cast in public, with the landlord's men watching. Reformers were hampered because people who still feared the excesses of the French Revolution resisted reform.

For fifteen years, riots and political unrest were ruthlessly suppressed. Still, people pressed for change, and some movement came from the Tory government. Socially concerned conservatives, such as Robert Peel, reduced the number of crimes punishable by death, reduced the restrictions on colonial trade with Europe, and removed restrictions on Catholicism in Ireland. *Peel*[188] also founded the first regular police force in England, which is why policeman are sometimes called "bobbies", a variant of his first name, Robert (Bob).

Then, in 1830, a combination of liberals from both parties defeated the Tories, and passed the Reform Bill (1832), the first step toward modern universal suffrage. The cities were better represented, and the vote, at first restricted to property owners, was expanded to include some men who paid high rents. The two-year struggle to pass the bill was an intense one. One author wrote, "The British people were the real heroes of the Reform Bill crisis. Middle-class and working-class leaders shared in a masterful organization and manipulation of public feeling.... By their determination and steadiness during a two-year crisis, the British people demonstrated that they were indeed ready for a constitutional change that broadened the base of political power" (Youngs et al, 307).

The Reform Bill of 1832 was the first of several voting reform bills in the nineteenth century. Two more laws expanded the franchise to nearly all males over the age of twenty-one. However, women were still denied the franchise. Despite the addition of different classes of voters, the two-party system continues in Britain, the USA and some Commonwealth countries. In England, Parliament is divided into those supporting the government and "His (or Her) Majesty's Loyal Opposition". In the nineteenth century, these two groups were the Whigs, who later became known as Liberals, and Tories, who were later called Conservatives. In the twentieth century, the Liberals were replaced by the Labour Party. Although smaller groups gain seats in Parliament, the legislative body is not a collection of separate political parties, but rather consists of the majority party, which in Britain is also the executive branch of government, and the "opposition", a collection of opposing parties.

Despite this rhetoric of "opposition", Liberals and Conservatives had a base of unity that underlay party politics and political discussions. Both the party in power and the party in opposition were loyal to the established ways and were desirous of national prosperity. This developed in the British people habits of compromise, of respect for the law, and of political good *sportsmanship[189], which continues today.

C) Help for the Working Classes—Relief, Bread, and Protection

In the two decades following the passage of the Reform Bill of 1832, several measures were taken to provide relief for the working classes. Part of the pressure for these changes came from a working class movement known as *Chartism[190]. The Chartists were the new urban industrial workers, especially the more active and radical workers who believed that the masses would vote for graduated income taxes and socialism. The Chartists called for universal suffrage, the secret *ballot[191], payment for members of Parliament, equal electoral districts, and annually elected Parliaments. Although none of these reforms was fully established in the nineteenth century, all but the last change was completed during the twentieth century.

Pressure for reform also came from the *Utilitarians[192], a middle-class group who believed that educated men will be led by their own self-interest to do what is best for humanity. Therefore, they believed that the government which governs best, governs least; and they also believed in establishing private educational institutions. Their efforts resulted in the New Poor Law (1834). This bill codified, centralized, and made more coherent the old tangle of public relief that came from the Elizabethan Poor Law (1601). As a result of the 1834 Bill, relief money went directly to families. The bill also tried to force people to work and to become more self-sufficient.

Another important measure was the repeal of the *Corn Laws[193] (1846). Free Traders wanted to eliminate the tariffs on imported grains and to make Britain a free-trade nation. The repeal of the Corn Laws helped the working classes by reducing the price of bread.

Also, the Factory Act of 1833 provided that salaried inspectors should enforce the law prohibiting children under the age of nine from working; children under the age of thirteen from working more than nine hours a day; and children under the age of eighteen from working more than twelve hours a day in factories. This act was followed by many others designed to protect workers. By the end of the nineteenth century there was a whole code of labor legislation, regulating hours of labor for everyone, giving special protection to women and children, and including provisions that made the employer responsible for helping workers injured in industrial accidents. Today this protection is known as Workman's Compensation.

D) Education—A Late Start

Like suffrage, welfare and labor reforms, educational reforms were sporadic but cumulative. The Victorian idea that education was not a government responsibility postponed a general education act until 1870. The issue was complicated by arguments between Anglicans and non-Anglicans over compulsory religious education. Finally, the 1870 Act laid the foundation for widespread compulsory, free public education. The religious differences were solved by exempting tax-supported schools from compulsory religious education. However, church schools were given public aid, a government support that continues today. By the end of the nineteenth century, illiteracy in Britain had generally been eliminated.

E) Ireland—Famine and *Home Rule[194]

In the 1840's, the "Irish potato famine" ruined the potato crop, which provided most of the food for the Irish poor. Tens of thousands of Irish died; and many more emigrated, mostly to the United States. The British government gave little direct relief; help was too little and too late. In the 1870's, *Charles Parnell[195] organized the Irish Nationalists in the English Parliament into a well-disciplined group that could often control the voting. In 1885, the English Prime Minister, *Gladstone[196], proposed a Home Rule Bill, giving the Irish their own Parliament. The Bill never became law, setting the stage for the Catholic Irish revolt in the twentieth century.

3. FOREIGN POLICY—PEACE AND IMPERIALISM

The basic unity underlying the nineteenth-century Liberals and Conservatives was evident in foreign relations. Most citizens agreed on the fundamental position of Britain: maintain the European balance-of-power, preferably by diplomatic rather than military action; seek no new territories in Europe; police the seas with the British navy; open world markets to British goods; and maintain the vast network of the British Empire.

During 1815 – 1914, Britain was involved in only one European war: the Crimean War (1854 – 1856). France and England joined as allies to resist Russian expansion into Turkey and the Near East. It was a typical balance-of-power war in which Britain played its traditional role of taking arms against a major power adding to its territory or its "spheres of influence". France and England successfully stopped the Russian invasion. A major result of this conflict was the disintegration of the Turkish *Ottoman Empire[197] and the addition of the *Balkan Region[198] to Europe. The Balkan States, with their deep-seated ethnic hatreds, continue to be a source of tension.

The Crimean War provided *Florence Nightingale[199], a remarkable young English woman, with an opportunity to provide a respectable career for women. Her organizational efforts to provide care to sick and wounded soldiers in the Crimea lay the foundation for the profession of nursing.

Imperialism was the one foreign issue which deeply divided the British political parties. *Disraeli[200] (1868,1874 - 1880), the Conservative Prime Minister, defended the greatness of the Empire, while his successor, Gladstone (1868, 1880 - 1885, 1885 - 1886, 1892 - 1894), the Liberal Prime Minister, attacked imperialism as un-Christian and unprofitable.

4. INTELLECTUAL LIFE IN NINETEENTH-CENTURY ENGLAND

Poetry and novels, including literary works written by women, flourished in nineteenth-century England. One can learn much of Victorian life from the literature: women from the works of *Jane Austen[201] (1775 - 1817) and *Charlotte Bronte[202] (1816 - 1855); the poorer classes from the works of *Charles Dickens[203] (1812 - 1870) and *Mrs. Elizabeth Gaskell[204] (1810 - 1865); politics and the life of the gentry from *Anthony Trollope[205]'s (1815 - 1882) novels, and the problems of the countryside from books written by *Thomas Hardy[206] (1840 - 1928).

Nineteenth-century British science flourished, but one major scientific theory clashed with religious dogma. Based on the ideas of *Charles Lyell[207] (1797 - 1875), a geologist known for his extremely careful and detailed observations of nature, *Charles Darwin[208] (1809 - 1882) constructed a theory of human evolution that contradicted traditional Christian thought. Darwin's On the Origin of Species by Natural Selection (1859) transformed western thinking about the natural and social worlds. Eighteenth-century thinkers viewed nature as part of a mechanical, "clockwork" universe. Darwin introduced the concept of change, which became transmuted by other Victorians into the idea of "progress", or social change for the better. Of course, the Victorians felt that they represented the perfect result of development, with other cultures being more "backward" and "primitive". Ironically, as traditional Christians fought the concept that human beings developed from other biological forms, they accepted the notion that other cultures were "backward", and in need of "civilizing" or being transformed to be like Victorian England.

Ⅷ. Nineteenth Century Imperialism

1. IMPERIALISM, OLD AND NEW

There were several important new elements in the imperialism of western peoples in the nineteenth century. First, it was a major part of political life, with goals, methods, and advocates known to all concerned with politics. Second, western imperial expansion was global. " *Geopolitics[209] ", the cumulative pressures of military and economic rivalries among the western nations, widened to Africa, Asia, and South America. Third, when capitalists and industrialists discovered that they were unable to market all of their products at home, they turned to markets abroad. Fourth, many Christian and secular missionaries honestly desired to make life better for all mankind.

2. THE BRITISH EMPIRE

The nineteenth-century British Empire had two distinct, if unacknowledged, divisions. In the first category were the white-dominated countries of Canada, Australia,

New Zealand and South Africa. The second category was subdivided into two parts: those territories that did not have a long documented history of civilization, such as territories in Africa and the *West Indies[210]; and those territories with a long tradition of civilization, such as Egypt, India and China.

A) White-dominated Countries

Countries in the first category were generally left alone, except for a heavy stream of British immigrants. The British North American Act (1867) established the present loose confederation of states in Canada; earlier, local governments had been granted to Australia (1855) and New Zealand (1856).

B) Countries without a Long History of Civilization

In the second category, those territories without a long history of civilization were often treated drastically. Many central African territories were acquired by treaty from European countries, including the Sudan, *Somaliland[211], *Kenya[212], *Uganda[213], *Zimbabwe[214], *Gambia[215], *Sierra Leone[216], the Gold Coast and *Nigeria[217], and new countries were formed that had little relationship to the cultures and people within their boundaries. This was particularly troublesome in Central Africa, as European-established borders cut through tribes, divided flourishing cultures and forcibly combined hereditary enemies. Many of the later tragedies, including genocidal slaughters in Africa, have their roots in this practice. British Territories acquired by treaty with other European countries included a variety of West Indian Islands, *Guyana[218] and *Honduras[219], and a large part of Central Africa. Although these territories regained self-rule in the twentieth century, many still use English as their official language, in part to avoid favoring one ethnic group over another.

The case of South Africa was different. In 1815, Britain acquired South Africa from the Netherlands by treaty. As the British moved in, the Boers, the descendents of Dutch colonists, grew discontented, particularly when English became the official language. A series of battles between the two groups of colonists escalated into the *Boer War[220] that ended in 1902. The Union of South Africa (1910) united several colonies under one government, and both English and the South African Dutch dialect were designated the official languages.

C) Countries with a Long History of Civilization

The remaining territories, those with a long history of civilization, were treated differently. Egypt was under French rule during much of the nineteenth century. The French had built and maintained the Suez Canal, which became increasingly important to the British as a short water route to Asia. When the Egyptians and Sudanese began to revolt against the Europeans, Britain turned to France for help in suppressing the riots. When France refused, British forces entered Egypt and remained.

For the first half of the nineteenth century, India continued to be governed by the commercial firm, the East India Company, in combination with local princes. Although the British brought central government and a system of transportation that stimulated development, they also repressed Indian industry in favor of British manufactured goods. Following a mutiny by the Indian army in 1857, India was placed under the direct rule of the British government which continued to exploit India.

3. ARGUMENTS OVER IMPERIALISM

The English people were not united about the practice of imperialism. Through the nineteenth and early twentieth century, the British debated their role.

A) Nineteenth-Century Arguments Defending Imperialism

One argument for the defense of imperialist expansion was "survival of the fittest", a phrase borrowed from the Social Darwinists who were people who tried to apply Darwin's concepts to human societies. Defenders of imperialism argued that, since Europeans were able to defeat the non-Europeans in war, they had shown that Europeans were more fit to survive in terms of evolution and progress. Therefore, Europeans would put order and prosperity into the lives of native people who were as yet unable to undertake leadership tasks and to assume moral responsibility.

Other European imperialists supported the theory of trusteeship, the most popular defense of imperialism, particularly among Anglo-Saxon people. They argued that Europeans would manage the government of native peoples until they were educated to take over their own affairs. Christian missionaries generally agreed with this argument. These missionaries were a major factor in the nineteenth-century expansion of the West. In non-developed countries, whole tribes nominally accepted Christianity, but continued to practice their native religions. The missionaries had only limited success in India and Japan. These civilized countries through thousands of years of civilization had deep-rooted beliefs.

The third argument supported imperialism as a defensive strategy: Europeans, outnumbered in a harsh world, had to organize and defend themselves against the non-European, non-white majority. One variation of the defensive argument involved increasing the number of naval bases and supply stations throughout the world so that the navy could protect the British Empire.

B) Nineteenth-Century Arguments Attacking Imperialism

Opponents developed many arguments against imperialism. The Social Darwinists believed that imperialism denied the struggle for existence that applied to humans as it applied to plants and animals. Each group of people had something to contribute to the world, and the deliberate destruction or suppression of any group harms the others and prevents true cultural evolution among human beings.

Other anti-imperialists questioned the economic benefits of overseas expansion. They argued that the only people who profited from imperialist ventures were the privileged minority in both the homeland and in the colonies.

Finally, anti-imperialists maintained that home country support for expansion rested on the ordinary man's vicarious satisfaction from national achievements, similar to the satisfaction in a local sport team's victory. Anti-imperialists disagreed with this motive, believing instead that human action ought to be rational and devoted to the greatest good of the greatest number of people, an idea expressed by the British Utilitarian philosophers, *Jeremy Bentham[221] (1748 – 1832) and *John Stuart Mill[222] (1806 – 1873).

IX. Twentieth-Century England: Crisis of Identity

1. EDWARDIAN BRITAIN—ABORTED CHANGE

The death of Queen Victoria and the succession of her son Edward (1841 – 1910) seemed to offer a much needed change to many Britons. Although political power no longer resided with the monarch, Queen Victoria had represented a tradition of empire that many now found outdated. British industry and mercantile power were facing severe challenges from other nations. British imperialism faced a strong rival in the United States. Europe was divided into hostile camps; Ireland was on the point of revolt. Women were pressuring for the right to vote, and large labor unions tried to force improvement through a series of strikes. The new Liberal government began a series of legislative acts to address these problems, but all progress halted as a result of war. An assassination of a minor official in the Balkans was the flimsy excuse for starting World War I (1914 – 1918).

2. BRITAIN AND WORLD WAR I—GLOBAL WARFARE

During World War I, ten million men died, fighting either for the Allies (Britain, France, Greece, Italy, Japan, Russia, *Serbia[223] and the United States) or the Central Powers (Austria-Hungary, Germany and Turkey).

A) The Desire for Territory

The causes of the war were already evident in the western nation-state system. Traditionally, nation-states have tried to increase their wealth, prestige and territory. By the early twentieth century, there was little room for European expansion except in the Balkan states of southeastern Europe, a major European gateway to Turkey and the Near East. Great Britain, the dominant world power, supported the existing balance-of-power and distribution of territories. Germany, growing in population and economic power, was a disturbing threat, which the British wished to neutralize. Other European countries looked greedily at neighboring territory where they once had claims, either through war or royal marriages. Since each nation thought it could profit by war, little was needed to start the global conflict.

B) The War—Devastating Losses

Although Japan fought the Germans in the Far East, along with troops from Commonwealth countries and the United States, the main conflict took place in Europe and on the world's major oceans. There were two European fronts or lines of opposing forces. The Eastern front primarily involved Russia, Greece and Turkey against the Central Powers, while the Western Front involved France and Britain against Germany. Although the Eastern front shifted territory as forces moved into and out of Russia and the Near East, the Western Front remained static for the entire war. This front consisted of trenches lined with barbed wire and protected by machine guns. There was little use of aircraft, but there was heavy use of poison gas.

At first, there was strong support for the war in England. Women harassed any healthy-looking young man in civil dress, giving him a "white feather" to symbolize the man's cowardice. The royal family changed its name from the Germanic House of Hanover to its current, more British-sounding name, the *House of Windsor[224]. Women entered the workforce to take the place of men fighting in the trenches. The income tax was extended to include the upper working classes. Some foodstuffs were available only in limited quantities. However, the years passed with no territorial gains; more and more men died or returned wounded or poisoned by gas.

Ironically, it was sea warfare that turned the tide of the war. Great Britain was supported by some of the Commonwealth countries, particularly Canada, Australia and New Zealand. The United States remained neutral for much of the war, seeing it as a European affair. This changed as a result of the battle for supremacy of the seas, which was both a military and an economic battle. Enemy merchant vessels were sunk by both sides. When German ships sank the USA merchant ships trading with the Allies, the losses provoked the United States to enter the war on the side of England—reminiscent of the events leading to the war of 1812, only now the United States fought with, not against, England. The influx of fresh American troops gave the victory to the allies, a victory that ultimately brought little lasting joy to any of the victors.

During the war, the British neglected the Irish, who went into a permanent state of rebellion. Southern Ireland, became the independent Republic of Ireland (also known as Eire) in 1922.

The Russian leadership lost more. An examination of the casualty lists gave a partial explanation. The British forces, including the troops from Commonwealth countries, totaled about 9 million men. Of these, one third were killed, wounded or taken prisoners. The Russian forces totaled about 12 million men. Of these, 10 million were killed, wounded or taken prisoners. The Russian people, infuriated by the losses, the irrationality of this imperialist war, the incompetency of their leaders, and the political system that empowered these leaders, revolted in 1917. The new socialist government withdrew from the war; *czarism[225] and the czar were obliterated from Russia.

C) The Peace—Further Devastation

Still, the Allied countries were the victors and determined the settlements during the 1919 Versailles Peace Treaty, settlements which had a lasting effect on Europe and the Near East.

The United States, represented by idealistic, peace-loving *Woodrow Wilson[226] (1856 – 1924), wanted a gentle settlement, similar to that imposed upon defeated Napoleonic France. Wilson also wanted to establish an international political organization, the League of Nations, to ensure that a global war would never happen again. He proposed a program of "Fourteen Points", which included open diplomacy, international disarmament, reduction or elimination of international tariffs and self-determination of nationalities. However, Wilson was not strong enough to impose this program on the allies who, mourning their losses and needing to justify the war to their peoples, gave the world a powerless League of Nations and a harsh peace.

Territories changed. Allied countries took portions of Germany, including control of the coal-rich *Saar basin[227]. Poland was reestablished as a country and given lands inhabited by important German minorities and other non-Polish speaking people. The Republic of Austria was formed, and many small, new countries were created in eastern Europe. Saudi Arabia became an independent country.

Control of non-European territory also changed through a system known as *"mandates[228]". Germany's colonies were given to the League of Nations, which promptly reassigned them to Allied countries who held control as a "mandate". The country holding a "mandate" was required regularly to inspect the controlled territory and to prepare it for independence. France and England divided control over German-held territory in Africa and the Near East. Japan was given the "mandate" to German holdings along the Pacific Rim. Japan promptly claimed the "mandated" holdings as Japanese territory. The League of Nations, lacking any means of enforcement, did nothing.

D) The Punishment of Germany

Land transfers were one major issue. Another issue was payment or reparations imposed on the Central Powers. It was primarily the German reparations that disturbed the future peace and the economy of the world. The Germans had to promise to pay for all the damage done to civilian property in Europe during the war. Ironically, the Germans were left without means to raise the money to make the payments. The German merchant fleet was given to the Allies. German territory was reduced, and her colonies were lost. Much of her coal went to France, Italy and Belgium. German sailors sank their own military ships, rather than gave them to the Allies. Finally, the Central Powers, with Germany singled out for special blame, were humiliated by being forced to say they were the only countries responsible for starting the war. The seeds for World War II had been planted.

3. INTERLUDE BETWEEN WARS (1919-1939)

A) The Postwar Depression

Britain at first seemed to emerge from World War I as a true victor: her trade rival, Germany, had been defeated, and the mandates added to her overseas dominions. At this point, Britain was at the peak of her power; she was a strong country surrounded and supported by strong allies, such as France, Italy, Japan and the Commonwealth countries. The events during the next thirty years dramatically reversed this situation.

Although the British Isles suffered no major material damage in World War I, the economic losses were very serious. Britain's post-war national debt was ten times that of 1914. Many British investments abroad had to be liquidated. Forty percent of the British merchant fleet had been destroyed. International trade on which Britain depended could not be restored rapidly in the unsettled postwar conditions.

One major result of the war was the effective competition from industrial plants of the United States, Canada and India. Germans, helped by US loans, renewed the industrial rivalry that had alarmed the British before World War I. Britain, the so-called "workshop of the world", could no longer give full employment to its millions of workers. They received meager unemployment payments, called "the dole", which was a form of relief. These workers were in no mood to accept a lower standard of living; they fought the war in the hope of a better future. Britain's economic decline was not catastrophic, but the dynamic growth of the economy slowed.

B) The Conservative and Labour Programs

Economic issues sharpened the differences between the Labour Party and the Conservative Party (Tories). The first casualty in this political struggle was the old Liberal party. Both Conservatives and Labour realized that twentieth-century Britain had to sell enough goods and services abroad to buy food and raw materials, but the two parties disagreed about how to achieve this goal.

Thwarted by high tariffs in the United States and elsewhere and by the world-wide drive to economic self-sufficiency, the Conservatives advocated protective tariffs against competing foreign goods. They also supported combining the Empire and the Commonwealth into a self-sufficient trade area. Under this system, raw materials produced in colonial and Commonwealth countries would receive preferred treatment in British markets in return for preferred treatment of British goods in the colonial and Commonwealth markets. The Commonwealth nations were reluctant to accept the less profitable role of producers of raw materials in exchange for British goods and services. Many of these countries wanted their independence and their own industries.

The Labour Party's solution to the economic problems was nationalization. The British government should purchase and operate key industries, paying just compensation to their private owners. Key industries suggested for nationalization were those organized on a large scale, including transportation, energy, coal, steel, machine tools, textiles, pottery and cutlery. As socialists, members of the Labour Party wanted nationalization because they believed that profits, rent and interest paid to the capitalist owners were forms of worker-exploitation and that exploitation would cease under nationalization. They argued that nationalization would enable British industries to produce goods more cheaply and efficiently.

Labour Party supporters also believed that British workmen, knowing that they were the real owners of their industries, would work longer and harder to raise production. This, in turn, would allow Britain to undersell her rivals in world markets.

C) Post World War Ⅰ Politics

During the twenty years between the two world wars, neither the Tories nor Labour were able to completely implement their ideas. Despite mounting tensions, most British remained law-abiding citizens. Reforms were instituted, such as expansion of voting rights to all men over the age of twenty-one and all women over the age of thirty (1918) and then to all women over the age of twenty-one (1928).

When the New York Stock Market crashed in October, 1929, the Great Depression spread around the world. Britain was forced to reduce social services, including money given to the unemployed. Britain went off the gold standard and dropped the value of the pound sterling. In 1932, Britain enacted protective tariffs and ceased payment on her war debts to the United States. By 1936, the economic and social questions faded before the threat of another war, fueled by the aggressions of Hitler in Germany, Mussolini in Italy, and the Japanese in China.

The unimportance of the monarchy to political events in Britain was demonstrated by the abdication of King Edward Ⅷ (1936), who wished to marry a woman considered ineligible because she was divorced and not from the nobility. When he abdicated as king "to marry the woman I love", his brother became George Ⅵ. The change in monarchs had no effect on the government.

D) Formation of the Republic of Eire (Most of Ireland Becomes a Separate Country)

In 1916, Irish nationalists, with German aid, staged an armed rebellion in Dublin. After the British subdued this "Easter Rebellion", Irish nationalists boycotted the British Parliament. Tired from their long war, the British were not ready to use force effectively. The Irish, who had created their own illegal parliament, were ready to fight. The extreme Sinn Fein, which means "ourselves alone" in Gaelic, split into two groups. The radicals insisted that all of Ireland achieve complete independence as a republic. The moderates were willing to allow the six northern Protestant counties to remain under direct British rule and were willing to accept dominion status, much like Canada, for the Roman Catholic counties. The moderates did obtain dominion status for the twenty-six southern counties, which were renamed the Irish Free State. The six northern counties, sometimes called Ulster, maintained the historical relationship with Great Britain which became the United Kingdom of Great Britain and Northern Ireland.

The Irish Revolution was a civil war between those Irish advocating a Free State and those advocating a republic. When the leader of the Free State group was assassinated, public opinion turned away from the republicans who had joined the Irish Parliament. The Irish Free State gradually and peacefully cut its ties with the United Kingdom. In 1948, Britain recognized the Irish Free State as the fully independent country, the Republic of Eire ("Eire" is Gaelic for "Ireland").

E) The British Commonwealth Between the Wars

In 1931, the Statute of Westminster gave self-government to the white-dominated countries in the Empire, which joined the organization called the British Commonwealth. Other colonial countries remained within the British Empire. Although Britain was unable to build a self-sufficient economic network among the Commonwealth countries, all of the Commonwealth countries fought on the British side during World War II. However, the independence movement gained strength in the colonial British Empire countries, particularly India.

4. BRITAIN IN WORLD WAR II

A) Move Toward War

The 1930's were marked by two very different trends. On the one hand, western nations were concerned with disarmament, notably through the World Disarmament Conference of 1932 and the London Naval Disarmament Conference of 1934. On the other hand, two centers of aggression developed: one in the Far East and one in Europe. While the western powers talked, Japan began a series of invasions into China. Despite Chinese appeals to the League of Nations, no help was sent. This gave encouragement to the Germans, who allied with Italy and set out to conquer their neighbors. At first the other European powers, particularly Britain, expected to solve this aggression through diplomacy, but when invasion followed invasion, France and Britain finally declared war on Germany in September, 1939.

B) Britain at War

Britain entered the European war with confidence. The French had a strong army, with powerful forces concentrated in a series of forts on the German border, known as the

*Maginot Line[229]. Britain, itself, believed it was protected by the English Channel and the North Sea. By May of 1941, the Germans and Italians controlled Europe. Fast tank divisions simply bypassed the French forts, cut off their supplies, and then destroyed them one by one. The remnants of the British and French armies in northern France were trapped between the English Channel and the German Army in Dunkirk, France.

The British and French soldiers resisted, in what was called their "finest hour". Instead of surrendering, as Hitler expected, the British fought back. When news of the trapped soldiers reached England, people, with no governmental prompting, set off in any small boat, capable of crossing the dangerous Channel waters—fishing boats, ferry boats, pleasure boats. This citizens' navy supplemented the small number of British navy ships and rescued 225,000 British and 100,000 French soldiers at Dunkirk.

Hitler sent an air fleet of bombers and fighters to Britain in preparation for an invasion. However, the Royal Air Force (RAF) was able to drive off many German planes in what is called the Battle of Britain. The Germans decided to destroy the supply ships from Canada and the United States through heavy *submarine[230] warfare. However, they did make one more attempt to force Britain to surrender by what is known as *"the Blitz"[231]. German bombers heavily attacked British cities, destroying one sixth of the housing in London, and causing great loss of life in all major English cities. Instead of weakening British resistance, the "Blitz", only strengthened it. British production of war materials continued. The King and Queen remained in their London residence, *Buckingham Palace[232], even though it was bombed. "The Blitz" lasted only from September, 1940 to May, 1941. Later bombing raids were sporadic until the final great bombardment of "vengeance weapons", or long range rockets that killed people and destroyed homes in the winter of 1944 – 1945.

*Winston Churchill[233], Prime Minster during World War II, expressed the spirit of wartime England. His first speech as prime minister candidly spoke to the British people about their difficult position. He said, "I have nothing to offer but blood, toil, tears and sweat". Then, after the rescue of the troops from Dunkirk, when the British still feared a German invasion, Churchill reaffirmed British resistance: "We shall fight on the beaches, we shall fight on the landing ground, we shall fight in the fields and in the streets, we shall fight in the hills; we shall never surrender".

Britain did not stand entirely alone. She served as a refuge for the remains of defeated European armies, such as the Polish air force, and as a home in exile for many European governments. She also was supported by Commonwealth forces, notably from Canada, India, South Africa, Australia and New Zealand. In 1941, this situation changed when the Japanese attacked Pearl Harbor, an American naval base in Hawaii. The British joined the Americans in declaring war on Japan. However, neither country had many troops or supplies in the Pacific. The Japanese occupied Hong Kong, Singapore, Malaya and *Rangoon[234], despite opposition from British and Commonwealth forces.

C) The End of the War

Finally, Hitler, like Napoleon before him, made the mistake of invading Russia. Once again, Russian resistance was heroic. The city of Stalingrad (Volgograd) has come to symbolize the determination of the Russian people. Although the city was surrounded, and the starving people fought with few weapons, Stalingrad successfully repulsed wave after wave of German attacks. Weakened by their losses in Russia, the Germans faced a new threat in Western Europe. An allied force of British, US and Commonwealth forces invaded Europe and drove the German army back to Germany, where they surrendered in May, 1945.

In Asia, the Chinese drove the Japanese out of China, and an allied army forced the Japanese back toward Japan. The horrors of the atomic bombs which annihilated the Japanese cities of *Hiroshima[235] and *Nagasaki[236] ended the war. The Japanese government surrendered in August, 1945.

D) Effects of the War

World War II was truly a world war, involving 57 nations and killing millions of people in many regions of the earth. The results of this global conflict were felt around the world. Western Europe, once the center of power, was weakened, and power shifted to the United States and the Soviet Union. The strain of sustained production and united resistance changed people's outlook and produced new concepts of national identity.

5. BRITAIN AFTER WORLD WAR II — DRAMATIC SHIFTS

In the second half of the twentieth century, Britain experienced profound changes. Some of the principal changes were acceptance of its role as a reduced military power, more autonomy for Scotland, Wales and Ireland, the independence of most Commonwealth countries, closer relationships with Europe, tense relationships with Ireland, changes in the degree of socialism, and challenges to the sense of national identity as immigration, for the first time since the Norman Invasion, brought marked cultural differences to Britain.

A) Reduced Military Power

After World War II, the United States replaced Britain as a major military power in the west. The loss of prestige was dramatized by the world response to the British-French invasion of Egypt in 1957. In the aftermath of an Israeli/Egyptian conflict, the French and British invaded Egypt on the pretext of maintaining order in *the Suez Canal[237], an important shipping route between Europe and the Far East. The entire world condemned the invasion, including staunch supporters of Britain like Canada and the United States. Humiliated, France and Britain withdrew. Since then, aside from attempts to maintain peace in Northern Ireland, British forces have served only as part of larger operations, such as those of the United Nations, or in small independent operations, such as the *Falklands[238] War in 1982, when Britain skirmished with Argentina for possession of small islands off the South American coast.

B) Independence of Most Commonwealth Countries

The period from 1947 to 1971 was characterized by the dissolution of the remains of the old British Empire. Commonwealth countries and countries held by mandate became independent, and some left the Commonwealth as well. The exodus began with India, Pakistan and Sri Lanka in the late 1940's; continued with most of the British-held African countries in the 1960's and the Pacific Island state, *Fiji[239], along with Caribbean islands in the 1970's. A few islands and small territories continue as dependencies. The Commonwealth itself was formally established in 1931 and continues today with 50 members who exchange information and contribute money toward joint development programs. The goals of the current Commonwealth include working towards peace through the United Nations, promoting personal freedom and racial equality, opposition to colonial domination, and reduction of the gap between wealthy and poor segments of humanity. These goals are very different from the early goals of the British Empire.

C) Irish Troubles—Tensions and Resolutions

The island of Ireland is divided into two countries. Located in the south, the larger country is the Republic of Ireland, or Eire, the Roman Catholic nation that fought free of British rule. The smaller country is Northern Ireland, a country of approximately 14,000 square kilometers, with a population that is forty percent Roman Catholic and sixty percent Protestant. In an age where the Anglican and Roman Catholic churches hold talks about reuniting, these Irish groups continue to hold ancient grudges, as the Protestant majority firmly dominates the Roman Catholic minority. Throughout the twentieth century, terrorism by both Catholics and Protestants was a problem in Northern Ireland and in England. Service in Northern Ireland is one of the most hazardous duties for the British army. Independent government for Northern Ireland (Home Rule) was repealed in 1972.

However, an historic accord in 1998 offered hope for the region. Irish leaders, from Northern Ireland and the Republic of Ireland, worked with British leaders to remove sources of discord. Northern Ireland was granted semi-autonomous rule, with representation of the Protestant majority and the Catholic minority in the Northern Irish government. The Republic of Ireland relinquished its claim to Northern Ireland. A Council was established to discuss matters of common concern to Northern Ireland and the Republic of Ireland. Political prisoners were released. British forces remained in Northern Ireland, but in reduced numbers and with reduced powers. In 1999 the leading Protestant party decided to begin the formation of a coalition government of Catholics and Protestants in Northern Ireland. A coalition government was formed, and warring factions have, for the most part, disarmed. The problems arising from Henry II's invasion of Ireland in the twelfth century seem to be finding resolution at the end of the twentieth century.

D) European Union (EU)—From Isolation to Integration

In contrast to the disintegration of the old British Empire under the stress of nationalism, Europe began a process of reducing national differences and of union into one community. At first Britain wished to remain independent. Then, abandoned by her major ally, the United States, during the Suez crisis in 1957, she turned to the European Economic Community (EEC) in 1962, only to be rejected because the French leader, *Charles DeGaulle[240], felt that the British were too independent and non-European. After the death of DeGaulle, Britain joined the EEC in 1973. On the whole, the British view their membership positively, although the changes from the old British system of money, adoption of the metric system and the EEC's restrictive agricultural policies caused discontent. As the EEC moves further toward a nation-state of Europe with a common currency and government, tensions can be expected to increase for the British resist further erosion of national independence. In 2008, Prime Minster Brown raised the question of dropping the British pound in favor of the euro, but there was still resistance. However, the train tunnel under the English Channel completed in 1994, known as the Chunnel, is a strong indication of British ties to continental Europe.

E) Changes in the Economy

Britain, at the end of World War II, had major economic problems. Shortages of food and domestic goods continued for several years after the war; food rationing, a system which required a purchaser to have government-issued *coupons[241] before buying, continued until the mid-nineteen fifties. Housing, destroyed by the German bombing, was in very short supply. Churchill's Conservative government, having brought the country through World War II, was replaced by a Labour government which implemented socialist solutions to these shortages and to the major problem of rebuilding the country.

These changes resulted in a series of "nationalizations", as major industries came under government, not private, control. In the five years after the war, the government took over the Bank of England, Civil Aviation, the National Coal Board, the bus and rail networks, as well as the supplies of electricity and natural gas. Perhaps the most far-reaching socialist measure was the inauguration of the National Health Service (1948), which promised free health care to all inhabitants of Britain. Confrontations between workers and government continued, but the British economy grew. The standard of living for ordinary citizens has risen greatly since World War II, aided by discoveries of natural gas and oil under the North Sea.

In the 1980's, the economy came under strain. The manufacturing sector declined as the service sector grew. In 1996, over sixty percent of the labor force was involved in service, less than thirty percent in manufacturing and construction, and slightly over one percent in agriculture. These transitions resulted in a high unemployment rate. The mounting expenses of the National Health Service caused a major drain of government funds. At this time, the Conservative government began to dismantle the socialist elements of the economy, while bringing other elements, such as education, under greater central control. Led by the first woman Prime Minster, Margaret Thatcher, the Conservative government "privatized", or returned to non-government control, the television, natural gas and electricity industries, and a variety of transport firms, including air, rail, and bus in the 1980's.

However, in 1997, British voters expressed dissatisfaction with these changes, by an overwhelming rejection of the conservative government. A Labour government, led by Tony Blair, won the national election and sought new solutions to economic problems. In 1997, a Labour government *referendum[242] in both Scotland and Wales asked if these countries wanted their own assemblies. The Scottish referendum offered the Scots the right to tax themselves. The Scots strongly supported this and formed the Scottish Parliament. The Welsh were not offered the right to tax themselves, and the vote was split. Still, a Welsh Assembly was formed.

However, foreign policy continued to be determined by the British Parliament in London. At the end of the century the British were uncertain as to how much their own government and the government of the European Community (EC) should directly control or shape the thriving British economy and industries.

6. BRITAIN AT THE START OF THE 21ST CENTURY

At the end of the twentieth century, Britain enjoyed a period of economic prosperity and peace. The 2001 terrorist attacks on the United States put an end to this. Prime Minster Blair followed President George W. Bush's lead, both in policies at home and in war abroad.

The major policy change was the Anti-Terrorism Crime Security Act of 2001, later supplemented by the 2005 Prevention of Terrorism Act. These acts gave police broader powers of surveillance and arrest. They represented a major erosion of civil liberties. The act is ironic because the year 2000 saw the Freedom of Information Act that gave the public greater access to government information and decision-making.

The war abroad was the invasion of Iraq. Blair, like George W. Bush, claimed that Sadam Hussein had weapons of mass destruction ready to use. Later investigations have been unable to find any support for these claims. Still, British troops were sent to Iraq. The war proved very unpopular in Britain, and Blair's support declined, despite the continuing economic prosperity.

In July, 2005 terrorist bombings shook the London underground transport system, killing 50 and injuring hundreds. Two weeks later, there were four more attempts, which were prevented In the summer of 2007, there were more attempts at bombings, which again were prevented.

In 2006, Blair called for a general election. The Labour Party was returned to power, but with a reduced majority. In 2007, Blair resigned, with Gordon Brown replacing him as Prime Minster and leader of the Labour Party. Britains remained opposed to the war in Iraq and uncertain about the economic climate.

7. WHAT DOES IT MEAN TO BE BRITISH?

A) Changes in Population

From the time of William the Conqueror to the mid-twentieth century, the flow of population was away from England. Throughout the colonial era, British emigrants settled worldwide, exporting their culture to the world. During the second half of the twentieth century, this changed under the influence of American and European cultures. Fewer people wish one another "the Best of British luck" or claim "There'll always be an England". Membership in the *Anglican[243] church has dropped.

Added to these strains has been the influx of people from the newly independent Commonwealth countries. After these new countries established their own identities, a number of people found themselves stateless. In 1968, immigration from Africa to Britain was measured at over fifty thousand a year. In addition, people of African descent also came from the Caribbean islands to England, drawn by the better economic environment. Seeking either a new home or economic opportunities, new people and cultures immigrated to Britain. Racial and ethnic problems and tensions, particularly in the larger cities, increasingly became a concern.

Wales and Scotland still assert their ethnic identify as well as their political autonomy. In 2001, about 21% of the Welsh said they could speak Welsh, although fewer than 60,000 Scots said that they could speak the Scottish version of Gaelic.

B) Summary: "There Will Always Be an England"

This phrase was often repeated during World War II to increase morale. But what is meant by "England" or the United Kingdom? It seems to be a collection of contradictions. It is an island attracting Romans, Celts, Anglo-Saxons and Normans in the first millenium; Pakistanis, Jamacians and Indians in the late twentieth century. It is a "garden" nation that prides itself on its industrial strength. It is a place where tradition and modernization go hand-in-hand. Footpaths from the medieval era are protected in the modern era, so that Britain has fine walking trails, despite its high proportion of urbanization.

The British Parliament, the so-called "Mother of Parliaments", conducts its business without a written constitution in a royal palace originally built by Edward the Confessor (1042 – 1066). Traditionally this building, the Palace of Westminster, serves as the assembly hall for Parliament, even though it is too small to hold all of its members, who watch the parliamentary debates on television. Members of the government party sit on one side of the hall, and opposition members sit on the other. The distance between them measures two-swords-length; yet parliamentary debates are broadcast to the entire country by television. The country is one of few to retain a monarch, but that monarch pays income tax like a common citizen. England abides by the common law dating back to the Anglo-Saxon era, but it has provided voting rights to all citizens over age 18. Great Britain created the imperialist British Empire and now sponsors the anti-imperialist Commonwealth of Nations.

Napoleon Bonaparte dismissed Britain as "a nation of shopkeepers". Yet these shopkeepers have changed the course of world history. By the end of the twentieth century English was either spoken as a native or as an auxiliary language by one sixth of the human race. Maintaining tradition while changing with the times, the product of two millennia of trial and transformation: the United Kingdom of Great Britain and Northern Ireland.

Appendixes

CHRONOLOGY OF BRITISH GOVERNMENT

MONARCH	DATE of RULE	COMMENTS
Germanic/Scandinavian Rule		
Alfred the Great	(871 – 899)	Anglo-Saxon Wessex Line
Edgar the Peaceful	(959 – 975)	Anglo-Saxon Wessex Line
Ethelred the Unready	(978 – 1016)	Anglo-Saxon Wessex Line
Canute	(1016 – 1035)	Scandinavian conqueror
Edward the Confessor	(1042 – 1066)	Son of Ethelred the Unready
Harold Godwinson	(1066)	Relative of Canute; chosen by Witan

CHAPTER 3 HISTORY OF THE UNITED KINGDOM

Norman French Rule

William I	(1066 – 1087)	William the Conqueror; French duke connected to the Wessex Line and favored by Edward the Confessor
William II	(1087 – 1100)	William Rufus, second son of William I
Henry I	(1100 – 1135)	Third son of William I
Stephen and Maud	(1135 – 1154)	Stephen was the grandson of William I; Maud (Matilda) was the daughter of Henry I

Angevin French-Plantagenets

Henry II	(1154 – 1189)	Son of Maud
Richard I	(1189 – 1199)	Oldest surviving son of Henry II known as Richard the Lionhearted
John	(1199 – 1216)	Second surviving son of Henry II who signed the Magna Carta
Henry III	(1216 – 1272)	Son of John
Edward I	(1272 – 1307)	Son of Henry III
Edward II	(1307 – 1327)	Murdered son of Edward I
Edward III	(1327 – 1377)	
Richard II	(1377 – 1399)	Murdered son of Edward III

Lancastrians

Henry IV	(1399 – 1413)	Grandson of Edward III
Henry V	(1413 – 1422)	Son of Henry IV
Henry VI	(1422 – 1461)	Murdered son of Henry V; uncles serve as regents

Yorkists

Edward IV	(1461 – 1483)	Grandson of Edward III
Edward V	(1483)	Murdered son of Edward IV
Richard III	(1483 – 1485)	Brother of Edward IV killed in battle

Tudors

Henry VII	(1485 – 1509)	Grandson of Edward III
Henry VIII	(1509 – 1547)	Son of Henry VII; selected by the Privy Council
Edward VI	(1547 – 1553)	Son of Henry VIII; uncles serve as regents
Mary I	(1553 – 1558)	Elder daughter of Henry VIII; selected by the Privy Council
Elizabeth I	(1558 – 1603)	Younger daughter of Henry VIII

Stuarts and the Commonwealth

James I	(1603 – 1625)	Grandson of Henry VII; also known as James V of Scotland (1567 – 1625)
Charles I	(1625 – 1649)	Son of James I; beheaded by order of the Rump Parliament
Oliver Cromwell	(1649 – 1658)	Lord Protector; chosen by Parliament and the army
Richard Cromwell	(1658 – 1660)	Exiled son of Oliver Cromwell

Restored Stuarts

Charles II	(1660 – 1685)	Selected by Parliament; chief minister of Parliament dominates the monarchy
James II	(1685 – 1688)	Younger son of Charles I exiled by Parliament
William III and Mary II	(1688 – 1702)	Rule by Mary, the elder daughter of James II, and her husband, William of Orange
Ann	(1702 – 1714)	Daughter of James II

Hanovarians (German Line)

George I	(1714 – 1727)	Grandson of James I; Robert Walpole (1721 – 1742) was the first Prime
George II	(1727 – 1760)	Son of George I

Prime Minister	Political Party
Robert Walpole (1721 – 1742)	Whig
Earl of Wilmington (1742 – 1744)	Whig
Henry Pelham (1744 – 1754)	Whig
Duke of Newcastle (1754 – 1756)	Whig
Duke of Devonshire (1756 – 1757)	Tory
Earl of Bute (1762 – 1763)	Tory

George III	(1760 – 1820)	"Mad King George", eldest son of George II

Prime Minister	Political Party
George Grenville (1763 – 1765)	Whig
Marquess of Rockingham (1765 – 1766)	Whig
William Pitt, the Elder (1766 – 1767)	Whig
Duke of Grafton (1768 – 1770)	Whig
Lord Frederick North (1770 – 1782)	Tory
Marquess of Rockingham (1782)	Whig
Earl of Shelburne (1782 – 1783)	Whig
Duke of Portland (1783)	Coalition
William Pitt, the Younger (1783 – 1801)	Tory
Henry Addington (1801 – 1804)	Tory
William Pitt, the Younger (1804 – 1806)	Tory
William Grenville (1806 – 1807)	Whig

	Duke of Portand (1807 – 1809)	Tory
	Spencer Perceval (1809 – 1812)	Tory
	Earl of Liverpool (1812 – 1827)	Tory
George Ⅳ	(1820 – 1830)	Eldest son of George Ⅲ
	Prime Minister	*Political Party*
	Earl of Liverpool (1812 – 1827)	Tory
	George Canning (1827)	Tory
	Viscount Goderich (1827 – 1828)	Tory
	Duke of Wellington (1828 – 1830)	Tory
William Ⅳ	(1830 – 1837)	Second son of George Ⅲ
	Prime Minister	*Political Party*
	Earl Grey (1830 – 1834)	Whig
	Viscount Melbourne (1834)	Whig
	Robert Peel (1834 – 1835)	Tory
Victoria	(1837 – 1901)	Granddaughter of George Ⅲ
	Prime Minister	*Political Party*
	Viscount Melbourne (1835 – 1841)	Whig
	Robert Peel (1841 – 1846)	Tory
	John Russell (1846 – 1852)	Whig
	Earl of Derby (1852)	Tory
	Earl of Aberdeen (1852 – 1855)	Peelite
	Viscount Palmerston (1855 – 1858)	Liberal
	Earl of Derby (1858 – 1859)	Conservative
	Viscount Palmerston (1859 – 1865)	Liberal
	Earl Russell (1865 – 1866)	Liberal
	Earl of Derby (1866 – 1868)	Conservative
	Benjamin Disraeli (1868)	Conservative
	William Gladstone (1868 – 1874)	Liberal
	Benjamin Disraeli (1874 – 1880)	Conservative
	William Gladstone (1880 – 1885)	Liberal
	Marquess of Salisbury (1885 – 1886)	Conservative
	William Gladstone (1886)	Liberal
	Marquess of Salisbury (1886 – 1892)	Conservative
	William Gladstone (1892 – 1894)	Liberal
	Earl of Roseberry (1894 – 1895)	Liberal
	Marquess of Salisbury (1895 – 1902)	Conservative
Edward Ⅶ	(1901 – 1910)	Son of Victoria
	Prime Minister	*Political Party*
	Arthur Balfour (1902 – 1905)	Conservative
	Henry Campbell-Bannerman (1905 – 1908)	Liberal
	Herbert Asquith (1908 – 1916)	Liberal
George Ⅴ	(1910 – 1936)	So n of Edward Ⅶ ; The Hanoverian monarchy is renamed the House of windsor
	Prime Minister	*Political Party*
	Herbert Asquith (1908 – 1916)	Coalition
	David Lloyd George (1916 – 1922)	Coalition
	Andrew Bonar Law (1922 – 1923)	Conservative

	Stanley Baldwin (1924 – 1929)	Conservative
	James Ramsay MacDonald (1924)	Labour
	Stanley Baldwin (1924 – 1929)	Conservative
	James Ramsay MacDonald (1929 – 1935)	Labour
	Stanley Baldwin (1935 – 1937)	Coalition
Edward VIII	(1936)	Eldest son of George V who abdicated
George VI	(1936 – 1952)	Second son of George V
	Prime Minister	*Political Party*
	Stanley Baldwin (1935 – 1937)	Coalition
	Neville Chamberlain (1937 – 1940)	Coalition
	Winston Churchill (1940 – 1945)	Coalition
	Clement Attlee (1945 – 1951)	Labour
	Winston Churchill (1951 – 1955)	Conservative
Elizabeth II	(1952 – to date)	Older daughter of George VI
	Prime Minister	*Political Party*
	Winston Churchill (1951 – 1955)	Conservative
	Anthony Eden (1955 – 1957)	Conservative
	Harold Macmillan (1957 – 1963)	Conservative
	Alec Douglas-Home (1963 – 1964)	Conservative
	Harold Wilson (1964 – 1970)	Labour
	Edward Heath (1970 – 1974)	Conservative
	Harold Wilson (1974 – 1976)	Labour
	James Callaghan (1976 – 1979)	Labour
	Margaret Thatcher (1979 – 1990)	Conservative
	John Major (1990 – 1997)	Conservative
	Anthony Blair (1997 – 2007)	Labour
	Gordon Brown (2007 –)	Labour

Study Questions

1. Describe how the sea influenced British history.
2. England was the first country to have a representative government. Why and how did this government evolve?
3. Discuss the causes and effects of colonization and imperialism.
4. Discuss the effects of the Industrial Revolution on English society.
5. In your opinion, which aspect of British history had the greatest effect on the development of the world as we know it?

Selected Bibliography

Brinton, Crane, John B. Christopher, and Robert Lee Wolf. *A History of Civilization*: *Prehistory to 1715*. Englewood Cliffs, New Jersey: Prentice Hall, 1958.
Brinton, Crane, John B. Christopher, and Robert Lee Wolf. Modern Civilization: *A History of the Last Five Centuries*. Englewood Cliffs, New Jersey: Prentice Hall, 1958.

Ergang, Robert. *Europe from the Renaissance to Waterloo*. Boston, Massachusetts: D. C. Heath, 1954.

Robbins, Keith. *The Eclipse of a Great Power: Modern Britain 1870 – 1992*, 2nd edition. New York: Longman, 1994.

Trevelyan, George Macaulay. *A Shortened History of England*. Baltimore, Maryland: Penguin Books, 1959.

Youngs, Frederic A. Jr., Henry L. Snyder, and E. A. Reitan. *The English Heritage*. 2nd edition. Arlington Heights, Illinois: Forum Press, 1988.

注 释

〔1〕伊比利亚人。
〔2〕凯尔特人的。
〔3〕腓尼基人,公元前 2000 年出现,公元前 1000 年时,居住在现今黎巴嫩和叙利亚的沿海平原一带。
〔4〕矽土,打火石。
〔5〕凯尔特人,罗马时代之前居住在英国和高卢等地,公元前 9 世纪时开始向中西欧扩展,语言及文化现存爱尔兰、苏格兰和威尔士等地区。
〔6〕日耳曼的。
〔7〕古希腊金、银币。
〔8〕马其顿。
〔9〕地中海的。
〔10〕凯撒,100—44 B.C.,罗马统帅,政治家,49—44B.C.为罗马独裁者。
〔11〕拉丁化。
〔12〕贡品。
〔13〕高卢,古代欧洲西部的一个地区,包括今日的法国、比利时、卢森堡,以及荷兰、瑞士、德国和意大利北部的部分地区。
〔14〕克劳狄一世,10 B.C.—A.D.54,罗马皇帝 41—54,在位期间扩大罗马版图。
〔15〕外籍军团士兵。
〔16〕巴斯。
〔17〕斯堪的纳维亚地区,包括挪威、瑞典;有时还包括芬兰、冰岛和法罗群岛。
〔18〕盖尔语,凯尔特语的一种。
〔19〕贝奥武夫。
〔20〕叙事诗,史诗。
〔21〕传教士。
〔22〕圣奥古斯丁,创建英格兰教会,并担任首任坎特伯雷大主教。
〔23〕罗马天主教。
〔24〕新教,16 世纪从罗马天主教分离出来。
〔25〕在俗教士。
〔26〕(主管教区下有自己的教堂和牧师的)堂区,牧区。
〔27〕修道院。
〔28〕什一税,罗马教会按人们收入的十分之一收取的捐税。
〔29〕9—10 世纪入侵英国的北欧人。
〔30〕实行丹麦法地区,指英格兰北部、中部和东部地区。
〔31〕阿尔弗雷德大帝,韦塞克斯王国国王。
〔32〕编年史。
〔33〕盎格鲁-撒克逊国王的议会,由国王亲自挑选的贵族和教士组成。
〔34〕笃信王,1042—1066 在位。
〔35〕11 世纪占领英国的法国北方人,912 年起,定居法国诺曼底地区。
〔36〕西敏寺,伦敦著名教堂,是国王加冕和著名人士下葬之所在。
〔37〕伯爵领地。
〔38〕(法)子爵。
〔39〕无债务的。
〔40〕国库。
〔41〕铸币,币制。
〔42〕神职人员。
〔43〕指 5 世纪中期由盎格鲁-撒克逊人定居英格兰开始至 1150 年期间的英语。
〔44〕变体。
〔45〕屈折变化,如英语中名词作复数时的词形变化。
〔46〕财政部。
〔47〕英国历史上到 1971 年为止的巡回审判庭,由一位从一县巡视到另一县的法官主持的特殊法庭。
〔48〕教会法。
〔49〕有教会背景的。
〔50〕坎特伯雷大主教,全英首席主教,由首相指派,并为君主加冕。

〔51〕补赎（一种包括悔罪、告解、自新等的圣事）。
〔52〕狮心王理查一世,1157—1199,亨利二世之子,1189—1199在位,中世纪的传奇人物,1191年领导第三次十字军东征。
〔53〕十字军东征,11到13世纪西欧基督教国家为从穆斯林手中收回圣地而组织的军事远征,第三次十字军东征(1189—1192),收复了某些失地,但没有收回耶路撒冷。
〔54〕赎金。
〔55〕奥古斯都,罗马帝国第一代皇帝(63B.C.—14A.D.),凯撒的继承人。
〔56〕禁制令,天主教中禁止某人参加圣事活动的宗教惩罚。
〔57〕开除教籍,逐出教会。
〔58〕大宪章,1215年英国大封建领主迫使英王约翰签署的保障部分公民权和政治权,限制皇室权力的文件。
〔59〕自由民。
〔60〕平民,无贵族称号的人。
〔61〕特权,特惠。
〔62〕封建领主的封臣或属臣。
〔63〕命令者,决策人。
〔64〕黑死病,14世纪蔓延于欧亚的鼠疫。
〔65〕腺鼠疫。
〔66〕乔叟(1342—1400),英国诗人,他用英格兰中部方言创作的作品使英语成为标准的文学语言。
〔67〕《坎特伯雷故事集》。
〔68〕因反对政府强征人头税而爆发的英格兰农民起义。
〔69〕农奴制。
〔70〕指在玫瑰战争中的兰开斯特王朝的成员。
〔71〕约克王朝成员。
〔72〕都铎王朝,1485年亨利七世到1603年伊丽莎白一世死为止。
〔73〕隶农。
〔74〕神学家。
〔75〕文艺复兴,14世纪到17世纪欧洲古希腊文学、艺术和思想的重新发现与繁荣。
〔76〕基督教世界。
〔77〕商行。
〔78〕教皇职权。
〔79〕路德宗教徒,路德提出宗教改革后的新教徒。
〔80〕星室法庭,都铎王朝的专政工具,专断暴虐,1641年被国会废除。
〔81〕"莫顿之叉",由英格兰坎特伯雷大主教和枢机主教莫顿(1420—1500)提出,即富者和穷者都必须交税,为亨利七世强行征税充实国库强辩。
〔82〕郡,行政区。
〔83〕享有自治权的市镇。
〔84〕资助人,赞助人。
〔85〕红衣主教。
〔86〕由奴隶、囚犯等划桨的桨帆并用的大木船。
〔87〕服饰,礼服。
〔88〕霍尔拜因(1497—1543),德国肖像画家和装饰艺术家,作品注重对象表面质感与装饰细节。
〔89〕选举权。
〔90〕选民。
〔91〕选举权。
〔92〕东正教,包括希腊、俄国、保加利亚、罗马尼亚等国的教会。
〔93〕反对教权干涉的。
〔94〕人道主义的。
〔95〕朝圣求恩巡礼,1536年英格兰北部反对亨利八世及宗教改革的起义。
〔96〕莫尔(1478—1535),英国政治家和作家,文艺复兴时期主要的人文主义领袖。
〔97〕泰伯恩刑场,英国伦敦一绞刑场(1300—1783)。
〔98〕圣帕特里克,爱尔兰守护神。
〔99〕安妮·博林(1507—1536),亨利八世的第二任妻子,伊丽莎白一世的母亲。
〔100〕克兰麦(1489—1556),英国新教教士,1532年被任命为坎特伯雷大主教。
〔101〕为渔翁得利而使相斗。
〔102〕符合帝王身份的。
〔103〕财政上地。
〔104〕西班牙无敌舰队。
〔105〕耶稣会会士。
〔106〕霍金斯(1532—1595),16世纪60和70年代参与西属印度群岛的奴隶贩运,1573年被任命为海军财政官。
〔107〕斯克尔顿(1460—1529),英国诗人和讽刺作家。
〔108〕英国诗人和布道家,玄学派诗歌代表人物。
〔109〕马洛(1564—1593),英国戏剧家,诗人,他的作品对莎士比亚的历史剧有深刻的影响。
〔110〕斯图亚特王室,1371年至1714年统治爱尔兰。
〔111〕采邑。

〔112〕哥特式建筑,12至16世纪之间流行于西欧的尖拱式建筑。
〔113〕抒情短诗,牧歌。
〔114〕邓斯塔布(1390—1453),英国作曲家,作有经文曲,弥撒曲和世俗曲。
〔115〕斯宾塞(1552—1599),英国诗人。
〔116〕培根(1561—1626),英国政治家和哲学家,他的激进哲学思想在他死后的一个世纪影响巨大。
〔117〕哈维(1578—1657),英国医师,生物学家,血液循环机制的发现者。
〔118〕吉尔伯特(1544—1603),英国物理学家,电磁学研究的先驱。
〔119〕塞西尔(1520—1598),英国政治家。
〔120〕罗利(1552—1618),英国探险家,作家,早期美国殖民者,曾将烟草和土豆带回英国。
〔121〕英王詹姆士一世钦定的《圣经》英译本。
〔122〕新教派,17世纪末遭迫害,很多人移民美国寻找宗教自由。
〔123〕1649年到1660年克伦威尔统治下的共和政体。
〔124〕贵格会。贵格会教徒反对暴力和战争,在教育和扶助他人方面卓有成就。
〔125〕首批清教徒移民,1620年乘"五月花"号到达马萨诸塞州的普利茅斯。
〔126〕哈得孙湾公司,1670年由皇家特许成立以商业掠夺为目的的殖民贸易公司。
〔127〕兰姆酒。
〔128〕酿酒商。
〔129〕印度地方行政长官。
〔130〕代表国王行使权力的总督。
〔131〕旧时英国军队中的印度兵。
〔132〕东印度公司,1600年在东印度群岛建立的进行殖民贸易的公司。
〔133〕王权神授说。
〔134〕在职人员名单。
〔135〕加尔文主义的,信奉16世纪宗教改革运动时加尔文倡导的神学学说的。
〔136〕圣礼。
〔137〕高教会,英格兰教会一支,强调与天主教的历史渊源。
〔138〕不信奉英国国教。
〔139〕盖伊·福克斯日(11月5日),英国人民在该日点燃篝火燃放烟花,纪念1605年盖伊·福克斯试图纵火烧毁伦敦议会。
〔140〕戒严法。
〔141〕劳德(1573—1645),英国高级教士,反对新教,镇压英格兰加尔文教派和苏格兰长老会信徒,导致国内宗教战争。
〔142〕保守者。
〔143〕长老会派,新教一派,信奉加尔文主义。
〔144〕英国金币。
〔145〕长期议会,1640年11月至1653年3月止,1659年曾短期复会,1660年最终解散,最初由理查一世召集,经历英国内战。
〔146〕大抗议书,1640年长期议会拟定的文件,提出改良主张。
〔147〕庇护所。
〔148〕英国查理一世时代的保皇党党员。
〔149〕公理会教徒,公理会教徒主张教会独立自主。
〔150〕残余教会,1648年英国共和国驱除约100名赞成与理查一世妥协的议员之后的长期议会,1660年解除。
〔151〕旧王统治结束新王尚未登基时的空位期。
〔152〕护民官。
〔153〕逗熊游戏,流行于16—17世纪的英国。
〔154〕皇家协会,英国最古老的、最有盛名的科学团体。
〔155〕理性主义的。
〔156〕启蒙运动,17世纪末到18世纪的欧洲知识界以推崇"理性"为人类知识和进步的关键,提倡宗教宽容的思想文化运动。
〔157〕蒲伯(1688—1744),英国诗人,为英国文学全盛时期的代表人物。
〔158〕非国教派人。
〔159〕雷恩(1632—1723),英国建筑师,设计了新的圣保罗大教堂(1675—1711),格林尼治天文台(1675)以及其他多座教堂。
〔160〕信教自由令。
〔161〕辉格党人,自由党的前身。
〔162〕托利党人,保守党。
〔163〕《权利法案》,1689年10月制定,确立新教王权统治及议会的最高权威。
〔164〕特许,豁免。
〔165〕选帝侯(德国有权选举神圣罗马帝国皇帝的诸侯)。
〔166〕汉诺威,德国一地区。
〔167〕沃尔波尔(1675—1745),英国辉格党人,首席财政大臣。
〔168〕雇佣兵。
〔169〕腓特烈大帝(1712—1786),在位期间扩大普鲁士版图两倍。
〔170〕寡头政治。
〔171〕狄德罗(1713—1784),法国启蒙思想家,

唯物主义哲学家和文学家。
〔172〕史密斯（1723—1790），苏格兰经济学家，哲学家，现代经济学的奠基人。
〔173〕人身保护令，传讯诉讼当事人出庭的令状，当事人得根据法庭裁决其拘禁是否符合法律程序。
〔174〕伯克（1729—1797），英国辉格党政论家。
〔175〕潘恩（1737—1809），英国政治作家，1744年移民美国，号召美国殖民地寻求独立，为《独立宣言》的起草奠定基础。
〔176〕卫理公会，一新教教派。
〔177〕不干涉主义，政府不干涉市场运作的理论和实践，后成为自由市场经济理论的核心概念。
〔178〕斯威夫特（1667—1745），爱尔兰讽刺作家，教士；《格列佛游记》的作者。
〔179〕艾迪生，英国诗人，剧作家，散文作家及辉格党政治家。
〔180〕菲尔丁，英国小说家，剧作家。
〔181〕贺加斯，英国画家，版画家。
〔182〕纳尔逊（1758—1805），英国海军统帅。
〔183〕威灵顿（1769—1852），托利党政治家，英国陆军元帅，首相（1828—1830）。
〔184〕四方联盟，英、俄、奥、普联盟，以击败拿破仑，并维持欧洲秩序。
〔185〕克里米亚战争（1853—1856），俄国与土耳其、英国、法国和撒丁王国之间的战争。
〔186〕《资本论》。
〔187〕《共产党宣言》。
〔188〕皮尔（1788—1850），保守党政治家，英国首相（1834—1835；1841—1846）。
〔189〕公平竞争原则。
〔190〕宪章运动，1837—1848年间争取选举和社会改革的民众运动。
〔191〕选票。
〔192〕功利主义者。
〔193〕谷物法，19世纪限制谷物进口和控制谷物价格的法令。
〔194〕爱尔兰自治，1870年至1921年爱尔兰民族主义者开展的运动，直到爱尔兰自由邦建立。
〔195〕帕内尔（1846—1891），爱尔兰政治家，民族主义者，爱尔兰自治领袖，英国议会下院议员（1875—1891）。
〔196〕格兰斯顿（1809—1898），英国自由党领袖，曾四次出任首相。
〔197〕奥斯曼帝国（1290—1922），奥斯曼为土耳其建立的军事帝国，版图包括小亚细亚和东南欧大部分地区，一战后瓦解。
〔198〕巴尔干地区。
〔199〕南丁格尔（1820—1910），英国女护士，近代护理学和护士教育创始人。
〔200〕迪斯雷利（1804—1881），英国托利党政治家，英国首相。
〔201〕奥斯丁，英国女小说家，著有长篇小说《傲慢与偏见》、《爱玛》等。
〔202〕勃朗特，英国女作家，代表作《简·爱》。
〔203〕狄更斯，英国作家，著有小说《大卫·科波菲尔》、《双城记》等。
〔204〕盖斯凯尔夫人，英国小说家，主要作品有长篇小说《玛丽·巴登》等。
〔205〕特罗洛普，英国小说家，著述甚丰，包括游记、传记、短篇小说等。
〔206〕哈代，英国小说家，诗人，代表作为《德伯家的苔丝》等。
〔207〕莱尔，苏格兰地质学家，他的著作《地质学原理》（1830—1833）影响了整整一代地质学家。
〔208〕达尔文，英国博物学家，进化论的创始人，进化生物学的奠基人，代表作是《物种起源》。
〔209〕地缘政治学。
〔210〕西印度群岛（拉丁美洲），包括大安的列斯群岛、小安的列群岛和巴哈马群岛。
〔211〕索马里兰。
〔212〕肯尼亚。
〔213〕乌干达。
〔214〕津巴布韦。
〔215〕刚比亚。
〔216〕塞拉利昂，非洲西岸的独立国家。
〔217〕尼日利亚。
〔218〕圭亚那。
〔219〕洪都拉斯。
〔220〕布尔战争（1899—1902），南非战争，英军击败布尔人，获得在南非的政治权利的战争。
〔221〕边沁，英国哲学家，功利主义哲学的代表人物，对19世纪英国思想有决定性的影响，特别是在政治改革方面。
〔222〕穆勒，英国哲学家，经济学家和逻辑学家，主要作品是《论自由》（1859）。
〔223〕塞尔维亚。
〔224〕英国（温莎）王室。
〔225〕沙皇制度。
〔226〕威尔逊，民主党政治家，美国第28任总统。

〔227〕萨尔盆地。
〔228〕托管地。
〔229〕马其诺防线,二战前法国在东部国境上所筑阵地防御系统,1940年德军进入法国,使防线失效。
〔230〕潜水艇。
〔231〕1940年的伦敦大空袭。
〔232〕白金汉宫,英国皇宫。
〔233〕丘吉尔(1974—1965),英国保守党政治家,著作家,首相(1940—1945)。
〔234〕仰光,缅甸首都。
〔235〕广岛,日本本州西南海岸城市,第二次世界大战末期遭美国原子弹轰炸。
〔236〕长崎,日本九州岛西岸城市,第二次世界大战末期遭美国原子弹轰炸。
〔237〕苏伊士运河。
〔238〕福克兰群岛(为英国所使用的称呼),原属阿根廷(阿根廷称之为马尔维纳斯群岛),1833年被英国占领,目前英、阿对其归属有争议。
〔239〕斐济群岛。
〔240〕戴高乐(1890—1970),法国总统(1959—1969)。
〔241〕配给券。
〔242〕全民公决。
〔243〕英国圣公会的。

CHAPTER 4 BRITISH ECONOMY

Dr. Steven D. Soderlund

I. Introduction

The United Kingdom of Great Britain, commonly called the United Kingdom (UK) or simply Britain, comprises four island nations off the European coast: England, Scotland, Wales, and Northern Ireland. The Act of Union from 1701 formally organizes the federation, prescribing English to be the official language, London to be the capital city, and the Pound Sterling (£) to be the unit of currency. In 1973 Britain joined with many other European nations to form the *European Community (EC)[1], which has evolved into the *European Union (EU)[2], a political and economic superstate that continues to grow in its authority, membership and economic promise. But now Britain has left the EU.

The British people enjoy a moderate climate and varied scenery, but their land has provided only modest natural resources for most of the past three centuries. Prosperity has come with inventiveness, urbanization and extensive trade.

II. Highlights of Britain's Economic Development

Britain's economic history involves three significant periods: the Period of Empire, the Period of *Decline and Retrenchment[3], and the Period of *Europeanism[4]. Briefly, the Period of Empire began soon after the Act of Union and culminated in a colonial trading empire which circled the globe. The subsequent Period of Decline and Retrenchment saw Britain relinquish its colonies and struggle to accommodate declining markets and industries. Finally, by 1990, having committed itself to the European Union, Britain arguably opened a new chapter in its economic development, the Period of Europeanism. Each of these periods is highlighted below.

1. THE PERIOD OF EMPIRE (1701-1944)

A sudden epoch of sustained growth in manufacturing began in Britain shortly after the Act of Union. This so-called "industrial revolution" involved the release of labor from widespread primary industries (agriculture, forestry, mining, and fishing), and its reactivation in manufacturing and service activities—mainly in fast-growing cities. Certain cities (especially London, Manchester and Birmingham) were centers of British growth and prosperity, first in manufacturing (especially textiles, clothing, steel, and engineering goods), then in service employments (including clerical, administrative, medical, financial and educational work). This pattern of adjustments in settlement and employment became a model of economic development that many nations would follow, often characterized by Graph I, which depicts the evolution of employment in primary, manufacturing and service activities.

Graph Ⅰ Britain's Development Pattern in Terms of Sectoral Employment ①

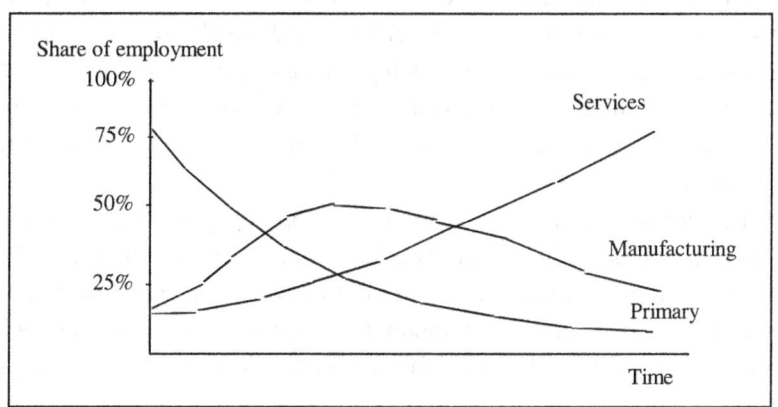

By around 1850, amidst its industrial revolution, the British economy employed about forty percent of its workers in primary activities, forty percent in manufacturing, and twenty percent in services. Subsequent years witnessed continuing division of labor and capital by sectors; by 1900 primary employment had fallen to less than 30% of the labor force. Meanwhile, London's population rose from about 500,000 in 1700 to almost 6,500,000 in 1900.

With limited domestic resources and markets, trade was a key to Britain's economic expansion. Being the first nation to experience the industrial revolution, Britain's dominance in manufactures helped it become the world's preeminent trading nation. Its trading empire (mainly subservient "colonies") eventually spanned the globe, leading to the famous saying that "the sun never sets on the British Empire".

While there was extensive trading among and between Britain's colonies, the flow of goods to and from Britain itself was vital to the colonial system. Britain's imports during the period consisted mainly of raw materials, food, tea, *spices[5], etc., while its exports were mainly manufactured items: cloth, clothing, ships, steel, engines, railroad equipment, etc. British entrepreneurs built railroads and warehouses all over the world to facilitate inland transportation and trade.

2. THE PERIOD OF DECLINE AND RETRENCHMENT (1944 – 1989)

Maintaining its empire required extensive military, diplomatic and administrative energies, which were quite expensive, many colonials yearned for independence from British rule. Encouraged by America's success after its colonial period, the independence movement gained strength all over the empire, triggering many regional wars and local

---

① Britain's development path was never so steady as seems implied in the diagram. Actual historical development included periods of advance, sometimes quick and sometimes slow, with many interruptions, including periods of stagnation and depression. There were two Great Depressions during the Period of Empire, one in the 1880s and one from the late 1920s through the 1930s.

Importantly, it remains something of a mystery as to what causes a nation or a city to step out on this British-type development path. Some nations and cities have yet to experience the churning social drama of "economic development" — in spite of their efforts to make it happen.

skirmishes, including the *Opium War[6] in China (1839 – 1842). By the early 20th century the cost of maintaining the empire had become problematic, and in the aftermath of World War II, when a war-damaged Britain could hardly afford its own rebuilding, most of the colonies managed to become independent nations, including the Asian nations of India, Pakistan, Burma and *Cambodia[7]. Today the British Empire is disbanded, and even *the British Commonwealth of Nations[8], its loosely assembled successor, shows weakening *cohesion[9].

During its Period of Decline and Retrenchment, Britain remained relatively prosperous, but lost its standing as the world's richest nation. Increasingly isolated, it became subject to the pressures of trade deficits, *currency fluctuations[10], and recessions. Its policy challenges (to maintain full employment, stable prices and a strong currency) proved especially difficult, forcing policy makers to shift back and forth between expansionary policies (for high employment) and contractional ones (to strengthen the currency). Commentators dubbed it the "Stop-Go" era. Meanwhile, there was widespread support for state-owned enterprises to ensure a steady flow of important domestic goods and services, including transportation (rail and air), medical care, utilities, oil and natural gas, and industrial steel.

During the 1950's and 1960's, as Britain struggled with its "Stop-Go" difficulties, countries on the European continent began experimenting with free trade agreements. At first this included only a few small nations (*Belgium[11], the *Netherlands[12], and *Luxembourg[13] whose mutual interests involved only two products: coal and steel). Eventually, however, more countries got involved, forming free trade associations and adopting collective trade restrictions, fixed exchange rates, and uniform standards. In 1973, when its domestic policies and economic circumstances seemed especially confounded, Britain joined a group of Western European nations in a free trade agreement that evolved into the European Union (EU), with its large, advanced, and open markets.

In the 1980's, under the leadership of *Margaret Thatcher[14]'s government, Britain reset its course with an energetic new domestic policy system emphasizing *privatization[15], modernization and balanced budgets. These policies seemed to stimulate income, growth and employment, giving Britain a new economic look. Meanwhile, EU markets became an increasingly vital component of British prosperity, so further national development seemed tied to European markets.

3. THE PERIOD OF EUROPEANISM (1990 – present)

By 1990, acknowledging a greater commitment to the European Union, Britain agreed to join the so-called European Exchange Rate Mechanism (ERM), which virtually pegged the Pound Sterling to other European currencies. After two years, however, Britain left the ERM, feeling that its Pound had been overvalued relative to the German Mark. The Pound was officially devalued, then allowed to float in currency markets so that it could realign itself on a more rational basis to other European currencies. As of January, 1999, most of Britain's EU partners are adopting a new currency, the Euro, which is intended to become the primary European currency. For the time being, however, Britain is opting not to participate in that venture, evidence of its lingering *nationalism[16] and ambivalence to European ventures beyond free trade.

At the outset of its Period of Europeanism Britain's economy featured growing productivity and advancing industries. The distribution of labor and capital among the primary, secondary and tertiary sectors had continued to follow the development pattern shown earlier. In 1990, for example, employment in primary activities involved barely 5% of the labor force (see Table A below), and less than 4% of the nation's capital stock. Only 1.5 of the labor force remained in agriculture. Meanwhile, tertiary (service) employments had expanded to a position of dominance.

Table A.

Composition of Labor Force		Composition of Capital Stock	
	% of total labor force	% of total capital stock	
Primary Employment	5.2	3.8	Primary Industry
Secondary Employment	23.1	26.1	Secondary Industry
Tertiary Employment	58.5	37.9	Tertiary Industry
HM Forces	1.1	32.2	Dwellings (providing housing
Self-employed	12.1		and other building services)
TOTAL	100	100	TOTAL

Source: Annual Abstract of Statistics 1996

Today the European Union is increasing its membership and its power over member states, thus exerting stronger and stronger influence over economic affairs. It has its own European Parliament, Central Bank and regulatory arrangements, and in many respects Britain opposes or reluctantly tolerates such impositions on its sovereignty. The overwhelming fact, however, is that Britain needs access to European markets for its continued prosperity. Thus, when all is said and done, the United Kingdom of Great Britain remains somewhat stubbornly a nation *unto[17] itself, proud and prosperous, inextricably bound to Europe, and worthy of special study. All these caused the Britain exiting from the EU.

III. Britain's Prosperity Today

With its advanced division and specialization of resources, Britain remains one of the world's wealthiest nations. Its Gross Domestic Product (GDP) in 1997 was 802 billion £ (or about 1.4 trillion US dollars). The regional distribution of GDP, shown in Table B for years between 1990 and 1996, reveals that England generates most of Britain's income. London alone accounts for more income than any of the other UK member states. Per capita GDP is lowest in Northern Ireland and Wales.

Table B. Gross Domestic Product, current prices, 1990–1996
(millions of pounds sterling and pounds per capita)

Year	United Kingdom	England	Wales	Scotland	Northern Ireland	London
*nominal [18] GDP:						
1990	478,886	401,346	20,306	40,231	10,166	69,737
1992	518,132	434,078	21,410	44,589	11,660	75,778
1994	580,135	484,358	23,774	49,720	13,091	84,686
1996	642,916	534,945	25,995	54,430	14,470	93,450
per capita GDP:						
1990	8,210	8,363	7,056	7,885	6,396	10,177
1992	8,822	8,973	7,387	8,724	7,205	10,975
1994	9,777	9,944	8,161	9,688	7,974	12,154
1996	10,711	10,897	8,899	10,614	8,700	13,210

Source: Office for National Statistics, *Regional Trends 33*, 1998 edition, 25 June, 1998.
http://www.statistics.gov.uk/statbase/

Table C provides an international perspective, showing GDP and per capita GDP (in US Dollars) for Britain and several other nations from 1980 to 1995. Britain's per capita income in 1995, for example, was £10,495, equal in spending power to $17,776 in the United States. Notice that the EU has GDP roughly equivalent to the United States, a sign of its importance as a proximate market for British goods and services.

Table C. Gross Domestic Products, 1980–1995, for Britain, Germany, Italy, the European Union, Turkey, and the United States
(based on purchasing power parity relative to the US)

Country	GDP (billions of $ US)				Per Capita GDP ($ US)			
	1980	1985	1990	1995	1980	1985	1990	1995
Britain	453	649	912	1,042	8,039	11,449	15,847	17,776
Germany	658	921	1,269	1,674	8,407	11,862	15,991	20,497
Italy	476	668	922	1,115	8,440	11,782	16,257	19,465
EU	2,873	4,036	5,623	6,925	8,083	11,246	15,426	18,612
Turkey	102	169	264	351	2,299	3,351	4,691	5,691
United States	2,708	4,017	5,490	6,995	11,892	16,844	21,966	26,438

Source: ECD, *National Accounts*, Main Aggregates, 1997.

The British economy features several significant imbalances not shown in Table C. One is regional disparities, already noted in Table B. Another involves disparities in household incomes, where a small fraction of households earn a disproportionate share of the nation's income. Table D shows the location of wealth and the large percentage of extremely wealthy households in 1999 – 2002. In 1996 – 1997, the top-erning 1% of households took 5% of the nation's total income while the lowest 15% got only about 4%

of the nation's income.

Table D. Distribution of Household Income, 1999–2002
(percent of households in each weekly income group)

Income Group (pounds/week)	United Kingdom	England	Wales	Scotland	Northern Ireland	London
Under 100	9	9	9	11	10	9
100–under 150	9	9	11	10	13	8
150–under 250	15	15	19	17	20	13
250–under 350	12	12	14	11	13	9
350–under 450	11	11	11	11	11	9
450–under 600T	14	14	15	14	13	10
600–under 750	10	10	10	9	9	10
over 750	20	21	11	16	12	33

Source: Office for National Statistics, *Regional Trends 38*, 2004 edition.
http://www.statistics.gov.uk/statbase/

Britain's overall economic performance typically fluctuates from year to year, which is widely seen as an organic feature of industrial economies. For example, in the past decade there have been a recession and a recovery, varying rates of inflation and some pesky trade deficits. Table E shows year-to-year rates of change for several economic indicators during the 1990s. Over that period GDP growth averaged 1.7% per year, but ranged from minus 2% (1991) to plus 4.3% (1994). Meanwhile, private consumption averaged a 2.0% growth per year and unemployment averaged 7.4%—though year to year changes have ranged widely, as shown.

Table E. British Economic Performance
(annual percentage changes except percent unemployment and interest)

Indicator	1990	1991	1992	1993	1994	1995	1996	1997	FORECAST 1998	1999
Real GDP	0.4	−2	−0.5	2.1	4.3	2.7	2.2	3.3	2.3	2.1
Private Consumption	0.6	−2.2	−0.1	2.5	2.8	1.7	3.6	4.6	3.6	2.6
Unemployment Rate	5.8	8	9.7	10.3	9.3	8.2	7.5	5.6	4.9	4.8
Consumer Prices	8.1	6.8	4.7	3	2.4	2.8	2.9	2.8	2.9	2.6
Hourly Earnings	9.4	8.2	6.6	4.5	4.8	4.5	4.4	4.4	4.9	3.8
Productivity	2.6	2.9	6.3	5	5.2	0.8	-0.8	1	0.6	0.7
Interest Rates	14.8	11.5	9.4	5.9	5.5	6.7	6	6.6	7.2	

Source: IMF, *World Economic Outlook*, May 1998.

The 1998 – 1999 readings in Table E were forecasts based on prior trends. Such forecasts suggested a bright future (with unemployment at a decade low of 4.9% and consumption rising by 3.6%). These projections seemed to be unfolding as predicted through July, 1998, as shown by the performance indicators in Table F.

Table F. Economic Indicators, July, 1998.

Indicator	Latest figures (updated 13 July, 1998)
Gross Domestic Product (GDP)	Up 0.5% in previous quarter and up 3.0% over year
Service sector output	Up 0.7% in previous quarter and up 4.1% over year
Industrial production	Up 0.8% in previous quarter and up 1.0% over year
Consumer spending	Up 0.9% in previous quarter and up 4.9% over year
Retail sales	Up 0.6% in previous quarter and up 4.3% over year
National investment	Up 3.8% in previous quarter and up 10.0% over year
Export of goods	Down 0.3% in previous quarter but up 3.3% over year
Unemployment	6.4% rate, an improvement from 7.3% a year before
Inflation	4.2%, up from 4.0% a year before

Source: British Treasury, *Economic Overview*, Latest Economic Indicators, updated July 13, 1998.

But shortly after that, in September, came an unexpected economic *downturn[19]. The so-called *"Asian Contagion"[20] moved into Europe and America, and with that a mood of gloom and worry quickly settled over the industrial economies. Stock prices fell precipitously in September, banks and investment houses began advising their customers to prepare for trouble, and the *IMF (International Monetary Fund)[21] and World Bank began speaking of a possible global recession. The British people have come to expect such episodic cycling in their economy.

Ⅳ. Britain's Economic System: A Unique Mix
1. ON ECONOMIC SYSTEMS

Economists for decades have tried to categorize national economies under such labels as Capitalist, Socialist, Democratic Socialist and so on. This effort to categorize has been interesting and understandable, but it has had its problems. First, there has been considerable disagreement about the essential features of the various systems. For example, many authors suggested that Capitalism was a system of economic organization based on free markets; others argued that Capitalism was a period of history during which the primary emphasis would be on saving and investment (focused on capital growth, hence the term Capitalism); and still others claimed that Capitalism was essentially a system of social relations wherein two constituent classes, workers and owners, inevitably vie for their shares. Some writers focused on the minimal state (*laissez faire[22]) to distinguish Capitalism, while others emphasized the need for energetic governmental participation in a capitalistic nation. Thus the effort to define categories consumed great energy, but yielded relatively little results.

Meanwhile, in practice, many nations around the world have evolved so-called "mixed economies", where markets, government, labor, constitutional procedures (Britain's so-called *"social contract"[23]), and international agencies operate simultaneously to shape national economic affairs. This is certainly the case in Britain, so in this section we will try to avoid words like Capitalism and Socialism, noting instead the components of Britain's unique Mixed Economy: relatively open markets, active government intervention, organized collective bargaining and lobbying, well-defined business structures, and adherence to global trading rules.

2. MARKETS AND GOVERNMENT

Being first and foremost a trading nation, Britain's prosperity has grown with access to global markets, where it has sold many of its competitively produced goods, including clothing, foods, motors, electronics, airliners, financial services, etc. Britain also relies on global markets to procure things that meet domestic needs, including foods, raw materials, automobiles, etc. To a large extent, Britain has also relied on markets to guide its domestic development, but here we encounter some of Britain's economic idiosyncrasies.

In theory market prices and quantities are determined by a complex interaction between profit-minded producers and goal-oriented buyers. Each side in exchange is sensitive to prices and *opportunistic[24] in behavior: other things being equal, suppliers are seen as producing and selling voluntarily—offering more at higher prices than at lower prices (a correspondence called "Supply"); meanwhile, buyers voluntarily purchase more at lower prices and less at higher prices (called *"Demand"[25]). When the two sides interact, market theory emphasizes the tendency for transactions to occur at a price which clears the market, i.e., a price at which the amount of a good being sold is equal to the amount being purchased. Any other price would tend to deteriorate in the direction of the market clearing price, the so-called *"equilibrium" price[26].

Expecting these dynamics, many economists predict that commodity prices will move toward their market-clearing levels. No *gluts[27], no *shortages[28], no central control.

The British tend to see markets in a positive light, but with reservations. They see the market system as a choice against alternatives like central planning or the authority of kings. In this view they favor markets, and as long as those markets work acceptably, *Britons[29] prefer that they be left alone. However, when markets do not perform satisfactorily, Britons traditionally favor intervention by democratic government. Consider some of the advantages and disadvantages of markets as commonly seen by Britons.

A) Perceived Advantages of Markets

First, among the advantages of free markets is that they graft well with political ideals of personal liberty and freedom. As market activity proceeds on the basis of voluntary contract, buyers are free to buy according to their own tastes. Meanwhile, suppliers are free to produce according to their instincts for profit. As the authority makes decisions in a market resting with individuals, markets fit well in nations where personal freedoms are protected and where contracts can be enforced by well-established courts of law.

Second, decentralized markets give rise to *"short-run efficiency"[30]. Not only are resources directed to meet people's wants, but as producers try to earn the highest possible profit, they strive to minimize costs and waste.

Third, markets tend to display "long term efficiency", as the profit motive continually invigorates human imagination to the task of meeting consumer wants at ever lower costs. When cost-reducing technologies are discovered, they tend to be adopted relatively quickly in a profit-oriented market system.

Next, compared to more centralized systems of authority (like representative democracy or bureaucracy), markets provide an excellent way of matching pertinent information to the task of decision making, each person taking charge of his or her own affairs. The market allows consumers to signal their wishes and producers cater according to profitability. Thus individual tastes and sophisticated technology are matched more or less spontaneously.

Finally, markets provide a means to fight against class discrimination. Most buyers do not care whether a product was made by a Christian or a Jew, a white or a black, a man or a woman, a *Chilean[31] or a *Brazilian[32]; it is the commodity's quality, usefulness and price that count. Thus markets can serve as a vanguard in the battle against discrimination and class oppression.

B) Perceived Disadvantages of Markets

Turning from advantages to disadvantages, the British feel that free markets also generate problems. One problem, for instance, arises when a market is "monopolized" by only a few suppliers. This translates into bargaining power, which allows such suppliers to extract extortionate profits from their "victimized" public. These profits also tend to promote lobbying for privilege and a reduced pace of innovation.

A second disadvantage of markets concerns fairness. Many people are left out of mainstream market prosperity, while others enjoy luxurious excess. Some people's dogs are better housed, fed and cared for in market economies than many people's children. Such striking disparities tend to violate the notions of fairness held by many British citizens and legislators.

A third disadvantage is that markets can be too quick in adopting innovations, inviting trouble. This is arguably the case with prescription drugs and farm chemicals, where slow, painstaking research can not identify pernicious long-term side-effects of new treatments before they are widely practiced.

A final disadvantage of markets is that voluntary contracts often disregard unwelcome consequences to third parties. When electric utilities choose to burn high sulfur coal, for example, an outcome (perhaps unintended) is acid rain, which kills trees and fish, in turn hurting a wide range of people. The market shows practically no concern for such third party pain and suffering (neither have central planners, for that matter). Cigarette smoking, foul auto emissions, and careless waste disposal are a few of the better-known items of third party concern these days.

Table G below summarizes the main points of this discussion. In general, the British see markets performing well in terms of efficiency and freedom, but not so well in terms of "fairness".

Appreciating the advantages and disadvantages of markets, the British have routinely intervened in their markets to achieve a more balanced income distribution and a more fair distribution of important goods and services. Active intervention sometimes takes the form of regulation, sometimes direct controls and state ownership, and sometimes government taxation and spending to meet important needs like police and fire protection, education, medical care, and social *infrastructure[34] (such as sewers, roads, water and flood control dams). Thus, markets and government are important components of

Britain's mixed economy.

Table G. Summary of Advantages and Disadvantages of Free Markets	
Advantages	**Disadvantages**
Short-term Efficiency 　Low cost production 　Production for wants and needs Long-term Efficiency 　Investment in sectors that generate high profits 　Human imagination directed to lowering costs of products with high demand Free contracts Impersonal producer-purchaser relations Relatively quick adoption of cost-saving methods Efficient, decentralized processing of information	Sellers can become powerful monopolists and *gouge[33] the consuming public Overly quick adoptions of farm chemicals, drugs and medical practice Nuclear energy Third party interests overlooked Pollution Health risks Many people unfairly left out of prosperity; low incomes for many of hard-working citizens

3. ECONOMIC INSTITUTIONS

Among the more famous of British economic institutions is the Limited Liability Company. The term "Ltd". appears in the name of such a company, signifying several things:

1. The company is treated as a "legal person" as it pursues the interests of its shareholders; thus it can sue and be sued in the nation's courts, but no suit against the company can claim more than the company's registered assets;

2. The company agrees to abide by the obligations imposed by the British Companies Act;

3. The company, registered with the nation's commercial authorities, can pursue business interests globally as a British subject.

All companies, including state enterprises, can qualify to become Limited Liability Companies.

Another key institution in the British economy is Parliament, which reserves the right to pass legislation regulating a wide array of economic affairs as it sees fit. Among other things: it can issue regulations controlling or influencing production or consumption; it can implement tax changes and spending programs; it can influence monetary policy; and it can nationalize resources or industries.

Related to the constitutional system are political parties and the press. Political parties represent economic policy stands before the electorate, thus serving as a means by which the electorate exerts its wishes concerning government economic activity. Meanwhile, the press reports to the public on anything it considers newsworthy, and in that way keeps the electorate informed on economic affairs and matters of policy.

Britain also has a highly institutionalized pattern of legislative lobbying and collective bargaining, with workers, employers and interest groups organized into political and bargaining units. Hundreds of thousands of British employers, for example, comprise the *Confederation of British Industry (CBI)[35], which represents employer interests in its consultations with government officials over matters of economic importance, including taxation and spending programs. Perhaps more importantly, the Confederation assists employers in their negotiations with trade unions. Meanwhile, trade unions, enjoy rights to bargain collectively on behalf of their members. Other interest groups are free to organize and work to influence politicians and policy.

Finally, of course, there are many international agencies that influence the British economy. First is the European Union, including the European Parliament and the European Central Bank. Next come several international banking and oversight agencies, such as the Organization for Economic Cooperation and Development (OECD), the International Monetary Fund (IMF), and the World Trade Organization (WTO). Britain finds itself increasingly subject to economic and trading rules promulgated by these agencies.

These are but a few of the institutions that shape the British economy today. They work continually to address difficulties, resolve disputes, and solve technical problems that impede national growth and prosperity.

4. STATE ENTERPRISES

Britain has a long history of state ownership in several industries: coal and steel, railroads, utilities, airlines, and the extraction and distribution of oil from North Sea coastal reserves. The state has also organized and controlled its health care industry to insure that everyone—irrespective of income—gets a fair chance for medical attention. Thus the state has participated actively in industrial affairs.

In the early eighties, as mentioned, many state-owned enterprises were deemed uncompetitive, and a process was begun under the Thatcher government to privatize. This policy of privatization has continued and expanded, resulting in a large stream of income for the government. Table H shows the major industries that have been privatized over the past twenty years. Note that the health care industry remains largely a state enterprise, though experiments with its so-called "liberalization" are also underway.

Table H. Privatization 1979–1991		
Name of Enterprise	Dates	Means of Privatization
British Aerospace	1981, 1985	Share issues
BAA	1987, 1988	Share issues
British Airways	1986	Share issues
British Gas	1986, 1988	Share issues
		New Regulatory System (OFGAS)
*Rover [36] Group	1984	Jaguar share issue
	1987	Rover Group sold
Britoil	1982, 1985	Share issues
British Petroleum	1979, 1981, 1983, 1987	Share issues
British Steel	1984, 1988	Share issues
British Telecom	1981, 1992	Share issues and
		New Regulatory System (OFTEL)
Cable and Wireless	1981, 1983, 1985	Share issues
Electricity Area Boards	1990	Share issues
Regional Water Authorities	1991	Share issues
		New Regulatory Agencies (OFWAT)
Electricity Generating Boards	1991	Share issues and New Regulator (OFFER)

Source: Hare and Simpson, eds, *An Introduction to the British Economy*, 1993, pp. 49–54.

Income from privatization has grown considerably over the years, starting at £ 370 million in 1980. The income from share sales grew to £ 8,184 million in 1993. The revenues will fall in the future unless more large equity issues are undertaken.

Today the British government, buoyed by its successes, continues to see privatization as a potentially gainful restructuring opportunity and source of funds. The 1993 privatization of British Rail has been the one source of controversy. Meanwhile, privatization has become a worldwide phenomenon, spurred by the World Bank, the IMF, and other economic policy and advisory agencies. In that context it is important to note that Britain's experience with privatization was neither so radical nor so heroic as the privatization experiments currently under way in Russia. Britain implemented privatization with a well-organized stock market, a historical experience with markets, Limited Liability Companies, and a competitive private sector.

5. REGULATION

As the British government implemented privatization, it continued to assert its role as a regulator of business. This especially involves what are called *"externalities"[37] of production—things like pollution that involve costs imposed by producers and consumers on society but not considered internally by those producers or consumers as costs. As British policy makers believe that such costs should be borne by the perpetrators, a regulatory environment has been implemented. For example, the state has tried to force producers toward the goal of environmental protection; firms must abide by pollution control regulations lest they lose the right to continue doing business in Britain.

Further, privatization was accompanied by the creation of several new regulatory agencies designed to ensure fairness in pricing and distribution. This is because the newly privatized companies often enjoyed monopoly power. Recall from Table H that new regulatory components accompanied the privatization of British Gas and British Telecom, among others. These are the so-called OFGAS and OFTEL, important policy institutions in modern Britain.

V. Consumer Expenditure

A key to national prosperity is the so-called "standard of living", which refers to how much consumption and leisure people enjoy. On this score the British are well-off indeed, as shown by spending data in Table I.

According to the data, Britishers on average devote less than half of their spending to housing, utilities, food and clothing. On average, therefore, they enjoy considerable discretionary spending that improves their quality of life, including on average spending a sixth of their income on leisure goods and services. The average expenditure per household for Britain overall is about £ 309, with the lowest national level being £ 293 in Scotland and the highest being £ 312 in England.

Table I. Average Household Expenditure by Commodity and Service, 1996—1997 (British Pounds per Week)

	United Kingdom	England	Wales	Scotland	Northern Ireland	London
Housing	49.1	50.8	46.2	39.3	29	61.7
Fuel, light, power	13.3	13.2	14.2	14.1	16	12.6
Food	55.1	55	53.8	56.1	60.2	57.9
Alcohol & tobacco	18.5	18.3	18.3	20.1	19.4	16.6
Clothing & footwear	18.3	18.5	15	17.1	22.7	19.9
Household goods & services	43.1	43.7	42.6	39.1	37.7	48.5
Motoring & fares	48.7	48.9	46.4	48.9	47.5	47
Leisure goods & services	49.1	50.3	44.5	41.7	43.4	57.6
Miscellaneous personal	13.8	14.2	12.2	11.2	14.4	16.2
Average Expenditure:						
Per Household	309.1	312.8	293.2	287.6	290.2	337.9
Per Person	126	127.5	123	118.2	109.9	135.1

Source: Office for National Statistics, *Family Expenditure Survey*.

Ⅵ. Industrial Structure and Output

Economists often characterize economies by the division of output among a nation's constituent industries. Table J shows estimates of output from each sector of the British economy in 1996.

Table J. Gross Domestic Product by Industry, Current Prices, 1996 (millions of pounds sterling)

Industry Group	United Kingdom	England	Wales	Scotland	Northern Ireland	London
Ariculture, forestry, fishing	11,790	9,023	474	1,642	651	97
Mining, quarrying, oil and gas	4,398	2,865	224	1,220	88	185
Manufacturing	137,006	114,715	7,420	12,103	2,769	11,178
Eectricity, gas, water	13,606	10,665	733	1,828	381	1,198
Construction	33,746	28,241	1,434	3,282	789	3,707
Hotels, catering, repairs	93,091	80,548	3,357	7,237	1,949	15,481
Transport, storage, communication	54,056	47,469	1,622	4,181	784	10,358
Financial and business services	164,282	146,445	4,528	10,780	2,530	38,476
Public administration & defense	38,244	30,835	1,949	3,709	1,751	5,227
Education, social & health services	81,876	67,046	4,025	8,250	2,555	10,909
Other services	24,713	21,047	912	2,160	594	5,319
Adjustment for financial services	−26,968	−23,953	−682	−1,962	−370	−8,685
Total GDP	629,841	534,945	25,995	54,430	14,470	93,450

Notice the relative strengths of manufacturing and financial services in this table. These are characteristically strong in Britain. Notice too that London, while contributing little in primary output (first two rows), makes a disproportionate contribution in financial services. London is one of the world's strongest financial centers.

Ⅶ. International Trade

As mentioned earlier, Britain has grown and prospered as a trading nation. But in the past two decades Britain has had to *reorient[38] its trading. Three things have influenced these adjustments: (i) the ascent of Britain's oil industry after production began in its North Sea district; (ii) the growing importance of trade with Europe; and (iii) a perceived loss in overall competitiveness for British manufacturing. Probably the most important of these, especially in the modern period of EU membership, is that continental Europe is its nearest, largest, and richest trading partner.

Over the past few decades Britain has exported about 30 percent of its GDP, a proportion that has been rising slightly but steadily in the past decade. While service exports have grown markedly, the composition of exported commodities in general has been stable over the past few decades. Manufactured goods continue to dominate the commodity stream, with around 80% of commodity export value. Exports of fuel have cycled a bit, hitting a high of 14% of total commodity exports in the early eighties, then abating to about 7% through the nineties.

By contrast, the stream of imported goods has changed markedly over the years. This is shown in Graph Ⅱ, where one quickly notices growth in finished manufactures, and declines in food, tobacco, beverages and basic materials.

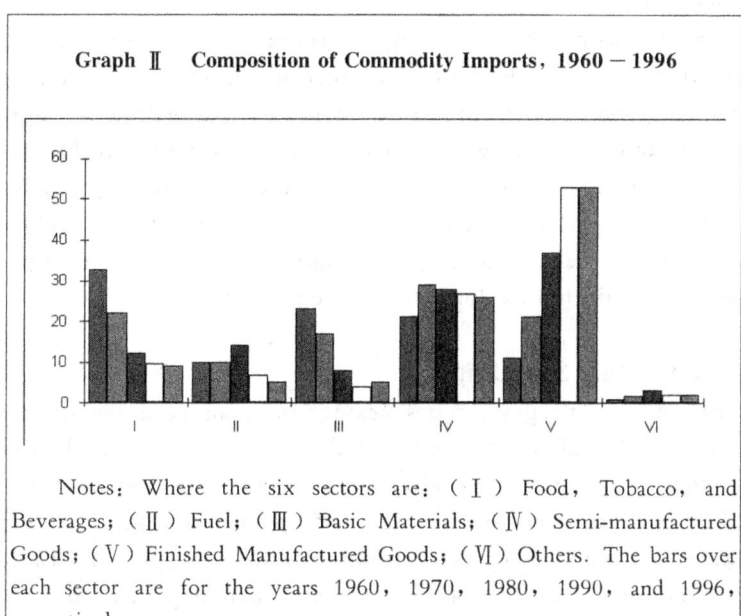

Graph Ⅱ Composition of Commodity Imports, 1960 — 1996

Notes: Where the six sectors are: (Ⅰ) Food, Tobacco, and Beverages; (Ⅱ) Fuel; (Ⅲ) Basic Materials; (Ⅳ) Semi-manufactured Goods; (Ⅴ) Finished Manufactured Goods; (Ⅵ) Others. The bars over each sector are for the years 1960, 1970, 1980, 1990, and 1996, respectively.

That Finished Manufactured Goods have become a growing import item is often read as a sign that Britain has lost in its competitiveness. One should note, however, that exports of finished manufactures have remained strong over the years, so it is hard to tell about overall competitiveness. Clearly, though, there is room for growth via imported substitution in finished manufacturing.

As shown in Table K, Britain's overall trade balance showed a slight deficit in 1997.

There was an overall surplus in services trade—owing in large measure to the UK's export of financial and information services—but there was an overriding deficit in traded goods. The net trade balance in 1997 was a £630 million deficit.

Table K. Exports, Imports, and Trade Balances, European Union (EU) and non-European Union (non-Eu), 2007
(millions of pounds sterling)

	Goods	Service	Total
Exports Eu	127,678	59,436	187,114
Exports non-Eu	93,025	88,198	181,223
Imports Eu	169,142	54,834	223,976
Imports non-Eu	140,813	51,028	191,841
Balance	−79,252	41,772	−37,480

Source: Office of National Statistics, *UK Balance of Payments*. Current Account: Transactions with the European Union and with non-Eu countries.

Britain is seen these days as a relatively small, open economy; its trade is significant, but it is such a small player in international markets that it has little control over the prices at which it sells. This is in stark contrast to the Period of Empire, when its traders had considerable pricing power.

Today's mix of British exports and imports reflects its new European orientation. In 2007, over half of exported goods went to destinations in other EU countries. Similarly, more of its imported goods came from the EU. Still, Britain maintains a significant global presence in transportation, finance, computer and information technology, scientific instruments and engineering products. About 13 percent of its exports went to North America in 1997. Meanwhile, less than 10 percent went to other developed countries, approximately 10 percent went to developing countries, and only about 2 percent went to OPEC countries (as Britain has its domestic source of supply).

VIII. Taxation and Public Spending

Britain's national tax program relies heavily on household income taxes, *Social Security Contributions[39] and the *Value Added Tax (VAT)[40], as shown in Table L. While total revenues have grown steadily in the past two decades, there is general satisfaction in Britain with its tax system, so a tax revolt of any kind seems remote.

These revenues are spent on a host of programs, as highlighted in Tables M and N. Table M shows the share of national government spending that goes to each of 11 programs. The combined expenditures on Social Security *pensions[41] and survivors' benefits, Health (the nationalized health care provider network), and Education and Science (public schools and support for higher education) amount to almost 60 percent of national government spending. The 2007 budget has similar expenditures for health and social security, but adds a line for debt interest, that results in small decreases in other areas.

At the local level, which involves barely a fourth as much money as national government spending, Education and Social Services again dominate—with almost 60 percent of local government expenditures. Police, fire and courts come next at about 18 percent of expenditures.

Table L. Government Revenue from Taxation			
	1978	1993	1996
Taxes on income			
Income tax	33	27	26
Corporation tax	5	7	10
Taxes on expenditures			
VAT	9	21	17
Tobacco	4	3	3
Oil	4	6	9
Alcohol	4	2	2
Other	7	5	8
Taxes on capital	2	1	1
Social Security Contributions	21	18	17
Community charges	11	10	7
Total	100	100	100
Total tax revenues			
(Billions of pounds)	57	211	286

Source: HM Treasury, Budget Report, March 1998.
http://www.hm-treasurv.gov.uk/pub/html/budget98/anexba.htm#tab9

Table M. National Government Spending by Category (% of total)				
	1978–1979	1984–1985	1990–1991	1992–1993
Defense	11.5	13	11.2	9.8
Trade and industry	4.7	3.9	2.3	2.2
Employment and training	1.7	2.3	1.5	1.4
Housing	4.6	4.3	4.1	4.4
Transport	7.1	3.7	2.5	2.6
Environmental services	3.8	3	3.7	3.7
Law and order	3.9	4.7	5.8	5.9
Education and science	14.2	13.3	14.5	13.3
Health	12.3	12.7	14.2	14.4
Social security	26.4	30.2	30.1	33
Other departments	9.8	8.9	10.1	9.3
Total	100	100	100	100

Source: Welham, Phillip, "Public Expenditure and Taxation," in *An Introduction to the UK Economy*, Prentice-Hall, 1996.

Table N. Real Net Current Expenditure of Local Government by Category (1993—1994 prices)					Percent of Total Spending 1994-1995
	1981-1982	1985-1986	1990-1991	1994-1995	
Education	17,756	17,948	21235	19,278	43
Personal social services	3,471	3,637	4727	6,870	15
Police, fire, courts	4,919	5,591	6,645	8,025	18
Highways and transportation	3,261	2,768	3,443	2,044	5
Housing	1,641	1,076	521	490	1
Libraries, museums	611	614	721	750	2
Recreation, parks, sports	1,060	976	1,097	1,115	3
Environmental health, waste	1,586	1,427	1,671	1,792	4
Planning, development	707	502	559	673	2
Revenue collection	263	238	720	524	1
Other	1,193	1,538	3,741	2,896	7
Total (millions of pounds)	36,468	36,315	45,080	44,457	100

Source: CIPFA, Financial and General Statistics (Annual)

IX. Economic Policy

Roughly from 1946 to 1982 British policy makers used *Keynesian[42] *countercyclical[43] economic policies. According to that policy, logic, fiscal and monetary controls provide the necessary policy tools to promote full employment, high incomes, price stability and stable growth. Monetary and credit policy could be used to control interest rates, prices and exchange rates. If exchange rates become problematic, the currency can be officially revalued or be floated—so that its value relative to other currencies would conform more closely to market forces of supply and demand. Meanwhile, fiscal policy—taxation and public spending—could be tuned to achieve full employment and balanced trade. If at full employment trade deficits mount beyond acceptable bounds, then the floating currency will weaken, stimulating exports and reducing imports. If particularly important industries should become compromised in the process, the government might opt to nationalize industries. It was all neat and tidy.

But British policy makers had trouble achieving their objectives. Under this policy system, when they cut taxes and increased spending to fight unemployment, then inflation would worsen and speculators would drive down currency values. Raising taxes to correct the falling currency and inflation resulted in higher unemployment and recession. Back and forth they went, promulgating Stop-Go policy: fiscal tightness—fiscal looseness, monetary tightness—monetary looseness. There seemed too few policy instruments to handle all the economic objectives.

When Margaret Thatcher's government came to power in 1979, the economic policy approach began to change. Keynesian thinking had by then fallen from favor, so a more institutional alternative was invented. At first this involved a brand of *"Monetarism"[44]—using the money policy to control inflation—and "fiscal conservatism"—to balance the budget. Flexible exchange rates were already in place, so the idea was to let the economy adjust to three imperatives: stable prices, balanced budget, and floating currency.

The immediate outcome was recession, but in time the result was economic accommodation. Slowly but surely the economy has adjusted. Meanwhile the policy of privatization was formulated and implemented. The Thatcherites envisioned a brand of prosperity which featured much less government intervention in markets.

By 1982, a political-economic doctrine called *"supply-side economics"[45] was catching on in America, and that provided a logic framework for Thatcherism. The idea was to attack social problems like unemployment, inflation and falling exchange rates with "privatization" and "stimulants to private investment". These supply-side policies, as they came to be called, have been based on tax cuts, reduced governmental influence and greater trust in the market system.

Of course, Britain's participation in the EU also helped to resolve its pressing economic problems by providing a market for exports. Britain liked that, but remained suspicious about relinquishing sovereignty. Europeanism progressed toward more open markets, easier migration of both capital and labor, and harmonized product standards among member states. In that environment British businesses had to face the ultimate economic discipline—competition from other European suppliers. That competition has been stiff, and it promises to get stiffer with the entry of members from Eastern Europe: Poland, *Hungary[46], the *Chech[47] Republic, and *Estonia[48]—where wages are much lower than in Britain.

In the aftermath of all this, Britain has become more comfortable with allowing market incentives to guide resource use and service delivery. Government intervention has become more focused and restricted. Finally, and most importantly, few people discuss British economic policy these days without reference to the European Union's evolution and the expanding role of emerging global markets. These provide the context for economic policy in Britain today.

Study Questions

1. Name and highlight the three eras of British economic development. Be sure to note Britain's varying fortunes in international trade through this historical sketch.
2. Describe the development pattern pioneered by Britain. Be sure in your description to include both settlement and employment patterns. Do you think that nation must travel the British-type path in the process of industrialization?
3. Drawing on data from Tables B and C, describe Britain's "prosperity" and how it is distributed. Which regions are most prosperous and which are least prosperous?
4. Using Table D, what fraction of households had income of £ 450 per week in 1999 – 2002? How does this proportion vary among Britain's constituent states and London?
5. Given the prominence of cities in modern economic affairs, find evidence showing the relative richness of London in the British economy. Verify too that London has a

high incidence of low income households. Why might this be?
6. Britain experienced a recession in 1991 – 1992. Characterize its recovery up to July, 1998. What global events have stirred worry about the recovery for the next couple of years?
7. What is a Limited Liability Company?
8. Describe some of the advantages and disadvantages of markets. How do some of the disadvantages translate into public policies in Britain?
9. Describe the main elements of privatization in Britain since 1980.
10. Wealth of UK is unevenly distributed. Please cite facts of 1996 – 1997 to show how big the gap was.
11. Judging from average consumer spending in Britain, would you say that Britons has a high or a low standard of living? Explain.
12. The Thatcher government brought some significant changes in economic policy. Characterize those changes.
13. Government spending in Britain is primarily devoted to meeting genuine human needs. Agree or disagree with that statement and explain your stand.

Selected Bibliography

Alford, B. W. E. *British Economic Performance, 1945 – 1975*. New York: Cambridge University Press, 1995.

Artis, Michael, Ed. *The UK Economy*, 14th Edition. New York: Oxford University Press, 1996.

Baker, David & Seawright, David. *Britain For and Against Europe*. New York: Oxford University Press, 1998.

Buxton, Tony, Chapman, Paul & Temple, Paul. *Britain's Economic Performance*. London: Routledge, 1994.

Cox, Andrew, Lee, Simon, & Sanderson, Joe. *The Political Economy of Modern Britain*. Lyme: Edward Elgar Publishing, 1997.

Hare, Paul & Simpson, Leslie. *An Introduction to the UK Economy*. New York: Prentice-Hall, 1996.

Holden, Ken, Matthews, Kent & Thompson, John. *The UK Economy Today*. Manchester: Manchester University Press, 1995.

Nankivell, Owen. *Economics, Society, and Values*. Brookfield: Avebury Press, 1995.

注　释

〔1〕 欧洲共同体。
〔2〕 欧盟。
〔3〕 经济衰退。
〔4〕 欧洲经济共同体第一主义。
〔5〕 香料,调味品。
〔6〕 鸦片战争。
〔7〕 柬埔寨。
〔8〕 英联邦(由英国和已经独立的前英帝国殖民地、附属国组成)。
〔9〕 凝聚力。
〔10〕 货币波动。
〔11〕 比利时。
〔12〕 荷兰。
〔13〕 卢森堡。

〔14〕撒切尔,英国首相(1979—1990)。
〔15〕私营化。
〔16〕民族主义。
〔17〕(古英语)相当于 to。
〔18〕名义上的。
〔19〕(商业活动的)下降趋势。
〔20〕亚洲经济形势的蔓延。
〔21〕国际货币基金组织。
〔22〕(法)自由竞争。
〔23〕(洛克、罗素等的)社会契约论。
〔24〕投机的。
〔25〕需求方。
〔26〕平衡价格。
〔27〕供过于求。
〔28〕供小于求。
〔29〕不列颠人。
〔30〕短期效率。
〔31〕智利人。
〔32〕巴西人。
〔33〕敲……竹杠。
〔34〕基础设施。
〔35〕英国工业联合会。
〔36〕英国制造的多用途越野车(商标名)。
〔37〕外在性。
〔38〕重新定向。
〔39〕为老年人、失业者和残疾人提供社会福利的社会保障制度。
〔40〕增值税。
〔41〕养老金,退职金,抚恤金。
〔42〕凯恩斯的。英国经济学家凯恩斯(1883—1946)认为失业和经济危机的原因在于有效需求的不足,主张国家干预经济生活并管理通货。
〔43〕逆周期性的。
〔44〕货币数量说,认为货币数量与商品价格成正比,与货值成反比,以及货币数量决定一国经济状况等。
〔45〕供给经济学,指通过减税等方法来刺激经济增长的政策。
〔46〕匈牙利。
〔47〕车臣。
〔48〕爱沙尼亚。

CHAPTER 5　BRITISH CULTURE

Gillian Masemore and Dr. Carol W. Pollard

Ⅰ. Introduction

The people of Great Britain include the English, Irish, Scots and Welsh. After Southern Ireland became an independent republic in 1948, the United Kingdom included Northern Ireland, England, Scotland and Wales. There are many differences among the ways these people live, depending on their geographic location and national traits. However, this introduction to contemporary middle-class culture will focus on the similarities shared by the British people.

Ⅱ. The British People—General Traits

At the start of the 21st century, nearly 61 million people lived in the United Kingdom. Generally, they tend to be a very reserved people. Since they are not immediately friendly and open with strangers, they seem to be difficult to get to know. They are not the kind of people to embrace friends with open arms and are offended by body contact, such as kissing and hugging, when meeting others. At an early age, children are taught to control their feelings and keep a *"stiff upper lip"[1]. Although this behavior is often perceived to be aloof, it is just a national trait.

Despite this very British reserve, the British are tremendously generous and hospitable. After being introduced, they will genuinely go to great lengths to make both friends and strangers feel at home.

The British have a wonderful sense of humor. The humor is a rather gentle, subtle humor, often directed against themselves, and the British enjoy making fun of their own customs, class system and even their government.

The British cherish their own space and privacy much more than Americans do. People who live in crowded apartment buildings or dense urban areas like to feel that their space is their own, so they do not usually mix freely with their neighbors. It is not uncommon for people to live next door to each other for years and never exchange more than a polite greeting or know anything about each others' private lives. When people travel by bus or train, however crowded the conditions, each person keeps to himself, reading a book or newspaper and rarely conversing with his fellow travelers. In fact, he might consider it to be quite an imposition if a stranger tried to strike up a conversation with him.

Since World War II, people from other countries have settled in Great Britain in search of a better life. By 2008, immigrants from India, Pakistan, Bangladesh, Africa, Poland and the British *West Indies[2] totaled eight percent of the population. Most immigrants settled in London or other urban areas. People of Asian or African descent have found it harder to *assimilate[3] into British life, although the better qualified immigrants from India usually earn more money and higher social status than those from Pakistan or Bangladesh. Bigoted white people call those with dark skins, Paki, a term of contempt. Even though many immigrants work hard and do very well, ethnic and racial prejudices continue to be a factor in contemporary daily life. Some British people are upset that foreigners have taken their jobs and their housing and are receiving health care that other British people have paid for.

1. MANNERS FOR A DENSELY POPULATED ISLAND

Good manners are very important to the British. Table manners are one of the first social behaviors taught to young children. Children are encouraged to sit straight, to keep their elbows off the table and never to talk with their mouths full of food! Even in the *immediate family[4], bad table manners are never tolerated. A knife and fork are used at the table, and food, except for bread, should never be picked up with one's hands. Manners outside the home are also important. Everyone says "Please" and "Thank you". It is still considered polite to use a person's title, such as Mr., Mrs. or Miss, unless you know the individual quite well.

Like Americans, the British people cherish their individual freedom. Generally the British tend to be sensitive to their neighbors' rights and freedoms. Since Britain is a small, densely populated country, people tend to put the good of the community above their own desires. An example of this would be the way the people in the United Kingdom always "queue" or line up to be served in a store or to board a bus, rather than pushing to the front of the line. Some people believe the British are a regimented people without a great deal of individuality. In reality, they have learned to get along well with their countrymen and do not need to express themselves publicly.

2. BRITISH PAGEANTRY AND ROYALTY

The British have been steeped in tradition for over one thousand years. Because they have been ruled by kings and queens, they dearly love the pomp and circumstance of royalty. Many events, from the Lord Mayor of London's parade to the opening of the horse races at Ascot, involve color and *pageantry[5]—golden coaches pulled by beautiful horses, surrounded by mounted cavalry in scarlet coats. In addition to this pageantry rooted in tradition, the British people are surrounded by reminders of royalty. They are defended by the Royal Air Force and the Royal Navy. Their letters are delivered by the Royal Mail. Criminals are sent to Her (His) Majesty prisons. Elite shops note in their advertisements if they sell to the royal family. Members of the royal family appear at the openings of new community facilities. The royal family provides a sense of stability when times are difficult or political parties change.

Throughout its history, British royalty has experienced a variety of difficulties, but a series of unfortunate events which occurred during the latter half of the twentieth century have jeopardized the status of the Royal Family. Particularly, the divorce between Prince Charles, Elizabeth II's heir to the throne, and his wife, Princess Diana, created a national controversy. Following the September 1997, death of Princess Diana, lovingly called "the People's Princess", many observers believe that the royalty will become more open and friendly to the British public.

Some people think that too much money is spent on maintaining the Royal Family. Others feel that the money is returned to the treasury when the many foreign tourists, eager to see members of the Royal Family, visit and shop in Britain. Other people like the fact that the king or queen bears the responsibility of pageantry, leaving the elected Prime Minister and his Cabinet time to concentrate on political issues rather than attending social functions.

Time will tell whether the monarchy will survive, but it has been a great force in the lives of the British *from time immemorial[6].

3. CLASS SOCIAL SYSTEM

England has traditionally been a country with a very rigid class system. The aristocracy is composed of the noble families, particularly the royal family, *lords[7], *earls[8], *barons[9], *viscounts[10] and the offshoots of these families. The upper class consists of large land owners and people with much inherited wealth. Until quite recently, most of the British political leaders came from the upper class.

Beneath the upper class, is a large middle class, which is also divided into upper-middle class and lower-middle class. The upper-middle class is comprised of professional people, including doctors, lawyers, clergymen, smaller land owners and people, who, over the years, acquired some wealth. The lower-middle class consists of white collar workers and shop owners. At the bottom of the class system is the working class which includes blue collar workers, such as factory workers, mechanics and shop assistants.

Although the class system has blurred considerably during the twentieth century, mainly because of universal education and an emphasis on an individual's ability, there is still an ingrained class consciousness in most British people. Class is still very important socially and in the work place. In order to succeed, it helps if one's father was in a good profession and if one attended a good private school.

Unlike America, where classes are divided mainly by the amount of money one has, money has very little to do with the class system in England. A working man may make a fortune, but he will never be accepted by the upper classes as one of their own. Similarly, if a member of the upper class should lose his money and have to live very frugally, he will unmistakably still be a member of the upper class!

Factors which separate the British classes include education, language patterns and regional accents, leisure activities and even food. Strangely, the class system is so ingrained that very few people strive to move out of their class. In fact, they will be ridiculed by their peers for trying to "better themselves" or for "not knowing their place".

4. EDUCATION—AN OVERVIEW

Most British children go to some kind of nursery school or day care facility between the ages of three and five. This early schooling is paid by the parents, unless the parents are unable to pay the fees. In this case, the children go to a free state school or day care.

Free primary schooling is available to children between the ages of five and twelve. Free secondary schooling is for students between the ages of twelve and sixteen. *Tertiary school[11] is primarily for students between the ages of sixteen and eighteen years who plan to enter the university or who choose some kind of vocational training.

Young people who leave school at sixteen may enter the workplace, or they might be apprenticed to a master, such as a brick layer, builder, or even a solicitor or an accountant. Some students prefer to work during the day and study for advanced degrees by enrolling in evening classes, but others study for a two-year *associate degree[12] or a three-year college degree. Some eighteen-year-olds will also go directly to work. About 75% of all British children will attend some form of higher education after secondary school.

At age eighteen, a student takes the "A" level (Advanced Level) examinations, a requirement to enter a university. A bachelor's degree is a three-year program. Both a master's and a doctorate require two additional years of education each.

Primary and secondary school students usually wear school uniforms. Before 8 am and after 3 pm, the streets fill with these students walking or cycling to and from schools. In urban areas they crowd the public transport system, chatting with their mates.

Free education has benefited all citizens, but essentially the school system is designed to keep the classes separate. The upper classes always send their young children to the good "public" schools, such as *Eton[13] or *Harrow[14], which actually are very expensive private schools. Some middle class children also attend these "public" schools; others attend less expensive "public" schools which also provide a very good education. However, the majority of students go to the state schools which are free. After graduation, the brightest students will attend a good secondary school, known as a grammar school, and may receive a scholarship to a good university. The less intellectually gifted will enter the *comprehensive schools[15], and many of these graduates who excel will continue into some form of higher education. Usually children from working class families will go to the comprehensive schools until age sixteen when they enter the work force.

5. THE HEALTH CARE SYSTEM

Britain has a National Health Care system (NHC). The form of this service varies slightly among the countries of the United Kingdom. For example, in England, only low income people may receive certain kinds of at-home care without any payment, while in Scotland all people may receive it without cost. The system employs a large number of people, and in 2007 their website claimed they saw a million patients every 36 hours. In general, all health care is free, because everyone contributes a specified amount of money each month from his/her wages to NHC. In addition to the doctors who provide general care, every small village has a clinic which cares for people with special needs: the very young, pregnant women and the elderly. A pregnant woman receives excellent prenatal care to ensure that her baby will be healthy. Beginning at birth, the baby receives regular check-ups and care. Although the very young and the very old receive free comprehensive health care, wage owners have to pay a small amount of money for their dental care, glasses and prescriptions.

British people buy medical insurance from private companies which allows them to have a surgical procedure whenever they choose. It also means that they can have a private hospital room, instead of sharing a ward with several other people.

6. FAMILY AND CHILDCARE

Young people in England will usually have several friends of the opposite sex before committing to one person. Because women now attend college and work equally with men, a couple may postpone marriage. They may choose to live together without marrying. Consequently, couples tend to have children later in life. Most couples restrict their families to one or two children because it is extremely expensive to raise children, particularly if the parents want their offspring to get a good start in life and to have a good education.

The ideal British family is the nuclear family, comprising father, mother, and children. Grandparents and other family members may or may not live nearby. However, throughout the second half of the twentieth-century, rising divorce rates have complicated this ideal. Many marriages end in divorce. Also, the numbers of lone parents, usually single mothers, have also increased.

The rising standard of living is an expensive one. In 2008, the government estimated that a household with two children was carrying about £100,000 in debt. This debt includes the mortgage on the house, loans such as car loans, and credit card debt. As a result, usually both husband and wife work. Working mothers will leave their children in day care centres or with relatives and friends. They will try to stay at home with their children until the youngest is three years old. Women still do more household chores and child care than men.

Problems with youth people are also increasing. Among European Union countries, Britain has one of the highest rates of teen pregnancies and teen problems, such as disruptive behavior, drunkenness, drug use, and vandalism. English teens are known for their materialism.

Concern about teen crime is only part of a British preoccupation with crime in general. Security cameras are everywhere, and people are concerned about burglary, theft, and vandalism. There is a small but consistent rise in the prison population. Even so, British police still are not routinely issued firearms. Small squads, usually based in London, may be heavily armed, but most police carry only a form of truncheon and, in some cases, a taser.

Despite worries and concerns, the British family is a close unit. Families usually share the evening meal and spend time together during the week and on holiday. They often will go out together for a meal, if only for a burger or fish and chips. Mobile phones keep members in touch with one another. Teens receive about £10 a week in pocket money.

7. HOUSING

The majority of British families live in single family houses. Since some of these homes share a common wall, they are known as *semi-detached[16] houses. Both houses and apartments, called flats, can be purchased or leased. Most single people and young married couples rent their homes until they have saved enough money for a down payment on a house of their own. Although housing is very expensive and will take a major portion of a person's income, most people strive to buy a house of their own. Real estate increases in value, so many times a young couple will purchase a small home hoping to sell it at a good profit after a few years and move into a large, better house.

Houses usually have a living room, dining room, kitchen, two to four bedrooms and one or two bathrooms. They have central heating. The average family owns at least one television set, a DVD player, a sound system, a washing machine, a vacuum cleaner, a microwave oven and small kitchen appliances, including a mixer, a blender and an electric kettle. Most will have satellite, digital, or cable receivers for the television. Over half have a home computer with an internet connection.

Outside the house, regardless of its size, is a small garden. The British are great gardeners and take great pride in their own piece of ground. Even a tiny area will be cultivated to grow bright flowers during the summer. Most English gardens have a lawn surrounded by flower beds. Roses, a favorite flower, grow very well in England, and many varieties have been developed. People living in a block of flats will usually plant flowers in at least one window box.

Public gardens are also very popular in England. Every town has one or more landscaped parks filled with trees, shrubs and flowering plants. There are usually wide lawn spaces for picnicking or playing games, as well as walking paths and benches. Sometimes these parks are huge, covering many acres, and sometimes they are a small green space where people can sit and relax.

8. FOOD IN HOMES AND RESTAURANTS

English food used to be fairly basic: meat, potatoes, and vegetables. Hotels will still serve foreigners the "traditional English breakfast" of bacon, sausage, eggs, beans, tomatoes, and toast. However, the merger with the European Union has brought a flood of fresh vegetables and fruits into the supermarkets. Immigrants from Asia and Africa have introduced some of their traditional foods.

Breakfast is usually cereal, juice, toast and coffee or tea. The children have milk. Children will carry a lunch to school or eat a light lunch furnished by the school. Adults at work often have a morning coffee break, which used to be the morning tea break. For lunch, they will usually nip into a local restaurant or takeaway near their work place. They may buy a sandwich from a nearby supermarket or corner shop. Adults at home may have a light lunch of soup, a sandwich, or sliced meat, a salad, and various kinds of bread or rolls

At one time, tea was always served in the middle or late afternoon, but, in today's busy world, most people take a short break for just a cup of tea. A full afternoon tea is only served during weekends and usually only when entertaining guests. A full or proper English tea consists of black tea from India or *Sri Lanka[17], served with milk and sugar. Tea is served with very thinly cut sandwiches, cakes and biscuits. If *scones[18] are served, they will be accompanied by thick, *clotted cream[19] and strawberry jam.

Dinner, the main meal during the week, is served in the evening. This meal used to be quite elaborate. As more wives work outside the home and there are more events going on in the evenings, dinner has become simpler; processed food has replaced home cooked food. Often dinner will come from the local Chinese or Indian takeaway. Curry is one of the most popular foods in England.

Sunday noon is generally a time for a large meal which both the nuclear and extended family members are expected to attend whenever possible. This meal usually consists of some kind of roast beef or lamb, cooked vegetables and roasted, baked or *mashed potatoes[20]. Since the English people enjoy sweet foods, the main course is nearly always followed by a dessert: a fruit *tart[21], pie, a *custard-like pudding[22] or cooked fruit with custard or cream.

A more elaborate meal includes several courses: an *appetizer[23], soup, fish, main course, dessert and cheese and crackers. Wine is served with each course, and strong, black coffee follows dessert.

Some people, especially the Scottish, have a different eating pattern. They consume a larger breakfast, eat their main meal at noon and have a *"high tea"[24] in the early evening. High tea is a meal which combines the food eaten at tea time with a light supper.

Many British restaurants serve good British food, while others serve foreign cuisine. Restaurants in London and other large cities are first class and serve food from almost any nationality found in the world. American fast food restaurants, such as McDonald's and Burger King, are also common.

The British are very fond of drinking beer, the largest-selling alcoholic beverage, although liquor and wine are also available. One very British tradition is the "Pub" or public house which is a combination of a bar and a restaurant. Every small village has at least one pub. Usually pubs are very old, quaint buildings, furnished with country antiques, because they have been public houses or small hotels for decades or even centuries.

Unlike drinking establishments in many other countries, the British pub is more of a social institution. It is a place to meet neighbors and friends, to talk or to play games, particularly darts and *skittles[25], a form of *bowling[26]. Children are not allowed in the pub, but outside there is often a small garden with tables and chairs where parents and children can eat and drink. Pub food is usually very good, although the menu is often casual and limited. Standard fare includes sandwiches, soups, hot meat pies, baked potatoes, bread and cheese. If one is traveling in Britain, it is a good idea to eat in a pub where traditionally the best and cheapest food is served.

9. RELIGION

Usually, the English do not attend church regularly. Many go to church at Christmas or *Easter[27], and almost everyone is married in church. The traditional religion in England is called the Church of England, a Protestant church created by King Henry VIII, when he broke away from Roman Catholicism in the sixteenth century. Before this historic event, the country was Roman Catholic, and a fairly large Catholic population still lives in the British Isles, particularly Ireland. There are hundreds of old churches in England, many of them built during the *Norman period[28]. Every small town and village seems to have one of these ancient square-towered churches which are still used today by the local *parishioners[29]. Since the influx of people from Africa, Asia and the British West Indies after World War II, many other religions and places of worship can be found, particularly in the large cities.

III. Entertainment

1. LEISURE

The British enjoy many activities such as gardening and horseback riding. Outside large cities it is always easy to hire a horse to ride. There are many horse shows during the year, and many of the larger contests are televised. Horse sports, such as *steeplechasing[30], *flat-track racing[31], *polo[32] and fox hunting are also popular. People also like to socialize and meet with friends. They will repair and improve their homes. This is called DIY (Do It Yourself) and there are DIY shops in most areas. People also like to go to the cinema and to eat out.

The British also love their automobiles and spend a good deal of time cleaning and repairing their cars. Reading, once a main activity, has lessened due to television and computers. All towns have a public library. Ticket holders can borrow books, DVDs, or audiotapes. They can use the internet or browse for information, with the help of library staff. Errand running often includes a visit to the library.

2. MASS MEDIA

For a long time, the only television programs in Britain were those produced by BBC, the British Broadcasting Company, and were funded by the sale of TV licenses. In 2008, the yearly fee for a colour TV license was £35.50; a black and white TV license was £5.50. Traditionally, BBC has presented high *caliber[33] programs, particularly excellent dramatizations of classical works of literature, discussions of topical interest and intellectual programs on the arts and sciences.

The BBC, which is sponsored by the national government, broadcasts radio and television programs for domestic and foreign markets. "BBC English" is famous throughout the world because it is the accent used by the BBC announcers. The BBC world service news has contributed to this fame. Formerly, educated people spoke "BBC English", but in recent times domestic local dialects and accents have become more popular. BBC broadcasts programs in Welsh to Wales, in Scottish to Scotland and in Irish to Ireland. In fact, local languages are now being taught as a second language in the local schools.

Today programs also come into Britain via satellite from all corners of the world. In addition, there are many domestic for-profit stations whose programs are funded through the sale of *commercials[34] shown throughout the programs. Commercial programming, especially sports, *sitcoms[35], comedy and game shows and popular singers, is less intellectual than the programming produced by BBC.

Everyone in Britain has at least one television, and people spend much time watching TV.

Television watching is so prevalent that when one man did not send in his fee, the authorities refused to believe that he did not watch television. They posted electronic equipment outside his home to check on him, and wasted days before they realized that he was telling the truth!

3. SPORTS—TYPES AND ATTITUDES TOWARD SPORTS

Most British enjoy watching and discussing sports events even if they do not actively participate. Most towns and villages have their own sports clubs for soccer, *rugby[36], *cricket,⁽³⁷⁾ tennis, and local teams will compete among themselves. Since everyone in England is encouraged to join a club, one need not feel inferior because of a lack of ability to play sports. Usually a club will have teams for all levels of players, and everyone has a chance to play and have fun. Many of the sports clubs also have social activities, serve alcoholic beverages, cater teas and dinners and offer other entertainment, such as table tennis, darts and video games.

Strangely, although the British are a nation of sports lovers and nearly everyone plays, watches and/or analyzes sports, they are not a competitive people. Unlike the famous American saying, "Winning isn't everything—it is the only thing!" the British refrain is, "It doesn't matter if you win or lose—it's how you play the game". Some people feel that it is "ungentlemanly" to constantly defeat your opponents—unless the game is soccer.

In the past, schoolboys were taught that if you took your sports too seriously and made your living by winning sports events, you were certainly no gentleman. The current fame and money earned by athletes have eroded this belief.

Professional sports are very popular, and England is host to several well-known sporting events. *Wimbledon⁽³⁸⁾, one of the favorite sporting events of the year, brings together the best tennis players from around the world. It used to be a very elite event, but now thousands of people attend. Many spectators wait all night outside the gate to buy a ticket.

Soccer is played throughout the British Isles. At the end of the year the *Soccer Cup Final⁽³⁹⁾ is held between the two teams with the best records. Tickets to the Cup Final, as well as to the earlier matches which determine the finalists, are almost impossible to buy. Excited fans often exhibit poor sportsmanship, and police may have to settle fights between gangs supporting rival soccer teams.

Two types of horse racing are extremely popular: flat racing and steeplechasing. The English Derby is one of the most important flat races, usually attended by the British monarch. The Grand National is televised worldwide because it is the world's greatest steeplechase. In this race, the jockeys and their horses compete on a four-mile track and jump over thirty-one fences. Some wealthy people also enjoy polo, a game played on horseback.

4. THE ARTS—THEATRE, MUSIC, AND FILM

In addition to television, live entertainment is very important in Britain where the theater is revered. Excellent theater companies perform in most major cities, including the London theater district. These *"repertory theater"⁽⁴⁰⁾ groups give wonderful performances, and enable young actors to gain valuable experience. Government subsidies keep ticket prices comparatively low.

Shakespearean theater continues to be popular, and Shakespeare's plays are always on stage somewhere in Britain. Originally, Shakespeare's plays were performed at the Globe Theater: a replica of the Globe Theater opened in London in 1997. Of course, Shakespeare's birthplace, Stratford-on-Avon, is the national center for staging his works.

Many cities also have other types of performing groups, including a symphony orchestra, a choral society, *jazz ensembles[41] and *amateur[42] dramatic groups. *Nightclubs[43] feature *stand-up comics[44], singers and other kinds of performers. Art galleries and museums are located throughout the country, an indication that the British revere their past and are extremely interested in it.

The British do not just look back; they look out and around. In the 1960s, the Beatles and other rock groups took American rock and roll and transformed it. Andrew Lloyd Weber did the same to the musical, with classics such as *Joseph and the Many Coloured Dream Coat* or *Cats*. Immigrants have brought new sounds and forms to the country. The three-week Edinburgh International Festival combines performances of classical theater, music, and dance with some of the most avant-garde music and drama in the world. Lists of music festivals in England will include many folk and traditional festivals, often designed for tourists, such as the acclaimed Bath Festival. You will also find many blues and jazz festivals as well. Scottish music festivals tend to stress traditional Scottish culture, but the list of Scottish festivals also includes the African Drum Village festival.

Major film studios located in England produce popular comedies and dramas. As a result of improved travel and technology, many modern films are made cooperatively with American or European companies.

5. SHOPPING

Although you hear many complaints about the service, it is very easy to travel in England because of its excellent bus and train transportation system and its large network of motorways. The car competes with rail and bus as a means of travel despite clogged streets and high urban parking fees. London has become so congested that it has instituted a congestion charge on all cars entering congested areas of the city.

Historically, English towns and villages were market centers. Today, large supermarkets and *shopping malls[45] have become popular. They are easily accessible by automobile and usually have large car parks where one can park free. They also provide many consumer goods in one place, including food, appliances, clothing and hardware. Since the smaller, independent shop-owners located in town centers cannot compete with the larger supermarkets and malls, their buildings have been taken over by business offices and small specialty stores, offering unusual items, especially cheese, wine, clothing, antiques and gifts.

6. PETS—KINDS AND ATTITUDE TOWARD ANIMALS

The British are known as a nation of animal lovers, and their animals are treated as important members of the family. Sick animals can be cured at the many veterinary hospitals, and most people will provide health care for their animals on a par with the care they give to their children. Nearly eighty percent of British families own a pet, usually a dog or a cat, although children will often keep small animals, especially *guinea pigs[46], rabbits or *hamsters[47]. Dogs are usually well-trained and travel with the family on shopping trips, where they can be seen patiently waiting for their owners outside shops, on buses and trains and even in restaurants, where they lie quietly under their owners' tables.

The welfare of animals has always been a concern to the British people. In fact, the first humane movement originated in England during the middle of the nineteenth century. At first, this movement was an attempt to prevent cruelty to horses, the main method of transportation. Later it was expanded to educate people about the proper care of animals and to enact laws to prevent cruelty to all animals.

The British humane movement has been accepted by many other countries, where laws are enacted to protect defenseless and endangered animals. Eventually legislation protecting animals became the basis for laws protecting British children. Originally these laws eliminated exploitative child labor, but today they protect children from any type of cruelty or abuse.

Modern animal activists are concerned about the overpopulation and exploitation of pets, particularly dogs and cats. They are also attempting to eliminate the use of animals for medical experimentation or for their furs. Some of these advocates want to stop all kinds of animal sports and shows, as well as the slaughter of animals for human food. Most people agree that animals should be protected from abuse, but they do not agree with the extreme views of the animal activists.

Before 2000 it was impossible to bring a cat or dog into Britain without leaving it in a kennel for six months quarantine to ensure it did not have rabies. To be in accord with EU practice, Britain now allows pets to enter without quarantine as long as they have met several rigid requirements.

7. HOLIDAYS

Several holidays are celebrated during the year in the United Kingdom. Easter, a religious holiday that has become commercialized, occurs in the spring. The Easter weekend begins on Good Friday, commemorating the *crucifixion[48] of Jesus Christ, and ends on Easter Sunday, celebrating Christ's *resurrection[49] from the dead. Easter Monday is also a holiday in England. Families usually gather for an Easter meal, and the children are given baskets filled with chocolate eggs and chickens. .

Each year there are two "Bank Holidays", one on a Monday at the end of May and the other on a Monday at the end of August. These holidays ensure that everyone has two long vacation weekends during warm weather.

*Guy Fawkes' Day[50] is celebrated on November 5th and commemorates a plot to blow up the Houses of Parliament in 1605. People build bonfires, and children make "Guys", life-size figures made with old clothes and stuffed with straw. When it is dark, these "Guys" are burned on the bonfires, and fireworks are set off.

Christmas, the largest holiday, was originally a religious holiday to celebrate the birth of Christ, but now it is more secular and commercial. Stores stock Christmas items earlier and earlier, and everyone is urged to buy presents for their family and friends. At Christmas everyone gives and receives presents, especially the children. Presents are placed under the Christmas tree or beside the children's beds where they can be easily seen when the children awaken. The children are told that Father Christmas, a fat, jolly old man with a white, bushy beard who wears a red suit, brings the presents. Children also hang up stockings, which are miraculously filled with small toys, nuts and fruit before Christmas morning. Usually on Christmas Eve there is a midnight religious service, but Christmas Day is a day for family dinners and parties.

*Boxing Day[51], the day after Christmas, is also a national holiday. In earlier times, wealthier people gave boxes of food and clothing to their servants or to poorer people in their neighborhoods on this day.

New Year's Eve is a big celebration. Actually in Britain, many businesses are closed for the week between Christmas, December 25, and New Year's Day, January 1. People attend boisterous parties and dances where they drink champagne to ring in the new year on December 31. Some people, especially the Scots, celebrate an old tradition called *"First Footing"[52]. These people believe that if a tall, dark man is the first person to set foot in your house on New Year's Day, you will have luck for the entire year. As a result, a tall, dark man, named the First Footer, is welcomed and given food and drink as he travels from house to house. In return, he gives a piece of coal to each household as a sign of good luck for the coming year.

8. SUMMER HOLIDAYS

It is unthinkable to the average British person that one would go through the entire summer without taking a vacation. It seems that everyone in the British Isles saves a good deal of money each year in order to have a summer holiday. The entire family discusses, plans and anticipates this holiday throughout the year. Sports players, bird watchers, garden lovers and people with other special hobbies can select a vacation which caters to their interests.

Many families go to the seaside on the eastern and southern shores where they camp or stay in a hotel or boarding house at night and spend their days on the long sandy beaches. Larger towns on the seaside provide all sorts of entertainment, including theater and *fun fairs[53].

Other families like to visit remote areas where they hike, ride horses, stay on working farms or go camping. Even though the population is dense, most of the people are concentrated in the major cities. As a result, much of the varied terrain in the British Isles is open space. The south of England is flat except for its rolling hills. Parts of Scotland and Wales are noted for their barren and low rocky mountains. The coastline of the British Isles is very rugged, especially on the western side, which has abundant rocks, cliffs and caves. Everywhere there are public footpaths which allow for excellent walking and hiking. People flock to the coastal areas, to Scotland, and to the Lake District. The Isle of Wight is a very active summer destination.

Recently, many British children will use their summer holidays to work in another country as an "au pair", a household helper and children's caretaker. This way they can perfect their speech in that country's language. More and more British families go to the continent on holiday, taking their car and camping with friends or going with a tour. Spain is a particularly favored holiday place.

The Chunnel, the tunnel under the English Channel linking England and France, was completed in 1996 and has made travel to the Continent faster and easier. However, the Chunnel has had a mixed reception in England. The British have always been very nationalistic and have cherished their island "separateness" from the European continent. Historically, they have been wary of the continental Europeans, and being linked so tangibly to France, although extremely convenient, it has been very difficult for some people to accept.

IV. Conclusion

The British Isles are covered with wonderful relics of the past—very old market towns; remains of walled cities and castles; ancient buildings and medieval churches; crumbling stone walls; and the mysterious presence of the large stone circles at Stonehenge and Avebury. Everywhere in the United Kingdom the past coexists with the present. Britain is also a very modern country which uses the latest technology. Older parts of major cities were rebuilt after the bombing destruction of World War II. Many of these towns and cities kept the essential flavor of their ancient past, but others preferred modern architecture.

Geographically and historically, the British tended to be an *insular[54] people. Today differences can be seen among people living in different regions of the country.

The British are a people who like order in their lives, and whose very being is based on their place in history, a history that surrounds them throughout their lives. At the same time they are a people who will seek ways to meld new technology and ideas into the established way of life. Although modern technology has changed their lifestyles, the basic character of the British people continues to cheer for the underdog, cherishes sportsmanship over competition and wants to do "the right thing".

Source

Office for National Statistics. The UK Statistics Authority. http://www.statistics.gov.uk.

Study Questions

1. How has the history of the United Kingdom contributed to the modern British character?
2. How has the geography of the United Kingdom contributed to the modern British character?
3. Compare Chinese cuisine with British cuisine.
4. Why do the British continue to support their monarchy?
5. Pets and gardens are important to the British people. What can you infer about the people from these two interests?

注　释

[1] 沉着的,感情不外露的。
[2] 西印度群岛。
[3] 被同化。
[4] 直系亲属。
[5] 盛大庆典。
[6] 自远古以来。
[7] 贵族,勋爵。
[8] 伯爵。
[9] 男爵。
[10] 子爵。
[11] 高等院校,提供高等教育课程,也可提供中等学校第六学级和职业教育的某些课程。

〔12〕准学士学位。
〔13〕伊顿公学,位于英格兰南部的一个小城镇。
〔14〕哈罗公学,英国哈罗城的一所著名的男生寄宿学校,创办于1571年。
〔15〕综合中学。
〔16〕半独立式的,与邻屋共一面墙的。
〔17〕斯里兰卡。
〔18〕烤饼,司康,一种源出英国,用大麦或燕麦面粉加糖、苏打、盐等烤制成的西点。
〔19〕固状奶酪。
〔20〕土豆泥。
〔21〕果馅饼。
〔22〕牛奶蛋冻布丁。
〔23〕餐前的开胃小吃或饮料。
〔24〕下午茶,通常为一小时;喝茶外,也可喝威士忌,吃点饼干之类的点心。
〔25〕撞柱游戏,一种很像保龄球的游戏。
〔26〕保龄球。
〔27〕(基督教)复活节,一般指春分月圆后的第一个星期日。
〔28〕指诺曼底公爵威廉1066年军事征服英格兰以后的时期。
〔29〕经常参加本区教堂的礼拜者。
〔30〕障碍赛马。
〔31〕平地赛马。
〔32〕马球。
〔33〕水准,程度。
〔34〕商业广告。
〔35〕情景喜剧,一种以固定人物为中心,故事相对独立的电视或广播系列剧。
〔36〕英式橄榄球运动。
〔37〕板球。
〔38〕温布尔登,位于伦敦附近,是著名的国际网球比赛地。
〔39〕足球杯决赛。
〔40〕保留剧目轮演剧团。
〔41〕爵士乐乐团。
〔42〕业余的。
〔43〕夜总会。
〔44〕以说笑为主的喜剧表演。
〔45〕大型步行区购物中心,备有停车场。
〔46〕天竺鼠。
〔47〕仓鼠。
〔48〕被钉在十字架上,受难。
〔49〕复活。
〔50〕盖伊·福克斯节(Guy Fawkes 为火药阴谋案的主犯,每年11月5日焚烧其模拟像以示庆祝)。
〔51〕节礼日,英国法定假日,在圣诞节次日,按习俗向雇员、仆人、邮递员等赠送匣装节礼。
〔52〕新年的第一位来客。
〔53〕英国的公共露天游乐场。
〔54〕具有岛民特征的。

CHAPTER 6 BRITISH EDUCATION

Dr. Carol W. Pollard

I. Introduction

The current British education system is highly complex; it consists of many types of schools and schooling. This complexity has resulted from British conservatism. When authorities changed the educational system, they tended to add new elements and alter existing ones, rather than to build everything anew.

Although this chapter is entitled "British Education", it will concentrate on English education. Welsh and Scottish systems were influenced by different religious and social values; therefore their systems have slightly different forms. This chapter will present the evolution of present-day institutions and regulations, particularly noting how people answered these questions: Who should be educated? Who pays for education? And what is the goal of education?

II. Medieval England — Church and Class

Before the *Norman Conquest[1] (1066), only boys from noble families received formal education, which was provided by the few existing schools or by itinerant tutors. After 1066, William the Conqueror's new government bureaucracy and his close ties to the bureaucratic Roman Catholic Church created a demand for more literate churchmen and clerks.

During the medieval period, Europe was united under the Roman Catholic Church. This Church was the custodian of knowledge and of education, as well as the main employer of literate men. Literacy was defined as reading and writing Latin, not English. Latin, the language of the *Roman Empire[2], had no native speakers, but all important European writing was in Latin. The importance of Latin can be seen in the written vocabulary of modern English, which has many Latin-derived words. Throughout medieval England and Europe, a young man seeking employment in the Church or in law or government had to read and write Latin. Since formal instruction in Latin was offered only through the church, most literate people were members of the church organization; such members were called clerics. If a merchant or government official wanted letters written or records kept, he would employ a cleric. The modern word "clerk" comes from the word *"cleric"[3].

1. ANSWERS TO QUESTIONS OF ACCESS, PAYMENT AND GOALS
A) Who Was Educated?

Formal instruction through schools and apprenticeships was primarily given to boys from middle-class families and the younger sons of the nobility. Children of peasant families had to work hard, and their parents could not afford to send them to school.

Noble families trained their eldest sons by sending them to another noble family to learn courtesy and fighting. Formal instruction was reserved for a very small percentage of the population.

B) Who Pays? — Donors and Parents

The Church-run schools were often partially funded by charitable donations given by wealthy individuals. At that time, people believed that charitable donations helped the donor to enter heaven after death. Such gifts contributed to the construction of schools, at both the secondary and the university levels.

However, the responsibility for educating a child rested with the family. Most parents did not send their children to school. Instead, the children learned skills by working alongside their parents. Peasant boys worked the land, or the mill, or the smithy beside their fathers. Peasant girls spun wool, wove cloth, baked bread, brewed beer, cared for dairy and poultry animals, cooked meals, cared for children, and tended vegetable gardens beside their mothers. Middle-class and upper-class girls also learned from their mothers, although such girls might also be taught to read and write in the family's language (English, French, Welsh, or Gaelic, the language of Ireland and Scotland).

Those families who did send their sons to school paid in several different ways. Wealthy families simply paid the tuition. Other families used church or aristocratic connections to find a scholarship position. An intelligent boy whose family lacked money or connections had little opportunity to go to school. He could not even learn by himself, since books were rare and expensive, and Latin was used only in the church or among educated people.

C) Goals of Education

Medieval Europeans did not believe in social change; therefore, education was not viewed as a means to improve society. Children were trained to replace their parents. Peasants did look to formal education as a means of improving their children's social status, but the nobility feared even this change. If a wealthy peasant managed to send his son to school, the son had few opportunities to use his education. Often, his only position was as a local priest. Such positions were poorly paid and without political power. Further, since priests could not marry or have legal children, the family as a whole could not advance. Even this opportunity was opposed by the nobility. They unsuccessfully tried to enact laws forbidding any peasants to be educated. The feudal church and the feudal nobility supported each other to preserve the *status quo[4].

2. EDUCATIONAL INSTITUTIONS: APPRENTICESHIPS AND UNIVERSITIES

Many institutions founded in medieval times, including apprenticeships and universities, exist today, although in very altered form.

A) Apprenticeships

Craftsmen, usually in the towns, could sign legal contracts of apprenticeships for their sons. The father selected a craft, such as weaving or carpentry, and signed a legal contract with a master in the trade organization (*guild[5]). The father paid the master, who thereafter provided housing and training for the boy. After six or seven years of obedient learning, the boy was granted journeyman status and received a small salary. Finally, the journeyman, usually in his twenties, approached the guild with a sample of his work and petitioned for status as a master. He could then start his own business and receive full payment for his work.

  This form of the apprenticeship system continued well into the twentieth century, until factory production and improved secondary education limited its usefulness. In the twentieth-century, apprenticeships were revised and included formal schooling.

B) Grammar and "Public" Schools

  "Grammar" schools originated in the towns and provided education for middle-class and upper-class boys. In 1179, the Roman Catholic Church ordered that a school should be built next to every *cathedral[6] (a church controlled by a bishop, a high-ranking church official). Further, the bishop was ordered to provide a school master to teach Latin grammar to *priests[7] and other people. Although these schools charged tuition, they also had scholarships. For example, since women were excluded from church positions and since vocal music was a part of the church service, boy singers were important. A boy with a good voice could receive an education in return for singing during the religious ceremonies in the cathedral. Such scholarships still exist today.

  These schools were often built through charitable donations given to educate local boys in Latin. These schools were known as "public" schools, since no tuition was required. However, the "public" grammar schools gradually accepted fee-paying students, who later dominated the schools. Winchester, founded by a donor in 1382, was originally intended to provide free education for local boys and boy singers, and only a few wealthy fee-paying students. Winchester boys were academically prepared for New College at Oxford University upon graduation. Eton, founded in 1440, followed the Winchester model. Its graduates went to King's College at Cambridge University, which was open only to Eton graduates. As with Winchester, the wealthy fee-paying students replaced the scholarship students. Such "public" schools soon became known as elite exclusive institutions for the sons of the wealthy. They were, and still are, the training ground of upper-class Englishmen and a synonym for snobbish elitism.

  The graduates of most grammar schools did not go to the universities. Instead, they went into apprenticeships or into their father's craft or trade. However, a small minority did continue their education in the chaotic and stimulating environment of a medieval university.

C) Universities: Oxford and Cambridge

  If medieval boys wished to attend an English university, they had two choices: Oxford and Cambridge. These universities still exist as prestigious institutions, although they are greatly changed. It is difficult to establish a date for the founding of these universities. Oxford gradually grew from a school associated with a local church, and Cambridge was founded by dissidents from Oxford. Slowly, the reputation of Oxford's teachers drew more and more students. As in the Greek academies of Plato's time (427? - 347 B.C.), the students paid the lecturers directly. The lecturers used the churches as classrooms, and the students found lodging in the town. There was an informal organization of teachers, called "the university", which acted like a medieval guild. The teachers often quarreled among themselves. A particularly bitter quarrel in 1209 caused one group to leave Oxford to found a university in the Cambridge area, where one lecturer had connections. On such a small event did the location of a major university depend. By 1300 A. D. , Oxford University had about 1,500 students, and Cambridge had about 500.

As more and more students came, charitable people donated money to pay for the students' room and board, establishing colleges where students could live while attending lectures. During the period 1316 to 1352, ten colleges were founded, each with its own rules, supported by its own income, and housing ten to twenty scholars. The scholars paid room and board fees to the college and tuition fees to the university, promised to obey the college rules, and were treated as lower members of the church organization. They even had their heads shaved like the church clerics.

There were no formal entrance or graduation examinations. Young men, fourteen or fifteen years old, simply were accepted into a college. They were usually sons of wealthy middle-class merchants and craftsmen, younger sons of nobles, and a few lower-class youths supported by scholarships. After attending lectures for four years, the young men were called *bachelors[8], like medieval knights in training. After another three years, they were termed *masters[9]. A candidate simply swore an oath that he had read the necessary books, and masters who knew him testified that he was qualified. Like a journeyman showing a sample craft item, the new master would give a sample lecture.

In the twenty-first century, versions of these universities have entrance and graduation examinations. Students are no longer considered to be members of a church organization. But the colleges of Oxford and Cambridge still have a high degree of autonomy, with individual identities and traditions, unlike residence halls in other universities. Although they are not the oldest of European universities, Oxford and Cambridge, with their centuries of eminence, still are prestigious and world-renowned.

The curriculum of medieval Oxford and Cambridge reflected the needs of the society. A university education prepared a young man for a career in the higher ranks of the church organization, for a career in the slowly expanding civil service, for further study in law (usually at the law center in London) or for study in medicine (usually in Italy where Italian universities profited from the knowledge of Arabic medicine).

The necessary readings fell into seven areas, known as the Seven Liberal Arts. ("Liber" was Latin for book). This phrase, the liberal arts, still is used for study in English, Philosophy, Music, Art and other *humanities[10]. The first three, the *trivium[11], consisted of logic; Latin, Greek and *Hebrew[12] grammar (the languages of the Bible); and *rhetoric[13]. These studies prepared the scholar to write *sermons[14] for church services and to study the Bible. The other four, the quadrivium, consisted of *arithmetic[15], *geometry[16], *astronomy[17] and music. They prepared the scholar to predict the dates of the lunar church festivals, such as Easter, and to prepare music for church services.

As the society changed, these subjects also changed. By the mid-nineteenth century, these universities became centers for science, culture and languages and became known for theoretical, rather than practical, approaches to their subject matter.

III. Renaissance Education

1. CHANGES: THE ENGLISH LANGUAGE, SELF EDUCATION, NEW SCHOOLS

During the *Renaissance[18] period (*Tudor[19] and *Stuart[20] (monarchies) several changes took place. English replaced Latin as an official language; people were banned from schools because of their religion; opportunities for self-education increased; and many new schools were founded. The goals of education and payment schemes for education remained unchanged, but questions arose about who should be educated.

A) English Language Problems

Throughout the medieval period, English was the despised language of the lower classes. When English began to displace Norman French as the language of the upper class, people had trouble communicating because of the many English dialects. People from the Northeast of England spoke a dialect influenced by Viking and Danish settlers; people from the North and Northwest spoke a Celtic dialect used by the early settlers; people from southern England spoke a dialect influenced by Norman French. Each region had its own vocabulary and pronunciation.

As long as English remained a lower-class spoken language, these variants posed no problems. When Henry VIII (1491 – 1547) established the Church of England, he also established English, not Latin, as the official language of the church, education, and government. The problem was to know which dialect of English to use. There was no standard for correct English, and no one to set the standard. When the major technological advance of the printing press reached Europe and mass production of books became possible, decisions about English had to be made. The first English printer, William Caxton (1422? – 1491), tried to decide which dialect to use, complaining that he could not please everyone. He finally settled on the dialect of southeastern England, since it was his native dialect and the dialect of London, the center of English political and commercial power. Other people tried to write English phonetically, putting the sounds of their own dialect onto the page. The result was wild variation in spelling. For example, William Shakespeare's name is spelled in four different ways on legal documents; he used two different versions himself!

To cope with this chaos, dictionaries appeared. The title of the first dictionary makes clear that it was intended for people who did not attend grammar school: "Ladies, gentlewomen and other unskillful persons" (1604). Twenty other dictionaries appeared in the next century. Despite such help, letters and other handwritten documents were often written phonetically in the writer's dialect.

B) Self Education

The printing press did more than establishing the London dialect as "English". Before Caxton, all English books were carefully and beautifully handwritten. A book might take a year or two to copy and would be very expensive. The rediscovery of movable type and the importation of paper-making from China meant that books were much cheaper, so that more and more people could afford them. In 1467, a bishop estimated that printed books cost one-fifth the price of handwritten books.

A book provides knowledge to a single individual, without any need for a teacher. Alone, a reader could directly encounter the writer's ideas. Further, the printing of books in English, instead of Latin, meant that a man or woman could learn the subjects directly, without attending "grammar" school. Even without a teacher, a person could study Aristotle, architecture or archery. Knowledge became more the property of an individual rather than belonging to a community.

This new knowledge was very important because, unlike medieval people, Renaissance people acknowledged that the world had changed. English ships explored the world; scholars rediscovered works by classical Greek and Roman authors and artists; and new religious ideas divided the European community. Changes were everywhere, and people needed to learn if they were to survive and succeed.

Self-education has been a marked feature of British life ever since the Renaissance, in modern times, knowledge may come from the open university, the public libraries or the Internet. Whether from the printed page or the electronic screen, Britons have learned to learn alone.

C) Religious Exclusions—Limits on Who Is Educated

Self-education was important in Renaissance England, not only because of the rapid changes taking place throughout the world, but also because of the division of Europe into *Catholic[21] and *Protestant[22] versions of Christianity.

Henry VIII separated England from Europe and the Roman Catholic Church, creating new educational problems. Henry's newly created Church of England (also called the Anglican Church) assumed responsibility for educational institutions previously controlled by the Roman Catholic Church. Since Catholicism threatened political stability in Renaissance England, Roman Catholic ideas and practices were forbidden.

In 1581, all students at Oxford and Cambridge Universities either swore loyalty to the Church of England or were dismissed. English, but not Scottish, universities were closed to Catholics and Protestants who disagreed with the Anglican Church. The Church of England's control extended to secondary education as well. Anglican bishops replaced Roman Catholic bishops as overseers of church-taught schools. However, many secular schools or non-religious schools were founded in the sixteenth century. They, too, came under church control. In 1604 *Parliament[23] enacted a law requiring that all teachers and private tutors be licensed by a Church of England bishop. At first this law was not strictly enforced. However greater control was exerted during the growing religious strife that finally erupted into the English Civil War, the Glorious Revolution of 1688, and suppression of the Stuart kings' rebellions. Religious differences meant political differences; political differences meant trouble.

Since the formal educational system was still based on the medieval clerical model, education was considered a part of the religious and political system. People who rejected the Church of England obviously did not attend Oxford or Cambridge, universities whose official role was the education of Anglican clergy. As a result, self-study was often the only education available for Catholics and dissident Protestants.

The importance of the Church of England in the English educational system did not diminish until the late 19th century. Today, church-run schools, particularly primary schools, are still important educational institutions. Religious education is still given in schools, although with an increasingly diverse population in England, children and teachers may seek exemptions from religious classes. Unlike the United States, where separation of religion and public education has been rigidly enforced, England has been comfortable with a much closer relationship between government institutions and religion.

2. RENAISSANCE PRIMARY, SECONDARY AND UNIVERSITY INSTITUTIONS

A) Primary and Secondary Schools

The 1604 Act of Parliament regulating all teachers was caused, in part, by the growing numbers of secular schools. Many new schools were small primary schools; they were called "petty" schools (from the French word for small, "petit") even though they were conducted in English. Petty schools taught small children the three "R"s: Reading, (w)Riting, and (a)Rithmetic. Since the teachers were often older women, the schools were also known as "dame" schools. The tuition fees for such schools were also small: a school in 1636 charged a penny a week for reading, two pennies for writing, and four pennies for writing and simple arithmetic. Yet even these fees were too high for most people. At this time, nearly 80% of the population lived in farm villages. One third of the population lived in poverty while another third barely escaped poverty. Poor farmers needed children to work on the farm, so education, even in the petty schools, remained unavailable to most children.

Middle class boys from Church of England households went to local primary and secondary schools. Boys from Catholic and dissenting Protestant households had a more exciting time. Since England contained a growing minority of Roman Catholics and dissenting Protestants, such as *Methodists[24], *Quakers[25], *Presbyterians[26] and *Unitarians[27], there were enough students to form "Dissenting Academies", schools that moved every few months in order to evade government repression. Graduates of these schools could attend Scottish or European universities. The "Dissenting Academies" and the Scottish universities were more progressive and provided more practical training, since they often included subjects such as geography, navigation and modern foreign languages and literatures.

Upper-class children were sent to the "public" grammar schools, which continued to teach Latin and Greek, preparing students for the seven Liberal Arts of the University. Grammar schools founded for the poor, such as Harrow (charted 1571), were converted to schools for wealthy children, as Eton and Winchester had been converted. The aristocracy, who made their money from landed estates, seemed to glory in useless learning. An educated man proved his education by using Latin quotations in his speech and writing. Knowledge of Latin was one way to distinguish higher from lower social classes.

B) Universities

a) English Universities

English universities continued to teach the medieval curriculum, designed for training clergy. However, they did add some disciplines by formalizing the tutorial system. A young man entering a college was assigned to a tutor, who oversaw his studies and his behavior. The university still provided lectures, but much of the learning took place in the colleges and the residence halls.

b) Scottish Universities

Three major Scottish universities were founded during this time. The oldest, Glasgow University, began in 1451. Then, the University of Aberdeen (authorized by the Roman Catholic Pope in 1494 – 1495) provided Great Britain with its first school of medicine. Finally, Edinburgh University was founded in 1582, when a Scottish lawyer provided 300 books as a nucleus for a library. These Scottish universities became very important, because they did not exclude students on the basis of religion.

IV. Eighteenth Century—What Is Correct English

Few changes took place in educational institutions in eighteenth-century England. The Anglican Church (Church of England) remained in control of teachers and universities; parents were responsible for paying for children's education; the wealthier lower classes managed to pay for their children to enter petty schools or to find scholarships in local grammar schools. Charitable schools did provide some education for poor children, but these schools stressed social division. Poor children were taught to "know their place" and "respect their betters", which meant they should be subservient to those from higher classes.

1. SCHOOLS FOR GIRLS

One of the few changes was the establishment of schools for middle- and upper-class girls; these young girls were taught a few academic subjects and many social subjects, such as dancing, the social ranks of the aristocracy, and how to enter a horse-drawn carriage gracefully.

2. DECREASED EMPHASIS ON RELIGION IN EDUCATION

Another change came in mid-century, when the Catholic Stuart rebellions ended, reducing religiously motivated political dissent. Dissenting academies were allowed to exist without government repression. Also, as secular institutions replaced religious ones, the clergy became less important in England. When English universities became social clubs for aristocratic youth rather than institutions for training clergy, their enrollments declined.

3. SEPARATION OF PROGRESSIVE AND PRESTIGIOUS EDUCATION

Finally, when clergy used English, not Latin, in church services, the medieval university curriculum with its emphasis on Latin became out-dated even for training clergy. Yet the curriculum was not changed. In the seventeenth century at Cambridge University, Sir Isaac Newton (1642 – 1727) revolutionized mathematics and physics. In the eighteenth century, Oxford and Cambridge slept. As a result, the most effective education came from the middle-class and Scottish institutions. The eighteenth-century inventors and scientists who paved the way for the nineteenth-century Industrial Revolution came from such backgrounds. James Watt (1736 – 1819), the developer of the steam engine, was associated with Glasgow University. Richard Arkwright (1732 – 1792), the inventor of the mechanical loom, was self-educated. Joseph Priestley (1733 – 1804), discoverer of oxygen, taught in a Dissenting Academy. Education for progress occurred in one group of institutions, while education for prestige took place in another group.

4. STANDARDS FOR CORRECT ENGLISH

The most influential change was unofficial, but far-reaching. As the English language became more important in government and in the arts, teachers were faced with the problem that still exists today: What is good English? Is it graceful and elegant? Is it clear or business-like? Is it balanced and orderly like classical Latin, or is it curt and direct? Are different dialects acceptable? Unfortunately, social prestige, rather than practicality, settled the dispute.

Teachers at the Dissenting Academies and the Scottish Universities trained middle-class students for practical careers. They argued that good contemporary writers furnished the best standard for good English. On the other hand, teachers at the "public" schools and at the English universities argued that Latin was the best model for good English. Since Latin was associated with the politically powerful upper-classes, Latin became the model for good English.

Ever since, the teaching of English has been made more difficult. The English language derives much of its written vocabulary from Latin, but its grammar is closer to Chinese than Latin. English retains a few inflections from its Anglo-Saxon roots, but is, like Chinese, a word order language. Like Chinese, it tends to change the tense and mode of verbs through added words. Latin indicates tense and function by word endings, not added words. Latin terminology could not describe many traits in the English language, such as phrasal verbs, e.g. "make up". Bewildered native speakers of English were taught meaningless confusing terms while, at the same time, they were not taught how to understand the many non-Latin features of English.

Further, the Latin-based scholars imposed Latin spelling upon English words. For example, they changed "dette" to "debt", because the Latin root contained a "b". They imposed Latin rules: do not split an infinitive ("to boldly go") and avoid double negatives ("I never saw nothing like it"). Since these rules are inappropriate for English, they made correct English more difficult, even for native speakers.

By the twentieth century, scholars understood much more about the linguistics and the nature of English, but the damage had been done. Without a central authority to determine what is correct and what is incorrect, no change could be made. Now that English is a world language, with many varieties such as British, American, Canadian, and Australian, regulation is impossible. If upper-class England had not been so fond of Latin, students of English, world wide, would have easier language studies.

V. Nineteenth Century — Class Struggle and Change

1. NEW ANSWERS TO OLD QUESTIONS

During the nineteenth century, English education was reformed, as a result of strong social pressure. The working classes fought for education as their right, not as a condescending gift from their "betters". Women agitated for university education. Communities began to understand the need for educated people and began to take control of education from the Anglican Church. Every aspect of education was affected.

All of Europe underwent many social upheavals after the French Revolution (1789 – 1799). England was no exception. As industry developed, relationships between workers and owners became strained. The medieval compacts between landowner and peasants provided some protection for the peasants, but the new factories and businesses offered no such protections. Agricultural England was smothered by the growing pollution from factories and mills, and ignorant farm children faced bleak prospects in life. However, educated people had a wider range of opportunities, with growing demands for factory managers, bookkeepers, shipping clerks and a host of positions requiring knowledge of writing, mathematics and foreign languages. The growing British Empire required bureaucrats to manage it.

Further, changes in thinking begun by the French Revolution led many to challenge the assumption that only aristocrats could hold important government positions. Perhaps the most influential result was the establishment of competitive examinations for positions in the vast British civil service. If schools promised advancement for their graduates, such schools had to prepare boys for these examinations. Proper education offered a way to a better life, and all classes were eager for it.

2. CHANGES IN WHO WAS EDUCATED

A) Who Was Educated—Self-Education

At the beginning of the nineteenth century, working-class men established Workingmen's Institutes and Subscription Libraries, where they could read and discuss ideas without instruction in respecting their "betters". By mid-century, these Institutes diminished, in large part because the Public Libraries Act (1850) permitted local governments to tax citizens to fund public libraries. Books loaned without charge became available to a wider variety of people. Since these libraries depended upon local funds, they were not uniformly distributed; wealthier communities and cities had more libraries. Still, the opportunities for anyone to be educated, regardless of class, expanded.

B) Who Was Educated—Primary and Secondary Education

Perhaps the most visible change in who was educated was the growing presence of girls and lower-class children. Parliamentary legislation governed all young children, not just boys. Working-class girls now were educated as well as their middle and upper-class counterparts. Law after law was enacted throughout the 19th century, requiring all children to attend primary school, although access to schools varied greatly with the wealth of the community. Parents were still responsible for tuition fees, although more and more funds became available to help pay for poorer children. Because no national system existed to ensure funding of education, poor children often were not educated. Teacher training was still influenced by the Anglican religion, since most teachers were trained in institutions run by the Church of England.

C) Who Was Educated—Universities

a) Oxford and Cambridge

During the nineteenth century new universities were founded, and the clergy-training, aristocracy-amusing Oxford and Cambridge were transformed into true educational giants. One cause of the transformation was the elimination of religious barriers. Now all intelligent young men could compete for entrance. Further, there was grudging acceptance of women as auxiliary members. In 1874, Girton College for Women was founded at Cambridge University; soon after, Oxford University founded Somerville and Lady Margaret Colleges for women. However, women were not granted Oxford degrees until 1920.

The university curriculum was transformed in the nineteenth century. Modern languages, the natural sciences (such as chemistry and geology), the social sciences (such as economics) and philosophy attracted bright minds. The shift in population and power from countryside to city meant that many of the aristocracy could no longer afford to support idle children. The universities still trained clergy and still retained their aristocratic flavor, but they became centers of learning and debate.

b) Red Brick Universities

New universities were also founded, such as the University of London (1828), established for the "youth of our middling rich people". These new universities were constructed out of the everyday cheap material used throughout England: red brick. Since Oxford and Cambridge had elegant stone buildings, the differences between the old and new were obvious. These nineteenth-century "red-brick" universities still exist. They have no religious affiliations and often have professional specializations, such as in law, architecture, and civil engineering. "Red-brick" universities are the true heirs of the Dissenting Academies. In addition, during the nineteenth century, schools, such as Sandhurst, were founded to train military leaders. Being aristocratic was no longer the requirement for leadership.

3. WHO PAID

Since the nine century, the problem of funding has dominated any discussion of education. If a society requires children to be educated, then that society must require someone to pay. The person or organization that pays often controls the educational system. When the Anglican Church and parents provided the education, they controlled it. During the 19th century, funding and control shifted from the church and parents to the national and local governments, who still control education in Britain.

In order to fund education, the English government first attempted to make businesses pay. The Factory Act of 1833 ordered factory owners to pay for two hours of schooling six days a week for all children under 13 years old. This was not a success. Then, the Elementary Education Act (1870) established a system that lasted, with some modification, until 1902. Local taxpayers elected school boards, which were responsible for local education. Parents paid whatever they could, and the school board provided supplements for families who could not pay the full cost. The boards also financed and built new schools.

At the end of the century, parliamentary legislation required school attendance and required that local schools accept all children, even if the parents could pay nothing. The Anglican Church continued to manage many of the village primary schools with the help of local funding. Although education varied with the wealth and commitment of the communities, these acts of Parliament were the first official recognition that education is not the responsibility of the church or family, but of the local community.

Ⅵ. Twentieth Century — Reform, Socialism and Conservatism

1. REFORM (1900—1945)

During the 20th century, educational opportunities continued to increase as more people were allowed into the educational system and as many new kinds of educational institutions were developed. Required tests were eased; children were given new ways to prove their qualifications for further education. At the same time, Great Britain was dramatically transformed from the head of an empire to part of the European Union. The resulting social changes also influenced education.

Through the first half of the 20th century, educational reform was an extension of the late 19th century: more educational opportunities for the poor, the handicapped, and women. The number of schools grew, especially elementary schools. In 1918, Parliament enacted laws requiring children to remain in school until age 14. Women were admitted to degree programs at Oxford and Cambridge Universities. Between 1900 and 1940, the number of university students was more than doubled, and a greater proportion of these came from the working classes. However, education still followed class lines; the majority of leaders came from the elite "public" schools, not publicly funded institutions. Some attempt was made to provide for uniformity: an act of 1917 required that a student seeking a secondary school certificate had to pass at least 5 subjects, including English, a foreign language, and science/mathematics.

The administrative governance of schools was determined by the Balfour Act (1902), which replaced local school boards with Local Education Authorities (LEAs). The LEAs are responsible for the primary and secondary schools in their regions. The 1902 Act strengthened connections between education and local governments. In addition, it gave LEAs the power to raise local taxes on real estate to pay for schools. Since 1902, the national government has controlled primary and secondary education by controlling the power of the LEAs. This control could take the form of "permissions". For example, LEAs were permitted to raise money for free meals provided to poor children between 1905 - 1986. (After 1986, other authorities resumed this task.) A 1944 Act permitted LEAs to provide nursery schools and many kinds of supplementary educational activities during summers and holidays. Since local communities were given permission, not funds, wealthier communities were more likely to provide these additional activities than poorer ones.

The national government could also require LEAs to perform certain duties. For example, a 1906 Act required LEAs to give medical examinations to all children in elementary school. A major statement of the national government's approach to education appeared in the 1944 Education Act. "It shall be the duty of the local education authority for every area, so far as their powers extend, to contribute towards the spiritual, moral, mental and physical development of the community by securing that efficient education shall be available to meet the needs of the population".

2. POST WORLD WAR Ⅱ — OPENING DOORS FOR EDUCATION (1945—1980)

The 1944 Education Act was an example of remarkable confidence and foresight. At that time, Britain was desperately fighting *the Axis [28] powers in World War Ⅱ. Yet

Parliament realized that after the war Great Britain would have to rebuild. The Education Act was an attempt to lay the foundation for a society in which social class was less important, and the educational system was ready to meet the postwar needs of the nation. The British approached post-war rebuilding through major funding of education. Returning soldiers and young children were the primary beneficiaries of the 1944 Act which dramatically increased funding for education.

A) Increased Government Funding

The Local Education Authorities were given increased funds to provide for the increasing numbers of children and for adult education. Pre-school or nursery school education was made more widely available. However, the most striking change came in university education. The goal was to enable all qualified people to attain a university education, regardless of their income or class. The numbers of university students, both men and women, rose sharply. Some institutions were raised to university status, and new universities were built. University students were given grants that paid not only fees for tuition, residence hall and food, but also a small stipend for other expenses.

Government funds were given to the University Grants Committee, an organization of academics and *civil servants[29] founded in 1919, that had advised the national government about higher education. This Committee totally controlled distribution of government funds to universities. Since the proportion of costs paid by the government jumped from 50% in 1946 to 75 - 90% by 1980, this was a remarkable example of funding without strong directives from the central government.

B) Founding of the Open University

In 1969, the Open University increased access to university education by allowing people to work and study in their own time. Its motto is "earning while learning". The Open University mails materials to students and assigns each a tutor. Materials are also found on-line, and students may conference with others via computer conferencing. In 2008, there were more than 220,000 thousand students enrolled, including 25,000 overseas students.

C) Reforms of National Examinations

A final reform, for which many school children were grateful, was a change in the secondary school structure and the 11 + examination. At the end of World War II, all eleven-year-old school children were required to take an intensive nation-wide examination to determine which children would be prepared for university entrance. Children achieving high scores were sent to Grammar Schools, which prepared them for higher education. Low-scoring children were sent to "Secondary Modern" schools, which prepared them for working-class careers.

A second series of examination, the O-levels, provided the sole remedy for students who did poorly on the 11 + examination. The O-levels, or GCE (General Certificate of Education) still exist as tests of general knowledge. However, the consequences to students have changed. Under the old system, Grammar School pupils might take exams in as many as 10 individual subjects, while Secondary Modern pupils took the few they could manage. Since most Secondary Modern pupils did poorly and needed money, they usually left school at age 15 or 16 years. However, those pupils from Secondary Modern schools who did well in O-levels were given the chance to study for a few years at a Grammar School. Grammar school graduates then took A-levels, advanced examinations in particular subject areas. Those doing well on A-levels usually proceeded to some form of higher education.

Gradually, the LEAs abolished both the 11 + examination and the segregation of students preparing for college from other students. By 1970, most LEAs had combined the two types of schools into one "comprehensive school". For twenty to thirty years, O-levels were the only compulsory national examinations.

3. MODERN ANSWERS TO OLD QUESTIONS—1980
A) New Influences on Education

At the end of the 1970's, several trends led to a new way of thinking about English education. First, the birth rate dropped and stabilized. With fewer births and longer life spans, children comprised a smaller percentage of the total population. Second, immigration from ex-colonies and Commonwealth countries led to a new ethnic diversity. Third, the government became increasingly concerned with financing its many social welfare programs. Fourth, the role of Britain within the European and world communities was changing. Beginning in 1980, Parliament reformed education through a series of Acts, which furnished new answers to the age-old questions.

B) Who Should Be Educated

Acts in the 1980's widened access for primary and secondary students with special needs, including both physical handicaps and learning disabilities. Schools were required to identify such students and to make every effort to include them in classes with other students.

Also, there was an attempt to provide a wider variety of "further education", post-seconday education outside a university. Further education may include training for A-level examinations outside of the grammar schools. Further education may also include study at further education and specialist colleges. The National Qualification Framework (NQF) has 9 levels of certificates and diplomas (including the higher education degrees) that students may achieve. In 2005 there were 4.5 million further education students. Some of these were taking a new version of the medieval Apprenticeship. This combines coursework with on-the-job training. In 2001, there were 266,000 young people in apprenticeships and other work-based learning programs in England and Wales. Continuing education is a growing field for adults. Indeed, education is becoming a major part of British life. By 2011, the government expects to extend compulsory education beyond 16 years of age. The education starts early, as parents are taking advantage of early education, with 64% of 3 - 4 year old children in school.

Application for entrance to a university is made through a central admissions system known as the Universities and Colleges Admissions System (UCAS). To enter a university, students must have an A-level standard of education, achieved by passing A-level examinations or their equivalents. The course of study usually concentrates on one or two subjects for three to four years. Then university students take lengthy examinations, which separate graduates by ability. Most desired is a first class Honors degree; second and third class Honors are good; an ordinary degree or pass is acceptable. Many universities use outside experts to grade these examinations, thus ensuring greater uniformity of degrees than in the United States. Although there are currently slightly more men than women in British universities, the gap in gender numbers continues to narrow.

C) What Should Children Learn—Uniformity of Education

Having opened education through wide access and varied institutions, Parliament became concerned with the content of education. Should all schools teach the same curriculum, with a uniform curriculum throughout England and Wales? The answer was yes. The 1988 Education Reform Act required all primary and secondary schools to teach the same topics, including English, mathematics, science, computer and information technology, history, geography, music, art, a foreign language, sex education, religious education, and physical education.

Schools are free to teach these subjects however they desire, but two controls ensure that schools adhere to standards. The first control consists of four examinations, at ages 7, 11, 14, and 16. Pupils need not fear these examinations as they feared the old 11 +, for these examinations affect schools more than pupils. Results are published, and schools with high scores are more likely to attract students.

The second control on uniformity is exerted by a national office of school inspection, which sends inspection teams to each school every four years. The teams report on the quality of education, the financial management, and the "spiritual, moral, social and cultural development" of the pupils. If a school is judged unsatisfactory, the LEA or the national government may dismiss or replace the school's governing board.

At the same time that uniformity was established and enforced, greater recognition was given to diversity. Welsh educators sought the autonomy possessed by Scottish educators. A separate Welsh Council has been established to oversee implementation of the national curriculum, and the Welsh language is included in the curriculum of Welsh schools. Also, religious diversity is recognized by permission for non-Christian parents to exempt their children from religious education. Parents are also allowed to exempt their children from sex education.

D) Who Pays

The costs of education are high. In 2005 – 2006, the annual cost for a primary school pupil was £3,150. The annual cost for a secondary school pupil was £4,070. These costs, however, vary from one district to another. Wealthier areas will spend more; poorer districts will spend less. The money to meet these costs comes from a variety of sources. Funding for primary and secondary schools reflects the historical growth of these schools. A few "public" schools are maintained solely through tuition from parents. Other schools are supported through tuition and funds from organizations, such as the Anglican or the Roman Catholic Church. More and more schools choose to receive direct grants from the national government. Other schools receive funds from the LEA. The 1988 Education Reform Act gives individual schools much more control over how funds are spent.

The LEAs raise funds by taxing property owners and businesses in their communities, by soliciting donations from parents, and by grants from the national government. Institutions of further and higher Education are funded directly from the national government and from tuition. Increasingly, parents are providing more and more of the funding. In return, the trend has been to give parents greater freedom of choice and more involvement in their children's education. Parents can choose which school to send their children to, and they have a greater influence on the governance of the school.

Increased payment from parents is particularly noticeable in university education. Before 1998, university tuition costs were paid by the student's LEA. After 1998, students or parents must pay increasing amounts. In 2009, the government limited this payment to £3,145 regardless of the program, but universities raised the amount by other small fees called "top ups". Overseas students pay triple this amount.

Traditionally, students chose to attend universities out of their home region, usually more than 150 kilometers away. The LEA provides poorer students with grants to assist with living expenses. These grants may provide over £2,800 for a year. However since a year's living expenses away from home were about £9,000 in 2008, students from poorer families usually live at home and may still need to borrow from the government-run Student Loan Company. Thus, for higher education, the trend is toward the medieval model: students or their parents pay for a university education. This means that poorer students have less opportunity for higher education. Also, several studies of English education show that despite efforts to make advancement independent of social class, a father's social class still greatly influences his children's educational level. A 1994 report from the Office of Population Censuses and Surveys found that 67% of full-time students in higher education had fathers in non-manual occupations, even though such fathers were only 36% of the whole population.

E) Goals for Education

Rapid changes, world wide, have forced most countries to reconsider the national goals of education. Great Britain is no exception. Earlier in the century, Parliament was concerned with ensuring that all citizens could enroll in needed educational programs. Having done so, Parliament and educators turned to questions of national goals. In doing so, the minor, but continuing problem of English standards reappeared.

The national goal of education has changed from goals stated in the 1944 Education Act, which stressed the development of the community and the needs of the people. Today, government policy places greater stress on employers' needs. The formerly independent Department of Education became the Department of Education and Employment. A government position paper, a White Paper, asserts that the first objective of the Department for Education and Employment is "To enable children, young people and adults to achieve skills and qualifications at the highest standard of which they are capable and to ensure progress toward the national Targets of Education and Training". These Targets are to "improve the United Kingdom's international competitiveness" by ensuring that employers provide employee development, that all citizens have access to education for their needs and aspirations, and that citizens become self-reliant and flexible.

When the government studied goals for education, the problems of English language goals arose. The 1988 Kingman Report recommended that teaching English should return to an 18th century idea. In addition to teaching Standard English, schools should also teach about language variation and should emphasize that dialects are not wrong, only different. The goals for English instruction should be effective communication and understanding of language.

Ⅶ. Conclusion

Nearly a thousand years ago, British education consisted of a few schools to train clergy and an apprenticeship system, organized by guilds, to train craftsmen. Some schools and universities still exist from these times, and apprentices still prepare for trades. However, now all children receive an education; many kinds of schools and universities provide opportunities for people of all ages to study a rich variety of subjects. Self-education through public libraries, the Open University and the Internet is easily accessible. Yet critical questions remain: What is the goal of education? Who pays for it? How is it best accomplished? If the goal of education is to supply a qualified work force, can British education remain free of demands from the European Union (EU), with its multi-national workforce? With technology changing the nature of work from year to year, who should be educated? The new answer may be: everyone, all the time. Adults must be trained and retrained to meet the continuously changing world. Who will pay for this training? The people themselves? The businesses they work for? The nation itself through taxes? Education transforms people and influences future events by doing so. British answers to the age-old questions about education will shape the nature of Britain in the 21st century.

Study Questions

1. How has religion influenced British education?
2. What are the methods used to pay for education? How do they affect who is educated?
3. How has the class structure influenced access to education?
4. How has the Latin language affected worldwide education in English?
5. How does the present English education system compare and contrast with the Chinese education system?
6. How have changes in technology changed the form of British education?

Selected Bibliography

United Kingdom Statistics Authority. Http://www.statistics.gov.uk.

Mackinnon, Donald, June Statham, and Margaret Hales. *Education, the UK: Facts and Figures*, rev. ed. London: Holder and Stoughton and the Open University, 1996.

Moodie, Graeme C. "United Kingdom", *International Higher Education: An Encyclopedia*, ed. Philip G. Altbach. V. 2. New York: Garland, 1991.

Lawson, John and Harold Silver. *A Social History of Education in England*. New York: Barnes and Noble, 1973.

注　释

〔1〕诺曼征服（指诺曼底公爵威廉于1066年对英格兰的军事征服）。
〔2〕罗马帝国（指公元前27年到公元476年的罗马奴隶制国家）。
〔3〕神职人员。
〔4〕（拉丁语）现状。
〔5〕中世纪的行会。
〔6〕（内设主教座的）教区总教堂。
〔7〕牧师。
〔8〕本科生。
〔9〕硕士生。
〔10〕人文学科。
〔11〕（中世纪大学的）三学科。
〔12〕希伯来语。
〔13〕修辞学。
〔14〕布道。
〔15〕算术。
〔16〕几何学。
〔17〕天文学。
〔18〕（欧洲14至16世纪的）文艺复兴。
〔19〕（英）都铎王朝。
〔20〕（英）斯图亚特王朝。
〔21〕天主教。
〔22〕（基督教的）新教派。
〔23〕（由上、下议院组成的）英国议会。
〔24〕卫斯理宗教会成员。
〔25〕公谊会教徒。
〔26〕长老会教友。
〔27〕（认为上帝只有一位并否认基督神权的）一位论者。
〔28〕轴心国（指第二次世界大战中德、日、意三国侵略同盟）。
〔29〕公务员。

CHAPTER 7　GEOGRAPHY OF THE UNITED STATES

Dr. John Way and Prof. Shen Peixin

I. Introduction

This chapter introduces the geography of the United States of America, a landmass mainly on the North American continent in both the western and northern hemispheres. The country comprises 48 contiguous states between Canada (north) and Mexico (south) plus Alaska, a massive peninsula in northwestern North America west of Canada, and Hawaii, an archipelago stretching over 2,400 kilometers in the Pacific Ocean.

In addition, the United States has political associates. In the Caribbean, there are the American Virgin Islands and the Commonwealth of Puerto Rico; in the Pacific there are island territories, such as American Samoa and Guam, along with the Commonwealth of the Northern Mariana Islands. Commonwealths have a greater degree of political independence than territories.

In 2008, the US population was estimated to exceed 306,000,000 with an annual growth rate of 0.88%. The greatest population growth has been in western and southern states and in or near major cities. The US population is becoming more racially diverse; in California, European-Americans no longer constitute the majority of the state's population. The American population is also aging. In 2008, the median age was the highest ever, 36.7 years, which reflects the large numbers of middle-aged Americans and a relatively low birth rate. Americans tend to live in smaller households; the average household size dropped from 2.63 people in 2000 to 2.57 people in 2007, with 26% of households occupied by one person.

The 9,826,630 square kilometers of the United States make it the fourth largest country in the world. The geography of the country contains many extremes since the 48 contiguous states lie between the cool latitude of 49 degrees 23 minutes north (part of Minnesota), and the tropical latitude of 24 degrees 33 minutes (Key West, Florida). The geography varies dramatically across this immense landmass. Consider the deeply dissected grandeur of the Rocky Mountains and the Brooks Range, the seeming endless kilometers of the flat Great Plains, one of the world's few temperate-climate rain forests, some of the planet's bleakest deserts, the vast Mississippi River system, the Great Lakes, the large, inland coastal waterway, and a line of rugged volcanic islands strung across the central Pacific Ocean. Truly, this is a land of contrasts.

II. Economic Activities

Each of the eight physiographic regions of the United States differs from the others in climate, surface features, and industry. Each region will be described separately in section IV. However, some overall generalizations can be made. The US economy today is dominated by the service sector; more than 75% of the work force is employed in a service industry, including education, entertainment, health, finance, insurance, real estate. Of these, the information-services sector overshadows others as a dominant segment of the US economy. The Gross Domestic Product (GDP), a measure of the total output of goods and services within the US borders, at the end of 2007 was $ 13.86 trillion dollars. Since 1976, the US has had a negative trade balance, importing more than it has exported.

1. AGRICULTURE

US agriculture produces over 40% of the world's corn (maize) and *soybeans[1] and over 10% of the world's wheat and cotton. Over half of the corn and soybeans are exported. The US produces nearly 20% of the world's beef, pork, mutton, and lamb; approximately 20% of total livestock production is exported. In 2007, agriculture contributed $ 1.2 trillion dollars toward the GDP, or less than 1%. Main agricultural areas are California, Texas, Florida, and the Midwestern states.

Although many Americans still retain a nostalgic picture of the independent small farmer, in fact most agriculture is run by large corporations. While the number of farms has declined, farm acreage has increased. Farming is often called agri-business, since it is highly mechanized and uses chemicals to control weeds and promote animal and plant growth, computer-derived planting schemes, and sophisticated genetic manipulation. However, there is growing concern about decreasing water quality for irrigation and increasing water pollution in agricultural areas.

Major crops include corn, soybeans, wheat, *alfalfa[2] (Lucerne grass), cotton, hay, rice, sorghum, and barley, along with various fruits and vegetables. Livestock output includes live cattle and beef, dairy products, chicken, live hogs and pork, as well as sheep, turkey, eggs, and farmed fish.

2. FISHING

In 2007, US commercial landings totaled 4.3 million metric tons, down 3% from the previous year. Of that total, finfish comprised 3.8 million metric tons (down 1%) and shellfish comprised 463 thousand metric tons (down 9%). Beset by overfishing and falling catches, and battered by imports from Asian, European, and Latin American *aquaculture[3], traditional American fishing continues in decline. Pollution is a problem of increasing concern as well; dumping of raw *sewage[4], industrial wastes, spillage from oil tankers, and blowouts of offshore wells are the main threats to the fishing grounds. There is some evidence to suggest that a management strategy, known as individual transferable quotas (ITQs) or individual fishing quotas (IFQs), may bring relief to the *beleaguered[5] fisheries industry.

3. FORESTRY

With a large forest resource and high production and consumption of wood products, the United States plays an important role in the forest product markets around the globe. Two-thirds of the country's forest lands, almost 200 million hectares, are classified as timberlands, i.e., forest lands used for the production of commercial wood products. Commercial timberland can be used for repeated growing and harvesting of trees. Of that timberland, Federal, State, and local governments own 27% and non-industrial private entities own 59%.

As the world's largest consumer of paper and paperboard (about 93 million metric tons in 2006), the US is supplied mostly by domestic production and imports from Canada. In 2006, the US solid wood industry manufactured about 92 million cubic meters of lumber and 30 million cubic meters of structural panel products. The forest products industry harvests more than 482 million cubic meters of softwood and hardwood timber annually.

4. MINING AND ENERGY SOURCES

The US mining industry comprises four main segments: oil and gas extraction, coal mining, metal ore mining, and nonmetallic mineral mining and quarrying. The US produces nearly 20% of the world's coal, copper, and crude oil, yet profits from this sector constitute less than 2% of the GDP.

Although the US exports petroleum, it is a major importer of petroleum and natural gas. The nation, comprising 5% of the world's population, consumes an estimated 25% of the world's energy resources. In 2007, carbon-based fuels provided over 86% of the nations' energy: petroleum (40%), natural gas (24%), and coal (23%); nuclear energy and renewable sources supply the rest. These energy sources fed the country's major consumption sectors: electric power (40%), transportation (29%), industrial (21%), and residential and commercial (10%).

In the US, *anthropomorphically[6] generated greenhouse-gas emissions, considered major factors in climate change, derive principally from the combustion of fossil fuels in energy use. Chief among these gases is carbon dioxide (CO_2), and increases in global atmospheric and oceanic temperatures have been attributed to a sharp rise in CO_2 levels over the past 50 years. Of the greenhouse gases produced by the US, energy-generated CO_2 emissions account for over 80%. For decades, the nation led the world as the number one emitter of CO_2, contributing 22% to the world's total.

5. MANUFACTURING

Manufacturing refers to businesses engaged in the mechanical, physical, or chemical transformation of materials or components into new products. American manufacturing includes food, beverage, and tobacco; textiles; apparel; leather and wood products; paper and printing; chemicals; plastics and rubber products; metals and fabricated metal products; nonmetallic mineral products; machinery; computers and electronic products; electrical equipment and components; transportation equipment; and furniture. Accounting for $1.5 trillion in GDP, manufacturing constitutes about 20% of the US economy, and, as a result, the US ranks as the largest manufacturing country in the world.

Of the nation's total labor force, estimated in 2008 at 154.9 million, manufacturing employs about 10%. Since reaching a high of 21 million workers in 1979, employment in this sector has declined steadily. A counterbalance to this drop has been an increase in compensation along with a dramatic rise in productivity. These factors, along with mounting competition in labor-intensive goods production from lower-cost foreign manufacturers have driven this decline. Yet, as job losses continue for less-skilled workers, high-skill job opportunities in US manufacturing increasingly exceed the supply.

6. TRANSPORTATION

The transportation sector, a major component of the US economy, ranks as the 4th most important expense after housing, health care, and food. Transportation-related goods and services totaled 11% of the nation's GDP in 2005. Overseen by the US Department of Transportation, this sector moves goods and people, employs millions of workers, generates revenue, and consumes materials and services produced by other segments of the economy. The sector also requires a wide range of services including for-hire freight carriers, private transportation providers, freight forwarders, logistics providers, and firms that service and maintain vehicles.

Passenger transportation, dominated by cars, pick-up trucks, vans, SUVs, and motorcycles, account for 86% of passenger miles traveled. The remaining 14% was handled by planes, trains, and buses. Public transportation networks of taxis, buses, trains, and subways are found primarily in cities. By contrast, freight transportation is handled by a variety of networks including truck, rail, air, ship, and pipeline. The largest carriers of freight, by weight, are trucks (60%), followed by pipelines (18%), rail (10%), ship (8%), and air (1%).

The first automobile roadway to span the lower 48, the Lincoln Highway was dedicated in 1913 to America's 16th president, Abraham Lincoln. Nearly a century later, the US is crisscrossed by a complex array of roads totaling more than 6,500,000 kilometers. Most are paved, designated with numbers, and maintained by local, municipal, and state agencies. However, a great many rural roads remain unpaved.

The National Highway System (NHS), comprising mostly two-land roads, represents 4% (260,000 km) of the country's roads. As the backbone of the nation's transportation network, the NHS carries more than 40% of the nation's traffic, including 75% of its heavy truck traffic and 90% of its tourist traffic.

Within the NHS, the Interstate (Highway) System, formally known as the Dwight D. Eisenhower National System of Interstate and Defense Highways, is a network of multi-lane, limited-access freeways or expressways named in honor of the nation's 33rd president who championed its creation. Officially completed in 1992, additional routes, spurs and bypasses are either currently under construction or remain on the drawing board. This system is both the largest highway network in the world, totaling more than 75,000 km, and the largest public works project in history.

Marked by the dramatic collapse in 2007 of an eight-lane, steel-truss-arch bridge that carried interstate traffic across the Mississippi River, the nation's transportation infrastructure displays widespread signs of aging. The condition of the system not only poses health and safety dangers, but increasing congestion on highways, railways, airports, and seaports, threatens the nation's security and the economy. Without significant federal policy changes and the infusion of large sums of money, the infrastructure will continue to deteriorate.

The majority of Americans have access to a car, and over half of the households have two or more vehicles. Most Americans drive to work alone; less than 15% share rides or *carpool[7]. As families move from the cities to the suburbs or countryside, *commuting[8] distances and times rise. Total vehicle miles traveled grew by nearly 3% a year from 1984 to 2004; however, this growth rate slowed in 2005 and 2006 and has declined since then in response to the sharp rise in gasoline prices.

US rail transport began in the 1830s, reached a peak in the 1920s, and subsequently declined as the automobile rapidly gained popularity. The emphasis shifted toward cargo as faster air transport came to dominate long-distance passenger travel. Most rail traffic today is concentrated within and between the coastal *megapolises[9] as commuters chose to avoid heavily congested highways. Public transportation networks of buses, trains, and subways similarly are found only in cities.

Air travel is important, given the mountains, deserts, and large distances between major population centers. Atlanta's (GA) Hartsfield-Jackson and Chicago's (IL) O'Hare headed the list as the top two busiest international airports in the world in 2008.

Boats are primarily used for freight transport. The most important waterways are the Mississippi River system and the Canadian-American St. Lawrence Seaway, which provide transport to and from the agricultural heartland of the country. America's busiest seaports are located in the south and east: South Louisiana, LA; Houston, TX; the New York City area, NY and NJ; New Orleans, LA; and Corpus Christi, TX.

Ⅲ. Rural, Suburban, and Urban Living Patterns

1. RURAL LIFE

American farmers have never been peasants. Historically, the countryside in America was inhabited by people who owned their farms. Of course, a small segment of the population either voluntarily worked on *ranches[10] and farms owned by someone else, such as the cowboys mostly in the west, and Africans imported as slaves who involuntarily worked on plantations mostly in the southeast.

As a result of the Industrial Revolution, many Americans moved from rural to urban areas for employment. During the 20th century those who remained in the countryside became more urbanized through the mass media, and they increasingly automated their farming activities. Today, the majority of the rural population lives in commuting distance of a city. Commuting enables many farmers to work in the city and to continue to farm part time, preventing the drastic decline in the rural population which occurred in remoter parts of the country.

Traditionally, the New England village was characterized by a grouping of white frame houses, a church, town hall, shops and large, stately homes centered around a grassy area called the "commons". Such towns were reproduced in sections of the northern Midwest. Less widely used was the pattern developed in central Pennsylvania and Maryland, where brick buildings, often a mix of residences and businesses, were closely packed together along a sidewalk lined with shade trees. The typical model of a small rural American town was the one which developed in the Midwest. It was based on a one-mile (0.6 km) square *grid plan[11]. The central business district was limited exclusively to commercial and administrative activities and contained closely built two or three-story brick buildings. Houses were built back from the street on spacious lots. These dwellings, railroads, factories and warehouses were peripherally located around the center of town.

Villages in New Mexico, Arizona, and southern California were built according to the traditional Latin-American plan with a central plaza dominated by a Roman Catholic church and encircled by low adobes or stone houses and shops.

2. SUBURBAN LIFE

After World War II, the American population increased; automobiles became more common; the interstate highway system was built; and housing in the cities became scarcer and more expensive. Consequently, housing developers constructed "bedroom communities" at the fringes of *metropolitan[12] areas; the first of these suburban housing developments was in Levittown, New York, built initially as "mass-produced" rental homes for World War II veterans. Suburbs are a transition zone between urban and rural communities. Houses are built near cities but are located in the countryside. Large malls or shopping centers and other service areas are located near these suburban developments. Given these circumstances, *suburbanites[13] believe that they have the best of living in the city and in the countryside. Generally, income and social status rise as the distance from the center of the city increases.

3. URBAN LIFE

To a foreign visitor, the American landscape may not seem harmonious. Unlike many cities in other countries, American urban centers are not well planned. Instead, cities tend to *sprawl[14] and merge with surrounding cities and towns, and even expand into adjacent states. By the end of the 20th century, approximately 75% of the United States population lived in cities and their nearby suburbs. Nowadays the countryside is economically dependent on the city. City location influences patterns of rural economy, rather than the reverse. Larger cities receive their water and energy from the countryside, and metropolitan areas want rural *disposal sites[15] for their increasing amounts of garbage. For many large rural areas, recreation, including tourism and camping, is the principal source of income and employment. During the weekends and vacation periods many city and suburban dwellers travel great distances and at great expense to the countryside or the coast for a "holiday".

Today, the most successful cities are centers for the production and consumption of services, particularly the information, managerial and recreational industries. The largest metropolitan areas are the headquarters for corporations which increasingly have global connections and investments.

Within these urban sites there have been man-made physical transformations of the land, shoreline and drainage systems. However, cities in the United States tend to be products of the historic period during their formative years rather than physical and social planning. In most cities the remnants of sharply defined immigrant neighborhoods in the 19th century are evident, even though specific ethnic groups may have shifted their location. During the last decades of the 20th century the later migrant groups, particularly Southern Blacks and Spanish-speaking Americans (sometimes called Hispanics or Latinos), live in the more impoverished neighborhoods of the inner cities.

It is important to note that six of the ten largest cities in America are located in the fastest growing region in the country, the Southwest. The southern states from the Carolinas in the east to California in the west contain more than half the population of the United States. They are collectively nicknamed the "Sunbelt" in contrast to the North which is called the "Snowbelt". These contrasts in climate are not to be confused with northeastern USA called the "Rustbelt" for its large number of abandoned factories.

A new type of city is emerging, one which caters to specific groups. For example, new urban areas which serve pleasure-seekers, vacationers and retirees have developed in Florida, Nevada, Colorado, Arizona and California. According to the 2000 census, these states are the fastest growing areas in the country.

At the same time, the nation's collective memory of an idealized agrarian life in the countryside is rapidly vanishing. Contemporary novelists, poets and painters as well as other professionals in films, television, country music and politics reinforce this national nostalgia. This ideal, combined with new technologies, mass media, an up-scaled transportation network, availability of land, credit, and a belief in mobility, has resulted in the merger of urban and rural life in the late 20th century.

4. MEGALOPOLISES

When urban sprawl is extensive, the result is a super city or megalopolis. Encyclopedia Britannica (1998) defines a megalopolis as "a small set of great constellations of polycentric urban zones, each complexly interlocked socially and physically with its neighbors".

One huge megalopolis follows the Atlantic Coastal from Portland, Maine, to Richmond, Virginia. It includes Boston, Massachusetts; New York City, New York; Philadelphia, Pennsylvania; Baltimore, Maryland; and Washington, D.C.

Another example of a megalopolis is the huge southern California sprawl from Santa Barbara to the Mexican border. Centered here, along the Pacific coast, is Los Angeles (also known as L.A.), the second largest city in America. Nicknamed the City of Angels, this cosmopolitan metropolis with its alluring *Mediterranean[16] climate is recognized as a preeminent point within the world-wide economic system, literally, a global city.

A discontinuous urbanized triangle in Texas which connects Houston, San Antonio, and Dallas-Fort Worth is another megalopolis. Houston, America's fourth largest city, is connected to the Gulf of Mexico by a man-made deep water channel and is the center of the country's rice and petro-chemical industries. The headquarters for *NASA (National Aeronautics and Space Administration)[17] is located nearby. Since NASA is responsible for space training, equipment testing and communications, Houston is nicknamed "Space City".

Three super cities are located in the Great Lakes region. One, with Chicago as its hub, embraces large segments of Illinois, Wisconsin and Indiana. The second, centered in Detroit, reaches into Canada and contains major areas of Michigan and Ohio. The third encompasses Buffalo, New York; Cleveland, Ohio; and Pittsburgh, Pennsylvania. These three super cities are expanding toward one another and may combine to form an even larger megalopolis. Looking further into the future, it is possible that the Great Lakes' super city conglomerate could join the Atlantic seaboard megalopolis via a corridor through central New York state to form an enormous super city.

As population increases, urban centers expand and new megalopolises arise. These "megaregions" typically interlink ground-transportation corridors with clusters and long chains of roughly continuous metropolitan areas. Emerging examples of this phenomena include the Front Range Urban Corridor, centered on Denver-Boulder, CO; the I-70 corridor in KA, MO, and IL; and the Peninsula comprising the cities in the southern two-thirds of FL.

5. SPECIFIC CITIES

Washington, D. C. , the nation's capital, is located on the Atlantic Coastal Plain between Maryland and Virginia in the humid *subtropical[18] climate zone. The most important and popular tourist attractions are the White House, US *Capitol[19], and the four presidential memorials for George Washington, Thomas Jefferson, Abraham Lincoln, and Franklin Roosevelt. The Smithsonian Institution, the world's largest educational and research organization, comprises 19 museums showcasing art, history, natural history, 9 research centers, the National Zoo, and the National Air and Space Museum.

New York City, New York, a part of the east coast megalopolis, is the most populated city in the United States and among the largest urban areas in the world. The *epitome[20] of a global city, The City of New York (NYC) influences global finance, commerce, culture, and entertainment. It is home to the Statue of Liberty, a gift from France commemorating the alliance between France and the United States during the revolutionary war. NYC, known around the world for its broad range of entertainment, includes the Great White Way—a thin strip of Manhattan containing more than 35 Broadway and Off-Broadway theaters offering nightly performances of small and large-scale musical and dramatic productions. In the early twentieth century, the *Harlem[21] area of the city was a creative center for African American music and art. Today, performances span the musical spectrum, ranging from opera, to musicals, to jazz, as well as all of the latest popular forms. The United Nations has its home here. New York's nickname is "the Big Apple", a phrase used by jazz musicians to explain the ultimate in achievement, size and excitement.

Miami, Florida is the southern-most city (exclusive of Hawaii). It serves as a gateway to and from the Caribbean Islands and Latin American countries. One is more likely to hear Spanish than English in many areas of the city. The Florida climate also attracts many tourists and retirees, particularly in winter.

Chicago, Illinois, the third most populated US city, is located at the intersection of southwestern Lake Michigan and the Chicago River, which makes it a major transportation hub and a financial center. Travel guides focus on Chicago's signature skyline, featuring record-high skyscrapers, unique profiles, and varied architectural styles. Heavy and light industries are highly developed, making Chicago the largest industrial city in the nation. Chicago has also been famous for its labor movements. Because thousands of workers protested there on May 1st, 1886, May 1st is now International Labor Day.

Las Vegas, Nevada is the fastest growing population center in the United States. Set in the barren desert, it is a gambling and recreational center. It is known for its garish buildings and advertisements.

Los Angeles (as known as L. A.), California, originally founded by the Spanish, was ceded to the United States after the Mexican-American War of 1848. One of the most diverse cities in the nation, L. A. is the west-coast's center for business, technology, culture, and international trade. Because of the city's vast area, its public transportation network is inadequate to serve the region. As a result, the city has an extensive network of roads, bridges, and overpasses, and the highest ratio of cars to people of any area in the world. A widespread and active fault system beneath the city periodically creates problems for the over 7 million daily commuters. After more than a century, L. A. continues to lay claim as the "entertainment capitol of the world", home to many of America's traditional industries, movie, television, and recorded music, as well as to some of the fast-growing trends in new electronic media. Many celebrities reside in and around the city, including some of the honorees in Hollywood's Walk of Fame, a line of bronze stars stretching along the famous sidewalks Hollywood Boulevard and Vine Street. L. A. is also the home of the Getty Center and its associated institutions comprise a focused effort for collecting, preserving, exhibiting, and interpreting high quality works of art, as well as using technology to research and preserve the world's masterpieces.

Seattle, Washington is located in spectacular natural surroundings on the edge of Puget Sound, between the Pacific Ocean and the Cascade Mountains. The city is known for its mild, rainy climate, its computer industry (Microsoft began here), and its position as a transportation center for travel to Alaska and the populated areas of the Canadian west coast.

IV. Physiographic Subdivisions of the United States

Eight regions of the United States are defined for the purposes of this chapter (Figure 1a & 1b, Table Ⅰ). Boundaries do not always follow the natural divisions of Earth's landforms. However, these regions do serve as convenient associations of states that have *commonalties[22] in terrain texture, rock type, *plate-tectonic[23] setting, and geological structure and history. In reality, several states lie within more than one region. A state was listed in the region that best described its landforms.

TABLE Ⅰ List of States within the 8 Physiographic Regions of the United States (US).

REGION NAME	US STATES
1. Atlantic and Gulf Coastal Plain	NJ, DE, MD, VA, NC, SC, GA, FL, AL, MS, LA, TX
2. New England	ME, NH, VT, MA, RI, CT
3. Appalachian Mountain Belt	NY, PA, OH, WV, KY, TN
4. Interior Lowlands	WI, MI, IN, ND, SD, MN, NB, KS, IO, MO, IL, OK, AR
5. Rocky Mountain Belt	MT, ID, WY, CO
6. Southwest	UT, NV, AZ, NM
7. Pacific Coast	CA, OR, WA, AK
8. Pacific	HI

*Refer to Table Ⅱ for the entire state name.

CHAPTER 7 GEOGRAPHY OF THE UNITED STATES

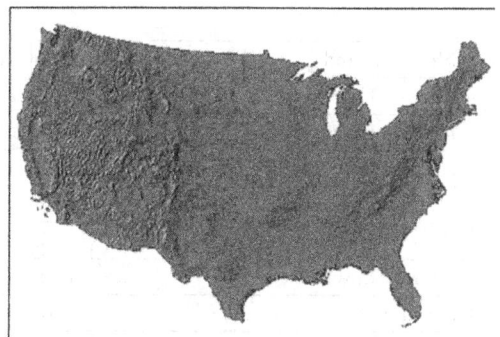

Digital Shaded Relief Image of the United States

Figure 1a This digital portrait faithfully reflects the geologic work of *tectonic[24] activity, *glaciers[25], rivers, volcanism, and other land-shaping processes. It is free of distortion and those vegetation and cultural features that mask *topographic[26] form on satellite images. The major *physiographic[27] regions of the US (Figure 1b. below) were recognized partly on the basis of important contrasts in topography.

The regional descriptions that follow comprise these parts: (1) its location and an overview of the region's dominant features; (2) a physiographic and *geologic[28] description; and (3) its significant mineral resources.

TABLE II List of Names of States in the United States				
(with their abbreviations, regions, rank in size, date of admission to US, and capitals)				
1. Alabama (AL)	Atlantic and Gulf Coastal Plain	29th	22nd	Montgomery
2. Alaska (AK)	Pacific Coast	1st	49th	Juneau
3. Arizona (AZ)	Southwest	6th	48th	Phoenix
4. Arkansas (AR)	Interior Lowlands	27th	25th	Little Rock
5. California (CA)	Pacific Coast	3rd	31st	Sacramento
6. Colorado (CO)	Rocky Mountain Belt	8th	38th	Denver
7. Connecticut (CT)	New England	48th	5th	Hartford
8. Delaware (DE)	Atlantic and Gulf Coastal Plain	49th	1st	Dover
9. Florida (FL)	Atlantic and Gulf Coastal Plain	22nd	27th	Tallahassee
10. Georgia (GA)	Atlantic and Gulf Coastal Plain	21st	4th	Atlanta
11. Hawaii (HI)	Pacific	47th	50th	Honolulu
12. Idaho (ID)	Rocky Mountain Belt	13th	43rd	Boise
13. Illinois (IL)	Interior Lowlands	24th	21st	Springfield
14. Indiana (IN)	Interior Lowlands	38th	19th	Indianapolis
15. Iowa (IO)	Interior Lowlands	25th	29th	Des Moines
16. Kansas (KS)	Interior Lowlands	14th	34th	Topeka
17. Kentucky (KY)	Appalachian Mountain Belt	37th	15th	Frankfort
18. Louisiana (LA)	Atlantic and Gulf Coastal Plain	31st	18th	Baton Rouge
19. Maine (ME)	New England	39th	23rd	Augusta
20. Maryland (MD)	Atlantic and Gulf Coastal Plain	42nd	7th	Annapolis

(Table Continued)

21. Massachusetts (MA)	New England	45th	6th	Boston
22. Michigan (MI)	Interior Lowlands	23rd	26th	Lansing
23. Minnesota (MN)	Interior Lowlands	12th	32nd	St. Paul
24. Mississippi (MS)	Atlantic and Gulf Coastal Plain	32nd	20th	Jackson
25. Missouri (MO)	Interior Lowlands	19th	24th	Jefferson City
26. Montana (MT)	Rocky Mountain Belt	4th	41st	Helena
27. Nebraska (NB)	Interior Lowlands	15th	37th	Lincoln
28. Nevada (NV)	Southwest	7th	36th	Carson City
29. New Hampshire (NH)	New England	44th	9th	Concord
30. New Jersey (NJ)	Atlantic and Gulf Coastal Plain	46th	3rd	Trenton
31. New Mexico (NM)	Southwest	5th	47th	Santa Fe
32. New York (NY)	Appalachian Mountain Belt	30th	11th	Albany
33. North Carolina (NC)	Atlantic and Gulf Coastal Plain	28th	12th	Raleigh
34. North Dakota (ND)	Interior Lowlands	17th	19th	Bismarck
35. Ohio (OH)	Appalachian Mountain Belt	35th	17th	Columbus
36. Oklahoma (OK)	Interior Lowlands	18th	46th	Oklahoma City
37. Oregon (OR)	Pacific Coast	10th	33rd	Salem
38. Pennsylvania (PA)	Appalachian Mountain Belt	33rd	2nd	Harrisburg
39. Rhode Island (RI)	New England	50th	13th	Providence
40. South Carolina (SC)	Atlantic and Gulf Coastal Plain	40th	8th	Columbia
41. South Dakota (SD)	Interior Lowlands	16th	40th	Pierre
42. Tennessee (TN)	Appalachian Mountain Belt	34th	16th	Nashville
43. Texas (TX)	Atlantic and Gulf Coastal Plain	2nd	28th	Austin
44. Utah (UT)	Southwest	11th	45th	Salt Lake City
45. Vermont (VT)	New England	43rd	14th	Montpelier
46. Virginia (VA)	Atlantic and Gulf Coastal Plain	36th	10th	Richmond
47. Washington (WA)	Pacific Coast	20th	42nd	Olympia
48. West Virginia (WV)	Appalachian Mountain Belt	41st	35th	Charleston
49. Wisconsin (WI)	Interior Lowlands	26th	30th	Madison
50. Wyoming (WY)	Rocky Mountain Belt	9th	44th	Cheyenne

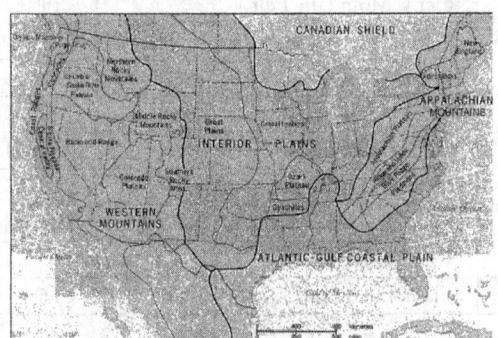

Major Physiographic Regions of North America

Figure 1b　The major physiographic divisions of the US based on terrain texture, rock type, plate tectonic setting, and geologic structure and history.

1. REGION 1: ATLANTIC AND GULF COASTAL PLAIN

The Coastal Plain stretches some 3,500 km, from Cape Cod, MA, in the northeast where it is narrowest, south to Florida, and westward to the Texas border (Figure 2). It continues south an additional 1,600 km beyond Texas into Mexico.

This *low-relief[29], sea-sloping coastal plain ranges from 150 to 300 km wide and covers portions of 17 states. With minor exceptions, elevations are below 150 m and more than half the region is less than 30 m above sea level. The *physiography[30] and abundant natural resources of this region facilitated its settlement and development during the nation's early history. Its fertile lowlands allowed for the cultivation of a wide range of agricultural products; the Southeastern Pine Forest provided a source of lumber; shellfish and fin-fish were accessible sources of protein; climates were generally agreeably mild; and its bays and sheltered coves provided safe harbors.

Coastal waters over this broad, low-relief portion of the continental shelf are extremely rich in *phytoplankton[31]. Abundant nutrients derive from both river runoff and the warm, northward-moving Gulf Stream water. In addition, depths are shallow enough, most less than 50 m, to allow substantial sunlight to penetrate the water. The *microscopic[32] *plankton[33] serves as the primary food supply for vast populations of fish, and for decades these world-famous plankton fields, including Georges *Banks[34] and the Grand Banks, have been the targets of fishing fleets from many nations. These *aquatic[35] resources have suffered recently from a combination of factors, including pollution due to ocean-pumping of wastes, over-fishing, and the application of technology used in locating schools of fish and in manipulating larger nets. Over the last several decades, much of the fishing industry in the northeast has closed, and the US has become increasingly more dependent on fish imported from abroad.

Geologically, the Coastal Plain comprises a *veneer[36] of young, unconsolidated sediment overlying older sedimentary rock units. Sediment is solid, fragmental material that originates chiefly from the *weathering[37] of rocks. These fragments are transported and deposited down-slope by water, wind, or ice. Sedimentary rock can be of two general types. One type, called *clastic[38] rock (e.g., sandstone and shale), results when grains of sediment are deeply buried, *compacted[39], and cemented together. The second type, called chemical rock (e.g., limestone and rock salt), forms as solids *precipitate[40] from aqueous solutions. Throughout the US Coastal Plain, gravel, sand, silt, and clay accumulate in rivers, beaches and *dunes[41], and tidal flats. Ultimately these sediments are carried offshore and deposited in the shallow waters of the marginal continental shelf. Beneath these sediments lies a thick sequence of older sedimentary rock units.

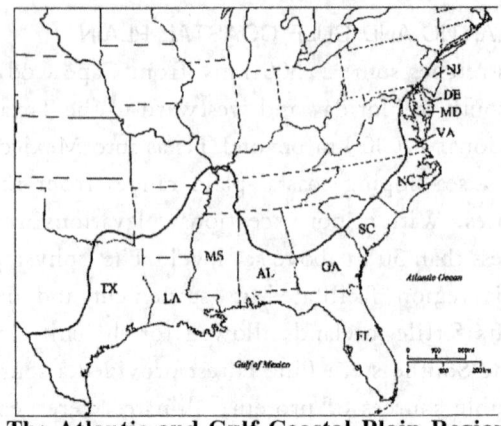

The Atlantic and Gulf Coastal Plain Region

Figure 2　The eastern and southern US states that lie within Region 1, The Atlantic and Gulf Coastal Plain.

　　Sedimentary rock formations, ranging in age from *Cretaceous[42] to Recent, comprise the eastern and southern Coastal Plain and extend offshore across the continental shelf. These formations were deposited on top of the much older, seaward-thinning edge of the continental crust. Together, these gently seaward-dipping rock units form a belt that roughly parallels the inner and outer margins of the coastal plain. The oldest, Cretaceous-age units are the farthest inland. Next is the belt of *Tertiary[43] formations, and the youngest, *Quaternary[44]-age units, comprise the present-day coastal belt. These units were deposited in virtually the same environments that we see throughout the continental coastal margin today. Since the beginning of Cretaceous time, the shoreline has generally receded, and the Coastal Plain has been built outward by the deposition of sediments derived from the erosion of the Appalachian and Rocky mountain belts farther up-slope.

　　Corresponding to the recent dramatic increases in crude oil and natural gas prices, the nation is turning its attention to the Coastal Plain and adjacent submerged shelf. The outer continental shelf (OCS), the gently sloping, 20- to 400-km-wide extension of the continent beneath deeper water marginal to the Atlantic, Gulf of Mexico, Pacific, and Arctic Slope of Alaska coasts, is estimated to contain substantial amounts of crude oil and natural gas resources. Continually improving technology along with higher prices encourages exploration and drilling in deeper and more remote locals. For example, thousands of platforms of various designs, often with multiple wellheads, currently operate in the Gulf of Mexico; some rigs produce in water depths exceeding 2,000 meters. However, the OCS waters are extremely sensitive ecologically, and these areas frequently are threatened by extreme meteorological conditions. Extraction of these domestic energy resources under such challenging conditions raise concerns among environmentalists of pollution, spills, and long-term changes to the ocean environment.

　　The abundance of oil and gas along the Gulf coast stretching from FL to TX, combined with easy access to shipping from the ports of Houston, TX, and New Orleans, LA, played a pivotal role in turning this region into a major center for natural gas processing, oil refining and petrochemical production. Additionally, the Strategic

Petroleum Reserve, the nation's emergency fuel store of petroleum maintained by the US Department of Energy, is located here. Designed to maximize long-term protection against oil-supply disruptions, several sites were engineered in subsurface salt domes to store more than 700 million barrels (159 liters each) of crude oil. Salt domes, huge masses of rock salt in the Gulf Coast region, serve as effective hydrocarbon traps and in this capacity as sealed storage chambers because of the impermeable nature of the mineral halite.

Complete drowning of the Atlantic Coastal Plain northward from Long Island, NY, occurred several times throughout the *Pleistocene[45] when ice sheets, each several kilometers thick, covered virtually all of Canada and much of the northern US. The weight of these masses of ice depressed Earth's crust. These effects were particularly pronounced along the northeast Atlantic coast. Today, the entire Coastal Plain off New England and the *Maritime Provinces[46] of eastern Canada remains *submerged[47].

Current global data indicate that sea level is rising on the order of 3 - 4 mm per year and will continue to do so into the foreseeable future. In general, the slope of the Coastal Plain is gentle, and rising ocean water will impact areas farther inland and dramatically change local coastlines over time. Sea-level rise combined with accompanying increases in storm surges are expected to pose significant threats to coastal metropolitan areas and require progressively greater expenditures to repair and replace infrastructure damaged as a result.

The boundary between the ancient and resistant crystalline rocks of the Appalachian *Piedmont[48] to the west and the much younger and softer rocks of the Atlantic Coastal Plain to the east is a narrow zone defined by connecting waterfalls on successive rivers up and down the coast. Called the "Fall Line", this zone represents the point where coastal tide-water influences cease and where up-stream navigation ends. Here also, the rivers can be most easily crossed. As a result of this physical boundary, this zone derived economic significance in the early history of the country. It is along this line of waterfalls that many colonial towns developed. Industries founded here harnessed the abundant river runoff for power. These towns grew, and today, they comprise a vital economic core region of large cities and seaports that extends along the Fall Line.

This densely urbanized corridor stretches more than 640 km virtually without a break from Boston, in southern MA, to Richmond in northern VA. It includes such well-known cities as New York, NY, Trenton, NJ, Philadelphia, PA, Baltimore, MD, and Washington, DC. (Such a set of interconnected cities today is known as a megalopolis, and this one has been nicknamed the "Boston-Washington" corridor.)

Farther south and west, approaching the terminus of the Appalachian Mountains, as the physical influence of the Piedmont disappears, the Fall Line becomes more subdued, and beyond AL, it eventually dies out. Yet, cities, such as Raleigh, NC, Columbus, GA, Montgomery, AL, Little Rock, AK, Fort Worth and Austin, TX, grew along the inner border of the Coastal Plain.

Along the Coastal Plain from VA to TX, the few natural harbors are small and shallow. Also, storms are common. As a result, far fewer cities were initially founded directly on the southern coast. Using modern technology, the US *Corps of Engineers[49] has been responsible for significant modifications to these coastlines. Cities like Corpus Christi, Galveston, and Houston, TX, New Orleans, LA, Mobile, AL, and Tampa, FL along the Gulf Coast, and Charleston, SC, Savannah, GA, and Miami, FL along the southeastern Atlantic coast have grown and become major US port cities.

Throughout this century, eastern and southern shores have served as the vacation destinations for large numbers of northeastern urban dwellers. Traditionally, the Atlantic coast beach areas swell to capacity in the summer, and southern coastal communities fill during the winter. Florida has attracted many retirees who seek relief from colder climates and harsh winters. More recently, however, these warmer, southern settings have become popular destinations for college students during their spring breaks. Increasing affluence and leisure time account for much of the recent development of year-round shoreline communities. Of growing economic impact are the new *condominiums[50] and townhouses, time-share resorts, and extensive family recreational theme parks that are springing up all along the eastern and southern coasts. However, expanding populations stress overtaxed resources of many low-lying coastal communities which are already constrained by the physical nature of the shoreline.

Another impact of growth relates to the violent storms that periodically ravage these coastlands. Intense tropical storms and *hurricanes[51] can strike either the Gulf or Atlantic shores between June and November. The lowland nature of the coastal plain, as well as its proximity to tidally dominated ocean waters, makes it particularly vulnerable to such storm-related hazards as extreme winds, huge wave surges, and extensive inland flooding which results from the copious rainfall. It is also not uncommon for a section of coast to be hit by several storms within a single season. Improved weather prediction has resulted in saving many lives, but has done little to reduce storm-related damage. Also, evacuating increasing numbers of people from these regions is a logistical nightmare. Reconstruction costs following storms continue to increase and deplete these communities' limited resources. Fierce *cyclones[52] also develop in winter along the Atlantic coast. These less *sensationalized[53] storms, nicknamed *"Nor'easters,"[54] generate gale-force winds that drive high seas landward from the northeast direction and often cause extensive coastal erosion.

The 2005 Atlantic hurricane season, the most active in recorded history, spawned six storms that hit the US, four of which were classified as major hurricanes. Hurricane Katrina smashed into the record books as being the costliest hurricane and one of the deadliest in US history and one of the strongest storms for the Atlantic Basin. Less than a month after Katrina devastated large parts of the central Gulf Coast region, Hurricane Rita made landfall near the Texas-Louisiana border. As the second hurricane of the season to reach Category 5 status (on the Saffir-Simpson scale) Rita marked the first time that two hurricanes reached Category 5 strength in the Gulf of Mexico in the same season.

However, it is Katrina that will be remembered for most catastrophic effects to a heavily populated portion of the Coastal Plain. High sustained winds, battering waves, and a 10 m storm surge inundated New Orleans, LA, and destroyed most structures on the Mississippi coastline. The federal flood protection system failed at more than fifty spots and every levee in the metropolitan area was breached. Floodwaters lingered for weeks, hampering rescue and recovery efforts, and three years later, thousands of displaced residents of this coastal area remain living in temporary housing.

In addition to large cyclonic storms, the Gulf Coast is subject to tornadoes. These violent, short-duration, rotating windstorms rank among nature's most destructive forces. As cooler, drier, low-pressure systems move from west to east across this low, flat area, they draw in warm, moist Gulf air. When conditions are optimal, these air masses clash and generate fierce thunderstorms, complete with lightening, locally strong winds, hail, and heavy rainfall. These squalls frequently spawn tornadoes over land or *waterspouts[55] over water, especially during afternoons and evenings in late winter through early spring.

Typically, coastal zones contain as much as 90% of all marine species. The northeastern tip of Maine's coast is slightly north of 45° N latitude. Key West, the southernmost point of the *conterminous[56] US, lies just one degree north of *the Tropic of Cancer[57], about 24.5° N. Variations in climate, physical coastal settings, tidal ranges, and ocean currents interact to create a variety of highly productive *ecosystems[58] across this latitudinal spread of nearly 21°. Over the years, many of these ecosystems have been considered a nuisance, a roadblock to growth and development. Huge areas of wetlands were drained, filled, and developed, or doused with *pesticides[59] and *herbicides[60] to eliminate unwanted pests, all in the name of progress. However, there is now a growing understanding of the importance of these fragile, coastal ecosystems, which leads to an increased resistance towards commercial development. Many small stretches of this coastline have been set aside as either municipal or state parks.

2. REGION 2: NEW ENGLAND

A majority of the New England Region (Figure 3) is characterized by rolling, heavily eroded, hilly uplands that are forested, *lake-strewn[61], and agriculturally uninviting. A central, north-south-trending lowland, the Connecticut River Valley, separates Vermont's Green Mountains and Massachusetts' Berkshire Hills to the west from New Hampshire's White Mountains and uplands of Maine to the east. This region can be considered as the northern part of the Appalachian Mountains which stretch from the southern US into Canada, but because it has many unique features, it deserves a separate description.

The New England and Appalachian Mountain Belt Regions

Figure 3　The eastern and northeastern US states that lie within Region 2, New England, and Region 3, the Appalachian Mountain Belt. (The Adirondack Mountain area, discussed within Region 4 Interior Plains and Highlands, is shown also.)

Summit elevations throughout most of the region lie below 450 m. Locally, however, peaks comprising rock far more resistant to erosion than the rocks of the surrounding terrain, attain elevations greater than 1,500 m. Such peaks are called *monadnocks[62], named for Mt. Monadnock in southern NH which stands some 600 m higher than its surroundings. Mt. Washington, located in the rugged and picturesque Presidential Range of the White Mountains in northern NH, stands 1,917 m in elevation and represents the highest point in the northeastern US. Here, *blizzards[63] strike in mid-summer and, in 1934, the weather station at the summit registered a wind gust at 370 km per hour, the strongest recorded anywhere on earth. Another monadnock, Mt. Katahdin, in north-central ME, is the northern terminus of the famed, 3,200-m-long Appalachian (hiking) Trail.

With the exception of the sedimentary rocks of the CT Valley, virtually the entire New England region is a crystalline terrain containing both *igneous[64] and *metamorphic[65] rocks. Generally, igneous rock originates as *magma[66], molten rock which forms deep in the Earth. Magma may ascend into the crust, where it cools slowly to form coarse-grained intrusive rock, e.g. *granite[67], or it may erupt onto the surface where it cools quickly and forms fine-grained or glassy extrusive rock, e.g. *lava[68]. Metamorphic rock derives from changes to pre-existing rock: sedimentary, igneous, or other metamorphic rocks. Exposed to deep burial or tectonic activity that results in elevated temperatures and pressures, these parent rocks undergo compositional and structural changes known as *metamorphism[69]. Folded and *faulted[70] *Precambrian[71], and *Paleozoic[72] metamorphic rocks, including *gneiss[73] *schist[74], *slate[75], *quartzite[76] and marble, have been intruded by large masses of granite and other igneous rocks.

Zones or layers of more resistant rock interspersed with less resistant units account for the irregular topography that has developed; the more resistant materials stand topographically higher than areas underlain with the less resistant rocks.

3. REGION 3: APPALACHIAN MOUNTAIN REGION

A band of narrow, tree-carpeted, parallel ridges stretches northeast to southwest through the center of a broad, extensive upland region in the eastern US. These forested ridges are separated from each other by broad, fertile valleys. Not surprisingly called Ridge and Valley, this unique landscape reflects its underlying buckled and wrinkled rock formations. This folded and faulted band of ridges and valleys forms the backbone of a nearly 2,000-km-long chain of highlands called the Appalachian Mountains (Figure 3).

The Appalachians of today are the remains of an ancient mountain complex that rose several hundred million years ago along the eastern margin of NA. The continent's ancient nucleus has remained stable and immobile for more than a billion years. These mountains extend across nearly 20 degrees of latitude and more than 30 degrees of longitude from Newfoundland, Canada, to central AL, and involve portions of 19 US states.

The deceptively tame and subdued topography of this mature mountain system we see today belies a long and tortured tectonic history. At its maximum extent, nearly 300 million years ago, these mountains must have rivaled the Rocky Mountains, the Alps, or perhaps even the Himalayas in stature and magnificence.

The Appalachian Mountains were uplifted by multiple collisions of both small and large crustal plates throughout a 200 million year period, and the rock sequences were squeezed, broken, and displaced many times.

Exposures closer to the east, where the tectonic forces were most extreme, display rock units that, in places, defy attempts to reconstruct their original position. Toward the west, stresses were not as severe, and it is only through close examination that some rock units can be shown to have been deformed at all. Not only does this mountain belt serve as a world-class model for structurally deformed sedimentary rock sequences, but it also remains as a classic area for a broad range of geologic and *geomorphic[77] studies today.

The northern portion of the Appalachians was previously discussed in the New England Region. South and west of the Hudson River, where the Appalachians broaden considerably, four roughly parallel mountain groups are evident: Piedmont, Blue Ridge, Ridge and Valley, and Appalachian Plateaus. Each is characterized by distinctive geologic structures, rock units and landforms; however, they are unified by the geologic history of the entire Appalachian system.

4. REGION 4: INTERIOR PLAINS AND HIGHLANDS REGION

An extensive interior-lowland region, uninterrupted by significant highlands, dominates the entire center of the US (Figure 4). It also includes much of the Mississippi River drainage basin, the largest in the nation. These lowlands stretch between the older Appalachian Mountain belt in the east and the younger Cordilleran mountainous complex in the west. To the north, they dominate a majority of the Canadian interior. To the south, they narrow, where they are bordered on the east by the Coastal Plains and on the west by the Basin and Range, extending through TX far into Mexico.

Generally, the bedrock of this central region in the US comprises nearly horizontal Paleozoic sedimentary rock units; sandstone, *shale[78], and limestone dominate. These sedimentary rocks, combined with the Precambrian crystalline basement below, create the great stable interior of the NA continent. Farther north toward Canada, the sedimentary rock cover thins and eventually disappears, leaving the crystalline basement rocks exposed as the *Canadian Shield[79].

Several intervals of Pleistocene *glaciation[80] affected much of the lowland region of the central US. Eroding and depositing as they relentlessly moved southward out of Canada, glaciers significantly altered the landscape in their paths, including the formation of the Great Lakes. These vast ice sheets spread huge volumes of eroded *debris[81] out across these lowlands as they melted and retreated.

Today, gigantic crystalline rock *boulders[82] sit isolated in the middle of farm fields. These boulders, called "haystacks", lie far from their Canadian sources and serve as reminders of the powerful capabilities of glaciers. However, the major effect of glaciation over much of the region was to level the land's surface. Its present low relief has come about not so much through wearing down of the high places as by filling in the low places with sediment transported by glacial (ice), alluvial (river), and eolian (wind) processes.

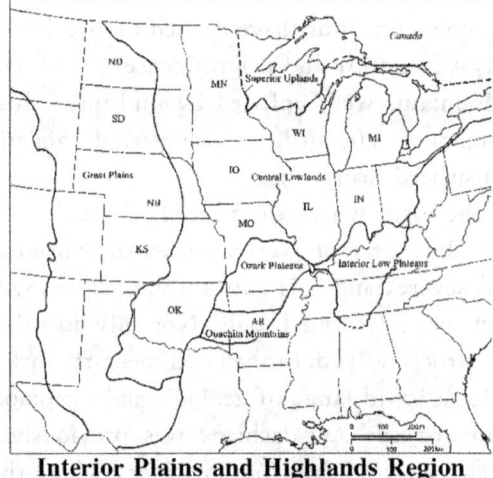

Interior Plains and Highlands Region

Figure 4   The central US states that lie within Region 4, Interior Plains and Highlands. (The Adirondack Mountains, discussed within this Region, are shown in Figure 3.)

This region can be subdivided into two large segments—the Central Lowlands in the east and the Great Plains in the west (Figure 4). Smaller subdivisions include: the Superior Upland (north-central), Adirondack Mountains (northeast), Black Hills (northwest), Ouchita Mountains (extreme south-central), Ozark Plateaus (south-central) and the Interior Low Plateaus (southeast).

The Coastal Plain's Mississippi Embayment separates the Quchita Mountains and Ozark Plateaus from the Interior Low Plateaus. This physiographic feature corresponds to a linear zone of crustal weakness at depth that originated as an incipient rift formed during super-continental breakup involving NA dating back some 750 million years.

The rift failed; however, the New Madrid seismic zone remains in the northern portion of the embayment. Periodic crustal movements, referred to as intraplate tectonic activity, reactivate this zone which extends into parts of six states, IL, MO, AK, KY, TN, and MI. Future seismic events have the potential to generate damaging earthquakes comparable to a series of three of the nation's most powerful temblors that struck the central Mississippi Valley during the winter of 1811 – 1812.

THE GREAT LAKES: The Great Lakes provide an excellent example of the direct effects of glaciation within this region. The basins now occupied by the Lakes Superior, Michigan, Huron, Erie and Ontario were scoured several times by advancing glaciers.

As Earth's largest group of fresh-water lakes, the Great Lakes contain approximately 95% of the fresh surface water in the US and about 18% of the world's fresh water. Together with the St. Lawrence River-Seaway, these interconnected lakes provide a natural route to the heart of the continent from the Atlantic Ocean. Of the five, only Lake Michigan lies entirely within the US; the other four are shared by the US and Canada. Among the chief lake ports are Chicago, IL, Milwaukee, WI, and Gary, IN, on Lake Michigan; Buffalo, NY, Cleveland, and Toledo, OH, on Lake Erie; and Duluth, MN, on Lake Superior.

Detroit, MI, another important port, lies on the St. Clair-Detroit River which connects Lake Huron and Lake Erie. These waterways facilitate the shipment of iron ore to steel-making centers, as well as wheat, corn and a variety of other crops, raw materials and manufactured goods to ports around the world. In addition, recreational sailing, boating and sport fishing appeal to increasing numbers of vacationers.

The Niagara River links Lake Erie with Lake Ontario and serves as a segment of American-Canadian border. Niagara Falls, at Buffalo, NY, is one of the nation's great scenic features. More water passes over these falls than over any other on the continent. Here, about midway between these lakes, river water drops over a substantial cliff, the Niagara escarpment, as two falls. On the Canadian side, the larger one spills over a rocky ledge of the Niagara limestone forming Horseshoe Falls. On the eastern shore, the remaining water flows across the cliff forming the American Falls. Downstream, the river flows through the 11 km steep-walled Niagara Gorge. Since glacial times, the falls have been retreating up-river, leaving behind an increasingly longer gorge. Today, the falls continue to retreat at an average rate of about a meter per year.

MISSISSIPPI-MISSOURI RIVER SYSTEM: The Mississippi River, along with its chief tributary, the Missouri River, together comprises the world's largest river system. Engineers estimate that it winds nearly 4,000 km from its source near the northern border of the US to its *delta[83] in the Gulf of Mexico. It is also one of the greatest trade waterways in the world.

The Mississippi-Missouri system, with more than 250 tributaries, drains over 40% of the continent's interior, an area estimated to be nearly 3,250,000 sq km. The Missouri River and its tributaries, including the Yellowstone and Platt Rivers, and the Arkansas and Red Rivers flow generally east, off the Rocky Mountains. The Illinois and Wabash Rivers flow south from the more recently glaciated Central Interior. The Ohio and the Tennessee Rivers flow generally west from the Appalachian Mountains. All of these rivers empty into the Mississippi River.

The Mississippi River drains one of the richest agricultural regions of the world. Flooding adds layers of fine-grained sediment and contributes to maintaining the fertility of the soils within its vast *floodplain[84] which *encompasses[85] at least a dozen states. Today, the national, state and local governments are playing increasing larger roles in river management and flood protection. Constructing dams, artificial channels and levees to prevent, or at least minimize flooding, has long been standard practice; yet these structures prevent natural re-nourishment of the floodplain and may fail with disastrous downstream consequences. Restricting or preventing development in floodplains is rarely a popular alternative. Establishing wildlife *reserves[86] in critical floodplain areas and wetlands is a strategy gaining acceptance, but these reserves are considered expensive.

From May through September of 1993, record flooding occurred across major portions of the Midwestern states of ND, SD, NB, KA, MN, IO, MI, WI, and IL. Referred to as the Great Flood of 1993, this protracted episode was one of the most significant and damaging natural disasters ever to hit the US. The flood was unusual in the magnitude of the crests, the number of record crests, the large area impacted, and the length of the time the flood waters lay across the region. Nearly 150 major rivers and tributaries flooded.

Although only 50 lives were lost, damages exceeded $15 billion, hundreds of levees failed, and tens of thousands of people were evacuated; many never returned to their homes. At least 10,000 homes were totally destroyed; hundreds of towns were affected with at least 75 towns totally inundated; and at least 6 million hectares of farmland were flooded and rendered unuseable for years. At the peak of flooding, all modes of transportation across the Midwest were impacted: barge traffic on the Missouri and Mississippi Rivers was stopped for nearly 2 months; bridges washed out or were not accessible; interstate highways and other roads closed; ten commercial airports were flooded; and all railroad traffic was halted.

Fifteen years later, in June 2008, much of this same region was hit again by record flooding with damages estimated in the billions. Late 19th century Midwestern American humorist, satirist, lecturer, and writer Samuel Langhorne Clemens, better known by his pen name Mark Twain, spent several years on the river as a riverboat pilot and spoke often of the "mighty Mississippi". Paraphrased here, he wisely noted: no one can tame, curb, confine, or tell that lawless stream where to go or make it obey. No one can bar its path with an obstruction which it will not tear down, dance over, and laugh at.

5. REGION 5: ROCKY MOUNTAIN REGION

For the impatient west-bound traveler who has just crossed thousands of kilometers of the American mid-continental lowlands, the fuzzy, barely perceptible images that begin to blur the sharp horizon dividing ground from sky offer the promise of heights often described using such terms as "splendor", "majesty" and "grandeur". A few kilometers closer, those images begin to sharpen. In step-like fashion, ghostly mountains rise from the ground like gray, rocky monoliths. Finally, the distance is close enough that the mind can fully comprehend what lies ahead. Stretching as far as the eye can see is an expansive panorama of massive, rugged terrain topped with jagged peaks reaching skyward. Except for a few billowing, bright-white clouds snagged by some of the highest pinnacles, the crest-line is sharply silhouetted against an intense, cloudless, azure western sky. The awesome magnificence of the elegant snow-capped Rocky Mountains rarely ceases to amaze and astonish the viewer.

The Rockies form a massive and complex mountain system that runs through the entire western US (Figure 5). It extends northward into Canada and AK, and, to the south, it becomes the Sierra Madres of Mexico. Even though the axis of this upland mass parallels the western edge of the NA continent, the belt comprises many smaller mountain ranges, each with its own particular geographic orientation. However, mountain ranges are only a part of the Rocky Mountain system. Numerous valleys, basins, and plateaus separate the ranges, each with its own isolated lowlands, lakes and river valleys. From the base of the mountains, to the highest alpine peaks, altitudes and climates create entirely different living zones for plants and animals.

Along their entire eastern margin, the Rocky Mountain uplands sharply contrast with the expansive lowlands of the western Great Plains. In CO, for example, Denver lies at the foot of the Front Range. Here, the Southern Rockies jut abruptly out of the flat, lowland floor and rise about 2,700 m in less than 50 km. The Front Range, a thick sequence of once horizontal *rock strata[87] that floor the Great Plains, were uplifted by crustal forces just as one might bend the edges of a paper-back book upward. Since then, these steeply tilted *strata[88] have been eroded, forming what geologists today call *flatirons[89]. To the casual observer, however, they might simply appear as sharply pointed *serrations[90] on a long knife blade that stands almost on edge.

Rocky Mountain Region

Figure 5　The western US states that lie within Region 5, The Rocky Mountains.

Beyond the Front Range lie the highest summits in the continental US. Jagged, glacially sculpted, snow-capped pinnacles reach heights far exceeding 3,000 m. Among these heights, glaciers, snowfields and their melt waters feed headwaters of many river systems. Running nearly north-south is a series of peaks, ridges and valleys that make up the great western continental divide. Rain falling to the west of this line moves into one of the rivers that drain west or southwest and ultimately reaches the Pacific Ocean. These include the Columbia and its main tributary, the Snake; also the Colorado and its principal tributary, the Green River. However, should the rain fall on the other side of the divide, it will move either east into the Missouri, Arkansas, or Platte rivers, all of which flow into the Mississippi River, or south into the Rio Grande River. Ultimately, these eastern and southern drainage systems empty into the Gulf of Mexico.

The rugged Rocky Mountain system which covers more than 460,000 sq km in the western US has a long and complex geologic history. This system can be broken into three sub-regions: Northern, Middle, and Southern Rockies, each comprising nearly a dozen distinct uplands. The Wyoming Basin, lying between the Middle and Southern Rockies, shares a common geologic history with the entire Rocky Mountain belt.

Within the Rocky Mountain system, one of Earth's largest volcanic provinces spans the continental divide between the Northern and Middle Rocky Mountains. The Yellowstone Plateau, a 2,400-m-high upland extending from northwestern WY into ID and MT, exposes evidence of repeated and extensive episodes of extrusive lava flows, all of which occurred within the last 2.5 million years. Covering some 900,000 hectares, Yellowstone National Park lies within the margins of a massive volcanic *crater[91] centrally located within the Plateau. Not at all obvious to park visitors, this basin-shaped *depression,[92] called a *caldera,[93] represents the collapse of the land's surface following a series of voluminous eruptions, culminating with a cataclysmic explosion about 630,000 years ago displacing, by some estimates, 6,000 cubic kilometers of material.

Today, volcanologists interpreting the geologic record recognize evidence of past eruptive events ranging on this order of magnitude around the globe. Labeling them supervolcanoes, such eruptions are capable of burying expansive areas with thick lava and ash, causing long-lasting changes in global weather patterns, e.g. initiating ice ages, and even threatening species with extinction. Geologists theorize that a shallow magma body, a stationary hot spot, comparable to that responsible for the Hawaiian Island archipelago, is the underlying cause of this episodic volcanic activity here in Yellowstone. Exposures of lava flows at Obsidian Cliff provide evidence of volcanism as recently as 59,000 years ago. Observations, beginning in 1923, indicate the basin rises and sinks measurably over time, rising as much as 7 cm/year since 2004 and demonstrating a caldera "at unrest".

Yellowstone captivates its more than 3 million visitors annually with an extensive array of thermal features, generated as ground-water moves through a subsurface plumbing system heated by its proximity to a magma chamber, perhaps as shallow as 5 – 6 km below the surface. Explosive *geysers[94], hot springs, bubbling mud holes and steam *vents[95], boiling sulfur pools, steaming hillsides and heated *seeps[96], unceasingly spew hot, mineralized waters onto the surface and vent nasty-smelling vapors into the air. At

Yellowstone, volcanism and *hydrothermal[97] features go hand-in-hand with earthquake activity. Small-magnitude earthquakes are common beneath the entire plateau; however, in 1959, a magnitude 7.5 temblor displaced land vertically along a 40-km-long fault up to 6 meters and modified fluid movement of many of the park's hydrothermal features.

Throughout the park, stream valleys carrying fast-moving waters from surrounding ice-covered peaks down-cut thick sequences of multiple rhyolitic lava flows, layers of columnar-jointed volcanic rock, and baked country rock. The scenic Yellowstone River carves a deep canyon, stepped with magnificent waterfalls and exposures of country rock, and stained in brilliant shades of red, orange, and yellow. The compelling high-country landscape of Yellowstone, though beautiful enough on its own, contains plants and animals that distinguish this western wilderness. The long list of indigenous plants and animals serves as a lexicon for the entire Rocky Mountain region. The park's importance as a wildlife *sanctuary[98] has grown steadily since it was declared America's first national park in 1872. Not only did this legislative action guarantee that this area of exceptional beauty and ecological importance would be set aside for the enjoyment of generations to come, it established a major conservation precedent for the entire nation.

6. REGION 6: SOUTHWEST REGION

A vast intermontane area lies between the Rocky Mountains and the Pacific coastal mountain chains (Figure 6). Four states are designated as the Southwest: Nevada (NV), Utah (UT), Arizona (AZ) and New Mexico (NM). Perhaps more than any of the other regions of the US, the Southwest inspires many lyric descriptions of its awesome landscapes, its glorious expanses and its colorful splendor. But the southwest can also be a harsh host, providing searing, unrelenting summer heat; violent, abrasive sandstorms; bitterly chilling desert nights; and formidable winter blizzards.

Today, extensive portions of the southwestern wilderness not under governmental or Native American Indian control are rapidly being developed. Often without regard for the long-term consequences desert landscapes are rapidly turned into *sleek[99], modern vacation resorts; huge, tree- and grass-lined retirement villages; *mammoth[100] irrigation projects required to keep the desert green; extensive *strip[101]-mine operations extracting coal for power generation; and modern, technological industries.

The spectacular scenery and dramatic natural settings of the Southwest are a product of its physiography. Aided by frost action, wind and gravity, water has been the principal player throughout the millennia. Weathering and erosion have sculpted spectacular canyons, massive cliffs, pinnacles and pedestals, sinuous *arroyos[102], *buttes[103] and *mesas[104], all of which comprise a medley of unique landforms so distinctively southwestern in appearance.

The Southwest is the driest part of the entire country, and it is possible to see here, more distinctly than anywhere else in America, the changes in plant and animal communities that occur as one ascends in elevation.

The Southwest encompasses two sizable physiographic segments, each with its own distinctive beauty, geologic history and contemporary essence: the Colorado Plateaus and the Basin and Range. However, physiographic boundaries are not limited by state boundaries. The Colorado Plateaus include portions of southwestern Colorado, and the

Basin and Range extends into southern Oregon, northeastern and southeastern California, northern Mexico and southwestern Texas. The adjacent Rocky Mountains include portions of northern Utah and northern New Mexico, and the Great Plains cover the eastern third of New Mexico.

Southwest Region

Figure 6 The southwestern US states that lie within Region 6, The Southwest.

This region experienced several intense periods of tectonic activity during the last 400 million years. Throughout the last 15 million years, the Southwest has undergone broad-scale uplift and east-west stretching. This extension of the Earth's crust created the present fault-block landscape. Volcanic cinder cones and *basaltic[105] lava flows covered portions of many blocks.

During the last few million years, widespread erosion under generally arid conditions has also shaped this unique landscape. Drainage runs *perpendicular[106] to the ranges; streams rise near the summits of the ranges and terminate in closed basins between them. These fast running, high-gradient streams pour out of confining upland gorges and discharge their high-yield sediment load directly onto the flat basin floors. Here, at the bases of mountains, large gravel *fans[107] form, grow and coalesce into thick aprons of coarse rock debris. Over time, alluvium accumulates in these basins and progressively buries the base of the range. Geologists estimate upwards of one-third of the tectonic relief lies buried beneath thick blankets of rock debris. This distinctive combination of physiography and structure is more extensively developed here than in any other part of the world.

7. REGION 7: PACIFIC COAST REGION

California, Oregon, Washington and Alaska: The Pacific Rim is perhaps the most scenic of all the US coasts. Here, quaint fishing villages, mill towns, Native American *reservations[108], *logging camps[109], farming communities, global shipping ports, and a few rapidly growing megalopolises coexist. The western edge of the continent comprises colorful, highly varied, magnificent landscapes, including expansive mountain ranges, white-sand beaches, rain forests, salmon-filled rivers, desert flats and fertile valley lowlands. The most extensive accumulation of lava sheets in the western hemisphere is located along the eastern margin of this region between the volcanic mountains and the Northern Rockies. Here, the combined thicknesses of these once fluid rocks are measured in hundreds of meters.

Pacific Coast Region

Figure 7a   The western US states that lie within Region 7, The Pacific Coast.

Mountain ranges stretch northward from southern CA through OR, WA, and Canada's British Columbia, and into the southeastern panhandle of AK (Figures 7a and 7b). However, it is the uniqueness of each of the many mountain ranges that characterize the Pacific Coast region. The height and ruggedness of its mountain peaks, the dissecting rivers with their rugged valleys and the intervening lowlands, all serve to separate, isolate, nurture, and protect the *myriad [110] living organism within their bounds. Its mountain chains and all that lies within possess exquisite beauty and prominence.

The massive granite mountains of the Sierra Nevada Range and the volcanic peaks of the Cascade Range run along the eastern margin of the coastal belt. Folded and faulted rock sequences span the shores of the Pacific and make up the Coastal Ranges of OR and CA and the Olympic Mountains in northwest WA.

A granite mountain complex in northern CA and southern OR, the Klamath Mountains, separates the Coastal Ranges. Still another granite ridge begins in the southern tip of CA and extends along the coast to form the Baja Peninsula in Mexico. Unlike the Appalachian mountain chain paralleling the east coast of the US, these Pacific ranges are geologically young and complex. Collectively, these ranges document recent tectonic forces actively pushing, pulling and tearing this edge of the continent. Some record collisions with other landmasses, severely folding, faulting, raising or lowering the land. Others result from episodes where molten rock rose from great depths and accumulated as massive magma chambers close to the surface where they cooled and crystallized very slowly. Later these igneous rock masses would be unearthed and uplifted into mountain belts. Still others chronicle multiple violent explosions at the surface that create great conical volcanic peaks out of mixtures of ash, cinders, and lava.

The mountain belts play a significant role in controlling the region's moisture. All of the east-directed Pacific Ocean air masses that move inland over the continent are forced aloft as they surmount the region's rugged mountain belts. As they rise, these masses cool, and the moisture carried inland from the ocean condenses and falls as precipitation on the western mountain slopes. Only the largest and strongest water-laden systems supply precipitation to the arid leeward lands east of the mountains.

Sheltered between the uplands, extensive foothills and intermontane valleys have become major centers for this region's agriculture. Mountain foothills serve as grazing lands for livestock, and lowlands floored with thick, rich soils are intensively farmed. However, irrigation is the key to agricultural success. Heavy winter snows typically form a valuable snowpack in the surrounding high mountains. Spring meltwater released into the rivers provides much of the region's irrigation requirements. Recent, unprecedented growth in the agriculture sector has created an increasing demand for water. As a result, water itself has become big business. Dams and reservoirs, canals and aqueducts, and pumping stations comprise vital components of a complex and highly regulated irrigation infrastructure.

Just as the mountain belts differ from west to east, so do America's Pacific and Atlantic coastlines. From California to Alaska, the Pacific coast is sharp, irregular and rock-bound and lined by vertical cliffs, imposing *headlands[111] and the occasional sheltered cove with its sandy or *cobble[112] beach. Cliffs drop precipitously into the surf, and isolated, wave-sculpted sea arches and stacks sit offshore and serve as reminders of past coastal margins. Clearly this coastline provides a dramatic contrast with the gently rolling, sandy lowlands and barrier island beaches of the Atlantic and Gulf coastal plains. Not even the rocky Atlantic coast of Maine approaches the ruggedness of the Pacific shoreline.

The entire region stretching from the Rocky Mountains to the Pacific Coast has formed since the middle of the Paleozoic Era, some 350 million years ago. However, much of the highly varied Pacific Coast region owes its existence to complex plate-tectonic processes operating throughout the last 65 million years. These processes involved the interaction of the westward-moving North American (NA) tectonic plate and the eastward-moving portions of the Pacific tectonic plate.

One frequently asked question by those unfamiliar with the geology of the US west coast—Will California ever fall into the Pacific Ocean? For those folks living farther east who may envy life in the Golden State, perhaps this idea has enduring appeal. Plus, all those images of massive mudslides and multi-million-dollar mansions toppling off steep coastal cliff tops carried by news media following severe storm activity serve to reinforce that concept. Such video footage of California landslides most often occurs in response to strong, low-pressure systems and months-long, storm-driven wave action accompanying El Niño events. Frequently, the unconsolidated bluffs along California coasts fail as they undergo erosion and cliff retreat, just as stream banks slump into the channel during flooding events. These surficial geologic processes reflect the influence of gravity upon over-steepened, unstable slopes.

Alternatively, the same question may arise within the context of earthquakes responsible for violent ground shaking, horizontal and vertical land displacement, and slope failure. From CA to AK's Aleutian Island Chain, the west coast of NA delimits a segment of the circum-Pacific seismic belt, better known as the "Pacific Ring of Fire". A direct result of plate tectonic activity, 90% of the world's earthquakes and 75% of the world's active volcanoes occur within this belt.

A wide zone of fractured and sheared rock, trending north-northwest/south-southeast, runs through western CA. Known as the San Andreas Fault System, this 1300-km-long band stretching from the Gulf of California to San Francisco demarcates the boundary between two of earth's 14 major tectonic plates—the NA (continental) Plate and the Pacific (oceanic) Plate. Each day thousands of earthquakes register seismic activity to a global network of monitoring stations as these two plates slide past each other at rates approximating 45 mm per year, about as fast as fingernails grow. That portion of the state corresponding to the Pacific Plate, western CA, moves northwest, up the coast, along the San Andreas fault relative to North American Plate. Geologists and geophysicists affirm that the horizontally directed plate motion here will not allow California to sink; however, Los Angeles and San Francisco will one day be adjacent to one another!

At several locations along the Pacific coast, sets of wave-cut marine terraces rise from the shore like giant steps, each higher level older than the last lower one. These expansive staircases demonstrate episodic coastal uplift over the last several million years. During periods of quiescence, the sea's relentless waves and currents ground coastal margins into flat plains. Periodically, a segment of the coast is uplifted, and the wave-cut platform is raised above sea level. Coastal erosion begins anew on a newly exposed portion of the coastline.

Glacial ice sculpted the Pacific Coast Region's mountains. Soon after the climate began its latest warming trend more than ten thousand years ago, glaciers and glacial ice sheets began their final retreat. Meltwaters choked with eroded rock debris and receding ice sheets deposited a mantle of glacial sediments across the lowlands. Once the landscape became ice-free, it was once again subject to all of those natural biologic, physical and chemical processes we see around us daily. Only in the region's highest mountains do glaciers currently exist. They remain because new snowfall in their headlands slightly exceeds the loss of ice and melting at lower elevations.

Periodically, and usually without much warning, earthquakes and volcanic eruptions—a result of plate interactions—plague the Pacific Coastal region. Thousands of earth-shaking events have been recorded within the historic past, and inevitably they will continue for millennia. In addition, *tsunamis[113] are generated by the earthquakes in oceanic and coastal regions. These waves move across deep ocean basins at speeds exceeding 970 km/hr. Upon reaching a shallow coast, these waves grow to heights exceeding 30 m as they crash onto shore. All of these natural geologic processes only become hazardous when humans get in the way.

Great Valley: Situated between the California Coast Ranges and the Sierra Nevada Range lies the Central or Great Valley of CA. This 80-km-wide *trough[115] stretches north-south for about 725 km, and was formed in conjunction with the uplift of the surrounding mountains. Most of the lowland lies less than 120 m above sea level. Since its formation, this trough has accumulated a great thickness of rich alluvium derived from river and glacial erosion of the surrounding highlands. Streams draining westward off the rugged Sierra Nevada Range carry large volumes of sediment out and onto the flat valley floor. Subsequent weathering of this thick mass of sediments has generated the valley's thick fertile soils.

Two major drainage basins carry mountain runoff from the northern thirds of the Valley into San Francisco Bay. Water supplies and runoff are generally abundant in the northern region, drained by the Sacramento River. The central San Joaquin Valley is drier, and this *watershed[116] is less productive. The southern third is semiarid to arid and subject to severe water shortages. In order to promote agriculture throughout the Valley, the rivers have been combined into a single system. Water courses of any consequence are dammed, and an extensive network of *aqueducts[117] and irrigation channels has been constructed. The economy of the entire Central Valley is dependent on carefully managed water resources.

As a result of its geology, topographic setting and climate, the Central Valley has become famous. Initially, the discovery of gold in 1848 in the foothills of the Sierra Nevada Range created a rush of prospectors and miners to the northern part of the valley. Responding to their needs, the port of San Francisco rapidly became a commercial point of entry to the goldfields. The increasing population stimulated a demand for a greater range of agricultural products, and soon agricultural settlements spread throughout the countryside.

The fertile soils, mild climate, and manageable water supplies facilitated the transformation of this region from one originally dominated by rural, single-family farms into one of the most productive agricultural regions in the world. Intensive, commercial development of this valley has extended into those areas that were once considered desolate. Population pressure, combined with increasing technology and wealth, has made even this region's deserts bloom.

Alaskan geographers apply the word "subcontinent" to this northwestern-most portion of NA, a landmass covering 1.5 million square km. It is bounded on the north by the Arctic Ocean, on the east by Canada's Yukon and Northwest Territories, on the south and southwest by the Gulf of Alaska and the Pacific Ocean, and on the west by the Bering and the Chukchi seas. East Cape, Siberia, lies only 33 km across the Bering Strait. On the southeast, the panhandle runs more than 800 km, and the Aleutian Islands on the southwest stretch more than 1,600 km across the Bering Sea. The curved nature of the Aleutian chain, known as a volcanic island arc, reflects its position at a convergent plate boundary. As the Pacific Plate descends (subducts) beneath the NA Plate, the ocean crust melts and forms magma. This magma eventually rises through the overriding plate and erupts to form a line of volcanoes.

Alaska (AK) serves as America's symbol of seemingly endless untamed wilderness. The native *Aleut[118] people referred to this region of NA as the "Great Land". The mere mention of the name Alaska evokes images of a region characterized as immense, vast, extreme, wild, remote, desolate, inhospitable, unpopulated, roadless, severe, magnificent and breathtaking.

AK claims extremes—the highest summit (Mt. McKinley, 6,194 m); the wettest slopes (SE AK); and the lowest winter temperatures (interior) in NA. The Aleutian Island chain is the longest *archipelago[119] of small islands in the world.

The world's largest carnivore, the Alaskan brown bear, inhabits Kodiak Island and the nearby AK mainland. Its far northern latitude provides eighteen to twenty-four hours of both summer sunlight and winter darkness. The nation's largest state, AK is more than twice the size of TX, and about one-fifth the size of the lower 48 states. AK contains 63% of the acreage in the US National Park Service system and 88% of the acreage in the US National Wildlife Refuge (NWR) system.

Yet, AK is a land that is full of endless contrasts: boundless ice fields and carpeted expanses of intertidal grasslands; thousands of white glaciers sparkling atop cloud-rimmed, lofty peaks and deeply flooded, jet-black, mist-shrouded coastal fjords; untapped gold deposits and rigs piping offshore crude oil southward to the lower 48; ocean waters teaming with fish and riparian wetlands sheltering mammals and waterfowl; protected old-growth, temperate rain-forest community and barren volcanic terrains covered with little more than cinders and ash; and skies sweeping the horizon, bright with the shimmering, delicately colored veils of the northern lights or pitch-black and filled with the infinity of stars.

To some, AK is a land evolving slowly as it emerges from the icy grip of the waning Ice Ages. But, AK is not an "Arctic" land; it displays a wide range of climates. Indeed, Point Barrow, the northern-most point on the Arctic Slope, is more than 1,900 km from the North Pole. Only the northern quarter of AK is *tundra[120] and falls within the northern Polar climatic zone. Along the state's entire southern coast, a subtropical climatic zone stretches from the Aleutian chain down to the southeast panhandle. This coast, one of the rainiest parts of the continent, is warmed by the huge clockwise-circulating Kuroshio *Current[121] that begins in the lower latitudes of the western Pacific Ocean.

The AK landmass is so varied and complex that this brief overview can do little more than address some of its principal characteristics. Four major geomorphic subdivisions are from south to north: (1) the Pacific Mountain System, including the Aleutian volcanic island chain, (2) the Interior and Western AK, (3) the Brooks Range, and (4) the Arctic (North) Slope (Figure 7b).

Between 1892 and 1954, some 12 million immigrant steamship passengers sailed under the Statue of Liberty into New York Harbor to Ellis Island, the nation's premier federal immigration station. However, the roughly 1,600-kilometer-wide Bering Land Bridge, linking Siberia and the Alaskan Peninsula, likely served as North America's first port of entry. During the Pleistocene, much of Earth's water was locked up in ice, and, as a result, sea level dropped as much as 90 m. Archaeological and anthropological evidence suggests that from about 40,000 to 13,000 years ago, the shallow Bering Strait was exposed providing a natural passageway for grazing animals and the humans who stalked them. Many scientists theorize that Native Americans descend from Asian people who moved into the Americas by way of this land bridge.

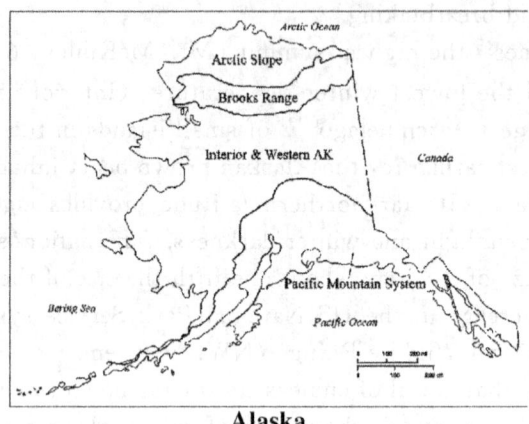

Alaska

Figure 7b Map of the Alaska within Region 7, The Pacific Coast.

8. REGION 8: PACIFIC-HAWAII

According to songs, legends and travel brochures, Hawaii is the "Paradise of the Pacific". Born from volcanic fires and glowing lava, Hawaii is the longest and oldest isolated archipelago on earth. America's 50th state is actually a chain of some 125 islands, *atolls[122], and *shoals[123] which stretches across the mid-Pacific Ocean in a southeast-Northwest line for nearly 2,400 km or 22° of longitude (Figure 8). These islands represent the tips of immense volcanic mountains that have grown upward toward the surface from abyssal depths.

The entire Hawaiian Island chain traces the movement of the Pacific tectonic plate to the northwest over the last 40 million years. During that time, a fixed *plume[124] of magma rising from deep within the Earth pumped massive amounts of molten rock through the crust. Geologists call such a point source of magma a hot spot. This hot spot generated a trail of volcanic mountains and islands in the westward-moving Pacific plate, much as a stationary welding torch would create holes, welts and bubbles if it were held beneath a slowly moving steel plate. This long line of now-extinct volcanic islands becomes progressively older to the northwest.

Located at the southeastern end of the Hawaiian archipelago are the eight Windward or High Islands. They extend over 600 km from Hawaii (Big Island) in the southeast to Niihau in the northwest and include Maui, Kahoolawe, Lanai, Molokai, Oahu and Kauai. Because they are the largest, geologically youngest and most populated, the Windward Islands are the most familiar islands in the Hawaiian chain. The rest of the islands, known as the Leeward Islands, comprise tiny, weathered, virtually uninhabited islands of hardened lava shoals flanked by coral reefs. This group constitutes the Hawaiian Islands National Wildlife Refuge. The total land area is 16,700 sq km, a figure which increases as volcanism and coral growth form new land.

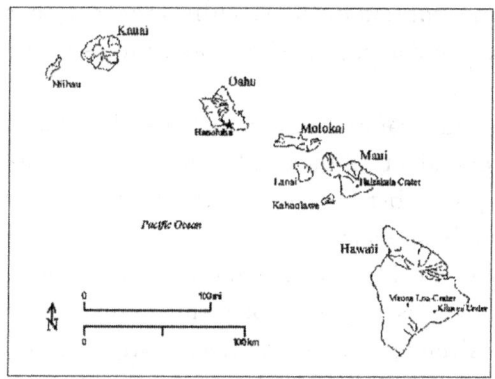

Hawaii Region

Figure 8　The Hawaiian islands that comprise Region 8, Hawaii Region.

In addition to volcanic eruptions which build new land, Hawaii has also been shaped by its exposure to the northeast trade winds which push moist ocean air across the coastal lowlands and up the mountains. From the mountains, fast-flowing rivers carry the water back down to the Pacific Ocean. Pounding surf, hurricane-generated storm surges and the occasional tsunami, huge ocean waves caused by local/offshore earthquakes, grind rocky headlands into sand which is then spread onto the beaches.

As a result of these timeless, relentless natural forces, Hawaii can make several unique claims. It contains the only tropical rainforest, the tallest sea cliffs and the most colorful beaches in all of the US, as well as the largest and most active volcano in the world. These islands offer an astounding biodiversity, ranging from marine coral reefs to rain-soaked jungles to high-altitude deserts, and almost every other imaginable ecosystem in-between. Rainfall contrasts are very pronounced between the windward, northeast sides of the islands and the leeward, southwest sides.

Altitude, amount of rainfall and age of the island surface are reflected in the magnitude of weathering and erosion displayed in various parts of the islands. The older islands to the northwest tend to display the most advanced stages of erosion. Here, thick, extensively *leached[125] (*lateritic[126]) soils underlie rain forests and elevated regions characterized by high rainfall, whereas *calcareous[127] (*alkaline[128]) soils have formed beneath the lower, drier grasslands and desert regions. Soils on the geologically younger islands to the southeast, if present at all, tend to be thinner and much less weathered.

Hawaiian beaches and shorelines reflect both the volcanic nature of the islands as well as the marine organisms that live in the shallow-water environments marginal to the islands. The magma, when it erupts on the surface, generates an iron- and *magnesium[129]-rich, black rock called basalt. Hawaiian black-sand beaches derive from the weathering of basalt, and its green beaches are concentrations of *olivine[130], a resistant green mineral that crystallizes in some basalt. Erosion of offshore reefs and beach-rock generates the small, light-colored coral and shell fragments and white grains of calcium *carbonate[131] sands that constitute some of the widely publicized beaches such as the one at Waikiki. Many of the island shorelines are rocky, devoid of long stretches of beaches, and consist of steep cliffs eroded into ancient lava flows. Sea stacks, caves and arches stand along the shores as tributes to the ongoing battle between land and sea.

Despite very high annual rainfall in much of the Hawaiian Islands, the fresh water supply is generally not abundant. Because of the volcanic nature of the islands, the soil and rock are highly porous. Most of the precipitation rapidly permeates the ground and collects as a thin layer of fresh water floating on salt water. Therefore, as in all island settings, fresh water is a valuable resource and requires careful management.

The economy of Hawaii is largely dependent on agriculture, the US military and international tourism. Although largely agriculturally based, less than 10% of the islands is cultivated and almost all of that land is used for raising sugar cane and pineapple. Half of the land is in pasture, about a third in forest preserve, 5% is in national parks, and the remainder is uneconomic. The islands lack economically important minerals beyond crushed stone and cement used for road-building and construction; the traditional fossil-fuel resources found in both AK and the lower 48 are not options.

Currently, more than 90% of Hawaii's energy comes from imported oil. Because of their favorable climate and geographical location, the Hawaiian Islands are well suited to both solar and wind power. Already, several energy projects harness alternative power, including *photovoltaic[132] arrays and wind turbines, but most are small in both scale and power output. Increasing solar and wind capabilities is underway, yet Hawaii's energy future lies in developing several other clean, abundant "renewables", including geothermal, pumped storage hydro, biomass, and landfill gas.

Hawaii has also been called the "Hub of the Pacific". Modern transportation has brought this state very close to the countries throughout the Pacific Rim. Honolulu International Airport is one of the busiest in the nation. In addition, there are seven deep-water commercial ports in Hawaii including the naval shipyard and military base at Pearl Harbor.

To avoid confusion with the state's name, the island of Hawaii is often referred to as the "Big Island", because it contains twice as much land area as the other islands combined. The island is roughly triangular, and virtually all of the population centers lie along the northeastern and western coasts. In sharp contrast, the southern third of the island is sparsely populated. Over the last several thousand years, lava has spread across this portion of the island and that threat continues today. Along the southern coast, South Point juts seaward and serves as the southernmost point both of the island as well as for the entire United States.

Geologically, the Big Island is the youngest landmass in the archipelago and one of Earth's most prodigious volcanic constructions. This volcano, typical of all those in Hawaii, is known as a shield volcano, because in profile their gentle slopes resemble a warrior's shield lying face up. Most of the island has formed from five shield volcanoes. Two of the most active volcanoes in the world today, Mauna Loa and Kilauea, dominate the southern half of the island. Located in the north-central portion of the island, the dormant shield volcano Mauna Kea is the state's highest mountain (4,194 m above sea level) as well as the highest point in the Pacific Ocean. Although Mauna Kea has not erupted in 3,600 years, it still could. When measured from their base on the sea floor to their summit, Mauna Kea and Mauna Loa qualify as the tallest mountains on earth and represent some 3 million years of active volcanism. Also classified as dormant is Hualalai to the west, which last erupted in 1801. Kohala, in the northwest corner of the island, is the smallest and the only one of the five considered extinct.

Climate, terrain, and elevation in Hawaii change dramatically over short distances; tropical beaches lay within 60 km of sub-Arctic, snow-clad volcanic mountain summits. On the flanks and coastal lowlands, abundant rainfall on the windward side waters the vast sugar-cane fields, groves of *macadamia nut[133] trees, a *cornucopia[134] of exotic fruits and brightly colored exotic flowers, while on the drier leeward side, commercial coffee plantations flourish. The island sustains cattle ranching as well. Parker Ranch, one of the largest and oldest individually owned cattle ranches in the US, is located near the north coast of the Big Island. A portion of its pastureland also serves as the site of the world's largest hybrid solar/wind energy project.

V. Geologic Processes Shape the Nation's Physical and Human Geography

The natural processes responsible for creating and shaping the land are not constrained by the "artificial" regional boundaries defined herein. In fact, the section lines drawn on these small-scale maps become fuzzy, imprecise linear tracts on the ground. Fundamental earth processes involving water, wind, ice, and tectonics modify the land inexorably over time and eventually transcend all artificially drawn boundary lines.

Increasingly, these natural forces impact lives, property, and ultimately the economy of the nation as the population grows and people spread into more sensitive, hazard-prone areas. Areas such as coastlines and wetlands, floodplains, volcanic foothills, and fault zones, are all subject to the whims of nature's fury. As a result, in spite of greater scientific understanding and advanced technological capabilities, costs in lives and property damage will continue to increase as more people develop infrastructure in harm's way.

Recent history provides powerful reminders the disregard nature has for human lives and the monuments they create. Examples illustrating severe regional impact include the (1) floods affecting much of the US Midwest in 1993 and again in 2008; (2) widespread destruction wrought by some of the worst hurricanes in the last 100 years (Galveston, TX, 1900, the deadliest; Andrew, 1992, the costliest; and, the recent Katrina and Rita, 2005, devastating much of the Gulf Coast, including the region's rich cultural heritage, and leading to civil unrest in New Orleans); (3) climate change illustrated in North America and Europe by the "Little Ice Age" (~1450 – 1850) including harsh winters, unusually short growing seasons, and highly variable rain and snow patterns leading to crop failure and famine, disease, and mass migrations; (4) notable volcanic eruptions in 1912, Novarupta, Katmai National Park, AK (world's largest twentieth century eruption) and in 1980, Mt. Saint Helens, WA; and (5) destructive earthquakes, including San Francisco, 1906, and the most powerful recorded earthquake in U.S. and North American history, the 1964 Good Friday temblor and ensuing tsunami in southern AK. In addition, the geologic record contributes substantial data that underscore the vulnerability of these areas over millennia as well as evidence of numerous examples of disasters of far greater magnitude that pre-date written history.

VI. Energy and Mineral Resources Required for a Modern Society

As the world's largest user of energy and mineral resources, it is important to recognize the broad spectrum of natural earth materials requisite to sustain the modern American society. The US uses them to generate its energy; build its infrastructure; fertilize its agriculture; and create the wealth that allows its citizens to buy goods and services globally.

Standing at 5% of the world's population, the US consumes 25% of global energy output. Traditional fossil fuel resources, coal, oil, and natural gas, as well as tar sands, shale gas, and oil shale, comprise the principal sources of combustible fuels for power generation. However, the US is heavily dependent on imported oil and gas, currently approximating 65% and 17% respectively, to feed the nation's ever-increasing thirst for energy. Uranium, a mined mineral, is the fuel for the nuclear power industry. Nuclear reactors currently generate about 20% of the nation's electricity. As energy costs surge, Americans seek to establish policies that move the nation toward energy independence, including (1) tapping remaining domestic supplies of traditional fossil fuels; (2) increasing insulation, improving the efficiency of existing technology, and practicing more conservation; (3) expanding the "greener" wind, solar, tide, geothermal, biomass, and hydro options; and (4) encouraging research and development of technologies that may not even being on the drawing board.

Non-fuel earth materials provide society with the raw materials used in construction, manufacturing, and industries necessary for continued economic growth. Stone, crushed rock, clay (brick), sand and gravel, concrete, iron and steel (nearly pure iron), asphalt, glass, and even recycled materials are fundamental in building and maintaining the nation's infrastructure—its highways, dams, skyscrapers, and houses. Mineral compounds enhance agricultural productivity. As fertilizers, they enrich soils and others are used in herbicide and pesticide synthesis. Minerals are basic raw materials in items we use every day, including dishes and flatware, cars and bicycles, and cameras and stereos. Much of the plastics used throughout our society today come originally from crude oil. Newer technologies often require uncommon raw materials, such as the rare metals platinum, gallium, and indium, increasingly used in solar panels, fuel cells, and light-emitting diodes (LEDs), as well as in familiar items like cell phones, computers, and flat-screen TVs. As with oil and natural gas, the US has insufficient domestic supplies of many mineral resources to meet current and anticipated demand and must turn to other countries to supply them.

VII. Summary: The United States—"A Land of Contrasts"

One approach in visualizing the breadth of variation the United States displays is to review some of the significant natural elements that comprise the fabric of the land and its people. We have described its mountains, rivers, shorelines, plains, valleys and plateaus.

CHAPTER 7 GEOGRAPHY OF THE UNITED STATES

We have identified those earth resources that serve humanity, including economic minerals, energy resources, soil, water and the flora and fauna that are important to the quality of the lives of its citizens. We have also addressed those natural processes that have the potential to impact society in remarkably negative ways, such as earthquakes, hurricanes, landslides, tornadoes and floods. So far, we have addressed overriding themes, including volcanism, glaciation and plate tectonics. However, a comprehensive analysis is beyond the scope of this chapter.

Picture the US as a land remarkably varied and often spectacular. Imagine a land of glacier-capped mountain peaks rising more than 6,000 meters to blazing hot desert floors lying more than 80 meters below sea level; sparkling clear, icy cold melt water streams and bubbling, frothy, sulfuric smelling hot springs. Pools of crystal-clear aquamarine cave ponds or lazy, slow-moving meandering rivers delivering millions of tons of sediment each year to the ocean; as well as the jagged, craggy rocky coasts and the smooth, silica-sand beaches of the shorelines strewn with accumulations of shell fragments, are all accessible in some corner of the USA. Alpine lakes, hot springs, calderas, canyons, caves, fjords, bayous, barrier islands, buttes and deltas, all dot the landscape.

The US has climates varying from *permafrost[135] to desert to tropical rain forest; it also holds an enormously varied flora and fauna of the *prairies[136], tundra, swamps and coral reefs. There are regions that regularly shake, roll, crack and separate with the continuously moving crustal plates, or that erupt violently, spewing ash and lava across the landscape. Vast wilderness refuges, systematically re-planted forests and woodlots, irrigated lands stretching as far as the eye can see, and natural and man-made wetlands are all examples of USA's co-existence with nature.

Within sprawling urbanized corridors, people are steadily trading concrete and asphalt for green space between cities and towns and *boroughs[137] and villages. There still exist isolated, single family farmsteads, small rural hamlets; but they compete with newly developed suburban communities, and modern megalopolises replete with cars, trucks, buses, shopping malls, skyscrapers, parking garages, slums, zoos, subways, congested streets, stoplights, headlights, streetlights, neon lights, government office buildings, colleges and universities, day-care centers, churches, *synagogues[138], *mosques[139], *cathedrals[140], corporate campuses, historic sites, noise, factories, tunnels and big crowds.

Industrious US workers give rise to vineyards, wheat fields, citrus orchards, genetically-engineered livestock, deep and open-pit mines, dredging operations, transcontinental pipelines, wind turbines, electricity-generating plants relying upon fossil fuel, hydro and nuclear energy, multi-level interstate highways, canals, covered bridges, railway networks, river ferries, sea ports, airports, petroleum refineries, meat-packing plants, automobile assembly lines, space-shuttle-launching centers, *cottage[141] industries, military installations, recreational theme parks, health-care facilities, banking/investment centers and research laboratories. Moreover, the US owns a richly diverse mix of indigenous cultures and people from around the world.

Study Questions

1. Construct the definition of a physiographic region by identifying those important factors that are used to characterize a particular region.
2. Compare and contrast the eastern and western coasts of the US relative to (a) erosional and depositional features characterizing the shoreline, (b) the dominant physical processes responsible for shaping them, and (c) the nature of the coastal regions relative to the North American Plate boundaries.
3. Compare and contrast the mountain belt along the eastern US with that of the mountain belt in the western US. Include (a) general age of the geologic units, (b) the shape of landforms, and (c) environmental problems associated with each of these major upland regions of the country.
4. Account for the presence of the broad central lowland portion of the US. Explain the relationship between this region and (a) the adjacent mountain belts, and (b) the continental shield of Canada to the north.
5. Describe the effects of Ice Age glaciation upon the eastern and western mountain belts as well as that of the US interior.
6. For each of the physiographic regions, identify a geologic hazard that has broad environmental and social impact to the residents and propose strategies to address those impacts.
7. Using Plate Tectonic theory, account for the following features along the Pacific Coast: (a) the San Andreas Fault, (b) Mt. Rainier in the Cascade Mountains in WA, and (c) the Aleutian Islands of southwest AK.
8. Support the premise that the physiography of the US has influenced where major populations are concentrated using specific examples from different parts of the country.
9. How does China's physical geography compare and contrast to the USA?
10. Which of the regions in the United States is the most habitable? Why?
11. Identify and rank the most important natural resources for each of the physiographic regions. Justify your conclusions.
12. How has the physical geography of the United States contributed to the spatial and social mobility in the country?
13. Define a "super city". Select one of the American super cities and explain why it became a megalopolis.
14. Why do individual American houses often differ within a neighborhood?
15. How and why have American urban and rural life merged?
16. Do you agree with the human-centered or the earth-centered environmentalists? Why?

Selected Bibliography

Fenneman, N. M., *Physiography of Western United States*. New York, NY, McGraw-Hill Book Company, 1931.

Fenneman, N. M., *Physiography of Eastern United States*. New York, NY, McGraw-Hill

Book Company, 1938.

Harris, A. G. and Tuttle, Esther, *Geology of National Parks*. Dubuque, IA, Kendall/Hunt Publishing Company, 3rd edition, 1984.

Hunt, C. B., *Natural Regions of the United States and Canada*. San Francisco, CA, W. H. Freeman and Company, 1974.

Patterson, J. H., *A Geography of the United States and Canada*. Toronto, ON, Oxford University Press, 9th edition, 1994.

Thornbury, W. D., *Regional Geomorphology of the United States*. New York, NY, John Wiley and Sons, Inc., 1965.

Bell, Daniel, *The Coming of the Post-Industrial Society*. NY: Basic Books, 1973.

Encyclopaedia Britannica, "The United States: Physical and Human Geography." Chicago, IL: *Encyclopedia Britannica*, 15th ed., 1998.

Konrad, Victor A. and others, *A Characterization of North America*. Commission for Environmental Cooperation. 1996 Draft.

Miller, G. Tyler, *Environmental Science*. Belmont, CA: Wadsworth Publishing Co., 1997.

US National Park Service, Department of the Interior. 1849 C Street Washington, D. C. USA. 20240

World Almanac and Book of Facts, Mahwah, NJ: Funk & Wagnall, 1996.

Web Addresses (URLs).

United States Department of the Interior (DOI), http://www.doi.gov/ This Executive Department is charged with handling the Nation's internal development and the welfare of its people.

United States Geological Survey (USGS), http://www.usgs.gov/ This Bureau stands as the sole science agency for the DOI.

United States National Park Service (NPS), http://www.nps.gov/ This DOI Bureau preserves the natural and cultural resources of the Nation's park system.

注　释

[1] 大豆。
[2] 〔植物(学)〕紫花苜蓿(豆科牧草,供作饲料)。
[3] 水产养殖。
[4] 污水,污秽物。
[5] 被围困的,处于困境的。
[6] 拟人法地。
[7] 几人合乘一辆车。
[8] 市郊间上下班交通。
[9] 特大城市,特大都市。
[10] (尤指美国、加拿大的)大牧场。
[11] (建)棋盘式街道布局。
[12] 大城市,大都会。
[13] 郊区居民。
[14] (指城市等)无计划地向外扩展(延伸)。
[15] 垃圾处理场地。
[16] 地中海的。
[17] 美国航空航天局。
[18] 亚热带的。
[19] 国会大厦。
[20] 缩影,象征。
[21] 纽约的一个黑人居住区。
[22] 共性。
[23] (地)板块构造的。
[24] 地壳构造上的。
[25] 冰川,冰河。
[26] 地形的。
[27] 地貌的。

〔28〕地质的。
〔29〕地势低。
〔30〕自然地理,地貌。
〔31〕浮游植物群落。
〔32〕用显微镜才可见的,极小的。
〔33〕浮游生物。
〔34〕浅滩,沙洲。
〔35〕水生的。
〔36〕层。
〔37〕风化(作用)。
〔38〕(地)碎屑状的。
〔39〕压紧的。
〔40〕使突然发生。
〔41〕(风吹积成的)沙丘。
〔42〕白垩纪(13,600 万年以前)。
〔43〕第三纪的。
〔44〕第四纪的。
〔45〕更新世。
〔46〕加拿大的沿海诸省。
〔47〕淹没的,浸在水中的。
〔48〕山麓地带。
〔49〕工程师队。
〔50〕(美)各户有独立产权的公寓(即所属房产为私有,草地、庭院等场地为公有)。
〔51〕飓风。
〔52〕旋风。
〔53〕耸人听闻的。
〔54〕即 northeaster,意为东北大风或暴风。
〔55〕海龙卷。
〔56〕相接的。
〔57〕北回归线。
〔58〕生态系统。
〔59〕杀虫剂。
〔60〕除草剂。
〔61〕布满湖泊的。
〔62〕残余山丘。
〔63〕暴风雪。
〔64〕(指岩石)火成的。
〔65〕变质的,变形的。
〔66〕岩浆。
〔67〕花岗岩。
〔68〕熔岩。
〔69〕变质作用。
〔70〕断层的。
〔71〕前寒武纪的。
〔72〕古生代的。
〔73〕片麻岩。
〔74〕片岩。

〔75〕板岩。
〔76〕石英岩。
〔77〕地貌学的。
〔78〕页岩,泥板岩。
〔79〕加拿大地盾。
〔80〕冰川作用。
〔81〕岩层。
〔82〕(经风雨或水侵蚀而成的)巨石。
〔83〕(河流的)三角洲。
〔84〕涝原。
〔85〕围绕,包围。
〔86〕自然保护区。
〔87〕岩石层。
〔88〕地层。
〔89〕熨斗,烙铁。
〔90〕锯齿状突起。
〔91〕火山口。
〔92〕洼地,凹地。
〔93〕(地)巨火山口。
〔94〕喷泉,间歇泉。
〔95〕排气口。
〔96〕小泉。
〔97〕(地)热液的。
〔98〕禁猎区,保护区。
〔99〕雅致的,豪华的。
〔100〕庞大的。
〔101〕露天开采(矿石)。
〔102〕(美国西南部)干涸的小河道。
〔103〕(美国西南部)孤山,孤峰。
〔104〕平顶山。
〔105〕玄武岩的。
〔106〕垂直的。
〔107〕扇状三角洲。
〔108〕印第安人居住地。
〔109〕(美国)(采木区的)新兴城镇。
〔110〕无数的,大量的。
〔111〕岬角(突入海中的高地)。
〔112〕大卵石。
〔113〕海啸。
〔114〕有危险的。
〔115〕低谷,天沟。
〔116〕分水岭。
〔117〕沟渠。
〔118〕阿留申岛人。
〔119〕群岛。
〔120〕冻土地带,冻原。
〔121〕气流。
〔122〕环状珊瑚岛。

CHAPTER 7　GEOGRAPHY OF THE UNITED STATES

〔123〕浅滩。
〔124〕地柱。
〔125〕沥滤。
〔126〕含有红土的。
〔127〕石灰质的。
〔128〕碱性的。
〔129〕镁。
〔130〕橄榄石。
〔131〕碳酸盐。
〔132〕光电伏特的。
〔133〕澳洲坚果。
〔134〕丰富,大量。
〔135〕(地)永久冻土。
〔136〕(北美的)大草原。
〔137〕自治的镇区。
〔138〕犹太教会堂。
〔139〕清真寺。
〔140〕大教堂。
〔141〕(度假)别墅。

CHAPTER 8   HISTORY OF THE UNITED STATES

Prof. Zhou Shulin and Dr. Carol W. Pollard

I. Introduction

The history of the United States is the story of a great nation that was carved out of a wilderness by a brave and freedom-loving people. The men and women who built the United States came from almost every part of the world. They represented many different nationalities, races and religions. Through the years, the people and their descendants have learned to live and work together in a multi-ethnic society and take pride in being Americans. The history of the United States tells how a people survived numerous challenges and hardships, including dangers in the wilderness, wars, social turmoil and economic depressions.

II. Native Americans

When he "discovered" America, Christopher Columbus named the people or Native Americans, "Indians" because he believed he had landed in India. It is generally believed that Indians wandered into North America from Asia 20,000 years or more ago. By the time the Europeans appeared, about 1,500,000 people were living in all areas of North and South America.

Indians in different regions developed different types of cultures. The foods and other resources available in each region largely determined the prevailing culture. For example, while the *acorn[1] was a staple food for California Indians, fish and sea *mammals[2] contributed the bulk of the food supply for eastern coastal tribes, and plant life and wild game comprised the diet for the Indians living on the *Great Plains[3]. Indian culture groups were also distinguished by many other characteristics. Language, clothing and architecture varied among native groups, as did crafts, weapons, and tribal, economic, social and religious customs.

The American Indians exercised an influence on the white civilization transplanted from Europe to the New World. Indian foods and herbs, methods of raising some crops, war techniques, vocabulary, a rich folklore, arts and crafts were among the general contributions of the Indians to their white conquerors.

Europeans, on the other hand, had a great and deleterious impact on the American Indians. When they began to explore the New Continent, they brought with them deadly diseases, including *small pox[4], which killed thousands of Indians in both North and South America. Europeans also introduced horses, guns and other technologies, which radically changed the lives of Native Americans.

III. Colonial North America

1. EXPLORATION AND EARLY SETTLEMENT

In 1492, Christopher Columbus, financed by the Spanish King and Queen, set sail westward, trying to find a short route to the East. He reached land on October 12, 1492, assuming he had arrived in the Far East. Actually he and his sailors had landed on San Salvador, an island east of North America. Columbus died in 1506, still believing that he had sailed to the Far East. But other Europeans realized he had arrived in an unexplored land which they called the New World.

The discovery of the New World caused great excitement in Europe . To many Europeans, the New World offered opportunities for wealth, land, power and adventure. Soon after Columbus' discovery, Europeans from several countries sailed across the Atlantic to explore America and to set up trading posts and colonies.

The Spanish and Portuguese spread out over the southern part of the New World in search of gold and other riches. The Spanish also established *religious missions[5] and other settlements in the West and South. By 1600, Spain and Portugal controlled most of the hemisphere from Mexico southward. All the Spanish colonies were royal property under the strict control of the Spanish King. The King found it more and more difficult to administer the distant colonies. As a result, the Spanish colonies in North and South America did not flourish.

At approximately the same time, the French and English were also exploring the New World. At first both nations sent only explorers and fur traders. But after 1600, they began establishing permanent settlements. The French settlements were chiefly in what is now Canada. The British settlements included the thirteen colonies along the Atlantic Ocean, and later, became the United States. The turning point in American history occurred when the English Navy defeated the *Spanish Armada[6] in a great sea battle (1588) and thereby gained control of the main sea routes.

Unlike the Spanish territories, the English colonies were not controlled directly by the British government. Instead, the monarch granted charters to private trading companies. These chartered companies induced people to emigrate permanently to America.

During the reign of King James I (1603 - 1625), the English-American colonies began to flourish. At that time, Great Britain was beset with religious disputes and economic problems. Many people who were forced to leave Great Britain immigrated to the thirteen English colonies, the beginning of the United States.

2. THE THIRTEEN BRITISH COLONIES

By the mid-1700's, the thirteen British colonies had been settled, stretching from what is now Maine in the north to Georgia in the south. They included the four New England colonies of Massachusetts, Connecticut, Rhode Island, and New Hampshire in the far north; the six Middle Colonies of New York, New Jersey, Pennsylvania, Delaware, Virginia and Maryland; and the three Southern colonies of North Carolina, South Carolina, and Georgia in the far south.

Virginia and Maryland were among the earliest British colonies. In 1607, the London Trading Company sent three ships with 104 people to the coast of Virginia, named in honor of the late Elizabeth I, the Virgin Queen. They built a settlement and named it Jamestown in honor of King James I. The Virginians demanded self-government. In order to attract more people to the colony, the London Company agreed, and in 1619, *the House of Burgesses[7], the first freely elected, representative legislature in America was established.

The founder of Maryland was a wealthy English Roman Catholic named Calvert. He intended to provide a place for Catholics who were persecuted in England. In 1649, *the Calvert family[8] granted religious freedom to people of both the Catholic and Protestant faiths.

A) New England

*Puritans[9], originally financed by the Virginia Company, founded the New England colonies. In 1620, a group of 132 *Separatists[10] (Puritans who had "separated" or left the Church of England) boarded the Mayflower and sailed for Virginia. The Mayflower was blown off course and landed in what is now Massachusetts, far to the north of Virginia. Since this group of people went to the New World for religious purposes, they were called Pilgrims. They founded Plymouth colony in 1620 and the Massachusetts Bay colony in 1630. Plymouth became part of the Massachusetts colony in 1691.

As time passed, a puritanical religious conformity was rigorously imposed on all people in Massachusetts. People who could no longer endure the life there began to move away, eventually settling in three other colonies in New England: Connecticut, Rhode Island, and New Hampshire.

The Puritans also contributed to American political life. While sailing to America, the Pilgrims wrote the Mayflower Compact which required that "just and equal laws" be applied to all male adults. Since the Pilgrims landed by mistake in Massachusetts, they were not under the authority of the London Company in Virginia. Instead, they governed themselves through their elected representatives. The New England states, including Maine and Vermont, which were created after the independence of the United States, are generally puritan in tradition. To this day, these New Englanders generally favor diligence, thrift, self-government and puritan morality—beliefs which form an important part of American national values.

B) The Middle Colonies

Originally, New York, New Jersey and Delaware were Dutch settlements, but after 1664 these three settlements became British colonies. In 1681, William Penn received a royal charter and became the *proprietor[11] of Pennsylvania. Penn was a member of the *Quakers[12], a *pacifist[13] religious group that had been persecuted in many countries. Penn adopted a tolerant policy, and Quakers and other settlers who sought freedom flocked to Pennsylvania.

C) The Southern Colonies

The large tract of land between Virginia and Florida called Carolina was given by King Charles II to eight proprietors in 1663. After 1663, British settlers, French Protestants and Americans from other colonies poured into Carolina. In 1712, North Carolina and South Carolina were established in the northern part of the Carolina territory, taking up approximately two-thirds of the land.

In South Carolina, rich landlords owned large *indigo[14] plantations. In order to find enough laborers to work on the plantations, the land owners brought large numbers of Africans to the colony as slaves. The first African slaves arrived in Virginia in 1619. By the late 1600's, they became the dominant labor force as far north as the *Chesapeake Bay[15] region.

The southern one-third of Carolina remained unsettled until 1772. Then *James Oglethorpe[16] of England founded Georgia and established the colony as a place of refuge for impoverished debtors from England.

3. LIFE IN COLONIAL AMERICA
A) Immigration

Most immigrants came from Britain and are sometimes known as WASPS (White Anglo-Saxon Protestants). However, the colonies also drew people from almost every other country of Western Europe. Settlers went to America for various reasons. Puritans, Quakers, Roman Catholics, and Huguenots (French Protestants) immigrated for religious reasons.

Other Europeans moved to America for economic reasons. Many poor people went to America as indentured servants. An indentured servant signed a contract before he left his home country agreeing to work for his master in America for seven years. In return, the master paid for the servant's transportation and provided him with food, clothing and shelter for the length of the contract.

The most important reason for making the dangerous ocean crossing was the availability of land. Europe was overpopulated, and land was very expensive. In most European countries primogeniture was the law; only the eldest son inherited all of the family's property. Thus, some of the immigrants to the British colonies were the second and third sons of the land-owning *gentry[17] class. In America land was plentiful and nearly free for the taking.

Some people immigrated to America involuntarily. For instance, prisoners from overcrowded English jails, Irish prisoners captured by the English in battle, and Africans captured in intertribal warfare were transported to America as laborers by European traders.

Immigration throughout the colonial period reflected distinctive lines of demarcation, characterized by varying nationalities in different time periods. During the 17th century most of the immigrants were English. Beginning in the second decade of the 18th-century a wave of Germans arrived in America; by 1770, approximately 250,000 Germans had immigrated to America, mostly settling in the Middle Colonies. The Scots-Irish and Irish immigration began on a large scale after 1713 and continued after the American Revolutionary War.

Through immigration and natural growth, the colonial population rose to 1.3 million by 1753. Despite the various backgrounds of the early immigrants, Americans of the mid-1700's (excluding African slaves) were said to have "melted into a new race of men".

B) Colonial Economy and Politics

Economically, the thirteen colonies developed rapidly. Though subsistence agriculture remained significant well into the 1830's, trade began to flourish during the colonial period. The colonies traded with the French, Dutch and Spanish, although they traded chiefly with Britain, whose manufacturing firms depended on raw materials from its colonies. In return the colonists received manufactured goods and were still under British royal rule.

However, because of the distance separating England and America and the powerful pressures exerted on royal officials by Americans, royal power was gradually weakened while the elected colonial governments gained political strength in the affairs of their respective colonies. By the mid-18th century most political power in America was in the hands of colonial officials.

Since most of the immigrants went to America because they were dissatisfied with their experiences in their home countries, they wanted to change old ideas and carry out reforms. They strongly rejected the old idea that government was an institution inherited from the past. They preferred to create a limited government for their own needs. To them, laws made in Britain were meaningless unless they were enforced. Since this was difficult to do, many Americans colonists simply ignored British laws. This independent attitude soon led to a clash between the Americans and the British government.

Ⅳ. The Founding of the United States

1. FRENCH AND INDIAN WAR (1753—1761)

Throughout the colonial period, Britain and France struggled for control of eastern North America. As settlers moved westward, both nations claimed the vast territory between the Appalachian Mountains and the Mississippi River. The struggle became fiercer and finally led to the outbreak of the French and Indian War (1754 - 1762), in which the English with their Indian allies eventually defeated the French and their Indian allies. In the Treaty of Paris (1763), the British gained control of what is now Canada and the upper Mississippi River Valley. After Britain acquired Florida from Spain in the same year, the British controlled all of North America from the Atlantic Ocean to the Mississippi River.

2. BRITISH POLICIES

The French and Indian War was a major turning point in American history. When Britain doubled its territory at the end of the war, the British government carried out a series of unpopular policies to control this vast region. These changes caused many Americans to seriously consider independence from England. One of these unpopular policies began in 1763 when the British government decided to station an army in North America. Two years later the British Parliament ordered the colonists to provide British troops with food and living quarters. In order to keep peace in North America, Britain sought to establish good relations with the Indians. To prevent the Indians from losing more land to the white settlers, Britain decided in 1763 to prohibit American colonists from settling west of the Appalachian Mountains, a policy which greatly affected the colonists' interest in territorial expansion.

Another problem caused by the French and Indian War was that Britain incurred heavy debts. To solve the problem the British Parliament passed taxation laws, which forced the colonists to pay their share of the cost of the war. The Sugar Act (1764) taxed molasses imported into the colonies. To enforce the Sugar Act, British officials claimed the right to search any person who was suspected of violating the law. Parliament also passed the *Stamp Act[18] (1765), which extended to the colonies the traditional English tax on newspapers, legal documents and other printed matter.

Many American colonists were bitterly opposed and hostile to these laws. As the colonists did not have representatives in the British Parliament, they argued Britain had no right to tax them. Besides, they feared that the new measures reflected a desire by the King to enhance his power. They also resented British efforts to tighten control over the colonial economy. In protest, the colonists organized a widespread boycott of British goods. In order to ease tensions the British Parliament repealed the Stamp Act (1766), but insisted that colonists obey all British laws. When Parliament passed the Townshend Acts (1767), which taxed lead, paint, paper, and tea imported into the colonies, the colonists boycotted English goods once again. As tensions between Americans and British grew, Britain sent troops to Boston and New York. On March 5, 1770, angry Boston citizens taunted a group of British troops. When the troops fired on the citizens, three Bostonians died and eight were wounded. Dubbed the *"Boston Massacre"[19], the incident was regarded as proof of British tyranny.

Faced with such opposition, Parliament repealed all provisions of the Townshend Acts (1770) with one exception, the tax on tea. Angry Americans vowed not to drink tea, and colonial merchants refused to sell it. On December 16, 1773, a group of American colonists boarded three East India Company ships for the explicit purpose of throwing the tea cargo into Boston harbor. This incident later became known as the "Boston Tea Party".

3. THE FIRST CONTINENTAL CONGRESS

Angered by Boston Tea Party, Parliament in 1774 passed a set of laws to punish the colonists. The laws included provisions that closed the port of Boston and required the colonists to provide British soldiers with food and lodging.

The colonists called theses laws "The Intolerable Acts". On September 5, 1774, twelve of the thirteen colonies, excluding Georgia, sent delegates to meet in Philadelphia for *the First Continental Congress[20]. The delegates called for an end to all trade with Britain until Parliament repealed the Intolerable Acts, and they drew up the Declaration of Rights and Grievances. When the Declaration of Rights and Grievances was sent to Parliament, it was rejected. King George III (1760 - 1820) had no intention of making concessions, and armed clashes between the two sides seemed inevitable.

4. THE SECOND CONTINENTAL CONGRESS

On April 19, 1775, British troops tried to confiscate the munitions of the Massachusetts militia. When fighting broke out, eight Americans were killed. Now the Congress faced the new task of preparing the colonies for war. On May 10, 1775, the colonial leaders met in Philadelphia for the Second Continental Congress. The Congress organized the Continental Army, and George Washington from Virginia was appointed commander-in-chief of the Army. To further mobilize people *Thomas Paine[21], a political theorist, published a 50-page pamphlet, "Common Sense". The pamphlet greatly helped to rally the masses of American people to the cause of independence.

5. THE DECLARATION OF INDEPENDENCE (1776)

As more and more Americans favored independence, there was an urgent need for a formal declaration to legitimize the movement. On July 4, 1776 the Second Continental Congress officially declared independence and formed the United States of America by adopting the Declaration of Independence, written by Thomas Jefferson of Virginia. The document declared that "all men are created equal" and are "endowed by their creator" with certain "inalienable rights" including "life, liberty, and the pursuit of happiness". (See Appendix for the Preamble to the Declaration of Independence.) In order to protect these rights, men organize governments, and governments derive their just powers only from the consent of the governed. However, when a government ceases to protect these rights, it is the duty of the people to change the government or to abolish it and to form a new one.

6. WAR FOR INDEPENDENCE (1776-1781)

When the American War for Independence began, the colonists were in an unfavorable position. They had a population of about 3 million while Britain had about 10 million. Under Britain's colonial policy American manufacturing was backward while Britain was the most industrialized nation in the world. Americans lacked a well-trained army, officers, equipment and money. They had no warships, in contrast to the British Navy, the strongest in the world, which had about 80 large warships. However, the Americans had several advantages over the British. The American cause was supported by France and other European nations that opposed Britain. Americans fought on their home territory while the British were fighting in an unfamiliar land thousands of miles away from home. Above all, the American soldiers had a high morale which the British soldiers lacked.

The War for Independence lasted more than six years. For quite some time after independence was declared, the Americans suffered severe setbacks. However, the situation began to change in 1777. Increasingly, the British government found it difficult to reinforce its troops and supply enough war materials for its army. France sent an expeditionary force of 6,000 men, and the French fleet cut off the British army's supply line. Finally in 1781, the combined armies of America and France defeated the British army. The peace settlement (1783) acknowledged the independence, freedom, and sovereignty of the thirteen states. The treaty granted the United States the land from the Atlantic Ocean to the Mississippi River and set the boundary between Canada and United States.

Ⅴ. Forming A New Nation

The original thirteen colonies became the first thirteen states of the United States. These states were determined to have a weak national government. In the Articles of Confederation the federal government was given the power to declare war and manage foreign affairs, but it was not allowed to collect taxes. Therefore, the United States was unable to pay the high national debt it incurred during the War for Independence. Also the government lacked the means for raising money to provide for national defense, and the federal government had no power to regulate the nation's trade. In addition, some states issued their own paper money. Revising the Articles of Confederation became an urgent issue.

1. THE CONSTITUTIONAL CONVENTION

Twelve states, except for Rhode Island, sent sixty-five delegates, including George Washington and *Benjamin Franklin[22], to Philadelphia's Independence Hall for a *Constitutional Convention[23]. Washington, because of his integrity and his leadership during the war, was chosen as chairman. Although Benjamin Franklin was 81 years old, he helped ease some of the difficulties among the other delegates with his kindly humor and wide experience.

The delegates debated long and hard over the contents of the US Constitution. Some wanted to strengthen the power of the federal government; others wanted to protect the rights of the states and demanded a weak central government. Some delegates wanted to exclude the West from statehood; other delegates favored statehood for the West. The Northern states favored protective tariffs and free labor while the Southern states wanted low tariffs and slavery.

All the arguments, with one exception, were settled through compromises. For example, representatives of small states, such as New Jersey, demanded equal representation in Congress with the large states while representatives of large states, such as Virginia, argued for proportional representation reflecting the population of each state. This debate threatened to go on endlessly until a Connecticut delegate came forward with convincing arguments for congressional representation in proportion to the population of the states in the House of Representatives and two representatives each from both the large and the small states in the *Senate[24]. The one issue that could not be satisfactorily resolved was the issue of slavery; Northern and Southern states could not agree on a compromise. The acceptance of slavery by the northern states contradicted the Declaration of Independence, which said, "All men are created equal...". Since this compromise was never fully accepted by the abolitionists, the controversy was settled a century later in the American Civil War (1861 – 1865).

On September 17, 1787, after sixteen weeks of deliberation, the delegates finally finished the new constitution. Franklin relieved the tension with a characteristic sally. Pointing to the half sun painted on the back of Washington's chair, he said, "I have often, in the course of the session . . . looked at that behind the President, without being able to tell whether it was rising or setting; but now, at length, I have the happiness to know that it is a rising, and not a setting sun".

2. THE UNITED STATES CONSTITUTION

Before the Constitution became law, it needed ratification by nine states. Americans who supported the new constitution were called *Federalists[25] while those who opposed it were called Anti-Federalists. The Anti-Federalists opposed the Constitution because it strengthened the powers of the national government and lessened the power of the states. *Alexander Hamilton[26], *James Madison[27], and *John Jay[28], who represented the Federalists, helped to gain much support for the Constitution through the *Federalist Papers[29], a series of letters to newspapers. The US Constitution was ultimately approved by all the states, and the first government for the United States was installed in 1789.

The first Congress of the new United States sent the Bill of Rights, the first ten amendments to the Constitution, to the states for their approval (1791). These ten amendments guaranteed individual freedom of speech, religion, the press, the right to trial by jury, the right to bear arms, the right to security from unreasonable searches and seizures and the right to avoid self-incrimination. The Bill of Rights also gave the states and the American people all rights not included in the Constitution as long as the state laws did not contradict federal laws. The Bill of Rights placed limits on what the government could do to its people. For most Americans it remains the most important part of the US Constitution.

The US Constitution also provided for *checks-and-balances[30] between the three branches of government. Each branch was given powers and duties that ensured that the other branches would not have too much power. The President (the Executive Branch) is head of the army, can propose and veto legislation, and execute laws passed by Congress (the Legislative Branch). The President has no power to dismiss Congress, and Congress can not remove the President from office without following legal procedures based on good reasons. Congress is responsible for writing national laws, printing money, enacting budgets and levying taxes. The US Supreme Court (the Judicial Branch) has the right to interpret the Constitution and determine whether the acts of the President and the Congress are constitutional. Thus, because the functions of government are divided, the US government is a "weak" form of government.

According to the Constitution, the President is elected by an Electoral College. The Electoral College comprises representatives of each state who cast their ballots based on the results of the national popular elections. In 1789, the Electoral College unanimously chose George Washington to be the first American president.

3. GEORGE WASHINGTON'S PRESIDENCY (1789—1797)

The new government faced serious financial problems, and the American people were divided about taxation. The debt incurred during the Revolutionary War posed a threat to finances in foreign affairs. In 1793, France went to war against Britain and Spain. Since France had helped the Americans in their War for Independence, it now expected the United States' assistance in its war. The United States also needed internal improvements such as roads and bridges, but the national government did not have any money. How to deal with the financial problems? The nation split into two groups. One group led by the *Secretary of the Treasury[31], Alexander Hamilton, wanted the government to take powerful action. Hamilton wanted to increase tariffs and tax domestic products, such as liquor. The government could use the tax money to pay the debts and make internal improvements. Hamilton also was in favor of a government-supported national bank to control government finances.

Another group, headed by the *Secretary of State[32], Thomas Jefferson, opposed government participation in economic affairs. Jefferson and his followers, mostly farmers and merchants, denounced Hamilton's plans. They were afraid that a strong central government with the power to tax would only benefit wealthy people. Jefferson also argued that the President and Congress had no power to establish a national bank because it was not written in the Constitution. Their way of interpreting the Constitution was known as the narrow or strict interpretation of the Constitution. Hamilton insisted that Congress and the President had such power for it was "implied", if not clearly written, in the Constitution. Hamilton and his followers interpreted the Constitution in a broad sense, known as the broad interpretation. Eventually Congress did establish the national bank. Jefferson was so angry that he resigned his position as Secretary of State and organized a new political party, the Democratic-Republican Party which became the forefather of today's Democratic Party.

George Washington and many other American leaders opposed political parties. However, in the 1790's, the disputes over government policies led to the establishment of two parties. Hamilton and his followers, chiefly Northerners, formed the Federalist Party, which favored a strong federal government and was generally sympathetic with Britain. Jefferson and his followers, chiefly Southerners, established the Democratic-Republican Party, which advocated a weak central government and was generally sympathetic with France.

The new government also faced problems in foreign affairs. In 1793, when France declared war against Britain and Spain, Americans were divided over which side to support. President Washington insisted that the United States remain neutral so that the nation could concentrate on its internal economic development. Neutrality in foreign affairs became a major theme in American foreign affairs for decades.

Gradually, the federal government became stronger. In 1795, Thomas Pinckney negotiated a treaty with Spain, which gave Americans the right to use the Mississippi River freely and settled the Florida border dispute between the two countries.

In 1796, Washington, "The Father of America", firmly refused to seek a third term as president and retired to his farm in Virginia. He set an example for future presidents; no president should serve more than two four-year-terms. The wartime presidency of Franklin Roosevelt (1933 – 1945) was the only exception to this rule.

4. THOMAS JEFFERSON AND JEFFERSONIAN DEMOCRACY

Jefferson, the third president, was elected in 1801 and again in 1804 following John Adams (1797 – 1800), Washington's successor. Jefferson was the first Democratic-Republican President, and his inauguration marked the beginning of the peaceful political transition from one political party to another in America.

Jefferson's political philosophy was known as Jeffersonian Democracy. Jefferson advocated a nation of small farmers. In his ideal society, people would lead simple yet productive lives and be able to direct their own affairs. Therefore, the national government should be weak and be an advocate of individual rights. He also promised to establish "a wise and frugal government which should preserve order among the inhabitants", but would "leave them otherwise free to regulate their own pursuit of industry and improvements".

Jefferson enjoyed extraordinary favor because of his idealism and his liberal ideas. To him, the plainest citizen was as worthy of respect as the highest officer. He taught his subordinates to regard themselves merely as trustees of the people. He favored "absolute acquiescence in the decisions of the majority" and opposed "every form of tyranny over the mind of man". Jeffersonian Democracy appealed to the great mass of people, and Jefferson earned himself the name of "a born popular leader".

A) The Louisiana Purchase

The first major action that President Jefferson took was the Louisiana Purchase, a purchase which doubled the size of the United States. The large area between the Mississippi River and the Rocky Mountains called Louisiana, originally belonged to Spain. In 1801, France, under the leadership of *Napoleon[33], acquired control of the land. Jefferson viewed French control of Louisiana as a danger to the United States. Also Jefferson wanted Americans to develop the Louisiana Territory for the benefit of American agriculture and commerce.

France, then at war with Britain, decided to sell Louisiana to the United States rather than allow the USA to become a British ally. The Louisiana Purchase (1803) added 2,144,476 square kilometers of territory to the United States. In 1804, Jefferson commissioned *Meriwether Lewis[34] and *William Clark[35] to lead an expedition through the Louisiana Territory. Lewis and Clark's adventures and detailed reports provided valuable information about the Indians, flora and fauna, and geography in the western territory. Equally important, their explorations gave the United States claim to the land to the Pacific Ocean.

B) The War of 1812

In 1803, Britain and France went to war again. Jefferson declared American neutrality. The British government, relying on its strong navy, which had more than 700 warships, manned by nearly 150,000 sailors and marines, prohibited all trade between France and neutrals, including the United States. The embargo directly affected America's interests and aroused indignation among Americans.

Though Britain had a strong navy, many sailors were so poorly treated that they deserted and found refuge on American vessels. The British Navy began to search American ships and forcibly remove British sailors. Moreover, British officers frequently impressed American seamen, seizing them and forcing them into British service. On June 18, 1812, when Congress declared war with Britain, the War of 1812 began.

The United States was barely prepared for war. First of all, Americans were not unified in their attitudes towards the war. Generally, while the South and West favored the war, New York and New England opposed it. Big bankers and merchants were strongly against the war, for they were afraid the war might end their profitable foreign business. As a result, New England bankers refused to lend money to the government, and the New England state governments refused to order their state militia into national service. When declaring war, America had fewer than 7,000 regular soldiers who were widely scattered along the Atlantic coast, near the Canadian border, or in the remote interior.

When the British Army captured Washington, D.C., and burned *the Capitol[36], Americans realized that their independence was at stake. Large numbers of volunteers rushed into service, fought bravely to stop the British offensive. On the night of September 12, 1814, the British fleet attacked Baltimore bombarding *Fort McHenry[37] throughout the night. Francis Scott Key, a young Maryland lawyer detained on a British ship, was greatly moved by the bravery and perseverance of the American soldiers. He was inspired to write *"The Star-Spangled Banner"[38], which became the national anthem of the United States in 1931.

The war, sometimes called the "Second War for Independence", continued indecisively for nearly three years. Ultimately, both sides agreed to the Treaty of Ghent on December 24, 1814, which brought peace and established a commission to settle boundary disputes.

VI. Nationalism and the Economy

1. NATIONALISM

Nationalism and increased feelings of self-confidence and unity grew among Americans after the War of 1812. Few would doubt America's ability to defend itself even against the powerful British Empire. The popular slogan was "Union and Liberty". The Federalist Party disintegrated, and the bitterness that had marked political disputes eased.

2. THE MONROE DOCTRINE

Before and during *James Monroe's[39] presidency (1817 – 1825) a series of revolutions occurred in Latin America, and, by 1822, the revolutionaries were successful. The United States recognized these revolutionary governments. In order to prevent France and Russia from helping Spain regain her colonies from the revolutionists, Monroe declared that any intervention in the affairs of those nations whose independence the United States had already recognized must be considered to be "the manifestation of an unfriendly disposition toward the United States". This speech (1825), which was later known as *"Monroe Doctrine"[40], was designed to secure the Pacific Northwest and Latin America from further European intervention. It later became a principle of US intervention whenever its national interests were threatened.

3. FURTHER PEACE

The peace that followed the War of 1812 enabled America to concentrate on domestic affairs. Historians sometimes called this period "The Era of Good Feeling" because the economy prospered, the nation expanded westward, new states entered the union and the nation gained two new territories between 1815 and 1820. In 1818 a treaty with Britain gave America the Red River Basin, north of the Louisiana Territory, and Spain ceded Florida to the United States in 1819.

4. THE AMERICAN SYSTEM

After the War of 1812, Americans realized the importance of a strong national economy. Henry Clay and other nationalists proposed economic measures that were called the "American System". They advocated higher tariffs to protect American manufacturers and farmers from foreign competition. With the growth of industry, more people would be employed; more employment would lead to greater consumption of farm products, and prosperous farmers would buy more manufactured goods. The "American System" was soon adopted.

In 1816, Congress enacted a high tariff and re-chartered the National Bank to give the government more control over the economy. The government also increased funding for the internal projects. The most important project was the National Road, connecting the eastern and western regions of the country from Cumberland, Maryland to Vandalia, Illinois.

5. THE NEW PARTY SYSTEM AND "COMMON MAN" POLITICS

Between the presidential elections of 1824 and 1840, a new political party system took shape. In the election of 1824, four Democratic-Republicans, including *John Quincy Adams[41] and Andrew *Jackson[42], wanted to succeed Monroe as President. Jackson received the most electoral votes, but he did not win a majority. As prescribed by the US Constitution, the *House of Representatives[43] had to decide, and the House selected John Quincy Adams to be president. Embittered, Jackson and his followers formed a separate wing of the Democratic-Republican Party, which soon developed into the Democratic Party. The result was a vigorous two-party system, which was adopted throughout the country, including the South and West. The control of public affairs became less exclusively the business of a small number of people from old and distinguished families in the East.

6. JACKSONIAN DEMOCRACY

Andrew Jackson was elected for two terms (1829 - 1837). Unlike the presidents before him, Jackson was born into a poor family who lived in a log cabin. Jackson gained support from Western farmers, *frontiersmen[44], city laborers and craftsmen. He promised to end the "monopoly" of government by the rich and to protect the interests of the "common man". He carried out the policy of equal political power for all, known as "Jacksonian Democracy".

The rise of "common men" was by no means unique in the Jacksonian era. Ordinary men had been increasing their wealth and social status ever since the colonial period. By the end of the 18th century, there had emerged in America an upper class of wealthy merchants and landowners.

In order to protect the interest of the "common man", Jackson launched a major crusade against the Second National Bank of the United States. The bank's duties included regulating the nation's money supply. Jackson believed that the bank operated as a monopoly that favored the wealthy. In 1832, Congress voted to re-charter the bank, but Jackson vetoed the bill. Soon he withdrew the government's money from the bank, and the bank collapsed.

However, Jacksonian Democracy did not bring about the "rise of every common man". It is true that in the 1820's and 1830's some ambitious and energetic young white men found opportunities in the relatively fluid society to achieve material success. With economic affluence they or their children soon gained both political influence and social prestige. However, only a limited number of men like Jackson emerged from the ranks of common men into the ranks of the elite. Instead, the great majority of common men in the Jacksonian era, as in those that preceded and followed it, established "middle class" respectability.

VII. Westward Expansion

1. THE THREE GREAT AMERICAN FRONTIERS

Many historians divide the westward expansion of the United States into three great frontiers. The first frontier was the eastern seaboard, from the Atlantic Ocean to the Appalachian Mountains, where the European colonists established the thirteen American states.

The Westward Movement is a term usually used to describe the second and third frontiers. The second frontier was the west of the early United States, the region between the Appalachian Mountains and the Mississippi River. After the Louisiana Purchase (1803) and the War of 1812 and the subsequent removal of the Indians, large scale western expansion into this region occurred. At that time the US government sold land cheaply to frontiersmen and their families, for as little as one dollar an acre if they would clear and farm the land. These incentives, along with improved transportation, the depleted farmland in the East as well as increased emigration from Europe motivated many families to move westward. Furthermore, from the late 1830's to the early 1840's the federal government forcibly removed Eastern Indian tribes to the Great Plains area west of the Mississippi River. This policy allowed settlers to move into Indian lands without fear of reprisals.

The third frontier was the Great West (Far West), stretching from the Mississippi River to the Pacific Ocean and can be subdivided into two sections: the territory between the Mississippi River and the Rocky Mountains and the region between the Rocky Mountains and the Pacific coast. In 1850 when California was admitted into the Union as the 31st state, the western movement had been completed. In 1810 only about 14% of Americans lived west of the Appalachian Mountains. By 1840, more than 1/3 of the American people lived in the West. By the 1830's the frontiers had flowed across the Mississippi into Iowa, Missouri, Arkansas, and eastern Texas. The land beyond, called the Great Plains, was dry and treeless, and the soil was relatively infertile. It was only during the latter half of the 20th century that this region became popular. Large numbers of people moved into the region after the government built large dams, which provided water for larger populations.

2. THE MEXICAN WAR (1846—1848)

After the Louisiana Purchase, new disputes arose between Mexico and the United States. America claimed that Texas, which belonged to the Spanish colony of Mexico, was included in the Louisiana Purchase while Mexico insisted that it was Mexico's territory. The Mexican government agreed to let Americans move into Texas as immigrants. By 1830 eastern Texas was occupied by nearly 20,000 whites and 1,000 Negro slaves. The American immigrants in Texas started their War of Independence in 1835 and declared themselves independent of Mexico in 1839. When Congress annexed Texas in 1845, Mexico severed diplomatic relations with the United States. In 1846, President *James Polk[45] sent *General Zachary Taylor[46] to occupy land near the Rio Grande River, claimed by both America and Mexico. Fighting broke out between the two sides, and on May 13, 1846 Congress declared war on Mexico. After the United States defeated the Mexican army, the Treaty of Guadalupe Hidalgo (1848) gave the United States a vast stretch of land from Texas west to the Pacific and north to Oregon. In return, the United States paid the Mexican government $15,000,000.

3. THE OREGON TERRITORY, ALASKA, AND HAWAII

The Oregon territory was a huge area whose ownership was disputed; the United States claimed that it had acquired Oregon in the Louisiana Purchase while Britain claimed Oregon as British since 1579. Since they were unable to agree on a line of division, the two countries agreed in 1818 to leave Oregon "free and open" to the citizens of both countries for a period of ten years.

During the 1830's and early 1840's, large numbers of American merchants, fur-trappers and missionaries moved to Oregon. They formed a provisional government, and in 1846, a treaty was signed by the two countries. According to the treaty, Britain gave up its claim to land south of 49 degrees latitude, establishing the western boundary between Canada and the United States, and the United States agreed that Britain could retain all of Vancouver Island and the right to navigate the Columbia River.

In 1841, organized groups of American settlers began to cross Nevada into California. Five years later, Americans in California revolted against Mexican rule. In the peace treaty of 1846 California became part of the United States. In 1848, James Marshall discovered gold in the northern part of California. Tens of thousands of newcomers joined the gold rush of 1849, sparking a huge migration of people westward.

In 1853 America bought 77,700 square kilometers of border lands from Mexico, paying $10,000,000. In 1867, Alaska was purchased from Russia for $7,200,000 which increased the land area of the United States by 20%. Alaska became a state in 1959. Hawaii, an independent kingdom since 1810, was annexed by the United States as a territory in 1898 at the request of the Hawaiian legislature. In 1960 Hawaii was admitted as the 50th state—the only state that lies outside North America.

4. THE SIGNIFICANCE OF WESTWARD EXPANSION

The New West did not have a great impact on political innovation in America, because state and local governments in the West were usually modeled after the East. Socially and culturally the West also tended to imitate the East. But because of its lack of local traditions, its interior position, and its need for military protection and improved transportation, the West was usually the most nationalistic section in America.

The problems and hardships that pioneers faced on the raw frontier encouraged them to develop individualism and resourcefulness. The settlers seldom felt the need to obey the rules and traditions which governed social mores in crowded neighborhoods. Among neighbors there might be some mutual help and charitable actions; however, the main trend was competition. Westerners showed great respect for the person who started from "scratch" and achieved success through competition. Relationships among people were rather "cold", cultivating a desire for self-reliance. Though the West did not produce a society of social and economic equals, it did demonstrate to the nation that all artificial barriers to advancement must be removed and that all people must have an equal chance to make their way in the world. This, together with the Puritan tradition of hard work, formed the foundation of the American value system.

VIII. The Industrial Revolution and Social Reforms

The Industrial Revolution began in Britain during the 18th century. This movement rapidly spread to America, and by the first half of the 19th century, American inventors were designing a variety of practical machines. The cotton gin (1793), invented by *Eli Whitney[47], became widely used in the 1800's. It enabled cotton growers to separate cotton fiber from the seeds as fast as 50 people could do the same work by hand. *Cyrus McCormick[48] invented the reaper (1834) which helped farmers to harvest grain much more quickly than before. Robert Fulton invented the steamboat (1807) which soon became the fastest and most important means of shipping goods. The telegraph (1837) was invented by Samuel Morse, which provided businessmen with a faster means of communication.

The period also witnessed a rapid development in transportation. New or improved roads, such as the National Road in the East and the Oregon and Santa Fe Trails in the West, made traveling and shipping goods by land much easier. Meanwhile, Americans built many canals. *The Erie Canal[49] (1825) opened a water passage from the *Hudson River[50] in New York to *the Great Lakes[51] in the Midwest. This important canal made it possible for boats to carry manufactured products to the West and farm products and raw materials to the East.

1. SOCIAL REFORMS (1830-1850)

During the Expansion Era, more and more Americans came to believe that social reforms were essential to improve their society. Churches and social groups set up charities to help the poor. People called *"Prohibitionists"[52], who were convinced that alcohol was the chief cause of poverty and other problems, persuaded thirteen states to forbid the selling of alcohol in the years between 1846 and the US Civil War. An amazing variety of reform movements flourished simultaneously in the northern states, which included advocating abolition of slavery, women's rights, *pacifism[53], prison reform, abolition of imprisonment for debt, improving the condition of the working classes, and a system of universal education.

A) The Women's Rights Movement

Early American women had few rights. They were excluded from the professions and public office; they were also denied the right to vote or to receive higher education. A married woman could not own property, and divorce was rare. When it did occur, the father received custody of the children no matter what the marital circumstances might have been.

It was even considered unfeminine for women to speak in public places. In 1840, a group of American women, including *Elizabeth Cady Stanton[54] and *Lucretia Mott[55], went as delegates to the World Anti-slavery Convention in London, but they were denied the right to participate These conditions and experiences provoked a women's rights movement that became an integral part of the general reform crusade.

In 1848 the first Women's Rights Convention met at Seneca Falls, New York. The delegates adopted a statement, which demanded that women "have immediate admission to all the rights and privileges which belonged to them as citizens of the United States".

In the years before the Civil War, women of the United States did make limited gains. A few states gave married women control over their own property, and two low-status professions, nursing and elementary education, were opened to them. In 1837 Oberlin College became the first co-educational college, and the first women's college, *Mount Holyoke[56], opened its doors.

B) Education Reform

In the early 1800's most of the good schools in the United States were expensive private schools. Poor children went to second-rate "pauper" or "charity" schools or just remained at home. The lack of public support, together with the fact that most teaching was done by low-paid untrained young men, left the mass of people in a state of semi-literacy. During the 1830's, Horace Mann, Secretary of Massachusetts' Board of Education, and other reformers began demanding education reform and better schools for all American children, an idea which won great support from the American people.

By the 1850's, the states were committed to making tax-supported public education available to all. By the 1860's, there were slightly more than 300 public schools in the United States, which admitted all children, not just those who were able to pay tuition. Excluding the southern states, a steadily growing number of children attended free public schools.

Higher education was less influenced by reform. The most notable development in higher education was the proliferation of private church-run colleges throughout the country. Between 1830 and 1850 about eighty religious colleges were founded.

C) The Abolitionist Movement

The Abolitionist Movement, named for those people who wanted to abolish slavery, was the most intense and controversial reform of the period. Beginning in colonial times, many Americans had demanded an end of slavery, and by the early 1800's, every Northern state had outlawed slavery. Meanwhile, since the plantation economy of the Southern states depended on slaves as a source of cheap labor, it was impossible for the majority of white Southerners to consider ending slavery. Because of different attitudes between the North and South, the question of whether to outlaw or allow slavery in new states became a paramount political and social issue in the 1800's. In the 1820's, under pressure from the abolitionists, mostly Quakers in the North, a small movement in the northern portion of the South began. The Quakers advocated payment to slave owners who freed their slaves. These freed Blacks would be sent back to Africa as colonists.

In the early stages of the movement, both Northern and Southern abolitionists believed African colonization would answer the question: what to do with so many freed black people? In 1817, abolitionists helped to organize the American Colonization Society, and in 1822 the first permanent settlement of free blacks from the United States was established in Liberia, West Africa. By 1860 only about 15,000 Blacks had migrated to Africa.

By the early 1830's abolitionists no longer argued in favor of this gradual transition; they demanded the immediate end of slavery. The leading figure of prompt and total abolition was William Lloyd Garrison, who began publication in Boston of a new antislavery newspaper, "The Liberator", in January, 1831. In 1832, Garrison organized the New England Anti-slavery Society, and a year later he helped to establish the national

American Anti-slavery Society. By 1840, a network of some 2,000 affiliated societies with 20,000 members was scattered throughout the North. In 1840, the disagreement over Garrison's effort to admit women to full participation in the organization, and the difference over gradual and immediate abolition caused a split in the anti-slavery movement. Thereafter, abolitionism was only loosely organized at the national level; the real power came from state and local groups. The movement did change some people's attitudes towards slavery. However, fundamental economic, political and social differences continued to divide the North and the South. The American Civil War (1861 – 1864) was the result of these regional differences.

IX. The American Civil War and Reconstruction

1. PRO-SLAVERY ARGUMENTS

To counteract the Anti-slavery Movement, Southern leaders designed an elaborate intellectual defense, presenting slavery as a positive good rather than a great evil. Some pro-slavery advocates cited both the Bible and Aristotle (384 – 322 B.C.) as authorities for their arguments.

A fundamental argument for slavery was based on a theory of the intrinsic biological inferiority of Negroes. Most whites, blind and deaf to the complexity of black culture, assumed that they were superior to blacks. Similar arguments were more "practical". Not only was slavery profitable, but it was also a matter of social necessity. In a lengthy poem published in 1856, William J. Grayson defended slavery as a better system than the wage slavery of northern industry. According to Grayson and his supporters, the factory system had created abuses and neglect far worse than those of plantation slavery. Within a generation these ideas had triumphed in the white South.

2. NEW STATES AND SLAVERY

A) First Missouri Compromise

Westward expansion intensified the debate on slavery between the North and South. In 1818 when the Territory of Missouri applied for admission to the Union, bitter controversy broke out over whether to admit it as a free or slave state. In either case, the existing balance between the eleven free states and the eleven slave states would be destroyed. The Missouri Compromise temporarily maintained the balance. Massachusetts agreed to give up the northern part of its territory. This area became the state of Maine, which entered the Union as a free state in 1820. In 1821, Missouri entered as a slave state. Now there were 12 free and 12 slave states. The Missouri Compromise also provided that slavery would be "forever prohibited" in the Louisiana Purchase, north of Missouri's southern border, except for Missouri itself. The Missouri Compromise satisfied many Americans as an answer to the slave question. But large numbers of reformers still called for complete abolition.

When the United States acquired Texas and other territories in the Southwest after the Mexican War, the renewed expansion of slavery became a possibility. The moral question of slavery became a political issue. Members of Congress became spokesmen for the various views about slavery. Some expressed the views of Americans who believed in the right to own slaves and urged that all the lands acquired from Mexico be opened to slave holders. Others, on behalf of people with strong antislavery beliefs, demanded that all the new regions be closed to slavery. Another group proposed that question be left to "popular sovereignty"; the settlers in each of the new states should decide whether or not slavery should be allowed.

B) Second Missouri Compromise

Congress had to decide whether California would enter the union as a free or a slave state. Again a compromise was reached. The Missouri Compromise of 1850 included a series of laws that made concessions to both the North and South. California was admitted as a free state, and the slave trade was abolished in the District of Columbia. To satisfy the Southerners, Congress ruled that when the territories of New Mexico and Utah became states, the residents would decide whether or not to allow slavery. Also this Missouri Compromise provided for the establishment of more effective methods for catching fugitive slaves in the North and returning them to their Southern masters.

C) Kansas-Nebraska Act

Most Americans accepted these ideas with great relief. The heated argument over slavery cooled, but only for a little while. Soon after, Congress began considering the creation of new territories in the area roughly between Missouri and present-day Idaho. On May 25, 1854, Congress passed the Kansas-Nebraska Act. This Act allowed the territory to be organized on the basis of popular sovereignty: that meant that the people of Kansas and Nebraska would decide whether or not to allow slavery. Because the Northern territory, Nebraska, was west of Iowa, a free state, few feared the development of slavery there, which pleased the Northerners; Kansas, to the south and immediately west of Missouri, a slave state, was another matter. Missourians seemed to think of Kansas as their own backyard, and Southerners endorsed the bill as a reasonable measure fair to the South.

Few, if any, American laws have had more far-reaching effects than the Kansas-Nebraska Act. Furious antislavery Americans denounced both Northerners and Southerners who had supported the act, but others firmly defended the act. Everywhere attitudes toward the slavery question hardened, and the possibility for further compromise disappeared. As a result, political and social turmoil swept through the country. In 1854, a group of antislavery Americans formed the Republican Party, a popular political party in the North. Many Democrats and *Whigs[57] who opposed slavery left their parties and became Republicans.

D) Dred Scott Decision

Before 1854, the stability of the two main political parties had helped keep the nation together. Now because of political differences, the country lost an important unifying force. In 1857, the US Supreme Court's famous Dred Scott decision weakened the court's influence in the North. Dred Scott was a Missouri slave who had been taken by his master some 20 years before to live in the Illinois and Wisconsin territories where slaves were forbidden. When Scott returned to Missouri as a slave, he sued for his freedom based on the argument that he had resided on free soil. Dominated by Southerners, the US Supreme Court decided that Scott was the property of his master and had no right to sue for freedom. Never before had the Supreme Court been so bitterly condemned. The Dred

Scott decision stirred fierce anger throughout the North and brought the nation closer to civil war.

3. THE ELECTION OF *ABRAHAM LINCOLN[58] (1860—1865)

In 1852, Harriet Beecher Stowe's novel *Uncle Tom's Cabin[59] was published. Immediately it became one of the most widely read books in America. This powerful work about the horrors of slavery helped stir antislavery feelings to a fever pitch. In the North, abolitionists stepped up their campaign against slavery. John Brown, who had struck a bloody blow against slavery in Kansas three years before, with the help of a group of followers, seized the federal arsenal at Harpers Ferry, West Virginia. Brown intended to organize a general slave uprising, but he did not succeed. Instead, he was captured and later hanged. Alarm ran through the nation. For many Southerners, Brown's actions confirmed their worst fears that there was an organized movement to end slavery. However, many Northerners thought of Brown as a martyr. These attitudes perhaps best showed how divided the United States had become in the 1850's.

The presidential election of 1860 was tense. Abraham Lincoln, the Republican Party candidate, won the presidency. Lincoln had been known as an opponent of slavery, and his election was unacceptable to the South. Southerners feared the new President would further restrict or even end slavery. On December 20, 1860, South Carolina seceded from the Union. In January 1861, Alabama, Florida, Georgia, Louisiana and Mississippi also seceded, and in February these six states formed the Confederate States of America. Later in 1861, Arkansas, North Carolina, Tennessee, Texas, and Virginia joined the Confederacy.

4. THE US CIVIL WAR (1861—1865)

In his inaugural address, President Lincoln refused to recognize the secession of the eleven southern states, considering it "legally void". His speech ended with a plea for restoration of the Union. But the South turned a deaf ear, and on April 12, 1861, Southern troops fired on Fort Sumter, a federal military port in Charleston, South Carolina. The bombardment of Fort Sumter released the explosive force of the sectional tensions that had accumulated during the preceding decade. War broke out. On April 15, 1861, President Lincoln issued a call for 75,000 men to serve in the militia for ninety days to put down what he called the "combinations" of men who had seized control of the seceded South. Early in May he asked for 42,000 more volunteers to serve a three-year enlistment. He also enlarged the regular army. Thousands upon thousands of Northerners responded to the President's call instantaneously, as secession from the union was regarded as illegal. The rebellion of Southerners had to be put down.

With comparable fervor, the people of the Confederacy rallied to the flag of secession, to the theory of states' rights and to the defense of slavery. Jefferson Davis was elected president of the Confederacy and immediately called for 100,000 soldiers. Thousands of Southern volunteers enlisted in the Confederate army. When the war began, Northerners expected a short and easy war for they had an overwhelming superiority in human and material resources. The 9.5 million people of the eleven Confederate States, including four million slaves, faced a population of twenty-two million in twenty-three Union States. Equally important, the Southern armies lacked supply and transportation lines. The North controlled 80% of the country's factories and most of the coal and iron. Approximately 22,000 miles of railroad traversed the North compared to 9,000 in the South. However, the South had better military leadership than the North and fought on southern soil much of the time. These were two major reasons why the "short, easy" war lasted nearly four long, bitter years.

However, the Union's advantages were not obvious at the beginning of the war. At first, the South gained the upper hand because the Confederacy was fighting a defensive war. The North was compelled not only to invade but also to occupy the South. Also the Southern commanders had the advantage of shorter supply lines. During the first two years, the Federal Army suffered repeated setbacks. As the war continued and as the Confederacy's prospects gradually disappeared under the increasing Union industrial and military strength, the South began to lose its early optimism. Confederate soldiers became discouraged and disaffected. While Union soldiers had adequate provisions and wages, Confederate troops often lacked food and clothing. Instead, they depended on captured Union supplies. Desertion became so widespread that by the end of 1863 one third of the Confederate Army was absent without leave (AWOL). Raging inflation, transportation shortages and a federal blockade of southern ports created extreme civilian unrest. However, the Confederacy's most serious problem was the growing indifference of many wealthy and powerful Southerners. The planter class resented the "usurpation" of their government, particularly policies that hurt their financial interests. A growing disenchantment with the Confederate cause was a major factor in the South's military collapse.

July 1863 was the turning point of the war. General Robert E. Lee, commander of the Confederate Army, marched northward into Pennsylvania hoping to capture Philadelphia. A strong Union force intercepted Lee's march at Gettysburg. In a three-day battle the Confederates made great efforts trying to break the Union lines. However, they failed after heavy losses. To commemorate the battlefield and soldiers' cemetery at Gettysburg, Abraham Lincoln gave a short speech in late 1863. Known as the Gettysburg Address, Lincoln ended with this important statement: "... and that government of the people, by the people, and for the people shall not perish from the earth".

On February 17, 1864, the Confederates abandoned Columbia, South Carolina's capital. On April 2, Lee abandoned his armies in Petersburg and Richmond, Virginia. A week later, when Lee was hemmed in by the Union force; he had no alternative but to surrender.

The four years of bloody fighting between the North and South had staggering effects on the nation. About 360,000 Union troops and perhaps 260,000 Confederate troops died; no other war in American history has taken so many American lives. It caused enormous property damage, especially in the South where many Southern cities, towns, plantations, factories and railroads lay in ruin.

5. THE EMANCIPATION PROCLAMATION

At the beginning of the Civil War, Lincoln's main goal was the preservation of the Union. But as the war continued, the complete emancipation of the slaves became a necessity. From the beginning of the war, Blacks had come over into the Union lines.

How to treat these "*contrabands[60] of war" as they were called? The Northern generals began to liberate the slaves. Meanwhile Lincoln edged toward emancipation. In March 1862, he proposed that federal compensation be offered to any state which began gradual emancipation. On July 17, 1862, a Confiscation Act was passed, liberating the slaves of all persons aiding the rebellion.

On January 1, 1863, Lincoln issued the Emancipation Proclamation. The Proclamation declared freedom for all slaves in the areas under Confederate control. He emphasized that this action was based on his war powers. The immediate effect of the Emancipation Proclamation was that large numbers of free Blacks joined the Union Army. The Emancipation Proclamation did not become law until January 31, 1865 when Congress ratified the 13th Amendment of the US Constitution, which completely abolished slavery in the United States.

6. RECONSTRUCTION

Toward the end of the Civil War, the North established terms under which Confederate states would be readmitted to the Union. These conditions, as well as the period following the war in the South, are called "Reconstruction".

Northerners had different opinions on Reconstruction policy. Presidents Lincoln and Johnson wanted to end the bitterness between the North and South and favored avoiding harsh treatment of the rebels. Lincoln had a flexible and pragmatic approach to Reconstruction. He only insisted that the South pledge future loyalty to the Union and emancipate its slaves. This attempt at reconciliation is often called Presidential Reconstruction. The Congress, led by radical members of the Republican Party, believed that the South should be punished for its rebellion. They favored military occupation of the South. They also wanted a policy that would ensure that Blacks received better treatment in the South than they had before the war, including voting rights for Black men. This is referred to as Congressional or Radical Reconstruction.

Lincoln was assassinated on April 1, 1865 by John Wilkes Booth, a crazed actor, who thought he was helping the South. Following Lincoln's assassination, Vice President Andrew Johnson became President. He tried to carry out Lincoln's policy of leniency toward the South. Although Johnson hated aristocrats and special privilege, he believed that Blacks were unfit for political equality.

Republicans in Congress tried to formulate their own plan to reconstruct the South. Their first effort was the 14th Amendment, which guaranteed basic civil rights to all citizens, regardless of race or ethnicity. Congress also passed the first Reconstruction Act (1867), which divided the South into five military districts. In 1870 Congress passed the 15th Amendment, once and for all forbidding *suffrage[61] discrimination on the basis of "race, color or previous condition of servitude". Under this legislation, new governments were established in all the former Confederate states.

Republicans in Congress did not trust President Johnson to enforce the Reconstruction legislation, which they passed in spite of his repeated vetoes. They tried to deprive him of as much power as possible. When Johnson continued to do all he could to block the enforcement of radical legislation in the South, the more extreme members of the Republican Party demanded his impeachment. In 1868, the House of Representatives impeached him, but the Senate voted against removing Johnson from office by the margin of a single vote.

As time passed, it became obvious that while white Southerners violently resisted all radical measures, Northerners were losing interest in reconstruction. White Southerners were hostile to Republican administrations for the next hundred years. In some places hostility to the new programs took on the form of white terror. The prototypical terrorist group was the *Ku Klux Klan (KKK)[62], which was organized in 1866 and rapidly spread across the South.

In May 1872, Congress passed a general *Amnesty Act[63], restoring full political privileges to all but about 500 Confederate sympathizers. Gradually, in one state after another, with differing degrees of fraudulent and forcible action, conservative Southern whites achieved victory at the polls. Thus, the old social order, based on white supremacy, returned to the South. The 12-year Reconstruction ended when President *Rutherford B. Hayes[64] finally withdrew Northern troops from the South in 1877.

During the three decades after the war, the civil rights of blacks disappeared under the pressure of white rule in the South and the force of the US Supreme Court decision to narrow the application of the Reconstruction Amendments. The fundamental problem of the Black person's place in American society has continued to haunt subsequent generations.

X. Industrialization, Capitalism, and Monopolies
1. INDUSTRIAL EXPANSION

America's industrial expansion was the most important post-war development. Prior to the Civil War, typical American industry was small. Hand labor was widespread, which limited the production capacity of industry. Since businesses lacked the capital for expansion, they only served a small market. During the postwar period, however, American industry changed dramatically. Hand labor was replaced by machines, and the productive capacity of industry increased tremendously. The value of goods produced by American industry increased almost tenfold between 1870 and 1916. American industrialization was larger in scale than that of other industrialized countries and transformed the national culture more profoundly. Its gross national product (GNP) was number one, indicating that the USA had the largest economy in the world.

Many interrelated developments contributed to the industrial growth of the United States. After the Civil War, Americans underwent a period of rapid advancement in science and invention, which enormously stimulated manufacture and speeded the economic process. The patent office recorded 36,000 patents during the years before 1860; in the next 30 years, 440,000 patents were registered; and in the first quarter of the 20th century, the number reached nearly a million. Among the inventions were the typewriter (1867), barbed wire (1873), the telephone (1876), the phonograph (1877), electric lights (1879), the automobile (1885), air brakes for trains (1868), steam turbines, the vacuum cleaner and countless others.

Invention was also the mother of new industries. For example, new processes in steel making and oil refining were the foundation of the *Carnegie[65] and *Rockefeller[66] enterprises. Of all the new products, the automobile had the greatest impact on the nation's economy. In the early 1900's, *Ransom Olds[67] and *Henry Ford[68] began turning out cars by mass production. Automobile prices dropped, and sales increased. The number of automobiles owned by Americans jumped from 8,000 in 1900 to almost 3,500,000 in 1916.

America's rich and varied natural resources played a key role in the development of its industry. In addition to coal and iron, America also has abundant valuable minerals including copper, silver and petroleum. Petroleum, the source of gasoline, became especially important after the automobile became more widely used in the early 1900's. Like the minerals, the timber of the northern Midwest and the far Northwest seemed inexhaustible. The nation's abundant water supply helped power the industrial machines. Americans used these natural resources with no thought of the possibility of their eventual depletion.

Another precondition to the growth of America's industry was the work force. People were needed to operate the factories and to buy the products. About 26 million immigrants, mainly from Southern and Eastern Europe, arrived in the United States between 1870 and 1916, and 20 million of them remained, mostly in cities where they worked in factories for modest wages. Immigration plus natural growth caused the US population to grow from nearly 40 million to about 100 million.

The expansion of the railroads was also basic to the economic growth of the United States during this period. In the postwar period the total mileage in railroads increased rapidly. During the 1880's, the great decade of railroad building, mileage leaped to 9,000 miles (14,500 kilometers) and to almost 200,000 miles (320,000 kilometers) in 1900. Most of this construction filled out the network east of the Mississippi. The high point in railroad development was in 1869, when workers laid tracks that joined the Central Pacific and Union Pacific railroads at Ogden, Utah. This event marked the completion of the world's first transcontinental railroad system, accounting for 1/3 of the world's railroad tracks. The railroads linked the United States from coast to coast, spurring economic growth. The railroads opened the West, connected the raw materials to factories and markets, and thus created a national market. At the same time they were themselves gigantic markets for iron, steel, lumber and other goods.

Improved sales methods also helped economic growth. Owners of big businesses sent traveling sales people to all parts of the country to promote their products. Enterprising merchants opened huge department stores in growing cities. For instance, *Marshall Field[69] in Chicago, R.H. Macy in New York, and *John Wanamaker[70] in Philadelphia established department stores which offered a large variety of products at reasonable prices. Other shop owners, including Montgomery Ward and *Richard Sears[71], began mail-order companies, chiefly to serve people who lived far from the cities. The companies published catalogs that showed their products, so that buyers could use the catalogs to order goods through the post office.

A) Monopolies

With the rapid development of industry, competing firms began to consolidate into large units capable of dominating an entire industry. The trend began during the Civil

War and gathered momentum after the 1870's. In 1882, John D. Rockefeller and his associates organized the Standard Oil Trust. A trust or monopoly was a new type of industrial organization in which the voting rights of a controlling number of shares of a firm were entrusted to a small group of men, or trustees, who were able to prevent competition among the companies they controlled. The stockholders benefited through the larger dividends they received. For a few years the trust was a popular vehicle for the creation of monopolies.

The Standard Oil Company was followed rapidly by other monopolies in cotton seed, oil, lead, sugar, tobacco and rubber. Soon businessmen began to carve out industrial domains for themselves. A 1904 survey showed that more than 5,000 previously independent companies had been consolidated into some 300 industrial trusts. From 1888 to 1905, 328 giant combinations or consolidated businesses were formed; half of them were monopolies in their industries. Other typical examples of consolidations included *Gustavus Swift's[72] meat-processing industry and Andrew Carnegie's iron and steel operation. In finance, too, the process occurred. *The House of Morgan[73] and its closest rival, Kuhn, Loeb and Company, controlled much of the nation's capital and credit supply. In the fields of transportation and communications, Western Union was the earliest of the large monopolies. It was followed by the Bell telephone system and eventually by the American Telephone and Telegraph Company (AT&T). In the 1860's, *Cornelius Vanderbilt[74] consolidated thirteen separate railroads into a single line connecting New York City and Buffalo, nearly 380 kilometers away. During the next decade the major railroads of the country were organized into trunk lines and "systems".

The monopolies had some favorable effects on the economy. They helped make possible efficient corporations that contributed greatly to economic growth. The monopolies also enabled businessmen to avoid sharp fluctuations in price and output by stabilizing sales. On the other hand, the monopolies gave some businessmen so much power that they could demand goods from suppliers at low cost, while charging high prices for their products. Monopolistic businessmen could also save money by reducing the quality of their products.

However, the workers, farmers and small businessmen strongly opposed monopolies. To them, the disadvantages outweighed the advantages. In the late 19th century, public resentment toward the trusts increased, and the large monopolistic corporations, bitterly attacked by reformers, became a hotly debated political issue. To break the monopolies, the government passed the Sherman Antitrust Act (1890), which prohibited monopolies in interstate trade and provided severe penalties for companies which did not comply. A decade later, President *Theodore Roosevelt[75] earned himself the nickname of *"trust-buster"[76] for his effective enforcement of the Sherman Antitrust Act.

B) Results of Industrialization

Industrial expansion had major effects on the lives of the American people. Establishing, expanding, and profiting from business opened up many opportunities for great financial gains. Some businessmen and investors were able to amass huge fortunes. The number of millionaires in the United States grew from about 20 in 1850 to more than 3,000 in 1900. Among the millionaires was a small group who accumulated fortunes of more than $100 million each, including Andrew Carnegie, Marshall Field, J. P. Morgan, John D. Rockefeller and Cornelius Vanderbilt.

America's middle class grew rapidly during this period. It included owners of small businesses, factory and office managers, and other city people who prospered well enough to live a comfortable life. Between 1860 and 1900, the richest 2% of American families owned more than a third of the nation's wealth, while the top 10% owned 75% of the wealth.

People who toiled in factories, mills and mines did not share equally in the benefit of the economic growth. They usually worked at least 60 hours a week for an average pay of about 20 cents an hour. Moreover, as technology improved, many workers were cyclically unemployed. In addition to low pay and unemployment, workers faced unhealthy and unsafe conditions in mines and factories, which had high accident rates. The poor lived in crowded slums known for illiteracy, crime, disease and poor living conditions. The gap between rich and poor people was enormous. The Labor Movement was the workers' response to industrialization.

C) The Labor Movement

As the tensions between employers and workers grew, national labor unions were organized. The first effective national labor union was the Knights of Labor, organized in 1869. The Knights believed in the unity of the interests of all workers, skilled or unskilled. They hoped to gain their ends through politics and education rather than through economic coercion. The Knights reached the peak of their influence in 1885, when they claimed a national membership of nearly 700,000. But its membership declined sharply after the Haymarket Riot (1886) when someone threw a bomb in Haymarket Square in Chicago during a labor dispute. When the bomb killed eight policemen and two other persons, many Americans blamed the disaster on the labor movement. * The Haymarket Riot[77] aroused anti-labor feelings and weakened the cause of unskilled workers.

As the power of the Knights declined, the leadership in the trade union movement passed to the American Federation of Labor (AFL). The AFL was organized in 1881 and reorganized in 1886. The AFL appealed only to skilled workers, and its objectives were those of immediate concern to its members: hours, wages and conditions of employment. It relied on economic weapons, chiefly the strike and boycott, and it eschewed political activity except for state and local election campaigns.

Unions were active in the 1880's. In 1886, there were nearly 1,600 strikes involving about 600,000 workers who demanded the 8-hour workday. The most famous strikes of the time included the railroad strikes (1877), the Homestead Steel Strike at Pittsburgh (1892) and the Pullman Strike in Pullman, Illinois (1894).

D) The Rise of Cities

With the explosive rise of industry, cities developed rapidly. The emergence of major cities occurred between 1860 and 1910. Population in the more than 2,500 incorporated towns grew from 6.2 million to 44.6 million, or from 19.8 to 45.7 percent of the nation's total population. After 1920, America was an urban nation.

In 1800 there were only six cities with more than 8,000 people. By 1890, there were

448 cities, and 272 of them had a population greater than 100,000. Even more striking was the rise of the American metropolis, big cities of more than half a million, which grew at an unprecedented pace in history. By 1900 there were six American cities as large as London and Paris, and three of them had a population of over a million. Chicago more than tripled its size between 1880 and 1900 when it had 1.5 million people, and New York grew from less than 2 million to nearly 3.5 million in those two decades.

Cities did not simply increase in number and expand in size; they rapidly changed their character, pattern, and structure. Until about 1870 the downtown business section huddled around a harbor with factories, banks, slaughter-houses, and retail stores side-by-side. Surrounding the business section were both slum streets as well as streets of wealth and fashion. It was the era of "walking cities", where proximity to work was most important. There was no central city of poverty with an outer rim of affluence. The segregated city of modern times with the poor living in the core of the city and wealthy people on the rim developed swiftly after 1870.

Smaller cities were often identified by economic specialization. There were beer cities, steel cities, textile towns, glass towns, even a candy town: Hershey, Pennsylvania. Albany, New York concentrated on shirts; Richmond, Virginia and Durham, North Carolina made cigarettes; and Dayton, Ohio was famous for producing cash registers, the very symbol of the urban culture.

2. THE PROGRESSIVE ERA

A strong spirit of reform swept through the United States during the late 1800's and early 1900's. This period is often called the Progressive Era, and the reformers were known as Progressives.

Actually, Progressivism was the response of various groups to problems raised by the rapid industrialization and urbanization that followed the Civil War: the rapid spread of slums and poverty; the exploitation of labor; the breakdown of democratic government in the cities and states caused by the emergence of political organizations allied with business interests; and a rapid movement toward financial and industrial concentration. Many Americans feared that their historic traditions of democratic government and universal economic opportunity were being destroyed by gigantic monopolies of economic and political power.

The numerous movements for reform at the local, state and national levels were motivated by common goals. Concern for the underprivileged and downtrodden, the restoration of government to the rank and file, and the enlargement of government power in order to bring industry and finance under popular control were major themes.

*The National Municipal League[78] (1894) united various city reform groups throughout the country. By winning elections, they overthrew corrupt local governments in New York (1894), Baltimore (1895), and Chicago (1896-1897). The vast majority of urban reformers fought for and won the same objectives: equitable taxation of railroad and corporate property, social reform, better schools and expanded social services for the poor.

The Progressives passed laws to prevent child labor and to protect women workers. They expanded charitable services to the poor and developed accident insurance systems to provide workmen's compensation to injured workers and their families.

The reformers gained public support not only from the poor but also from many middle class and some upper class Americans who elected people to Congress who favored their views. The three Presidents elected after 1900, Theodore Roosevelt, *William Howard Taft[79] and *Woodrow Wilson[80], supported many reform laws. Roosevelt called for a "square deal" for all Americans, and established the Bureau of Corporations (1903). When the Bureau found that a business was violating the Sherman Antitrust Act, the government sued. During Theodore Roosevelt's presidency, government brought suits against more than 40 companies.

His successor, President Taft, helped further the cause of reform because he brought twice as many suits against businesses as Theodore Roosevelt did. He also called for a federal income tax and an increased role for the professionally-trained civil service in running government programs. The reform movement flourished under President Wilson (1913 – 1921). Two amendments to the Constitution proposed during Taft's administration were ratified in 1913. The 16th Amendment gave the federal government the power to levy an income tax. The 17th Amendment provided for the election of United States Senators by the people rather than by state legislatures. In 1914, Congress passed the Antitrust Act, which struck another blow against monopolies. The Tariff Act of 1913 and the Federal Reserve Act, which modernized the national banking system, were some of the reform measures passed during Wilson's presidency.

However, Progressivism had its limits. Some of its policies allowed big business to evade many regulations. Progressives presided over one of the worst periods of race relations in the US history. Segregation became the law in the South, and violence in the region against Blacks escalated. In response, Blacks began to move to northern cities in large numbers, a migration which has changed American history.

XI. The United States Becomes a World Power
1. IMPERIAL FOREIGN POLICY

Before the 1890's, most Americans agreed with George Washington that their country should remain aloof from foreign affairs. In comparison to European nations such as France, Germany, and England, America was weak militarily and had little influence on international politics. Among Europeans, American diplomats had the reputation of being bumbling amateurs. The German leader, Otto Von Bismarck, summed up the Europeans' attitude toward America when he said, "A special Providence takes care of fools, drunkards, and the United States".

However, during the 1890's and 1900's, when the United States had become a great power and an imperialistic country, America's historic attitude of isolationism declined. Numerous publicists said that America ought to act like a world power to assert its influence in international affairs. There were advocates of sea power who argued that future national security depended upon a large navy supported by bases throughout the world Social Darwinists said that the world was a jungle where international rivalries were inevitable, and that only strong nations could survive. Added to these arguments were those of idealists and religious leaders who claimed that Americans had a duty to "take up the white man's burden" and to carry their superior culture and the blessings of Christianity to the backward peoples of the world. Gradually, the United States began to change its foreign policy.

The United States built up its armed forces during Theodore Roosevelt's presidency. Roosevelt insisted that the country back up its diplomatic efforts with military strength. His slogan was "Speak softly and carry a Big Stick". In order to meet its needs of rapid economic expansion, America strongly desired foreign trade, especially in the Far East. And, increasingly, America claimed dominance in the Caribbean region. It was against this background that the United States went to war with Spain.

2. SPANISH AMERICAN WAR (1898)

For nearly 400 years, Cuba, Puerto Rico, the Philippines, Guam, and other overseas territories were ruled by Spain. Cuba, a rich Caribbean island near Florida, had long been coveted by the Americans, especially by pre-Civil War Southerners who had wished to add Cuba to the US as a slave state. America offered 100 million dollars in exchange for Cuba, but Spain refused the offer. However, America businessmen invested heavily in Cuba and controlled the country's economy and foreign trade. Trade between the two countries flourished in the 1890's. In 1895 when Cubans revolted against their Spanish rulers, Americans were sympathetic with the Cubans. Yet, there was no reason for America to send troops to aid the Cuban rebels.

The United States remained neutral until February 15, 1898 when the United States battleship "Maine" was blown up in Havana Harbor. Americans blamed Spain. On April 25, 1898, Congress declared war on Spain at the request of President * William McKinley[81]. The war with Spain lasted only four months and ended with Spain's defeat. According to the December 10, 1898 treaty, Cuba was transferred to the United States for temporary occupation, a preliminary step to Cuba's independence. In addition, Spain ceded Puerto Rico and Guam in place of a war indemnity, and America purchased the Philippines for $20,000,000. Although Puerto Rico became a part of the United States as a result of the Spanish American War, it has preferred to retain its Commonwealth status, and has its own independent government. Puerto Ricans, nearly four million in number, are considered US citizens, but they cannot vote in national elections. However, they do send a non-voting representative to the US Congress.

Militarily speaking, the Spanish-American War was so brief and relatively bloodless that it might have been a passing episode in modern history. However, its political and diplomatic consequences were enormous because it catapulted the United States onto a new road of imperialism.

3. THE UNITED STATES AND WORLD WAR I (1914—1918)

A) The USA in World War I

When World War I began, the US repeatedly stated its neutrality. Believing themselves to be secure and immune, the great majority of Americans adhered to the Monroe Doctrine: they should stay out of the war unless their rights and interests were violated. While German-Americans and Irish-Americans supported Germany and her allied countries, British and French Americans sympathized with the Allies. Moreover, neutrality benefited America's economy because America was trading with all of the belligerents, primarily Britain and France.

But increasingly, German acts of aggression brought the USA closer to joining the Allies. When a German submarine sank the unarmed British ship, the Lusitania, without warning (1915), 128 American passengers were killed. Germany promised to stop attacks on defenseless civilians, but four months later German submarines began sinking American merchant ships. The Germans suspended unrestricted submarine warfare for a time, and, when it resumed, the US declared war on Germany on April 6, 1917. In addition to the menace to America's overseas shipping and German violations of American neutrality, was the fear of what a German victory would mean to the future of the U.S.

Mobilization for war in America occurred in two stages. In 1917, the national government relied mainly on voluntary and cooperative efforts. After 1917, the government established complete control over every phase of the economy, including railroads, food and fuel. The National Defense Act (1916) and *the Selective Service Act[82] (1917) strengthened the US Army. To finance the war, existing taxes were increased, and new taxes were levied. The American people rallied around the government, and approximately 2 million men volunteered for military service. The spirit of patriotism grew to a fever pitch throughout the country. People bought Liberty Bonds, which raised billions of dollars to help pay the cost of the war. Fiery patriotic songs, such as "Over There" and "You're a Grand Old Flag" raised the spirits of the public and the doughboys, the popular nickname for American soldiers.

The American Expeditionary Force of nearly 2,000,000 soldiers played an important part in the war. In their first major battle, American soldiers drove the German force out of Chateau-Thierry. They also helped to halt the German drive toward Paris during the second battle of the Marne After their supply lines were cut, the German Army retreated to its homeland, and the war ended in November 1918.

B) The Treaty of Versailles

In January 1919 the victorious Allies held a conference at the Versailles Palace near Paris to negotiate the peace terms. In order to ensure that the US had a decisive role in shaping a lasting postwar agreement between the warring countries, President Wilson led the American delegation to Versailles. He wanted the Allies to adopt his Fourteen Points, which included freedom of the seas, removal of trade barriers, arms reduction and readjustment of the European borders based on self-determination. Finally, Wilson proposed the League of Nations, an international organization to preserve peace.

In the meantime, the Allies were determined that Germany should be divided and made to pay the cost of the war. They adopted the Treaty of Versailles, which ignored many of Wilson's Fourteen Points. One exception was the adoption of *the League of Nations[83]. However, America did not join the League because the US Senate failed to ratify the Treaty of Versailles, fearing that the League would infringe on US sovereignty.

XII. The Post World War I Period
1. ISOLATION

After World War I, isolation once again dominated American popular opinion. However, total disengagement from world affairs was impossible. As the world's greatest manufacturing and exporting nation, imperialist America could not return to its traditional isolation. America's policies during the 1920's effectively promoted its overseas trade, and American exports more than doubled during this decade. Encouraged by favorable tax laws, American investors penetrated foreign markets as never before. The US vied with the British and French for oil in the Near East and developed copper mines in Chile. America continued its Open Door Policy around the Pacific Rim.

Because these ventures were done in the name of profit, and not for military or political gains, military force was rarely invoked except for minor instances in the Caribbean. Using this approach, the American government could appease isolationists and pacifists while still pursuing an active foreign policy.

2. IMMIGRATION

A significant change in attitude and legislation about immigration occurred during the 1920's. In 1920 nearly 800,000 immigrants came to the USA. In 1921 emergency legislation was passed to severely limit this number to 164,000 people. These laws reflected fears of labor unions, business groups and native organizations, which had opposed cheap immigrant labor for many years.

People from Northwestern Europe were given preference, while the number of people migrating from Eastern and Southern European countries was restricted. Partly this reflected a response to the "Red Scare", the fear that after the Russian Revolution of 1917 communism would spread to the USA. Institutionalized prejudices against Asian immigrants had begun a generation before, but the 1921 immigration law totally excluded people from Asia, who were regarded as "aliens ineligible for citizenship". The end of free and open immigration, like the disappearance of the frontier, lessened the competitive and mobile character of American life.

3. THE BOOMING ECONOMY

In many ways, the 1920's laid the foundation for modern America. During this decade the American economy soared to spectacular heights as a result of favorable government policies, advances in technology, mass production and scientific management to increase productivity. The GNP (Gross National Product) grew from nearly 73 billion dollars in 1920 to over 104 billion dollars in 1929, and per capita income rose from $672 in 1922 to $857 in 1929.

Two conservative American presidents, *Warren Harding[84] (1921 – 1923) and *Calvin Coolidge[85] (1923 – 1929), adopted policies that favored business. Harding's slogan was "Less government in business and more business in government".

New techniques and technology enabled American manufacturers to produce faster and cheaper. The assembly line dramatically increased the production of cheaper automobiles. The number of registered automobiles nearly tripled between 1920 and 1929 from 8 to 23 million vehicles. The automobile industry triggered growth in related industries, such as steel, road construction, gasoline sales and tourism. Electricity from improved generators became the major source of industrial and household energy. Electrical appliances such as radios, washing machines, vacuum cleaners and refrigerators became standard equipment in American homes. Mass advertising and installment buying changed American patterns of consumption.

4. MIGRATION TO THE CITIES

In 1920 for the first time, the US Census reported that the majority of Americans lived in urban areas. Amusements in the city included movies, plays, sports events and nightclubs. Nightclubs and radio programs featured music, including the unique contribution of Black American musicians nicknamed "jazz". Shorter working hours gave people the leisure time to learn to play. By 1929, one out of five American families had an automobile, allowing them to travel farther from their homes.

5. WOMEN'S SUFFRAGE

While some states had allowed women to vote since the middle of the 19th century, the 19th Amendment to the US Constitution (1920) granted all American women the right to vote. Some women demanded their own apartments, as well as the right to drink whiskey and smoke cigarettes. Women changed their hair and clothing styles. Short "bobbed" hair and short skirts worn with rolled-down stockings replaced long hair and the full-length dresses of earlier days. Women who disdained conventional dress and behavior and who adopted the new styles were called *"flappers"[86]. Later in the 20th century when women demanded other reforms, they were inspired by the activists in the 1920's.

6. PROBLEMS IN THE POST-WORLD WAR I ERA (1918-1941)

Changes in the 1920's created problems as well as benefits. Many Americans had problems adjusting to the impersonal, fast-paced life in the cities. This disorientation led to the decline of strong family relationships and to a rise in divorce, juvenile delinquency, crime and other anti-social behavior.

The 18th Amendment to the Constitution (1919) is known as "Prohibition", because it prohibited the sale of alcoholic beverages in the United States. The primary intent of the amendment was to keep men at home, rather than becoming intoxicated at taverns and bars. Moreover, many people believed that alcoholism was the root cause of poverty. But the majority of Americans ignored Prohibition. They drank at *"Speakeasies"[87], illegal nightclubs, and bought illegal liquor from *"bootleggers"[88]. One unforeseen problem was that bootleggers joined gangs in order to protect their lucrative territories. The result was that gang warfare and other criminal activities rose dramatically. Prohibition was finally repealed by the Twenty-first Amendment (1933).

Many people, especially those living in provincial areas, resented the post-war changes. These Americans clung to the social mores of the agricultural past; their identities and moral values were rooted in traditions associated with family, church and community. Traditionalism led to the revival of religious *fundamentalism[89], which insisted that the Bible must be accepted as literal truth. Fundamentalists rejected the concept of biological evolution and attacked those who taught Charles Darwin's Origin of Species (1859). Several southern states passed laws prohibiting the teaching of evolution. The Ku Klux Klan, a white *supremacist[90] group which began during Reconstruction, was revived because the organization seemed to have easy answers to difficult questions. By the 1920's in the North and South it had about 5 million members who blamed the nation's problems on "outsiders", including Blacks, Jews, Roman Catholics, foreigners and political radicals.

A major problem caused by the economic boom of the 1920's was the uneven distribution of wealth. In 1929, the combined income of the richest 0.1% equaled that of the poorest 42%, including coal and textile workers, seasonal laborers, and most Blacks, who experienced hard times. Moreover, the prosperity of the 1920's was as unsound as it was uneven. Consolidation of businesses often led to speculation in land and stocks instead of productive investments.

Disaster struck in 1929 with a worldwide stock market crash. Financial institutions had to close because they had made bad loans and, therefore, did not have their customers' money. The Great Depression that followed the stock market crash was marked by deflation, no growth, and high unemployment.

7. PRESIDENT FRANKLIN ROOSEVELT (1933—1945) AND THE NEW DEAL

In the early days of the Great Depression, President *Herbert Hoover[91] (1929 – 1933) promised that prosperity was "just around the corner". As the depression worsened, the presidential election of 1932 approached. The Republicans nominated Hoover, and the Democrats chose *Franklin Delano Roosevelt (FDR)[92]. Roosevelt's program of "Relief, Recovery and Reform" was popularly known as *"the New Deal"[93], a program that significantly and dramatically increased the national government's intervention in the economy.

Born into a wealthy family, Roosevelt graduated from Harvard University. In 1921, an attack of poliomyelitis (polio) left him permanently crippled and unable to stand or walk without braces. However, he never lost his courage, optimism or desire for a political career. His personal struggles transformed the once supercilious young man into one of the most outgoing political figures of the century and one of the most influential and controversial US presidents.

The nation was suffering from an acute banking crisis when FDR took office (1933). Before FDR implemented his New Deal to restart the economy, he told the American people that they "had nothing to fear, but fear itself". In the hundred days between March and June 1933, Congress passed a series of laws with unbelievable speed. The Emergency Banking law allowed the federal government to strengthen and re-open fiscally sound banks under the Federal Reserve System. Soon deposits exceeded withdrawals in these banks. Americans were obliged by law to cash in their gold for paper currency, taking the dollar off the gold standard. Eventually the American currency stabilized at 60% of its former value, increasing both the price of commodities and stocks. By June 1933 the stock market rose 15%.

The Roosevelt administration provided work rather than welfare. The Civilian Conservation Corps (CCC), one of the most popular New Deal agencies, created jobs for unemployed men aged eighteen to twenty-five. They worked in a variety of jobs in national forests, parks, and recreational areas and in soil conservation projects for a nominal pay of $30 a month. Some of these jobs were planting trees, eliminating stream pollution, building facilities and increasing the size of the national forests.

Congress passed legislation to refinance mortgages to help home and farm owners who faced mortgage foreclosures. In 1933 – 1934, the Farm Credit Administration refinanced 20% of farm mortgages, and the Farm Bankruptcy Act of June, 1934, enabled farmers who had lost their farms to regain them. The Home Owners Loan Corporation refinanced about 1/6 of all home mortgages.

The Trade Agreement Act gave the president power to negotiate low tariff agreements in order to revive foreign trade. The Beer and Wine Revenue Act legalized the alcoholic beverage industry, ending Prohibition.

Agricultural prices had fallen faster than industrial prices. The Agricultural Adjustment Act (1933) increased farm income by controlling production. Benefit payments were made to farmers who agreed to regulate their plantings according to a national plan, marking the beginning of an era when farmers received subsidies from the federal government to improve their economic status.

New programs were initiated to regulate stock exchanges and investment banking. The Federal Deposit Insurance Corporation (1933) guaranteed the safety of small bank deposits. The Banking Act (1935) altered and strengthened the Federal Reserve System. In 1936, the Tennessee Valley Authority (TVA) acquired 5 dams and in the next two decades built 20 new dams in the Tennessee Valley. This innovative legislation provided flood control, cheap electricity and rehabilitated one of the most poverty-stricken regions in the country.

Another important program was the Social Security Act (1935), which laid the foundation for a national system of old-age, unemployment and disability insurance, financed largely by employer and employee contributions. Social Security assured modest supplemental retirement allowances for most workers at age 65, and by 1938 every state had some form of unemployment insurance.

In the election of 1938 conservatives regained control of Congress, and the era of the New Deal ended. However, the New Deal was a major turning point in American history because it established the federal government's strong role in the nation's economic affairs, particularly in the areas of currency, banking and credit. Ending the Great Depression and taking responsibility for the social and economic welfare of the American people made Roosevelt popular with the majority of voters. These are some of the reasons why they elected him to an unprecedented four terms (1932 – 1945).

XIII. World War II

1. ISOLATIONISM AND NEUTRALITY

While the *totalitarian[94] regimes in Japan, Germany and Italy expanded their territories in the 1930's, the United States remained neutral. Many Americans wanted to help Britain, but they also wanted to stay out of the war. With the reluctant approval of FDR, Congress enacted a series of neutrality laws which prohibited trade or credit to any belligerent. After Germany's invasion of Poland (1939), Congress allowed belligerents to purchase munitions on a "cash-and-carry" basis.

In the spring of 1940 when Germany invaded Denmark, Norway, Netherlands, Belgium and France, public opinion changed. Many believed that the countries that threatened Europe's security also threatened the United States. When German air attacks on Britain began in the summer of 1940, fewer Americans remained neutral. In September 1940, Congress voted immense sums for rearmament and passed the first peacetime conscription bill in American history.

While the war in Europe intensified, tensions increased in Asia. Seeking to improve her strategic position, Japan announced a "New Order" in which Japan would exercise hegemony over all the Pacific area. When Japan joined the Berlin-Rome Axis (1940), the United States imposed an embargo on scrap iron and steel exported to Japan. Relations between Japan and the US grew tense. However, the Japanese air raid on the US Naval Base at Pearl Harbor in Hawaii on December 7, 1941, was the immediate cause of America's entrance into World War II (WWII). Three days later, Germany and Italy declared war against the US, and Americans entered the war with virtual unanimity.

2. AMERICA ENTERS THE WAR (1941-1945)

Once war was declared, the United States quickly mobilized its manpower and industries. By the end of 1943, approximately 65 million American men and women were engaged in war-related occupations. The Office of War Mobilization established priorities to channel scarce raw materials into the most essential types of production, controlled prices, and allocated war supplies to the nation's armed forces and allies. By the end of 1944, US production was twice that of all the Axis countries combined. Much of this production was in new technology, including radar, sonar and radio-directed *proximity fuses[95].

General * Dwight D. Eisenhower [96], the European Supreme Commander, coordinated the *"D-Day"[97] invasion of Northern France by American and British forces. By August 1944, Paris was retaken, and on May 8, 1945 Germany surrendered.

In the summer of 1945, when the Japanese government refused to surrender, President *Harry Truman[98] (1945-1953) decided to drop the deadly atomic bomb on two Japanese cities, *Hiroshima[99] and *Nagasaki[100], killing nearly 300,000 people. On September 2, 1945, Japan surrendered on the US battleship Missouri, ending World War II.

3. RESULTS OF WORLD WAR II

America's entrance into the war ended the national economic depression. Unlike other nations that had fought in the global conflict, the US was never bombed or invaded. As a result, farms, cities, industries and the infrastructure in the United States remained intact. New technologies developed during the war, including computers and atomic power, were converted to peacetime uses.

Thousands of Americans returned home, married and had children, a phenomenon known as the *"Baby Boom"[101]. These war veterans demanded education, employment, housing and a better life for themselves and their descendents.

At the end of WWII, the United States joined the United Nations (UN). Although the UN is an international organization based on Wilson's idea of the League of Nations, it was redesigned by President Roosevelt and British Prime Minister Winston Churchill before the end of WWII. It comprises a General Assembly, a forum for all member states; a Security Council with five permanent members representing China, France, Russia, the United Kingdom and the USA; and the secretary-general who is responsible for the administration of the UN.

The US also funded the Marshall Plan, which provided money and technical assistance to reestablish the economies in devastated European countries, including Germany and Italy. Germany was divided into four zones: the British in the north, the

French in the central region, the Russians in the east, and the Americans in southern Germany. The Japanese retained their emperor, but were under American military control because the Japanese, like the Germans, were prohibited from reestablishing an army. Both countries were required to hold democratic elections for their respective prime ministers and parliamentary representatives.

The only nation that emerged from the war with its military and economic power enhanced was the United States. During the postwar period, the US produced 60% and exported 30% of the world's total market.

XIV. The Post World War II Period (1945 – 1989)
1. THE COLD WAR

In modern jargon, a "Hot War" means actual fighting. The "Cold War", a term popularized by Winston Churchill in 1946, means alternative forms of warfare that rely on limited violence and ideological, economic and political methods. It was a war because the USSR's avowed purpose was a world socialist revolution while the USA tried to maintain the existing governments.

As a world power after World War II, US foreign policy changed from isolation into intervention to maintain the balance-of-power. More and more it tended to act as the world's policeman. Immediately after the war, East-West rivalry centered on Eastern and Central Europe, where American hopes for a capitalist world order collided with Soviet ideology and security needs. On the one hand, the Soviet Union was determined to create a buffer zone by establishing friendly neighbors in order to prevent invasion from the West and to concentrate on internal economic development. On the other hand, the USA insisted on national self-determination and an "open door" policy in these buffer countries. Hence, a cold war between the two sides was inevitable.

A) The Containment Policy

When several socialist countries emerged in Eastern Europe, America's fear of Communist control in Western Europe and other parts of the world grew daily. The US decided to prevent the expansion of Communism with a policy known as the "Containment Policy" or "Containment". The purpose of containment was to block the Soviet effort to flow into "every nook and cranny available to it in the basin of the world", according to Secretary of State, George Kennan, a primary author of the policy. A corollary to the containment policy was the *"Domino Theory"[102], which assumed that if one country joined the Soviet Block, its neighbor would join and so on until whole regions would be under Soviet control. It was America's responsibility to prevent any country from joining the Soviet Block. The United States committed itself to counter-revolutionary politics by economically assisting any nation merely because it was anti-communist.

In 1947, Britain declared that it could no longer afford to send aid to Greece and Turkey. President Harry Truman requested and received $400 million from Congress for military aid for these two countries to resist Communism. This policy became known as the "Truman Doctrine", a form of containment.

In 1947, Secretary of State, George Marshall, proposed a plan for the economic rehabilitation of Europe. The Marshall Plan revitalized the economy of Western Europe and cut the strength of the Western European Communist Parties. In 1948, Truman proposed his Point Four Program, which extended the same aid and technical assistance to the world's developing nations. In large part, Truman's program was an attempt to persuade developing nations to side with the United States rather than with the Soviet Union.

In 1949, America, Canada and ten European countries joined the North Atlantic Treaty Organization (NATO). They agreed that an armed attack on one of the member states would be an attack against all of the member states. The first commander of the NATO forces was an American, appointed by Truman.

B) The Korean War (1950–1953)

The Korean War was a result of Cold War frictions. After World War II, Korea was divided at the 38th parallel into the Soviet-supported north and the American-supported south. When the Korean War broke out in 1950, Truman sent American troops to reinforce the south, which was the nation's first military engagement of the cold war. When the American troops entered the north, China dispatched the Chinese People's Volunteers to North Korea to protect itself from possible invasion. Negotiations between the opposing forces began at Panmunjom in July 1951, but the talks and war dragged on until 1953. In the same year, prisoners were exchanged, and an armistice, which confirmed the 38th parallel as Korea's dividing line between North and South Korea, was signed.

C) The Red Scare and McCarthyism

The fear of communism was also demonstrated inside America during the post-war era. Based on the belief that communism was being advocated by Americans in positions of influence and leadership, Truman signed an *executive order[103] (1947) which required federal employees to take a loyalty oath to the United States. Also in 1947 the House Committee on *Un-American Activities[104] began searching for Communists among Hollywood screen writers, directors and actors. The most prominent people, known as the "Hollywood Ten", went to jail. A larger number of writers, directors and actors who were suspected of "disloyalty" for being Communist Party members were eventually "blacklisted", and barred from working in the film industry.

In part, Truman's actions were intended to deprive the Republicans of the political issue of communism in America. Also Truman sought public support for his anti-Soviet foreign policy by over-dramatizing the domestic menace. This prompted Congress to pass the McCarran Internal Security Act (1950). Communists and communist-front organizations had to register with the US *Attorney-General[105]. By 1951, some 2,500 alleged security risks were dismissed from federal employment without due process, but no espionage ring was uncovered.

In 1953, Julius and Ethel Rosenberg were arrested, tried, convicted and electrocuted for treason, because they were accused of transmitting atomic secrets to the USSR. The Russian Secret Service, the KGB, released records at the end of the Cold War indicating that Julius Rosenberg was guilty, but his wife was not.

The post-World War II Red Scare became a modern witch hunt for communists, commonly known as *McCathyism [106] named for Joseph McCarthy, a junior senator from Wisconsin. He began his crusade in 1950 with a list of 205 people he believed were communists. The elections of 1954 ended McCarthyism. Unfortunately, the cost was high. Sections of the government had been demoralized, and individual lives and careers had been destroyed.

D) John Kennedy (1961-1963) and the Cuban Missile Crisis

*John Kennedy[107] hoped to increase America's influence in the world. He continued the containment policy and redesigned the foreign aid program by paying more attention to the economic development of underdeveloped countries. He increased America's missile and bomber forces, as well as the size and capability of the army.

In April, 1961 Kennedy launched an abortive invasion of Cuba to overthrow the pro-Communist *Fidel Castro[108] by Cuban forces that had been secretly trained and supplied by the US. The Cold War and the Cuban situation reached a critical point in 1962 when the US learned that the Soviet Union had installed *ballistic missiles[109] in Cuba capable of attacking the United States. Kennedy ordered a *naval quarantine[110] of Cuba to prevent Soviet ships from delivering additional missiles to the island. After five tense days, the USSR agreed to dismantle its missile bases and to withdraw its troops from Cuba.

E) The Vietnam War

Apart from the Cuban Missile Crisis, the major US foreign dilemma in the 1960's was Vietnam. America's involvement actually began in 1954 when the French colonists were defeated by the Vietnamese communist forces led by Ho Chi Minh. Earlier, America had sent substantial economic and military aid to the French, but after the French defeat, American aid shifted directly to Ngo Dinh Diem, the anti-Communist dictator in South Vietnam. The rationale for American involvement was consistent with the containment policy and the domino theory.

Following Eisenhower, John Kennedy *covertly[111] and overtly increased the American military presence in Vietnam. After Kennedy's assassination (1963), President Lyndon Johnson (1963-1969) sent more than 500,000 soldiers to Vietnam and ordered sustained US bombing of North Vietnam (1965). Large sections of the countryside were contaminated and *defoliated[112] by a combination of bombing and herbicide spraying. Much of the transportation system and industrial capacity of North Vietnam was destroyed.

When *Richard Nixon[113] became president (1969-1974), he decided to end the war through a policy called "Vietnamization". Vietnamization meant the gradual replacement of American troops by Vietnamese troops. Even though the fighting spread to Cambodia in 1970, Nixon continued his policy of "Vietnamization". Systematic withdrawal of US troops reduced American ground forces to fewer than 70,000 by 1972.

The Vietnam War had profound effects on American society and US foreign policy. President Johnson refused to run for a second term in 1968 because the war was unpopular with a large portion of Americans. The war had polarized many of America's young people who increasingly become more disillusioned and radical during the war.

As public distrust of the government's foreign policy increased, Americans showed growing concern over the neglected areas of domestic policy. Cities had deteriorated; the environment was polluted; and welfare rolls increased. Inflation, the direct result of the cost of the Vietnam War, was the worst the nation had experienced since WWII.

The consequences of the Vietnam War were not limited to the domestic economy. The war had adverse effects for the US internationally as well. While the US devoted billions of dollars annually to military expenditures, the Japanese economy, based on a relatively small military investment, developed at an unprecedented rate. Japan invaded the American domestic markets and undercut US sales abroad. Eventually, as foreign confidence in the dollar sagged, US currency was devalued when it was allowed to float on the international market in 1971.

Ironically, the war eroded respect for the military so that young Americans regarded military service as corrupt and ignoble. European nations, while applauding the US withdrawal, doubted America's reliability, and revolutionary leaders in the developing nations mocked America's policies.

F) Richard Nixon and *Detente[114]

As Nixon distanced America from the Vietnam War, he searched for a better-focused foreign policy. Nixon, and his Secretary of State, Henry Kissinger, began a kind of balance-of-power diplomacy by reducing tensions between the United States and the two major communist nations: China and the Soviet Union. He was the first president to visit Beijing since the founding of the People's Republic of China. In February 1972, Nixon and Kissinger met with Chairman Mao Zedong and Premier Zhou Enlai, to discuss matters of mutual concern. This visit led to the establishment of diplomatic relations between China and the USA in 1979. In May 1972, Nixon was the first American president to consult with Soviet leaders in Moscow about trade, cooperative space programs, cultural exchanges and other areas of mutual interest.

Nixon's actions were significant because he recognized that the world had changed since World War II. International politics during the post-war period had been dominated by the conflict between the two super powers, the United States and the Soviet Union. Nixon acknowledged the existence of several power blocks, the limits of American power, and the need for America to find ways to coexist within these political realities.

2. DOMESTIC ISSUES
A) The Economy

Following WWII the United States entered the greatest period of economic growth and the longest period of peaceful prosperity in history. By 1970, the gap between the living standards in the US and the rest of the world had become a chasm; with 5% of the world's population, America produced and consumed about 25% of the world's goods.

Several factors contributed to this prolonged economic growth. Massive federal expenditures for the military during WWII had catapulted the American economy out of the Great Depression (1930 – 1939). Due to the tensions generated by the Cold War, defense spending represented the single most important stimulant to the postwar boom. Military-related research also helped spawn new industries, particularly chemicals, electronics and aviation.

Since most of the other major industrial nations of the world had been physically devastated during WWII, American industry had a virtual monopoly over international trade. Technological innovations, particularly the computer, contributed to the "automation" of the workplace, creating spectacular increases in productivity. For example, in 1945 it took 310 man-hours to make a car, but by 1960 it only took 150 man-hours.

The postwar population explosion and a purchasing frenzy created consumer demands for houses, automobiles and highways. However, the new prosperity was not universal, because agriculture continued to be a problem. Technological and scientific innovations contributed to the overproduction of staple crops. When this forced food prices down, small farmers were not able to earn enough money, and they sold their family farms to large land-owners and agricultural corporations. Elsewhere in the economy, disparities between richer and poorer Americans were evident. By the late 1950's, the richest 5% of the population made more money than the poorest 40%.

By 1960 some 600 businesses, or 0.5% of all American corporations, earned more than half of all the US corporate income. Significantly, during the postwar period, global *conglomerates[115] and multinational corporations transcended national boundaries and controlled many enterprises that were totally unrelated to their parent companies.

B) The Civil Rights Movement

Black Americans developed new strategies in their continuing fight for equality. One of these strategies was legal challenges to existing laws. For many years, white people used the doctrine of "separate but equal" to justify educational segregation between the races. However, Black schools were poorly funded and supported. Black groups supported Mr. Brown who wanted his daughter to attend the white elementary school in his neighborhood. Brown sued the Board of Education in Topeka, Kansas. In a momentous decision on May 17, 1954, the US Supreme Court ruled that the "separate but equal" doctrine was unconstitutional and must end.

Another strategy was organized protest. In 1955, Rosa Parks, a Black woman, refused to move to the rear of a bus to make seating space available for white passengers, triggering the Montgomery, Alabama bus boycott. This event marked the beginning of the Civil Rights Movement of the 1950's and 1960's, which dominated domestic politics. Increasingly Blacks, joined by Whites, staged non-violent demonstrations to dramatize their demands for civil rights and equality. In the South, racial segregation existed in schools, restaurants and hotels. In the North, the issues were better housing and employment for Blacks.

SNCC (The Student Non-violent Coordinating Committee) cooperated with *Martin Luther King's[116] SCLC (Southern Christian Leadership Conference) in sit-ins, *teach-ins[117], freedom rides, boycotts, demonstrations, marches and other non-violent civil disobedience activities. Their activities gained widespread public acceptance. Increasingly, many white people became convinced that Black demands were both legitimate and moral.

Martin Luther King, the leader of the nonviolent movement, had been influenced by the American philosopher, *Henry David Thoreau[118] (1817 – 1862), and the Indian nationalist and spiritual leader, *Mohandas Gandhi[119] (1869 – 1948). He led 250,000 people, both Blacks and Whites, down *the Mall[120] in Washington, D.C. on August 28, 1963 in the largest civil rights demonstration in US history. Standing in front of Abraham Lincoln's statue, King delivered one of the memorable speeches of the century entitled, "I Have a Dream".

Not all Blacks were nonviolent, and rioting frequently erupted in Black neighborhoods. In the 1960's the Black Power Movement emerged, advocating Black pride, solidarity and control of institutions. New organizations such as *the Black Panthers[121] grew out of the movement. However, Black Power was more of a slogan than a philosophy.

In 1964, Congress passed the first of a series of Civil Rights Acts. The law protected the voting rights of minority people. It also stated that no federal money would be given to any business, employer or labor union, which discriminated against people because of their race, ethnicity, religion, gender, age, disability or national origin. The Equal Employment Opportunity Commission (EEOC) was established to enforce fair labor practices. The Civil Rights Acts increased educational opportunities, particularly for Blacks and other minorities. In general, the economic gap between many Blacks and Whites decreased but persisted, and city ghettoes remained intact.

C) Women's Rights

The passion and success of the Black Movement in the 1960's encouraged activists to renew the struggle for equality for women. The groundwork had been laid during WWII when women worked in the factories while men fought overseas. Although feminists were divided between moderate reformers such as Betty Friedan and radicals such as Kate Millett, they were united by a set of demands, particularly for an end to job and wage discrimination, liberalization of abortion laws, and federal and state support for child-care centers.

Modern *feminists[122], like their predecessors, faced ridicule, hostility, and even abuse. The Civil Rights Acts, passed by Congress and approved by the President, prohibited gender discrimination, and these laws were upheld by the US Supreme Court. Under Title IV of the Educational Amendment Act (1972) colleges were required to ensure equal opportunity for women. One feminist stated, "If the 1960's belonged to Blacks, the next ten years are ours".

Women's growing presence in the labor force assured them of a greater share of economic and political influence. During the 1970's over half the married women and 90% of the female college graduates were employed outside the home. One economist called this development, "the single most outstanding phenomenon of this century".

D) Youth Culture

The *Youth Culture[123] was a very different kind of protest in the 1960's. Alienated by the Vietnam War, racism, political and parental demands, and new technologies, young people grew disillusioned with the government and other institutions representing the status quo. A growing feeling emerged that something was fundamentally wrong, not just with the political system, but with the entire structure of American life and values. By the mid 1960's there was a full-fledged youth revolt on college campuses across the country. The political movement was known as *the New Left[124] to distinguish itself from the "Old Left", which espoused *Orthodox Marxism[125] and had embraced Stalinism in the 1930's. The cultural revolt was known as the *counterculture[126], and some of its participants were called "Hippies".

Students for a Democratic Society (SDS) pursued the ideal of participatory democracy and inspired many college students to take political action. The group gained national attention when they demonstrated in support of the Civil Rights Movement and against the Vietnam War. After the assassination of Martin Luther King(1968), a strike led by the SDS forced the temporary closing of Columbia University. In 1969, Black youths with guns intimidated the Cornell University administration into making concessions. Following America's 1970 invasion of Cambodia, student protests erupted on hundreds of campuses across the country.

Other young people, especially disillusioned, affluent Whites, adopted the life style of the Counterculture for non-political reasons. Long hair, blue jeans, tie-dyed shirts, sandals, mind-altering drugs, rock music, and cooperative living arrangements, which shocked their parents were more important than revolutionary ideology.

Opinion polls indicated that the majority of the nation's youth were as traditional as their parents. Even on the most politicized campuses, the New Left and the Counterculture appealed to a distinct minority of students. Nevertheless, these two student movements had a lasting impact on American attitudes toward sex, marriage, work, leisure, careers, education, and war.

E) Progressives in the White House (1961-1969)

When John F. Kennedy became president (1961 - 1963), he became a symbol of youth, vigor, intelligence, wit and reform. He gave hope to the young and the disadvantaged as he boldly spoke of moving the country forward. He had a long list of proposals for economic growth and full employment. He supported civil rights and a substantial cut in federal income taxes. He advocated medical care for the aged (Medicare), federal aid to education, and the creation of the Department of Urban Affairs to improve life in American cities. Kennedy's supporters in Congress passed legislation which outlawed the poll tax in federal elections; initiated a large urban renewal program; increased the minimum wage; and assisted workers threatened by automation. However, Kennedy was assassinated before he could complete his agenda. Widely unpopular while he was the president, Kennedy was regarded by many Americans as a martyr and a saint after his assassination.

As specified by the US Constitution, Vice President *Lyndon Johnson[127] became president. Johnson was a very clever politician who had spent years in Congress and knew how to win votes for his programs. He also wanted to enact Kennedy's unfinished legislation promptly. He called his administration *"the Great Society"[128], and the result was a flood of new laws. Some of the most notable legislation were: the Civil Rights Acts (1964 and 1965); tax reductions; aid to education; a *food stamp[129] program for needy families; Medicare; establishment of new national parks; elimination of air and water pollution; new automobile safety standards; beautification of highways; and millions of dollars for reducing poverty, urban redevelopment and inexpensive public housing.

In spite of Johnson's remarkable domestic record, he and his advisors were stymied by the Vietnam War. Johnson decided not to run for a second term, and Richard Nixon was elected president.

F) The Watergate Scandal

Richard Nixon had to resign in August 1974 as the result of the Watergate Scandal, one of the biggest political scandals in the history of the United States. Watergate is the name of a large apartment building in Washington, D.C.. In an office in the Watergate building was the headquarters of the Democratic National Committee (DNC).

In order to find out if Senator Ted Kennedy, the youngest brother of the assassinated president, John Kennedy, would run for the presidency, as well as other campaign activities, Nixon approved of a plan to burglarize the DNC's office.

After the five burglars were caught, it was discovered that they had connections with Nixon. From the start, Nixon was personally involved in the cover-up, denying any knowledge of illegal activities. He used his presidential powers to discredit and block the Watergate investigation. Most alarmingly, during the course of the investigation it was discovered that the burglary was only one small part of a large pattern of corruption and criminality sanctioned by the Nixon White House.

By March 1974 the Watergate crisis and other crimes had forced the resignation of more than a dozen officials, including the vice-president for graft. When it became apparent that Congress would use its constitutional impeachment powers to remove him from office for "high crimes and misdemeanors", Nixon resigned.

The erosion of public confidence generated by the Vietnam War, combined with the Watergate Scandal, renewed public cynicism toward a government which had systematically lied to its people. However, when Vice President Gerald Ford was sworn in as Nixon's successor, the nation had weathered a profound constitutional crisis. The Watergate scandal demonstrated that no citizen is above the Constitution, including the president of the United States. Also the American public became interested in the personal life of the president. Since Watergate, no American president or his family could escape the scrutiny of the mass media and the public.

G) Stagflation

Between the late 1960's and the early 1970's, the American economy underwent *"stagflation"[130], an unorthodox combination of *stagnation[131] or recession and inflation. Several factors contributed to this situation, including the Vietnam War and America's loss of technological superiority. In retaliation for the massive aid the US sent to Israel in 1973, OPEC (Organization of Petroleum Exporting Countries) in the Middle East announced that it would not sell oil to nations supporting Israel and that it was raising its prices by 400%.

In 1970 the GNP (Gross National Product) declined, and in 1971 American imports exceeded exports. Inflation increased in 1973 – 1974, aggravated by the large deficit in foreign trade caused by importing expensive petroleum. By 1979 annual inflation was more than 13%, and unemployment hovered around 7%. Although Presidents Nixon, Ford and Carter tried various ways to *remediate[132] stagflation, none of them was successful.

3. RONALD REAGAN (1981—1989): THE REAGAN REVOLUTION

Reagan presided over a peaceful and prosperous America. To a degree unmatched since FDR's New Deal, *Ronald Reagan[133] imprinted his personal brand on the 1980's. It was not that Reagan possessed a master blueprint for American society. Instead, Reagan believed in a few basic ideas. He possessed a traditional view of the role of government in society. He agreed with President Jefferson who said, "The government that governs best governs least".

Reagan believed that the "monkey" of big government was bad and should be lifted from the American people's backs. Reagan limited the size of the US government and, by reducing income taxes, allowed people to spend and invest more of their own money. To compensate for this loss of revenue, the Reagan government reduced funding for education, social services and scientific research. However, since military spending increased sharply, the government still did not have enough money. The government borrowed heavily, greatly increasing the national debt.

The US government borrows money by issuing bonds and promises to repay buyers of these bonds both their original investment plus interest. The national debt is closely related to the number of bonds the government issues. Usually, a government borrows heavily during a national crisis, such as wartime; in contrast to the Reagan administration that borrowed during prosperous years to pay for the increasing military expenses. Under Reagan, the American national debt increased from 907.7 billion dollars in 1980 to 2,857 billion dollars in 1989. Interest payments rose from 74.9 billion in 1980 to 240.9 billion in 1989. Since the interest on the bonds must be paid before the debt can be reduced, Americans continue to pay back this debt through their taxes.

His foreign policy, based on his monolithic world view, brought the United States into a new Cold War era. The Reagan administration centered its anti-communist crusade in Latin America, unlike other postwar administrations, which had primarily focused on Europe and/or Asia. Since the Monroe Doctrine (1823), the great world powers had quarreled over Latin America. In addition, the United States feared revolutionary anarchy in the region. This is why Reagan was determined to oust Nicaragua's Sandinista's government. Meanwhile, the United States expanded its military presence in neighboring Honduras. In October 1983 Reagan invaded Grenada, a small Caribbean island. The pretext was to protect American medical students in Grenada, but, in reality, the invasion was to eliminate Cuba's communist influence on the island.

During the end of his presidency, Reagan abruptly changed his foreign policy and moved toward détente. In 1987, the administration that had launched the biggest military buildup in history signed a major arms-control treaty with the Soviet Union. According to the treaty, both countries would reduce the number of their intermediate-range missile forces.

This sudden thaw in the Cold War was a result of many factors. Both countries needed to solve urgent domestic economic problems. Moreover, they finally acknowledged the world was not bipolar. Rapid developments in the Pacific Rim areas, the robust economies in Japan and Germany and the projected European Union reshaped their domestic and foreign policies and priorities. The Cold War was over.

4. THE PERSIAN GULF WAR (GULF WAR)

When Iraqi forces occupied and annexed Kuwait in 1990, nearly the entire global community moved to drive the Iraqis from Kuwait and to restore Kuwait's sovereignty. Out of vital interests of the United States in the Middle East, President *George Bush [134] forged an international coalition under the *auspices [135] of the United Nations to force Iraqi forces to withdraw from Kuwait, In the ensuing Gulf War the U.N. forces, led by the U.S., Britain, and France, quickly restored Kuwait's sovereignty.

To the immense relief of Americans who had feared that thousands might perish in the war, only 148 Americans were killed and 467 were wounded in the short Gulf War. The war was also inexpensive for Americans because wealthy UN allies which did not send combat forces largely paid the 30 billion dollars needed to finance the war. Even though the Persian Gulf War scarcely resembled the Vietnam War in any way, President Bush announced that Americans had finally overcome the *"Vietnam syndrome". [136]

The involvement of the United States in the turbulent politics of the Middle East after the Cold War period is a good example to show that America will continue to use its activities not to fight communism but to defend its economic interests.

XV. Modern Times

1. BILL CLINTON (1992—2000)

George Bush ran for a second presidential term in 1992. Republican Bush expected to be reelected, based on his popularity generated by the victory in the Gulf War. He was opposed by *Bill Clinton [137], a democrat and former governor of Arkansas. Clinton's campaign focused on the domestic economy, rather than foreign policy. His decision was partly influenced by Ross Perot, a third party candidate, who advocated balancing the budget.

Perot's idea won support from many voters who were weary of paying taxes to reduce the national debt. This debt was the highest in American history due to a combination of factors including the "War on Poverty", the Regan Tax cuts, and the Cold War containment policy.

In order to pay for these programs, the United States issued bonds and borrowed from commercial banks and foreign investors who demanded prompt repayment of their loans. Money was also borrowed from Social Security, the national retirement fund for American workers, which was not repaid. Many Americans feared that there would not be enough money in the Social Security fund for their retirement. Clinton capitalized on the voters' dissatisfaction and promised to balance the budget. In an upset victory he became president (1992) and was reelected for a second term in 1996.

Due to a series of fortunate events, including the end of the Cold War, Clinton and the Republican Congress announced that there would be a budget surplus in 1998. Clinton and some members of Congress wanted to use this surplus to restore the Social Security fund. Other members of Congress believed that federal taxes should be lowered to provide an immediate tax break.

A second reason for Clinton's popularity was a strong economy. Both the national unemployment and the inflation rates were low during his presidency. This phenomenon was contrary to a historic belief that when unemployment was high, inflation was low, and when unemployment was low, inflation was high.

In reality, the strong economy was a result of many factors. The Federal Reserve closely controlled interest rates, which banks use to borrow and lend money. Clinton's Secretary of the Treasury, Robert Rubin, was a Wall Street financier who had excellent business skills and friends who gave him good advice. The Republican Congress passed legislation which empowered the states to assume responsibilities which were formerly administered by the federal government, including welfare for people below the poverty level. Additionally, foreign and domestic investors poured large sums of money into American businesses. Basically, Clinton agreed with Congress that "The era of big government was over".

Another reason for Clinton's economic success was the expanding global economy. American businesses were closely related to the country's political and military involvement throughout the world. American businesses often invested in developing countries where usually labor was cheaper and taxes were lower. As a result, the United States became the largest producer and seller of goods in the world market after WWⅡ.

These circumstances, combined with the US open trade policy, leadership in the technological revolution, quality control of products, and leadership in international economic organizations, such as NAFTA (North American Free Trade Agreement), placed the United States in a successful position in the global marketplace by the end of the 20th century.

The foreign policy of Clinton administration was, on the whole, cautious and tentative, partly due to the rapidly changing character of the world order. Clinton presided over a historic agreement between Israel and the Palestinian·Liberation Organization to end their long struggle over the lands Israel had occupied in 1967. His administration reached an agreement with Ukraine for an elimination of the nuclear weapons that had been positioned there when the republic had been part of the Soviet Union. After months of resisting involvement in a bloody civil war in Bosnia (part of the former Yugoslavia), he agreed early in 1994 to NATO (North Atlantic Treaty Organization) air strikes and other military actions against the aggressors in the conflict. But there was as yet no replacement of containment for American foreign policy.

The last years of Clinton's administration were marred by charges of sexual misconduct against him. Despite his achievements, Clinton was impeached by the US House of Representatives but later *acquitted [138] by the U.S. Senate.

This scandal only gave greater influence to people called the religious right or the Christian right. This is the term given to a loose coalition of fundamentalist and conservative Christians. Although they do not have a shared set of beliefs, in general they hold some of the following ideas. Despite the founding fathers' firm separation of church and state, they assert that the United States is a Christian country. They argue that the Bible takes precedence over scientific findings, and so want to prevent the teaching evolution in schools and are skeptical about global warming. They are ready to adopt a "holy" war against Muslims, despite Clinton's support of Muslims in the Balkans. Some are racists who feel the Bible justifies white dominance. They vehemently oppose abortion and any teaching about sexuality or family planning in schools. They are very troubled by the increasing recognition of homosexual partnerships by some state governments and businesses.

2. George W. Bush (2001—2009)

Clinton's scandal thus created problems for his Vice President, Al Gore, when he ran for president against *George W. Bush[139]. Bush received the support of the Christian right. Despite this support, the 2000 presidential election was so close that it was not decided for a month after the official election day. The decision was due in part to a conservative US Supreme Court. Although Al Gore had more popular votes, George W. Bush, the son of ex-President George Bush, became president because he had more electoral college votes.

George W. Bush kept his promises to the Christian right. He supported the Faith-Based and Community Initiative that provided federal government money for religious charities. He opposed scientific research with *embryo stem cells[140] that President Clinton had approved. He cut off aid to the United Nations Population Fund because it supported birth control and abortion. He also refused to abide by the *International Kyoto Protocol[141] on carbon emissions and refused to abide by the Nuclear Arms limitation treaty. He sponsored major tax cuts that favored the wealthy. He did sponsor the No Child Left Behind attempt to improve elementary and secondary education.

On September 11, 2001 Al-Qaeda terrorists seized control of several airplanes. They crashed two into the World Trade Center towers in New York City and crashed one into the Pentagon, U.S. military headquarters outside Washington D.C. A fourth plane was crashed by the passengers before it could harm others. Three thousand people were killed. This event has become known as 9/11.

George W. Bush responded by declaring war on terrorism. The Al-Qaeda leadership was based in Afghanistan. After the Afghan government, controlled by Islamic fundamentalists, repeatedly refused to arrest or expel Al-Qaeda, a coalition force led by the US invaded Afghanistan and overthrew its government.

The initial response of the US public was complete support of President Bush, enabling him to obtain approval from Congress for many of his programs, including expanded powers for Federal government security agencies.

President Bush and some of his advisors claimed that Iraq also supported terrorism and was building weapons of mass destruction (WMD). Although U.N. fact finders were unable to find such weapons, the U.S., with forces from a few other countries, invaded Iraq in March, 2003. They deposed and later executed its president, Sadam Hussein.

The Iraq war was a disaster of enormous proportions. Instead of removing Sadam Hassein and replacing him with a more favorable ruler, the U.S. and Britain found themselves in the middle of fighting factions; Sunni Muslim versus Shiite Muslim, Kurds versus Iraqis, and everyone against the United States and Britain. The war sucked in all available U.S. troops and ten billion dollars a month.

Despite liberal groups attempts to use the internet to counter the grassroots campaigns of the Christian right, George W. Bush was re-elected by a very slight margin in 2004. Americans tend to keep presidents in the middle of a war, and the economy was holding steady. The next four years brought the bitter results of his earlier policies.

Iraq was the major problem. The war was costly, in terms of money and soldiers killed or injured. There were scandals over the false reports of WMD, over U.S. private companies operating in Iraq, over torture by private companies, and over the treatment given wounded U.S. soldiers. There was concern over reports of illegal detention and torture of prisoners held in the Guatanamo Bay prison. This was not on U.S. territory, although operated by U.S. forces, and the Bush administration claimed it was not subject to U.S. law. This claim was finally overturned in federal court and U.S. citizens became aware of torture done by their military.

In 2005 Hurricane Katrina devastated the U.S. Gulf Coast, particularly the city of New Orleans, a city loved and admired by the rest of the country. The response of authorities to those *evacuated [142] from the city and to those struggling to rebuild was incompetent at best. The office of Homeland Security, formed to respond to large scale disasters, spent much money but accomplished too little. The Bush appointees who headed the response were not qualified for the job. Since *evacuees[143] from New Orleans found refuge with relatives, friends, church groups, and other support groups all over the country, people became well acquainted with the incompetent response.

The final year of the George W. Bush administration saw a major collapse of the American and world banking system. This was initially caused by the bursting of a "housing bubble" in which speculators had driven up prices to unsustainable levels. When it became apparent that many home owners would not be able to repay their mortgage loans, the financial institutions who had bought these loans faced large losses, which forced many of them to seek help from their government. The resulting crisis soon spread to other parts of the economy, causing many *layoffs[144]. The response of the Bush administration was to provide more federal government funds for the financial institutions, not the ordinary people who would lose their homes.

The administration of George W. Bush began with a nation at peace, a budget surplus, a strong economy and a respected place in the community of nations. In 2008, the nation was at war, the federal debt was so large it would take generations to pay, people were losing their homes, and high prices were causing most Americans to struggle to meet expenses and debts. The U.S. was hated and distrusted abroad. The Al-Qaeda terrorists responsible for the 9/11 attacks had not been brought to account for their actions.

3. Barack Hussein Obama (2009—2017)

Democrat *Barack Obama[145] was elected president in 2008, defeating Senator John McCain with 52% of the popular vote. Obama appealed to blacks and other minorities, women, urban voters, and young voters. College students waited in line for hours to vote for him. His call for change brought out many first time voters.

Obama is the son of a Kenyan lawyer and an American mother. He was raised in Hawaii, but traveled extensively. With a degree in political science from Columbia University and a law degree from Harvard University, he went to Chicago, Illinois, where he worked as a community organizer and as a law professor. He was elected to the Illinois state senate and then to the United States Senate. In a sharply fought campaign, he defeated Hiliary Clinton, the wife of Bill Clinton, for the Democratic nomination for president. (He later appointed her to be Secretary of State, a major position in his administration.) He then faced Senator John McCain in the general election. With his chosen candidate for Vice President, Senator Biden, he campaigned on a platform calling for an end to the Iraq War, massive help to end the economic crisis, and a new approach to universal health coverage. He won a clear majority of votes. However, Obama was faced with great challenges: a nation in economic turmoil; a nation in an unpopular, unjustifiable war; a nation that must change in many ways in order to be true to the "American dream".

XVI. Conclusion

Though comparatively a young nation with a history of a little over two hundred years, the United States is a great nation and was the only super power at the end of the 20th century. It continues to play a leading role in the world's economy, politics, technology and popular culture. As a nation formed by immigrants, America still accepts people from around the world who are seeking a better life.

Some Americans use their freedom better than others. America is a country where it is easy to win and easy to lose. Compared to other countries, the United States of America has the most billionaires, but it also has the highest percentage of its population in prison.

Appendixes

A) In Congress, July 4, 1776

Declaration by the Representatives of the United States of America

When in the Course of human Events, it becomes necessary for one People to dissolve the Political Bands which have connected them with another, and to assume among the Powers of the Earth, the separate and equal Station to which the Laws of Nature and of Nature's God entitle them, a decent Respect to the Opinions of Mankind requires that they should declare the causes which impel them to the Separation.

We hold these Truths to be self-evident, that all Men are created equal, that they are endowed by their Creator with certain unalienable Rights, that among these are Life, Liberty, and the Pursuit of Happiness That to secure these Rights, Governments are instituted among Men, deriving their just Powers from the Consent of the Governed, that whenever any Form of Government becomes destructive of these Ends, it is the Right of the People to alter or to abolish it, and to institute new Government, laying its Foundation on such Principles, and organizing its Powers in such Form, as to them shall seem most likely to effect their Safety and Happiness. Prudence, indeed, will dictate that Governments long established should not be changed for light and transient Causes; and accordingly all Experience hath shewn, that Mankind are more disposed to suffer, while Evils are sufferable, than to right themselves by abolishing the Forms to which they are accustomed. But when a long Train of Abuses and Usurpation, pursuing invariably the same Object, evinces a Design to reduce them under absolute Despotism, it is their Right, it is their Duty, to throw off such Government, and to provide new Guards for their future Security. Such has been the patient Sufferance of these Colonies; and such is now the Necessity which constrains them to alter their former Systems of Government. The History of the present King of Great Britain is a History of repeated Injuries and Usurpations, all having in direct Object the Establishment of an absolute Tyranny over these States. To prove this, let Facts be submitted to a candid World.

B) Declared effective March 4, 1789

Preamble to the Constitution of the United States

We, the People of the United States, in Order to form a more perfect Union, establish Justice, insure domestic Tranquility, provide for the common defence, promote the general Welfare, and secure the Blessings of Liberty to ourselves and our Posterity, do ordain and establish this Constitution for the United States of America.

C)   **Abraham Lincoln's Address at Gettysburg 1863**

Four score and seven years ago our fathers brought forth on this continent a new nation, conceived in liberty and dedicated to the proposition that all men were created equal.

Now we are engaged in a great civil war, testing whether that nation or any nation so conceived and so dedicated can long endure. We are met on a great battlefield of that war. We have come to dedicate a portion of that field, as a final resting-place for those who here gave their lives that that nation might live. It is altogether fitting and proper that we should do this.

But, in a larger sense, we can not dedicate—we can not consecrate—we can not hallow—this ground. The brave men, living and dead, who struggled here, have consecrated it, far above our poor power to add or detract. The world will little note, nor long remember, what we say here, but it can never forget what they did here. It is for us the living, rather, to be dedicated here to the unfinished work which they who fought here have thus far so nobly advanced. It is rather for us to be here dedicated to the great task remaining before us—that from these honored dead we take increased devotion to that cause to which they gave the last full measure of devotion—that we here highly resolve that these dead shall not have died in vain—that this nation, under God, shall have a new birth of freedom—and that government of the people, by the people, for the people shall not perish from the earth.

D)   **Presidents of the United States of America**

President's Name	Political Party	Terms of Office
1. George Washington	Federalist	1789 – 1797
2. John Adams	Federalist	1797 – 1801
3. Thomas Jefferson	Dem.-Rep *	1801 – 1809
4. James Madison	Dem.-Rep *	1809 – 1817
5. James Monroe	Dem.-Rep *	1817 – 1825
6. John Quincy Adams	Dem.-Rep *	1825 – 1829
7. Andrew Jackson	Democratic	1829 – 1838
8. Martin Van Buren	Democratic	1837 – 1841
9. William Henry Harrison	Whig	1841
10. John Tyler	Whig	1841 – 1845
11. James Knox Polk	Democratic	1845 – 1849
12. Zachart Taylor	Whig	1849 – 1850
13. Millard Filmore	Whig	1850 – 1853
14. Franklin Pierce	Democratic	1853 – 1857
15. James Buchanan	Democratic	1857 – 1861
16. Abraham Lincoln	Republican	1861 – 1865
17. Andrew Johnson.	Republican	1865 – 1869
18. Ulysses Simpson Grant	Republican	1869 – 1877
19. Rutherford Birchard Hayes	Republican	1877 – 1881
20. James Abram Garfield	Republican	1881
21. Chester Alan Arthur	Republican	1881 – 1885

(Table Continued)

22. Grover Cleveland	Democratic	1885 – 1889
23. Benjamin Harrison	Republican	1889 – 1893
24. Grover Cleveland	Democratic	1893 – 1897
25. William McKinley	Republican	1897 – 1901
26. Theodore Roosevelt	Republican	1901 – 1909
27. William Howard Taft	Republican	1909 – 1913
28. Wooldrow Wilson	Democratic	1913 – 1921
29. Warren Gamaliel Harding	Republican	1921 – 1923
30. Calvin Coolidge	Republican	1923 – 1929
31. Herbert Clark Hoover	Republican	1929 – 1933
32. Franklin Delano Roosevelt	Democratic	1933 – 1945
33. Harry S. Truman	Democratic	1945 – 1953
34. Dwight David Eisenhower	Republican	1953 – 1961
35. John Fitzgerald Kennedy	Democratic	1961 – 1963
36. Lyndon Baines Johnson	Democratic	1963 – 1969
37. Richard Milhous Nixon	Republican	1969 – 1974
38. Gerald Rudolph Ford	Republican	1974 – 1977
39. Jimmy Carter	Democratic	1977 – 1981
40. Ronald Reagan	Republican	1981 – 1989
41. George Bush	Republican	1989 – 1993
42. William Jefferson Clinton	Democratic	1993 – 2001
43. George W. Bush	Republican	2001 – 2009
44. Barack Hussein Obama	Democratic	2009 –

*Dem.-Rep. Party is now the Democratic Party.

Study Questions

1. Americans have always believed that government should play a limited role in society. What are some of the reasons for this belief?
2. America has been called a nation of immigrants. Why did people migrate to the United States?
3. Most countries have problems with the relations between people of different ethnic, racial, or national origins. What are some of the reasons why the US has had a difficult time in dealing with race relations?
4. The three most important documents in American history were the Declaration of Independence, the US Constitution and the Gettysburg Address. What did each of these documents contribute to American democracy?
5. The US was on the winning side in the three great wars of the 20th century—World War Ⅰ, World War Ⅱ, and the Cold War. Was the US just lucky or were there other reasons for this?
6. Select one event in American history and explain why you think it was important.

Selected Bibliography

Brinkley, Alan. *American History: A Survey*. New York: McGraw-Hill Colleage, 1999.
Morris, Richard Brandon. *Encyclopedia of American History*. 6th ed. New York: Harper & Row, 1982.
Davidson, James West et al. *Nation of Nations: A Narrative History of the American Republic*. 3rd ed. New York: McGraw Hill, 1998.
Shi, Tindal. *American*. Brief Third edition, Vol. 1 – 2. New York: W. W. Norton & Company, 1993.

注　释

〔1〕橡树果。
〔2〕哺乳动物。
〔3〕大平原(北美中西部的河谷地区和平原)。
〔4〕天花。
〔5〕传教团设立的机构(如教堂、学校、医院等)。
〔6〕(西班牙)无敌舰队。
〔7〕美国独立战争前弗吉尼亚州的议会。
〔8〕卡尔弗特家族。卡尔弗特(1580—1632),英国殖民地开拓者,下院议员,马里兰殖民地的创建者。
〔9〕清教徒。
〔10〕宗教上的分离主义者。
〔11〕(美国独立前,英王特许独占某块殖民地的)领主。
〔12〕贵格会教徒(基督教新教教友派的别称)。
〔13〕和平主义的,爱好和平的。
〔14〕木蓝属植物(能提取靛蓝)。
〔15〕切萨皮克湾(大西洋的海湾)。
〔16〕奥格尔索普(1696—1785),英国将军,创建美国佐治亚州的殖民地。
〔17〕英国出身低于贵族的中上阶层。
〔18〕印花税法(英政府1765年颁发的对北美殖民地人民征收直接税的法令,规定殖民地的法定文件、商业凭证等都需加印花税票)。
〔19〕波士顿惨案(1770年3月5日波士顿居民反对殖民地统治和经济勒索,遭当地英国驻军屠杀)。
〔20〕第一次大陆会议(1774—1789年间英属北美13个殖民地的代表会议,独立战争期间的立法机构)。
〔21〕潘恩(1737—1809),美国作家,政治理论家。

〔22〕弗兰克林(1706—1790),美国资产阶级革命时期的民主主义者、作家。
〔23〕立宪会议。
〔24〕参议院。
〔25〕联邦主义者。
〔26〕汉密尔顿(1755—1804),美国联邦党领袖,担任美国首任财政部长(1789—1795),提出建立国家银行和加强中央政府等施政方针。
〔27〕麦迪逊(1751—1836),美国第四任总统(1809—1817),宪法主要起草人,1812年美英战争中任总司令。
〔28〕杰伊(1745—1829),美国最高法院第一任首席法官(1789—1795)。
〔29〕《联邦党人文集》指杰伊、麦迪逊、汉密尔顿三人分别写给报刊的信件后来被收集成册出版的书。
〔30〕制约和平衡。
〔31〕财政部长。
〔32〕国务卿。
〔33〕拿破仑一世(1769—1821),法国皇帝(1804—1815)。
〔34〕刘易斯(1774—1809),美国探险家,曾与克拉克率探险队进行首次直达太平洋西北岸横贯大陆的考察(1804—1806)。
〔35〕克拉克(1770—1838),美国军人,探险家,曾与刘易斯率探险队对广大西北地区进行探险(1804—1806),对开发密苏里准州作出贡献。
〔36〕国会大厦。
〔37〕位于巴尔的摩的麦克亨利要塞。
〔38〕《星条旗永不落》。
〔39〕门罗(1758—1831),美国第五任总统,为独霸美洲提出欧洲各国不得干涉美洲事务的

主张。

〔40〕门罗主义。1823 年门罗提出的美国外交政策原则,口号是"美洲是美国人的美洲"。

〔41〕亚当斯(1767—1848),美国第六任总统(1825—1829),当过外交官,门罗总统的国务卿(1817),一贯反对扩展奴隶制。

〔42〕安德鲁·杰克逊(1767—1845),第二次反英战争时期的将军,于 1829—1837 任美国第七任总统。

〔43〕众议院。

〔44〕(美国)边疆居民,边疆开发者。

〔45〕波尔克(1795—1849),美国第十一任总统(1845—1849),兼并得克萨斯。

〔46〕泰勒(1784—1850),美国第十二任总统(1849—1850),墨西哥战争中的美国英雄。

〔47〕惠特尼(1765—1825),美国机械工程师,发明家,轧棉机的发明者,设计并生产装配步枪用的互换零件,对工业影响很大。

〔48〕麦科马克(1809—1884),美国工业家,发明家,收割机发明者(1831)。

〔49〕伊利运河(五大湖区的一个人工河道)。

〔50〕美国纽约州东部的哈得孙河。

〔51〕五大湖(北美洲中东部湖泊群)。

〔52〕禁酒论者。

〔53〕和平主义。

〔54〕斯坦顿(夫人)(1815—1902),美国女权运动领袖,在纽约召开第一次妇女权利大会(1848),通过争取妇女选举权等提案。

〔55〕莫特(夫人)(1793—1880),美国女改革家,反对奴隶制度,从事女权运动。

〔56〕美国第一所女子学院,位于新罕布什尔州。

〔57〕(自由党的前身)辉格党。

〔58〕林肯(1809—1865),美国第十六任总统(1861—1865),共和党人,反对蓄奴制,后被刺杀身亡。

〔59〕《汤姆叔叔的小屋》,美国女作家斯托夫人所著长篇小说。

〔60〕南北战争时逃入(或被北军带入)北军战线内的黑人。

〔61〕选举权,参政权。

〔62〕三 K 党,美国南北战争后不久成立于南部的白人秘密组织,迫害黑人等少数民族。

〔63〕对反政府政治犯的特赦法令。

〔64〕海斯(1822—1893),美国第十九任总统(1877—1881)。

〔65〕卡内基(1835—1919),美国钢铁实业家,曾致力于慈善事业,创办图书馆和卡内基基金会等。

〔66〕洛克菲勒(1839—1937),美国洛克菲勒财团的创始人,创办美孚石油公司。

〔67〕奥尔兹(1864—1950),美国发明家,汽车制造商,设计奥尔兹汽车,首创流水线装配法。

〔68〕亨利·福特(1863—1947),美国汽车制造商,创办福特汽车公司(1903),生产 T 型汽车,发明装配线生产法,使美国成为汽车大国。

〔69〕菲尔德(1834—1906),美国商人,开设芝加哥马歇尔·菲尔德纺织品公司。

〔70〕沃纳梅克,美国早期百货商店的创办人之一,以善于使用广告闻名。

〔71〕美国商人(1863—1914),开创珠宝首饰邮购业务,创办美国著名百货商场 Sears。

〔72〕斯威夫特(1839—1903),美国企业家,铁路冷藏车之发明人,组织斯威夫特公司(1885)。

〔73〕摩根(1837—1913),美国金融家,铁路巨头,组建摩根公司(1895)。

〔74〕范德比尔特(1794—1877),美国航运和铁路巨头。

〔75〕西奥多·罗斯福(1882—1945),美国第二十六任总统(1901—1909)。

〔76〕企图解散托拉斯的人。

〔77〕秣市骚乱,1886 年 5 月 4 日发生在芝加哥秣市广场的警察镇压抗议工人群众的暴力事件。

〔78〕全国市政联盟。

〔79〕塔夫脱(1857—1930)美国第二十七任总统(1903—1913),推行反托拉斯法,实行金元外交政策。

〔80〕威尔逊(1856—1924),美国第二十八任总统(1913—1921),民主党人,倡议建立国际联盟。

〔81〕麦金利(1843—1901),美国第二十五任总统(1897—1901),共和党人,发动美西战争,吞并夏威夷,曾对华提出门户开放政策。

〔82〕义务兵役制条例。

〔83〕国际联盟。

〔84〕哈定(1865—1923),美国第二十九任总统(1921—1923),任内使国会通过建立联邦政府预算制度等法案。

〔85〕柯立芝(1872—1933),美国第三十任总统,(1923—1929),对内实行不干涉工商业政策,对外推行孤立主义,任内美国经济繁荣。

〔86〕20 世纪 20 年代行动与衣着不受传统约束

的年轻女子。
[87]（美俚）非法经营的酒店。
[88]（美俚）偷卖（贩、酿、运的）酒商。
[89] 正统派基督教。
[90] 至上主义者。
[91] 胡佛（1874—1964），美国第三十一任总统。
[92] 福兰克·罗斯福（1882—1945），美国第三十二任总统，（1933—1945），民主党人，推行"新政"，二战中对建立反法西斯同盟作出重大贡献。
[93] 新政，罗斯福在20世纪30年代实施的内政纲领名称。
[94] 极权主义者。
[95] 感应引线（指炮弹、导弹等的无线电感应装置，可在接近目标的特定范围内引爆）。
[96] 艾森豪威尔（1890—1969），美国第三十四任总统（1953—1961）。
[97] 第二次世界大战中盟军在法国北部的进攻日，即1944年6月6日。
[98] 杜鲁门（1884—1972），美国第三十三任总统，下令对日本广岛和长崎实施原子弹轰炸（1945）。
[99] 广岛（日本本州岛西南岸港市）。
[100] 长崎（日本九州岛西岸港市）。
[101] 二战后，1947—1961年美国的生育高峰。
[102] 多米诺骨牌理论。原为政治术语，指一个倒下会引起连锁反应而全部倒下。
[103] 美国总统之行政命令。
[104] 反美活动。
[105] （美）司法部长。
[106] 麦卡锡主义，指美国共和党参议员麦卡锡于1951—1954年间发动的反共以及迫害民主进步力量的法西斯行径。
[107] 肯尼迪（1917—1963），美国第三十五任总统，1963年11月23日在达拉斯市遇刺身亡。
[108] 卡斯特罗，古巴共产党第一书记，1959年推翻巴蒂斯政权后曾在政治、经济等方面进行一系列改革。
[109] 弹道导弹。
[110] 海军封锁。
[111] 偷偷摸摸地。
[112]（尤指用化学喷雾或燃烧弹）毁掉。
[113] 尼克松（1913— ），美国第三十七任总统。1972年2月访问中国，与周恩来总理在上海分表联合公报，开辟了中美关系正常化的道路。
[114]（法语）国际紧张关系的缓和。
[115] 联合大企业。
[116] 马丁·路德·金（1929—1968），美国黑人牧师，著名黑人民权运动领袖。1964年获诺贝尔和平奖，1968年被种族主义分子枪杀。
[117] 对引起争论的政治或社会问题进行讨论或辩论的宣讲会。
[118] 梭罗（1817—1862），美国作家，超验主义运动代表人物，主张回归自然，反对蓄奴制和美国侵略战争。
[119] 甘地（1869—1948），印度民族解放运动领袖，首倡非暴力抵抗运动。
[120]（美国华盛顿国会大厦与华盛顿纪念碑之间的）草地广场。
[121] 黑豹党人。创建于1966年的美国黑人政党成员，主张以武力获取权力。
[122] 女权主义者。
[123] 反传统文化（1960's—1970's），美国青年中形成的一种文化群落，表现为反传统的生活方式和思想道德观念。
[124] 新左派，20世纪60年代美国兴起的以大学生为主的激进的社会政治改革运动。
[125] 正统的马克思主义。
[126] 即 Youth Culture。
[127] 林顿·约翰逊（1908—1973），美国第三十六任总统（1963—1969）。
[128] 伟大社会，美国总统约翰逊于1964年提出的以社会福利为主要内容的施政纲领。
[129] 政府发给或以低价供给穷人食品的票证。
[130] 经济滞胀。
[131] 停滞。
[132] 矫正。
[133] 罗纳德·里根（1911— ），美国第四十任总统（1981—1989）。
[134] 乔治·布什（1924— ），美国副总统（1981—1984，1985—1988），美国第四十一任总统（1989—1993）。
[135] 支持。
[136] 越战综合症（对战争的恐惧、厌恶、憎恨等情绪）。
[137] 克林顿（1946— ），美国第四十二任总统（1993—2001）。
[138] 宣告无罪。
[139] 乔治·W·布什（小布什，1946— ），美国第四十三任总统（2001—2008）。
[140] 胚胎干细胞。胚胎干细胞具有自我复制并分化为人体各种功能细胞的潜能，被广泛应用于生物学各个领域，具有潜在的医

学应用前景。
〔141〕京都议定书。为了控制全球二氧化碳排放，联合国141个成员国于1997年12月在日本签署了京都议定书。定于2005年2月16日正式生效。
〔142〕撤离。
〔143〕被疏散者。
〔144〕停工。
〔145〕奥巴马（1961—　），美国第四十四任总统（2009—2017）。

CHAPTER 9 BRITISH AND AMERICAN GOVERNMENT

Lawrence Thomas Farley

I. Introduction

It is often said that comparison is the starting point for all analysis. Only by comparing can we bring out the similarities, the contrasts, the parallels and the discontinuities that make things interesting and understandable.

The governments of Britain and the United States grew out of the same historical and cultural milieu. The British and American people share a similar language and a common philosophical heritage. Yet the Americans have evolved a very different form of government.

Indeed, by many measures British and American government are polar opposites. Britain is a *unitary[1] *monarchy [2] lacking a formal written constitution and has highly disciplined political parties. The United States is a federal republic with a written constitution and has undisciplined political parties. Britain has a strong central government with little separation of power among the *legislative [3], *executive [4], and *judicial [5] functions of government. The United States has a weak central government with strict separation of powers between the legislative, executive, and judicial branches of government.

It should come as no surprise that British and American politics are mutually incomprehensible even among well-educated people in the two countries. Most Britishers have absolutely no idea what a primary election is about or what state governors do. Most Americans are completely baffled over *by-elections[6], *parliamentary whips[7], and *backbenchers[8].

Because British and American politics are so radically different and yet are set in a common historical and philosophical milieu, we have an excellent opportunity to reap exciting analytical rewards. Therefore, this chapter is going to be conceptual in focus. It will not examine names, dates, places, and events except insofar as they illustrate major concepts. It will not catalog the institutions and structures of British and American government. Rather, this chapter seeks to develop the conceptual tools that will make these institutions and structures meaningful to the reader.

In this chapter, we will examine the politics of the U.S. through the prism of the fundamental concepts that have shaped its forms of government. First, the concepts of politics and government will be developed followed by *political legitimacy[9], *absolutism[10] and *constitutionalism[11]. Then the forms of democracy will be explored along with theories of representation. This will take us to a consideration of elections, political parties, assemblies, and *bureaucracies[12].

II. Politics

1. THE BEGINNINGS OF POLITICS

The political traditions of the Britain and the U. S. date back about twenty-five centuries to the ancient Greeks. Most of the vocabulary of politics is derived from the Greek language. Of course, the meaning and significance of the words have evolved considerably over the centuries. Nevertheless, it was the ancient Greeks who were the pioneers of Western political thinking, and their influence remains very great today

The word politics comes from the Greek word polis which means "town". We often see this usage of polis in place names, for example, Indianapolis (the capital of the state of Indiana) means "Indian town". So the word politics refers to the public affairs of towns— the first organized governmental entities in ancient Greece.

The word government comes from the Greek word kubernete which refers to the steering oar used on early Greek ships. Thus, to govern is to steer or to direct the public affairs of a political entity. China is not the only country where a ruler is sometimes referred to as the "helmsman" of the ship of state.

A remnant of the original Greek word is seen in the adjective *gubernatorial[13]. For example, if someone is running for the office of governor in one of the American states, it may be said: "She is a candidate in the gubernatorial election". Gubernatorial elections are important in the U. S. because several recent presidents, including Carter, Reagan, Clinton, and Bush were state governors before they became president.

2. THE ROLE OF GOVERNMENT IN POLITICS

A government is a social institution within which politics takes place. Governments are different from other social institutions because the political process is authoritative. Governments can compel a person's behavior by the threat of force or by the use of force. Other social institutions such as business corporations, churches, private clubs, and universities are not authoritative. They cannot use compulsion to force people to behave in certain ways. Americans who work for a company, belong to a church, are members of a clubs, or students at a university are not subject to the authoritative jurisdiction of those organizations. If they don't like the rules, they have the exit option—they can quit. They obey the rules and policies of these organizations only if they choose to obey. Since they are free to terminate their connection to these organizations, these organizations do not have compulsory jurisdiction over them.

America has a long tradition of private, non-governmental organizations and associations. Historically, most of the economic, religious, recreational, and educational dimensions of life in this country have operated outside of government control So, the distinction between authoritative governmental institutions and voluntary private institutions is very clear and very obvious.

In other countries with long *statist[14] traditions where the government owns or controls all social institutions—business enterprises, churches, clubs, and schools—these institutions are governmental and are, therefore, authoritative. In such countries the compulsion of the political system extends to virtually all dimensions of social life. If the exit option is not available, no institution can be entirely voluntary.

CHAPTER 9 BRITISH AND AMERICAN GOVERNMENT

3. SEPARATING THE GOVERNMENT FROM PRIVATE ISSUES

A major theme that runs throughout American history is the division line separating the public from the private sphere. Government is seen as having a limited role in society. Many people see politics both as a way to solve important societal problems and as a problem in itself that should be limited and contained as much as possible.

We will define politics as *the authoritative allocation of values[15]. The political process is authoritative. It can and will compel your behavior. If you do not obey the rules laid down by the political process, there are police, prison guards, and soldiers to ensure your obedience. Your participation in government as a citizen is not voluntary. Unlike private social institutions, you cannot resign from the political process.

Many Americans are angry these days with all the laws, rules, regulations, and taxes imposed upon them. They are tired of police, lawyers, and courts. They are infuriated by *pettifogging bureaucrats[16] and the fines and prisons that stand behind them. So imagine an angry American citizen saying this: "That's it! I quit! I'm not going to take any more bullying from my government! I'm moving to Australia!" Of course, when he arrives in Australia, he will discover that he is subject to the compulsory jurisdiction of the Australian political system. The Australian system has even more regulations and higher taxes than the U.S. Also, unlike the U.S., voting is compulsory in Australia. If you fail to vote, you will be fined. If you refuse to pay the fine, you are put in prison.

4. THE GOVERNMENT AS AN AUTHORITY

Thus, politics is authoritative. The political system has compulsory jurisdiction over its citizens. But what does it do with its authority? This brings us to the second part of the definition of politics. The political system allocates values. Values such as wealth, status, and opportunity are allocated by the political system. Wealth is collected through various systems of taxation and then redistributed through government spending programs. Status is conferred by governments through the grant of licenses, charters, and permissions. Opportunity is allocated primarily through the provision of educational opportunity. (In the U.S. about half of American youth receive some college training; in Britain about twenty percent; worldwide about one percent.)

A) Allocation: Some Get More and Some Get Less

In any system of allocation there are winners and losers. Some people get more and some get less. But win or lose the process is compulsory. For example, many people in Scotland remain angry that most of the enormous oil wealth produced in recent decades just off the Scottish coast did not stay in Scotland. Rather, much of the oil revenue has been taken by the British government and distributed largely for the benefit of the English. The Scots are losers in the authoritative allocation process whereby North Sea Oil wealth is being distributed. But win or lose, they are bound authoritatively to accept the result.

Some people in Pennsylvania, a state in the northeastern U.S., are distressed that taxpayers in Pennsylvania pay more in federal taxes to Washington, D.C., than they receive back in federal spending in Pennsylvania. In some years Pennsylvania has only received 93 cents in federal spending in Pennsylvania from every dollar sent to the federal *treasury[17]. The people of Pennsylvania are losers in the federal government's *budgetary[18] process. Wealth is literally being taken out of Pennsylvania and is sent to other states. In some years California, for instance, has received as high as $1.25 in federal spending for every dollar sent to Washington in federal taxes. Californians are winners, and Pennsylvanians are losers. Pennsylvanians and the citizens of other states have been losing for decades. This is one reason why millions of Americans have followed the money and moved to California.

To review, politics is the authoritative allocation of values. The political institutions we call governments can use compulsion to allocate values such as wealth, status, and opportunity. The political system does not allocate these values equally. Some people win, and some people lose. But whether they win or lose, the government can use police, prisons, and armies to command their obedience.

"Wait a minute!" you are saying. "This is all true enough but most people don't obey their government because they're afraid. They support it willingly. They don't need a policeman watching them to obey the law". Why do people willingly accept their political system? To explore the answer the reader will have to examine the next section.

III. Political Legitimacy
1. GOD

The oldest and by far the most important source of political legitimacy during recorded history is God. God, defined in the Christian, Jewish, and Islamic traditions as the all-knowing, all-powerful creator of the universe, has been a central figure in Western politics. In all three of the great Western religions, God is depicted as choosing the persons who are to rule mankind. They, in turn, are required to obey God's laws, foster the spread of God's church, and to carry out any divine instructions. This concept, often called the divine right of kings, is quite clear. God speaks to the king, and the king speaks to the people. By obeying the king the people are obeying God.

$$God ==> King ==> People$$

If people believe that this is the way the universe is structured, if they believe that their government is carrying out God's orders, then they are likely to obey their government.

Technically, this kind of government is called *theocracy[19]. Theos in Greek means God. (We see the same Greek root in theology—the study of God—and in atheist—someone who does not believe in God.) The second part of "theocracy", the-cracy, also come from Greek and means rule by. So "theocracy" means rule by God.

Until the twentieth century most kings and emperors in nearly all countries ruled by some kind of divine right. The ruler was the vital link connecting God to the people. The ruler was God's agent on earth. To show disrespect to the ruler was to show disrespect to God.

To this day, the British monarchs utilize the divine right principle. It was God that chose the British royal family, the *House of Windsor[20], to rule over Britain. Contemporary British coins continue to carry the abbreviated legend deo gratia regina—queen by the grace of God. She is queen not by the grace of the parliament, not by the grace of the voters, but by the grace of God. When the present queen, Elizabeth II, dies or abdicates, the new king will receive his crown from the head of the Church of England, the *Archbishop of Canterbury[21].

By the early twenty-first century the theocratic source of legitimacy has waned considerably in importance. Only a few countries can be described as pure theocracies. In Iran members of the *Islamic clergy[22] fulfill the role of intermediaries between God and the people. Many Iranians believe that God speaks to the clergy, and the clergy tell the people what God wants them to do. Thus, by obeying the laws of the Iranian government, many Iranians believe that they are carrying out God's wishes.

While no longer the dominant source of political legitimacy, the divine will remains relevant to the political process. Many elected politicians in the United States claim that their programs and policies are congruent with God's wishes. References to God appear in virtually every major speech given by every modern American president and presidential candidate.

Theocratic legitimacy does not require a belief in a Western-style personal God. The laws of nature or the laws of economics can fill the same role as God. Indeed, any transcendent reality that is accepted by people can serve as a substitute for God. For example, if a people believe that a free market economic system is the best way to order the material world and if their government proclaims its devotion to free market economics, the citizens are more likely to support and obey their government.

In summary, if people believe that their government is carrying out God's will or the laws of nature or the laws of economics, they are more likely to support and obey that government.

2. EXCELLENCE

The second source of political legitimacy in the Western world is excellence. If people believe that the most excellent people are running the government—the best qualified, the best trained, the most skilled, the most sincere—then it stands to reason to obey their orders.

Most people accept the logic of turning to experts and specialists for guidance. However, we follow the guidance of physicians, lawyers, accountants, insurance agents, auto mechanics, investment counselors and others, if, and only if, we believe that they are excellent in what they do. If we have doubts about their qualifications, their training, their skill, or their integrity we will probably not follow their advice.

A) Aristocracy

Technically, this kind of government is called *aristocracy[23]. Aristos in Greek means the best. So aristocracy means rule by the best. People obey aristocratic governments because they believe that the best people are in charge. For many centuries people in China willingly obeyed Confucian aristocrats because they had proven that they were the best people to rule by achieving the highest scores on the imperial examinations.

Throughout most of British and American history a handful of aristocrats, blessed with formal education and experienced in managing wealth, have been the rulers. It is easy to forget that until the nineteenth century most people were illiterate, were steeped in ignorance and superstition, had never traveled more than a few kilometers from where they were born, and had never handled money. The idea that the people, the great ignorant masses, should tell the government what to do was regarded by both aristocrats and commoners alike as simply absurd. It was sensible and logical for the masses to defer to those with education and experience in managing wealth to operate the government.

If aristocrats prove themselves to be inept and corrupt, then they are no longer, by definition, aristocrats. They are not the most excellent. People are unlikely to obey them.

Aristocratic governance remains a powerful source of political legitimacy. If ruling elites are able to provide stability and high living standards to their people they are likely to receive broad support from the citizenry. If the people believe that the best and brightest leaders are running the government and that they are doing a good job, the people are likely to support and obey that government.

However, in many countries including Britain and the U.S., aristocratic legitimacy is becoming less and less important. Many voters are coming to believe that the "best and brightest" are congenitally unable to understand and appreciate the needs of the average person. These voters suspect that aristocrats use the government to enrich themselves at the expense of the general public.

The decline in aristocratic legitimacy is largely a product of the rise of the third and greatest modern source of political legitimacy, the will of the people.

3. THE WILL OF THE PEOPLE

The third and most important source of political legitimacy in the world today is the will of the people. If people believe that their government is carrying out the people's wishes, then the people are likely to support and obey that government. The logic is both circular and compelling. By obeying a government that is carrying out their wishes, the people are in essence obeying themselves.

$$people ==> government ==> people$$

Technically, this kind of legitimacy is called democracy. Demos in Greek means people. So "democracy" means rule by people.

For most of the past twenty-five centuries democracy has been dismissed as a silly idea. The notion that the crude, illiterate masses could tell the government what to do was simply ludicrous. Democracy, if attempted, would surely degenerate into mob rule and *anarchy[24].

It is only in the last two centuries—with the coming of mass public education and near universal literacy—that democracy has begun to achieve some credibility. Today, the average urban factory worker in Britain and the U.S. has a better education, is better traveled, and has handled more money than the typical aristocrat of three centuries ago.

The most important political trend in the world over the past one thousand years has been the increase in the level of public participation in the political process. Slowly at first but with increased speed in recent centuries, people have demanded the right to participate in the process that authoritatively allocates values.

A) British Democracy and the Monarchy

Britain's experience with rising public participation is typical. In the Middle Ages the rural land owning gentry classes demanded a consultative role in the king's government.

During the Renaissance the commercial classes in the burgeoning towns and cities struggled to join in the consultative process that evolved into parliament. With the coming of the Industrial Revolution, a new class of entrepreneurs and technical specialists entered the political process and helped to make parliament the dominant governmental institution. In the nineteenth century the working class and in the twentieth century women and minority groups became full participants in politics. Now that virtually all of the people have a role in the political process, their will has become supreme.

The will of the people became the dominant source of political legitimacy in the twentieth century and has virtually eclipsed the ideas of theocracy and aristocracy. Every government in the world today claims to be democratic. Even the most brutal military dictatorships claim to be carrying out the will of their people.

The rise of democratic legitimacy has spelled the end for most monarchies. A monarchy is a government led by a king, i.e. a person who wears a crown. Until the twentieth century most countries were monarchies. The titles varied—king, queen, emperor, empress, duke, duchess, count, countess, baron, baroness, * emir[25], *sultan[26], or *shah[27]. A republic is a government the head of which is not a king, i.e. he does not wear a crown. The head of state of a republic is usually called a president.

Some examples of monarchies and republics in the early 21st century:

Monarchies	Republics
Britain	USA
Japan	Germany
Saudi Arabia	France
Thailand	Russia
Spain	Iraq
Malaysia	Israel
Netherlands	Vietnam
Kuwait	Brazil
Canada	

Two centuries ago there were only a few republics in the world. Today, only about ten percent of countries are monarchies. Interestingly, Europe, the continent that pioneered the ascent of democratic legitimacy, is the continent with the greatest number of monarchies today.

How do monarchies survive in a democratic age? In the past monarchies relied on theocratic and aristocratic legitimacy. Those monarchies that could not make the transition to democratic legitimacy were swept away and replaced by republics. The surviving monarchies, with Britain as a prime example, succeeded because they shifted from absolute to constitutional rule.

IV. Absolutism and Constitutionalism

The second most important political trend during the last one thousand years, deriving from expansion in participation, is the gradual placing of limits on what governments can do to their people. The concept of putting limits on the government is called *constitutionalism[28]. Thus, constitutional government is limited government. Constitutionalism is not about limits that are placed on the freedom or opportunities of the individual citizen. It is about limitations that are placed on the government. Absolute government is unlimited government. An absolute government can do whatever it likes to its people. No government is totally absolute. There are always some limitations—if only the fear by the rulers of assassination or rebellion.

Absolute and constitutional government are the opposite ends of a continuum. On one end is absolute or unlimited government and on the other end of the scale is constitutional or limited government. All governments can be placed on the scale. Historically, governments have been moving slowly from the absolute end to the constitutional end of the scale.

```
       absolutism                                    constitutionalism
       (no limits)                                    (many limits)
       /_____/
```

As an example of absolute government, let's look at one of Britain's most famous kings, King Henry VIII (1509 - 1547). There were very few limits to Henry's power. In most matters his word was law. If, while looking out the window of his palace, he saw a commoner walking by whose appearance annoyed Henry, Henry could have the man arrested and executed immediately. However, if the man was a member of the gentry class, the hereditary aristocracy, Henry's power was limited. Dating back to the *Magna Carta[29] (1215), there were legal limitations upon what Henry could do to members of the aristocracy. An aristocrat was entitled to a trial and to a jury composed of fellow aristocrats. The law stood between Henry and some of his *subjects[30]. The law limited Henry's power.

```
       absolutism                                    constitutionalism
       /____x_____/
            Henry VIII
```

Law is an important constitutional limitation on government. People living under absolute government see law as simply the commands of the rulers. But people living under constitutional governments see law as a protection from arbitrary government action.

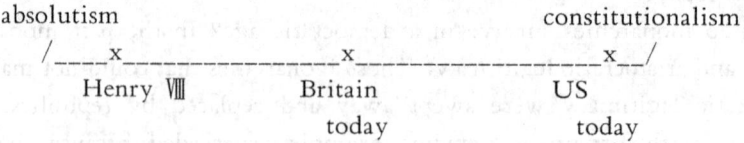

```
       absolutism                                    constitutionalism
       /____x_____x_____x__/
            Henry VIII      Britain              US
                            today                today
```

1. UNITARY AND FEDERAL GOVERNMENT

Within the worldwide movement toward constitutionalism, two forms of national government have emerged: unitary and federal government. Of these two forms of government, federal government is typically the more constitutional because it sets more limits on the powers of a national government.

In a unitary government there is a pre-existing central government which creates and controls smaller, local units of government.

Diagram of a Unitary Government

((((= = = = = = = = = = = =>   ((((
central government   small units of government

About ninety percent of national governments in the world are unitary in form. Britain has a unitary government. The central government in London, from time to time, has created local governments. These local governments, variously named shires, *regional councils[31] and districts councils, depend entirely upon the central government—the British government—for their powers. The government in London can create, reshape, reorganize, or abolish these local units of government.

What distinguishes unitary from federal government is the direction of causality as shown in the diagram above. It is the central government that causes the local units of government to exist. The local units of government cannot oppose or seek to reform the central government without risking their abolition by the central government. Therefore, they do not constitute a limitation on the powers of the central government. The local units of government are the creatures of the central government—not its controllers. In a federal government the small units of government pre-exist. It is the small units that come together to create a central or "federal" government.

Diagram of a Federal Government
small government units = = = = = = = = = = =>central or "federal" government

Only about ten percent of countries in the world today have federal governments. The United States is a federal government. The central government of the United States, the so-called "federal" government in Washington, D.C., is the creation of the states. In 1787 a group of independent states, each a former British colony, held a convention that led to the creation of the current United States.

The states are the owners of the United States. They created it. Only they can change it. The Washington, D.C., government is powerless to change its structure. Any amendment to the structure of the United States requires the approval of three-fourths of the states. Indeed, the states could, if they wish to, call a new convention and abolish the United States. Each state would then be completely free to go its own way as a separate country.

There are a number of examples of members of federations breaking away and becoming separate countries. Singapore had been a member state of the Malaysian federation but seceded to become a separate *sovereign state[32]. The two members of the Czechoslovak federation—the Czech and the Slovak republics—agreed to abolish Czechoslovakia and to create two new countries—the Czech Republic and Slovakia. One of the members of the Canadian federation, the province of Quebec, has considered withdrawing from Canada.

Typically, the small units that together create and control a federal central government are themselves unitary governments. Each of the fifty states in the United

States has a unitary government. This is true of most of the small units, variously called states, provinces, republics, or cantons, in federations. One exception was the Russian republic in the former Soviet Union. The Russian republic, one of the fourteen members of the Soviet federation, was itself a federation. Thus, Russia was a federation within a federation.

Because all of the fifty states in the United States have unitary governments, the citizens of the United States have experience with both forms of government—unitary and federal. Citizens of Britain have experience only with unitary government and are usually puzzled and confused about the differences between unitary and federal government.

For Americans the federal form of their national government is seen as an important mechanism for limiting the power of that government. The Washington, D. C., government possesses only the powers granted to it by the states. The states control the national government and, by amending the national constitution, the states can override any law enacted by the central government.

The United States government, the central government of the American federation, is a weak government. The British government, like the governments of other unitary regimes, is strong. The United States government possesses a limited set of powers and cannot acquire additional power on its own. It depends on the fifty states for its structure, its powers, and even its existence. The British government is all-powerful in Britain. It defines its own powers. It creates and dominates all other governmental units in Britain.

The United States government is a structurally weak government because the group of states that created it wished it to be weak. The fifty US states today continue to keep it weak. There are several reasons for this. First, there is a widespread belief that local government is better and more democratic than a national government. The government in Washington, D.C., is seen as distant from the real needs and problems of people. Because the United States is a large and very diverse country, the solution to a problem in one part of the country might not work in another part of the country.

Second, Americans are afraid that a strong government may become tyrannical. Because of the unhappy experience of the American colonies with what they saw as a tyrannical central government in London, the newly established United States was provided with a weak central government. The states granted to the national government (the United States) only those powers that were seen as necessary for protecting the national interest. All other powers were to be retained by the states. This preference for a weak central government continued to strengthen in the early twenty-first century with a majority of Americans believing that "big government" is a threat to their liberties.

V. Democracy

With the rise to dominance of the will of the people as the principal source of political legitimacy and the increasing demands of the people for government that is more constitutional, it is important that we analyze democracy in greater detail.

1. GREEK ORIGINS OF DIRECT DEMOCRACY

Dating back to the time of the ancient Greeks, Western thinkers have defined two basic types of democracy. The first, direct democracy, has rarely been put into practice.

Many Americans have no experience whatever with direct democracy and do not know what it is. The second type of democracy, indirect or representative democracy, is widely used around the world and, for most people, it is the only kind of democracy they know.

In direct democracy the people themselves operate the government in a hands-on fashion. They do not choose other people to run the government for them. With direct democracy the people themselves are the government—they perform all legislative, executive, and judicial functions of government.

Ancient Athens, one of the leading city-states of ancient Greece, experimented with direct democracy for a brief time. Every few weeks a meeting was held of all the citizens of Athens. This meeting was the government of Athens. Each citizen was free to stand up at these meetings and to propose new laws. For instance, one citizen might rise and propose that the tax rate be raised by 5%. After the proposal was debated the meeting would vote on the proposal. If a majority of the citizens in attendance voted "yes", the proposal became law. Another citizen might stand up and propose that the *admiral[33] in command of the Athenian navy be fired. The proposal would be debated, and if a majority voted "yes", the admiral was dismissed. Another citizen might rise and accuse his neighbor of a crime. Witnesses would be called, evidence presented, and speeches made. The accused person would be convicted of the crime if a majority of the citizens at the meeting voted "guilty".

Thus, Athens had a direct democracy. The citizens did not choose representatives who then formed a government and conducted the government on behalf of the citizens. The citizens themselves directly conducted the government. The citizens were the government.

2. MODERN DEMOCRACY

A contemporary example of direct democracy in the United States is the New England Town Meeting form of government. New England, in the northeastern corner of the U.S., has many small rural towns. In some of these towns a meeting of the residents is held about twice a year. The meeting is the government of the town. They do not elect a town council to run the town for them. Everyone is "elected" and serves as a member of the council. Within limits set by state law, the citizens of these towns are free to offer proposals regarding town laws (including taxes) at the town meetings. If a majority of the citizens at a meeting vote "yes", then a proposal becomes law.

The New England Town Meeting, like the assembly in ancient Athens, can operate successfully because there are only—at most—a few hundred people involved. To hold a similar sort of town meeting in New York City would no doubt be chaotic and unworkable.

Is direct democracy suitable only in small political entities? No, there are several forms of direct democracy that have been developed in the U.S. (but not in Britain) that do work when millions of citizens are involved. These forms of direct democracy are called *initiative[34] referendum, and *recall[35].

A) Initiative

An initiative is a process begun (initiated) by citizens whereby the citizens themselves directly make law. Typically, one citizen or a group of citizens draft a possible law. Then other citizens sign *petitions[36] in support of the proposed law. If a sufficient number of signatures is obtained, then the proposed law is put on the ballot at the next general election when the citizens vote either "yes" or "no". If a simple majority votes "yes", the proposed law becomes law.

For example, imagine that a group of university students in one of the U.S. states that permits initiatives are angry about the high tuition they must pay. So, one day, a group of students writes a proposed law—a law that bans tuition payments and that requires the state government to pay the entire cost of university education. Next, they collect several hundred thousand signatures of citizens who support their proposed law. If sufficient signatures are collected—in many places five percent of the registered voters must sign—the proposed law is put to a vote in the next election. If the voters say "yes", the proposal becomes law.

It is important to note that no legislature or parliament is involved in the initiative process. The voters by-pass the elected institutions of government that normally make law. It is easy to see why the elected politicians who serve in state legislatures are often hostile to initiatives.

Initiatives are not permitted in Britain nor are they allowed at the federal level in the U.S. Only about a third of the states in the U.S. permit initiatives. A famous example of the use of the initiative came in the 1970's when the voters in California voted themselves a huge tax cut.

Initiatives are very popular with interest groups. Commercial interests, farmers, labor unions, professional groups, sportsmen, and minority groups use initiatives to further their interests. Every group that wants lower taxes, government subsidies, protection from competition, or exemption from certain laws may launch an initiative drive. Of course, the voters are often suspicious of the motives behind initiative campaigns and vote "no".

The initiative process is nearly a pure form of direct democracy, i.e., the people themselves are directly making law.

B) Referendum

A referendum differs from an initiative in that a governmental unit takes the initiative to launch the process—not the citizens themselves. In a referendum a unit of government—a city council, a state legislature, or a national parliament—refers a matter to the voters for a decision. Instead of the elected representatives of the voters approving or rejecting a measure, the measure is put on the ballot at the next election for the voters to decide themselves.

In some countries, such as France, the President is able to use referenda to by-pass the national parliament by putting questions directly before the voters. The British parliament has always been hostile to all forms of direct democracy but in recent times has been forced to conduct referenda on thorny questions such as Scottish separatism and British participation in European institutions.

There is no *provision[37] for referenda in the U.S. constitution, so there are no referenda at the federal level in the U.S. However, most of the fifty states do permit referenda. Often, a referendum is used by state and local governments as a way for elected representatives to avoid controversial issues. Instead of a city council voting to enact higher taxes, they may refer the matter to the voters in a referendum. Thus, the officials escape responsibility for raising taxes. If the voters vote themselves higher taxes, they have only themselves to blame.

C) Recall

The recall election is similar to an initiative in that the citizens begin the process. An initiative is launched by citizens to create a new law while a recall election is launched by citizens to oust an elected representative from office. A recall election is a procedure whereby the voters can remove an official from office at any time.

Like an initiative, a recall begins with a petition campaign. If a sufficient number of signatures are collected, typically about five percent of the registered voters, a special election is called. The citizens then vote either "yes" or "no" to recall (oust) the official from office. If a majority vote "yes", the official is removed from office immediately. A second special election is then held to fill the vacancy.

Britain does not have recall elections nor does the U.S. at the federal level. Most of the fifty states in the U.S. do provide for recall elections at the local level.

A recall election amounts to a peaceful rebellion against a member of the government. It is a constitutional procedure since it holds elected officials directly accountable to the voters at all times and not only at regularly scheduled elections.

Ⅵ. Indirect or Representative Democracy

Indirect democracy is the kind of democracy with which all Americans are completely familiar. With indirect or representative democracy voters choose individuals to run the government on their behalf. Beginning at about age six, American children begin electing representatives to their schools' student governments. By the time they are adults these citizens accept without question the concept of indirect democracy.

Representative Assemblies in Britain and the U.S.

	Name	Length of Term in Office
	Upper House	
Britain:	*House of Lords [38]	lifetime
US:	*Senate [39]	six years
	Lower House	
Britain:	*House of Commons [40]	not more than five years
US:	House of Representatives	two years

What is not clear in the minds of most Americans citizens is the precise role of elected representatives. What are elected representatives supposed to do? Citizens are often angered when politicians campaigning in elections make promises and then, after they are elected and assume office, offer reasons why they will not keep the promises. Is it the function of representatives simply to do what the voters want them to do, or should representatives provide them leadership? Should representatives do things that the people do not want the government to do, but which, in the opinion of the representatives, are good for the people?

In essence, there are two theories of conceptualizing what representatives are supposed to do. One is called the *delegate theory[41] and the other the *trustee theory[42].

1. THE DELEGATE THEORY OF REPRESENTATION

In the delegate theory the job of a representative is to find out what the citizens wish and then to carry out their wishes. A delegate simply serves as an agent for his master—he receives instructions and then implements those instructions. For example, delegates to the *General Assembly[43] of the United Nations cast the vote of their countries at General Assembly sessions, but the delegates do not decide how to cast the votes. Instead, each delegate is instructed by his or her government on how to cast the country's vote. Delegates obey the orders of the people who send them.

For example, under the delegate theory the job of a member of the U.S. Congress would be to find out what the people of his district want him or her to do and then to go to Washington, D.C., and do it. Under the delegate theory, a congressional representative is simply a conduit to bring the demands of his or her constituents into the halls of government. The delegate theory reflects the democratic source of political legitimacy where the will of the people is the foundation of government.

2. THE TRUSTEE THEORY OF REPRESENTATION

In the trustee theory the representative uses his own best judgment to do what he believes is in the best interest of the citizens—whether or not the citizens agree. A trustee uses his own experience and wisdom to do what is best for the people and the country.

The trustee theory has its roots in the aristocratic source of political legitimacy. Clearly, the best people—the aristocrats—should use their own best judgment to act on behalf of the mass of people. Since ordinary people do not understand complex matters such as law, budgets, and foreign policy, representatives must use their own experience and wisdom in making decisions.

When representatives are elected in competitive elections there is a strong tendency for them to behave as delegates. They know that if they behave too much as trustees they may offend too many voters and therefore may lose the next election. Members of the U.S., House of Representatives, who serve terms in office of only two years, behave mainly as delegates. They are continually running for re-election and feel obliged to carry out the voters' wishes. Members of the U.S. Senate, who serve six-year terms, are better able to behave as trustees. Especially during the first few years of their term, senators are freer to use their own judgment because they know that voters have short memories. However, toward the end of their six-year terms senators begin to behave more as delegates in order to please the voters. Members of the U.S. Supreme Court, who serve lifetime terms, are completely free to behave as trustees since they never face the voters in an election. Many local judges in the U.S. are elected, and therefore must take more account of the wishes of the voters if they desire to be re-elected.

Elected representatives in Britain and the U.S. face a dilemma. If they behave as delegates and simply obey the latest public opinion *poll[44], they are condemned by the public for failing to show leadership. But if they take bold, unpopular positions on controversial issues—if they show leadership—they are condemned by the public for ignoring the will of the people.

In practice, most elected representatives behave as delegates on some issues and as trustees on others. With issues that are highly salient to the voters in their district they behave as delegates, because they know they may be defeated in the next election if they don't. With issues that are not relevant to their district, the representative is largely free to behave as a trustee.

VII. Elections

The concept of election is a very old one in the Western world and dates back some three thousand years ago to biblical times. The election or selection of certain individuals to rule the government (or to live in heaven) was made by God. God did the electing. The so-called "elect of God" were the people selected by God to do important things and to enjoy God's special favor.

Typically, a group of aristocrats—kings and priests—would claim that God had told them of His electoral decisions and they, in true theocratic tradition, would carry out the divine will. In recent centuries, with the rise of democratic legitimacy, the power of election has shifted from God to the mass of people. Some people in the West still believe that God remains central to the electoral process asserting vox dei, the voice of God, is heard in vox populi, the voice of the people.

There are two basic kinds of elections: candidate and issue. Candidate elections are an essential part of representative democracy while issue elections derive from direct democracy.

Candidate elections in Britain and in the United States are quite different. In Britain the party organizations choose the candidates, and the voters select between the various parties' candidates at a general election. The winner of a general election is elected to office; for example, the winner becomes a member of parliament.

In the U.S. there are normally two stages in a candidate election. The first stage is a primary election. In a primary election the citizens who are affiliated with a particular party vote to choose the persons who will be the candidates of their party in the general election. Voters who identify themselves as Democrats will choose among the Democrats who are seeking the Democratic Party's nomination, and Republicans will vote to choose from among the Republicans seeking the Republican Party's nomination. Citizens who identify themselves as independents, those who have no party affiliation, do not vote in primary elections.

It should be stressed that no one is elected to office in a primary election. Rather, the winners of a primary election face each other as candidates of their respective parties in the general election held later.

Many Americans are quite critical of the absence of primary elections in the British system. It is feared that when party bosses choose the candidates, rather than the voters, it is the party bosses who will control the candidates after they are elected to office.

Issue elections are rare in Britain and uncommon in most of the states of the United States. The initiative and referendum, discussed above, are two types of issue election where the voters decide matters of policy rather than having elected representatives decide for them.

1. PARTIES

Individuals run as candidates in elections and individuals are elected to office. However, a group of individuals pooling their efforts, resources, and connections have a better chance of being elected. In the British context a party is a group of people who wish to win elections and to control governments. In the American context a party is a group of people who wish to win elections.

Parties in Britain, influenced by political trends on the European continent, often claim to represent a particular ideology and can thus be said "to stand" for something. Even so, major British parties never forget that winning elections is important and frequently adjust their ideological principles to suit the current tastes of the voters. Since most voters are *moderate[45] or *middle of the road[46] in their political views, the parties must offer similarly moderate policies if they wish to win.

Of course, most parties have members who are *ideological zealots[47]. They believe that ideological purity is sacred and should not be compromised merely to win elections. When zealots take control of a party, it usually loses elections and keeps losing until moderates in the party, those who wish to win elections, regain control.

The left-wing of the Labor Party in Britain kept the party true to its leftist principles through much of the 1980's and lost a series of elections to the Conservative Party, which was better able to appeal to moderate voters. In the 1990's the Labor Party jettisoned many of its ideological scruples in hope of winning elections and returned to power.

In the United States the parties have minimal ideological content. This is not readily apparent because most active members of American political parties are inspired by strongly held ideological views. Nevertheless, most party activists realize that other activists and voters with different ideological views must be accommodated inside the party if the party is to have a chance of winning elections.

2. PARTY AND GOVERNMENT

In the U.S. the sole significant function of a political party is the winning of elections. After the election the victorious party plays a limited role in the operation of the government. Party leaders find it almost impossible to discipline the elected members of their party, since it is the voters in the next primary election, not the party leaders, who will decide the names to be on the next general election ballot.

In Britain, and in most of Europe, a party which wins an election takes over control of the parliament and thereby takes control of the institutions of government. The parliamentary whips are party leaders whose job is to ensure that the elected members of the party obey their party leaders in the manner that they cast their votes in parliament. No such discipline exists in the U.S. The president may be of a different party than the party that holds a majority in the two houses of the Congress. In any event, since the party leadership cannot effectively discipline the members of the party elected to the Congress, the parties cannot be said to control the Congress—much less the government. To understand this important difference between American and European politics, we must first examine the concept of assembly.

VIII. The Assembly Model

Social institutions reflect the ascendant organizational models of their time. Perhaps the extent to which institutions are influenced by ideas and models of organization is not widely appreciated. Each era seems to regard its conceptual models as "common sense" and does not see them as models at all.

Throughout history Western governments have been organized in accordance with the dominant organizational concepts of the time. In the Middle Ages governments were *hierarchical[48] organizations held together by ties of kinship or of personal fealty. Knights were *vassals[49] of dukes, who were vassals of kings, some of whom were vassals of emperors. Over the centuries a new organizational model emerged: the assembly model. Assemblies such as the British parliament gradually took powers away from the royal hierarchies.

Assemblies—parliaments, legislatures, congresses, conventions—are found in virtually all countries in the early twenty-first century. Nearly every country in the world either has a parliament or has had one in recent years. Yet, strangely, the assembly as a theoretical model is little understood. Indeed, as a form of organization it has not only been ignored, but it has been increasingly scorned.

However, the assembly model is a fully articulated organizational model with an honored tradition of scholarship behind it. The assembly model has the following basic elements:

The members of an assembly are equipotent, that is, none has a special leadership function. There is a minimum of hierarchy. The members select officers, e. g., the Speaker, from their own members for a fixed term. Such officers often surrender their power to vote and are considered *primus inter pares[50]. There is overlapping task competence; that is, every member can perform ALL the tasks of the organization. Every member can make motions, speak, and vote. The organization has a non-specific structure. It can form itself into a committee of the whole, break-up into standing or *ad hoc committees[51], or sit as a court. There is no necessary limit to the size of the group nor are there exclusive channels of communication between members of the group.

The organization functions by way of directive correlation whereby individuals working independently or in groups support and facilitate the work of others toward the achievement of a joint aim.

Assemblies are underpinned by the democratic ethic of the French Revolution; that is, political legitimacy arises from the will of the people. The legitimacy of an assembly derives from the manner in which it is constituted—not from what it does or accomplishes. If an assembly is regarded as fairly and freely constituted, then what it does or does not do is valid. It should be noted that assemblies are not justified on the grounds of efficiency and effectiveness—the twin principles of modern bureaucratic organizations.

There is a growing recognition that assemblies are poorly understood as organizations. Nelson Polsby, America's leading student of legislatures, declares, "Legislatures are badly understood as organizations because they are atypical as organizations in the flatness of their authority structure and in the internal legitimacy which they confer upon conflict, bargaining and coalition building".

IX. Conclusion

The governments of Britain and the US are quite different. The British government is a unitary monarchy with strongly disciplined political parties and few formal constitutional restraints on its powers. The U.S. government is a federal republic with weak political parties and many constitutional restraints on the powers of the central government.

There are some similarities between British and American government. Both claim the will of the people as the source of political legitimacy, and both use indirect or representative democracy as the means for the people to express their will. However, the British system tends more toward the trustee concept of representation, and the U.S. system tends more toward the delegate concept of representation. In the U.S. political system, at the state and local level, direct democratic techniques such as initiatives, referenda, and recall elections are increasingly used.

Some people in Britain and in the U.S. arrogantly believe that their respective forms of government are the best in the world. Can they both be correct? The fact that the British and American political systems are so radically different in form, and yet they are seen as strongly legitimate by the citizens of each country, leads us to one conclusion. All countries can evolve their own legitimate, democratic political systems in keeping with their own traditions and culture. The evolution of a political system can be made smoother if people take the time to compare other political systems with their own.

Appendixes

A) Glossary (Specialized terms used to describe contemporary US and UK politics)

Terms: US

bill: A bill is a proposed law that is being considered by a legislature. Only members of the legislature may propose bills.

议案：交由立法机构审核的议案。例：只有立法机构人员能够提出议案。

civil disobedience: Civil disobedience refers to the sincere and deliberate breaking of a law to draw attention to the unfairness of a law. Persons engaged in civil disobedience do not resist the police and accept whatever penalty is ordered by the courts. e.g. Anti-war demonstrators engaged in civil disobedience to protest against the war.

蓄意地违法：以文明的违抗引起对法律不公正之处的注意。参与蓄意违法行动的人并不与警察对抗，并接受法庭所决定的任何惩罚。例：反战示威者通过蓄意违法的方式来反对战争。

electoral college: The electoral college is a group of delegates representing the fifty states which selects the president and the vice-president. These delegates usually vote according to the popular vote in their home states. If a candidate receives the most votes from the voters in Illinois, the delegates to the electoral college from Illinois will cast their votes for that candidate. e.g. The electoral college meets in December to elect the president and the vice-president.

选举团：这是由50个州所选出的代表而组成的团体，将由这个团体选出正副总统。这些代表通常根据其所代表州的民意来选举总统。如果一位候选人得到的来自伊利诺斯州的选票最多，伊利诺斯州的代表则将投这位候选人的票。例:选举团在12月碰头,以选出正副总统。

filibuster: A filibuster is an effort to stall, delay, and ultimately block the consideration of a bill by the US Senate through the making of many long speeches. A filibuster may continue for weeks or even months until the Senate decides it must move to other business. e.g. The bill was filibustered to death.

阻挠议事的行动:通过许多冗长的发言来拖延,并最终妨碍美国参议院对一项法案的审议。妨碍可持续数周甚至数月,直到参议院决定开始进行另一项事务。例:这项议案被延误直至最后不了了之。

fiscal year (FY): The fiscal year is the official accounting period for the federal budget. It runs from October 1 through September 30. Fiscal year is often abbreviated FY. e.g. The budget for FY99 is the first budget in decades to be in balance.

财政年度:是官方对联邦政府的预算进行结算的一段时间。财政年度(美国)从10月1日至第二年的9月30日。财政年度通常缩写为"FY"。例:99财政年度的预算是数十年以来第一个平衡的预算。

focus group: A focus group is a technique used by election campaign organizations to measure the reaction of the public to specific themes, issues, and advertisements used during an election campaign. Typically, about a dozen people—chosen at random—are assembled and probed for their reactions to what has been done by a candidate in a campaign or to what a candidate may do in a campaign. e.g. The focus groups indicate that foreign policy is not an important issue with the voters this year.

焦点组:竞选运动组织用此方法来衡量公众对某个主题或事件的反应,也是一种在竞选运动中使用的广告。通常由随意选出的12人组成,来调查他们对某一候选人在竞选运动中已做或也许会做的事情的反应。例:焦点组指出,对选举人来说,外交政策在今年并不重要。

Freedom of Information Act: The Freedom of Information Act is a federal law enacted in 1967 which requires federal government agencies to make open to the public all documents and information which they possess. Only information which pertains specifically to national security or to privacy is exempt from the law. e.g. The journalist used the Freedom of Information Act to force the government to release the documents.

信息自由法案:这是一项在1967年通过的联邦法令,要求联邦政府机构对公众公开他们所有的文件及信息,只有与国家安全与机密有关的信息被排除在此项法令之外。例:记者利用信息法来要求政府发布文件。

grand jury: A grand jury is a panel of citizens who evaluate the evidence submitted to it by a prosecutor and decide if the prosecutor should bring charges against persons suspected of crimes. Grand juries do not decide guilt or innocence—they only bring charges which must then be tested in a trial. e.g. The grand jury is looking into corruption in the police department.

大陪审团:一个公民团体,他们评审由检察官提交的证据,并决定该检察官能否对犯罪嫌疑人提出控告。大陪审团并不决定犯罪嫌疑人是否犯罪,只提交要在接下来的法庭上接受审理的控告。例:大陪审团正在调查警务部门的腐败情况。

impeachment: Impeachment is a charge brought by the US House of Representatives against an official in the judicial or executive branches of the federal government. In essence, the House of Representatives sits as a grand jury considering the evidence against a president, vice-president, or a federal judge. If the House of Representative votes a charge of impeachment against an official, the US Senate conducts a trial and decides the guilt or innocence of the accused official. e.g. A committee of the House of Representatives voted to impeach President Nixon in 1975—but he resigned before the full House of Representatives could vote on the impeachment.

弹劾:指由众议院对联邦司法或行政部门的某个官员提起的诉讼。实质上是由众议院议员组成大陪审团,对不利于总统,副总统或联邦法官的证据进行审核。如众议院议员投票赞成对某官员的弹劾,参议院进行审理以决定该官员是否有罪。例:1975年,众议院议员投票赞成弹劾尼克松总统,但是他在投票之前辞了职。

iron triangle: An iron triangle is a powerful relationship between members of the Congress, the bureaucrats in federal government agencies and certain interest groups. For example, the Congress appropriates the money for the federal highway bureaucrats who then issue multi-million dollar contracts to road construction companies which then contribute millions of dollars to the re-election campaigns of congressmen helping to ensure the re-election of those congressmen who then work to appropriate more dollars for the highway program, etc. e.g. Many people think that iron triangles are a threat to democracy.

铁三角：这是指国会议员，联邦政府机构的官员及某些利益集团成员之间牢不可破的关系。例如，国会给联邦高速公路的官员拨款，公路官员于是和道路建筑公司签订数千万美元的合同，然后建筑公司再捐几百万美元给国会议员以帮助他们再度竞选成功，接着国会议员又给公路项目拨更多的款，等等。例：许多人认为，铁三角是对民主制度的威胁。

judicial review: Judicial review is the power of the courts to rule whether actions taken by the legislative or executive branches of the government are consistent with the powers granted to those branches by the US Constitution. e.g. The Supreme Court ruled that the law passed by the Congress was contrary to the US Constitution and is therefore null and void.

司法审查：这是法庭的权力，用以判定政府的司法行为或行政部门所作的行为是否与美国宪法相符。例：联邦最高法院裁定，国会通过的一项法律违背了美国宪法，所以是无效的。

leak: A leak is secret or confidential information that is given surreptitiously to the media or to another branch of the government to influence public opinion or public policy. e.g. Someone in the White House leaked the contents of the document to a reporter from *The New York Times*.

泄露：指机密情报被偷偷地泄露给新闻媒介或政府的另一部门，以对公众舆论或政策造成影响。例：白宫有人把文件的内容泄露给了纽约时报的一名记者。

lobbying: Lobbying refers to activities designed to influence the decisions made by public officials. Most lobbying is completely legal and involves providing information and the making of election campaign contributions. e.g. Lobbying by the tobacco industry blocked the bill that would have raised cigarette taxes.

游说：指以影响政府官员的决定为目的而进行的活动。这些活动许多是完全合法的，并与提供信息和竞选捐款有关。例：烟草行业的游说阻止了提高烟草税率议案的通过。

pork: Pork refers to wasteful government spending on projects within the district represented by an elected official for the purpose of making the official more popular in his district and, therefore, more likely to be re-elected. A significant amount of the federal budget is pork. Of course, what is a worthy project in one's own district is pork if it is in someone else's district! e.g. That new stadium is pure pork!

政治恩惠：政府对已当选的官员所代表的区内某些项目上的所作的过多的支出，目的在于使该官员在其所在的区内更得人心，由此有可能再次当选。联邦预算中有着数量可观的政治恩惠。当然，一个项目在某人所在区是值得进行的，而在他人所在区就成了政治恩惠。例：那个新建的体育场是个纯粹的政治恩惠。

primary election: A primary election is an election wherein the voters choose who the candidates will be in the general election. Thus, no one is elected to office in a primary election. Rather, the winners in a primary election win spots on the general election ballot. e.g. She may have finished first in the primary election but she doesn't have a chance in the general election.

初选：选民选出参加大选的候选人。由此可知，官员并不是在初选中选出的，但是初选中的胜利者可以在大选投票中赢得点数。例：可能她已通过初选，但她没有机会在大选中获胜。

spin: Spin refers to efforts by government officials or by candidates to influence the way that news is reported by the media. e.g. The President's staff tried to put the best spin on the bad news coming from Wall Street.

编造：指政府官员或候选人力图对媒介的新闻报道施加影响。例：总统的工作人员试图对华尔街的坏消息尽量掩饰。

think tank: A think tank is a non-profit policy research organization which tries to influence public policy through education instead of through lobbying. e.g. After he was fired by the President he got a job with one of the think tanks.

智囊团：这是一个非赢利性的政策研究组织，利用学识而不是游说的方法来对政府的政策施加影响。例：他被总统解雇以后，在一个智囊团里找到一份工作。

turnout: Turnout is a measure of the proportion of the potential voters who actually do vote. In most elections in the US a majority of the citizens who are eligible to vote do not vote. Thus, the turnout is a major determinant of who wins elections. A high turnout usually helps the Democrats while a low turnout usually helps the Republicans. A higher percentage of older citizens tend to turnout than younger citizens. Wealthy citizens turnout in greater proportions than poor citizens. e.g. The rainy weather kept the turnout down in yesterday's election.

实际投票率:在美国大多数选举中,大部分有资格投票的公民并不投票,这样,投票率是一个决定胜负的重要因素。通常,高投票率对民主党有利,低投票率对共和党有利,年长的和富有选民比年轻的和贫穷的选民更愿意投票。例:雨天造成昨天的选举投票率低下。

veto: A veto is the formal rejection by the president of a bill passed by the Congress. e.g. President Reagan vetoed the bill which would have raised taxes.

否决:指总统对已被国会通过了的议案进行否决。例:里根总统否决了提高税率的议案。

Terms: UK

Back-bencher: A back-bencher is someone who does not have a position of importance in the parliament. In the House of Commons the members of parliament who are ministers in the government or who are leaders of the opposition parties sit on the front benches. Everyone else sits on the back benches. e.g. She was getting tired of being a lowly back bencher.

(尤指英国下院的)普通议员:在国会中没有重要席位的人。在下议院中,部长级的国会会员及反对党的领袖坐前排,其余的人坐后排。例:她已厌倦了当一名地位低下的普通议员。

By-election: A by-election is a special election held to fill a vacant seat in the House of Commons. Every time a member of the House of Commons dies or resigns there must be a by-election to fill the seat. Since by-elections are held between the general elections they are seen as important indicators of how well the parties are doing with the electorate. e.g. The Tories hope to gain a seat in tomorrow's by-election in Liverpool.

(尤指英国下院的)补缺选举:这是一个专门的选举,以填补下议院的空缺。每次当下议院中有人死亡或辞职,就会有一个补缺选举来填补空缺。因为这种选举是在大选之间进行的,所以被看做是该政党与选民之间相处好坏的重要标志。例:托利党人希望在明天利物浦的补缺选举中取得一个席位。

collective ministerial responsibility: According to the principle of collective ministerial responsibility, all the ministers in a government are responsible for the actions of individual ministers. e.g. While the disaster was the fault of the Defense Minister, the Prime Minister felt obliged to resign—citing the principle of collective ministerial responsibility.

部长团体职责:根据此项规定,所有政府的部长应对每一个部长的行为负责。例:因为这场灾难是国防部长的错误所致,根据部长团体职责这一条文,首相应该辞职。

constituency: A constituency is an electoral district. Each constituency has a name and each constituency elects one member of the House of Commons. e.g. Mrs. Thatcher spent the weekend campaigning in her constituency.

选区:指选举区域。每一选区都有一个名称,并从中选出一名下议院议员。例:撒切尔夫人周末在她的选区中竞选。

devolution: Devolution refers to the shifting of power from the central government to regional or local governments. Historically, most power in the United Kingdom has been centralized in London. In recent years there has been a trend to devolve more power to the regional and local governments. e.g. Most people in Scotland want more power devolved to local governments in Scotland.

权力下放:指中央政府将权力下放给地方政府。从历史上讲,英国的大多数权力集中在伦敦,近些年来,有一种向地方政府下放更多权力的趋势。例:大多数苏格兰人希望他们的政府能有更多下放给他们的权力。

dissolution: Dissolution refers to the dissolving of the House of Commons in preparation for a general election. Usually, it is the Prime Minister who requests the Palace to dissolve the parliament and to call for a new election of members to the House of Commons. e. g. If the Prime Minister loses the vote of confidence it will lead to dissolution.

解散：这里指解散众议院为大选做准备。通常由首相请求白金汉宫解散议会并要求举行新一轮下议院的选举。例：如果首相失去信任投票（指英国议会以多数票对首相及其内阁的政策表示信任的投票），议会将被解散。

division lobbies：When members of the houses of parliament vote they walk into one of two lobbies—a "yes" lobby or a "no" lobby. Thus, a house "divides" into two groups—one group disappearing into the lobby on one side of the chamber and the other group disappearing into the lobby on the other side of the chamber. Tellers at the doors to the lobbies count the number of members who pass into the lobbies. e. g. The Prime Minister led the members of her party into the yes lobby.

英国议院的两个分组投票厅：当议会议员们投票时，他们将走进两个分组投票厅中的一个："赞成"厅，或"反对"厅。这样，议员们便分为两组，一组进入议院会议厅的这一边，另一组进入议院会议厅的那一边，每一个投票厅的入口处都有人计算进入本厅的人数。例：首相率领她的政党成员进入了"赞成"厅。

Downing Street：The Prime Minister's official residence is located on this small street in London. e. g. As yet there has been no reaction from Downing Street regarding the fall in North Sea oil prices.

唐宁街：首相府邸坐落在伦敦的这条小街上。例：目前，唐宁街还未对北海石油价格下跌作出反应。

free votes：Most members of the House of Commons vote the way they are told to vote by their party leaders. Occasionally, members of parliament are allow a "free vote" and are free to vote either "yes" or "no" as they individually see fit. e. g. The Prime Minister decided to make the vote on the death penalty bill a free vote.

自由投票：多数下议院议员按照其党派领导的旨意进行投票，但偶然地，国会议员也会被允许进行"自由投票"，可以根据个人意见投"赞成"或"反对"票。例：首相决定对死刑议案进行自由投票。

front-benchers：Front-benchers are the leaders of the parties in the House of Commons. Members of the government cabinet sit on the front benches on one side of the chamber while the leaders of the opposition parties sit on the front benches opposite the government benches. e. g. The government's front-benchers cried "Shame! Shame!" at the leader of the opposition.

（英国）议会的前座议员：通常指下议院中的党派领袖。政府内阁成员坐在议院会议厅一边的前座，而反对党首领坐在政府对面的前座。例：政府中的议会前座议员对反对党首领叫道："不要脸，不要脸！"

MP：MP is an abbreviation for Member of Parliament. e. g. Our local MP is coming to visit our school.

国会议员的缩写。例：本地的国会议员将访问我校。

The Palace：Buckingham Palace is the official London residence of the Queen. When the Prime Minister goes to "The Palace", it means the Prime Minister is going to a meeting with the Queen. e. g. The Palace had no comment on the behavior of the Princess.

白金汉宫：这是女王在伦敦的官方府邸。首相"进宫"指首相前往觐见女王。例：白金汉宫对公主的举动尚未发表意见。

peer：A peer is a member of the House of Lords. Some peers inherit their seats in the House of Lords while others are given "life peerages" by the Queen which cannot be inherited. e. g. After retiring from the House of Commons the Queen made Mrs. Thatcher a life peer.

上议院议员：有的议员通过继承得到他们在上议院的席位，其他人则是被女王册封为"终身议员"。"终身议员"是不能被继承的。例：从上议院退休后，撒切尔夫人被女王封为"终身议员"。

PM：PM is an abbreviation for Prime Minister. The Prime Minister is the leader of the majority party in the House of Commons. e. g. The PM was deeply discouraged by the results of the Glasgow-Hillhead by-election.

首相的缩写：首相是下议院多数党的领袖。例：首相对格拉斯哥－西尔海德的补缺选举结果极为失望。

quango：Quango stands for quasi-autonomous non-governmental organization. In practice, most quangos are governmental bodies with some degree of independence. For example, the University Funding Council is responsible for allocating funds to universities. e.g. Mrs. Thatcher thought there were too many quangos and abolished many of them.

准自治的非政府组织:实际上,多数该类组织为具有一定独立性的政府团体,例如大学基金理事会负责给大学分配资金。例:撒切尔夫人认为准自治的非政府组织太多因此取消了许多。

Tory: A Tory is a member of the Conservative Party. e.g. The Tories were soundly defeated in the last election.

托利,指保守党员。例:在上届选举中,托利党人彻底失败。

vote of confidence: A vote of confidence is a formal vote taken by the House of Commons expressing confidence or no confidence in the government of a particular Prime Minister. Should a government lose a vote of confidence it is obliged to resign or to request a dissolution. e.g. The government survived the vote of confidence by a single vote.

信任投票:这是下议院用来考察对政府的某位特定首相是否有信任而进行的正式投票。如果某政府在信任投票中失败,则应辞职或要求解散。例:政府在信任投票中以一票险胜。

B) United Kingdom—Government Structure

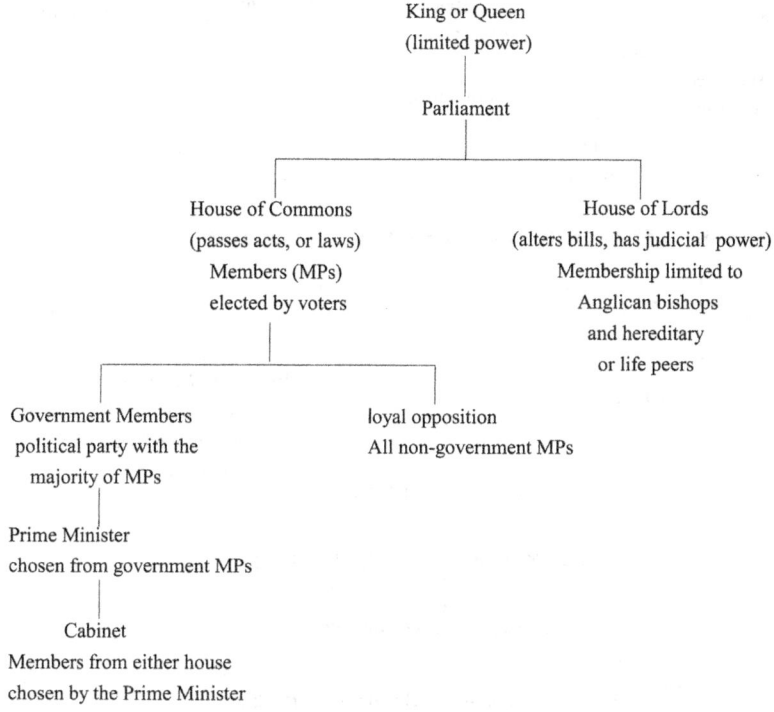

United States—Government Structure

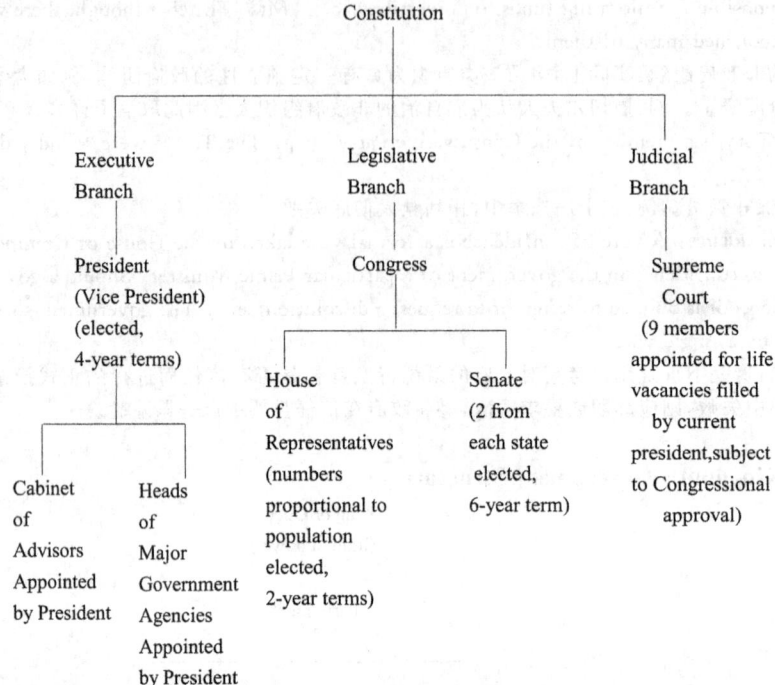

C) **United Kingdom—How an Idea Becomes Law** (Passage of a Bill)

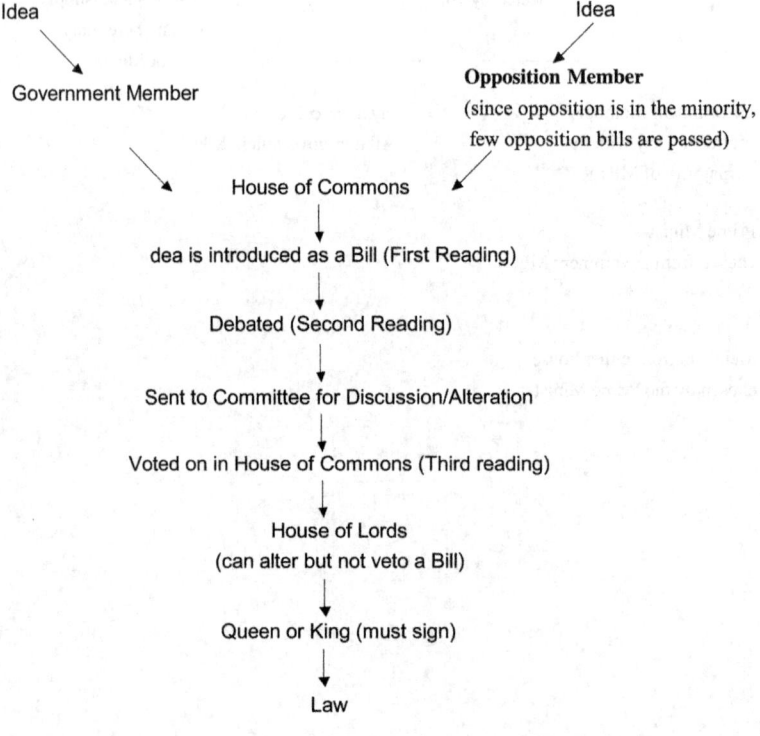

United States—How an Idea Becomes Law

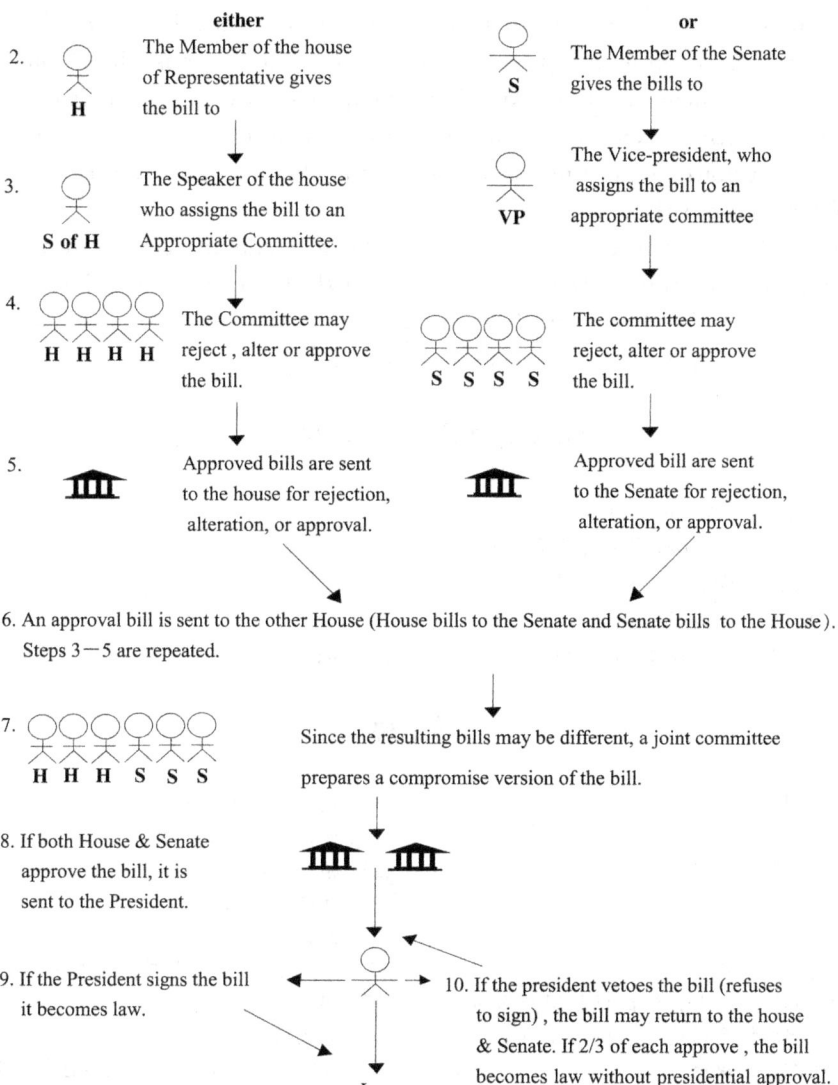

Study Questions

1. Do you think there is any connection between the progression from theocratic to aristocratic to democratic legitimacy and the progression from absolute to constitutional government? Explain.
2. Compare the merits and demerits of unitary and federal systems of governments. What sorts of countries might find unitary government more suitable? Which would find federal government more suitable?

3. Some people argue that unitary governments have the best chance of holding large, diverse countries together. Others argue that federal systems are better at holding such countries together. What is your opinion? Why?
4. Many Americans believe the British government is less constitutional than the American government. They think that there are many more limitations placed on what the American government can do to Americans compared to what the British government can do to its citizens. What arguments might the British make that their government is just as constitutional as the American government? (Hints: respect for traditions; the role of opposition parties).
5. Looking at the two houses of the British Parliament and the two houses of the US Congress, do you think members of the British Parliament or of the American Congress are more likely to behave as trustees of the voters best interests (rather than as delegates reflecting the voters immediate wishes)? Why?

Selected Bibliography

Hamilton, Alexander and others. *Federalist Papers*.
Hofstadter. *The American Political Tradition*.
Huxley, Aldous. *Brave New World*.
Mill, John Stuart. *On Liberty*.
Tinder, G. *Political Thinking: The Perennial Questions*.

注　释

[1] 中央集权制的。
[2] 君主国。
[3] 立法的。
[4] 行政的。
[5] 司法的。
[6] 英国下院的补缺选举。
[7] (英)(政党在议会中有权执行党纪及敦促本党议员出席议会讨论等的)组织秘书。
[8] 英国下院的普通议员。
[9] 政治合法性。
[10] 专制政体。
[11] 立宪政体。
[12] 官僚政治。
[13] 州长的。
[14] 中央集权论的。
[15] 权威对价值的分配。
[16] 讼棍式的官僚。
[17] 财政部。
[18] 预算拨款的。
[19] 神权政治。
[20] 英国王室。
[21] 坎特伯雷大主教。
[22] 伊斯兰教神职人员。
[23] 精英统治。
[24] 无政府状态。
[25] 酋长。
[26] 苏丹(某些伊斯兰国家统治者的称号)。
[27] 伊朗国王的称号。
[28] 立宪政体,宪政。
[29] 大宪章,1215年英国大封建领主迫使英王约翰签署的保障部分公民权和政治权的文件。
[30] 臣民。
[31] (英)(市、镇、等)政务委员会。
[32] 主权国家。
[33] 海军元帅。
[34] 公民立法提案权。
[35] (美)(由公民投票对官员的)罢免,罢免权。
[36] 请愿。
[37] 规定,条款。
[38] 上议院。
[39] 参议院。

〔40〕下议院。
〔41〕代表参政制度。
〔42〕受托参政制度。
〔43〕联合国大会。
〔44〕民意测验。
〔45〕（政见）温和。
〔46〕折中主义。
〔47〕意识形态的狂热者。
〔48〕等级制度的。
〔49〕封臣。
〔50〕（拉丁语）同级（或同辈中）居首位者。
〔51〕特别委员会。

CHAPTER 10　THE ECONOMY OF THE UNITED STATES

Dr. Philip Sprunger

I. Introduction and Overview

The United States has the world's largest economy. The combined private and public sectors of the economy currently produce over 14 *trillion[1] US dollars worth of goods and services every year. Plentiful natural resources, a well-educated work force and an extensive infrastructure give the majority of Americans a high standard of living. Despite this wealth, a percentage of the American population is poor, and the American economy faces a continuous set of challenges.

The American unit of money is the dollar ($), and each dollar is worth 100 cents, or pennies. Money values are written in the following form: $ 10.53, which represents 10 dollars and 53 cents. Paper money or "currency" goes from $ 1 to $ 10,000 bills, although bills over $ 100 rarely circulate. Coins range from one cent to one dollar.

II. History and Growth

The economy of the United States is best defined as a mixed economy. A mixed economy is one in which the production of goods and services is divided between a privately-owned sector and a government-owned or public sector. In addition, the government regulates, taxes and *subsidizes[2] the private sector. Although this is a mixture of capitalism and socialism, the economy has been, and continues to be, dominated by the capitalistic private sector.

The growth of total output in the economy, measured by the Gross Domestic Product (GDP), has progressed at a rate of about 3.4% per year between 1959 and 2006 (see Figure 1 for samples at 10-year intervals). However, this rate of increase has not come with perfect regularity. The growth rate of outputs has followed a pattern of higher growth rates (expansions) followed by *contractions[3] (recessions). For example, in 1973 GDP grew by 5.8%. Then in 1974 it fell by 0.5%, and by 1976 the economy was once again growing at an above-average 5.3%. However, during this post war period, a clear trend of decreasing average growth rates has emerged. From 1946 to 1970 the economy grew at a 3.6% average rate, but from 1970 to 1995, the average rate has been 2.7%. While this growth rate is considerably smaller than the 10% GDP growth rates of modern China, the absolute dollar amount of growth is still quite substantial. Slowing economic growth rates are a point of political concern, even though the American economy continues to expand on both an absolute scale and on a per capita basis.

Figure 1　Some Selected Years of GDP Growth Rates

Year	Yearly Increase in GDP, Adjusted for Inflation
1975	-.2%
1985	4.1%
1995	2.5%
2005	3.1%

Source: *The Economic Report of the President*, 2008 (Table B-2)

Over time, the composition of the nation's output has slowly moved from agriculture to manufacturing to services. Agriculture once dominated the economy of the United States, but the proportion of the population which works in the farming sector has declined *precitously[4] this century (see Figure 2). At the same time, increases in productivity have boosted output per farmer so much that today's 1.9% of the labor force (about 4.8 million people) produces more food than ever before.

Figure 2　The Role of Farming in the Economy

Year	Percentage of Population in Farming
1900	41%
1930	21.5%
1970	4.0%
2000	1.9%

Source: *The 20th Century Transformation of U.S. Agriculture and Farm Policy*, United States Department of Agriculture Electronic Information Bulletin Number 3, June 2005 by Carolyn Dimitri, Anne Effland, and Neilson Conklin.

Like agriculture, the manufacturing sector has both expanded its gross output and decreased the number of workers and their share of the labor force during the twentieth century. Between 1970 and 1990 the percentage of the work force that was employed in manufacturing, such as the automobile and computer industries, has declined by about 52% while the percentage of workers employed in service industries, such as legal and restaurant services, increased by 53%. This shift in the work force occurred largely because technological improvements in manufacturing allowed a greater output of goods with a smaller work force.

III. Commercial and Nonprofit Firms

The private sector of the American economy produces the vast majority of its goods and services. Firms vary in size from one to tens of thousands of workers and produce output for American consumers and other firms, the government and for export to other countries. This section will discuss how American firms are legally organized, the role of competition, and how business is financed.

1. BUSINESS ORGANIZATION

American businesses fall primarily into three methods of organization. The simplest and most common organization is the *sole proprietorship[5], which accounts for approximately three-fourths of all American firms. The other one-fourth of American firms are set up either as partnerships or as a corporation. Each of these methods of organization has its strengths and drawbacks, so that each business must examine its own situation when determining its legal structure.

Sole proprietorship is the quickest and easiest way to form and begin a business. Sole proprietorships are owned by a single person, who is legally and financially responsible for the business. A single person may be the owner, manager and only worker for the proprietorship. Or the owner, or "proprietor", may hire employees to manage the business and produce the output. This type of business structure is both quick and relatively inexpensive to set up, and it is often the first organization for a business. However, the speed of expansion is limited by the owner's ability to borrow money for equipment, building and training purposes. In addition, the owner is legally *liable[6] for all debts and losses *incurred[7] by the business. This puts the owner's entire wealth at risk, and induces many successful proprietors to convert their businesses into a partnership or a corporation.

A partnership is another option for a firm, because the firm is owned by two or more "partners," who jointly control the business. By combining the resources of more than one person, partnerships generally have more financial power than sole proprietorships. Each partner can contribute a different skill to the business, which allows for greater specialization. Often law firms are established as partnerships; each partner lawyer has a specialty, such as contract or tax law. On the downside, the partners must be able to work together, or managerial disputes may arise. Like sole proprietorships, liability is a major issue. Should the partnership incur losses, creditors may pursue payment from each partner's private wealth until the debts of the partnership are paid.

The corporation is the third major type of business in America, and most of the largest firms choose this organization. Although only one-fifth of American businesses are corporations, their impact is much greater because they produce 90% of the private sector output. A corporation usually has many owners. Each owner owns a small part of the firm in the form of "shares" of stock which entitles the shareholder to a percentage of the corporation's profits, depending on the number of shares they own. For example, a corporation may be divided into 1,000 shares. If it earns $50,000 profit in the year for its shareholders, then each owner of a share will receive a *dividend[8] of $5. However, corporations must pay income taxes on their profits before giving any dividends to their shareholders. Each dollar of corporate profit is actually taxed twice because shareholders must also pay a tax after receiving the dividends.

Despite this shortcoming, large companies prefer the corporation structure. Corporations can usually find money more easily than the other two types of business organizations. Corporations can either borrow money from banks or issue bonds, or they can sell new shares of stock. People like to own shares in corporations because the shareholders are never responsible for liability or bankruptcy losses. However, the shares become worthless if the corporation fails, and the money the shareholder invested is lost.

2. THE STOCK AND BOND MARKETS

Corporations issue and sell shares of stock to investors. Stock owners earn dividends on the stock as long as they choose to keep their shares. However, these shares may be sold at any time to another person. This is done in special financial markets, known as stock markets. The largest and most famous American stock market is the New York Stock Exchange (NYSE). Located on Wall Street in New York City, the NYSE centralizes the trading of stock of over 3,000 corporations, and more than a billion shares are bought and sold there each day. The price of shares is determined by the market forces of supply and demand, rather than the initial issue price the owner paid for the shares. Generally, prices rise and fall based on the changing expectations that investors have for the future profits of each corporation.

Bonds are another important type of security traded in financial markets. A bond is a security in which the seller, or issuer, agrees to pay the owner of the bond a stated amount of money at a stated time in the future. The issuer also promises to pay a certain percentage of interest to the owner each year. Durations for bonds range from 1 months to 50 years, and the major issuers of bonds are corporations and the American national, state and local governments. Simply stated, bonds are loans from investors to corporations or governments.

Like stocks, owners of bonds can sell them to other investors, rather than waiting for the bonds to mature, the time when the issuer repays the face amount of the loan to the current owner. Like stocks, the price of bonds is set by the market forces of supply and demand. Depending on the market, a $1,000 bond may sell for more or less than this *face amount [9], the monetary value at maturity which is recorded on the front of the bond.

Such a bond may sell for more than $1,000 if its interest rate is higher than other bonds. Or it may sell for less if its stated interest rate is lower than other bonds. When compared to the bond market, a bond is more attractive when its interest rate is higher; it is less attractive when its interest rate is lower. Another reason why the value of a bond might fall is the fear that the bond issuer may fail and never repay the bond at maturity.

Stock and bond markets are important for corporations, governments and investors. The local, state and national governments sell bonds to fund capital projects or to fund budget deficits. Corporations sell stocks and bonds because they represent a legal source of money which they can use for expansion, research or operational expenses. Investors purchase stocks and bonds as a form of savings and sell them when they need money or if they think their market investments will lose money in the future. Without these organized markets where buyers and sellers can exchange stocks and bonds, it would be much harder for firms to find financial backers for their businesses.

3. NONPROFIT FIRMS

Some American firms are specifically designed to not earn profits. These "nonprofit" firms have more *charitable[10] goals, such as promoting a religion, helping poor people, or providing a service that is not provided by the profit sector. Nonprofit organizations include the Christian churches, universities, and museums. These firms do not have owners who receive dividends; instead, they spend all the money they earn. The government supports nonprofit firms by exempting them from paying most taxes.

Many nonprofit firms sell goods and services, but they usually require additional sources of money. Some receive donations; others, such as universities, receive part of their funding from the government. To keep their costs down, nonprofit firms also rely on volunteers, people who work for no wages. In order to live, volunteers have another job for which they are paid; are retired and receive a pension; or are supported by other members of their family. Volunteers support the goals of the nonprofit firm and want to contribute to its success; in this way they maximize the scope of the firm's mission. Millions of Americans serve as either part-time or full-time volunteers in nonprofit organizations each year.

4. BANKING

Banking is an important industry in the American economy. Banks, which are almost always organized as corporations, provide the easiest method for saving and borrowing money. People who want to save money deposit their money in banks; banks reward these savers by giving them interest on their money and other special services. Banks lend this money to firms, households, and governments which want to borrow money. They charge these borrowers higher rates of interest than those they pay to the savers. The difference, known as the *"spread"[11], between these two different interest rates is the bank's money. Banks use some of this money for salaries and other operational expenses, but the remainder of the money is the bank's profit.

There are more than 10,000 banking firms in the United States. Even the smallest towns have one or more banks. Although banks are privately owned, the federal government regulates banking. The Federal Deposit Insurance Corporation (FDIC) is a government agency which insures saving deposits in banks. Individual savers can get back their deposits in the event that their bank fails. For this reason, Americans believe that their banks are the safest place to save money. Although banks rarely fail, an increased number of them did collapse in the 1970's and 1980's. By the end of the twentieth century, bank mergers became more common. The result was the creation of very large banks and their branches which manage billions of dollars of deposits and loans annually.

In addition to saving and lending money, American banks provide a service called a *"checking account"[12]. A checking account allows its owner, either a firm or an individual, to deposit money in a bank and write checks as payment for goods and services. The recipient of the check, either a firm or an individual, gives the check to a bank for currency or as a deposit in a checking account. Within a few days the original bank receives a digital image of the check; withdraws the stated amount from the payer's checking account; and sends this amount to the second bank. Similarly an electronic debit card can also be used to access the checking account money at stores that have the electronic processing equipment. Periodically, the checking account owner receives a bank statement which includes the checks and debit card transactions the owner recently used as payment. In this way, the owner can monitor personal and business financial transactions. Loss and theft are nearly eliminated through this process. It is no surprise that almost every American adult has a checking account.

A third service banks provide are credit cards, an increasingly common form of payment in America. A bank issues a credit card when it determines that a person is financially able to repay loans made through the credit card. Then the person gives the card to a merchant as payment for a purchase. In turn, the merchant receives the money from the bank which issued the card. The bank puts this purchase on the cardholder's account. A cardholder has the option of either paying the bank each month or extending the payment over a longer period of time by paying interest to the bank. Toward the end of the twentieth century Americans owned more than 800 million credit cards, and many individuals owned and used more than one card. Credit cards are also used extensively for purchases at internet merchants.

Ⅳ. Households

American households have a range of work patterns, incomes and lifestyles. By international standards, nearly all are wealthy, although there is a considerable range of income across American families. Some are very poor and others very rich. This section will discuss the income, employment and savings patterns of U.S. households.

1. INCOME DISTRIBUTION

On average, Americans earn $ 45,790 (2007) for every person living in the United States. This is roughly five and a half times the world average. However, this income is not distributed equally, and many people earn much more or much less. American families of two or more people earn a median average of $ 62,359 (2007), which means that one half of families earn more and one half of families earn less. In some cases all of this income is earned by one worker in the family. Often, however, families have both a father and a mother that earn wages. About 73% of adult males and 60% of adult females have jobs. For women, this has been a substantial increase since 1950 when only 35 percent of adult females had paying jobs. In the past, explicit discrimination against women allowed employers to openly pay women a lower wage than men who worked the same job. That type of discrimination is now illegal and female wage rates are rising, but women continue to, on average, earn about three fourths of male salaries.

Despite America's high levels of average income, 37 million of America's 299 million residents live in poverty. Poverty is defined as those who have an income of less than three times the cost to buy food for the family. For example, a family of four people earning less than $ 20,650 is said to be living in poverty. The poorest 20% of Americans earn only about 3.4% of all income earned, while the wealthiest 20% of Americans earn over 49.7% of all income.

The poverty and wealth of the United States is not distributed evenly by race, geography or age. There are 24.5% of African-Americans living in poverty, compared to only 10.5% of white Americans. Some, though not all, of this difference reflects differences in education levels between the races. Part of the difference is also usually attributed to racial discrimination, which reduces economic opportunity for minority groups.

Poor people are most concentrated in the southern states. Over 20% of the residents in the southern state of Mississippi live in poverty while only about 7 percent of the residents of the state of New Hampshire live in poverty. Within each state, the poor tend to be most concentrated in rural areas and in city centers. Wealthier Americans are most concentrated in suburbs, which are smaller towns that surround cities and allow their residents to work in the city without actually living in it. These suburbs have become both day is healthy. All modern apartments have some form of central heating, and the more expensive apartments will also be air conditioned.

2. HOME OWNERSHIP

Owning a home is part of the American Dream. However, houses are expensive, and a purchase requires a *down payment[51] and a bank loan or a *mortgage[52]. Homes are either single family dwellings or *condominiums (condos)[53], apartments which are owned, not rented. Buying the first home is seen as an important accomplishment. It also means that the person is willing to pay local real estate taxes which support the local school district and other community institutions. A home purchase also gives the owner economic power because houses usually increase in value over time and provide *collateral[54] if the owner wants to borrow additional money from a bank or another lending institution.

Houses are important indicators of social class in America. The location of the house, the building materials, the size of the house and the amount of land surrounding the house immediately convey information about the owner's status in American society. Since most people spend a lot of time and money on making the inside and outside of their homes as attractive as possible, a large home improvement industry is thriving in the United States.

The quality of furnishings and appliances inside the home is also important an indicator of social class. A typical middle class kitchen would have a sink, stove, refrigerator, dishwasher, *blender[55], microwave oven, toaster oven, *chopper/shredder[56] and an electric garbage disposal. Most homes would have several television sets, a DVD player and a stereo radio/player which accepts audio cassettes or CD's.

Many houses have more than one phone: one in the kitchen, one in the living room and perhaps one in a bedroom. Usually a child will have a phone in his/her bedroom with a separate telephone number. It is common for a child to have his/her own cell phone. Another reason why many American houses have more than one phone line is the increased use of personal computers which are connected by telephone to other computers outside the home. One room in an American house may be solely designated as "the computer room" or a study, while other rooms may only be used for a hobby such as a sewing room, a greenhouse or a library. Larger American homes also contain a "family room" which is where the family members congregate for group activities: watching TV, playing games or entertaining friends.

Outside, American houses frequently have *porches[57] or *balconies[58] and a garage. In small towns, suburbs or rural areas houses are usually surrounded by a yard of grass and flower and vegetable gardens. Most home owners spend a considerable amount of time during the summer weekends cutting the grass, planting flowers and making their yards beautiful.

Ⅶ. Pets

Americans are very attached to their pets, especially cats and dogs. In the past, dogs were the most common pets, but today, since many people live in apartments and work during the day, cats are now the most popular pets. Other pets are birds, fish, rabbits, *gerbils[59] and *hamsters[60]. In recent years snakes and *reptiles[61], including into a fund, which is then used to pay a retirement pension to that firm's retirees. The amount of the pension is determined by length of employment with that firm and by the pre-retirement wage of the employee, rather than the success of the investments in the fund. If the fund's investment profits are low, then the firm must put in more money to cover the needs of the promised retirement benefits. A typical pension benefit is one quarter to three quarters of the employee's pre-retirement wage. This was once the dominant form of pension in the United States, but recently a second type called *defined contribution[17] pensions have become popular.

Defined contribution pensions are essentially mutual fund investments that cannot be spent until retirement. In this type of pension, both the worker and the employer regularly put money into that worker's retirement account. The account is then invested like a mutual fund and grows until the worker is ready to retire. The money from a worker's account is then paid out to him or her during retirement.

A final large component of household savings comes in the form of home ownership. Two thirds of all American families own their own home. Most purchase their homes by borrowing the money from a bank for a period of 30 years using what is called a mortgage loan. By the time most people retire, they have paid back the mortgage and own their homes without debt. The owner can then live in his or her house without having to pay rent, or can sell the home and spend the money. The average home in the United States is now worth over $200,000 (about three years of income for an average family), so the purchase of a home provides a large quantity of savings for most households. Houses have become physically larger as well. In 1970 the average house was 128 square meters, and it has now risen to 234 square meters.

V. Government and the Economy

Government in the United States is divided into three levels: federal, state and local. Each level has its own budget. When added together, these budgets are huge, derived primarily through some form of taxation. This tax money is spent on a wide range of programs and services which cost trillions of dollars annually. These financial activities, as well the regulation of the economy, are the major roles of the American government discussed in this section.

1. THE FEDERAL GOVERNMENT

The federal government is the largest and most powerful of the three levels of government in the United States. By 2007, the federal government had a budget of $2.8 trillion, or about 20% of America's $14 trillion GDP.

The federal government plays many roles in the American economy. It is a major purchaser of goods and services, such as military equipment, interstate highways and buildings. It also transfers money and other resources to needy Americans, particularly to the poor and to retirees. Not only does it produce currency, but it also controls the supply of money in circulation and the interest rates banks may charge for lending money. It also regulates the work environment in the areas of health, safety and environment and promotes competition and fair business practices. The following sections discuss some of these important roles.

A) Federal Taxation, Deficits and Debt

In order to finance its many activities, the federal government taxes both firms and households. Modest amounts of money are raised from *tariffs [18] on imports and from excise taxes on products such as tobacco and gasoline. However, as of 2007, the vast majority of federal receipts came from three sources: income taxes paid by households (45%); income taxes paid by corporations (15%); and *payroll taxes [19] paid by workers (35%). To ensure that these taxes are paid, the government assigns the collection and enforcement to its agency, *the Internal Revenue Service [20] (IRS).

Individuals pay income taxes, based on a percentage of their total annual income earned from wages, rent, interest and profit. In addition to income, these percentage rates depend on personal circumstances. For example, larger families pay lower income taxes. The American tax structure is called *progressive [21] because the percentage that a person pays varies from 0% for low income people to nearly 35% for the wealthiest Americans. Corporations also pay income taxes, depending on their level of profits.

In recent years there has been a public debate about replacing the progressive system with a *flat tax [22] on incomes. A flat tax means that all Americans would pay the same percentage rate on their incomes, excluding the poorest people; payroll taxes, based on wages, are current forms of the flat tax. Payroll taxes are based on a percentage of wages earned (15.3%). An employer pays half of the wage tax, and the employee pays the other half.

Since 1969, the federal government has had a budget deficit. In other words, the government has spent more money than it has collected every year since 1969 with the exceptions of 1999 to 2001. To make up this deficit, the government borrows money by issuing and selling bonds. After their maturity date, which ranges from 30 days to 30 years, the government is obligated to buy back the bonds for their original face value (see Figures 3).

Figure 3 The Federal Budget *Deficit [23]

Year	Yearly Federal Government Deficit (in billions)
1965	− $14
1975	− $53
1985	− $212
1995	− $164
2005	− $318

Source: *The Economic Report of the President*, 2008 (Table B−78).

The national debt, or the accumulation of all debt owed by the federal government, was over $10 trillion or a little less than two-thirds of the GDP. Approximately 9% of the total federal budget pays for the interest of some $237 billion on the national debt. In the 1990s there had been growing political pressure in the country for the federal government to balance its annual budget. That led to the three years of balanced budgets from 1999 to 2001, but that pressure has subsided and is not currently a point of major political focus.

B) Welfare and Aid to the Poor

Although the United States is a very rich country, there are many poor people who have low incomes. Providing for the poor is a joint venture between the federal and the fifty state governments. Collectively, these programs are known as "welfare". Welfare is a distinctively different program from unemployment benefits, money paid to those who are temporarily or permanently unemployed. Unemployment benefits are based on 40 - 60% of the worker's wages and may be paid for 26 weeks.

Some welfare programs involve cash payments to the poor. The largest of these programs is Temporary Assistance for Needy Families (TANF). Under TANF, cash is given to poor families, generally headed by a single mother, who have children living at home. Although it is partially funded by the federal government, TANF is administered by the state governments with each state providing different levels of cash support. Typical benefits levels for a family of three are between $300 and $400 per month, and about 4 million Americans received payments for some part of the year. TANF benefits are not meant to be permanent and are limited to 5 years total per person. Another large cash program is *Supplemental Security Income[24] (SSI), which provides a minimum income level for poor people who are either disabled or elderly.

In addition to cash payments, poor Americans are entitled to receive *"in-kind"[25] benefits from the federal government. Instead of cash, "in-kind" programs provide needed goods and services to low income households. *Medicaid[26], the largest of these programs, pays for the medical care of the poor, including elderly people who cannot afford long-term nursing care. In 2005, Medicaid cost $276 billion to care for nearly 20% of the American population, or 58 million people.

Another important in-kind program for the poor is the Food Stamp Program that gives on average about $100 per recipient per month. Poor people are issued food stamps, a special type of money (typically electronic cards) that is only accepted for the purchase of food at grocery stores. Store owners redeem the food stamp money from the federal government, and the federal and state governments *reimbursed[27] the grocery store owners for $29 billion in 2005. In 2007, the combined cash and in-kind welfare programs comprised about 9 percent of the federal budget, or $254 billion.

One problem with these US welfare programs is the fact that recipients have little incentive to seek employment once they receive the benefits. To qualify for these types of programs, a household must have an income which falls below levels determined by the government. If a person who receives welfare finds employment, the household's income would increase, and the person's benefits would be reduced or eliminated. Under this system, a welfare recipient's income may be too high for Medicaid but too low to pay for America's expensive private health system.

C) Government Regulation

Regulations define how legislation is to be implemented. Both the American federal and state governments impose regulations on the design, production and disposal of many types of goods, including food and medicine. These regulations increase production costs, which are ultimately paid by the consumer. However, these prices can be justified if the improved benefits of the goods offset the costs of regulations.

The design of products is regulated by the government for two major reasons. First, regulations protect the health and safety of the consumer. For example, manufacturers of medicine are required to use caps that young children cannot open, and automobile manufacturers must place seat belts in all of their cars. These safety regulations apply not only to products made in the USA, but also to imported goods.

Second, the regulation of product design is meant to reduce the amount of pollution that the user of the product imposes on other people. To this end, automobile manufacturers must meet *myriad[28] design specifications for car engines in order to reduce the quantity of car emissions and to reduce the environmental damage caused by these emissions. Regulations also require a special quality of gasoline that does not unduly pollute the air for use in heavily populated areas of the country. Environmental regulations are mainly under the jurisdiction of the federal government's agency, the Environmental Protection Agency (EPA).

The government also regulates the methods of production for almost all goods. The primary reason is to protect the safety of the workers. Worker and workplace safety is supervised by the government's Occupational Safety and Health Administration (OSHA). OSHA is involved in all aspects of safety, from the quality and design of ladders to workers' injuries and illnesses which may be related to their jobs. The EPA also monitors and regulates production methods to prevent pollution from a wide range of sources, including factory smokestacks and liquid discharges into lakes, rivers and oceans.

By federal law, employers are required to pay a minimum wage to all workers. In 2009, the minimum was $7.25 per hour. Firms that paid their employees more than the minimum wage were not directly affected by this legislation. However, firms that paid less than the minimum wage had an increase in their wage costs. The rationale for the federal minimum wage law is to ensure that a worker will receive a basic income. When Congress increases the minimum wage from time-to-time, workers are compensated for rising consumer prices. Many people argue against the minimum wage because they believe that the government is interfering with the market economy. According to these critics, after the minimum wage increases prices, some firms hire fewer low-skilled workers, which then causes the unemployment rate to rise.

Employers are also mandated to pay hourly workers 50% extra per hour for any time that exceeds more than 40 hours a week. Pay for the extra time is called "overtime" pay. For example, a firm must pay an employee earning minimum wage $290 for a forty-hour week. If the employee works 50 hours, the firm must pay $10.87 per hour for the 10 extra hours of overtime plus the 40 hours for a total of $398.70.

In addition to the design and production of goods, the federal government regulates the disposal of solid waste created by both consumers and producers. *Garbage landfills[29] must control pollutants which *contaminate[30] the water supply. Restrictions on *radioactive[31] and other toxic wastes are stricter, which significantly increases their disposal costs. Nevertheless, Congress and the American public generally agree that the gains in safety have offset these costs.

The purity of food and medicine is monitored and regulated by the Food and Drug Administration (FDA). Producers of food are required to meet purity guidelines, accurately measure nutrient values and clearly print this information on the food packaging. The FDA requires extensive testing of a new medication to ensure that consumers will not suffer from any harmful side effects from this drug. In most cases, the drug is first tested on animals and later on human volunteers. After these requirements are met, a process which could last for several years, the pharmaceutical company receives approval from the FDA and can begin selling the drug to the public.

D) The Money Supply

Beginning in 1913 with the creation of *the Federal Reserve System[32], the federal government has controlled the supply of money in the United States. The Federal Reserve System is a special group of 12 regional banks that monitor and control the supply of money in the country for the government. The system also regulates and assists private banks in their day-to-day operations. The Federal Reserve System is operated by a Board of Governors who are appointed for 14-year terms by the President of the United States. These governors are given this long tenure to minimize political pressure on monetary policy by either the President or the Congress. The chairman of the Federal Reserve System's Board of Governors is often viewed as one of the most powerful economic policy makers in America.

The money supply in America can be measured in several ways. A popular and simple measure is to add the dollar value of all coins and currency in circulation to the balances currently held in checking accounts. This total value is simply called the M1 measure of money. As this measure changes, interest rates on bonds change, and, eventually, money increases, leading to higher prices. Higher prices are called inflation which has undesirable effects on the economy. To avoid inflation, the Federal Reserve System allows the money supply to increase only enough so that this increase does not cause more than a few percentage points of inflation each year.

Creation of M1 money is done in two ways. The most basic method occurs when the government prints currency. A second and more complicated method is the control of checking account deposits. When people deposit money into a checking account, the bank will lend some of that money in order to earn interest. By regulating how much deposited money the bank can lend, the Federal Reserve can control the growth of dollar deposits in these checking accounts. Thus, private banks create the checking-deposit portion of M1 money by lending money to people. Another measure called M2 is broader and includes more types of monetary banking balances. As of 2008, the M1 supply of money in circulation was about $1.5 trillion and the M2 supply of money was about $8 trillion.

The Federal Reserve can also increase the supply of money by buying bonds held by the public. These purchases give money to individuals or firms which increases the amount of money in circulation. Or the Federal Reserve can reverse this process by decreasing the supply of money by selling bonds to the public. These sales take money out of circulation. Buying and selling bonds are called "open market operations" and are closely watched by investors and bankers. Buying bonds decreases interest rates on short-term bonds, and selling bonds increases the interest rates. The Federal Reserve's decisions to buy or sell bonds have an important impact on the economy. Firms which want to borrow money to buy capital equipment will have to pay more interest when the rates are higher; therefore, they may reduce or postpone their purchases until the interest rates are lower.

E) Social Security and Medicare

Beginning as a result of America's great economic depression in the 1930's and continuing through the 1960's, the federal government developed a comprehensive program of payments and benefits for retired workers and their spouses. This program can be divided into two major categories: Social Security and Medicare. Social Security pays cash to retired workers, and Medicare provides them with medical care. With a few exceptions, every American aged 65 and older qualifies for both Social Security and Medicare. Combined, these programs for the elderly account for a major portion of the federal government's budget and are growing (see Figure 4).

Figure 4 Size of Social Security and Medicare Programs

Year	Expenditure on Social Security and Medicare
1950	$ 1 billion
1960	$ 11 billion
1970	$ 36.8 billion
1980	$ 152.1 billion
1990	$ 352.4 billion
2000	$ 607 billion
2010	$ 1,114 billion (estimated)

Source: U. S. Government Printing Office. Budget of the United States Government: Historical Tables Fiscal Year 2009. http://www.gpoaccess.gov/

At the start of the 21st century, almost all American workers were required to pay 7.65% of their wages to fund Social Security and Medicare. Employers also had to pay an equal amount on behalf of their employees. Since more Americans retire and live longer, money collected today is used to pay current retirees. This trend will continue to put pressure on the federal government's budget as the ratio of workers to retirees continues to shrink.

2. THE STATE AND LOCAL GOVERNMENTS

Each state and city has its own government that has the power to tax its residents and spend money on their behalf. These smaller governments use somewhat different methods of levying taxes than does the federal government. They also spend their money differently. This section describes some of the differences.

A) Taxation

Although the federal government has a budget that is larger than all the state and city (also called "local government") governments combined, the state and local governments do together spend about $ 1.7 trillion, which is equal to about two thirds of the federal budget. The federal government currently provides 20% of the money for these budgets, so the rest must be raised from taxes.

Like the federal government, many state and local governments tax the incomes of workers and corporations. But this represents only 15% of the state and local revenues. Instead, these regional governments rely on property taxes and sales taxes to generate the bulk of their money, with each providing 20 – 25% of their revenues. Property tax is a tax that an owner pays on the value of land and the buildings on the land. The government sets a percentage rate of tax, for example, 2%, which then means that each property owner must pay 2% of the current value of the property each year. This rate of tax can be adjusted up or down each year based on the spending needs of the government.

The sales tax is another important form of tax revenue for state and local governments. This tax is a percentage rate that people pay on the dollar value of their purchases. For example, the state of Pennsylvania has a 6% sales tax. A buyer of a $200 television must then pay a tax of $12. In an effort to reduce the burden of the tax on poor people, many governments do not charge the tax on goods considered necessary for basic living, typically food, clothing and medicine. Additionally, extra taxes are often placed on the purchase of other less necessary goods, such as cigarettes and alcoholic beverages.

B) State and Local Government Expenditures

State and local governments spend the majority of their money on three types of spending: education, welfare for the poor, and road construction.

Fully one third of state and local government spending is for education. The local governments provide free education to children between the ages of 5 and 18. The state governments assist the local governments for those costs, and they also provide subsidies to public universities. Privately-funded schools also exist alongside these public schools and universities. But students must pay tuition at these private schools, so the majority of students are in the public schools.

State governments provide welfare to the poor in partnership with the federal government, which provides much of the money for these programs (described in section V.1.B). Not including health care expenditures for the poor, this represents about 7% of state and local spending, but this figure will grow as more of the responsibility for welfare is switched to the states.

Road construction and maintenance also represents a large part of state and local expenditure at slightly over 6% of total expenditures. Nearly every road and highway is paved and must be regularly repaired and cleared of snow in the winter. The remainder of the budgets includes police and fire protection, park maintenance and other local services.

VI. International Trade

All countries of the world engage in some forms of trade with other countries. Trade allows countries to consume goods that they otherwise could not and to produce and sell goods that would not sell at home. This section deals with what and how much the U.S. trades with other countries, as well as the United States' major trade negotiations and policies.

1. QUANTITY OF TRADE

The world economy has become increasingly globalized in recent years, and the United States economy is no exception. Since 1970, exports have gone from 6% of GDP to about 11% of GDP. Although this is a much smaller percentage of GDP than many other countries (see Figure 5), the large size of the American economy puts the U.S. at or near the top of world trade for the absolute dollar value of exports and imports.

Figure 5   Exports of Various Countries

Country	Percentage of GDP Exported (2004)
Japan	12%
United States	7%
China	20%
United Kingdom	35%
Switzerland	33%

Source: Steven Husted and Michael Melvin. *International Economics*. Pearson Education, Inc. (Boston), 7th ed. 2007.

Major exports of the United States include machines and transport equipment (49%), chemicals (12%), motor vehicles (9%), food (6%), and aircraft (5%). Together, they total more than $800 billion (2003). For imports, the largest components are machines and transport equipment (41%), motor vehicles (13%), mineral fuels (13%), and clothing (5%). In some cases, such as food, the U.S. is a major exporter but not a major importer, which reflects a comparative advantage in production for the United States. Here, the vast amount of available space and productivity of the American agricultural sector leads to surplus production for trade. In other cases, such as automobiles, the U.S. is a both a major exporter and importer. There, the products are different from brand to brand, and the import and export patterns reflect the desire of people to drive both American and foreign cars.

Geography places an important role in international trade, and as result, America's number 2 and 3 trading partners are Canada and Mexico, respectively (see Figure 6). The North American Free Trade Agreement (NAFTA) also contributes to the importance of trade with these two countries. Recently, China has moved into first place in imports to the United States, although exports to China ($61 billion in 2003) are much smaller than the imports from there.

Figure 6   Trading Partners of the United States

Largest Export Markets	2007 Exports in Billions of Dollars
Canada	$213
Mexico	$119
China	$61
Japan	$58
Largest Importers to the U.S.	2007 Imports in Billions of Dollars
China	$323
Canada	$313
Mexico	$210
Japan	$145

Source: *United States International Trade Commission*. 2008

2. TRADE POLICIES

One hundred years ago the United States restricted trade through very high tariffs—often higher than 50%. Tariffs are a tax on the value of imports into the country. Over the years, however, the United States has become an advocate of freer trade and has lowered tariffs to a current average level of less than 3%. Some political leaders in the United States worry that the U.S. has run a merchandise trade deficit for every year since 1976. A merchandise trade deficit occurs when the dollar value of imported goods is larger than the dollar value of exported goods. It is not clear that such a deficit is particularly unhealthy for the economy, and in part is the result of the desire of foreigners to invest money in the United States. As a result, American policy continues to favor freer trade, with the persistence of the trade deficit a secondary consideration. In some cases, the U.S. sets individual trade policies with various countries. Its main policy of this type is the granting of Most Favored Nation (MFN) status to many countries. MFN status gives a country the lowest tariff rates offered by the U.S. Those countries not granted MFN status must pay much higher tariffs on imports to the U.S. than MFN countries.

A second important component to U.S. trade policy is participation in multi-country trade treaties. The two major trade treaties of this type are the North American Free Trade Agreement (NAFTA) and the World Trade Organization (WTO).

NAFTA is a 1993 agreement with the neighboring countries of Mexico and Canada to eliminate all tariffs on goods that are produced and exchanged within these three countries. In the agreement, all tariffs were eliminated over ten years, and exports and imports rose for all three countries. When the treaty was signed, many Americans were concerned that too many manufacturing jobs would relocate from the U.S. to Mexico, causing economic stress to *displaced workers[33]. As a result, the federal government has agreed to assist and help retrain any American workers who lost their jobs as a result of NAFTA. So far, there have only been minor job displacements attributed to the treaty.

The second, and much larger, trade treaty in which the U.S. participates is the WTO. The WTO is an international agreement involving over 100 countries who desire to see a decline in global tariffs. First established in 1947, the WTO has gone through eight distinct rounds of negotiations, and as a result, member countries have seen average tariffs fall dramatically, coupled with dramatic increases in the volume of exports and imports. The WTO organization that developed the agreements monitors and *arbitrates[34] disputes that arise over the agreement.

Ⅶ. Problems and Challenges for the U.S. Economy

Despite a massive economy and a largely wealthy population, many people are concerned about certain aspects of the U.S. economy. This section will discuss some of the more prevalent worries of Americans concerning the economy.

One main concern has been the slowing of the economy's growth rate, which was discussed in section II above. The move from growth rates in the 3 – 4% range to the 3% range means that current generations are improving their standards of living at a much slower pace than earlier generations of Americans. On the other hand, per capita incomes have never been higher than they currently are, despite the slowdown in growth. One fear is that with low growth rates, it becomes easier to slip into an actual economic contraction, which generally leads to increases in unemployment for workers. Currently, about 6% (2008) of Americans who want to work are unemployed. This is considered low by the standards of other industrial countries. But during recessions in the 1970's and

1980's it was sometimes close to 10%. Concern over economic growth rates has ensured that the impact on growth is considered whenever the federal government considers changes to economic policies.

Another area of concern is the persistent budget deficit that the federal government has been running (see section VI). There are two main concerns people have with the deficit. The first is that government borrowing is *"crowding out"[35] borrowing by firms which would use the funds for productive factories and equipment. If the government uses savings to cover its deficit instead of allowing firms to borrow it, then over time industrial productivity and profitability will be slowed. A second worry is that the large debt being incurred by the government will have to eventually be repaid, and that the burden for this debt will fall unfairly on future generations.

A future challenge that is related to federal budget deficits involves the generation of people born between 1946 and 1964, popularly called the *"baby boom"[36] because they were born following the end of the Second World War. This group of people is the largest generation ever born in the U.S. and they are more numerous than the younger people born after 1964. This new group is sometimes called the *"baby bust"[37] because births per year fell dramatically relative to the baby boom years. The issue is how the smaller baby bust generation will be able to pay for Social Security and Medicare costs for the baby boom when they begin retiring around the year 2010. Either the baby bust generation will have to pay much higher taxes, or Social Security and Medicare costs will have to be reduced. This is certain to be an area of growing political controversy over the next 10 to 15 years.

As discussed in section IV.1, many Americans are poor, despite the country's overall prosperity. In addition to the current suffering of the poor, there is a tendency for poverty to pass through generations. That is, the children of the poor receive lower quality education and have fewer economic opportunities. Thus, they frequently grow up to be poor adults, contributing to a cycle of poverty. There is not a strong consensus on how this cycle of poverty can be broken, and the growing gap between the rich and the poor is likely to be a continuing problem.

Finally, many fear that inflation will cause problems in the future. Inflation is an increase in most prices. Currently the inflation rate has been varying between 2% and 3% per year, which means that prices have, on average, been increasing by 2% to 3% every year. This is considered to be a low and desirable rate of inflation. However, in the 1970 and early 1980's, inflation was more commonly in the 5% to 10% range. Inflation is unpopular with people who have saved money because after prices increase, those savings can not buy as many goods as before. Past problems with inflation have frequently involved a disruption in the oil markets of the Middle Eastern part of the world. American dependence on oil (much of it imported) as an energy source, means that increases in the price of oil cause increases in production costs for most industries, which leads to price increases for most goods.

Despite worries that people have about the U.S. economy, most Americans are generally positive about the economy and their own futures.

CHAPTER 10 THE ECONOMY OF THE UNITED STATES

Study Questions

1. Growth has slowed in the U.S. economy, but the overall level of GDP and income per capita is higher than it used to be. Is it better to have high incomes that are growing slowly, or lower incomes that are growing more quickly?
2. Fewer Americans work on farms than did in the past. Does this mean that Americans grow and eat less food than before?
3. What is the best way to save money: putting the money in a savings account, or investing it in the stock market? Why might different people choose different answers?
4. Does America have many poor people? What government help is available for someone who is poor?
5. Does the U.S. federal government balance its budget in most years? Why do Americans worry about this issue? What is the difference between budget deficits and the national debt?
6. Why does the U.S. federal government regulate businesses? Is such regulation good or bad for the country, or does it depend on whom you ask?
7. What is Social Security? It is very expensive; why would Americans want such an expensive government program?
8. Does the United States have any economic worries? What do you think the most serious problem is? Why?

Selected Bibliography

Arnold, Roger A. *Economics*. Thomson Higher Education, 8th ed., 2008.
The Economic Report of the President. (Published annually by the U.S. Government Printing Office)
Husted, Steven and Michael Melvin. *International Economics*. Pearson Education, Inc. (Boston), 7th ed., 2007.
Statistical Abstract of the United States. (Published annually by the U.S. Government Printing Office)

注　释

〔1〕（美）兆（即百万个百万）。
〔2〕资助。
〔3〕经济收缩。
〔4〕急转直下地。
〔5〕单独经营者。
〔6〕负有（法律）责任的。
〔7〕惹起，引起。
〔8〕红利，股利。
〔9〕票面价值。
〔10〕慈善的。
〔11〕差额。
〔12〕支票活期存款账户。
〔13〕银行存折。
〔14〕（投资等）生息。
〔15〕（美）共同基金（一种投资公司形式）。
〔16〕把（钱等）投入集合资金。
〔17〕从雇员的工资中按一定比例提取，雇主做适当补贴，共同组成雇员的养老金。
〔18〕关税。
〔19〕所得税。
〔20〕国内税收部门。
〔21〕累进的。

〔22〕统一税。
〔23〕赤字,逆差。
〔24〕补助救济金。
〔25〕以实物,以货代款。
〔26〕医疗辅助计划。
〔27〕偿还。
〔28〕无数的。
〔29〕垃圾掩埋法。
〔30〕污染。
〔31〕放射性的。
〔32〕联邦储备系统(美国范围内的银行系统,1913年建立)。
〔33〕失业工人。
〔34〕仲裁。
〔35〕挤掉。
〔36〕1946—1965年间的美国生育高峰。
〔37〕生育低谷。

CHAPTER 11   AMERICAN SOCIETY

Dr. Renuka Biswas and Dr. Greg Walker

I. Introduction

American society is a system of components: individuals, families, groups, organizations and communities. For instance, individual Americans compose their society. All American families form this society too. Families comprise the smallest unit of the society that socializes and maintains the individual. Similarly, all groups, organizations and communities that exist inside the geographic boundaries of the United States provide purposes, ideals and distinctiveness to the American society. Some theoreticians think the United States is a society of groups, organizations, and communities of individual Americans who have different backgrounds, life-styles, economic status and political and social ideas and ideals. It is a multi-cultural, multi-racial, multi-rational and multi-religious society. These theorists believe that heterogeneity is the core of American society.

Other societies and people think America is a white (*Caucasian[1]) society and completely ignore its multi-cultural, multi-ethnic and multi-racial characteristics. Because white Euro-Americans dominate the society, other groups do not always assert their American identity. For example, an African-American woman did not respond to the call of a Frenchman at the American Express Office of Paris, who called her an "American lady". Instead, she looked around for a white American woman. When the Frenchman again asked her "Aren't you an American?", she was embarrassed and said, "Yes". There seems to be a tendency for minority people to identify with their ethnicity or race such as, "I am a Puerto-Rican," or "I am Chinese," or "I am Black". Descendents of Europeans would usually say "I am an American". The whole world seems to perceive white Americans as the only true Americans, thereby disregarding the society's multicultural and multiracial nature. Nevertheless, at home all Americans believe that American society is the social system to which they all belong.

II. Individuals

When discussing the American people, one fact should always be kept in mind. Because of multi-cultural, multi-ethnic, multi-religious and varied socioeconomic backgrounds, growth, development, work, lifestyles and social status will differ among individuals from birth to old age. When someone claims, "We Americans think this way" or "We Americans do this," the question is, "Which Americans?" because Americans with different backgrounds usually do things differently.

On the other hand, universal education and media exposure have developed some *commonalties[2] in actions and ideas. Generally, American values include rugged individualism; freedom of speech and religion; democratic ideals; free enterprise; competition, achievement, success orientation; acceptance of other's differences; legal social-political rights; respect of private property; welfare of children, the sick or disabled and the elderly; and faith in science and technology. In the United States, laws and regulations are made on the basis of these values.

1. CHILDREN

Anyone who is born within the geographic boundaries of the United States is legally an American citizen. It does not matter if the child's parents are American citizens or legal or illegal residents. Immediately at birth, the newborn is registered by the US Health Department as "American". The birth certificate, issued by the Health Department, also includes the child's gender, *ethnicity[3], race and religion. The father's and mother's names and their marital status are indicated. For instance, a child of an unwed mother may bear the surname of one parent or both parents. A child of married parents is usually given the father's surname although some modern parents opt to give their child a different surname.

A) Socialization

At birth the child is socialized by both parents and *extended family[4] members. Americans use different socializing methods and goals for boys and girls; boys get preference. In 1988, 82% of college students surveyed said they want their first child to be a boy. The male child is encouraged to participate in vigorous activities such as running, tumbling, jumping and fighting. Boys are expected to be physically strong, aggressive, competitive and successful.

Conversely, the female child is encouraged to participate in quieter activities such as playing with dolls and kitchen utensils with some limited running and jumping. Girls are expected to be submissive, dependent, beautiful, caring, and able to please and serve others. Girls develop non-aggressive, non-assertive, submissive and dependent behavior. Traditionally, girls ideally develop slender bodies, disregarding their physical strength and health. Despite widespread ideas promoted by the women's liberation movement of the 1960's and 1970's, the majority of American families still socialize children to play traditional roles of men and women. However, in recent years, girls have also been encouraged to participate in sports and gymnastics and have been encouraged to achieve and succeed.

B) Effect of Ethnic Background

Although the mother plays the major role in child care, children learn their world view from their ethnic background. For instance, a child in a *Sioux[5] Indian, Chinese, or Mexican American family first learns to position himself/herself within the cultural group before he/she positions himself/herself in society. In contrast, Euro-American children are taught that they are individuals, and secondarily, that they are a part of the family or group. Euro-American children are usually allowed to behave more freely as individuals and grow up in a more permissive environment than children born in an ethnic group which stresses the importance of the family and the group. From a very early age (2 - 1/2 years) American children are encouraged to make small decisions for themselves, unlike many other countries where the mother would make the decision for them. For example, a mother of young children might ask them, "What would you like to eat for dinner?" Most American children are toilet-trained before the age of 3. Many children by age 3 or 4 go to nursery school or to a federal *Headstart program[6] which is designed to assist in the cognitive development of disadvantaged children. Children develop the concept of "self" between the ages of 3 and 5. They understand their separate identity from others and develop some sense of their ethnicity as well as their religious, social and economic status in society. When children are unable to be properly cared for by their families, the government provides organizations and services to care for those children.

C) Government Agencies

Federal and state governments sponsor child welfare organizations which play an important part in child rearing in the United States. These Child Welfare Agencies promulgate rules for parents and other care givers. Child abuse, including physical, sexual and emotional harm, inflicted by parents or relatives, is taken very seriously. It is reported that a million young American children are victims of child abuse and child neglect annually. Abuse and neglect are two causes for removing children from their homes. These children are then placed with other acceptable family members or in a *foster home[7] where the care givers are given money by the government to raise the children. Children in foster care may be allowed to return to their parent's home if the parents have made changes in their behavior and family environment. If these changes do not occur, some of these children may be adopted by their relatives or sent to a new family by Child Welfare Agencies. The federal and state governments represent the American society and expect the family environment and treatment of a child to be conducive to healthy growth and development. However, children who move from foster home to foster home often experience many problems during their development and later in their adult life.

American children are usually consumers of goods, as opposed to children in many other countries who are producers of goods. In other countries children often work long hours for very low wages in order to help support their families. In the United States, children with unemployed parents or parents without adequate resources receive cash benefits from the government. This assistance program is called public assistance or simply "welfare". In addition, poorer families may be eligible for help under Medicaid, a federal program which provides or subsidizes health care for needy people.

2. ADOLESCENTS (TEENAGERS)

The opportunities and education of American children vary, depending on their social and economic status. Poorer communities receive less money for public schools unless the individual state governments allocate tax money to equalize the funding between poor and rich school districts. Without a tax subsidy, poorer children often do not have the educational background necessary for employment after graduation from high school. Since many children from the lower socioeconomic class drop out of school during their preteen or teenage period, they became even more disadvantaged.

During the pre-teen and teenage transition period American children face one of their most difficult times. They are exposed to illegal drug use, are pressured to engage in sexual activity, and encounter increased societal demands for appropriate social behavior.

This is also the age when young people strive for independence from parental control. They may demonstrate an identity crisis by participating in activities which are very different from those prescribed by their parents and the adult community, such as listening to popular music, wearing unusual clothing and hairstyles, body piercing, and experimenting with drugs and sex. A foreign visitor may be amazed at the sight of teenagers with *punk hairdos[8], shaven heads, even *dreadlocks[9] hairstyles. Both boys and girls may wear extremely oversized shirts and pants.

Some American teenage girls become pregnant and are ill-prepared to assume child care responsibilities. The mass media glorify sex but do not educate teenagers about parental responsibilities. Child abuse, neglect and abandonment often occur when teenage children cannot perform adult parent roles. Some schools, religious organizations and communities provide programs about sex education and parenting for unwed teenage mothers in order to help them cope with their responsibilities. Unfortunately, although birth control devices are available, some teens do not use them.

It is important to remember that teenagers' behaviors represent their different ethnic and economic backgrounds and socialization patterns. An Euro-American adolescent's behavior may differ from the adolescent behavior of a Native Indian, African, Asian or Mexican-American.

3. ADULTS

People between the ages of 18 to 29 are called young adults, and people between the ages of 30 and 50 are called adults. Young adults move out of their parents' homes and try to live independently. By this age they have completed their formal education, and they have entered the work force. They either get suitable positions, or if they are unable to find a suitable position, they take any available job and later switch to something else. Americans constantly search for better positions, better salaries and better jobs.

Adult Americans have a great deal of stress in their lives. Many work more than 40 hours per week, in more than one job. American women have additional stress. They highly value their physical beauty. Looking young and beautiful is important socially, and it is sometimes jokingly said that American women never age. This agelessness comes from using cosmetics, exercising, and sometimes having surgery. Also when both husband and wife work outside the home, women have more physical and psychological strains since they still have primary responsibility for managing the house and caring for the children. This situation is easing somewhat as now more husbands share household duties with their working wives. If a husband stays home to manage the household and to care for the children, he is termed a "house husband".

For American men, their earning capability is the standard by which they are measured. The more they earn, the more prestige they receive, not only from the family members, but also from the group, organization or community to which they belong. Their success as adults is measured by their economic resources and prestige. Increasingly, American women are also concerned about their earning capacity, although it is a secondary issue. This pressure for success can cause health problems for both sexes

Adult Americans may also be involved in many other activities. Parents are involved in all aspects of their children's lives, including activities in the parent-teachers association at the children's schools. Parents also provide transportation for their children to and from such things like music lessons, sporting events, shopping, or meeting with friends. Adults may join a union or a professional organization at work and they also may become active in their community's activities. These activities may be related to their religious faith, politics, ethnicity or neighborhood. Some organizations may be harmful, like the Ku Klux Klan (KKK) which threatens minority groups.

4. OLDER AMERICANS

Compared to the elderly population in many countries, American elderly are more healthy and active because the entire society has become more health conscious. One may hear people discussing healthy activities and nutrition at social gatherings or in family discussions. After age 50, people are usually more conscious about health issues. Older women become concerned about menopause because it is believed that at menopause women lose their physical beauty, youthfulness, energy and sexuality. Many women feel undesirable and unattractive in a youth-centered society.

Middle-aged people, ages 50 to 65 plan for an enjoyable retirement, and sometimes their employers assist and counsel them in retirement matters. This is also a time when some people are lonely because their adult children have moved away. This phenomenon is called the *"empty nest syndrome"[10]. Nonetheless, they accept the condition as a natural part of raising a family, especially if their children are employed elsewhere.

5. OLD AGE

The standard of living for the elderly is different for different socioeconomic groups. For instance, wealthy people can enjoy their retirement by traveling and enjoying a variety of leisure activities. Poorer people usually remain where they have lived all their lives, and some elderly people become poorer after retirement. Ethnicity may influence attitudes toward old age. For example, South Asian elders may not strive to look younger or like to talk about sexual enjoyment during old age.

Working Americans pay social security taxes, and after retirement these workers receive monthly social security payments from this fund. The purpose of Social Security is to supplement pension or retirement benefits workers receive from their employers. If handicapped or elderly people did not pay into the social security fund for the prescribed ten years, they will receive a supplemental security income (SSI). People aged 65 and older also receive health benefits in the form of Medicare which is financed by federal taxes. Many also purchase supplemental medical insurance through Medicare or from private insurance companies.

Americans are living longer. "The oldest old people, age eighty-five and over, are the fastest growing segment of the population; their numbers will increase six fold over the next century," according to sociologist John J. Macionis. Since people over age 65 receive money from Social Security and for health care through Medicare, politicians and younger people have raised concerns about the rising expenses for these benefits in the twenty-first century. At that time there will be fewer people paying federal taxes and more people receiving benefits. Interestingly, Macionis noted that as the median income decreased among young people, it increased among elderly people.

Elderly people have become politically active and influence national policies and social conditions. As a result, educational, recreational and health programs and facilities have been specifically developed for elderly people. Multi-storied apartment buildings, housing complexes, *nursing homes[11] and hospitals have the latest technology to help older people. Buses and other forms of transportation are specially equipped for those who use a wheelchair or have difficulty walking. Instead of adult children taking care of their elderly parents, social agencies employ other people to take care of them. Many older people prefer to live independently, and even after they are unable to completely care for themselves, they can remain at home and receive assistance from one of the federal or state welfare agencies.

III. Families

American families are usually composed of a father, mother and children. Although this kind of family is a *nuclear family[12], diversity occurs because of the multi-ethnic nature of the society. Some families include grandparents, and Native American families often include members of the extended family. Other families may be single-parent families headed by an unwed mother, a divorced mother or father, or a widowed mother or father. There are some same-sex families: two men or two women living together as a couple. They may have their own children from earlier marriages, or they may adopt children. Two women living as a couple may choose to have children by *artificial insemination[13]. A *surrogate[14] mother may carry a child for a couple who cannot have children of their own.

Family means a great deal to Americans, and family values are cherished. Public discussions on various issues related to family welfare and family values often occur. The family social unit provides love, affection, security, safety, morality and identity to its members. Families link children with the larger society by teaching them societal norms and orientation for work and relationships. Most American families are in the middle class. According to Melvin Kohn, "Middle class parents tolerate a wide range of behavior and show concern for the intentions and motivations that underlie their children's actions. Working-class parents by contrast stress behavioral conformity". It is in the family that children learn how to learn and behave, what to do when they become adults, and how to relate to others in their social groups and in society.

IV. Groups

1. PRIMARY GROUPS: FAMILY AND PEERS

*Primary groups[15] are families and peer groups. In these two groups people relate to one another very intensely, demanding loyalty, emotional ties, togetherness, and mutual help. Members feel responsibility and ownership towards each other and to the group as a whole. Peer group influence is very strong among American young people. Beginning at about age 12 and continuing throughout adolescence, the impact of peers is stronger than the influence of the family. Since peers allow teenagers to escape adult supervision, some deviations from parental norms and life styles may occur.

2. SECONDARY GROUPS

Secondary groups are larger and more impersonal; they could be social clubs, neighborhood organizations, college organizations, and church or work-related organizations. Most Americans belong to one or more groups, and usually these groups are task oriented and fulfill the need of the members to complete these tasks. In time, some of these secondary groups may become more like a primary group to some of the individual members. In schools and colleges young people belong to clubs which focus on academics, hobbies or social relationships. Younger people may join the *Boy Scouts[16] or Girl Scouts in order to learn skills such as leadership or wilderness survival. In addition to learning democratic decision-making at home and at school, children also learn this process in all the groups they join.

3. NEIGHBORHOOD GROUP—AN IMPORTANT KIND OF SECONDARY GROUP

Americans of all ages may also belong to one or more neighborhood groups, whose goal is to improve the community. It is important to know that all these community projects are done voluntarily and without payment. Projects may include raising funds for charity or some improvement to the neighborhood. Improvements may include cleaning up roadside litter or forming a neighborhood crime prevention unit. Many adults belong to organizations like the *Lions[17], *Elks[18], *Rotary[19], American Association of University Women, or business and professional clubs which basically provide education and services. Special interest clubs focus on gardening, reading books, photography, sports and other hobbies. Political groups work for their political goals and objectives, and members actively participate in local, state and federal election campaigns. Other members of groups disseminate information about treatment and prevention of illnesses such as cancer, heart disease, lung diseases, *arthritis[20], *polio[21], AIDS or *cerebral palsy[22] and other physical deficiencies.

4. RESPONSE TO DISASTERS

When natural disasters strike such as fire, flood, famine, earthquakes and epidemics, the American people quickly respond by forming groups informally and formally to mobilize resources to help victims. This remarkable trait of the American people can be recognized even when a disaster strikes people in another country. Many Americans will send money and supplies, and some Americans will even volunteer their services to help the victims.

V. Organizations

1. RELIGIOUS ORGANIZATIONS

During their lifetimes, Americans belong to many organizations. A first and fundamental organization is usually the local church or a religious organization, which is often part of a larger national or international religion. Often local churches select their own leaders from those approved by the larger organization. However, although the local church may be part of an international organization, American churches may differ from churches in other countries. For example, the *Roman Catholic Church[23] is directed by the Pope in the *Vatican City[24] located in Rome, Italy. In the United States, some people, especially women, don't subscribe to all the ideas and ideals propagated by the Pope, particularly those forbidding abortion or birth control devices.

Protestant churches usually have international associations to guide and control the activities of their different denominations, and most of the Protestant churches are affiliated with the World Church Organization, whose headquarters is in Switzerland. Many Jewish Americans came to the United States in order to escape religious persecution in Europe, especially during the period of religious and ethnic *genocide[25] during the first half of the twentieth century. Many American Jews support the Jewish country, Israel; this greatly influences US policy in the Middle East.

Most non-African *Muslim[26] Americans originally came from countries in the Middle Eastern, South and South East Asia. They are guided by the *Koran[27] and the religious authority of their native countries. Black American Moslems are also guided by the Koran, and some are also guided by the teachings of the Black leader, Elijah Mohammed, and his disciples. This has been a reaction to racism and racial oppression.

Local religious temples and national organizations rule the activities of other religious groups like Buddhists, *Zen Buddhists[28], *Hindus[29], *Sikhs[30], *Bahais[31] and *Jains[32]. In addition to these major religions, there are other smaller religious sects in the United States.

Religious organizations serve as centers for worship, social activities, and coordination of volunteer activities. In addition, since Americans often move from one city to another in search of a better job, churches provide a place where new residents can find people who share their beliefs and concerns.

Some of the larger religious organizations in the United States in 2005 were:

African Methodist Episcopal Church (Protestant, Primarily African American)	2.5 million
Jewish 5.3 million, Church of Jesus Christ of Latter Day Saints (*Mormon)[33]	5.5 million
The Episcopal Church (Protestant, from English Anglican Church)	2.5 million
*Evangelical[34] *Lutheran[35] (Protestant)	7.5 million
Jehovah's Witnesses (Protestant)	1 million
Muslim/Islamic	2 million
*Presbyterian[36] Church (Protestant)	3.2 million
Roman Catholic Church	67 million
*Baptist[37] (Protestant)	34 million

Source: *Time Almanac 2005*

Although religious organizations and government organizations are separate, as required by the US Constitution, religious organizations often exert pressure on the government to enact laws in accordance with their beliefs. The large numbers of Americans involved in churches, enable them to lobby the government effectively.

2. EDUCATIONAL ORGANIZATIONS

Educational institutions are the second most important organizations in Americans' lives. More and more people not only attend college for four years, they also return for adult education. Graduates of a college often correspond with each other and return to the college for reunions with other college graduates. Moreover, colleges and universities serve as a cultural and information center for a community. "High tech" industries, using the latest technology, often cluster near a university. University sports teams, particularly American football and basketball, often attract many spectators.

3. WORK-RELATED ORGANIZATIONS

Work-related organizations are very important formal organizations, providing the work places in which millions of people are employed. Many corporations such as General Motors, AT&T, and IBM are highly bureaucratic with many layers of management. Workers are represented by national organizations, for example, the American Medical Association (AMA) for doctors, and the American Federation of Labor and the Congress of Industrial Organizations (AFL-CIO) for both blue and white collar workers.

The United States government, the largest employer in the nation, is a huge, complex organization modeled like a pyramid. Although the United States' president is frequently considered to be the highest authority, he is constrained by checks-and-balances prescribed by the American Constitution. The federal government in conjunction with the state and local governments constitute the governing structure of the USA.

4. SPECIAL INTEREST ORGANIZATIONS

The Social Security Administration, the largest organization in the United States government, administers Social Security, S.S.I., Medicare, Medicaid and other benefits for all of the American people. All Americans receive a social security card from the Social Security Administration. This card has the individual's social security number on it. This number is very important because it is used for identification purposes; education, employment, health and other kinds of insurance, and for all legal documents.

Americans belong to many other kinds of national organizations which represent their individual interests. Some of these groups are "self-help" groups, such as *Alcoholics Anonymous[38] (AA), whose nearly 2,000,000 members work together to escape addiction to alcohol. Other groups, such as *Greenpeace[39] which also has nearly 2,000,000 members, work to improve the environment. Some organizations support a particular point of view. The 4,300,000 members of the National Rifle Association (NRA) promote gun ownership and safety. Nearly every hobby, every kind of work, and every disease, has a national organization that disseminates information and supports its members. Some of the better known organizations are the American Medical Association (AMA); the American Association of Retired Persons (AARP); the National Organization of Women (NOW); the National Association for the Advancement of Colored People (NAACP); and the American Federation of Labor and the Congress of Industrial Organizations (AFL-CIO). These and many other organizations influence policy decisions in the United States directly through their members or indirectly by lobbying members of Congress.

VI. Socioeconomic Classes, Status and Roles

Since the American socioeconomic classes are stratified, class regulates the individual's life and social contacts. For instance, children born to the Rockefeller, DuPont, Ford or Kennedy families will have social contacts that will bring enormous educational and social opportunities which are not available to people born in a middle or lower class family. The lowest class lives below the poverty level, a number calculated every year by the federal government. It is based on the price of consumer goods, the household income and the number of people in the household. In 1998, the US government considered a three-person family at the poverty level if their total income was less than $13,650 per year. The lowest class consists of very poor people who rarely move out of their social class. However, through achievements and success, social mobility is possible in America.

1. SOCIAL STATUS AND WEALTH

A small percentage of the American population controls the majority of wealth. The middle class, which is nearly 80% of the population, controls the remainder of the nation's wealth. By the end of the twentieth century, approximately thirty-nine million people were categorized as lower class and had very little or no wealth.

In 2005, the annual percentage of households at various incomes were as follows:

Households earning under $15,000	$15,000 - $24,999	$25,000 - $34,999	$35,000 - $49,999	$50,000 - $74,999	$75,000 - $99,999	$100,000 and more
8.9%	10%	14.6%	10.7%	16%	13.5%	21.8%

The higher the income, the more likely that at least two household members work.

2. SOCIAL STATUS AND PRESTIGE

Status and social prestige are synonymous. People in the highest social class enjoy more prestige and have a higher status in the society than a middle class school teacher earning a moderate income. In addition to social status and prestige based on wealth, sociologists also analyze other kinds of social status. Every person has more than one status; everyone has a status-set. In this set some positions may be high while others are lower. For example, the Director of General Motors has higher status in his company and in society, but he may be an ordinary member of his club or church where other people hold a higher status than he does. In this way, American people assume many different levels and kinds of statuses in their status set.

3. SOCIAL AND GENDER ROLES

Social roles also vary. A mother performs certain role sets for her children. At the same time she assumes other role sets for her husband, other members of her family, co-workers and neighbors. In other words, the same person may be playing many role sets. In less technologically developed countries there are fewer role sets for an individual to play.

Gender determines status and roles in all societies. Males are often assigned higher status roles than females. Traditionally, women assumed homemaker and caregiver statuses and roles, and males assumed achievement, provider and leadership statuses and roles. As a result, women did not have any significant roles in the economic, social and political matters outside of the home before the 20th century. Women were treated like children who were not allowed to sign legal documents, to own property, to make contracts, or to vote.

Nonetheless, some women became active in social movements and campaigned for the abolition of slavery, for children's rights, and finally for women's voting rights. In

1920, the 19th Amendment of the US Constitution gave women the right to vote. Approximately fifty years later the Equal Rights Amendment (ERA) was passed by Congress. This proposed amendment to the United States Constitution stated that equality of rights under the law shall not be denied or abridged by the United States or any state on account of sex. Despite wide support from the public, this amendment was not approved by three-fourths of the states. Therefore, it was not added to the Constitution. However, the women's movement which sponsored the ERA irreversibly changed gender roles, improved the educational and employment opportunities for women, and generally promoted gender equality in America.

In spite of these changes, women who advocate equal treatment still encounter resistance, hesitation, and outright opposition in all segments of society. Many modern women are often victims of sexual harassment and secure inferior salaries and positions when compared to men who have equal education or experience. Some women continue to rely on *Affirmative Action[40], a controversial government policy which provides equal opportunity for women and minority groups. However, compared to the situation before the women's movement in the 1960's and 70's, there is much more flexibility in both the roles of American women and men today.

Because of the *feminist movement[41], modern American women have become involved in all fields of work. At the end of the 20th century, US presidents have increasingly demonstrated sensitivity towards a woman's ability to assume important leadership roles. Sandra Day O'Connor was appointed to the US Supreme Court by President Ronald Reagan and became the first woman *Supreme Court Justice[42]. President Clinton appointed Janet Reno to the position of US *Attorney General[43] and Madeline Albright as US Secretary of State. Each was the first woman to hold that office. Even in some Protestant religious organizations, women are now ordained as ministers, a role traditionally reserved for men. The American military is also adapting to the changing roles of women, and recently American women have been commissioned as high ranking military officers and have served as astronauts in the space program.

Ⅶ. Race and Ethnicity
1. RACE

As a biological concept, race is considered meaningless in the modern world (Robert Songs). Historically, biologists and anthropologists categorized people as follows:

People of European Background	Caucasians or Whites
People of African Origin	Negroid or Blacks
People of Eastern Asia (Mongolia, China, Japan and Korea)	Mongoloid or Yellow
People of South and Southeast and West Asia, and Australia	Austroid or Brown.

These classifications included skin color as well as facial features and hair texture. However, when contemporary scientists identified many more variables, they concluded that human beings cannot be classified in such rigid categories. They also found connections between the survival needs of nomadic people in various environments and gradual genetic changes. There is no pure race as Adolph Hitler (1889 - 1945) claimed. Race is actually a social concept propagated during the European colonization of countries and the domination of indigenous people. The colonizers tried to justify and legitimize their ill-treatment of native people by exploiting their differences. The slave trade, oppression of people in colonized countries and exploitation of foreign wealth and resources were contrary to Christian ethics; therefore, Europeans used these racial categories to justify their behaviors. Today these categories are used as social concepts without any biological significance.

In the United States, race is a very important issue. Race guides the behavior, education, opportunities and resources of Americans. Dominant Euro-Americans have traditionally held political and economic power. Since many Euro-Americans consider the United States as their country, psychologically they do not seem to accept minority Americans who constitute the other 20% of the population. By the end of the twentieth century the American racial/ethnic population was approximately:

Race	1980	1990	2000
Euro-Americans	194,713,000	208,710,000,	225,532,000
Black	26,683,000	30,486,000	34,658,000
Native American	1,420,000	2,065,000	2,402,000
Asian	3,729,000	7,458,000	11,245,000
Hispanic	14,609,000	22,354,000	31,366,000

The *Declaration of Independence* proclaimed that all men are created equal and have rights to life, liberty and the pursuit of happiness. Thomas Jefferson, who wrote the *Declaration of Independence*, owned slaves. Others who signed this document also had slaves and held negative attitudes toward a large number of Black African-Americans formerly called Negroes. In his book *American Dilemma* (1944), Gunner Myrdal wrote about the disparity between American laws and the treatment of minority people of non-European backgrounds.

According to Jan Robertson, two factors have shaped the conditions of non-Europeans in the United States. First, their cultural differences from the European Americans excluded them from equal participation in American society through formal and informal barriers. Second, historical circumstances prevented their participation as equal partners in the society. This meant that Black Africans who were imported as slaves and Asians who were imported as *coolies[44] were not usually treated as equals by their owners or employers.

2. AFRICAN-AMERICANS

Beginning in 1619 Africans were imported to the United States as slaves to work on the cotton, tobacco and sugar plantations. Racist ideology motivated the slave trade and become more powerful and color conscious as slavery became more and more rooted in the economy. African slaves were called Negroes and *stereotyped[45] as subhuman, innately irresponsible, stupid, lazy and promiscuous. They were not allowed to marry, be educated or work independently. Since they were not allowed to practice their cultural activities or speak their native languages, they lost much of their African culture and language. They worked long days, did not have much of a family life, and were lynched for violation of the rules set by their owners. They lived in poor accommodations and lacked adequate food.

Slavery was outlawed in 1780 in the northern states. At the end of the US Civil War (1865), slavery was abolished everywhere in the United States. Inequalities and oppression continued, however. Legal segregation slowly ended, beginning with President Truman's directive (1948) to end segregation in the US military and the US Supreme Court decision (1954) in the case of Brown vs. the Board of Education of Topeka, Kansas. The Civil Rights Movement led by Martin Luther King, Jr. finally desegregated the South in the 1960's. The Civil Rights Acts (1964 – 1965) integrated minorities, women and other disadvantaged people into the work force. In spite of these laws and Affirmative Action which gives preferential treatment to women and minorities, discrimination in employment and housing still exists. By the 1990's more educational and employment opportunities for African Americans and other minorities became available. However, because Affirmative Action has been controversial since its inception, it has been challenged and/or eliminated in some states.

A large segment of the Black African-American population is trapped in ghettoes, areas in a city where minority groups live, often because of pressures from the majority group. Unemployment, poverty, infant mortality, and a lower status in society are common in ghettoes. As members of an underclass since the days of slavery, only a limited number of educated Blacks enjoyed the moderate economic gains between the 1970's and 1990's.

3. HISPANICS (LATINOS)

*Hispanics[46] or Latinos, especially people from Mexico, Puerto Rico and Central America who are predominately Catholic, also often live in poverty in ghettoes. Mexicans, commonly called "Chicanos", are the largest group of Hispanic immigrants. At the end of the 20th century nearly 2,000,000 Americans were born in Mexico. Originally Mexicans populated Texas, New Mexico, Colorado, Arizona and California. After the Mexican War (1848), these lands were seized by the United States, and the Mexicans living there became citizens of the United States. In addition to the descendents of these Mexican-Americans, many more Mexicans have legally immigrated to the United States. Large numbers of illegal Mexican immigrants are migrant workers who provide a constant source of labor for the United States. Many harvest fruits and vegetables; others work in sweat shops doing hard factory labor for little pay, as domestic workers with families, or in businesses and factories. Since they are poorly paid, poorly educated and poorly trained, these illegal immigrants and many legal Mexican immigrants constitute a large underclass living on a subsistence level income in ghettoes. By the late 1990's their median income was 68% of what an Euro-American earned, and approximately 29% of Mexican-Americans were in utter poverty.

Comparatively, Americans from * the Commonwealth of Puerto Rico[47] who immigrate to the United States often live in even worse conditions. Their income is only 46 cents for every dollar a Euro-American earns. Moreover, 43% of Puerto Ricans live below the poverty line. Although the Commonwealth of Puerto Rico has been a possession of the United States since 1917, it has not developed as rapidly as mainland United States.

All inhabitants of Puerto Rico are American citizens, although their island is not a state. Because they can move freely to the American mainland, Puerto Ricans gravitate to the mainland in search of a livelihood or even public assistance, but most of them remain in the most impoverished conditions.

Americans from Central American countries, such as Guatemala, Nicaragua, or Costa Rica, also face prejudice, discrimination and economic impoverishment. Their economic problems can be attributed to a lack of education, work skills and language issues and skills. Since most Cuban immigrants were well educated, had resources and a higher socioeconomic status in Cuba, they adapted socially, economically and politically in the United States.

4. NATIVE AMERICANS (AMERICAN INDIANS)

The terms "Native Americans" or "American Indians", refer to hundreds of "nations" (groups), including the *Zuni[48], *Pueblo[49], *Cherokee[50] and Sioux Indians. These groups lived in North and South America thousands of years before the Europeans arrived. Leaving Asia, they crossed *the Bering Strait[51] and spread throughout the Americas. They were hospitable to the Europeans who first came late in the 15th century, but unfortunately these Europeans were not. They drove Native Indians from their habitats and pushed them to areas that were not suitable for survival. As a result of relentless wars, confrontations, intentional genocide by the Europeans, and European diseases, millions of Native Americans gradually vanished. By the end of the twentieth century about 2,000,000 Native Americans had merged with mainstream American life or lived on 267 *reservations[52]. Reservations are living areas specifically allocated to Native Americans by the United States government. The majority of these areas are located in the western part of the United States and are often unsuitable for human habitation. The Indian cultures were shattered; their food sources were gone; there were no available employment opportunities. The Indians were forced to accept public assistance for food, clothing, and other necessities. Many treaties were made with Native American tribes, but most of these treaties were broken whenever it was beneficial to the Euro-Americans. Native Americans were unfairly treated, and it was not until 1926 that they were granted United States citizenship.

Approximately 50% of the Native American population lives below the poverty line. Those above the poverty line have a median income that is the lowest in the United States. In recent years, as Native Indians have become more conscious of their culture and traditions, they are making greater efforts to preserve and revive them. They are also trying to improve their educational, social and economic conditions. Some of the groups have succeeded in reclaiming their original land or have received compensation for their lost land. Because Native Americans are governed by their own laws and are exempt from laws restricting gambling, some tribes have opted to build gambling casinos on their reservations and have become wealthy from the gambling profits.

5. ASIAN-AMERICANS

Asian-Americans, the fourth major minority group in the United States, numbered about thirteen million people in 2008. Large immigration of Asians began with Chinese laborers in 1839. Chinese males built railways and urban infrastructures, worked in mines, and provided other needed services. Many Euro-Americans could not understand or tolerate the Chinese workers who had a different language and culture. Prejudice and discrimination against them reached a critical stage when the genocide of the Chinese in Los Angeles occurred. Due to enormous pressure from the public, the Chinese Exclusion Act of 1882 barred future immigration. The early Chinese immigrants became small businessmen, domestic workers or farmers. Usually they lived in isolated urban "China Towns" where they retained their culture, language and dietary habits. Not until 1942 were the Chinese once again legally allowed to immigrate to the United States.

After 1882, Koreans and Japanese filled the need for cheap labor on the plantations in Hawaii and farms in the western part of the continental United States. They were treated no better than the Chinese by the Euro-Americans. Eventually, they earned a living by working in agriculture, landscaping, small businesses and domestic work. During World War II, Japanese-Americans were interned in camps and lost their property. After the war, they moved to all parts of the United States and gradually became the most affluent Asian-Americans.

Currently, Philippinos and Asian Indians are also affluent groups. Although Philippinos were American nationals prior to 1935, they experienced the same kind of prejudice as the Chinese, Japanese and Koreans. When the United States gave independence to the Philippine Islands, the government hoped that the Philippinos would be motivated to remain in the Philippines. The Philippines were included in the barred Pacific Zone in the Immigration Act of 1917. As a result of this act, immigration of Philippinos and Asian Indians was forbidden until 1965 when the immigration restrictions for these groups were lifted. Since 1965, hundreds of Philippinos and Asian Indians have moved to the United States. Because most of these immigrants were educated professional people, they had relatively few difficulties in entering the mainstream of American society.

VIII. Other Social Issues
1. HEALTH CARE

All societies have a pattern of health care and treatment. These patterns indicate how the society cares for individuals, because illness is an individual issue. In the United States, an individual's treatment of illness is paid through health insurance which is mainly funded by the insured persons. People who are unable to buy health insurance are often covered by a program known as the Medicaid Program.

The health care system in the United States is highly developed because it is based on modern technology. But the cost of this medical treatment is so enormous that Daniel Shore, a reputable journalist, once said, "Don't get sick in America". Medical costs have skyrocketed; one in every ten dollars goes for health care. Pressure for profit, governmental programs of Medicaid and Medicare, escalating hospital costs and extensive testing for medical diagnosis and treatment contribute to this ever-increasing health care cost. About 35 million Americans, including many children, cannot afford health insurance. This disparity between the advanced medical technology and its lack of availability to millions of Americans who cannot afford health care emphasizes the economic and social conditions of the underclass. Many efforts are currently being made to contain health care expenses and to provide health care for the uninsured.

Since the causes of various illnesses such as heart disease, cancer, lung disease, *diabetes[53], AIDS and other diseases are widely discussed through television, newspapers, magazines, books, and the Internet, people tend to emphasize preventive measures. For instance, legislation barring smoking in public places, buses, and airplanes resulted from public awareness that cigarette smoke is dangerous for people's health. The United States has placed some restrictions on tobacco companies' products and advertisements. The Food and Drug Administration (FDA) regulates the quality and kind of food sold by retailers. Whenever any problem regarding food occurs, the items are removed from the grocery shelves. For health-conscious Americans many health and exercise centers are available. Control of various kinds of pollution such as air, water and noise pollution is regulated by the federal government as preventive measures to ensure the public's health. Some experts claim that not only pollution but the depletion of resources will have a drastic impact on people's health and population dynamics in the future.

2. POPULATION, IMMIGRATION, AND DEMOGRAPHIC CHANGE

By the end of the twentieth century, the total population of the United States was over 260 million people; it continues to increase through birth, prolongation of life and immigration. The birth rate decreased in the 1980's and 1990's to 1.8 children per family. Some segments of the American society are adamantly opposed to abortion or even planned parenthood as methods of birth control. Some people are afraid that the ratio between Euro-Americans and non-Euro-Americans will change the *demographics[54] of the country because minorities have higher birth rates. Not only has the birth rate declined, but the death rate has also declined.

Because of improvements in the health care system and medical treatment as well as people's heightened consciousness about health, the average *life expectancy[55] has increased. By the end of the twentieth century infant mortality had also declined. For minority Americans the rate was 23.1 per thousand births; for Euro-Americans the rate was 12.0 per thousand births. Longevity and lower death rates are not the only cause for the population increase in the United States; immigration is also a factor.

The number of immigrants has increased dramatically. On one hand, immigration has charged the USA with immense vitality and productivity. On the other hand, immigration has created problems. In 1965 the immigration laws were changed to allow more people to come to America. The number of Asians rose from 3 million to 5 million in one decade. Asians and Hispanics living in America legally sponsor their relatives who want to immigrate. These new immigrants sponsor other family members creating a chain reaction. In addition, illegal immigrants, especially those from Mexico, have also increased the population. In the 1990's some restrictions were placed on the number of legal immigrants, and border security between Mexico and the United States was strengthened. Nevertheless, it has been estimated that 3 million people illegally entered the US in 1996.

The Commission on Population Growth estimated that even if the current birth rate remains low, by the year 2020 the US population will be 307 million people. A population increase could cause crowding in urban areas. Increased demands for housing, food, water, electricity and gas could also cause serious problems nationally and internationally. Currently, one American baby uses the same number of resources used for 50 babies in Asia. Americans use a third of the world's energy, and they produce one-half of the global pollution. Although the US population growth impacts the ecology of the world, abortion is a controversial national political issue.

3. *DEVIANCE[56]: CRIME AND THE CRIMINAL JUSTICE SYSTEM

A) Deviance

Socially disapproved behaviors are termed "deviance". Deviant behaviors are violations of the social norms. It is important to remember that what is deviant behavior in one country may not be deviant behavior in another country. For instance, smoking *marijuana[57] may be considered deviant behavior in America, but in India some people use marijuana in their drinks. Deviant behavior demonstrates that social control through the socialization process sometimes fails.

Some causes of deviance are pressure from deviant friends, absence of appropriate care in childhood, and an individual's reaction to discrepancies in the opportunities provided by the society. Biologists and psychologists argue about other causes of deviance. Whether the causes are biological or psychological, society reinforces the social norms by demonstrating the consequences of the deviance to the people in the society. Delinquent and criminal activities, two extreme forms of deviance, are punished by law.

Drug and alcohol abuse, *prostitution[58], gambling, gang fights, physical and sexual assaults, burglary, *vandalism[59], destruction of property, extortion, *treason[60], murder and *arson[61] are considered to be deviant behavior in the United States and are punishable by law. All of these crimes disrupt the social order and could harm both the criminal as well as other people.

B) Violent Crime

Crimes of violence, which increased during the 1990's, are the most feared crimes in the US. Guns and other weapons are readily available in America and contribute to the homicide rate which is without parallel in other modern industrial societies. In 1990 there were more murders in Detroit or Chicago or Los Angeles than in all of England. Property crimes are more common, and by the end of the twentieth century, one occurred on average every three seconds. Increases in crime statistics can be attributed to improvement in reporting crimes as well as the increase in the population. Higher crime rates also reflect more extensive criminal activities, particularly *drug trafficking[62] and drug use since the United States became the biggest world market for illegal drugs by the 1990's. Statistics on violent crimes, such as murder and rape, are widely reported. People fear that strangers will attack them, but research indicates that violent crimes happen more among people known to each other.

C) Victimless Crime

Victimless crimes such as prostitution, public drunkenness, vagrancy, *curfew[63] violations, *loitering[64], gambling and drug offenses constitute approximately one-third of all arrests. Although the federal, state and local governments spend large amounts of money to control victimless crimes, they are difficult to eradicate.

Evidence is hard to find. Offenders often do not respect laws relating to these crimes, and therefore do not have a sense of guilt. Although some petty offenders are arrested and punished, hard core offenders usually evade arrest.

D) White-Collar Crime

White-collar crimes are usually committed by people in the higher socioeconomic class. White-collar crimes refer to offenses like fraud, *embezzlement[65], false advertising, copyright violation, swindling, stock manipulation, price fixing and tax evasion. The President's Commission on Law Enforcement and the Administration of Justice found that the total cost of white collar crime is almost three times that of other crimes. Frequently, these crimes are either not detected or not reported. Even when criminals are arrested, they usually avoid punishment and tend to be less censured by the public. One reason why this happens is that judges often consider social status when sentencing the violator. A judge may justify a light sentence by saying, "He (the white-collar criminal) has suffered enough". Not all crimes are detected, and not all of these are reported to the police. Then, police do not always make arrests. When the police do make an arrest, the government's prosecutor may not gain a *conviction[66]. Finally, a conviction does not always mean imprisonment.

E) Hate Crimes

A relatively new category of crime is *"hate crime"[67], which is defined as words or actions motivated by the race, religion, ethnicity or sexual bias of the victim. Such words or actions violate the Civil Right Act (1965), and can be punished by fine or imprisonment. Not all people who are found guilty of such crimes are imprisoned. Some are merely fined or ordered to provide a set number of hours of service to the community.

F) Criminal Justice System

Violent crimes, victimless crimes, and white-collar crimes are all tried in the criminal justice system, which assumes that the defendant is innocent until proven guilty. The defendant is usually represented by a lawyer who refutes the accusations of the prosecuting lawyer representing the government. The social status of the offender is a major factor which determines if the defendant will be prosecuted. In other words, the higher the social status, the less apt the offender is to be prosecuted. Preferential treatment of people in the criminal justice system raises questions about the fairness and equality of the system.

IX. Social Changes and Global Connections

In the nineteenth century, Tocqueville, a French sociologist, observed the long-term trends in America and concluded that the country would experience "the gradual progress of equality". During the last half of the twentieth century, the trend toward equality has become more rapid. There are many reasons for this, including modern technological developments, the pervasive use of television and computers, the global economy and rapid global travel. Ethnic barriers are breaking down as more interracial and inter-ethnic marriages occur, and educational opportunities for all segments of the population increase.

The people of the United States are a diverse population. Following democratic ideals and constitutional law, more Americans seem to be more willing to accept these diversities. The rise of movements dedicated to the rights of minority people and women have influenced public policy and legislation. Both public and private organizations are moving away from centralization of power and decision-making.

There is also an increasing awareness of all ethnic groups in America to encourage people to revive and conserve their ethnic and cultural heritage. In a multi-ethnic festival an observer could see African, Asian, European and South American groups participating together as they displayed their clothing, songs, dances, food and crafts side-by-side. A change in attitude toward ethnic diversity is only one area of change in American society; the moral view of society is also changing.

What was considered scandalous behavior 50 years ago is now almost commonplace. The increasing number of working women is one factor contributing to the changes in sexual morality. Men and women are interacting in the workplace providing increased opportunities for pre-marital and post-marital relationships. Children born to unwed mothers are now considered legitimate. Since no-fault divorce has become the norm, the number of divorces has increased slowly. As a result of these and other socioeconomic factors, tension that exists in social interactions among different people appears to be declining. Not only are there changes in the moral view, but there are also changes in the direction of the work force.

A rising concern in America is the loss of manufacturing jobs to countries where workers are paid lower wages. Although Americans lost these manufacturing jobs, they gained jobs in the high-tech and service industries. By the beginning of the twenty-first century, young Americans could find employment, but some earn much more than workers a few decades earlier and some earn much less.

Exportation of manufacturing jobs from the United States to other parts of the world has had a great global impact. Not only did it provide jobs to people around the world, but it also introduced American goods, life styles and standards to them. As a result American technology and consumer goods are in high demand. These transactions of goods and services have created a mutual dependency among the participating nations. Americans are wearing shoes and T-shirts manufactured in China and driving cars made in Japan and Korea. The Chinese, Japanese and Koreans are wearing blue jeans, eating hot dogs or Kentucky Fried Chicken and drinking a Coke or a Pepsi. Software made in India by American companies is used in the USA, while American-made IBM machines are widely used by businesses in India.

The economic globalization of the world has moved nations closer to each other. This globalization also has an equalizing element, as the American life style and consumption pattern are adopted by people throughout the world. Why is this happening? One answer could be that America's multi-cultural heritage, mass media and political and economic policies provide the basis for the world's people to identify with American society.

Study Questions

1. Why is the United States a multi-racial, multi-ethnic multi-cultural and multi-religious society?
2. Despite these differences, how do Americans develop commonality in their thinking?

3. How does an American child learn democratic ideals and decision-making?
4. Which social changes have occurred in the United States recently?
5. How have civil rights movements and global connections affected the social changes in the USA?

Selected Bibliography

Anderson, Ralph E. and Irl Carter. *Human Behavior in the Social Environment*. Chicago: Aldine, 1991.

Caplow, Theodore. *American Social Trends*. New York: Harcourt, Brace & Jovanovich, 1991.

Lidz, Thodore. *The Person: His and Her Development Through the Life Cycle*. New York: Basic Book, 1976.

Macionis, John J. *Society, the Basics*. Upper Saddle River, New Jersey: Prentice Hall, 1996.

Reiman, Jeffrey. *The Rich Get Richer and the Poor Get Prison*. New York: Wiley, 1984.

Robertson, Jan. *Sociology*. New York: Worth Publishing, Inc., 1984.

Toffler, Alvin. *The New Wave*. New York: Morrow, 1980.

Vago, Steve. *Social Change*. Upper Saddle River, New Jersey: Prentice Hall, 1996.

注　释

[1] 高加索人,白种人。
[2] 共同性,一致性。
[3] 种族特点,种族渊源。
[4] 大家庭(如与祖父母、已婚子女等共居的数代同堂家庭)。
[5] 苏人(美国南部和加拿大北部的印第安人,即达科人)。
[6] 启智计划,启智方案(指1965年美国国会通过的改善贫困儿童学前教育环境及提前教育计划)。
[7] 寄养家庭。
[8] "朋克"发式(牙买加黑人、雷盖乐师等的一种发式)。
[9] (常用复数)"骇人"长发绺(牙买加黑人、雷盖乐师等的一种发式)。
[10] 空巢综合症(指因子女成年离家后所产生的孤独寂寞情绪)。
[11] (尤指接纳年老体弱者的)私人疗养院。
[12] 核心家庭,小家庭(指只有父母及其子女两代人的家庭)。
[13] 人工授精,人工孕。
[14] (人工授精的)代孕妇。
[15] 首属群体(指成员直接接触,具有最亲密和最持久关系的群体,如家庭,子女)。
[16] 男童子军。
[17] (1917年成立于美国的)国际狮子会俱乐部。
[18] 美国慈善互助会。
[19] 扶轮社(各地专业人员及商人所组成的以社会服务为宗旨的国际社团)。
[20] 关节炎。
[21] 脊髓灰质炎。
[22] 大脑性麻痹。
[23] 罗马公教会,天主教会。
[24] 梵蒂冈(罗马教廷所在地)。
[25] 种族灭绝。
[26] 穆斯林教。
[27] 《古兰经》。
[28] 禅宗教徒。
[29] 印度教徒。
[30] 锡克教徒。
[31] 巴哈依教徒。
[32] 奢那教徒。
[33] 摩门教。
[34] 主张"因信称义"的基督教新教(如美以美会,浸礼会)。

〔35〕路德教的以"因信称义"为教义的。
〔36〕长老派的。
〔37〕浸礼会教友。
〔38〕匿名戒酒协会。
〔39〕绿色和平组织。
〔40〕（鼓励雇佣少数民族成员及妇女等的）赞助性行为，积极措施。
〔41〕（起源于20世纪70年代的）女权运动。
〔42〕最高法院首席法官。
〔43〕司法部长。
〔44〕（尤指旧时印度、中国等东方国家的）苦力。
〔45〕使固定概念，使定型。
〔46〕西班牙（或墨西哥）裔美国人。
〔47〕波多黎各（美国一个自由联邦，实行自治）。
〔48〕祖尼人。
〔49〕普韦布洛人（定居于美国南部及墨西哥北部的印第安人）。
〔50〕（北美印第安人）切罗基人。
〔51〕白令海峡。
〔52〕印第安人居留地。
〔53〕糖尿病。
〔54〕人口统计数据。
〔55〕预期寿命。
〔56〕离轨，异常。
〔57〕大麻。
〔58〕卖淫。
〔59〕破坏他人或公共财产的行为。
〔60〕叛国罪。
〔61〕纵火罪。
〔62〕毒品贩卖。
〔63〕宵禁。
〔64〕游荡。
〔65〕挪用公款，侵吞财产。
〔66〕定罪，判罪。
〔67〕攻击性犯罪。

CHAPTER 12   AMERICAN CULTURE

Dr. Judy Brink

I. Introduction

The major determinant of culture in America is social class. This chapter will concentrate on the category representing the majority of Americans, the middle class. The middle class can be further divided by the various regions: North, South, East, or West, and by the specific location of a person's dwelling, that is urban, suburban, or rural.

II. Materialism and the Mass Media

Consumerism is one of the characteristics that defines and unifies Americans. When reading a magazine or newspaper, listening to the radio, watching TV, a video or a movie, or browsing on the Internet, Americans are exposed to advertisements which encourage them to buy, buy, buy. A good way to study American values is to see how advertising companies use these values to influence consumer spending. Americans are told that buying a brand of perfume or a car will make them young and sexually desirable; preparing a certain food for a family member or a pet will make them love you; and washing your children's clothes with a particular *detergent[1] will make you a good mother.

Materialism is central to American values. Young American children learn at a very young age to value owning things and to experience pleasure when buying or being given something. The importance of consumerism is reflected in the large amount of money spent each year on gifts and greeting cards. These gifts and cards are usually given to a person to celebrate *a rite of passage[2]. A rite of passage marks the transition between one important stage in life and another. Shopping is also a unifying experience as virtually all Americans shop in the same chain stores. Identical chain stores, like *Sears[3] or *Wal-Mart[4], are easily accessible no matter where a person lives in the United States.

Television has made a profound impact on Americans, and TV has been incorporated into almost every aspect of American life. More Americans watch the news on TV than read newspapers, and Americans watch other people discuss controversial issues on *talk shows[5] rather than discuss them with their friends and neighbors as they did in the past. Television programs are geared to appeal to specific groups based on age, sex, ethnicity or a special interest. Many middle class Americans have *cable TV[6] in their homes and pay a monthly fee to view a variety of special channels on history, home repair, nature, sports, music, old movies or the arts.

Television has been combined with digital video disk (DVD) player. *Camcorders[7] allow families to record their own tapes of family activities which are then viewed on the VCRs by themselves or by distant relatives to whom the tapes have been sent. Children are especially fond of watching their favorite TV programs or movies over and over again. Advertisers take advantage of their interest by promoting clothes, food, toys, posters and other *memorabilia[8] which feature pictures of film and TV heroes and heroines. It was thought that people would prefer to watch films in their homes rather than going to the theater, but that has not been the case. Attendance at movie theaters has reached record-breaking levels in recent years. Likewise, there have been predictions that people who watch TV will not read as much as they had in the past. This also has not been the case, because book and magazine sales have also increased.

III. Individual Style and Personal Rites of Passage

One of the myths that Americans choose to believe is that "Anyone can grow up to be President", an expression which symbolizes that through their own efforts individuals can control their own destinies. The reality that individual choices are limited by social class, gender, race and ethnicity is ignored or minimized by most Americans.

1. INDIVIDUAL STYLE

The majority of Americans attempt to create a unique identity for themselves by making careful decisions. Each person makes many choices: what food or clothes to buy; which transportation to use or music to enjoy; where to live and work; and even how much education or how many jobs they will have.

For example, a man could choose to live in a small town, become a *mechanic[9] after graduating from high school and define himself as a "country boy", one who wears jeans, listens to Country and Western music, eats country fried steak, drinks beer, drives a *pickup truck[10] and goes hunting. His brother, who graduated from college, could choose a different life style as a *"Yuppie"[11], Young, Urban, Professional, in the city. With a high paying job he could wear suits, listen to classical music, eat *sushi[12], drink fine wine, drive a *BMW[13] automobile and play golf.

In the same way that each person strives to be a unique individual, each generation strives to define itself as different from the previous one. This is known as the generation gap. Part of the American obsession with the "new and better" results when young people create a style that is different from their parents. For example, the *"Hippies"[14] of the 1970's shocked their parents by growing long hair. In the 1990's the children of the "Hippies" find a new way to shock their parents by dyeing their hair green and being *tattooed[15].

Most Americans create an individualistic style within these generational parameters. The trend setters of the younger generation are primarily the actors and musicians made famous by mass media, and teenagers spend a great deal of time and money attempting to emulate the "style" of their favorite stars. This, of course, requires the constant consumption of new clothes, *cosmetics[16] and *accessories[17] which fuels the demand for new products, a vital characteristic of a capitalistic economy.

2. PERSONAL RITES OF PASSAGE

A) Birthdays and Aging

All Americans have personal celebrations which designate important times in their lives. Ritualized rites of passage include birthdays, weddings, anniversaries, birth of a baby and funerals. Age is a very important determinant of behavior in America, and the celebration of birthdays reflects how age is viewed throughout a person's lifetime. Children are in a hurry to grow up because youth is associated with restrictions on behavior. Since a child longs to be "old enough" to stay awake later and participate in the games and activities of older children, a birthday is an important occasion which brings greater prestige and more privileges. Children's birthdays are celebrated with a party which includes birthday cards, gifts and a special cake with lit candles, one for each year of life. Usually very young children's parties are family affairs, but older children invite their friends. The climax of the party is when everyone sings "Happy Birthday to You". Then the birthday boy or girl makes a secret wish and simultaneously blows out all of the candles in order to make the wish come true.

After childhood, birthdays become less important although close friends and relatives still give cards and gifts. Some birthdays are more important because they signify ages which represent major behavioral changes: 16 when you can legally drive a car; 21 when you can legally drink alcohol; 30 when you know you are growing older; 40 when you are considered to be middle aged; and 65 when you are a "senior citizen" eligible for Social Security checks.

Americans dislike growing older because old age is associated with declining health and decreased independence. They deal with this sensitive issue in two ways: humor and avoidance. Often adults are given humorous birthday cards which make fun of how old they are, and frequently people make jokes about how much they dread turning 30, 40 or 50. Another way people handle the fear of growing older is to ignore their birthdays or refuse to tell others their real ages. This sensitivity to age is why it is considered very impolite to ask an American adult's age. Among very old but healthy adults, who are proud to be 95 or 100 years old, this attitude is reversed. It is an established practice for someone celebrating his/her 100th birthday to receive a birthday card from the office of the President of the United States.

B) Weddings

Weddings are elaborate celebrations, closely associated with many traditions. The bride is given a party called a "wedding shower" at which her female friends and relatives give her gifts. The groom is entertained at a "bachelor party" at which his male friends and relatives celebrate his last night as a single man. Usually the wedding is held in a church or *synagogue[18], but it is both a religious and a legal ceremony. After the wedding ceremony, a reception is held in a hotel, a restaurant or a home. Guests eat, drink, dance and toast the happy couple, wishing them a successful marriage. Each year on their wedding anniversary married couples celebrate by giving each other cards, gifts or sharing a romantic dinner at an expensive restaurant. Since the 25th and 50th year anniversaries are special occasions, they are celebrated with large parties attended by relatives and friends. Second and even third marriages have become more common, a result of the increased divorce rate and the longer life span of many Americans. A recent and interesting phenomenon is for Americans over the age of 65 who are either divorced or widowed to remarry. At any age a wedding is seen as a joyous time because it is commonly believed that a good marriage is the basis for a happy life. In contemporary America *gay[19] and *lesbian[20] couples have publicized their controversial demand to legally marry, arguing that marriage is a basic human right.

C) Births

Another joyous time is the birth of a baby. The middle class views pregnancy as a medical event which requires careful monitoring by a doctor. First time expectant parents are encouraged to attend birthing classes where they are trained in "natural child birth", making it possible for the husband to participate in the birth by coaching the mother through the labor and birth process. Female friends and relatives give presents to the mother-to-be at a *"baby shower"[21]. Some people prefer to wait until the child is born to give their gifts.

As with most events in contemporary American lives, having a baby is commercialized, requiring the purchase of new clothes and toys and special baby food and furniture: crib, playpen, highchair, car seat and a "changing table", a specially designed table for changing the baby's diapers and storing the necessary supplies. A recent trend is for professional women to delay having a baby until their education is completed and their careers are well established. This delay has resulted in higher rates of infertility and therefore lower birth rates. Since there are fewer American babies available for adoption, some couples who want children are unable to have them. It also suggests why many Americans adopt Chinese baby girls.

D) Deaths

In many ways, death, the last rite of passage, is the most difficult for Americans. Just as Americans fear old age, many are also phobic about death. Instead of saying the word death, Americans tend to use the euphemistic phrase, "passed away". People are reluctant to write their wills or plan their funerals.

Death rituals usually have three components: the *visitation[22], the funeral and the *interment[23] of the deceased person. After a person dies, either at home or in the hospital, the funeral director takes the body to a funeral home where it is prepared for burial. Friends and family members come to "view" the corpse which is "laid out" in an open casket and to extend their sympathy to the deceased's family. A recent trend has shortened the viewing period from three days to one or two days.

A funeral, frequently conducted by a religious leader, is either held in a church or at the funeral home. If the deceased is buried, it is common for mourners to follow in their cars, the hearse which contains the corpse, to the place of burial. At the cemetery, a shorter eulogy is given by the presiding religious leader before the closed casket is lowered into the ground. This tradition is changing as more Americans want their bodies to be *cremated[24] or donated to medical centers for research. In any case, friends express their sympathy by sending cards, flowers or a donation to an appropriate charity. Neighbors often help the bereaved family by providing food, taking care of children or pets, and attending to other details, including driving to the airport to meet people coming to the funeral.

Generally Americans believe that they have control of their lives. They are disturbed by death because they feel that they have lost control. Recently several states have legalized living wills which allow people some choices in the level of medical treatments that will be taken in order to prolong their lives. With the advancement of medical technology, people fear that their lives will be artificially prolonged and that they will be kept alive in a *vegetative[25] state by machines. To prevent this treatment, people who are physically and mentally healthy write living wills which instruct their physicians and *next-of-kin[26] about kinds of medical treatments and interventions they will accept or reject when they are seriously ill and can no longer make these decisions. In this way Americans have a voice in their medical treatment even if they are incapacitated.

Ⅳ. Manners

1. IMPORTANCE OF GOOD MANNERS

Good manners are very important to Americans. In crowded cities a well mannered person does not intrude into others' private space. Most Americans dislike coming into physical contact with strangers, and an accidental touch requires an apology. Strangers should avoid eye contact because staring is considered an invasion of privacy. When meeting someone you know, you are expected to greet them briefly and informally since city people are usually in a hurry. In rural areas where people do not rush as much, people take the time for more lengthy greetings. Even strangers receive a friendly "Hello". Another common greeting is "How are you?" Actually the person doesn't want to know about your medical condition, but is only being polite. The normal response is "I'm fine", or "I'm okay". This social situation is similar to the one in China when one is asked "Have you eaten yet?" Americans value friendly, courteous and informal relations. Most adults prefer to be addressed by their first names; titles such as Mr., Mrs., Ms., Dr. or Professor are routinely only used by children, in professional settings, and in certain areas of the southern USA.

2. PUNCTUALITY

Punctuality is very important, particularly in the work place. Since being late implies that you do not value a person's time, tardiness is often construed as an insult and can result in anger or even dismissal from your job. You should always apologize if you are late, and you must include a valid reason, such as traffic, weather or a family emergency, when you make an apology.

3. THE AMERICAN "THANK YOU"

One interesting aspect of contemporary American culture is the constant use of the phrase, "Thank you". These words are used in almost every social exchange no matter what the relationship is between the two people: strangers, friends or family. "Thank you" is expected when anything is physically handed to you such as when a sales clerk gives you change after a purchase or when the paperboy hands you a newspaper.

When information is exchanged, such as asking for directions, or during a phone conversation, the recipient of the information is obliged to say "Thank you". Another appropriate and necessary time to respond with a "Thank you" occurs after you receive a compliment, such as "This was a delicious meal" or "That's a very pretty dress". To not say this is interpreted as rude and implies disrespect. Arguing that the meal was not delicious or that the dress is not pretty suggests that the person who gave the compliment has faulty reasoning which could result in a misunderstanding.

Dining at a restaurant, a common situation, illustrates how often the phrase is used. In all of the following situations one is expected to say "Thank you": when one is seated by the hostess; handed the menu; given the salt and pepper; when the food arrives; when the waitress asks if everything is OK; and when presented with the check and the change.

4. FRANKNESS AND PRIVACY

There is a complex set of rules which governs what sort of conversation is appropriate, but the most important one is that Americans are direct and frank. For example, when a host offers something to a guest, the guest is required to respond honestly. A "No, thank you" is not a polite refusal, but represents the guest's genuine intention.

Because Americans project an attitude of friendliness, honesty and informality, it might seem that they are willing to discuss anything. American concern for privacy is very important, and many personal topics are not appropriate for conversation between casual acquaintances. It would be considered inappropriate and impolite to ask about someone's age, religious preference, medical history, why they are not married, why they do not have children, or how much they earn.

V. Food and Meals

1. MEALS

Most Americans eat three meals a day: breakfast, lunch and dinner. Traditionally, the preparation of food was the primary responsibility of the wife/mother. Even though there have been some changes in sex roles because most women work outside the home, buying, cooking and serving the food and cleaning up after meals are still primarily done by women and girls.

A) Breakfast

Breakfast is often a hurried meal, eaten at different times by each family member, since each person in the household usually has a different work/school schedule. Cereal with milk, toast or *doughnuts[27] are typical breakfast meals, but there may be time on weekends for a hot meal which could include a combination of eggs, *waffles[28], pancakes, bacon, sausage, ham and potatoes. Although many adults drink coffee or tea, children drink fruit juice or milk because it is thought that the caffeine in coffee or tea is not good for their health. A recent trend is for fast food restaurants like McDonald's to sell breakfast, and some people buy breakfast on their way to work and eat their food in their cars.

B) Lunch

Lunch is usually eaten at the work place or school. Typical foods eaten at lunch time are sandwiches, such as hamburgers, hotdogs, ham-and-cheese combination or roast beef; soup such as *chili[29], chicken noodle or vegetable; and fruit and vegetable salads. Children may bring a packed lunch, consisting of a sandwich, fruit and dessert, and buy milk, juice or a soft drink. Others buy their meals at the school *cafeteria[30] which serves hot and cold meals for a modest price. Large companies allocate time for a "lunch hour" when employees may eat wherever they choose, and some companies provide cafeterias for their employees.

C) Dinner

Dinner, the evening meal, was traditionally the one meal during the day when the entire family ate together, and some families still continue this tradition. Since dinner is often the largest meal of the day, it may consist of several dishes. If soup is served, it is served first, followed by the *entree[31] which consists of meat and vegetables. Popular meat dishes are beef, chicken, pork or fish. If potatoes are not served, *pasta[32], noodles and rice will be substituted. Typical dinner vegetables are peas, corn, carrots and *broccoli[33]. Salads made from raw *lettuce[34], tomatoes, *celery[35] and carrots may accompany the entree. The meal usually ends with a sweet dessert such as ice cream, pie, cake or cookies.

2. REGIONAL VARIATIONS

Regional variations determine how food is cooked. In the North and Midwest most food is *bland[36], seasoned only with salt and black pepper, while in the Southwest the food is often more *spicy[37] because it is cooked with red pepper. Each area of the country has food specialties—the Northeast for *lobster[38]; the South for *pecan[39] and *key lime pie[40]; and the Southwest for Mexican food. Food also varies according to ethnicity. People from all over the world have immigrated to the United States, and many people continue to cook food according to traditions they brought with them from their homelands. In large cities one can find Chinese, Indian, Mexican, Italian, Middle Eastern, Thai and Japanese restaurants.

Chinese *cuisine[41] is very popular in America. Because the majority of early Chinese immigrants to the USA were from the area near Guangzhou, Cantonese cooking was the most familiar to Americans, but later, when Americans were introduced to foods from Hunan and Sichuan, they also became popular. Many native Chinese will be disappointed when they eat in the typical Americanized Chinese restaurant because the food has been cooked to suit the American taste.

3. SCHEDULING MEALS

Today, different work and leisure schedules sometimes make it difficult for the family to eat together. The traditional family meal is often replaced by a meal in a restaurant or a *staggered[42] meal at home when individual family members heat their own dinners in the microwave oven. A large fast food industry makes it affordable for familles to eat out, and a wide variety of frozen dinners which can be purchased ready-to-eat and heated in an oven or microwave for a few minutes have contributed to the decline of traditional family dining.

4. SNACKING

Americans eat more than meals: snacking is very popular. Snacks can be *crunchy[43] and salty such as potato or corn chips, popcorn and *pretzels[44], or they can be sweet such as cookies, cake, ice cream and soft drinks. Commercially prepared snack food is available for sale not only at supermarkets or grocery stores, but also at gas stations or in *vending machines[45]. Many Americans are overweight because advertisers and retailers tempt people to consume high calorie snacks, especially in the evening when people are watching TV.

5. ALCOHOLIC BEVERAGES

Alcoholic beverages are enjoyed by many Americans. In the 1950's and 1960's *cocktails[46] made with *gin[47], whiskey or vodka were popular, but since the 1980's consumption of beer and wine has become more common. Although most states do not allow people under the age of 21 to purchase or drink alcohol, this law is routinely broken. Teenagers either use an illegal identification (ID) to lie about their ages, or convince older friends to purchase the alcoholic beverage for them. Drunk driving is a very serious problem among adults, especially for teenager drivers. In order to alleviate this problem among adults, bars which serve alcohol now have a custom called a "designated driver". One member of the group who has gone out together refrains from drinking alcoholic beverages during the evening so that he/she is able to drive everyone home safely.

6. CIGARETTES

Cigarette smoking used to be very common among Americans, but since the US *Surgeon General[48] has required that serious health warnings be displayed prominently on cigarette packages, many people have quit smoking. There is an entire industry which produces a variety of measures to help smokers quit. Americans believe that non-smokers are affected by cigarette smoke, a condition called "second-hand smoke". Smoking is banned on all domestic airlines and in most American public buildings. Restaurants are required by law to have a non-smoking section, and you can request non-smoking rooms in hotels and motels. It is considered polite to ask permission from others before smoking near them, and it is common for non-smokers to request that smokers do not smoke in their homes or cars.

Ⅵ. Housing

1. RENTED HOUSES OR APARTMENTS

Houses in America can either be owned or rented from a landlord. People in urban areas or people who cannot afford to buy a house often live in rented apartments. Renters sign a legal *lease[49], agreeing to comply with the landlord's requirements including an advanced payment of one month's rent before moving in. The renter also has rights which are written in the lease. It is important for the renter to know if the landlord will provide *off-street parking[50] and pay the utilities: heat, water, electricity and garbage disposal.

Smaller or efficiency apartments consist of a small kitchen, a bathroom and a room which is a combined living room, dining room and bedroom. Larger apartments will have a separate living room, more than one bedroom and possibly a dining room. Kitchens will always be equipped with purified hot and cold water which is why Americans drink water that comes directly from the spigot. Often the landlord furnishes the kitchen with a sink, a stove and a refrigerator and furniture in the other rooms. If not, the apartment is advertised as "unfurnished". Bathrooms will have a sink, toilet and a shower and sometimes a bathtub because most Americans believe that taking a shower or a bath once a day is healthy. All modern apartments have some form of central heating, and the more expensive apartments will also be air conditioned.

2. HOME OWNERSHIP

Owning a home is part of the American Dream. However, houses are expensive, and a purchase requires a *down payment[51] and a bank loan or a *mortgage[52]. Homes are either single family dwellings or *condominiums (condos)[53], apartments which are owned, not rented. Buying the first home is seen as an important accomplishment. It also means that the person is willing to pay local real estate taxes which support the local school district and other community institutions. A home purchase also gives the owner economic power because houses usually increase in value over time and provide *collateral[54] if the owner wants to borrow additional money from a bank or another lending institution.

Houses are important indicators of social class in America. The location of the house, the building materials, the size of the house and the amount of land surrounding the house immediately convey information about the owner's status in American society. Since most people spend a lot of time and money on making the inside and outside of their homes as attractive as possible, a large home improvement industry is thriving in the United States.

The quality of furnishings and appliances inside the home is also important an indicator of social class. A typical middle class kitchen would have a sink, stove, refrigerator, dishwasher, *blender[55], microwave oven, toaster oven, *chopper/shredder[56] and an electric garbage disposal. Most homes would have several television sets, a DVD player and a stereo radio/player which accepts audio cassettes or CD's.

Many houses have more than one phone: one in the kitchen, one in the living room and perhaps one in a bedroom. Usually a child will have a phone in his/her bedroom with a separate telephone number. It is common for a child to have his/her own cell phone. Another reason why many American houses have more than one phone line is the increased use of personal computers which are connected by telephone to other computers outside the home. One room in an American house may be solely designated as "the computer room" or a study, while other rooms may only be used for a hobby such as a sewing room, a greenhouse or a library. Larger American homes also contain a "family room" which is where the family members congregate for group activities: watching TV, playing games or entertaining friends.

Outside, American houses frequently have *porches[57] or *balconies[58] and a garage. In small towns, suburbs or rural areas houses are usually surrounded by a yard of grass and flower and vegetable gardens. Most home owners spend a considerable amount of time during the summer weekends cutting the grass, planting flowers and making their yards beautiful.

VII. Pets

Americans are very attached to their pets, especially cats and dogs. In the past, dogs were the most common pets, but today, since many people live in apartments and work during the day, cats are now the most popular pets. Other pets are birds, fish, rabbits, *gerbils[59] and *hamsters[60]. In recent years snakes and *reptiles[61], including *iguanas[62], have become popular with young people.

There is a huge pet industry in the United States which manufactures special food, toys, beds and even clothing for pets. Many people treat their pets more like children than animals, and it is a common practice for dogs and cats to sleep with their owners. Americans believe that petting cats and dogs is soothing and can extend a person's life. Nursing homes have "pet therapy" when visitors can bring cats and dogs to visit the old people who are not allowed to keep pets.

The majority of Americans become outraged when they see anyone abusing an animal which is a criminal offense. *Veterinarians[63], specially trained doctors authorized to medically treat animals, encourage dog and cat owners to have their pets *neutered[64] to prevent reproduction in order to diminish the current pet overpopulation in America. It is ironic that although Americans are so concerned with the well-being of their own pets, many other dogs and cats do not have any food or shelter. Sometimes these stray animals are temporarily housed in an animal shelter, but eventually most of these homeless animals do not find owners and are *euthanized[65] rather than have them forage on their own in the wild where they suffer from cold weather, hunger and disease.

Ⅷ. Leisure Activities

Leisure activities can be classified as those activities in which individuals and groups of people participate when they are not working. Many American social activities are organized by groups of people who share an interest. Groups are organized by institutions such as schools or churches and by national organizations, such as the Boy Scouts of America, but many groups are organized by individuals acting on their own.

1. SPORTS

Sports are a good example of a group leisure activity. Many teams are organized for those who want to participate in baseball, American football, golf, soccer, basketball, bowling, tennis or other group sports, by schools, churches, businesses or neighborhoods. Teams are organized into leagues which are defined by age, ranging from pre-school children to senior adults. Americans are very conscious of age, and activities are often organized to include only those of a similar age. Americans are also very competitive, and children of both sexes are encouraged by their parents to compete in sports as a way to develop desired personality characteristics. As well as participating in sports, Americans love to watch professional teams play; there are hundreds of cable sports channels. The most popular sports are American football which is played in winter and baseball which is played in summer.

2. GROUPS

There are many other types of groups which organize social activities: groups organized by people who share a single interest such as gardening, canoeing or breeding dogs; groups who want to do charitable work such as the Rotary International Club or volunteer firemen; and groups for individuals who are seeking help or guidance such as *Alcoholics Anonymous[66] and *Parents Without Partners[67]. Children also participate in many group activities, and parents often find it difficult to budget time and transportation so that each child can be delivered to and picked up from each scheduled event.

3. FAMILY ACTIVITIES

Other leisure activities are solely family activities. Most Americans live in nuclear families consisting only of parents and their children. Since *extended family[68] relatives often live very far away, relatives are able to meet each other only for special occasions such as birthdays, anniversaries or family reunions. Family members who live close by can meet more informally and often share meals and participate in everyday activities together such as shopping or watching TV.

Americans often plan a family vacation, and there is a huge leisure industry in the USA which caters to families who want to spend a week having fun. Some families visit large amusement parks such as Disney World; others go to the ocean or a lake, or camp in the countryside. Many families own a small house or cabin located in a wilderness area where family members spend their leisure time hunting, fishing or relaxing.

Day-to-day family leisure activities include going to a restaurant for dinner, shopping, seeing a movie and watching television or a DVD movie at home. Families often enjoy *barbecuing[69] and eating outdoors either at a public park or in their backyard. Some leisure activities are usually done with a few friends. Shopping malls have become places of entertainment as well as *retail outlets[70]. Teenagers especially enjoy spending time at the mall playing video games in the *arcades[71], seeing a movie, or simply walking around with their friends. Adults, particularly young adults, often spend their leisure time drinking, talking and listening to music with their friends in a bar or at informal parties in their homes or attending concerts or movies with friends. Friends frequently meet to play cards, take walks or simply to chat.

4. INDIVIDUAL

Americans value having the time and privacy to spend in individual activities, and many people enjoy solitary leisure activities such as reading, gardening, walking, playing with a pet, listening to music or watching TV. Most homes have more than one television set, and it is common for one person to watch a program in one room while other family members watch a different program elsewhere in the house. Some Americans are very concerned with keeping themselves fit, and they often walk, jog, and use exercise equipment at home or at commercial *fitness clubs[72].

5. THE IMPORTANCE OF TRANSPORTATION

Americans value their leisure time, and many working adults think of childhood and retirement as carefree times of life when individuals have few work responsibilities and can participate in many leisure activities. Many American leisure activities involve some form of transportation such as a car, bicycle, motorcycle, *roller skates[73], *skateboard[74], boat, raft, *kayak[75] or canoe. Sometimes it seems that Americans spend more time on wheels than on their feet! ,

Two important characteristics of Americans, a concern with saving time and a love of automobiles, have resulted in many businesses allowing their customers to purchase an item or a service from their cars. Americans can do their banking, buy beer, pick up their dry cleaning, see a film at a drive-in movie or eat a meal without leaving their car. Cars are also being equipped with such amenities as *cellular phones[76] and CD players. Owning a car is a necessity in much of the country because public transportation is only available in large cities, and it is common for a family to own two or even three cars.

Americans know that relying on cars, rather than public transportation, is expensive and harmful to the environment, but they believe that the freedom and mobility obtained by driving a car is worth the cost. A car represents independence: the ability to go where you want, when you want to go. Passing the driver's test in order to acquire a driver's license at age 16 is a major rite of passage for young Americans. A teenager often works at a job in the evenings, on weekends and during the summers so that he/she can afford to buy and maintain a car. When older Americans have to give up driving due to poor eyesight or other physical problems, they are often bitterly resentful of losing their cherished independence.

IX. Holidays

Americans celebrate three kinds of holidays: official, secular and religious. Since official holidays are sponsored by the national government, many businesses, including banks and the post office, are closed on these days. The seven official holidays are New Year's Day, Martin Luther King Jr.'s Birthday, President's Day, Memorial Day, Independence Day, Labor Day and Thanksgiving. These holidays are occasions to reinforce patriotism and to celebrate American ideals such as courage, hard work, liberty, honesty, tolerance and love of God and family.

1. OFFICIAL HOLIDAYS
A) New Year's Day

New Year's Day, which occurs on January 1, is an internationally celebrated holiday. In America the main celebration actually takes place on New Year's Eve when family and friends gather together to "toast in the New Year" at parties which are held in homes, businesses, nightclubs or restaurants. At New Year's Eve parties people usually wear very fancy clothes, and women often buy a new dress just for this occasion. People drink, dance and eat until a few minutes before midnight when they watch the final countdown to the new year on television. This is broadcast *live[77] from Times Square in New York City where thousands of people gather to celebrate. At midnight people make a new year's resolution, drink champagne and wish each other a "Happy New Year". Children, who are usually allowed to stay up late, bang pots and pans or set off fireworks to celebrate the new year. Generally, New Year's Day is a family day when people eat special "good luck" food such as pork and *sauerkraut[78] or black-eyed peas and watch parades and football games on television.

B) Birthday of Martin Luther King, Jr.

Martin Luther King Junior's Birthday, the newest official holiday first celebrated in 1986, also occurs in January. This holiday was established to honor Dr. King, a Nobel Peace Prize winner, who was assassinated in 1968 while leading a non-violent campaign to gain civil rights for Black Americans. Speeches and special television programs memorialize Dr. King and his ideals on his birthday. This celebration is tied into Black History Month during which Black Americans celebrate their unique cultural heritage by educating themselves and others about the contributions of Black Americans. Martin Luther King Day is an attempt to make up for the many decades of prejudice and discrimination that erased the Black experience from American Culture and to help educate people in order to combat prejudice.

C) Presidents' Day

Presidents' Day, the third Monday in February, honors two of the greatest American presidents: George Washington, the first American president, affectionately called "the Father of His Country", and Abraham Lincoln, the president during the American Civil War (1861 - 1865). Flags and pictures of these presidents are publicly displayed, and school children attend assemblies where they learn about Washington and Lincoln. Sometimes the children are taught the importance of honesty through the legend of the young Washington who confessed to cutting down a cherry tree by saying, "I can not tell a lie". *The Gettysburg Address[79], Lincoln's most famous speech which emphasized national unity, is often read or memorized by students. Although most adults enjoy having the day off, there are no special national celebrations on Presidents' Day.

D) Memorial Day

*Memorial Day[80] is celebrated on the last Monday in May and is a day to honor the dead, especially those who died defending their country. The day is marked by watching parades, listening to speeches, and decorating graves with flags and flowers. People often decorate their homes with American flags, and it is traditional for families and friends to get together for a picnic. Memorial Day weekend is considered to be the beginning of summer.

E) Independence Day (Fourth of July)

America's National Day is officially called "Independence Day" because the Declaration of Independence, written by Thomas Jefferson and signed by the Second Continental Congress on July 4, 1776, stated that the thirteen American Colonies were independent from England. The common name of this holiday is "the Fourth of July" which is celebrated by patriotic speeches and music, parades, and public and private displays of the American flag. Large fireworks displays are shown on TV, but most communities have their own fireworks displays.

F) Labor Day

Labor Day, a day to honor American workers, is celebrated on the first Monday in September. Labor Day's long weekend is considered to be the end of summer season, and people usually celebrate it with family dinners or picnics.

G) Thanksgiving

Thanksgiving always occurs on the fourth Thursday in November and is celebrated to give thanks to God for his blessings. According to legend, in 1621, the first Thanksgiving was in celebration of the first harvest by the *Pilgrims[81], the first English settlers in Massachusetts, and their Native American friends who had helped them to survive the harsh conditions in the New World. Many Americans travel long distances to be with their families for Thanksgiving, causing major traffic congestion on the highways and at the airports. Thanksgiving is a day when extended family members gather for a dinner of roast turkey, stuffing, sweet potatoes and pumpkin pie, traditional foods believed to have been eaten by the Pilgrims on the first Thanksgiving. People decorate their homes for the occasion by displaying colored "Indian" corn and symbols of the harvest such as corn shocks, brightly colored autumn leaves and pumpkins. The President broadcasts his annual Thanksgiving Day speech, and people watch parades and football games on TV.

2. UNOFFICIAL SECULAR HOLIDAYS

Since secular holidays are not as important as official or religious holidays, they are primarily celebrated by children or specific groups of adults. The five secular holidays are Valentine's Day, *Saint Patrick's Day[82], April Fool's Day, Mother's Day and *Halloween[83].

A) Valentine's Day

*Valentine's Day[84], which is celebrated on February 14th, is associated with romantic love and is primarily celebrated by couples who are dating, engaged or married. Homes, schools and shops are decorated with red hearts and cupids, the symbols of Valentine's Day. These symbols can be traced to Greek mythology, which believed that *Cupid[85], the son of Venus, the goddess of love, and Mars, the god of war, would shoot his arrows into people's hearts, causing them to fall in love. Couples exchange cards and gifts on Valentine's Day. Men often give red roses, the symbol of love, or elaborately wrapped packages of chocolate candy to their wives and sweethearts. Valentine's Day parties are occasions for dating couples to wear their best clothing and dance together for an evening. School children also exchange valentine greeting cards with their classmates and teachers. These valentines are placed in a specially decorated box, and one child is designated as the "postman" who walks around the classroom delivering the cards. The children usually also have cookies, candy and a beverage.

B) St. Patrick's Day

St. Patrick's Day is celebrated on March 17 to honor the *patron saint[86] of Ireland, the homeland of the Irish who immigrated in large number to the USA in the nineteenth century. It is said that on this day "Everyone in America is Irish". The largest festivities are held in New York City which stages a parade along Fifth Avenue, but many people throughout the country celebrate with small parties. Since green represents Ireland's verdant countryside, on this day people often wear green; some schools, shops and homes are decorated with *shamrocks[87], a green three-leafed *clover[88] representing good luck; and some bars serve green beer.

C) April Fool's Day

April Fool's Day is always April 1. This day to play jokes on people to make them look foolish may have originated during the time of ancient Rome, although no one really knows for certain. During the Middle Ages most Christian countries celebrated the start of the new year with a festival beginning March 25 and ending April 1. When the modern calendar was adopted in England during the eighteenth century, the new year began on January 1, but some practical jokers continued to give mock gifts on April 1. After playing a joke on someone, the prankster says, "April Fool!" Having a sense of humor is very desirable to Americans, and the two correct responses to a prank are to laugh and to congratulate the person for successfully deceiving you.

D) Mother's Day

Mother's Day, which celebrates the importance of the family, occurs on the second Sunday in May. On this day people honor their mothers by sending them flowers, gifts and greeting cards. The holiday began in 1907 when Anna Jarvis asked her church in Philadelphia, Pennsylvania to hold services to honor all mothers on the anniversary of her mother's death. As with other American holidays, this one has been highly commercialized, and now there are "Mother's Day" cards for wives, sisters, grandmothers, virtually any female relative. If people can not take their mothers to dinner at a restaurant, they will telephone their mothers, making this one of the busiest days of the year for the telephone companies.

E) Halloween

Halloween originated in pre-Christian Europe where October 31st was All-Hallows-Eve, the night when the ghosts of the dead walked the land. In order to placate these spirits, gifts of food were left on the doorstep outside the house. In America this ancient custom has been transformed into a charming holiday for younger children who wear masks and costumes. After choosing a favorite character from a book, film or television program, the child, accompanied by an adult or an older sibling, will dress like that character and go *"trick or treating"[89]. Children knock on people's doors asking for a treat—usually candy—so they will not play a trick on the inhabitants of the house. Usually these "tricks" are ringing the doorbell or rubbing soap on a window. Recently trick or treating has become unsafe in certain regions of the country. Some people have contaminated the treats, and now some communities are sponsoring parties or parades on Halloween as alternative activities. Halloween has also become a commercial holiday. People buy "ready made" costumes, and commercial decorations are replacing the traditional jack-o'-lantern, a pumpkin which is carved with a frightening face and illuminated by placing a candle inside.

3. CHRISTIAN RELIGIOUS HOLIDAYS

Since most Americans are Christians, the religious holidays most often celebrated are Christmas, which celebrates the birth of Christ, and Easter, which marks His resurrection. As these holidays become increasingly more elaborate and secular, many people, who are neither Christians nor religious, participate in these holidays by exchanging greeting cards and gifts and by decorating their homes, shops and work places.

A) Christmas

Christmas is a holiday season which begins at Thanksgiving and ends on New Year's Day. It is a special time for children who believe that if they are good, Santa Claus, who lives at the North Pole, will visit them on Christmas Eve, December 24th. Santa arrives in his sleigh pulled by eight reindeer, bringing the children presents and placing them under the Christmas tree. Children often leave a snack for Santa to thank him for his generosity to them. Since adults go to great pains to ensure that young children believe this story, the truth is often revealed by another child, either a sibling or a classmate.

Almost every building in America is decorated with symbols of the Christmas season such as colored lights, holly, green wreaths, *mistletoe[90] and a Christmas tree, which is an evergreen placed inside the home and decorated with lights, colored balls and other ornaments. Gaily wrapped gifts from relatives and friends are placed under the tree and are not opened until Christmas Eve or Christmas Day.

During the Christmas season many parties are held at the work place or with friends and family members. Christmas Day, December 25th, is usually celebrated only with family members. After the presents are opened, the family has a Christmas feast of turkey or ham "with all the *trimmings"[91]. Despite the importance of these secular customs, Christmas is a religious holiday, and special Christmas Eve services take place in churches where children often *reenact[92] the Christmas story, and Christmas hymns are sung.

B) Easter

The date for Easter changes every year, but it is always celebrated on a Sunday between March 22nd and April 25th. Although many people attend church on Easter to remember the resurrection of Jesus Christ, this holiday is also rapidly losing its religious character. Children are told that when they are sleeping, the Easter *Bunny[93] will bring them Easter eggs and baskets of candy. Since the eggs and baskets are hidden, the children have great fun looking for them on Easter morning. Again adults go to great lengths to keep the "secret" from their children that there is no Easter Bunny (Rabbit). But by the age of six or seven most children know that it is their parents who have provided the baskets filled with jelly beans, chocolate eggs and bunnies and the red, blue, purple, green and yellow dyed chicken eggs. Today, some adults buy commercially prepared eggs and baskets or take their children to Easter egg hunts sponsored by a mall, church or other organizations.

C) Conflicts over Religious Holidays

Because the US Constitution legally requires the separation of church and state, the conflicting religious and secular natures of Christmas and Easter are causing problems in America. The current solution is a compromise which allows school children to sing secular Christmas songs such as "Jingle Bells", but not religious songs such as "O Little Town of *Bethlehem[94]". The federal post office sells both religious and secular Christmas stamps. Government buildings may display secular symbols such as a Christmas tree or the Easter Bunny, but not a *creche[95] or a *crucifix[96] which are religious symbols.

4. JEWISH RELIGIOUS HOLIDAYS

In addition to religious holidays celebrated by the Christian majority, other religious holidays are also celebrated by large groups of Americans, affecting the communities where these groups are found. In the fall, Jewish-Americans will leave school or work for their New Year and *Day Atonement[97] (Rosh-Hashanah and Yom Kippur). In midwinter, Jewish-American children are given gifts on *Hanukkah[98]. Such children often receive gifts twice, on Hanukkah from family and on Christmas from friends! The Jewish *Passover[99] is celebrated near the time that Christians celebrate Easter. In an effort to emphasize acceptance of all religious holidays, not simply Christian holidays, businesses will sometimes display both Christian and Jewish holiday symbols at midwinter and in the spring.

Chinese-Americans celebrate the Spring Festival. Since the majority of Chinese-Americans live either in New York or California, the largest Chinese Lunar New Year celebrations occur in these two states. Many Americans are familiar with the traditional festivities shown on TV including the famous "Dragon Dance".

Ⅹ. American Values

Americans are future-oriented and value that which is new and modern. Young is better than old, and an active life is better than a passive one. The ideal American is individualistic, pragmatic, achievement oriented, competitive and hard-working; more sharp witted than intellectual. This ideal American does well in school, has many friends and acquires special work and leisure time skills. After college graduation, a young American lives independently for a period of time, then falls in love, marries, owns a house, has children and is a faithful spouse, a devoted parent and an honest, law-abiding citizen. In old age the ideal is to stay healthy and to live independently so as not to be a burden on one's children. Most of all, the ideal American is happy and healthy. This is the American Dream.

Study Questions

1. What evidence indicates that the consumption of material goods is becoming more important in America?
2. Why do Americans value youth more than old age? How does this idea compare to the current attitude in China?
3. Why is owning and driving a car so important to Americans?
4. Why would older Americans prefer to live alone rather than with their children?
5. Why do Americans ignore how sexism, racism and social class limit their options?

Selected Bibliograph

Althen, Gary. *American Ways: A Guide for Foreigners in the US*. Yarmouth, Maine: Intercultural Press, 1992.

Lanier, Alison. (Revised by C. William Gay). *Living in the USA*, 5th ed. Yarmouth, Maine: Intercultural Press, 1996.

Stewart, Edward C. and Milton J. Bennett. *American Cultural Patterns: A Cross-Cultural Perspective*. Yarmouth, Maine: Intercultural Press, 1991.

Wallach, Joel and Gale Metcalf. *Working with Americans: A Practical Guide for Asians on How to Succeed with US Managers*. New York: McGraw-Hill, 1995.

注　释

〔1〕洗涤剂。
〔2〕为人生进入一个主要阶段(如成年、结婚、死亡等)所进行的仪式。
〔3〕美著名连锁购物中心。
〔4〕美著名连锁超市。
〔5〕脱口秀,谈话类节目。
〔6〕有线电视。
〔7〕摄像机(尤指小型摄像机)。
〔8〕纪念品。
〔9〕机修工。
〔10〕轻型卡车。
〔11〕雅皮士。
〔12〕寿司。
〔13〕宝马(一种德国产名牌轿车)。
〔14〕嬉皮士。
〔15〕文身。

〔16〕化妆品。
〔17〕(妇女的)装饰品(如手套、手提包等)。
〔18〕犹太教会堂。
〔19〕男同性恋。
〔20〕女同性恋。
〔21〕(美)为即将分娩的妇女举行的送礼会。
〔22〕(美)葬礼前的守夜。
〔23〕土葬或火葬。
〔24〕火葬。
〔25〕植物人状态的。
〔26〕最近的亲属。
〔27〕油炸圈饼。
〔28〕奶蛋烘饼,华夫饼。
〔29〕香辣酱。
〔30〕自助餐厅。
〔31〕正菜。
〔32〕意大利面食(如通心粉、细面条等)。
〔33〕花椰菜。
〔34〕莴苣。
〔35〕芹菜。
〔36〕不辣的。
〔37〕辛辣的。
〔38〕龙虾。
〔39〕美洲山桃。
〔40〕翅果酸橙馅饼。
〔41〕菜肴。
〔42〕用餐时间错开的。
〔43〕松脆的。
〔44〕一种纽结状的椒盐饼。
〔45〕(出售饮料、食品等的)投币式自动售货机。
〔46〕鸡尾酒。
〔47〕杜松子酒。
〔48〕公共卫生局医务长官。
〔49〕租约。
〔50〕指马路以外的停车场所,如后院、与邻居房子之间的空地或私人车库。
〔51〕预付定金。
〔52〕抵押贷款。
〔53〕(美)所属房产为私有、庭院等公用场地为共有的一种公寓。
〔54〕担保品,抵押品。
〔55〕搅拌器。
〔56〕切菜器。
〔57〕门廊。
〔58〕阳台。
〔59〕沙鼠。
〔60〕仓鼠。
〔61〕爬行动物。
〔62〕美洲的大蜥蜴。
〔63〕兽医。
〔64〕阉割。
〔65〕使安乐死。
〔66〕防酒精中毒协会(美国的戒酒团体)。
〔67〕单亲协会(由单身父母组成的互助团体)。
〔68〕大家庭(如与祖父母或已婚子女同住的几代同堂家庭)。
〔69〕野外烧烤。
〔70〕零售店。
〔71〕长廊商场(有屋顶的店铺街)。
〔72〕健身房。
〔73〕溜冰鞋。
〔74〕溜冰板。
〔75〕美式帆布艇。
〔76〕(美)手机。
〔77〕实况转播。
〔78〕酸泡菜。
〔79〕1863年林肯在该地阐述民主主义精神的演说。
〔80〕阵亡将士纪念日。
〔81〕1620年到达北美创立普利茅斯殖民地的英国清教徒。
〔82〕圣帕特里克节(3月17日,爱尔兰人节日,圣帕特里克是爱尔兰人的守护神)。
〔83〕万圣节。
〔84〕情人节。
〔85〕爱神。
〔86〕守护神。
〔87〕酢浆花(爱尔兰的国花)。
〔88〕苜蓿。
〔89〕"不给吃的,可要捣蛋喽"(万圣节时孩子们到人家门前说的戏语)。
〔90〕(用作圣诞节悬挂饰物的)槲寄生小枝。
〔91〕(主菜之外的)花色配菜。
〔92〕再次展现。
〔93〕兔子。
〔94〕伯利恒,耶稣诞生地。
〔95〕基督诞生塑像(描绘基督在马槽中诞生的情景,常于圣诞节陈列)。
〔96〕耶稣受难像。
〔97〕(犹太教)赎罪日。
〔98〕修殿节(犹太纪念节日之一)。
〔99〕逾越节(犹太历7月14日至21日)。

CHAPTER 13 EDUCATION IN THE UNITED STATES

Prof. June Almes

I. Introduction

Education in the United States has always reflected the historical, political, social, cultural and economic conditions in the country. This chapter introduces the background of several contemporary educational issues which resulted from the dynamic combination of these factors. European settlers who came to the thirteen American colonies adopted three distinct systems of formal education for their children, depending on their geographic location. The three geographical regions were New England, the Middle Atlantic and the South.

1. THREE MODELS OF BASIC EDUCATION IN THE UNITED STATES

A) New England: Universal Education

In New England the goal was to promote universal education. Puritans, heirs to the Protestant Reformation, believed that the individual should read the Bible, instead of relying on a clergyman to interpret the book. Since the Bible was an integral part of the people's everyday life, reading was stressed. This helps explain why the New Englanders introduced universal education.

At first only boys went to the local public elementary school, first to sixth grade, but later girls were included. In order to support these primary or grammar schools, New England citizens paid a real estate tax on their property. The money was given to elected representatives, collectively known as a *school board[1], who were responsible for building and maintaining the one-room school house and also for hiring, paying and occasionally firing the school's teacher who *boarded [2] with his students' families on a rotating basis.

The New England model of community-supported, universal education was transplanted to the West in the late eighteenth century through the enactment of *the Northwest Ordinances[3], national laws which required that each new community donate land for a school building.

The concept of education as preparation for a religious and moral life became less important when the powers of church and state were separated following the adoption of the Bill of Rights (1791). However, the New England model continues to profoundly influence American education's goal of universal literacy. Moreover, each community, called a school district, still provides tax money and elected school board members who are responsible for spending this money on the schools within the district.

B) Middle Atlantic States: Vocational Education

A second form of education developed in the Middle Atlantic colonies where Benjamin Franklin and others recognized the need for *vocational education[4] in order to prepare children for adulthood by teaching them practical skills or a trade. These secular goals gradually replaced the religious focus of the New Englanders, and vocational training continues to be one of the choices American high school students may select.

C) Southern States: Tutorial System for the Wealthy

Today, the third form of education, the tutorial system adopted by the Southern colonies, is not as important as the New England or the Middle States' models. Originally the tutorial system was designed to educate wealthy children. The tutor came to the plantation and taught the children what their parents wanted them to learn. Some wealthy southern boys were sent to Europe to complete their studies.

In the early days of the nation, southern black children and children from poor white families received no formal education and were expected to work as soon as they were able. Later, when universal education was imposed on the Southern States, white and black children legally went to different schools which were "separate but equal". In 1954 the US Supreme Court overturned the unfair "separate but equal" doctrine in the case, Brown versus Board of Education, Topeka, Kansas, dramatically changing the racial patterns of modern US education. By the end of the twentieth century almost 40% of all American children attending publicly funded schools were from minority groups: Native Americans, Asian Americans, African Americans and Hispanics or Latinos.

Today the southern tutorial system has been modified and renamed "home schooling". About one-third to one-half million American children are tutored at home by their parents, who are required to teach a curriculum developed by their local school district. A school administrator periodically tests the home-schooled children to ensure that they have learned the prescribed curriculum.

There are several reasons why home schooling is becoming more popular in modern America. Since some white parents do not want their children to associate with children from minority racial and ethnic groups who attend the public schools, these parents either teach their children at home or send them to more expensive private schools. Religious parents may prefer home schooling to safeguard their children from effects of a drug culture and its associated violence occurring in some American schools.

Finally, the increased popularity of home tutoring parallels both the rising levels of education of parents and the increasing use of home computers. Computers allow children at home to search and study thousands of data bases, including museums, libraries, newspapers, and magazines, as well as to communicate with other users connected to the World Wide Web (www).

2. PRESCHOOL EDUCATION

Another important educational development was introduced in the 1960's during the Civil Rights Movement when President Lyndon Johnson called on Americans to join the "War on Poverty". Federal tax money was allocated for Head Start, a preschool program which provided fundamental education and nutritious meals for poor young children.

Today the middle class continues to support preschool education because the majority of American mothers have joined the work force. Middle-class parents can choose the *Day Care Center[5] where they want their children to be educated, although these families are often limited by the high costs of preschool education or long waiting lists.

3. ORGANIZATION OF BASIC EDUCATION

Basic education is free and mandatory in the United States. Basic education includes Kindergarten through twelfth grade, popularly known as a K – 12 education. K – 12 education is divided into two administrative categories: elementary and secondary schools. Elementary school includes the primary grades (grades K – 3) and the intermediate grades (grades 4 – 6). Younger secondary school students attend either middle school (grades 6 – 8) or junior high school (grades 7 – 9) and older students attend a senior high school until they have completed the twelfth grade.

Regardless of the state, the local school district or the age of the student, some characteristics are evident in American basic education. Usually the legal length of the school year is 180 days, which begins after American Labor Day in September and ends in June. This schedule originated when the majority of Americans were farmers, and children were needed to help harvest the crops during the summer season.

4. AN AVERAGE DAY

School begins between 8 and 8:30 a.m. and ends at 3 p.m. Some students can walk to their local schools, but most children ride a school bus. All students eat lunch in the school cafeteria because it is too difficult and expensive for them to go home at midday.

The school day begins with a principal, teacher or student broadcasting "opening exercises" over a loud speaker. "Opening exercises" include announcements about special events for the day, the lunch menu, and music or poetry to motivate the children to do their best throughout the school day.

Teachers prefer to teach subject matter, such as reading, social studies, mathematics and science, in the morning when the students are rested and alert. They believe subjects, such as art, music and physical education should be taught after lunch when the students have shorter attention spans. Scheduling these subjects according to the teachers' preferences is difficult; this is why many school districts have adopted a *"staggered schedule"[6]. A staggered schedule is a five day cycle when different subjects are taught at different times. Beginning on the sixth day the cycle is repeated.

Elementary children usually stay in their *self-contained classroom[7] for their academic subjects. Secondary pupils move from classroom to classroom, but their teachers remain in the same room, sometimes called the "home room". Even elementary children go to other rooms for classes which require special equipment, such as art, music and physical education.

When weather permits, elementary students go outside for *recess[8], a time to socialize and play games with their friends on the school playground. Playgrounds are furnished with sturdy equipment, especially swings, slides and *seesaws[9].

Classrooms are usually furnished with a blackboard or a whiteboard, a bulletin board, portable desks and chairs, a *storage cupboard[10], television and at least one computer. Additional equipment, such as a VCR, can be borrowed for scheduled periods of time from the central storage room. Frequently Kindergarten classrooms have a bathroom, and many elementary, art and science classrooms have water. Since teachers and students prefer cheerful rooms, they devote time and energy decorating them. Often they make colorful decorations which reflect holidays and other special events, or the teacher will display an excellent student's work. A large, thriving industry, which produces commercially made classroom decorations and other types of learning materials, caters to teachers.

Teachers record a student's progress quarterly on a report card which the student takes home for a parent to read and sign. At the end of the school year students are allowed to keep their report cards.

The school curriculum is enriched in a variety of ways. Older students may travel and study in a foreign country. Guest speakers, particularly people in the local community who have a special talent or hobby, are invited to discuss their knowledge with a large group of students at an assembly program or with a smaller group of students in a classroom. Children who bring items from their travels or collections are permitted to share them with classmates. Teachers often take their students on field trips; younger students walk around the community, and older students travel longer distances on a bus to historic and scenic places.

5. EXTRA-CURRICULAR ACTIVITIES

Extra-curricular activities are an important feature of American education. Girls and boys voluntarily participate in sports; American football, baseball, soccer, basketball, hockey, track and golf are the most popular sports. Schools which have a swimming pool sponsor competitive and *intramural[11] swim meets. Students may also join a club to be with others who share their interests, such as collecting stamps or coins, playing chess or computer games, speaking a foreign language, acting in a play or performing in the orchestra or band.

6. PARENTAL INVOLVEMENT

Parental involvement depends on individual parents. Mothers, more than fathers, visit the schools for a variety of reasons. Parents belong to a group called the PTO, Parent-Teacher Organization, or PTA, Parent-Teacher Association. PTO's and PTA's are national organizations with local *chapters[12] which raise money to purchase equipment, library books and other items which benefit local school children. Members volunteer their time to help teachers supervise students during special events.

All parents are invited to the school for parent-teacher conferences. During the conference a teacher will evaluate a child's progress for a parent who then is able to ask questions and to provide background information about his/her child to the teacher. Schools sponsor an "open house" during National Education Week in November. Students' work is displayed throughout the school building, and parents and teachers chat informally about matters of mutual interest. Parents of successful children tend to volunteer or visit the school more often than other parents.

7. HIGH SCHOOL GRADUATION

Graduation from school is a major rite of passage. Graduation ceremonies are held when a student leaves elementary school, middle or junior high school and senior high school. The most important ceremony occurs when students graduate from senior high school, a line in American society which separates childhood and adulthood.

A dance, or *prom[13], is held on the Saturday after final examinations. Girls buy special dance gowns, and boys rent *tuxedoes[14]. A boy buys his date a *corsage[15] and takes her to an expensive restaurant where they eat dinner before going to the prom. Sometimes a group of graduates will rent a *limousine[16] which they will drive to the prom. The dance hall is decorated with flowers and *crepe paper [18] will play popular, romantic songs. After dancing for several hours, the graduates and their dates will change into casual clothing. Many will continue to celebrate at a classmate's home or visit a scenic place to watch the sunrise.

The graduation ceremony is held the following week. Graduates, each wearing a *flat cap[19] with a tassel and marching to traditional music, walk into the auditorium. Joyful family members and friends watch the graduation procession. Sometimes a religious leader will begin the ceremony, followed by a guest speaker who talks about adulthood and the future. Students who have attained special honors are recognized. Then the presiding school official reads the graduates' names in alphabetical order, according to surname. Individually seniors receive their high school diplomas and congratulations from school officials. At the conclusion of the ceremony, graduates move their tassels to the other side of their caps, cheer, throw their hats in the air or release balloons. The orchestra plays recessional music as the graduating seniors march out of the auditorium, followed by their family and friends who congratulate them. Later in life classmates organize a class reunion every five or ten years to celebrate their high school graduation anniversaries.

II. Issues in American Basic Education
1. DECENTRALIZATION

The most important characteristic of American education is decentralization. The states, and, to a lesser extent, local school districts, are responsible for the education of the children in their jurisdiction. Compared to other nations which centralize educational authority in the capital city, America's system is unique. Decentralization was a direct result of the United States Constitution, based on the New England model which required local financial support and supervision. The authors of the Constitution did not include education. Instead, they delegated this responsibility to each state as stated in Amendment X of the Bill of Rights: "The powers not delegated by the Constitution, nor prohibited by it to the States, are reserved to the States respectively, or to the people".

The federal government does have important political and economic interests in education. The executive branch provides information through its US Department of Education. Congress provides money and legislation for national education needs. The US Supreme Court rules on the constitutionality of laws affecting education. In the past the Supreme Court has ruled on *desegregation[20], school prayer, articles in student newspapers and the school board's powers.

The advantage of each state being responsible for its own system of education is that there is strong state and local control by the elected representatives. Interested individuals and lobby groups know their representatives and frequently communicate with them about current legislation.

One disadvantage is that the federal government can not require the states to mobilize their educational resources to meet a national crisis. Since each state has its own academic curriculum, the nation cannot decide what American children should learn. One compromise is to allow the individual to choose the curriculum track he/she wants to study in high school. Usually there are at least three tracks: academic, vocational and general studies.

2. NO CHILD LEFT BEHIND

The national government became more involved in K – 12 education in 2002 when Congress passed the No Child Left Behind (NCLB) legislation during the George W. Bush administration. NCLB provided funding for schools whose students passed national reading and mathematics tests. The law has had a sweeping impact on American education because it affects what students are taught, the tests they take, the training of their teachers, and the way money is spent on American education.

Charles Finn, a leading American educator and supporter of NCLB, believes that 5 myths have developed about NCLB. Myth One, NCLB allows the federal government to control schools. Finn objects to this myth because states are free to forego federal money if they do not want federal intervention. However, no state has left the program yet. Myth Two, NCLB is not sufficiently funded. Finn disagrees because nearly all legislation from Washington, DC lacks sufficient funding. Myth Three, NCLB will fix the problems of American schools. Finn reminds us that NCLB follows an educational theory called "standards based instruction" that says: State what children should know; measure their progress; and use rewards and punishments to help them succeed. Achieving this goal of NCLB, not solving all of the problems of American education.

Myth Four, the standardized testing required by the NCLB gets in the way of real learning. Finn believes that accountability made possible by standardized testing is appropriate as long as the test is an honest measure of a solid curriculum. Myth Five claims certified teachers are better than non-certified teachers. Finn argues that there is no solid evidence that teacher certification is necessary.

Like Charles Finn, advocates of NCLB claim that the law holds schools accountable, empowers parents and is helping to close the achievement gap in American schools. Many critics, including those who agree with the goals of the law, dislike the "one size fits all" approach to education that overemphasizes testing and does not provide enough money to schools to achieve success.

In fact, better schools have improved and poorer schools have declined since NCLB has passed. Debate continues to rage over whether the law is a way to improve academic achievement or not, and, if it is, how can the law be changed to make it more effective.

3. FUNDING

American basic education is largely subsidized by state and local property taxes, and to a lesser extent by the federal government. People who pay taxes on their property and do not have children in school believe that the system is unfair because they do not receive direct benefits from their tax dollars. Major inequities arise because wealthy suburbs have excellent funding for excellent schools while rural and urban school districts have fewer funds for salaries, textbooks and equipment and buildings. Rising inflation and new educational programs increase the cost of schooling which is paid by the tax payers at a time when their daily living expenses are also increasing. Frequently tax rates are debated at all levels of American society, particularly before local, state and national elections.

4. MASS EDUCATION

Throughout their history Americans have valued education and have been willing to allocate tax money to provide free public education for all of their children. Influenced by Thomas Jefferson's ideas, they believe that a literate citizenry is necessary when voters elect their national, state and local officials.

However, the concept of mass education has caused several problems. One criticism is that basic education in the United States caters to the "least common *denominator[21]", meaning the teacher gives attention to the slower learners while the brighter students become bored and lose interest in learning.

A related issue involves *"mainstreaming"[22], a program which allows physically and mentally handicapped children to attend the same classes with children without these problems. While parents of handicapped children want their children to be included, other parents are concerned that their children are not receiving the best possible education because the teacher spends a great deal of time helping the disadvantaged students. Moreover, the costs for educating the handicapped exceeds the costs for educating other children.

5. CRIME

Crime does occur inside and outside American school buildings, especially harassment, bullying, petty theft, robbery, aggravated assault and vandalism. However, the majority of American children neither perpetrate nor experience crimes during their years in school.

Contributors to school crimes include drugs, television, films, music, the single-parent family, working mothers, child abuse, mass education, accessibility of guns, peer pressure and a permissive, materialistic society.

Responses to crime vary among school districts and even among schools in one school district. An administrator of a school which experiences high rates of crime may lock the school doors to prevent intruders from entering the building. Local and state police may be asked to patrol inside and outside the school building. Visitors may be required to register at the principal's office. Of course, teachers supervise children throughout the school day including lunch time and recess. Still, concerned parents may escort their children to and from school or move to a less troubled school district. They may also send their children to a private school or teach them at home.

At the national level, Congress has enacted laws which make guns more difficult to obtain. At the state level, adults who are convicted of selling drugs to children are sent to prison. In spite of these kinds of remedies, many American schools continue to be plagued by crime.

6. CURRICULUM

Outspoken advocates with opposing ideas about what children should learn in school can be found in each of the fifty states. Some people believe that schools should only teach the basic subjects, "reading, writing and arithmetic". They would eliminate all "frills" such as driver training and controversial subjects related to attitudes and values. Their opponents argue that at appropriate ages students should learn how to drive a car, explore attitudes and values other than those taught at home and study sex education in order to understand how the AIDS disease is transmitted.

A related controversy involves learning strategies. Some American educators claim that learning factual knowledge is a waste of time since facts change quickly in the modern world. Therefore, students should learn how to learn. *John Dewey[23], an American educator and philosopher, believed that students should learn how to solve problems based on the scientific method: defining the question, developing the hypothesis, gathering the information and testing the hypothesis. The process begins again when the question is reformulated based on the new evidence.

Other American educators disagree. They argue that school-age students need to learn basic information before they can solve problems. During Ronald Reagan's administration, *A Nation at Risk* (1981) was published. This book, which advocated that American schools return to a basic curriculum of reading, writing, mathematics and computing, was widely acclaimed.

7. "MELTING POT" AND "MULTICULTURALISM"

Another divisive issue is the "cultural wars". Traditionalists support the "melting pot" theory, a belief that the diverse racial, ethnic and religious populations in America can be unified. Supporters of the "melting pot" idea believe that the primary responsibility of public schools is to "Americanize" its students. The ideal curriculum would teach civic values, social skills and the English language as well as American history and biography. In that way, all Americans, regardless of their differences, can share the national identity.

Beginning in the 1960's Congress passed a series of Civil Rights laws which legally and economically empowered minority groups. These multicultural groups demanded that the curriculum taught in basic and higher education be revised to give more emphasis on previously neglected or excluded non-elite groups.

The American intellectual historian, David Hollinger, in his book, *Postethnic America: Beyond Multiculturalism*, distinguished sharply between biology and culture, complaining that multiculturalism too often assumed that a person's values depended on skin color. Instead, he offered an inclusive vision of a dynamic, pluralistic society which appreciates multiple identities and accepts the formation of new groups as part of the normal life of a democratic community. However, this concept has not resolved the issue of multiculturalism in American society. Therefore, the debate continues about ethnic studies in the school curriculum.

8. TECHNOLOGY

The widespread use of technology in the United States, especially television and the home computer, often circumvents formal education. Research suggests that most American children spend more time watching television, and, to a lesser extent, playing computer games than learning in the classroom. As a result, critics complain that Americans are not able to concentrate for long periods of time and that they are becoming more passive learners. The problem with passive learners is that they only learn what they are told to learn and do not question or integrate ideas. In fact, there is a popular and humorous name for this phenomenon, a *"couch potato"[24].

Some critics believe that two societies exist in America: the "haves" and the "have-nots". The "haves" are more affluent and can afford the latest technologies for their children. Since the "have-nots" and their children do not have these advantages, the gap between these two groups is widening, creating new societal problems.

On the other hand, technology in the schools has allowed students, regardless of their economic situation, to learn new ideas and information by using the new machines and methods.

9. CHOICE OF SCHOOL

In recent years, there has been a new issue in education. Most American parents believe that their local public schools are doing a good job of educating their children. However, a growing number of politicians and other leaders along with a number of parents believe that American public schools are not preparing young people to compete internationally. Parents are also concerned with safety, with moral issues, and with local control of curriculum. As a result, four major alternatives to traditional public schooling have been developed. These alternatives are the focus of national controversy.

Two of the major options are private schools, primarily sponsored by religious groups, and home schooling. *Vouchers[25] set amount of money provided by the government from education budgets are a third alternative. Parents selecting this alternative can place their child in any school of their choice, public or private. The parents would give the chosen school the vouchers, which the school would return to the government for the set amount of money. Unpopular schools would receive fewer vouchers and less money. The voucher alternative primarily benefits children in urban areas, with many choices of schools.

A fourth alternative is a charter school, a public school paid by tax dollars collected by the local school board. Unlike the traditional public school, the charter school is allowed to hire teachers who have not the state requirements for teachers. A charter school may also set its own curriculum, as long as it loosely meets state curriculum requirements. Parents of children in charter schools exert greater control over their children's education, but the quality of charter schools varies dramatically.

In addition to these four major choices, two variations may also occur. If the majority of children in a school are failing state examinations, the state will take control until test scores improve. Also to foster particular skills, such as science and the arts, and to improve the diversity of racial and ethnic groups in the school, a community may establish a *magnet school[26]. A magnet school in mathematics would be designed to attract talented mathematicians from a wide area in order to foster their special skills. Any student may apply for admission, but only the most talented are accepted.

III. Higher Education

1. HISTORY

The foundation for free, universal education was established in the eighteenth and nineteenth centuries. By the twentieth century free education was available to all American children from Kindergarten to twelfth grade, an education which prepared people for farm or factory jobs. Today, this amount of education is no longer considered sufficient.

In 1996, President Bill Clinton announced that every American citizen needed at least two years of education after high school, a K－14 education. His announcement reflected the changes in the national economy caused by the postwar shift from manufacturing to service. It also reflected the belief of a majority of employers and employees that post-secondary education can provide better educated workers who should be paid higher salaries.

Even in Colonial America the need for specialized higher education was evident. Harvard University, the first American institution of higher learning, opened in 1636. Most of the early colleges were founded by religious sects in order to train their clergymen.

In 1862, Congress recognized the need to improve agriculture and mining by passing the Land Grant Act which allowed money raised from the sale of public land to be used to establish the state university system. Located in every state, these universities continue to train their students in new methods and technology. Graduates spread the ideas to local farmers and miners, creating a stronger technical *infrastructure[27].

Military schools were established to improve officer training, notably the army's US *Military Academy at West Point[28], New York in 1802 and the US Naval Academy, at Annapolis, Maryland in 1825. As K－12 education became more universal, there was also an increased demand for trained teachers. Specialized teacher training colleges or "normal schools" originated in the late nineteenth century to meet this need.

During the first half of the twentieth century the majority of these specialized, single-purpose institutions became multi-purpose colleges and universities. Of the approximately 3,000 institutions of higher learning in the United States today, only a few single purpose institutions survive.

Beginning in the nineteenth century, women and Black Americans demanded access to higher education. To meet their demands, institutions were established solely for the purpose of educating these groups. Today, nearly all institutions of higher education have an "open admissions" policy. This policy allows women and minority groups, as well as white men, to attend most American colleges or universities.

2. FUNDING

By the 1950's three changes in funding greatly influenced American education. First, the United States Congress passed the G.I. (Government Issue) Bill of Rights in 1944 which provided benefits for members of the armed forces who served their country in World War Ⅱ. One of these benefits was that federal tax money paid for their education. Many young people, who normally would not have gone to college before the war, took advantage of this opportunity to train for new careers. Reasons why these *veterans[29] needed higher education were directly related to World War Ⅱ. Wartime technology altered the post-war job market by eliminating wartime industries and creating new kinds of employment. Many of these former military people reconsidered their career goals based on their war experiences. "Baby Boomers", the children of these veterans, expected to go to college, a demand which succeeding generations of Americans continue to make.

A second way World War Ⅱ altered funding for higher education resulted from a new involvement of universities in non-academic activities. In order to defeat Germany and Japan, leaders in the government, the military and industry decided to allocate money and resources to university researchers who could develop advanced techniques and materials even though there might not be an immediate benefit. This partnership between the "government-military-industrial complex" and the universities is still common in America today. The Internet was developed by the US Department of Defense and several universities, a modern example of this type of cooperation. Easy access to these resources and to other researchers is one reason why many scholars throughout the world travel to America to study. Not only do these scholars contribute to their homelands, but they also contribute to the quality of life in the United States.

A third change in funding and emphasis occurred in 1957 during the "Cold War" when the USSR launched Sputnik, the first space satellite. Since the US government thought that the USSR was technologically more advanced than America, Congress allocated millions of dollars to education, believing that improved education meant improved technology.

This federal money was given to the fifty states in two ways: block and categorical grants. Each state received *block grants[30], or sums of money that could be spent wherever state and local authorities saw a need. Each state also received categorical grants, or sums of money that could only be spent as Congress directed, for basic and higher education. Categorical grants provided money to universities under the National Defense Act, which provided tuition, housing, books and a stipend to worthy students selected by participating colleges and universities. As a result of this legislation, thousands of Americans were able to graduate from college at the tax payers' expense.

In the latter half of the twentieth century, Community Colleges were established to meet the increased demands by Americans for higher education. These two-year colleges originally educated students who lived in the local community and who wanted additional training at a low cost before entering the work force. However, as the idea became more popular and the community colleges offered a variety of academic programs, students traveled to distant community colleges to pursue their special interests. Now some of these community college graduates transfer to a four-year institution to continue their studies.

Unlike basic public education which is free, the cost of higher education is expensive because it is paid by the student or the student's parents. Historically, higher education in the United States was the way for an individual to enter a profession. In order for more Americans to achieve this goal, public and private resources consistently have been allocated to higher education. State support varies for colleges and universities, depending on three funding categories. Public or state owned institutions are the least expensive. State supported institutions are somewhat expensive. Privately owned institutions are the most expensive.

Recently, shrinking levels of public support have occurred even at the public institutions. Although scholarships, fellowships, assistantships and low interest loans are available to college students, critics believe that increasing numbers of middle class families will not be able to afford higher education for their children in the future unless public support is increased.

3. UNDERGRADUATE EDUCATION
A) Selecting a College

American college students have many choices. During the senior year in high school a student selects one or more colleges and applies for admission. Reasons for selection vary. Most applicants know someone who attended the institution, heard good reports about its programs or simply can afford its fees.

Some select a college because they can live at home and drive to classes. Many Americans have never lived independently from their families until they go to college. This is a problem for freshmen living on campus who have to take personal responsibility for their daily life for the first time. Colleges provide printed material giving information and advice, such as a college catalog and a directory of local businesses. An *orientation[31] for new students includes a walking tour of the campus and presentations by college administrators, teachers and counselors.

B) Dormitory Life

Dormitory rooms include a bed, desk, and storage space for each student. Students who have telephones in their rooms must pay for their long distance calls. Communal bathrooms and sometimes kitchens are located on each floor, and washers and dryers are located in the basement. Dormitories have a common room where residents can congregate to watch television, attend meetings, use the computers or buy snack foods and drinks from *vending machines[32]. Dormitories also have study areas where conversation is limited.

Hall managers living in dormitories perform several functions. They are counselors for students who have problems. They are responsible for the safety and security of their students and buildings. They act as a liaison between the college administrators and students, and they hold seminars about topics of mutual interest.

Students may have only as few as one or as many as five room mates. To demonstrate their individuality and to delineate their private spaces they decorate their rooms with photographs, *posters[33] and other memorabilia. Many students bring their televisions and sound systems which make dormitories noisy. Colleges which do not have adequate dormitory space allow upper-classmen to move into private housing off campus. Upper-classmen may park their automobiles on campus if they live in the dorms. Some students go home on weekends to see their families, eat home cooking or work at a part-time job.

C) Extra-curricular Activities

Extra-curricular activities are available to both residents and commuters because all students pay an annual activity fee. At the beginning of the academic year, colleges distribute a calendar of events which lists special programs, including convocations, art displays, drama and music programs. "Homecoming" is a weekend when graduates return to campus to reminisce with their classmates and watch a parade consisting of marching bands and decorated *floats[34] preceding a college sports event. Colleges provide a sports *arena[35] and sport and fitness equipment. Larger universities make a profit from televised football games, and their teams are enthusiastically supported by their alumni and local communities.

Colleges which do not have a central computer laboratory available for student use will provide computers in the dormitories and student rooms. Several colleges require freshmen to buy computers which can be purchased at a discount in the student book store. The majority of American college libraries are automated, and computer data bases are rapidly replacing printed materials. Colleges have been wired for *closed circuit television[36], and more affluent institutions have their own television studios and stations.

D) Academic Work

During the first week of classes professors give their students an outline of the course, course requirements and evaluation procedures. A student then decides to remain in the class or to replace it with another one. The result is that each student has a different schedule which can cause problems. To remedy this situation, students are assigned an advisor, a professor in their academic discipline. It is the student's responsibility to contact his/her advisor about academic problems such as scheduling and failing grades.

Students also select when they want to graduate. Some people decide to graduate early by enrolling in additional courses during the academic term or summer school. Since approximately 25% of American college students begin college when they are over thirty years old, many of these "non-traditional" students want to graduate as quickly as possible.

Other students attend college for a longer period of time in order to raise a family, work at a full-time job or take a course twice, hoping to raise their original grade. Those who enjoy the carefree campus life postpone their graduation as long as possible.

E) Rigidity and Flexibility in American Undergraduate Education

American colleges are a mixture of rigidity and flexibility. Rising costs have made them more rigid about demanding payment. Rising costs have also prompted colleges to provide a variety of scholarship programs, each with different application deadlines and requirements.

Many students with different needs and abilities make course scheduling for individuals very difficult. Latecomers may not be able to enroll in popular courses which close early in the scheduling process. Specialized courses may have *prerequisites[37], for example, a student may be required to complete a course in calculus before enrolling in a physics class. Freshmen are often bewildered by the many forms and the bureaucracy of a university.

On the other hand, a student is free to make choices. For example, a student is responsible for selecting an academic major. A student also chooses a course schedule to meet his/her individual needs. Some students want morning classes in order to participate in afternoon sports. Some prefer afternoon classes so they can sleep later in the morning. Others select evening classes because they work during the day.

4. GRADUATE EDUCATION

Graduate education terminates with either a master's or a doctorate degree. A student can usually receive a master's degree after completing the course work and a master's thesis, usually a two-year program. It is difficult to determine how long a doctoral student needs to complete the course work, research, writing and defense of the *dissertation[38], but most American universities set a maximum of seven years.

5. ADULT AND CONTINUING EDUCATION

One reason why adult and continuing education is becoming more popular in America is because Americans are living longer and retiring earlier. Another reason is that many Americans are convinced that they should continue their education throughout their lives. Finally, changing technologies and the changing economy sometimes force out-dated industries to close. Unemployed workers will seek education in newer technologies so they can find work.

Colleges and universities provide most of the post-secondary education, including adult and continuing education. However, alternative programs and courses for adults are also available. It is difficult to categorize these programs because they are designed to meet a wide variety of adult needs and interests.

One major trend has been for corporations and other large institutions to provide a wide range of *"in house" courses[39] for their employees. "In house" courses meet a special institutional need, such as learning about interpersonal skills or how to plan for retirement. The employer and/or employee pays for these courses with the expectation that better informed employees will make better informed decisions in the workplace.

A second trend has been for non-academic educational institutions to offer courses. Religious organizations and churches sponsor continuing education for their adult members at no cost. Public institutions, especially libraries and museums, offer courses related to their specialty, such as local history. Students may or may not pay a fee, depending on the teacher and the materials used during the course.

A third trend has been for organizations and institutions to provide profit-making courses and programs to special interest groups. Many travel agencies offer educational trips for sports-minded people, including hunters, fishermen and skiers, as well as people with hobbies, such as gardening, photography and *archeology[40]. Music lovers and intellectuals enjoy the stimulating programs and lectures at places like Chautauqua, New York. *Elderhostel[41] is an organization which caters to people over age fifty. People who enroll in Elderhostel programs decide when and which courses they would like to study at home or abroad and pay a reasonable fee for their instructor, room and food.

During the summer, local secondary schools may invite the public to study language, mathematics and computer courses for a modest fee. Correspondence schools provide degrees to people who prefer to study at home, although the reliability of the school should be investigated by the student before paying any money.

Certainly, it is possible to find almost any type of continuing education in the United States today.

Ⅳ. Conclusion

Education in the United States reflects American history, politics, economy, society and culture. Ideas about education have survived whenever they could be adapted to meet the needs of the society. One idea has prevailed throughout American history: education is the key to achieving the American Dream.

Study Questions

1. How has education in the United States reflected American history, politics, economy, society and culture?
2. How are American and Chinese education systems similar? How are these two systems different?
3. Why do Americans believe that education is the key to achieving the American Dream? Is this belief justified?
4. Discuss the advantages and disadvantages of mass education.
5. Select one of the educational issues and explain how the issue reflects contemporary American society.

Selected Bibliography

Moss, George. *America in the Twentieth Century*. Upper Saddle River, NJ: Prentice Hall, 1997.
World Almanac and Book of Facts. Mahwah. NJ: Funk and Wagnall, 1996.
Hollinger, David. Postethnic America: *Beyond Multiculturalism*. NY: Basic Books, 1995.
Nation at Risk. Washington, D.C.: US Government Printing Office, 1981.
Bell, Daniel. *The Coming of the Post-Industrial Society*. NY: Basic Books, 1973.

注　释

〔1〕学校董事会。
〔2〕搭伙，包管膳食。
〔3〕西北法令。
〔4〕职业教育。
〔5〕日托所。
〔6〕将上课时间错开的课程表。
〔7〕学生在固定的教室里上课。
〔8〕课间休息。
〔9〕跷跷板。
〔10〕教师存放书本或其它物品的贮藏柜。
〔11〕校内的。
〔12〕全国性组织的地方分会。
〔13〕(美)(大学、高中的)班级舞会。
〔14〕男式半正式晚礼服。
〔15〕(女用)紧身胸衣。
〔16〕豪华轿车。
〔17〕(装饰用)绉纸。
〔18〕碟片播放员。
〔19〕带边的帽子。
〔20〕废除种族隔离。
〔21〕一般水准。
〔22〕(残疾人)转入正规班级。
〔23〕杜威(1859—1952)，美国哲学家、教育家和心理学家，实用主义哲学学派创立者之一。
〔24〕电视迷，指终日躺在沙发上边看电视边吃土豆片的青少年学生。
〔25〕此处指美国部分州政府给予的教育津贴。有些家庭可用此津贴送孩子上学费比公立学校昂贵的私立学校。
〔26〕(美)有特色的重点学校，因而对学生具有很大的吸引力。
〔27〕基础结构(如运输、动力、通讯、教育等设施)。
〔28〕西点军校。
〔29〕退伍军人。
〔30〕(美)(联邦政府发给州或地方的)固定拨款。
〔31〕迎新情况介绍。
〔32〕(出售饮料、食品的)自动售货机。
〔33〕招贴画，海报。
〔34〕彩车。
〔35〕室内运动场。
〔36〕闭路电视。
〔37〕先决条件。
〔38〕学位论文。
〔39〕现场培训。
〔40〕考古学。
〔41〕为老年人安排各种活动的组织。

后　　记

　　上世纪 90 年代末,我的一位美国朋友 June Almes 教授来华教学,在中国国内未能找到一本令人十分满意的英美概况教材,于是她约我和 Carol Pollard 以及沈培新等教授与她共同策划,编写一本内容较新、客观性较强的英美概况书。凭着自己对英美背景知识的浓厚兴趣、多年来相关知识的积累及相关课程的教学经验,我欣然应允。随后的几年中,全书从初稿撰写到最后定稿,每一章都经过专家审核,有些章节反复修改,甚至重写。此外,为便于中国读者阅读,还加了一些中文注释。现在,参编此书的中外教授、专家们多年来辛勤工作的结晶——《新编英美概况教程》一书终于由北京大学出版社出版,与广大读者见面了。

　　读者阅读此书,如能在获得大量真实客观的英美社会、文化背景知识的同时,学到一些地道的英语,June Almes、Carol Pollard 等教授和我将会感到十分欣慰,这也是我们当时写此书的初衷之一。

周叔麟
2004 年 2 月于南京